GLOBAL ISSUES

2021 Edition

Sara Miller McCune founded SAGE Publishing in 1965 to support the dissemination of usable knowledge and educate a global community. SAGE publishes more than 1000 journals and over 800 new books each year, spanning a wide range of subject areas. Our growing selection of library products includes archives, data, case studies and video. SAGE remains majority owned by our founder and after her lifetime will become owned by a charitable trust that secures the company's continued independence.

Los Angeles | London | New Delhi | Singapore | Washington DC | Melbourne

GLOBAL ISSUES

SELECTIONS FROM *CQ RESEARCHER*

2021 EDITION

$SAGE | **CQPRESS**

FOR INFORMATION:

CQ Press

An Imprint of SAGE Publications, Inc.

2455 Teller Road

Thousand Oaks, California 91320

E-mail: order@sagepub.com

SAGE Publications Ltd.

1 Oliver's Yard

55 City Road

London EC1Y 1SP

United Kingdom

SAGE Publications India Pvt. Ltd.

B 1/I 1 Mohan Cooperative Industrial Area

Mathura Road, New Delhi 110 044

India

SAGE Publications Asia-Pacific Pte. Ltd.

18 Cross Street #10-10/11/12

China Square Central

Singapore 048423

Printed in the United States of America

ISBN: 978-1-5443-8688-1

This book is printed on acid-free paper.

Acquisitions Editor: Anna Villarruel

Editorial Assistant: Lauren Younker

Production Editor: Astha Jaiswal

Typesetter: Hurix Digital

Proofreader: Lawrence W. Baker

Cover Designer: Candice Harman

Marketing Manager: Jennifer Jones

SUSTAINABLE FORESTRY INITIATIVE

Certified Chain of Custody
Promoting Sustainable Forestry
www.sfiprogram.org
SFI-01028

20 21 22 23 24 10 9 8 7 6 5 4 3 2 1

Contents

Annotated Contents

CONFLICT, SECURITY, AND TERRORISM
U.S. – Iran Relations

President Trump's withdrawal from the landmark 2015 Iran nuclear deal and his crippling economic sanctions against Tehran have added more volatile elements to an already tense Middle East. Trump wants to force Iran to permanently halt its nuclear and ballistic missile programs and stop supporting Shiite militants fighting Sunni governments across the region. The sanctions, while causing suffering for many Iranians, have united the country behind its defiant clerical leadership. Tehran has sought to raise the stakes of the confrontation and encourage global pressure on Trump to lift his sanctions by downing a U.S. drone and harassing foreign oil tankers in the Persian Gulf. American officials also accuse Iran of attacking Saudi Arabia's oil installations. So far, Trump has not responded militarily, but neither has he relaxed the sanctions. As long as they remain in place, experts say, Iran will likely continue its provocations. The standoff between Washington and Tehran will not end peacefully unless the two sides start talking about their differences, experts add.

Measles Resurgence

The number of measles cases in the United States has reached a 27-year high—a startling development for a disease that the World Health Organization declared eradicated in the country in 2000 as a result of widespread vaccine use. And the problem is global: 110,000 deaths from measles were reported worldwide in 2017, the most recent year for which global estimates are available, up from fewer than 90,000 in 2016. In the United States, experts attribute the measles resurgence to reduced vaccination rates for children whose parents believe—against all scientific evidence—that the vaccine for measles, mumps and rubella (MMR) is unsafe or that the disease poses no significant health risk. Most of the U.S. cases occurred in insular, underimmunized communities and have been linked to travelers bringing measles back from countries with large measles outbreaks. In some states, policymakers are eliminating or narrowing exemptions for mandatory vaccinations of children attending public schools, and health officials are pushing back against skepticism about the safety and necessity of vaccines.

The New Arms Race

In recent years, the United States and Russia have withdrawn from several major agreements developed over 40 years to control the spread of nuclear weapons, citing violations by the other side. Those treaties created a climate of strategic stability, minimizing the chances of nuclear war. Without them, a new arms race, reminiscent of the Cold War years, has begun, as both sides develop ultramodern, super-fast weapon systems capable of delivering a nuclear device anywhere on the globe within 15 minutes. U.S. and Russian military leaders also have embraced doctrines that maintain that a limited nuclear war using small, tactical nuclear weapons can be won. The last remaining treaty limiting U.S. and Russian nuclear arsenals will expire next February unless both countries agree to extend it. President Trump says he prefers to negotiate a broader pact that includes China, but Beijing has said it is not interested, and critics say a year is not enough time to negotiate such an ambitious accord. Meanwhile, a stalemate in talks over North Korea's denuclearization has added uncertainty to the future of arms control, as has the U.S. withdrawal from an international agreement halting Iran's development of nuclear weapons.

Cyberwarfare

Cyberwarfare has become a crucial battleground between nations. This largely hidden conflict, which has echoes of the Cold War struggle between Western democracies and communist nations, involves a range of activities: from online disinformation campaigns to the use of sophisticated computer worms to disrupt or commandeer government and commercial computer systems. Russia, the United States, China, Iran and other nations all have probed and hacked into other countries' computer systems. Some U.S. officials worry about a "cyber Pearl Harbor," in which an enemy launches a surprise cyberattack to disable key public utilities such as the power grid. But other analysts believe the greater danger lies in the way Russia manipulated social media to spread disinformation and worsen political divisions in the 2016 U.S. election as it worked to boost the campaign of President Trump. U.S. intelligence officials say that Russia is at it again, and experts warn that new technologies such as 5G high-speed wireless and artificial intelligence make defending against cyberattacks even harder.

Zoonotic Diseases

The pandemic circling the globe is only the latest instance of a disease that jumped from animals to humans, known as a zoonotic disease. COVID-19 likely came from a bat; AIDS, severe acute respiratory syndrome (SARS), Ebola, West Nile and Lyme disease also originated in animals. Zoonotic disease outbreaks have been occurring more often since the 1940s as an expanding human population pushes deeper into forests for hunting, agriculture, mining and housing. Demand for exotic meat also brings live wildlife to food markets, where they can transmit viruses to other animals and humans. How to prevent the next pandemic is a matter of vigorous debate: Some scientists are pushing for more research into animal viruses, while others stress stopping human activities, such as deforestation, that can spur contagion. Conservation groups urge a ban on the wildlife trade, but critics say that will only encourage a black market. Some researchers and environmentalists say preserving wilderness and biological diversity is key to preventing more outbreaks.

INTERNATIONAL POLITICAL ECONOMY
European Union at a Crossroads

Amid the United Kingdom's Brexit crisis and a surge in populism throughout Europe, the 28-nation European Union (EU) is facing renewed questions about its future. Nationalist-populist governments rule in Italy, Hungary, Poland and Greece, and populist parties are posing stiff challenges in France and Germany, the EU's most powerful members. A slowing economy and worsening relations with the Trump administration, which calls the EU a foe on trade, present additional challenges to the Union. But many political analysts believe the EU remains strong, noting that the U.K.'s expected departure from the federation has chastened foes of European integration and led them to drop their drives for Brexit-style secessions in other countries. The EU also has drastically cut illegal migration from Africa and the Mideast—a major source of populists' anger. Nevertheless, many experts say next month's elections for the EU's Parliament will be crucial. They predict a strong showing for populists, who would be in a position to keep the EU from becoming more powerful.

US Foreign Policy in Transition

After more than 70 years as the standard-bearer of multilateral engagement and constructive diplomacy, the United States is undergoing a dramatic foreign policy shift that has led some to question whether the nation is giving up its global authority. Departing from the approach of previous presidents, who tended to cooperate with allies through multilateral agreements to promote democracy, free trade and environmental protection, President Trump is championing an "America First" policy aimed at protecting U.S. jobs and interests. Preferring to rely on his instincts and personal rapport rather than professional diplomats, he has ended U.S. participation in several major international treaties, praised authoritarian leaders and waged a trade war against key economic partners. Trump's supporters say he is using America's economic and political might to its advantage and trying to prod uncooperative allies—particularly in Europe—to do more to protect their own security interests. But critics say Trump's conduct has isolated the United States internationally and undermined the nation's claim to moral leadership.

China's Belt and Road Initiative

Dozens of countries in Asia, Africa, Europe and elsewhere are embracing China's Belt and Road Initiative (BRI), a $1 trillion program aimed at building a vast system of transportation, energy and telecommunications networks linking China to resources and markets worldwide. So far, 117 nations have received more than $400 billion in loans and investments from Beijing, whose state-owned construction companies are building roads, bridges, power plants and other projects. Chinese President Xi Jinping says the program seeks to help China and other countries strengthen their economies. But the massive infrastructure project—the largest in history—has sparked concerns that China is trapping poor nations in debt with the goal of forcing them to surrender strategic assets and that Xi's ultimate objective is to create a new world order in which China's norms and priorities prevail. To counter the BRI, the United States is readying a $60 billion development program that it argues will help recipient nations grow without becoming burdened with debts they cannot repay.

Hidden Money

Tax evasion and money laundering are generating major headaches and revenue losses for governments across the globe. In this shadow economy, wealthy investors and others use offshore tax havens and shell companies to hide money and avoid tax collectors. Drug cartels and other criminals, meanwhile, launder money by buying real estate or putting illicit gains in legitimate businesses. According to one estimate, the amount of hidden money worldwide tops $10 trillion. In response, experts are urging more cooperation among governments. The United States is seeking to collect more information on the overseas financial accounts of U.S. citizens, and other nations want Washington to share more data about their citizens' accounts in U.S. banks. But the Trump administration opposes a proposal that would require multinational companies to disclose their earnings in each country and pay a global minimum tax. And with U.S. states competing to attract businesses, the United States has become one of the largest tax havens in the world.

Supply Chains at Risk

President Trump's approach to trade policy—using import tariffs and other punitive measures as leverage when negotiating international agreements—is forcing many companies to restructure their global supply chains, which often took decades to develop. International trade rules established after World War II, combined with technological breakthroughs such as robotics, cloud computing and software, have resulted in intricately connected worldwide supply chains that have cut costs and boosted profits. The shifts also have cost thousands of U.S. manufacturing jobs. Trump says his strategy will change that, but many companies and economists say imposing tariffs at levels unseen since the 1930s will not rein in rivals such as China, the world's second-biggest economy and America's biggest trading partner in 2018. As U.S. companies scramble to find non-Chinese suppliers and brace for lower profits, they warn that the cost of the tariffs eventually will mean higher consumer prices. And China has retaliated by imposing its own tariffs on U.S. goods or halting purchases of American farm products, triggering fears of a prolonged "cold" trade war between the two countries.

RELIGIOUS AND HUMAN RIGHTS
Global Migration

The world is witnessing the highest numbers of migrants on record, nearly 272 million in 2019, more than triple the number in 1970. Advocates of immigration restrictions say migrants steal jobs and sometimes abuse a system designed to provide asylum for the truly persecuted. But human rights advocates say nations are shirking their responsibility to provide refuge to those experiencing persecution and violence. Citing a broken system in which asylum-seekers sometimes disappear into the United States, the Trump administration is limiting those who can seek asylum. It also is taking aggressive steps to end what President Trump calls a "very serious crisis" at the U.S.-Mexico border. Migrant advocacy groups say Trump has manufactured a crisis, and statistics show illegal immigration from Mexico is in a long-term decline. Governments often seek to stem migration by providing aid to improve the economies of origin countries. Experts say the solution is not so simple, because it takes at least a generation before rising income encourages people to remain at home.

Global Protest Movements

Protest movements swept the globe last year—so widely that some experts said there were more protests, and more protesters, in 2019 than at any other time in history. Millions of citizens in dozens of countries took to the streets to protest a host of grievances, ranging from higher consumer prices to government corruption and social inequality. Thousands died; national leaders were forced from office. Experts differ on whether the wave of protests is a sign of failing democracy or of healthy citizen empowerment. But the deadly global spread of the coronavirus this year halted most street protests, at least temporarily, as governments enforced social distancing restrictions in hopes of preventing further infections—and perhaps in some cases in hopes of breaking the protests' momentum. Many movements took their campaigns online, but how successfully remains to be seen. Social media enables protesters to organize effectively and promote their causes widely. Yet some observers argue that a social media campaign dissipates quickly if organizers cannot meet their followers' expectations.

Christians in the Middle East

The number of Christians in the Middle East has been falling for more than a century, due mainly to emigration and lower birth rates. But the decline has intensified since the early 2000s, as Christians and other religious minorities have faced increased persecution and violence due to wars in Iraq, Syria and Yemen, the rise of extremist groups such as the Islamic State and instability following the Arab Spring democracy movements that began in 2011. Tension also has been rising between Iran and Saudi Arabia, which represent opposite sides of Islam's Sunni-Shiite divide and where religious restrictions remain among the most severe in the world. While some exiled Christians are trying to return to their old homes, experts are not optimistic that the outflow from the region will slow; nor do they expect the Middle East to become more hospitable to religious minorities. Experts say the plight of these minorities reflects a dangerous lack of pluralism and respect for human rights in many of the area's societies.

ENVIRONMENTAL ISSUES
Extreme Weather

Climate scientists say that rising global temperatures caused by greenhouse gas emissions are making some extreme weather events increasingly likely and severe. They predict that heat waves, wildfires, hurricanes and other weather-related disasters will continue to set records and send damage costs soaring, even as countries around the world pledge to reduce emissions in response to global warming. Climate change skeptics, including President Trump and some conservatives, say fears that carbon emissions are making severe weather more frequent and more destructive are largely groundless, and administration officials are taking steps to minimize the role that climate science plays in setting government policies. Recent trends in extreme weather have led many experts to ask whether initiatives such as the financially troubled National Flood Insurance Program should continue to subsidize repeated rebuilding in disaster-prone areas. Some experts believe people living in such areas should be encouraged to leave. Others disagree, saying people have the right to live where they choose.

Climate Change and Health

Scientists warn that a warming planet threatens human health. A United Nations agency estimates climate change will cause 250,000 additional deaths annually between 2030 and 2050. The threat is multifaceted. Prolonged droughts are causing malnutrition in Africa, while extreme heat is leading to spikes in heat stroke in places as diverse as Baltimore and Paris. Across the globe, changing climes are worsening allergies and increasing the deadly reach of illnesses such as malaria, dengue fever and West Nile virus. But consensus is lacking about what to do. Some experts argue the threat is exaggerated because people will adapt to the changing climate. Others say nations must quickly reduce carbon emissions to limit global warming and protect human health.

Environmental activists are amplifying that message. One survey found that respondents ranked climate change as the top threat in 13 of 26 countries polled. In the United States, however, only 27 percent of Republicans—versus 83 percent of Democrats—view climate change as a major threat.

Fuel Efficiency Standards

President Trump is significantly reducing federal fuel efficiency and emissions standards for vehicles to below those set by the Obama administration. The Obama regulations required automakers to build vehicle fleets that would average about 54 mpg by 2025. The Trump rule cuts the requirement to about 40 mpg by 2026. Trump has also revoked a waiver that allowed California to set stricter standards, which are followed by several other states. The Trump administration contends its rule will save consumers billions of dollars in vehicle costs and will spur a move to new, cleaner and safer vehicles. Opponents say the rule will endanger public health and accelerate climate change by putting into the air more pollutants and greenhouse gases that cause global warming, especially carbon dioxide. The battle over the standards has divided automobile manufacturers and led a coalition of states headed by California, along with a dozen environmental groups, to sue to block the Trump administration's fuel efficiency and emissions rollback.

Preface

In this pivotal era of international policymaking, scholars, students, practitioners and journalists seek answers to such critical questions as: Will climate change set off a global health catastrophe? Is a denuclearization agreement with North Korea possible? Can companies adjust their global supply chains to Trump's tariffs and still grow? Students must first understand the facts and contexts of these and other global issues if they are to analyze and articulate well-reasoned positions.

The 2021 edition of *Global Issues* provides comprehensive and unbiased coverage of today's most pressing global problems. This edition is a compilation of 16 recent reports from *CQ Researcher*, a weekly policy brief that unpacks difficult concepts and provides balanced coverage of competing perspectives. Each article analyzes past, present and possible political maneuvering, is designed to promote in-depth discussion and further research and helps readers formulate their own positions on crucial international issues.

This collection is organized into four subject areas that span a range of important international policy concerns: conflict, security, and terrorism; international political economy; religious and human rights; and environmental issues. *Global Issues* is a valuable supplement for courses on world affairs in political science, geography, economics and sociology. Citizens, journalists and business and government leaders also turn to it to become better informed on key issues, actors and policy positions.

CQ RESEARCHER

CQ Researcher was founded in 1923 as *Editorial Research Reports* and was sold primarily to newspapers as a research tool. The magazine was renamed and redesigned in 1991 as *CQ Researcher*. Today, students are its primary audience. While still used by hundreds of journalists and newspapers, many of which reprint portions of the reports, *Researcher*'s main subscribers are now high school, college and public libraries. In 2002, *Researcher* won the American Bar Association's coveted Silver Gavel Award for magazine excellence for a series of nine reports on civil liberties and other legal issues.

Researcher writers—all highly experienced journalists—sometimes compare the experience of writing a *Researcher* report to drafting a college term paper. Indeed, there are many similarities. Each report is as long as many term papers—about 10,000 words—and is written by one person without any significant outside help. One of the key differences is that the writers interview leading experts, scholars and government officials for each issue.

Like students, writers begin the creative process by choosing a topic. Working with *Researcher*'s editors, the writer identifies a controversial subject that has important public policy implications. After a topic is selected, the writer embarks on one to two weeks of intense research. Newspaper and magazine articles are clipped or downloaded, books are ordered and information is gathered from a wide variety of sources, including interest groups, universities and the government. Once the writers are well informed, they develop a detailed outline and begin the interview process. Each report requires a minimum of ten to fifteen interviews with academics, officials, lobbyists and people working in the field. Only after all interviews are completed does the writing begin.

CHAPTER FORMAT

Each issue of *CQ Researcher*, and therefore each selection in this book, is structured in the same way. A selection begins with an introductory overview, which is briefly explored in greater detail in the rest of the report.

The second section chronicles the most important and current debates in the field. It is structured around a number of key issues questions, such as "Can Iran's economy survive under Trump's sanctions?" and "Does the BRI increase the chances for military conflict between the United States and China?" This section is the core of each selection. The questions raised are often highly controversial and usually the object of much argument among scholars and practitioners. Hence, the answers provided are never conclusive, but rather detail the range of opinion within the field.

Following those issue questions is the "Background" section, which provides a history of the issue being examined. This retrospective includes important legislative and executive actions and court decisions to inform readers on how current policy evolved.

Next, the "Current Situation" section examines important contemporary policy issues, legislation under consideration and action being taken. Each selection ends with an "Outlook" section that gives a sense of what new regulations, court rulings and possible policy initiatives might be put into place in the next five to ten years.

Each report contains features that augment the main text: sidebars that examine issues related to the topic, a pro/con debate by two outside experts, a chronology of key dates and events and an annotated bibliography that details the major sources used by the writer.

ACKNOWLEDGMENTS

We wish to thank many people for helping to make this collection a reality. For many years, Thomas J. Billitteri, former managing editor of *CQ Researcher*, gave us his enthusiastic support and cooperation as we developed this edition. Now, Kenneth Fireman, managing editor of *CQ Researcher*, is carrying on the tradition of helping College Editorial with our new edition texts. He and his talented editors and writers have amassed a first-class collection of *Researcher* articles, and we are fortunate to have access to this rich cache. We also thankfully acknowledge the advice and feedback from current readers and are gratified by their satisfaction with the book.

Some readers may be learning about *CQ Researcher* for the first time. We expect that many readers will want regular access to this excellent weekly research tool. For subscription information or a no-obligation free trial of *Researcher*, please contact CQ Press at www.cqpress.com or toll-free at 1-866-4CQ-PRESS (1-866-427-7737).

We hope that you will be pleased by the 2021 edition of *Global Issues*. We welcome your feedback and suggestions for future editions. Please direct comments to Anna Villarruel, Sponsoring Editor for International Relations, Comparative Politics, and Public Administration, CQ Press, an imprint of SAGE, 2600 Virginia Avenue, NW, Suite 600, Washington, DC 20037; or send e-mail to *Anna.Villarruel@sagepub.com*.

—*The Editors of CQ Press*

Contributors

Jonathan Broder is a Washington-based reporter and editor. He was a senior writer for *Newsweek*, a senior editor at *Congressional Quarterly* and served as a foreign correspondent in the Middle East, South Asia and the Far East for the *Chicago Tribune*. Broder's writing also has appeared in *The New York Times Magazine*, *The Washington Post*, *Smithsonian* and the *World Policy Journal*, among other publications. He previously reported for *CQ Researcher* on financial services deregulation and on India.

Lola Butcher is a journalist who covers health care policy and business issues, trends and controversies. Her work has appeared in *Undark, Knowable, Fast Company, TheAtlantic.com, Salon, Neurology Today, Managed Care* and other publications. She is a member of the Association of Health Care Journalists and a graduate of the Missouri School of Journalism.

Sarah Glazer is a New York-based freelancer who contributes regularly to *CQ Researcher*. Her articles on health, education and social-policy issues also have appeared in *The New York Times* and *The Washington Post*. Her recent *CQ Researcher* reports include "The Israeli-Palestinian Conflict" and "Universal Basic Income." She graduated from the University of Chicago with a B.A. in American history.

Reed Karaim, a freelance writer in Tucson, Ariz., has written for *The Washington Post, U.S. News & World Report, Smithsonian, American Scholar* and other publications. He is the winner of the Robin Goldstein Award for Outstanding Regional Reporting and other journalism honors. He is also the author of two novels, the most recent of which, *The Winter in Anna*, published by W. W. Norton & Co., is set at a small town weekly newspaper. He is a graduate of North Dakota State University in Fargo.

Rachel Layne is a Boston-based freelance journalist whose work has appeared in outlets including *CBS, USA Today, HBS Working Knowledge* and *MIT Technology Review*. She also spent 20 years at *Bloomberg News*, where she covered multinational corporations, among other roles.

Melba Newsome is a health, education and general interest writer. Her work has appeared in national publications such as *The New York Times, Bloomberg Businessweek, Oprah, Playboy, Reader's Digest, Time, Good Housekeeping* and *Wired*.

Stephen Ornes is a freelance science and medical writer in Nashville, Tenn., whose articles have appeared in *Scientific American, Discover, New Scientist, Science News for Students, Cancer Today, Physics World* and other

publications. His book, *Math Art: Truth, Beauty, and Equations* (Sterling Publishing), was published in April 2020.

Sara Toth Stub is a Jerusalem-based U.S. journalist who has written for *The Wall Street Journal, The Atlantic, U.S. News & World Report* and other publications. She usually covers business, culture and travel.

Bill Wanlund, a former Foreign Service officer, is a freelance writer in the Washington, D.C., area. He has written for *CQ Researcher* on abortion, intelligence reform, the marijuana industry and climate change as a national security concern.

Charles P. Wallace was a foreign correspondent for 35 years, working for United Press International, the *Los Angeles Times* and *Time* magazine on virtually every continent. He won the Business Journalist of the Year award in 1999 for economic reporting on Europe. He previously reported for *CQ Researcher* on global fishing controversies.

Global Issues,
2021 Edition

U.S.-Iran Relations

Is a military conflict inevitable?

By Jonathan Broder

By Jonathan Broder

Iranian Supreme Leader Ali Khamenei and Islamic Revolutionary Guard Corps members participate in a graduation ceremony at the Khatam al-Anbia Air Defense University in Tehran on Oct. 30, 2019. Khamenei has urged a "resistance economy" in the face of U.S. sanctions.

From *CQ Researcher,*
November 15, 2019

THE ISSUES

On the moonlit night of June 20, 2019, U.S. fighter jets, laden with precision-guided bombs and rockets, were in the air over the Arabian Sea while U.S. Navy warships below prepared missiles for an attack. Their targets: a trio of radar and missile installations in Iran.

Earlier that day, President Trump had ordered the attack in retaliation for Tehran's downing of an unmanned U.S. spy plane flying in what the Trump administration said was international airspace over the Persian Gulf—an assertion strongly denied by Iranian officials, who said the drone was in Iranian airspace and ignored several orders to leave.[1]

But 10 minutes before the strike was to commence, Trump abruptly called it off, explaining later he deemed the likely deaths of some 150 Iranians during the attack a disproportionate punishment. "We were cocked and loaded to retaliate last night on three different sites," Trump tweeted the next day.[2]

Trump's last-minute decision to abort the attack underscores just how close the United States and Iran came to a military clash after more than a year of escalating tensions. Yet, despite what now appears to be Trump's reluctance to use force against Iran, the two nations remain on a dangerous course toward armed confrontation unless they step back from their respective approaches, say independent analysts and former officials of both countries.

For Trump, who prides himself on being the first U.S. president to seriously confront Iran, a step-back would mean relaxing

Iran Arms Militants Across Middle East

In the struggle between Sunni and Shiite Muslims in the Middle East, Iran—a Shiite theocracy—has armed and trained Shiite militants in Lebanon, Yemen and Iraq and also backed Sunni armed groups opposing Israel in the Gaza Strip. Saudi Arabia—a Sunni theocracy—supports groups fighting Iran's proxies. Although all Middle Eastern countries have mixed Sunni and Shiite populations, only Iran, Iraq and Bahrain are predominantly Shiite, but Bahrain is ruled by a Sunni monarch. About 90 percent of the world's Muslims are Sunnis. Oman's population is predominantly of the Ibadi sect of Islam but also has some Sunnis and Shiites.

Iran supports the following proxies in:

Lebanon — Shiite **Hezbollah** (Party of God) possesses more than 100,000 missiles, threatening Israel, and has a powerful political party in parliament.

Yemen — Shiite Houthi militants toppled the Sunni-led government in 2014. (The Saudis lead a Sunni Arab coalition trying to restore the government.)

Syria — Hezbollah and Iran's Al Quds special forces trained, armed and funded more than 100,000 Shiite fighters who helped Shiite President Bashar Assad fend off a Sunni rebellion. Some anti-Assad rebels have been supported by Saudi Arabia, the United States, Qatar and Turkey.

Iraq — Shiite militias killed hundreds of American troops during an eight-year U.S. occupation, but later helped expel the Islamic State, an extremist Sunni group that had seized much of northwestern Iraq.

Gaza Strip — Hamas, an Islamist Palestinian organization that rules the area, and Islamic Jihad, a militant Palestinian group, both are predominantly Sunni.

Sources: Seth G. Jones, "War by Proxy: Iran's Growing Footprint in the Middle East," Center for Strategic and International Studies, March 11, 2019, https://tinyurl.com/y2j5xn3y; "Mapping the Global Muslim Population," Pew Research Center, Oct. 7, 2009, https://tinyurl.com/y49kadm7

his so-called "maximum pressure" strategy of harsh economic sanctions aimed at forcing Tehran to permanently end its nuclear program and scrap long-standing regional security policies. For Iran's clerical leaders, whose long historical memory stretches back to the 1953 CIA-organized coup that toppled their country's democratically elected prime minister, a change would mean tempering their own escalating campaign of "maximum resistance" to the sanctions, which Tehran regards as yet another U.S. effort at regime change.

Both sides insist they do not want a war. Yet domestic political pressures, regional allies' security concerns and Trump's unpredictability continue to hinder diplomatic efforts to broker talks between the two countries. If the U.S.-Iran standoff persists, some analysts fear a military confrontation is inevitable, potentially sparking a wider regional war that would send world oil prices soaring and usher in a global recession.

The latest round of U.S.-Iran tensions began building in May 2018. That's when Trump pulled the United States out of a landmark 2015 agreement between Iran and six world powers, under which Tehran had curtailed its nuclear program in return for relief from international sanctions imposed between 2010 and 2015. The sanctions sought to pressure Iran to curb its nuclear ambitions. Calling the accord "the worst deal ever negotiated," Trump imposed much harsher restrictions, flexing America's economic and financial muscle in an effort to make Tehran choose between economic collapse or new talks toward a more stringent accord.[3]

But Iran rejected any new negotiations unless Trump first returned to the 2015 agreement and lifted his sanctions. And Tehran fought back by harassing and seizing foreign oil tankers in and near the Persian Gulf, downing the U.S. drone and deliberately breaching some provisions of the 2015 accord.

Iran has been plagued by sanctions since 1979, when the United States first imposed them after Islamic militants seized the U.S. embassy in Tehran, the country's sprawling capital, and held 52 American diplomats hostage for nearly 15 months. After the hostages were released in 1981, the United States lifted those sanctions, but reimposed unilateral trade restrictions and embargoed U.S. military sales to Iran in the 1980s

and '90s in an effort to force Tehran to stop building ballistic missiles and supporting regional militant groups Washington regarded as terrorist organizations. Since the mid-2000s, U.S. and international trade sanctions have aimed to convince Iran to limit its nuclear program.

Trump's latest sanctions tightened restrictions on Iran's oil sales and targeted Iranian Supreme Leader Ali Khamenei, other top political figures and Iran's Islamic Revolutionary Guard Corps, triggering a major escalation in the standoff that jolted world oil markets. A Sept. 14 drone-and-cruise-missile attack devastated two major Saudi Arabian oil facilities, instantly cutting global oil supplies by 5 percent. Iran-aligned Houthi rebels in Yemen claimed credit for the attack as part of their ongoing war with the Saudis, but the Trump administration blamed Iran, which denied responsibility. After weeks of deliberation, Trump imposed sanctions on Iran's Central Bank and a development fund. In addition, the president ordered a secret cyberattack on Iran's communications system, U.S. officials say. But Trump kept a U.S. military response off the table.[4]

The attack on the oil infrastructure of Saudi Arabia, the world's largest oil exporter, appeared to be primarily in response to a Trump administration vow to halt Iran's oil exports, say Iran analysts. "If one day they want to prevent the export of Iran's oil, then no oil will be exported from the Persian Gulf," Iranian President Hassan Rouhani warned last in December 2018.[5]

Iran is being driven to take such risks by the impact of Trump's sanctions on the country's oil exports, a major source of Iran's hard currency earnings, analysts say. In April of last year, just before Trump withdrew from the nuclear deal, Iran exported 2.5 million barrels a day, earning about $60 billion annually, according to Adnan Mazarei, an expert on Iran's economy at the Peterson Institute for International Economics, an independent Washington think tank. Today, he estimates, the sanctions have reduced Iran's oil exports to around 300,000 barrels per day, dropping its earnings to around $12 billion this year.

Correspondingly, Mazarei says, since the sanctions kicked in, Iran's rial currency has lost about 70 percent of its value against the dollar. Inflation runs about 42 percent annually, he says, and the average unemployment rate stands at nearly 12 percent, with youth unem-

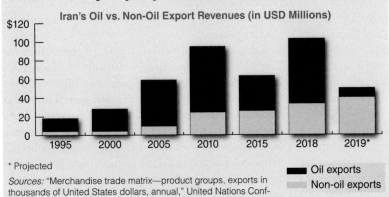

Iran's Dependence on Oil Exports Declines

In an effort to make the economy less reliant on oil exports, which are targeted by U.S. sanctions, Iran gets a growing share of its export revenue from non-oil exports.

Iran's Oil vs. Non-Oil Export Revenues (in USD Millions)

(bar chart showing years 1995, 2000, 2005, 2010, 2015, 2018, 2019 with y-axis from $0 to $120; Oil exports (black) and Non-oil exports (gray))*

* Projected

Sources: "Merchandise trade matrix—product groups, exports in thousands of United States dollars, annual," United Nations Conference on Trade and Development, https://tinyurl.com/y3x68yw3; Esfandyar Batmanghelidj, *Bourse & Bazaar*, Aug. 19, 2019, https://tinyurl.com/y6akna4c

■ Oil exports
□ Non-oil exports

four decades. The sanctions have not sparked mass demonstrations against the regime. Though polls show a majority of Iranians blame the Rouhani government's economic mismanagement and corruption for the country's fiscal woes, a growing percentage blame the United States and have rallied around their clerical leaders.[7]

"The regime's narrative about why Iran faces difficulties has shifted from the things that [Iranians are] doing wrong to the difficulties outsiders have created for us," Mazarei says. "So U.S. responsibility for the sanctions and current conditions has become far more prominent in the minds of ordinary Iranians. And that has created social solidarity."

Driving the administration's sanctions policy are a dozen demands that would dismantle Iran's strong military position in the region, which the United States, its Persian Gulf allies and Israel view as a threat. Formulated last year by Trump's hawkish then-national security adviser John Bolton and Secretary of State Mike Pompeo, the key requirements include a permanent end to Tehran's nuclear program, as well as termination of both its ballistic missile development and its support for Shiite proxy militias in Lebanon, Syria, Iraq and Yemen. Analysts agree that those proxies have helped shift the regional balance of power in Iran's favor by extending its influence far beyond its borders. (*See Graphic.*)[8]

Trump fired Bolton in September after sharp disagreements over signs the president was straying from Bolton's hard line and softening his position on Iran, among other issues. But even with Bolton no longer in the White House, Trump's demands and the sanctions remain.

"If we want to get to a point where Iran's proxies are weaker and the regime doesn't have the resources that it needs to destabilize the Middle East, it will require economic pressure," says U.S. Special Representative for Iran Brian Hook, the administration's top official dealing with Tehran. "There is no other way to accomplish that goal."

Among the Democratic candidates vying for their party's presidential nomination, Sens. Elizabeth Warren

U.S. State Department Special Representative Brian Hook is the Trump administration's top official handling affairs with Iran.

ployment at 27 percent. The International Monetary Fund (IMF) forecasts that Iran's economy will contract by 9.5 percent in 2019.[6]

Trump's sanctions also have blocked international banks from conducting transactions in dollars with Iran, significantly curtailing imports of medicine and food. Although those items were exempted from the sanctions, foreign suppliers and banks have backed away from exporting them to Iran. (*See Short Feature.*)

Yet experts say the Iranian economy, for now, is not about to collapse, because it has diversified over the past

and Amy Klobuchar and South Bend, Ind., Mayor Pete Buttigieg have said they would unilaterally return to the 2015 nuclear deal if elected. Former Vice President Joe Biden has made his return conditional on Iran's full compliance with the agreement, while Sen. Cory Booker has said he will seek "a better deal."[9]

Analysts say the administration's policy of relying on economic sanctions, combined with Trump's reluctance to use military force, has only encouraged greater Iranian defiance and heightened the chances of an eventual military confrontation.

"Iran is incentivized to make riskier decisions, such as conducting additional significant attacks on Saudi oil infrastructure," according to an October analysis by the Eurasia Group, a Washington-based political risk consultancy. "Tehran could also cross, either intentionally or accidentally, Trump's main red line: the death of U.S. service members."[10]

Ryan Crocker, who served as U.S. ambassador to five Arab and Muslim countries over a 40-year State Department career, says the intractability of current tensions between the United States and Iran can be traced to Trump's failure to observe one of the most basic equations in international security affairs: matching means with ends.

"President Trump has shown himself to be a national security minimalist who is not likely to rush to war," says Crocker. However, he adds, "He and his team are pursuing maximalist ends by demanding the Iranians give up their nuclear ambitions, their missile program and their support for regional proxy forces. Those things are absolutely integral to the Islamic Republic's basic essence."

Crocker continues: "When we put things like that out there as demands, what the Iranians hear is that this isn't about de-escalating tensions and finding common ground; it's about removing the Islamic Republic. So they're going to deliver a maximalist response that our minimalist president isn't prepared to deal with."

Amid these challenges, here are some key questions being asked about the increasingly fraught U.S.-Iran relationship:

Can Iran's economy survive under Trump's sanctions?

Ali Safavi, an exiled Iranian opposition figure living in Washington, D.C., insists the clerical regime in Tehran is close to collapse.

"Today, the Iranian regime is at its weakest point," says Safavi, a member of the Mujaheddin e-Khalq, the oldest and best organized Iranian opposition group. "It is extremely vulnerable."

He attributes the regime's fragility largely to Trump's economic sanctions, which ban any individual, company or country from doing business with Iran from the United States. Trump has said his goal is to block Iran's oil exports, viewed by Washington as the lifeblood of the Iranian economy. And over the past year, Trump has steadily intensified those sanctions, targeting Iran's Central Bank, the country's leaders and its elite Islamic Revolutionary Guard Corps, the regime's most powerful military organization but branded by the U.S. government as a foreign terrorist organization. Iran's long-standing problems of corruption and malfeasance compound the impact of the sanctions, experts say.

The resulting inflation and weakening of the rial sparked widespread anti-government protests and strikes in 2017 and 2018, Safavi says, eroding the Iranian leadership's grip on power. Videos from last year's street demonstrations captured angry mobs hurling insults at police and chanting "Death to inflation! Death to unemployment!"[11]

But an *NPR* report from Tehran last August told a different story. "Morning Edition" program host Steve Inskeep said: "Stores are well-stocked, though prices have soared through inflation. New stores and restaurants have opened to serve the elite, even if they're not always full of customers. New buildings are under construction, even if the progress on some has been slow." The government appears firmly in charge, Inskeep said, and he saw no anti-government protests while he was there.[12]

Iran experts say the country's economy is a mixed picture. Trump's sanctions have hit hard, they say, denying the government billions of dollars in oil export revenues and drastically limiting Tehran's ability to pay subsidies and fund public projects. Major foreign companies operating in Iran, such as German automaker Mercedes Benz and France's Total gasoline company, have fled the country. The sanctions also have denied Iran access to the global financial markets, where the U.S. dollar is the premier trading currency.

Spikes in inflation and unemployment have hit ordinary Iranian households the hardest, economists add. The Peterson Institute's Mazarei says food inflation is running at about 60 percent, significantly weakening

Iranians' View of U.S. Worsens

The share of Iranians who view the United States unfavorably rose from 71 percent in July 2014 to 86 percent in August 2019, a year after President Trump imposed new sanctions on Iran. The share of Americans who view Iran unfavorably has generally remained above 80 percent since 2001.

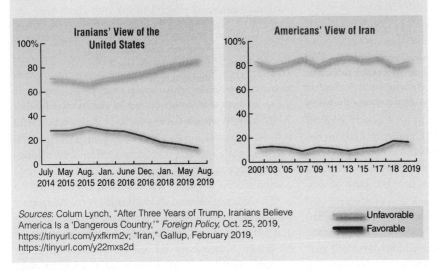

Sources: Colum Lynch, "After Three Years of Trump, Iranians Believe America Is a 'Dangerous Country,'" *Foreign Policy*, Oct. 25, 2019, https://tinyurl.com/yxfkrm2v; "Iran," Gallup, February 2019, https://tinyurl.com/y22mxs2d

sanctions for another five years, that's going to be a big problem. The current economic situation is not sustainable for another five years. Eventually, the Iranians will have to strike a deal with the United States if [Iran is] going to get its economy back on track again."

Other analysts agree the sanctions have hurt Iran badly, but question predictions that it is headed for economic collapse. Barbara Slavin, director of the Future of Iran project at the Atlantic Council, a Washington think tank, notes Tehran has roughly $100 billion in foreign currency reserves and negligible foreign debt. More importantly, she says, the regime reduced its heavy dependence on oil exports in the 1980s—from 90 percent to 30 percent today—by increasing exports of petrochemicals, manufactured goods and agricultural products. Those exports are expected to bring in an estimated $40 billion this year, Mazarei says, thanks largely to Iranian expertise at smuggling, honed during 40 years of various international sanctions regimes.

Iran also continues to export oil to China, which is defying Trump's sanctions by using its renminbi currency as payment. Analysts tracking the movements of Iranian tankers say Tehran also is believed to be selling its oil to Turkey and Syria, illustrating the challenge Trump faces in zeroing out Iranian oil exports.[13]

"Iran is the most experienced country in the world in resisting sanctions," says Sayed Hossein Mousavian, an Iranian policymaker and nuclear negotiator and now a visiting research scholar at Princeton University.

Iranian manufacturers and merchants have eased the impact of the sanctions somewhat by finding other suppliers willing to risk doing business with them, says Esfandyar Batmanghelidj, an economist and publisher of *Bourse & Bazaar*, a London-based Iranian business journal.

Iranians' ability to purchase chicken, meat and other basic food items. He says rents have risen sharply. And while salaries have gone up around 20 percent over the past year, Marzarei says, the raises offset only half of the overall inflation rate of 42 percent, resulting in a significant loss in real income.

"The issue now is going to be how the government finances itself and its deficit from domestic sources," Mazarei says. "They've had to borrow considerably from the commercial banks and from the Central Bank. But eventually, the sustainability of this operation will require the printing of money in significant amounts, and therefore higher inflation. And that means further reduction in real income."

Some independent analysts believe Iran's economy risks collapsing into Venezuela-style hyperinflation and serious social unrest if sanctions continue into a second Trump term.

"If Iran has to deal with the current economic situation for another year or so, that's one thing," says Ariane Tabatabai, an Iran analyst at the RAND Corp., an independent think tank that works closely with U.S. policymakers. "But if Trump is re-elected and Iran has to deal with the

The government also has been able to stabilize the currency and slow inflation, he adds, by creating financial mechanisms that encourage Iranian exporters to repatriate their dollar earnings from abroad.

"The economy is much more resilient than Washington would have us believe," says Batmanghelidj. "The question is not whether there's an economic crisis today; it's whether that crisis remains in place a year from now. Only then will we know whether the sanctions are going to have a full impact on Iran's decision-making."

Has the expansion of Iranian influence shifted the balance of power in the Middle East?

Since its 1979 revolution, Iran has sought to fill the various power vacuums that emerged from the Palestinian-Israeli conflict, the U.S. invasions of Afghanistan and Iraq and ongoing upheavals in the region.

Iran's moves into these troubled areas reflect not only a drive for greater regional influence but also the latest chapter in a centuries-old struggle for supremacy within Islam between the Shiite sect, centered in Iran, and the Sunnis, led by Saudi Arabia. And layered on top of their religious rivalry are the long-standing ethnic tensions between the region's Arab populations and the predominantly Persian Iranians.

Analysts say Iran has expanded its influence relatively cheaply by cultivating mostly Shiite militias across the region to resist the Sunni-led Arab monarchies in the Persian Gulf, which have been aided by the United States and Israel. In Syria, Saudi Arabia tried unsuccessfully to blunt Shiite proxies by backing a hard-line coalition of Sunni extremist groups that included Jabhat al Nusra, the Syrian affiliate of al Qaeda.[14] Iranian-supported militants now form a network of formidable proxy forces, extending from Lebanon on the Mediterranean Sea, across the vast Levantine steppe of Syria and Iraq and down to Yemen on the southern tip of the Arabian Peninsula.

"They're building these militias, training them, arming them, making sure there's a certain degree of loyalty to Iran," says Trita Parsi, author of several books on post-revolutionary Iran. "These alliances have a common religious bond and a strong ideological bedrock. They're more than just temporary political marriages based on money."

Saudi Arabia's efforts to counter Iran by financing its own proxy forces have largely failed because many of those groups, such as al Qaeda, also want to overthrow the Saudi monarchy, Parsi adds. "Within six months, those forces are using those funds to attack Saudi Arabia," he says.

But Iran and its proxies have yet to prevail over Israel. "The Iranians have a healthy respect for Israel's ability and willingness to respond militarily to Iran's provocations," says Jarrett Blanc, a former senior State Department official who oversaw implementation of the 2015 nuclear accord. "So they often pull back their proxies in Syria and Lebanon" when they come under Israeli attack. Such redeployments appear to be tactical retreats, aimed at preserving resources to fight another day, he says.

Michael Connell, director of the Iran studies program at the U.S. government's Center for Naval Analyses in Washington, said Tehran's support of proxies stemmed from its recognition after the 1980-88 Iraq-Iran war that its regular army, hobbled by international sanctions imposed after the 1979 Iranian revolution that prevented military modernization, was no match for technologically superior enemies. So Iran cultivated Shiite proxies to confront common enemies, teaching them what Connell called a "deterrence based model of attrition-based warfare," characterized by suicide bombings and small attacks to raise opponents' risks and costs.

"The goal is to inflict a psychological defeat that inhibits an enemy's willingness to fight," Connell said.[15]

Iran has armed and trained these proxies in:

- **Lebanon**—Hezbollah (Party of God), a Shiite group founded after Israel invaded that country in 1982. The group has launched guerrilla attacks and suicide car bombings against Israeli and U.S. facilities in Lebanon, eventually driving the United States and Israel out. The group today has more than 100,000 missiles that pose a serious threat to Israel, experts say, and has formed a powerful political party in Lebanon's parliament.

- **Gaza Strip**—Hamas, an Islamist Palestinian organization that rules the area, and Islamic Jihad, another militant Palestinian group, even though both are Sunni.

- **Yemen**—The Houthis, members of the Zaydi Shiite sect, who toppled the government in 2014 and

HUSSEIN FALEH/AFP via Getty Images

An Iraqi woman protests corruption in the Iran-supported government in Baghdad in November 2019. Militias backed by Iran have joined Iraqi government forces in attempting to suppress such demonstrations.

seized its weapons and medium-range missiles. Accusing Iran of engineering the overthrow, the Saudis have led an Arab military coalition with U.S.-supplied weapons and intelligence support in a deadly campaign to restore the ousted government to power. Some experts say the Houthis initially had no military relationship with Iran but later turned to Tehran and Hezbollah for help after the Saudi-led offensive triggered a dire humanitarian crisis. Houthi missiles repeatedly have struck inside Saudi Arabia, even reaching the capital Riyadh. The Houthis claim they launched the September attack on Saudi oil facilities.

- **Syria**—Hezbollah fighters, often called "Iran's Foreign Legion," who poured across the border into Syria in 2012 at Tehran's request to help embattled President Bashar Assad, a member of the Shiite Alawite sect. Since then, Hezbollah has helped train, arm and fund more than 100,000 Shia fighters, who have fought alongside Syrian government troops and with Russian air support against Sunni rebels, some of which are backed by the United States and Saudi Arabia.[16]

- **Iraq**—Shiite militias that killed hundreds of American troops during the eight-year U.S. occupation of that predominantly Shiite country. Later, fighting as government forces—ironically with U.S. air support—these groups helped expel the Islamic State, an extremist Sunni group that had overtaken huge swathes of

northwestern Iraq in an effort to establish a religious state known as a caliphate.

Analysts say that after U.S. forces toppled Iraqi leader Saddam Hussein—a Sunni and Iran's arch enemy—in 2003, the election of a pro-Iranian, Shiite-led Iraqi government ended Baghdad's role as a regional check on Iran and swung the region's balance of power toward Iran.

The Trump administration says U.S. sanctions have constrained Tehran's ability to fund its proxies in the region. "We can't overstate the significance of this development," says the State Department's Hook, citing a Hezbollah appeal for donations in March and reports of financial shortages affecting pro-Iranian groups in Syria, Iraq and the Gaza Strip. "We're making a lot of progress in that direction."

But Middle East experts say Hezbollah routinely seeks donations and was doing so before Trump imposed his sanctions. And Tehran's support for its proxies remains a top strategic priority, they say. "We haven't seen any evidence that Iran has stopped supporting these groups," so Trump's sanctions are not achieving one of his key strategic goals, says the RAND Corp.'s Tabatabai.

Moreover, these experts say, such support is relatively cheap compared to the hundreds of billions of dollars Saudi Arabia has spent on weapons and the estimated $200 million a day it is spending to pursue its war in Yemen.[17] A 2018 U.S. State Department report estimated that since 2012 Iran spent some $16 billion supporting its proxies in Iraq, Syria and Yemen and provides $800 million a year to Hezbollah and Palestinian groups.[18]

Meanwhile, recent anti-government protests in Lebanon and Iraq against government corruption and the lack of economic reforms are challenging Iran's standing among the Shiite communities in those countries. In Iraq, Iran-supported militias and predominantly Shiite government forces have fired on the protesters in recent weeks, killing at least 319, according to an Iraqi parliamentary committee.[19] And in Lebanon, Iran-aligned Hezbollah has sided with the government against the demonstrators, even though many of the protesters are Shiites.

The result, analysts say, is an unprecedented confrontation with the same Shiite communities that had looked to Iran for arms and training but are now rising up against their pro-Iran leaders, who did not translate Tehran's military and political successes into economic gains.

"Simply puts, Iran's resistance narrative did not put food on the table," said Hanin Ghaddar, an expert on the Shiites at the Washington Institute for Near East Policy, a think tank.[20] Ghaddar and other Middle East analysts say it is unclear whether Iran's proxies can restore order and Tehran's standing in Lebanon and Iraq.

Israel poses the biggest challenge to Iran's regional dominance, regularly bombing proxy-controlled Iranian missile stores in Syria and Iraq. And Israeli military intelligence closely tracks Iranian convoys moving arms overland to Iraq, Syria and Lebanon and pre-emptively strikes any looming threat.

"If someone rises up to kill you, rise earlier and kill him first," said Israeli Prime Minister Benjamin Netanyahu, quoting an ancient dictum from the Talmud.[21]

Is war inevitable between the United States and Iran?

It is impossible to predict whether war will break out between the United States and Iran. But growing fears on the part of world leaders, regional experts and oil industry analysts demonstrate that they see such a conflict as likely unless something dramatic changes the course of events.

As tensions mount over Trump's crippling sanctions and Iran's escalating belligerency, desperate diplomatic efforts have been initiated to halt an apparently inexorable march toward a major conflict in the Persian Gulf, where nearly a quarter of global oil supplies originate.

First, European leaders last year created a barter mechanism to allow businesses to sell Iran food, medicine and other humanitarian supplies without going through the dollar-dominated global financial system. But companies, fearing U.S. sanctions nonetheless, have backed away. Then French President Emmanuel Macron tried unsuccessfully to arrange a meeting between Trump and Iranian President Rouhani on the sidelines of the recent United Nations General Assembly in New York.

Experienced former diplomats and Iran experts say a dangerous escalatory spiral is now in motion. Trump insists he wants to avoid a military clash, fearful that it would sink his 2020 re-election chances. So he has

responded to Iran's provocations with more sanctions and nonlethal cyberattacks.

But the sanctions pose what former IMF senior executive and diplomatic troubleshooter Hossein Askari calls an "existential threat" to thousands of impoverished Iranians. Among the Iranian leadership and ordinary citizens, experts say, that threat has stirred the country's centuries-old Shiite code of resistance and martyrdom, all but guaranteeing more provocative Iranian behavior and growing chances of a war.

"The idea that you can conduct economic warfare against Iran without that leading to military confrontation and costs to the United States is unrealistic," says Iran expert Parsi, noting that Secretary of State Pompeo last year advised Tehran to bow to U.S. demands "if your people want to eat."[22]

"You can't conduct that degree of economic warfare and expect nothing will happen," Parsi says.

Many Iran experts regard Iran's harassment and seizure of several foreign tankers this past spring as warning shots. And the highly destructive attack on Saudi oil facilities, they say, was meant to provide Washington and its Arab allies a taste of what Iran is willing to do if war breaks out. To make sure the Trump administration got the message, Iranian Foreign Minister Javad Zarif pledged "all-out war" if Iran is attacked, putting at risk the rest of Saudi Arabia's oil infrastructure and the roughly 70,000 U.S. troops in Iraq and the Arab sheikdoms in the Persian Gulf.[23]

Patrick Theros, a former U.S. ambassador to Qatar, said the attack on the Saudi oil facilities was consistent with Iran's asymmetrical warfare doctrine. Unable to defeat U.S. forces using conventional means, Iran aims to hurt the United States indirectly by targeting the world economy's dependence on Persian Gulf oil and gas.

As the standoff with Iran intensifies, some military analysts say the Trump administration still has several options short of war to pressure Iran into compliance. Sabahat Khan, a senior analyst at Dubai's Institute for Near East and Gulf Military Analysis, said these include Trump's standing offer for negotiations, a proposal Iran adamantly refuses to accept unless sanctions are lifted first. Another is more sanctions, Khan said, and a third is cyberattacks targeting Iran's oil production and critical economic infrastructure.[24]

But Chas Freeman, a former U.S. ambassador to Saudi Arabia, says without a diplomatic breakthrough, punitive measures will only draw increasingly belligerent responses from Iran, especially now that they believe Trump will not respond militarily. At some point, Freeman worries, Iran's actions will cross a line that will leave Trump no option but a military response.

Freeman compares Trump's maximum pressure strategy against Iran to President Franklin D. Roosevelt's embargo on oil and rubber sales to Japan in the 1930s, aimed at halting Tokyo's military expansionism in East Asia. As with Iran, Freeman points out, the sanctions hardened Japan's resolve to resist U.S. intervention in regional affairs. Eventually, in a desperate bid to remain a major Asian power, Japan attacked the U.S. Navy in Hawaii, drawing the United States into World War II.

Freeman calls Iran's escalating provocations against Trump's sanctions "a very clear warning of what we know from past history—namely that if you corner a country, even if it's not your military equal, at some point you pay a price for that." At some point, he adds, "You get attacked."

BACKGROUND

Repeated Invasions

The United States has never fully understood modern Iran, neither as a monarchy nor as the Islamic Republic. The most glaring example is the unquestioning faith that successive U.S. administrations placed in the durability of the Iranian monarchy and its role as America's policeman in the Middle East.

In December 1977, President Jimmy Carter memorably praised Iran as "an island of stability" in the turbulent region. Within days the first demonstrations erupted in what became a revolution that eventually would end the monarchy, send Shah Mohammad Reza Pahlavi into exile and transform Iran into the virulently anti-American Islamic Republic.

Iran scholars rank the Iranian revolution as one of the three most consequential events in the Middle East during the 20th century, the other two being the collapse of the 500-year-old Ottoman Empire after World War I and the creation of Israel in 1948. And like those events, the shock waves from Iran's revolution continue to reverberate across the globe.

"Virtually no part of the world has been untouched by the revolution's repercussions because of its effect on oil prices, on the patterns of terrorism and modern warfare, on Third World politics and on the emergence of religious fundamentalism, not only within Islam," wrote Robin Wright in her 1989 book on post-revolutionary Iran, *In The Name of God: The Khomeini Decade.*[25]

Today, 40 years after the revolution, the crisis over the Islamic Republic's nuclear program, its ballistic missile development and its push for Middle East dominance underscore the revolution's enduring impact and Iran's geostrategic importance.

For Iranians, however, that is nothing new. Since ancient times, Iran—a geographic and cultural bridge between the Middle East and India—has been central to the military, religious and cultural history of the region. Many scholars say modern Iran's deep suspicion of outsiders is the legacy of centuries of repeated foreign invasions and meddling in its internal affairs.

That history began in the fourth century B.C. when the Persian Empire, Iran's predecessor, stretched from modern day Bulgaria in the west to northern India in the east and Egypt in the south. Alexander the Great conquered Persia as he drove his armies east to India. In the seventh century A.D., the Arab conquest of Persia opened the way for the spread of Islam to Central and East Asia.[26] The Turks overran Persia in the 11th century, followed by Genghis Khan's Mongol army in the 13th century and Tamerlane in the 14th century.

In the 16th century, Persia's Safavid monarch, Ismail, claimed to be a direct descendent of the Prophet Muhammad's cousin, Ali, and declared Shiism the country's official religion. It was a transformative move that gave Persians a separate religious identity from their mostly Sunni Arab neighbors.[27]

Since then, Persians established close clerical bonds with Shiite communities in Lebanon, Syria and Iraq—a relationship that has helped the modern Islamic Republic enlist them as proxies in its struggle against rival powers.

Modern Meddling

In the early 20th century, the British and Russian empires targeted Persia in their "Great Game" competition for dominance over Central Asia, forcing the Persians in 1905 to cede a sphere of influence in northern Iran to Russian control and the oil-rich south to the British. But by the end of World War I, Britain emerged as the sole colonial power in Persia.[28]

To secure its control over the oil fields, London offered to make Persia a British protectorate, but the Persian parliament rejected the plan. Britain withdrew its personnel from the country in 1921, after supporting a coup by Col. Reza Khan, commander of the Persian Cossack Brigade and an ardent nationalist.[29]

In 1925, Reza Khan became shah, or monarch, and his eldest son, Mohammad Reza, heir to the throne. Shah Reza took the surname Pahlavi, establishing his new dynasty. In 1935, at the shah's behest, the parliament changed the country's name from Persia to Iran.[30]

Shah Reza pursued a vigorous modernization campaign and sought closer relations with Nazi Germany, which, unlike Britain and Russia, had not meddled in Iranian affairs or occupied its territory. When World War II began, Reza declared neutrality.[31] But British and Soviet forces occupied Iran in 1941 to secure the Trans-Iranian Railroad for carrying critical British and U.S. military aid from India to the Soviet Union. The British remained suspicious of Shah Reza's pro-German sympathies and forced him to abdicate, putting his pro-British son on the throne.

Middle East scholars say the young shah's willingness to assist the Allied war effort laid the foundation for Iran's close ties with the West, particularly the United States.

Roots of Revolution

The first major crisis in Iran's relations with the West began in 1951, when the lawyer Mohammad Mosaddegh was elected prime minister. Soon after taking office, he introduced a wide array of political and economic reforms and nationalized Iran's British-controlled oil industry. After diplomacy failed to obtain a compromise, the CIA, convinced by the British that Mosaddegh was a communist sympathizer, helped to overthrow him in a coup that became a turning point in Iran's modern history.[32]

Although the shah introduced many reforms, some of which lifted restrictions on women, he also created the notorious SAVAK secret police force, trained by the CIA and Israel's Mossad intelligence agency, to quash challenges to his rule. It soon became Iran's most hated and

feared institution, responsible for the torture and murder of thousands of the dissidents.[33] (*See Short Feature.*)

During the administration of Republican President Richard M. Nixon, the shah bought huge quantities of sophisticated U.S.-made weapons, establishing Iran as Washington's Persian Gulf policeman.[34] The administration of Democratic President Jimmy Carter discouraged any questioning of the arrangement, and U.S. officials overlooked the anti-shah anger and resentment that was building in the country's mosques.[35]

Leading the opposition was Ayatollah Ruhollah Khomeini, an outspoken senior Shiite cleric whose arrest in 1963 for an anti-shah speech sparked riots in which government troops killed up to 400 of his followers.[36] Exiled the following year, Khomeini eventually moved to Paris. As protests in Tehran intensified, the shah declared martial law and banned all demonstrations.

On Sept. 8, 1978, government troops opened fire on a large crowd of protesters in Tehran, killing nearly 100 people. The deaths stunned the nation, destroying any possibility of reconciliation. Strikes and massive anti-shah protests spread. "That's the point when it turned into a revolution," said Gary Sick, an Iran expert who served on the White House's National Security Council during the administrations of Gerald Ford and Carter and is now a professor at Columbia University in New York.[37]

Carter's advisers were split over the worsening situation in Iran, Sick recalled. One camp favored the shah's abdication and formation of a new pro-Western government of senior military officers and moderate clerics, with Khomeini as its figurehead. The other side advocated a military crackdown by the shah's forces.

While Washington debated its options, the shah convinced opposition politician Shapour Bakhtiar to serve as prime minister while the shah went abroad "on vacation." On Jan. 16, 1979, Bakhtiar assumed leadership, and the shah and his family flew to exile in Egypt, ending 2,500 years of monarchist rule in Iran.[38]

On Feb. 1, 2019, Khomeini flew to Tehran, where he was met by up to 3 million Iranians celebrating in the streets. He denounced the Bakhtiar government as illegitimate. "I shall kick their teeth in," the cleric proclaimed. "I appoint the government."[39]

A few days later, Khomeini named a provisional revolutionary government. His supporters took control of government buildings, TV and radio, and Bakhtiar fled

CHRONOLOGY

530 B.C.-A.D. 1501 *Persian Empire falls to a succession of foreign invaders; Iran adopts Shiite Islam.*

332 B.C. Alexander the Great conquers the Persian Empire, which stretched from modern-day Bulgaria in the west to northern India in the east and Egypt in the south. A succession of rulers will try to restore the Persian Empire to its original boundaries, but it never regains its immense size.

636 Islamic rule begins after Arabs conquer Persia, which stretches from modern Georgia in the west to western Afghanistan in the east.

1501 Persia's Safavid dynasty declares Shiism the state religion.

1900s-1948 *Persia becomes constitutional monarchy; after discovery of oil, Britain and Russia occupy the country during world wars.*

1907 Democratic reforms establish a constitutional monarchy, under which the shah, or king, shares power with an elected government headed by a prime minister.

1908 British discover oil in southern Persia and form the Anglo-Persian Oil Co.

1914-18 Persia declares neutrality in World War I, but is occupied by Russian and British troops to prevent Germany from capturing its oil fields.

1921 Military commander Reza Khan seizes power in British-backed coup.

1925 Khan is crowned Shah Reza Pahlavi, and his oldest son, Mohammad Reza, is proclaimed crown prince.

1935 Persia is renamed Iran.

1941-45 British and Russians again occupy Iran during World War II because of Shah Reza's pro-German sympathies; Reza abdicates; his pro-British son is crowned shah.

1950s-1960s *The Iranian government nationalizes the oil industry, provoking a CIA coup.*

1951 Lawyer Mohammed Mosaddegh is elected Iran's 35th prime minister by parliament and nationalizes Iran's oil industry. . . . Power struggle erupts between Mosaddegh and Shah Mohammad Reza.

1953 Shah dismisses Mosaddegh, sparking riots that force the shah to flee the country. . . . Mosaddegh, accused by Britain of having communist leanings, is overthrown in a coup orchestrated by the CIA and British intelligence; the shah returns.

1957 The shah creates the SAVAK secret police, which becomes notorious for torturing and killing dissenters.

1963-77 Shah undertakes modernization campaign and loosens restrictions on women; Iran becomes Cold War ally of the United States.

1978-1995 *Islamic revolution transforms Iran into bitter U.S. foe.*

1978-79 Iranian revolution, directed by ultraconservative cleric Ayatollah Ruhollah Khomeini from exile in Paris, begins. Shah and family go into exile. . . . Khomeini returns, declares Islamic Republic. . . . Militants take 52 Americans hostage in U.S. Embassy; Washington severs diplomatic ties with Tehran.

1980-81 Iraq-Iran war begins. . . . Iran releases U.S. hostages after 444 days in captivity.

1982 After Israel invades Lebanon, Iran creates Shiite Hezbollah militia to resist Israeli occupation.

1983 Iran-backed Hezbollah militants launch truck-bomb attacks on U.S. Embassy and U.S. Marine barracks in Lebanon, killing more than 300 people. The group also takes 25 American civilians in Lebanon hostage.

1985 To win the hostages' release, Reagan administration secretly and illegally sells arms to Tehran, using payments to fund anti-communist guerrillas in Nicaragua.

1988-89 Iraq-Iran war ends in stalemate. . . . Khomeini dies; Ayatollah Ali Khamenei becomes Iran's supreme leader.

1990-95 United States imposes sanctions on Iran over its alleged support for terrorism.

2000-2010 *U.S. invasions of Afghanistan and Iraq enable Iran to extend its regional influence.*

2001 After Sept. 11 terrorist attacks in the United States, a U.S.-led coalition invades Afghanistan to stamp out al Qaeda terrorist group, the perpetrators of the 9/11 attacks; with Iranian help, Sunni extremist Taliban government is toppled in Kabul. . . . President George W. Bush ignores Iranian outreach for better relations.

2002 Bush brands Iran, Iraq and North Korea as an "axis of evil," sparking outrage in Iran. . . . Tehran begins construction of its first nuclear reactor.

2003 U.S. invades Iraq, ousting Saddam Hussein, Iran's Sunni archenemy. . . . Elections in Iraq bring Iranian-backed Shiite government to power, expanding Tehran's influence there.

2007-10 After the International Atomic Energy Agency predicts Iran can develop a nuclear weapon within eight years, the United States imposes additional sanctions on Iran; the following year, the United Nations Security Council adds international sanctions.

2011-Present *Iran accepts an international deal that lifts nuclear-related sanctions, but President Trump withdraws and reimposes sanctions.*

2013 Iran and six world powers begin negotiations toward a nuclear accord.

2014 Shiite Houthi tribesmen in Yemen overthrow the government, prompting a Saudi-led military campaign to oust the rebels, who later align with Iran.

2015 Iran, the United States and five other nations sign the landmark Joint Comprehensive Plan of Action curtailing Iran's nuclear program in return for sanctions relief.

2018 Trump withdraws the United States from the nuclear deal and reimposes tough sanctions on Iran, demanding Iran accept a far more stringent accord; Iran refuses.

2019 U.S.-Iran tensions spike after attacks on foreign tankers in the Persian Gulf, Iran's downing of a U.S. drone and drone-and-missile strikes on Saudi oil facilities.

to Paris. Iranians overwhelmingly voted for the establishment of an Islamic theocracy.[40]

Hostage Crisis

The first phase of the Iranian revolution, which lasted until Khomeini's death in 1989, was marked by a violent purge of the shah's associates and by the November 1979 takeover of the U.S. embassy in Tehran by militant students. Enraged that the U.S. government had allowed the shah to come to the United States for cancer treatment, the students captured 52 American diplomats and held them hostage for 444 days, despite an aborted rescue attempt by the U.S. military in 1980. The U.S. Treasury froze $12 billion in Iranian assets here and abroad.[41]

After lengthy negotiations brokered by Algeria, the hostages were released on Jan. 20, 1981, the day Republican Ronald Reagan was inaugurated as president. Since then, the two countries have had no official diplomatic relations, and the hostage affair

cemented the Islamic Republic as an implacable foe in the minds of most Americans.

Bettmann/Contributor/Getty Images

Blindfolded American diplomats are paraded outside the U.S. Embassy in Tehran on Nov. 4, 1979. Militant students held 52 Americans hostage for 444 days before releasing them on the day Ronald Reagan became president.

Iranian Women Defy Mandatory Hijab Laws

Government imposes 10-year sentence for removing a headscarf in public.

In late September, Iranian intelligence agents arrested three relatives of Masih Alinejad, a U.S.-based Iranian dissident in what human rights groups called a bid to intimidate the U.S.-based activist. Alinejad, 43, leads a popular campaign against the Islamic Republic's laws requiring women and girls to wear a hijab, or headscarf.

Those arrested include the brother of Alinejad, whose women's rights campaign has alarmed the conservative clerics who run Iran's courts, as well as the brother and sister of Alinejad's former husband. After the three were interrogated about Alinejad's activities, the brother-in-law was released with a warning: Any contact with the feminist activist will be considered a crime. The status of the other two detainees is unclear.

"These arrests are a blatant attempt by the Iranian authorities to punish Masih Alinejad for her peaceful work defending women's rights," Philip Luther, Amnesty International's Middle East research and advocacy director, said in a statement.[1]

In 2014 Alinejad denounced Iran's compulsory hijab law on Facebook, calling it discriminatory, and encouraged Iranian women to post photographs and videos of themselves removing their headscarves. The campaign caught on, and Iranian women began removing their headscarves in public and demanding the law be repealed.[2]

Alinejad later created a website, My Stealthy Freedoms, from which she launched a second campaign—"White Wednesdays"—which asked Iranian women to gather weekly in public wearing white hijabs and then remove them.

Both campaigns have gone viral on social media, gaining a widespread following among Iranian women and girls, and unnerving Iran's conservative courts. The regime's religious police routinely break up the protests and arrest the demonstrators. According to Iran's Tasnim news agency, police last year described those arrested as "people who have been deceived by the 'My Stealthy Freedoms' movement." An Iranian judge said anti-hijab protesters had been influenced by foreign groups and "industrial recreational drugs."[3]

Until recently, the anti-hijab protesters received two-month jail sentences and the equivalent of a $100 fine for violating the Islamic dress code. But in July, the courts increased the sentence to 10 years for removing a hijab in public or sending photos or videos to Alinejad's website. Bails have been set as high as $110,000.[4]

"If the authorities thought this would scare off Iranian women, they were wrong," said Alinejad, who left Iran in 2009 and now lives in Brooklyn, N.Y. She said she gets 2,000 messages a day from Iranian women showing themselves removing their headscarves.[5]

Iran's conservative religious leaders who came to power after the 1979 Islamic revolution imposed compulsory hijab laws. That did not sit well with many Iranian women, who had enjoyed new rights under the rule of Shah Mohammad Reza Pahlavi. On March 8, 1979—the day after Iran's new clerical rulers imposed the new law—some 100,000 women, many accompanied by their husbands, brothers and fathers, marched through the streets of Tehran to protest the rule.[6]

Although the shah had also imposed authoritarian policies and brutal police methods, women were allowed to leave their heads uncovered. The shah also:

• Provided free education to girls as well as boys, and allowed women to attend Tehran University.

• Granted women the right to vote and run for public office.

During the next decade, Iran exported anti-American Islamic extremism across the Muslim world. In 1983, Iranian-backed Hezbollah militants bombed the U.S. embassy and Marine barracks in Lebanon. They later murdered the CIA's Beirut station chief and held hostage 25 U.S. civilians working in Lebanon. U.S. efforts to gain their release would spawn the Iran-Contra scandal, in which the Reagan administration secretly sold weapons to Iran—in violation of U.S. law—in exchange for the hostages' freedom. Proceeds from the sale were used to fund anti-communist Contra guerrillas in Nicaragua, violating a congressional ban on such payments.[42]

- Allowed women to petition for a divorce and gain child custody, eliminating antiquated statutes that permitted men to unilaterally divorce their spouses with a simple verbal declaration and automatically gain child custody.

- Required men to go to court to take a second wife.

- Raised the legal age when girls could marry from 13 to 18.[7]

After the revolution, the new, ultraconservative religious government kicked women out of government and judicial positions and required them to cover their heads in public. Family laws again made wives the property of their husbands, removed restrictions on polygamy, allowed girls to be married at nine years of age and reimposed the death-by-stoning penalty for women convicted of adultery.[8]

Since then, Iranian women have clawed back some of their rights, according to Haleh Esfandiari, former director of the Middle East program at the Wilson Center, a Washington think tank. Iran's women's movement, she said, is one of the most dynamic in the Muslim world.[9]

That movement scored its most recent victories in October, when the regime allowed women to pass their Iranian citizenship on to children with non-Iranian fathers and lifted a ban on women attending soccer games. The soccer ban sparked international outrage in September after Sahar Khodayari, a 29-year-old sports fan, set herself on fire to protest her prosecution for appearing in public without a hijab after being caught sneaking into a soccer match dressed as a man. She died from her burns.[10]

"To say that these concessions were granted reluctantly by Iran's misogynistic rulers would be an extreme understatement," wrote Jason Rezaian, a *Washington Post* columnist and former Tehran bureau chief who was imprisoned with his Iranian wife in 2014 for 18 months on charges of espionage. "But a prolonged and principled commitment by activists inside Iran and their supporters in the international community of human rights advocacy to extend women's liberties is paying off."[11]

In February, Alinejad met with Secretary of State Mike Pompeo in Washington and urged him to speak out more forcefully against Iran's discrimination against women.[12]

"I fear the Trump administration will cut a deal with Tehran that ignores human rights, emboldening the clerical regime to crack down on domestic opposition without concern for international pressure," she later said.[13]

—*Jonathan Broder*

[1] "Iran: Family of women's rights activist arrested in despicable attempt to intimidate her into silence," Amnesty International, Sept. 25, 2019, https://tinyurl.com/y5tctqs4.

[2] "Masih Alinejad," Human Rights Foundation, 2019, https://tinyurl.com/yht2lopv.

[3] "Iranian women defiant against compulsory hijab," *Deutsche Welle*, June 2, 2018, https://tinyurl.com/y49om7pq.

[4] *Ibid.*

[5] Masih Alinejad, "My Brother Ali Is Iran's Latest Hostage," *The Wall Street Journal*, Oct. 6, 2019, https://tinyurl.com/y2pe38po.

[6] Pip Cummings, "The day 100,000 Iranian women protested the head scarf," womenintheworld.com, Sept. 15, 2015, https://tinyurl.com/y34owyj2.

[7] Haleh Esfandiari, "The Women's Movement," *The Iran Primer: Power, Politics and U.S. Policy* (2010), p. 45.

[8] *Ibid.*

[9] *Ibid.*

[10] Farnaz Fassihi, "Iran's 'Blue Girl' Wanted to Watch a Soccer Match. She Died Pursuing Her Dream," *The New York Times*, Sept. 10, 2019, https://tinyurl.com/yyubwg6l; "Iran Adopts Amendment Allowing Women To Pass Citizenship To Children," *Radio Farda*, Oct. 2, 2019, https://tinyurl.com/y2qw92ux.

[11] Jason Rezaian, "Women in Iran need America's help. Why won't we give it to them?" *The Washington Post*, Oct. 8, 2019, https://tinyurl.com/y5a5roka.

[12] "Pompeo Tells Iranian Rights Activist of U.S. Support" *Radio Farda*, Feb. 5, 2019, https://tinyurl.com/yez9ktvs.

[13] Alinejad, *op. cit.*

Also during the decade, the United States was drawn into conflict with Iran during the 1980-88 Iraq-Iran war, the Middle East's longest and bloodiest armed struggle. Iraq initiated the war by invading Iran to prevent Tehran from inciting Iraq's predominantly Shiite population to revolt. The United States provided Iraq with intelligence and chemicals to produce poison gas, which the Iraqis used against the Iranians. In addition, after a Kuwaiti oil tanker struck Iranian mines in the Persian Gulf, the Reagan administration placed Kuwait's entire tanker fleet under the U.S. flag and sent Navy warships to escort them in and out of the gulf. In 1987,

Iranians Say Sanctions Block Critical Medicines

"People are losing their lives."

D r. Ghader Daemi Aghdam, the director of a Tehran pharmacy, has the difficult job of informing many customers that he cannot fill their prescriptions. The reason: U.S. sanctions on Iran.

"Out of every 20 people, we have to tell at least 10 that we have run out of medications they need," Aghdam said.[1]

Although the Trump administration asserts that medicine, food and other humanitarian goods are exempt from the U.S. sanctions on Iran, economists and Iran experts say international banks and foreign suppliers have stopped selling Tehran any items—even humanitarian goods—in order to avoid any risk of violating American sanctions.

"Even if an item is not under U.S. sanctions, banks and foreign vendors shy away from doing business with Iran because they're afraid they could still fall afoul of the U.S. and lose access to the U.S. market," says Adnan Mazarei, an Iran expert at the Peterson Institute for International Economics, a Washington think tank.

President Trump reimposed economic sanctions on Iran after he pulled the United States out of a 2015 international agreement limiting Iran's nuclear activities. Trump said he did so in hopes that it would force Tehran to return to the negotiating table for a more stringent agreement halting Iran's ballistic missile programs and support for violent proxy groups in the region, as well as its nuclear activities.

Although humanitarian items are supposed to be exempt from the sanctions, pharmacies, clinics, hospitals and their patients across Iran face growing shortages. Most imports of medicines or ingredients needed to manufacture local versions of drugs have halted. Meanwhile, imports of lifesaving medical equipment, such as lasers, X-ray machines and blood centrifuges remain under sanction because the United States considers them dual-use items that can be used for civilian and military purposes.

Iran experts say the sanctions have hit the economy hard overall but have been particularly devastating for those struggling to secure medicines. Even if people can find medicines, the country's soaring inflation rate, last gauged at more than 40 percent, puts them beyond the reach of most Iranians, whose median monthly salary is around $1,200.[2] Economists say many have taken second and third jobs to afford their prescriptions—if they can be found. Others have been forced to forgo treatments to avoid financial ruin.

A woman named Sarah, who declined to give her last name, told *The Washington Post* she must buy imported nutritional supplements for her elderly father, who suffers from macular degeneration, an age-related deterioration of the retina. Before the sanctions, she said, the supplements cost around $7. Once the sanctions kicked in last November, however, the supplements disappeared from many pharmacies and cost $70 where they could be found.

"All the prices have gone up," she said, "and we can't find many products anymore."[3]

Muhammad Sahimi, an Iranian-born chemical engineering professor at University of Southern California, said a relative in Iran cannot find medicine for her multiple sclerosis at any price. Sahimi and his wife, an Iranian-educated medical doctor, are still in touch with medical colleagues in Iran.[4]

"Every single member of this network has been telling us the same thing: that the shortage of critical medicine is so severe that people are losing their lives," he said.[5]

Without official statistics on how many Iranians have died from sanctions-related shortages of medicine, data on the number of people suffering from various diseases help define the scope of the shortage. According to Iranian health officials, 5.2 million Iranians have diabetes, more than 248,000 have cancer, and some 70,000 have Alzheimer's disease. Another 23,000 suffer from

U.S. warships destroyed two Iranian oil rigs in the Persian Gulf after Iranian missile attacks on several reflagged tankers. And after an Iranian mine badly damaged a U.S. Navy destroyer in 1988, U.S. air and naval forces sank or crippled half of Iran's naval ships.[43]

The war ended in 1988 after a U.S. warship shot down an Iranian civilian airliner over the gulf, killing all 290 people aboard.[44] Exhausted after eight years of fighting and convinced the airliner downing signaled the U.S.' entry into the conflict, Khomeini accepted a U.N-

thalassemia, a genetic blood disorder; 7,000 suffer from multiple sclerosis; and some 6,000 are registered AIDS patients, although experts believe that number is low.[6]

To help alleviate the medicinal shortages, the Trump administration could issue clearer guidelines to banks and vendors for handling humanitarian exports to the Islamic Republic, says Ariane Tabatabai, an Iran analyst at the RAND Corp., a Washington think tank. But the administration says that is Tehran's problem, not Washington's.

"The burden is not on the United States to identify the safe channels" for humanitarian exports to Iran, Brian Hook, the administration's point man on Iran, told reporters at a briefing last November. "The burden is on the Iranian regime to create a financial system that complies with international banking standards to facilitate the provision of humanitarian goods and assistance."[7]

But Tabatabai and others point out that the administration used the threat of sanctions to quash a European plan to activate just such a channel—a so-called special purpose vehicle—that the Europeans created to use barter rather than dollar transfers to facilitate humanitarian trade with Iran. The Trump administration said the vehicle could undercut the effectiveness of sanctions, not only on Iran, but on other countries in the future. Facing U.S. sanctions on them, the Europeans backed away from their plan.

In a later briefing, Hook lashed out at Iranian officials for portraying the administration's exemptions for medicines as disingenuous. "The regime's attempts to mischaracterize these humanitarian exemptions are a pathetic effort to distract from its own corruption and mismanagement," he said. "The regime has enough money to invest in its own people."[8]

Nevertheless, the sanctions have fostered deep resentment toward Washington among ordinary Iranians, many of whom had expressed admiration for the United States after the U.S.-brokered 2015 nuclear accord lifted nuclear-related sanctions and allowed foreign goods to flow into Iran. Now, polls show, a majority blame the United States for seeking to prevent humanitarian products from reaching Iran.[9]

"It's remarkable how poisoned public opinion has become in Iran toward the United States," says Esfandyar Batmanghelidj, an economist and publisher of *Bourse & Bazaar*, a London-based Iranian business magazine. "My big concern is that the United States may not be able to repair its image in Iran at the end of this episode. I don't think there's an awareness in Washington of how detrimental it is to take a population that admired the U.S. and then tarnish America's image to no obvious end. That's the political impact that Washington needs to worry about."

—*Jonathan Broder*

[1] Somayeh Malekian, "As US sanctions hit Iran, residents complain of medicine shortages," *ABC News*, June 25, 2019, https://tinyurl.com/yxwke2lx.

[2] "Average salary in Iran 2019," Salaryexplorer.com, undated, https://tinyurl.com/y59s47q6.

[3] Erin Cunningham, "Fresh sanctions on Iran are already choking off medicine imports, economists say," *The Washington Post*, Nov. 17, 2018, https://tinyurl.com/y7b4ejx4.

[4] Muhammad Sahimi, "Economic Sanctions will Kill Tens of Thousands of Innocent Iranians," Lobelog.com, July 30, 2019, https://tinyurl.com/y3aqttoc.

[5] *Ibid.*

[6] "Concerning statistics of diabetics in Iran," Khabaronline.ir, Jan. 1, 2019, https://tinyurl.com/y5cglst6; "Iran, Islamic Republic of," International Agency for Research on Cancer, World Health Organization, 2018, https://tinyurl.com/y5h5gsvf; "70,000 people in Iran have Alzheimer's," *BBC Persian Service*, May 6, 2018, https://tinyurl.com/yydqjomc; "Thalassemia Patients at Passage of Suffering and Hope," *Islamic Republic News Agency*, May 1, 2019, https://tinyurl.com/yysmp7bn; "MS Statistics in Iran," alef.ir, June 1, 2019, https://tinyurl.com/yxd4kcaq; and "The latest AIDS statistics in Iran and the world," Shahid Beheshti Medical Sciences Agency, Nov. 5, 2018, https://tinyurl.com/y4xtyko7.

[7] Cunningham, *op. cit.*

[8] *Ibid.*

[9] "Iranian Public Opinion under 'Maximum Pressure,'" Question No. 8, Center for International and Security Studies at Maryland, Oct. 1-8, 2019, https://tinyurl.com/y3n48t8a.

brokered ceasefire, ending the war he had pledged to wage until Iran's total victory.

After Khomeini's death in 1989, hard-liner Ayatollah Ali Khamenei ascended to the supreme leader's post, and moderates Akbar Hashemi Rafsanjani and Mohammad

Khatami served as president from 1989 to 2005. The two presidents allowed Iranians more freedoms and improved relations with other countries, including the United States.

In 1995, Democratic President Bill Clinton tightened sanctions, banning all U.S. trade with Iran, in response to what the United States called Tehran's "malign" activities in the region. The embargo undermined Iran's moderates, whose reforms were already under attack from Khamenei and his supporters in parliament. By the end of Khatami's second term, a deep political rift had opened between Iran's moderates and conservatives.[45]

In 2001, the Sept. 11 terrorist attacks led to a short period of cooperation between Iran and the United States. Iran had long opposed Afghanistan's Taliban regime and the al Qaeda terrorists it harbored, both strict Sunni fundamentalist groups who regarded all Shiites as heretics. Tehran condemned the 9/11 attacks and quietly provided special forces to help the U.S. military topple the Taliban.[46] Iran also helped the United States form a new pro-Western Afghan government.[47]

But Republican President George W. Bush ignored Tehran's assistance and in his first State of the Union speech in 2002 lumped Iran with Iraq and North Korea as part of an "axis of evil." He threatened U.S. military action to block their nuclear programs. But Iran persisted, volunteering to arm, train and support 20,000 Afghan troops under a U.S.-led program. American officials never responded to Iran's offer.[48]

After the U.S. invasion of Iraq in 2003, Iran—fearing it was next—made a sweeping offer to address the issues dividing Washington and Tehran. But the Bush administration did not respond to that offer, either.[49] Instead, the United States and Israel launched a cyberattack on Iran's nuclear program, using the Stuxnet virus to destroy scores of centrifuges used to enrich uranium.[50]

Shifting Policy

In 2005, Mahmoud Ahmadinejad, the hard-line mayor of Tehran, was elected president of Iran. As U.S. troops became bogged down by insurgencies in Iraq, Iran shifted policy and threw its support behind Iraqi Shiite militias fighting the Americans. Over the next four years, the militias killed hundreds of U.S. troops.

When Democratic President Barack Obama took office in 2009, he reached out to Iran in a broadcast. "My administration is now committed to diplomacy that addresses the full range of issues before us," Obama said.[51] The top issue was Iran's nuclear program, which U.S. and Israeli officials suspected was aimed at developing a nuclear weapon.

But Israel threatened Obama's diplomatic effort, letting the administration know it planned to bomb Iran's nuclear infrastructure before it became too advanced. Obama repeatedly dispatched senior U.S. officials to Jerusalem to argue that an attack would spark another Mideast war that inevitably would involve the United States. But Israeli Prime Minister Netanyahu argued that Iran's response would be limited. Besides, he added, an Israeli strike would not only derail Iran's nuclear program but also spark the overthrow of the Tehran regime.[52]

The administration did not know whether Netanyahu was bluffing. So as U.S. spy satellites watched Israel openly prepare for an attack, Obama chose another strategy: secret negotiations with Iran. In late 2010, two top White House aides flew to Oman, where they quietly hammered out a framework for negotiations with Iranian officials representing Khamenei.[53]

In 2013, prospects for better relations with Iran brightened after moderate Rouhani was elected president and indicated during a trip to the U.N. General Assembly that his government was ready to engage with the United States.[54] A few days later, Secretary of State John Kerry and Iranian Foreign Minister Zarif met to discuss how to follow up on the framework agreement reached in Oman.[55]

Their meeting launched intense negotiations for a nuclear accord between Zarif and Kerry and the foreign ministers of Russia, China, Britain, France, Germany and the European Union. On July 14, 2015, after two years of talks, they signed the Joint Comprehensive Plan of Action (JCPOA), under which Iran agreed to curtail its nuclear program in return for relief from international sanctions. The U.N. Security Council endorsed the deal, giving it the imprimatur of international law.[56] The United States, however, kept its non-nuclear sanctions in place.

Israel and Saudi Arabia castigated the accord, noting that it failed to address non-nuclear threats, such as Iran's ballistic missile program and its support for proxy forces across the region. Trump adopted that view as he campaigned for the 2016 Republican presidential nomination and pledged to withdraw the United States from the agreement if elected.

Trump made good on that promise in May 2018, despite repeated U.N. certifications that Iran was in full compliance with the agreement's provisions. Six months later, Trump reimposed crippling economic sanctions on Iran, reigniting the hostility and distrust that had poisoned U.S.-Iran relations for nearly 40 years.

CURRENT SITUATION
Escalating Standoff

Washington and Tehran are now locked in an escalating standoff that could explode into a major Middle East war unless the two sides can reach a diplomatic solution, warn many former officials and regional experts. But the chances of negotiations taking place anytime soon seem remote.

For now, both countries, as well as Iran's rival Saudi Arabia, have stepped back from the brink, sobered by September's suspected Iranian attack against Saudi oil facilities. But Trump's overall strategy of strangling Iran's economy remains in place, as has Tehran's unyielding resistance. If those policies persist, a military confrontation is more likely than not, observers say.

"That's why we've got to be very, very careful," says former Ambassador Crocker. "The law of unintended consequences is always in force in the Middle East."

In early 2019, Iran hoped the Europeans would maintain the economic investments and other benefits promised by the nuclear deal and also sought to gain leverage by gradually reviving its nuclear program, in deliberate violation of the 2015 accord. The breaches could be reversed if the Europeans came through, Tehran said. But the U.S. sanctions proved too intimidating for the Europeans to move ahead with the plan for a special trade-financing mechanism using barter instead of U.S. dollars.

U.S.-Iran tensions have intensified significantly since April, when the Trump administration refused to renew waivers that allowed eight countries to continue buying Iranian oil.[57] The waivers had gone to Tehran's biggest customers—including China, India and Japan—whose oil purchases had helped insulate Iran's economy from the sanctions. With the cancellation of those waivers, the administration signaled its intention to shut down Iran's oil sector and maximize Iran's pain.

"We're going to zero across the board," said Pompeo as he announced the end of the waivers. "How long we remain there . . . depends solely on the Islamic Republic of Iran's senior leaders."[58]

Despite a subsequent plunge in Iran's oil sales and severe economic hardship for ordinary Iranians, the sanctions have had no apparent effect on Tehran's national security policies, according to Iran experts. "On the contrary, instead of Iranians backing down, coming to the negotiating table and begging on their knees for mercy, they have counter-escalated in almost every area of contention with the United States," says Iran expert Parsi.

Following Trump's withdrawal from the JCPOA last year, Tehran has gradually breached restrictions on Iran's nuclear program in an effort to pressure the accord's European signatories to come up with the JCPOA's promised economic benefits. In the most recent breach, President Hassan Rouhani said in November that Iran would accelerate its nuclear enrichment activities by injecting uranium gas into centrifuges at its underground Fordow facility. Under the JCPOA, Iran agreed to halt nuclear enrichment at that facility and use it for research. Meanwhile, Iran said it added dozens of advanced centrifuges to its uranium enrichment efforts, shortening the time needed to produce enough highly-enriched nuclear fuel for a bomb.[59]

Iran experts say Tehran also continues to support its Middle East proxies, as evidenced by the Sept. 14 drone-and-cruise-missile attack on Saudi oil facilities and Iran's recent moves to enhance the range and accuracy of missiles it has given Hezbollah, the Houthis and the Iraqi Shiite militias. "Even in the worst of times economically, those efforts are not underfunded," says Crocker. With an unpredictable Trump at the helm of U.S. forces, he adds, "national security remains Iran's paramount priority."

Trump's October announcement that he was implementing his decision last year to withdraw U.S. troops from Syria has created yet another political vacuum for Iran's Shiite proxies to fill, say Arab affairs analysts. Obama had deployed around 2,000 U.S. special operations forces to northeast Syria in 2014 to help Kurdish forces fight the Islamic State. The U.S. pullback will give the Iranians "the operational space to expand their

Will U.S. sanctions force Iran to the negotiating table?

YES — Djavad Salehi-Isfahani
Professor of Economics, Virginia Tech

Written for *CQ Researcher*, November 2019

Since May 2018, Iran's economy has taken a serious beating due to U.S. sanctions. After contracting by 4.9 percent in 2018, Iran's economy will contract by 9.5 percent this year, according to the International Monetary Fund. Since 2012, sanctions have cost a total of about half a trillion U.S. dollars, nearly the same as Iran's GDP.

Iranian leaders are under increasing pressure to restore economic growth. But they believe the Trump administration's primary objective is Iran's capitulation or regime change, and the leadership is divided on the benefits from dialogue with the United States and on how badly Iran needs to end the sanctions.

Iran's Supreme Leader, Ayatollah Ali Khamenei, who has been advocating a "resistance economy" for 10 years, sees proximity to the West as undermining Islamic values. He is optimistic that the economy can function with—and even benefit from—very low oil exports. Employment data for the first half of the Iranian year (March 21 to Sept. 20) support his optimism: About 800,000 more people are working in Iran now than when sanctions began in 2018, and the unemployment rate has dropped by 2 percentage points.

The jump in jobs and output is not surprising, because the economy has unused capacity that is being used to replace imports. Devaluation in 2018 also raised average prices of imported goods by 2 to 3 times, making local production more profitable. But such recovery has its limits.

Pressure from U.S. sanctions is unlikely to abate, at least not until 2021 and then only if Trump loses the 2020 election. Serious obstacles to long-term recovery remain. Investment as a share of GDP has declined, from about 20 percent in 2011 to about 14 percent in 2018. This level of investment is barely enough to keep up with depreciation of existing capital. Having lost its major source of revenue from oil, the government is unlikely to take the lead in an investment-fueled recovery. The equally cash-strapped private sector cannot count on much help from the banking system, which is still recovering from a decade-long crisis of insolvency.

Unless the government can overcome these challenges and the economy begins to bear fruit soon, pressures from the decade-long stagnation will strengthen those who argue for re-engaging with the West. But this may not be enough to bring Iran to renegotiate the nuclear deal anytime soon.

NO — Esfandyar Batmanghelidj
Founder, Bourse & Bazaar

Written for *CQ Researcher*, November 2019

The Trump administration has been adamant that its "maximum pressure" sanctions are bringing the Iranian economy to the brink of collapse. But even as the country grapples with the harsh realities of a 9.5 percent contraction in GDP in 2019, the pending recovery of the Iranian economy is easy to demonstrate across four basic datasets.

First, Iran's foreign exchange market has stabilized. Since early May, the Iranian rial has regained around 30 percent of its value against the dollar. The value of the rial has remained stable after the Central Bank of Iran implemented new oversight systems, even as geopolitical tensions reached new highs this past summer.

Second, while inflation remains high and continues to erode the purchasing power of Iranian households, the recent recovery of the rial has seen inflation grow at the slowest pace since the reimposition of sanctions 18 months ago. The consumer price index rose at an annual rate of only 6.1 percent in September. As economist Djavad Salehi-Isfahani recently observed: "Price stability is necessary for economic recovery, and the trend in inflation is in the right direction for Iran."

Third, Iran's purchasing manager's index, which measures whether the manufacturing sector is expanding or contracting, has exceeded 50 in five of the last seven months. An index greater than 50 reflects an expansion in manufacturing activity compared to the previous month. Iran's assembly lines keep whirring, and Iran continues to produce goods for export.

Finally, Iran's non-oil exports are projected to reach a record level this year—more than $40 billion—exceeding oil exports for the first time. Oil exports will be limited to around $10 billion in 2019 after the Trump administration revoked key sanctions waivers. The recourse to non-oil trade means Iran will continue to earn vital foreign currency, further reducing dependence on an oil industry that rarely accounted for more than 20 percent of Iran's GDP.

In short, the harm the Trump administration has inflicted on so many Iranian households does not, in fact, equate to fundamental vulnerability in the Iranian economy.

growing network of Shiite foreign fighters, who can be mobilized and moved throughout the Middle East," the RAND Corp.'s Tabatabai and her colleague Colin P. Clarke said after Trump first announced the Syria withdrawal last year.[60]

Other analysts say Trump's recent statement that the situation in Syria has "nothing to do with us" also sends the message to Saudi Arabia, Israel and other U.S. allies in the Middle East that Washington will no longer block Iran's designs on the region.[61]

De-Escalating Tension

Meanwhile, Iran's preference to avoid a military confrontation has been evident in the care it has taken not to kill or wound any Americans in the region and by denying responsibility for the most aggressive incidents. The Trump administration also has kept its responses to those incidents below the threshold of war.

In June 2019, when Tehran acknowledged downing the unmanned U.S. surveillance drone, Iranian officials pointed out that they had refrained from shooting down an accompanying U.S. Navy P-8 maritime patrol aircraft carrying 35 crew members.[62] After Trump cancelled retaliatory airstrikes on Iran, he launched a nonlethal cyberattack that wiped out Iran's database for tracking ship traffic in the Persian Gulf. It was Trump's answer to suspected Iranian attacks in May, which Iran denied, that damaged several foreign tankers in and around the Persian Gulf.

After the attack on Saudi oil facilities, Trump resisted hawkish lawmakers' calls to retaliate militarily against Iran, mounting instead another cyberattack on Iran's "propaganda" infrastructure, U.S. officials said. "You can do damage without killing people or blowing things up; it adds an option to the toolkit that we didn't have before, and our willingness to use it is important," said James Lewis, a cyber expert with the Center for Strategic and International Studies, a centrist Washington think tank.[63]

Iran also appears to be exhibiting similar caution with Saudi Arabia. When two explosions ripped gaping holes in an Iranian oil tanker sailing off the kingdom's Red Sea coast on Oct. 11, 2019, the state-run National Iranian Oil Co. that owns the ship initially claimed the Saudis had fired two missiles at the tanker, raising fears of

FAYEZ NURELDINE/AFP via Getty Images

Saudi Arabian Defense Ministry spokesman Turki bin Saleh al-Malki displays pieces of what he said were Iranian cruise missiles and drones recovered from a September 2019 attack that targeted the Saudi oil infrastructure. Iran has denied involvement.

Iranian retaliation. But later, the company said the origin of the explosions was unclear.[64]

Rouhani and Zarif now say a foreign government carried out the tanker attack, but they have stopped short of naming the government. "All this shows that Iran wants to de-escalate the tension," said Imad K. Harb, the head of research at the Arab Center, an independent Washington think tank that focuses on Middle East issues.[65]

Apparently, Saudi Arabia—which has been sobered by Trump's lack of military response to the attack on its oil facilities—also wants to reduce tensions. Crown Prince Mohammed bin Salman, the kingdom's de facto ruler, reportedly asked Iraq's prime minister to see if Iran's leaders would be willing to de-escalate tensions.[66] "The political and peaceful solution is much better than the military one," Prince Mohammed told *CBS*' "60 Minutes" in September 2019.[67]

Some Arab affairs analysts say the best way to reduce regional tensions is for Iran and Saudi Arabia to negotiate maritime security in the Persian Gulf and an end to the war in Yemen. One aspect of that conflict appeared to be resolved in November, when separatists in Southern Yemen, backed by the United Arab Emirates, signed a peace agreement with the ousted Saudi-backed Yemeni government, which had made the southern port city of Aden its interim seat. In August, the separatists seized Aden in a move that split the Saudi-led Arab coalition fighting the Houthis and opened a fresh front in Yemen's civil war. Prince Mohammed said the peace agreement, which gives the separatists and other southern groups half the seats in any new Yemeni cabinet, opens the way for a broader peace accord between the Saudi-backed government and the Houthis.[68]

But in the wake of the September attack on the kingdom's oil facilities, distrust remains a major hurdle to any Saudi-Iranian reconciliation. "Efforts at de-escalation must emanate from the party that began the escalation and launched attacks, not the kingdom," an official Saudi statement said.

OUTLOOK
Continued Standoff?

Middle East analysts agree negotiations are unlikely between the Trump administration and Iran before the 2020 U.S. elections. As long as the administration maintains its sanctions and Tehran continues to regard them as unacceptable, Iran probably will not come to the table.

Another obstacle to negotiations: President Rouhani's reform movement is expected to lose seats in Iran's parliamentary elections in February to hard-liners who reject any engagement with the United States, according to Iranian journalist and political analyst Saeid Jafari. And if Trump wins re-election, U.S. and Iranian experts agree, the administration's standoff with Iran will probably continue, with neither side in any hurry to enter into talks.[69]

The Peterson Institute's Mazarei says the sanctions eventually will force the Rouhani government to print more money, boosting inflation. But Tehran appears confident that the public, already accustomed to hardship, will weather the additional loss in real income, he says. "So we're talking about survival with considerable amounts of pain," he says.

Former ambassador Crocker agrees. "If President Trump's gamble is that the unhappiness of the Iranian population will lead to regime-destroying unrest, he's deluded," Crocker says. "The more damage our pressure does to the economy, the tighter the solidarity around the leadership becomes."

Public opinion polls in Iran support Crocker's analysis. A survey in May 2015—a few months before the JCPOA was signed—by the University of Maryland's Center for International & Security Studies showed that 26.3 percent of Iranians cited foreign sanctions and pressures as the major cause of Iran's economic woes. By October 2019, that number had grown to 37.5 percent.[70]

Even if a Democratic president returns the United States to the Iran nuclear deal and lifts the sanctions, Tehran anticipates that any new round of negotiations would include pressure for tighter restrictions on its nuclear program, missile development and support for regional proxies, says the RAND Corp.'s Tabatabai. Thus, she expects Iran to continue breaching the nuclear deal in order to accumulate leverage in future talks.

No matter who wins the U.S. election, analysts agree Iran likely will continue swaying elections in Lebanon and Iraq and providing military muscle for its proxies where Shiites are fighting for power or confronting Israel. At the same time, Israeli military strikes against those proxies in Lebanon, Syria and Iraq will continue, the analysts say. Likewise, military experts expect Iran to continue developing its missile capabilities, a far cheaper and more realistic national security option than trying to build up a modern air force while under sanctions.

Finally, veteran diplomats say, unless U.S. policy changes dramatically, the coming years likely will be marked by a deep distrust among America's allies of U.S. trustworthiness. Trump's abandonment of Kurdish allies in Syria has forced allies such as Israel and the Gulf Arab states to question, for the first time, long-standing U.S. security commitments. Others, like Turkey and Egypt, have turned to Russia for weapons.

It will take years to rebuild U.S. credibility, these diplomats say. "We've lost our political leverage in the region," says former ambassador Freeman. "We're in a world now where no one wants to put all their eggs in our basket."

Former IMF senior executive Askari predicts that tensions between the United States and Iran will continue to build, pushing both countries closer to a military confrontation they say they want to avoid.

"Time is not on the side of better Iran-U.S. relations," he said. "Distrust of the U.S. has ballooned among leaders in Tehran after the U.S. tore up the nuclear deal and exited the agreement. War, or an accidental war, is much more likely today than reconciliation and fruitful relations."[71]

NOTES

1. Michael D. Shear, Helen Cooper and Eric Schmitt, "Strikes on Iran Approved by Trump, Then Abruptly Pulled Back," *The New York Times*, June 20, 2019, https://tinyurl.com/y3r85vfg.

2. *Ibid.*; Michael D. Shear *et al.*, "Trump Says He Was "Cocked and Loaded" to Strike Iran, but Pulled Back," *The New York Times*, June 21, 2019, https://tinyurl.com/y47kclts.

3. "Editorial: Trump is inching closer to blowing up the Iran nuclear deal," *Los Angeles Times*, Jan. 13, 2018, https://tinyurl.com/yg37b385.

4. David E. Sanger and Julian E. Barnes, "The Urgent Search for a Cyber Silver Bullet Against Iran," *The New York Times*, Sept. 23, 2019, https://tinyurl.com/y5swrnd5.

5. Babak Dehghanpisheh, "If Iran can't export oil from the Gulf, no other country can, Iran's president says," *Reuters*, Dec. 4, 2018, https://tinyurl.com/yb6aqbm5.

6. "World Economic Outlook, October 2019: Global Manufacturing Downturn, Rising Trade Barriers," International Monetary Fund, October 2019, p. 60, https://tinyurl.com/y5xcnc7a.

7. Nancy Gallagher, Ebrahim Mohseni and Clay Ramsay, "Iranian Public Opinion Under 'Maximum Pressure,'" School of Public Policy, University of Maryland, Oct. 16, 2019, https://tinyurl.com/yyl9vh8u.

8. Michael R. Gordon, "U.S. Lays Out Demands for New Iran Deal," *The Wall Street Journal*, May 21, 2018, https://tinyurl.com/y9mwc2d9.

9. Nahal Toosi, "Democrats want to rejoin the Iran nuclear deal. It's not that simple," *Politico*, July 20, 2019, https://tinyurl.com/y6tdruyf.

10. "Diplomatic breakthrough remains unlikely, but war risk has fallen," Eurasia Group, Oct. 3, 2019, accessible to subscribers.

11. Asa Fitch and Aresu Eqbali, "Iranians Protest Economic Woes as New U.S. Sanctions Loom," *The Wall Street Journal*, Aug. 6, 2018, https://tinyurl.com/y566lte4.

12. Steve Inskeep, "Reporter's Notebook: Here's How Iran Is Functioning In The Face Of Sanctions," *NPR*, Aug. 27, 2019, https://tinyurl.com/y6r6kzbd.

13. Anjali Singhvi, Edward Wong and Denise Lu, "Defying U.S. Sanctions, China and Others Take Oil From 12 Iranian Tankers," *The New York Times*, Aug. 3, 2019, https://tinyurl.com/yyaeb7lp.

14. Kim Sengupta, "Turkey and Saudi Arabia alarm the West by backing Islamist extremists the Americans had bombed in Syria," *The Independent*, May 12, 2015, https://tinyurl.com/yj6l42lc.

15. Robin Wright, ed., *The Iran Primer: Power Politics, and U.S. Policy* (2010), p. 70.

16. Seth G. Jones, "War by Proxy: Iran's Growing Footprint in the Middle East," Center for Strategic and International Studies, March 11, 2019, https://tinyurl.com/y2j5xn3y.

17. David Ottoway, "Saudi Arabia Yemeni Quagmire," Wilson Center, Dec. 15, 2015, https://tinyurl.com/y45qvtac.

18. Iran Action Group, "Outlaw Regime: A Chronicle of Iran's Destructive Activities," U.S. Department of State, Sept. 25, 2018, https://tinyurl.com/y57ssy88.

19. Mohammed Tawfeeq, "Iraq protests death toll rises to 319 with nearly 15,000 injured," *CNN*, Nov. 10, 2019, https://tinyurl.com/y3hnjd37.

20. Hanin Ghaddar, "Iran is Losing the Middle East, Protests in Lebanon and Iraq Show," *Foreign Policy*, Oct. 22, 2019, https://tinyurl.com/yyybhnvy.

21. Benjamin Netanyahu, Twitter post, Aug. 24, 2019, https://tinyurl.com/y5slk6kh.

22. Brendan Cole, "Mike Pompeo says Iran must listen to U.S. 'if they want their people to eat," *Newsweek*, Nov. 9, 2018, https://tinyurl.com/yb84zjvx.

23. Sune Engel Rasmussen, "Iran's top diplomat warns of 'all-out war' if his country is attacked," *The Wall Street Journal*, Sept. 19, 2019, https://tinyurl.com/yysjkqlz.

24. Sabahat Khan, "What are Washington's options for a military faceoff with Iran?" *The Arab Weekly*, Oct. 6, 2019, https://tinyurl.com/yya7nr4t.

25. Robin Wright, *In the Name of God: The Khomeini Decade* (1989), p. 22.

26. Janet Afary, Khosrow Mostofi and Peter William Avery, "Iran," *Encyclopedia Britannica*, Oct. 30, 2019, https://tinyurl.com/yypl9pt3.

27. *Ibid.*

28. *Ibid.*

29. *Ibid.*

30. "Iran During World War II," Holocaust Encyclopedia, United States Holocaust Memorial Museum, undated, https://tinyurl.com/y3gcbh6k.

31. *Ibid.*

32. Stephen Kinzer, *All the Shah's Men: An American Coup and the Roots of Middle East Terror* (2003).

33. Gregory F. Rose, "The Shah's Secret Police Are Here," CIA.gov, Sept. 18, 1978, https://tinyurl.com/y4cb545c.

34. Jeb Sharp, "The US and Iran, part II: the Shah and the revolution," *Public Radio International*, Oct. 26, 2004, https://tinyurl.com/y35fgx59.

35. *Ibid.*

36. Wright, *In the Name of God*, *op. cit.*

37. Sharp, *op. cit.*

38. Dan Geist, "A Darker Horizon: The Assassination of Shapour Bakhtiar," *PBS Frontline*, Aug. 6, 2011, https://tinyurl.com/y3dp4le5.

39. "Ruhollah Khomeini," *New World Encyclopedia*, Aug. 31, 2019, https://tinyurl.com/y58s2t58.

40. Geist, *op. cit.*

41. "Iran hostage rescue mission ends in disaster," History.com, updated July 28, 2019, https://tinyurl.com/y5k572dy; Kate Hewitt and Richard Nephew, "How the Iran hostage crisis shaped the US approach to sanctions," The Brookings Institution, March 12, 2019, https://tinyurl.com/ydtuoh6u.

42. *Ibid.*; Roland Matthews *et al.*, "The Iran-Contra Affair," *Encyclopedia Britannica*, Feb. 7, 2019, https://tinyurl.com/yybd44ks.

43. Alex Chadwick and Mike Shuster, "U.S. Links to Saddam During the Iraq-Iran War," *NPR*, Sept. 22, 2005, https://tinyurl.com/y5rblfga; "Iraq-Iran War—The Tanker War, 1984-87," GlobalSecurity.org, undated, https://tinyurl.com/y5cp5tjm; and Stephen Andrew Kelley, "Better Lucky Than Good: Operation Earnest Will as Gunboat Diplomacy," Naval Postgraduate School, June 2007, https://tinyurl.com/y5nzgn3t.

44. *Ibid.*

45. Wright, "The Challenge of Iran," in *The Iran Primer*, *op. cit.*

46. Barbara Slavin, "Iran helped overthrow Taliban, candidate says," *USA Today*, June 9, 2005, https://tinyurl.com/y2kojl7o.

47. James Dobbins, "Engaging Iran," in Wright, *The Iran Primer*, *op. cit.*, p. 203.

48. *Ibid.*

49. *Ibid.*

50. Ronen Bergman and Mark Mazzetti, "The Secret History of the Push to Strike Iran," *The New York Times Magazine*, Sept. 6, 2019, https://tinyurl.com/y3b855hk.

51. Paul Reynolds, "Obama offers Iran 'new beginning,'" *BBC*, March 20, 2009, https://tinyurl.com/ch4n7r.

52. Bergman and Mazzetti, *op. cit.*

53. *Ibid.*

54. Rick Gladstone, "Iran's New President Preaches Tolerance in First U.N. Appearance," *The New York Times*, Sept. 24, 2013, https://tinyurl.com/yxwy2qss.

55. Julian Borger, "Breakthrough hailed as US and Iran sit down for nuclear deal discussion," *The Guardian*, Sept. 26, 2013, https://tinyurl.com/y2jl4yeo.

56. "Iran deal set to become international law," *CBS News*, July 17, 2015, https://tinyurl.com/yye3lre5.

57. Rebecca Kheel, "Trump removes sanctions waivers on countries buying oil from Iran," *The Hill*, April 22, 2019, https://tinyurl.com/y6mv8qvp.

58. *Ibid.*

59. Parisa Hafezi, "Iran further distances itself from 2015 deal by fueling Fordow centrifuges," *Reuters*, Nov. 5, 2019, https://tinyurl.com/y36zha4r; David E. Sanger and Richard Perez-Pena, "Iran Adds Advanced Centrifuges, Further Weakening Nuclear Deal," *The New York Times*, Nov. 4, 2019, https://tinyurl.com/y58o2ylo.

60. Colin P. Clark and Ariane M. Tabatabai, "Withdrawing From Syria Leaves a Vacuum That Iran Will Fill," *Foreign Affairs*, Jan. 8, 2019, https://tinyurl.com/yadqbxu7.

61. Peter Baker and Catie Edmondson, "Trump Lashes Out on Syria as Republicans Rebuke Him in House Vote," *The New York Times*, Oct. 16, 2019, https://tinyurl.com/y566t2f6.

62. Bozorgmehr Sharafedin, "Iran says it refrained from shooting down U.S. plane with 35 on board: Tasnim news," *Reuters*, June 21, 2019, https://tinyurl.com/y6n37d5w.

63. Idrees Ali and Phil Stuart, "Exclusive: U.S. carried out secret cyber strike on Iran in wake of Saudi oil attack: officials," *Reuters*, Oct. 16, 2019, https://tinyurl.com/y6pj5wwe.

64. Tom O'Connor, "Iran said another 'state' was behind a missile attack on its oil tanker," *Newsweek*, Oct. 15, 2019, https://tinyurl.com/yy6dtmvf.

65. Imad K. Harb, "Saudi Arabia and Iran may finally be ready for rapprochement," *Al-Jazeera*, Oct. 16, 2019, https://tinyurl.com/y4cybe9z.

66. Farnaz Fassihi and Ben Hubbard, "Saudi Arabia and Iran Make Quiet Openings to Head Off War," *The New York Times*, Oct. 4, 2019, https://tinyurl.com/y4e6raxo.

67. Norah O'Donnell, "Mohammad bin Salman denies ordering Khashoggi murder, but says he takes responsibility for it," "60 Minutes," *CBS*, Sept. 29, 2019, https://tinyurl.com/y3cpj73x.

68. Reuters, "Yemen's Government Signs Peace Deal With Southern Rebels," *The New York Times*, Nov. 6, 2019, https://tinyurl.com/y5fgquur.

69. Saeid Jafari, "Have Iran, US slammed door on nuclear negotiations?" *Al-Monitor*, Oct. 7, 2019, https://tinyurl.com/y3bmdyhz.

70. "Iranian Public Opinion Under 'Maximum Pressure,'" Center for International and Security Studies at Maryland, University of Maryland, Oct. 1-8, 2019, https://tinyurl.com/y3n48t8a.

71. Hossein Askari, "What Will it Take for Iran and the US to bury the Hatchet?" *The Globe Post*, Oct. 5, 2019, https://tinyurl.com/yyojogwh.

BIBLIOGRAPHY

Books

Barrett, **Roby C.**, *The Gulf and the Struggle for Hegemony: Arabs, Iranians, and the West in Conflict*, **Middle East Institute, 2016.**
A former State Department Arabist and adviser to U.S. special operations forces explores the histories of Iran and the Persian Gulf emirates and their turbulent relations with each other and the West.

Glaser, Charles R., and Rosemary Kelanic, eds., *Crude Strategy: Rethinking the US Military Commitment to Defend Persian Gulf Oil*, **Georgetown University Press, 2016.**
Essays by political scientists, historians and economists explain the implications of maintaining or withdrawing the U.S. military presence in the Persian Gulf.

Kinzer, Stephen, *All the Shah's Men: An American Coup and the Roots of Middle East Terror*, **John Wiley and Sons, 2003.**
A former *New York Times* foreign correspondent analyzes the ongoing foreign policy implications of the CIA's 1953 coup that toppled Iranian Prime Minister Mohammad Mosaddegh.

Parsi, Trita, *Losing an Enemy: Obama, Iran, and the Triumph of Diplomacy*, **Yale University Press, 2017.**
A Middle East adviser to former President Barack Obama provides an insider's look at the negotiations that produced the 2015 nuclear deal.

Wright, Robin, ed., *The Iran Primer: Power Politics and U.S. Policy*, **U.S. Institute of Peace, 2010.**
Experts analyze the Islamic Republic's government and military institutions and U.S. policy toward Iran.

Articles

Askari, Hossein, "What Will it Take for Iran and the US to bury the Hatchet?" *The Globe Post*, **Oct. 5, 2019, https://tinyurl.com/yyojogwh.**
An Iranian-born international relations professor outlines the steps needed for a U.S.-Iranian rapprochement.

Gordon, Michael R., "U.S. Lays Out Demands for New Iran Deal," *The Wall Street Journal*, May 21, 2018, https://tinyurl.com/y9mwc2d9.
The Trump administration presents a dozen conditions for a new agreement that would lift U.S. sanctions.

Harb, Imad K., "Saudi Arabia and Iran may finally be ready for rapprochement," *Al-Jazeera*, Oct. 16, 2019, https://tinyurl.com/y4cybe9z.
A Middle East expert details the compromises that Iran and Saudi Arabia will need to make to end their destabilizing rivalry for regional dominance.

Inskeep, Steve, "Reporter's Notebook: Here's How Iran Is Functioning In The Face Of Sanctions," *NPR*, Aug. 27, 2019, https://tinyurl.com/y6r6kzbd.
The host of *NPR*'s "Morning Edition" reports that Iran is surviving U.S. sanctions—so far.

Khan, Sabahat, "What are Washington's options for a military faceoff with Iran?" *Arab Weekly*, Oct. 6, 2019, https://tinyurl.com/yya7nr4t.
A Middle East analyst presents various ways in which U.S. military action against Iran could unfold.

Sanger, David E., and Julian E. Barnes, "The Urgent Search for a Cyber Silver Bullet Against Iran," *The New York Times*, Sept. 23, 2019, https://tinyurl.com/y5swrnd5.
In a bid to avoid a shooting war, the United States is retaliating against Iranian provocations in cyberspace.

Reports and Studies

"Outlaw Regime: A Chronicle of Iran's Destructive Activities," Iran Action Group, U.S. Department of State, Sept. 25, 2018, https://tinyurl.com/y57ssy88.
The Trump administration alleges a long list of Iranian illicit activities and support for terrorist operations.

Dizaji, Sijjad F., and Mohammad R. Farzanegan, "Do Sanctions Really Constrain Iran's Military Spending?" *Bourse & Bazaar*, Nov. 26, 2018, https://tinyurl.com/y6lezn5u.
Two scholars show that President Trump's unilateral U.S. sanctions are squeezing Iran's military budget, but broader international sanctions have had the strongest impact.

Esfandiari, Halah, "Iran and the Women's Question," Atlantic Council, Feb. 4, 2019, https://tinyurl.com/y4jg8s82.
An Iranian scholar traces the movement for women's rights in Iran since the 1979 revolution.

Jones, Seth G., "War by Proxy: Iran's Growing Footprint in the Middle East," Center for Strategic and International Studies, March 11, 2019, https://tinyurl.com/y2j5xn3y.
An international security expert analyzes the spread of Iranian influence across the Middle East via its network of Shiite militias in Afghanistan, Iraq, Lebanon, Syria and Yemen.

Katzman, Kenneth, "Iran: Internal Politics and U.S. Policy and Options," Congressional Research Service, May 30, 2019, https://tinyurl.com/yxbgctpo.
The research arm of the U.S. Congress examines the political rivalry between Iranian moderates and hardliners over policy toward the United States.

THE NEXT STEP

Iranian Proxies

Abdul-Zahra, Qassim and Joseph Krauss, "Protests in Iraq and Lebanon pose a challenge to Iran," *The Associated Press*, Oct. 30, 2019, https://tinyurl.com/y35hboqv.
Iran is trying to contain protests against governments they support in Iraq and Lebanon, with little success.

Bachner, Michael, "Iran said increasing Hamas funding to $30m per month, wants intel on Israel," *The Times of Israel*, Aug. 5, 2019, https://tinyurl.com/y5ecbf7p.
An Israeli television network reports that Iran plans to increase by fivefold the amount of money it provides each month to Hamas, a militant Palestinian group, in exchange for information about Israeli missile capabilities.

Sakelaris, Nicholas, "Houthi rebels claim they shot down a U.S. drone Friday," *UPI*, Nov. 1, 2019, https://tinyurl.com/y2dmddly.
Iranian-backed Houthi rebels in Yemen say they shot down an unmanned U.S. aircraft carrying out spying activities along the border with Saudi Arabia.

Rising Tensions

Lawson, Sean, "Why Did the U.S. Cyberattack Iran's Propaganda Network?" *Forbes*, Nov. 1, 2019, https://tinyurl.com/yyhrk884.
The United States responded to an alleged Iranian strike on Saudi oil facilities by launching a cyberattack on Iran's online propaganda network, which utilizes both humans and bots to spread pro-Iranian views on Twitter, Facebook and Instagram.

Schmitt, Eric, and David E. Sanger, "Trump Orders Troops and Weapons to Saudi Arabia in Message of Deterrence to Iran," *The New York Times*, Oct. 11, 2019, https://tinyurl.com/y64pfz4t.
The United States announced a further deployment of 3,000 troops to Saudi Arabia in response to increased Iranian attacks in the Gulf region.

South, Todd, *et al.*, **"What war with Iran could look like,"** *Military Times*, June 4, 2019, https://tinyurl.com/yxbym9hd.
Military experts speculate that a U.S. war with Iran would differ from the 2003 invasion of Iraq, lead to thousands of deaths and play out on multiple fronts, including through proxies and cyberwarfare.

Sanctions

"Iran: Sanctions Threatening Health," Human Rights Watch, Oct. 29, 2019, https://tinyurl.com/y2zjcjzt.
According to a report by Human Rights Watch, U.S. sanctions have hindered Iran's ability to import medicine and medical equipment, even though the sanctions specifically exempt such humanitarian imports.

Chiacu, Doina, and Daphne Psaledakis, "U.S., Gulf countries impose joint Iran-related sanctions on 25 targets," *Reuters*, Oct. 30, 2019, https://tinyurl.com/y6exz726.
The United States and several Middle Eastern countries issued new sanctions on businesses, banks and people linked to Iran's support for militant networks.

Mortazavi, Negar, "Trump renews sanction waivers to allow Russia, China and Europe to continue nuclear work in Iran," *The Independent*, Oct. 31, 2019, https://tinyurl.com/yxsvw9vz.
The Trump administration will continue to issue sanction waivers that allow companies from Russia, China and Europe to collaborate on Iran's civilian nuclear program, even as foreign policy hawks in the United States call for ending these exemptions.

Women's Rights

Alijani, Ershad, "Iranian police arrest more women for the 'crime' of dancing," *France 24*, Oct. 31, 2019, https://tinyurl.com/y2z5ce2x.
Iranian officials detained several female dancers who had tens of thousands of followers on Instagram for "obscene content creation."

Cranley, Ellen, "Fans are calling out an Iranian music streaming site for erasing women from their own album covers," *Insider*, Sept. 30, 2019, https://tinyurl.com/yxd6qdqy.
A music streaming site in Iran is removing images of female artists from album covers in order to comply with the country's strict censorship policy, which forbids women to appear with their heads uncovered.

Panja, Tariq, "Iranian Women Allowed to Attend Soccer Game for First Time Since 1981," *The New York Times*, Oct. 10, 2019, https://tinyurl.com/y5b54vmn.
Following weeks of outcry after a female soccer fan self-immolated to protest exclusionary policies, Iran allowed women to attend an international soccer match, but required them to sit in a separate section from the men.

For More Information

Arab Center Washington, 800 10th St., N.W., Suite 650, Washington, DC 20001; 202-750-4000; arabcenterdc.org. Independent think tank that produces academic research, policy papers and events focused on U.S.-Arab relations.

Atlantic Council, 1030 15th St., N.W., 12th Floor, Washington, DC 20005; 202-778-4952; atlanticcouncil.org. Independent think tank with several Iran-related programs; produces policy studies and hosts symposia and conferences.

Carnegie Endowment for International Peace, 1779 Massachusetts Ave., N.W., Washington, DC 20036-2103; 202-483-7600; carnegieendowment.org. Nonpartisan think tank whose Middle East program offers analysis and symposia focusing on political, economic and strategic developments in Iran and the Arab world.

Center for Strategic and International Studies, 1616 Rhode Island Ave., N.W., Washington, DC 20036; 202-887-0200; csis.org. Centrist think tank with a comprehensive Middle East program that holds conferences and generates Iran policy papers and country studies.

Center for Strategic Studies, 52 E. Pasteur St., Tehran, Iran; +9821-6445-3046; css.ir/fa. Official research arm of the Iranian president's office; produces policy papers.

Institute for Near East and Gulf Military Analysis, Dome Tower, Cluster N, Office 1306, Jumeirah Lake Towers, Dubai, United Arab Emirates; +971-4-399-8355; inegma. com. Arab think tank and consultancy that provides clients with expertise in political risk, energy security and defense trade.

Institute for Political and International Studies, Corner Shaheed Aghaei Street and Shaheed Bahonar Avenue, Niavaran, Tehran, Iran; +9821-2280-2656; ipis.ir. Official thank tank of the Iranian Foreign Ministry; produces policy studies and hosts lectures, conferences and roundtable discussions.

RAND Corp., 1200 S. Hayes St., Arlington, VA 22202; 703-413-1100; rand.org. Branch of California-based think tank that provides policymakers with objective analysis of political, economic and military events in Iran and the Arab world.

United States Institute of Peace, 2301 Constitution Ave., N.W., Washington, DC 20037; 202-457-1700; usip.org. Congressionally funded think tank that conducts research and policy analysis on Iran and Arab countries and briefs congressional staff and U.S. officials.

A patient with measles, a highly contagious disease, rests at the Amazon Tropical Medicine Foundation in Manaus, Brazil. In the first three months of 2019 the number of measles cases worldwide rose 300 percent compared to the same period in 2018, according to the World Health Organization.

From *CQ Researcher,*
September 13, 2019

2

Measles Resurgence

Can experts reduce skepticism about vaccines?

By Melba Newsome

THE ISSUES

Rachel's seven children range in age from 1 to 15. After her oldest received the vaccine for measles, mumps and rubella (MMR) when she was 18 months old, the child was hospitalized with a 106-degree fever. Despite her doctor's assurance that the vaccination was blameless, Rachel was unsatisfied. Information from an anti-vaccine advocacy group convinced her that vaccines were harmful, so she did not vaccinate her youngest children.

Rachel, who asked that her real name not be used, is an Orthodox Jew living in Brooklyn's Williamsburg neighborhood, where vaccination rates among the ultra-Orthodox community have dropped precipitously. Visitors from places where measles was spreading, such as Israel, enabled the disease to get a foothold in Brooklyn.[1] Similar conditions caused outbreaks in Rockland County, N.Y., and Ocean County, N.J. Washington state has had two outbreaks and 86 reported cases this year.[2] One was traced to an exposure at Sea-Tac Airport in Seattle and the other to Clark County in southern Washington, where only 78 percent of 6- to 18-year-olds are vaccinated.[3]

The World Health Organization (WHO) declared measles eliminated in the United States in 2000, but recently skepticism has arisen—fueled largely by misinformation on the internet and a campaign by high-profile critics—about the safety, efficacy and necessity of vaccines.

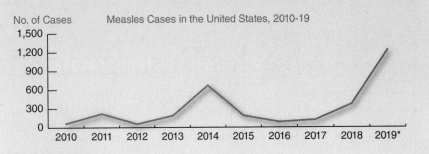

U.S. Measles Cases Spike in 2019

The number of measles cases in the United States this year reached 1,241 by Sept. 5, more than three times the number in all of 2018, according to the Centers for Disease Control and Prevention. The last spike in measles cases in the past decade occurred in 2014, with much of the increase resulting from an outbreak among unvaccinated Amish communities.

Measles Cases in the United States, 2010-19

No. of Cases

1,500 / 1,200 / 900 / 600 / 300 / 0

2010 2011 2012 2013 2014 2015 2016 2017 2018 2019*

* Through Sept. 5.

Source: "Measles Cases and Outbreaks," Centers for Disease Control and Prevention, U.S. Department of Health and Human Services, Sept. 9, 2019, https://tinyurl.com/y39perlm

states are eliminating exemptions from mandatory vaccination policies for schoolchildren, and health officials are using a variety of strategies to overcome skepticism about the necessity and safety of vaccines.

Measles is transmitted by direct contact with infectious droplets or spread through the air for up to two hours after an infected person breathes, coughs or sneezes. Babies, young children, pregnant women and people with compromised immune systems are at greatest risk. Measles is so contagious that a single child in a pediatric oncology clinic in Shanghai infected 23 other children; nearly 22 percent of them died and more than half suffered severe complications.[5]

Before the measles vaccine was introduced in 1963, about 4 million people in the United States contracted the disease annually, says Dr. Sandra Fryhofer, a member of the board of trustees of the American Medical Association. Of those who caught measles each year, 500 died, 48,000 had to be hospitalized and about 1,000 developed chronic disabilities from acute encephalitis, an inflammation and swelling of the brain that can cause hearing loss, pneumonia and brain damage, she says. "Worldwide, it killed between 2 and 3 million people annually," she says.

Before the development of vaccines, thousands of people each year were sickened, impaired and even killed by common illnesses such as measles, mumps and chicken pox. Vaccines have led to the decline or eradication of many of those diseases, leading to public complacency about the dangers of diseases such as the measles, says Dr. Anthony Fauci, director of the National Institute of Allergy and Infectious Diseases (NIAID), a division of the National Institutes of Health that conducts and supports research on infectious diseases.

A sign in the Williamsburg section of Brooklyn in New York City tells people who have been exposed to the measles or who have symptoms of the disease not to enter the building. Earlier in 2019, Mayor Bill de Blasio declared a state of emergency during a measles outbreak in the city's ultra-Orthodox Jewish community.

Immunization rates are down, particularly in certain communities, and the incidence of measles among the unvaccinated has been on the rise, reaching the highest level since 1992 during the first eight months of this year. Infectious disease experts say unless this trend reverses, the disease is poised to return full force this school year.[4] Some

Most Americans Support Mandatory Measles Vaccine

As the number of measles cases rises in the United States, Americans overwhelmingly support requiring that all children be vaccinated against the disease, a stricter rule than exists in most states today. A similar percentage say they have been vaccinated for measles, and 87 percent believe the vaccine is safe.

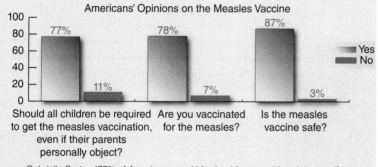

Americans' Opinions on the Measles Vaccine

Source: Gabriella Borter, "77% of Americans say kids should get measles shot even if parents object: Reuters Poll," Reuters, May 7, 2019, https://tinyurl.com/y3qcxdkr

streaming service after Rep. Adam Schiff, D-Calif., complained to Amazon CEO Jeff Bezos that it contained misleading information about vaccines.[11]

Despite the overwhelming scientific consensus that the MMR vaccine is safe for healthy children, reluctance to have children vaccinated continues to pose a public health challenge—and is not limited to the United States. The WHO calls such "vaccine hesitancy" one of the top 10 threats to global health and a serious hurdle to the worldwide eradication of measles.[12]

In the United States, all states have requirements for schoolchildren to receive the MMR vaccine, but 45 states allow parents to opt out for medical, religious or philosophical reasons. Many parents who oppose vaccines have done so using the philosophical and religious exemption.

Linda Fentiman, a professor at Pace University School of Law and author of *Blaming Mothers: American Law and the Risks to Children's Health*, says anti-vaxxers are "disproportionately people with more education, more wealth or more time. They typically cluster in groups, and the word spreads about how to claim exemptions."

But Richard Moskowitz, a family physician specializing in homeopathic medicine, has a different view. In his book, *Vaccines, A Reappraisal*, he wrote that making vaccines mandatory poses significant risks of disease, injury and death, deprives citizens of genuinely informed consent and prevents parents from making health care decisions for their own children.

"If you cannot voluntarily decide when and for what reason you are willing to risk your life or the life of your child, your unalienable right to life and liberty has been taken from you," said Barbara Loe Fisher, co-founder and president of the National Vaccine Information Center, a group based in Sterling, Va., that lobbies for vaccine safety reforms and for informed consent protections for parents.[13]

Although health officials in New York declared on Sept. 3, 2019, that the measles outbreak there had ended, by Sept. 5, 2019, 1,241 measles cases have been reported nationwide, with cases in 31 states, according to the latest report from the U.S. Centers for Disease Control and Prevention (CDC).[6] Of those who caught measles this year, 130 people have been hospitalized and 65 have suffered complications such as pneumonia or encephalitis.[7]

Moreover, preliminary data from the WHO indicates measles is on the rise worldwide, with reported cases up 300 percent in the first three months of this year over the same period in 2018.[8] A 43-year-old Israeli flight attendant and mother of three contracted the disease in March after flying from New York City to Israel. She suffered brain damage, fell into a coma and died on Aug. 13, the third measles death in Israel since 2018.[9]

Public health officials blame this year's measles outbreaks on anti-vaccine groups and misinformation spread via the internet, social media and through documentaries such as *Vaxxed: From Coverup to Catastrophe*. This film was written, produced and directed by Andrew Wakefield, a British researcher who is best known for writing a 1998 article in the British medical journal *The Lancet* linking vaccines to autism, which has since been discredited.[10] Amazon removed *Vaxxed* from its video

Fisher was referring to vaccines in general, and neither Fisher not Moskowitz gave examples of children dying from getting the MMR vaccine. In fact, the MMR appears to be one of the safest vaccines available, according to data from the National Vaccine Injury Compensation Program, a federal program that compensates people who have been injured by vaccines.

An anti-vaccine parent holds up a prescription document as she waits to enter a hearing about vaccines before the Senate Committee on Health, Education, Labor & Pensions in March, 2019. While some celebrities and internet activists help spread the idea that vaccines are unsafe, most Americans support mandatory vaccinations for schoolchildren.

John Leddy swings his 2-year-old daughter, Vanessa, with wife Christy Lambertson, at a park in Culver City, Calif. When the couple found out that the day care center they were considering for their daughter had a low measles vaccination rate, they decided not to enroll her there.

Between 2006 and 2017, some 101 million doses of the MMR vaccine were distributed in the United States, but only 123 people were compensated for an injury from the vaccine during that period, according to the program's database.[14]

While many vaccine opponents believe vaccines are unsafe, others make a different argument: Parents are best positioned to determine whether their child needs a particular vaccine and are better qualified than health experts or public health agencies to decide what is in their family's best interests.[15]

But Fentiman says it is not that simple. "No matter how much a parent tries to educate themselves, most are not physicians and aren't able to assess the risk because there is so much misinformation," she says. In addition, "When a parent decides not to vaccinate their child, other children are . . . being put at risk."

Several well-known people, ranging from President Trump—before he took office—to Hollywood celebrities, have at times used their highly visible platforms to spread doubts about vaccine safety and oppose mandatory vaccinations. In June 2019, actress Jessica Biel lobbied California state legislators against a proposed bill that would make it more difficult to claim a medical exemption, arguing that vaccine decisions should be left to parents, not mandated by the state. Other performers who have opposed mandatory vaccinations include Robert DeNiro, Jenna Elfman, Jim Carrey and Juliette Lewis.

"Celebrities have always had an exaggerated and often unwarranted influence on society," said Andrew Selepak, a media professor at the University of Florida. "That we place such high value on the uninformed opinions of celebrities is one problem, but the bigger problem is when we act on these uninformed opinions and it puts ourselves or others in danger."[16]

In 2014, before entering electoral politics, Trump, a Republican, lent credence to the discredited claim that vaccines can cause autism, tweeting: "Healthy young child goes to doctor, gets pumped with massive shot of many vaccines, doesn't feel good and changes— AUTISM. Many such cases!"[17] Shortly before he was sworn in as president, Trump met with vaccine skeptic Robert F. Kennedy Jr., who later said Trump asked him to lead a commission on vaccine safety. However, the commission was never formed.[18]

But after this year's measles outbreaks, the president urged parents to vaccinate their children. "They have to get the shots. The vaccinations are so important," Trump told reporters in April. "This is really going around now. They have to get their shots."[19]

Dr. Dean Blumberg, chief of pediatric infectious diseases at UC Davis Children's Hospital, says Trump's mixed message is harmful. "You need clear, consistent messaging. One slip-up and we're back to the conspiracy theories," says Blumberg. "Every time a respected public figure waffles on the issue, that is a definite setback that will take years to overcome."

In addition, if the Trump administration succeeds in its effort to overturn the Affordable Care Act, insurance companies will no longer be required to pay for federally recommended vaccinations with no out-of-pocket costs, making them unaffordable for many families, wrote University of Connecticut law professor John Aloysius Cogan Jr. in a piece for the medical news website *Stat*.[20]

U.S. health officials are using a variety of strategies to improve measles vaccination rates and halt the disease's spread, starting with repeatedly debunking widespread misinformation. Fauci, of the NIAID, says it is important to involve community and religious leaders and health care workers so skeptics can get reliable information from their peers rather than from government officials.

"Public health officials can't pejoratively confront them because that will turn them off," says Fauci. "We have to present the communities with the facts in a measured way and get them to understand that they need to make health decisions based on facts, not on distorted and false information."

BACKGROUND

Foundations Laid Early

Vaccines can be traced to 10th-century China, when the first precursor of today's immunizations was used to guard against smallpox.[21]

In 1796, English country doctor Edward Jenner inoculated an 8-year-old boy with pus from a cowpox lesion on a milkmaid's hand. Six weeks later, when Jenner infected the boy with smallpox, the disease failed to take hold, laying the foundation for modern vaccinology.

A painting by Georges Gaston Mélingue shows the first vaccination, performed by English doctor Edward Jenner, who is inoculating 8-year-old James Phipps in 1796 using pus from a cowpox lesion on a milkmaid's hand.

Christophel Fine Art/Universal Images Group via Getty Images

The 20th century ushered in the modern age of immunology with vaccines against pertussis, also called whooping cough, in 1914, diphtheria in 1926 and tetanus in 1938. By the late 1940s, vaccines were being mass-produced, allowing the implementation of disease control policies on a much broader scale.

Following a record-setting polio outbreak of almost 58,000 cases in 1952, medical researcher Jonas Salk announced he had developed a vaccination for the dreaded disease, which frequently caused paralysis and was often fatal. The polio vaccine was introduced in 1955, followed by the measles vaccine in 1963. Vaccines against mumps and rubella followed in 1967 and 1969, respectively. All three were combined into the MMR vaccine in 1971.

Every February the CDC updates its recommendations on who should receive vaccines, at what age, how many doses, the length of time between doses and what combination, if any, of vaccines should be given. While the CDC's recommendations are not mandatory, states typically use the CDC schedule as the basis for requiring children to be vaccinated before they can attend public schools. All 50 states and the District of Columbia require public school students to be vacci-

CHRONOLOGY

900s-1920s *Early efforts to immunize against disease are developed.*

900-1000 The variolation technique—deliberate infection with a disease—is developed in China to inoculate against smallpox.

1796 After noticing that milkmaids who contract cowpox appear immune to smallpox, English scientist Edward Jenner inoculates an 8-year-old boy with pus from a cowpox blister on the hand of an infected milkmaid. The boy does not contract smallpox. Two years later, Jenner publishes his work on the development of a smallpox vaccine.

1800 Benjamin Waterhouse, a Harvard professor of medicine, performs the first vaccinations in the United States on his children and works to encourage public immunization.

1885 French biologist Louis Pasteur prevents rabies in a 9-year-old boy with a live rabies vaccine. . . . Spanish physician Jaime Ferrán develops a live cholera vaccine, the first immunization against a bacterial disease.

1898 Greater regulation of pharmaceutical companies and advances in microbiology lead to increased vaccine safety and production.

1899 British military uses early version of typhoid vaccines during the second Boer war.

1902 After 22 children die from contaminated diphtheria and smallpox vaccines, Congress enacts the Biologics Control Act to establish government oversight of the purity of biological treatments.

1914 U.S. scientists develop vaccines for typhoid, rabies and tetanus.

1915 Vaccine against pertussis (whooping cough) is approved.

1923 Diphtheria vaccine is licensed.

1940s-1960s *Scientists develop additional vaccines.*

1945 The first influenza vaccine is approved in the United States for military use, and in 1946 for civilian use.

1949 The last case of smallpox in the United States is reported. . . . A combination vaccine to immunize against diphtheria, pertussis and tetanus is licensed.

1952 The worst polio epidemic in U.S. history results in 57,628 reported cases.

1954 American scientist John Enders and pediatrician Thomas Peebles isolate the measles virus in cell culture.

1955 American scientist Jonas Salk licenses the first polio vaccine. . . . Six years later, Albert Sabin's oral polio vaccine is licensed for use in the United States.

1962 The Vaccination Assistance Act allows the Centers for Disease Control and Prevention (CDC) to launch mass immunization campaigns.

1960s-2000 *As more vaccines are developed, questions are raised about the safety of immunization.*

1963 Measles vaccine is introduced.

1964 The U.S. surgeon general creates the Immunization Practices Advisory Committee to review the childhood immunization schedule and recommend newly licensed vaccines.

1966 The CDC announces the first national measles eradication campaign. . . . Two years later the incidence of measles has fallen by more than 90 percent.

1967 The U.S. Food and Drug Administration approves the mumps vaccine.

1971 A combined measles, mumps and rubella (known as German measles) vaccine (MMR) is developed.

1977 The Department of Health, Education and Welfare launches the national Childhood Immunization Initiative, which aims to achieve 90 percent vaccination levels among all U.S. children.

1980 The United Nations' World Health Assembly certifies that the world is free of naturally occurring smallpox.

1986 The Department of Health and Human Services establishes the Vaccine Adverse Event Reporting System to accept reports of suspected adverse reactions to vaccines against measles, mumps, rubella, polio, pertussis, diphtheria and tetanus.

1988 Congress establishes the National Vaccine Injury Compensation Program to compensate victims of vaccine-related injury or death.

1998 British medical journal *The Lancet* publishes a study linking vaccines to autism, an article it retracts 12 years later.

2000-Present *Despite advances in vaccines, immunization rates fall and measles makes a comeback in some areas as new controversies and fears arise about vaccine safety, largely spread via the internet.*

2000 The CDC declares measles eradicated in the United States.

2005 The CDC announces that rubella is no longer regularly found in the United States.

2014 U.S. measles cases spike to 667—up by more than threefold from the previous year's total—much of it due to an outbreak among unvaccinated Amish communities.

2018 Measles cases start to rise, up threefold from 2017.

2019 The CDC reports 1,241 measles cases in the United States as of Sept. 5, the highest number in 27 years. . . . The World Health Organization lists reluctance to undergo vaccination as one of the 10 greatest threats to global health.

nated, while allowing exemptions for medical reasons. Forty-four states and the district allow exemptions based on religious grounds and 15 states allow exemptions for personal, moral or other beliefs. Five states—New York, California, Maine, Mississippi and West Virginia—do not allow religious or philosophical exceptions.[22]

According to the CDC, children should receive the MMR vaccine shortly after their first birthday and a second dose between the ages of 4 and 6. This schedule confers immunity to measles, mumps and rubella to 97 percent of vaccinated children. The remaining 3 percent may still contract one of those diseases, though often with milder symptoms.

While vaccines have saved millions of lives over the years, some people have, in fact, been injured by vaccines. The federal government in 1986 established the National Vaccine Injury Compensation Program to compensate people injured by vaccines. By establishing the program, the government also exempted vaccine manufacturers from liability for injuries caused by vaccines. The program's online database indicates that the MMR vaccine is extremely safe compared to other vaccines: Of the 4,400 people compensated for injuries caused by the 3.5 billion vaccine doses distributed in the United States between 2006 and 2017, only 123 were compensated for injuries due to the MMR vaccine.[23]

Vaccines have often stirred controversy, with public reactions ranging from awe to skepticism and outright hostility.[24]

In 1998, the British medical journal *The Lancet* published a paper by Wakefield asserting a link between the MMR vaccine and autism, a condition characterized by challenges with social skills, repetitive behaviors, speech and nonverbal communication. Many parents seized on the study as proof that the vaccine was dangerous. But in 2010, after years of controversy, *The Lancet* retracted the paper, saying that several elements were incorrect. Wakefield later lost his medical license in the United Kingdom.[25]

Nevertheless, many anti-vaccine activists still cite that article as evidence that vaccines are dangerous. Experts say the internet and social media have greatly increased the ability to spread misinformation, taking a once-fringe issue mainstream.

In addition to the many sincere anti-vaccine activists, more nefarious actors have used social media to spread the message, Blumberg says. "This anti-vaccine message has been amplified by Russian bots because it creates conflict and creates discord," he says. "It's not surprising that the Russians would want U.S. children to be vulnerable to disease."

In addition, during a 2015 GOP presidential primary debate, candidates Trump, Ben Carson and Sen. Rand Paul all voiced concerns about vaccine safety. Trump told the story of a 2-year-old who allegedly became autistic after

"Herd Immunity" Acts As Shield

It protects those who cannot be vaccinated due to health reasons.

The term "herd immunity" refers to indirect protection from an infectious disease that occurs when a community or a population has near-universal immunity to the disease. It is usually achieved when a certain proportion of individuals in a particular population have been immunized, reducing the incidence of infection and thus protecting the population from new infection. [1]

With herd immunity, people who have not themselves been immunized have a lower risk of infection if the virus or disease is introduced into that community. In other words, vaccinations protect not only the immunized individuals but also those with whom they come in contact. Thus, if vaccination rates remain high, the disease becomes rare and may be eliminated altogether. "When a high percentage of people in the community are vaccinated, those vulnerable people who can't get vaccinated are protected because the virus has no place to spread," says Dr. Anthony Fauci, director of the National Institute of Allergy and Infectious Diseases.

This community immunity, as it is also known, only works for diseases spread directly between people, such as measles, mumps and rubella. It does not work on tetanus, for example, which is caught from bacteria in the environment.

In the case of measles, most Americans born before the 1970s became immune by contracting and surviving the virus. The first measles vaccine was developed in 1963, and the combined measles, mumps and rubella (MMR) vaccine was introduced in 1971. [2]

To achieve herd immunity, all 50 states, the District of Columbia and several U.S. territories require that children entering schools and child care receive the MMR vaccine. That raises the question frequently asked by vaccine skeptics: Why does failing to vaccinate a child pose a risk to him or her and others if the child is protected through herd immunity?

The answer, experts say, is that vaccination is the best protection against a disease. In addition, unless the unvaccinated individual stays in one location, surrounded by the same people, he or she cannot rely on the herd for protection. Traveling to a place with lower vaccine coverage puts the unvaccinated at risk. [3]

While vaccine-preventable diseases such as measles are rare in the United States, they are still prevalent elsewhere in the world. The recent measles outbreaks in Washington state and in the ultra-Orthodox communities in New York and New Jersey occurred after vaccination rates dropped

being vaccinated. Carson—a neurosurgeon—expressed concern that bundling vaccines like MMR might be dangerous and Paul, an ophthalmologist, suggested that mandatory vaccines infringed on parental freedom.[26]

"We are in a constant battle between what's true and not," says Dr. Robert McLean, President of the American College of Physicians. "The anti-vaxxer stuff is always a challenge because, even when you present [parents] with the facts, they don't believe them. They think they're selective facts."

CURRENT SITUATION
State Exemptions

Several state legislatures are reassessing their vaccine waiver policies after a dramatic increase in nonmedical exemptions has been shown to be associated with outbreaks of vaccine-preventable disease.[27]

On Jan. 25, 2019, Washington Gov. Jay Inslee, a Democrat, declared a state of emergency in all counties in response to more than two dozen confirmed cases of measles in the state. Months later, the state enacted a law that eliminated personal and philosophical objections to the MMR vaccine for children in public and private schools and day care centers.[28]

In New York state, a bill introduced by Democratic Sen. Brad Hoylman to discontinue the religious exemption for immunizations for public school students became law in June.[29]

On May 25, 2019, Maine enacted one of the country's toughest vaccination laws, removing all nonmedical exemptions. "It is my responsibility to protect the health and safety of all Maine people, and it has become clear that our current laws do not adequately protect against the risks posed," Democratic Gov. Janet Mills said in a written statement. Doctors and pediatric primary care

and infected travelers brought the virus into the United States, where it took hold in undervaccinated populations.

In addition, some people cannot be vaccinated for health reasons, such as being ill, taking medication that weakens the immune system, being allergic to the vaccine or one of its ingredients or having had a serious reaction to a vaccine in the past. Others are too young to be immunized. Such individuals are most vulnerable to infection and must rely on others for protection.

That protective shield is pierced or compromised when vaccination rates fall below those required to trigger herd immunity. The rate differs according to the disease, but it typically ranges between 90 percent and 95 percent. Because measles is the most infectious of the vaccine-treatable diseases, 93 percent to 95 percent of the population must be immunized for herd immunity to work. For a less contagious disease, such as polio, only 80 percent to 85 percent of the population would need to be vaccinated.

Before the MMR vaccine was introduced, every person with measles would infect another 10-15 people, leading to a rapid spread of the disease. Even a slight decline below the herd immunity threshold puts others at risk, with potentially disastrous consequences. In one 2015 case in China, a single baby with measles infected 23 other children in a pediatric oncology clinic, with a fatality rate of nearly 22 percent.[4] The children were too young to be fully vaccinated, and because they had cancer, their immune systems were compromised, so they were doubly at risk.

A study published in the journal *JAMA Pediatrics* found that a 5 percent reduction in MMR vaccination rates resulted in a threefold increase in annual measles cases. [5]

"Herd immunity through high vaccination rates helps minimize transmission of disease to the unvaccinated and people who are at the highest risk of severe infection," says Dr. Sandra Fryhofer, a member of the board of trustees of the American Medical Association. "Vaccines not only protect the child or adult who receives them but also the health of the community."

—Melba Newsome

[1] Paul Fine, Ken Eames and David L. Heymann, "'Herd Immunity:' A Rough Guide," *Clinical Infectious Diseases*, Vol. 52, Issue 7, April 1, 2011, pp. 911-916, https://tinyurl.com/ydz8mozw.

[2] "Vaccine History: Developments by Year," Children's Hospital of Philadelphia, undated, https://tinyurl.com/y47ds566.

[3] "Measles, Mumps and Rubella (MMR) Vaccination: What Everyone Should Know," U.S. Centers for Disease Control and Prevention, undated, https://tinyurl.com/y7joyjwh.

[4] Y.L. Ge *et al.*, "Measles outbreak in pediatric hematology and oncology patients in Shanghai, 2015," *Chinese Medical Journal*, June 5, 2017, https://tinyurl.com/y3762tax.

[5] Nathan C. Lo and Peter J. Hotez, "Public Health and Economic Consequences of Vaccine Hesitancy for Measles in the United States," *JAMA Pediatrics*, September 2017, https://tinyurl.com/yxfywubx.

givers will now determine if a child should receive a medical exemption and the Maine Center for Disease Control will report on the safety and effectiveness of vaccines in an effort to increase transparency. Unvaccinated students will have until 2021 to receive vaccinations required for school.

Given California's experience with such laws, they may not solve the problem of vaccine avoidance. After a measles outbreak that began at Disneyland in 2014, the state eliminated all religious and personal belief vaccine exemptions in 2015.[30] But parents exploited another provision in the law, says Catherine Flores-Martin, executive director of the California Immunization Coalition, an advocacy group in Sacramento that promotes full immunization in the state.

"Some found doctors willing to write medical exemptions so that their children would not get vaccinations and still be in school," she says. "We know this because they shared information on the internet, Facebook and other social media sites about where parents could find a vaccine exemption-friendly doctor."

California State Sen. Dr. Richard Pan, a Democrat and a pediatrician, introduced a bill to require that a doctor's waiver be approved by state health officials.[31] Both measures have been strongly opposed by anti-vaccine advocates, including Kennedy, and groups such as the Informed Consent Action Network and Parents United 4 Kids. Actress Biel traveled to the state Capitol in Sacramento to lobby against the new legislation. Opponents say these provisions violate patient-doctor relationships and infringe on medical freedom.

Dorit Reiss, a UC Hastings law professor, has written extensively about the vaccine requirements and testified

Should nonmedical vaccine exemptions be eliminated?

YES
Sandra Fryhofer, M.D.
Board Member, American Medical Association; Liaison to the Advisory Committee on Immunization Practices

Written for *CQ Researcher*, September 2019

Immunization programs are credited with having controlled or eliminated the spread of epidemic diseases, including measles, smallpox, mumps, rubella, diphtheria and polio. That public health success is in jeopardy today as a growing number of parents are refusing to vaccinate their children based on long-debunked claims about vaccine safety, efficacy or necessity.

According to the Centers for Disease Control and Prevention (CDC), the United States has the highest number of measles cases since the disease was considered eradicated nearly 20 years ago. This recent outbreak is the result of declining vaccination rates.

The scientific evidence is overwhelming that vaccines are among the safest and most effective medical interventions. Vaccines prevent death and illness from preventable diseases, such as measles, and safeguard public health by helping to prevent the disease from spreading to others in close contact. When individuals opt out as a matter of convenience, personal preference or misinformation, they put themselves and others at risk—particularly children too young to be vaccinated, cancer patients and other immunosuppressed patients who cannot be vaccinated.

To protect communities, it is vitally important that policymakers eliminate nonmedical exemptions from required childhood immunizations and physicians grant exemption requests only when patients cannot receive vaccines for medical reasons. And, given the declining child vaccination rates, the American Medical Association supports legislation, regulations, programs and policies that encourage states to eliminate all nonmedical exemptions from mandated pediatric immunizations.

Nonmedical vaccine exemptions have doubled in the past 20 years. The process for obtaining personal-belief exemptions varies by state, with some requiring education about the risks and benefits of vaccines before an exemption can be granted and others allowing a parent to simply check a box on a school form. Allowing personal-belief exemptions lends credence to the disproven claim that vaccines are unsafe or cause health problems.

Broad vaccine exemption policies take us down a dangerous path to compromising public health. People who cannot be vaccinated due to medical reasons rely on community or "herd" immunity to prevent disease. At least 93 percent of the population

NO
Michael Sussman
Civil Rights Lawyer for Vaccine Opponents

Written for *CQ Researcher*, September 2019

The difficulty with eliminating nonmedical vaccine waivers is vividly illustrated by a pending vaccine exemption case in New York state.

In early fall 2018, a measles outbreak developed in several New York counties. Public health authorities failed to utilize the measures and means permitted by state law to quell such outbreaks. They did not quarantine or isolate those infected with measles. The outbreak spread, and in early December a county health commissioner barred all unvaccinated children from all public and private schools, even though there was no evidence that these children had contributed to the spread of the disease. In addition, state law allows that if a case of measles occurs in any school, unvaccinated children could be barred from that school for several weeks.

In March 2019, Rockland County Executive Ed Day declared a public health emergency, ordered all unvaccinated children with religious exemptions to remain indoors and barred them from any public place. Apart from the obvious enforcement issues, this ban was both troublingly overbroad and under-inclusive at the same time. Unvaccinated adults were not included because it would be too expensive and disruptive, Day's lawyer told a state Supreme Court justice. And more than 1,000 healthy children were stigmatized and isolated by Day's order. The Supreme Court enjoined Day's ban, so Day began vociferously lobbying state legislators to repeal the religious exemption to vaccinations. His message—and that of bill sponsors—was quite blunt: People claiming religious exemptions were frauds; no religion prohibits vaccinations, and those claiming the contrary were pretenders.

This direct assault on sincerely held religious beliefs continued in the legislature, where lawmakers repealed the 55-year-old religious exemption, without any legislative hearings, tossing 26,000 children out of their schools without a strategy for educating them. This includes special-needs children whose educations are protected by federal law.

I am challenging the repeal of the religious exemption, because the legislative debate makes it clear that the discussion was dominated by an animosity toward religion—indeed, the outright denigration of people of religious faith, invalidating the state's action. Motive matters,

needs to receive the measles vaccine to guard against the spread of the disease.

Some parents say they should be free to make medical decisions on behalf of their children, but they also have a responsibility to do what's in the best interest of their child and the community at large. We cannot allow misinformation and persistent rumors about vaccines to take us backward in this fight to eradicate disease.

and those who spoke made clear that their very belated response to the ebbing outbreak was intended to signal that people who hold religious views contrary to those of the majority should be damned. That is not what a constitutional democracy looks like. It is more like the establishment of a state religion, which is prohibited, quite strictly, by the First Amendment.

before the California State Senate judiciary committee in support of the current law and the proposed change. "No court, state or federal, has ever struck down an immunization law, because parental rights have never been absolute," says Reiss. "They have always been limited. Vaccine mandates are especially natural because they protect the welfare of the child and the safety of others."

Not all such legislative efforts have been successful. Democrats in the Oregon Legislature abandoned a bill to end nonmedical exemptions after Republicans walked out of the Capitol to block its passage. In Alabama the Senate failed to pass a bill introduced in May that would have removed religious exemptions. And in Florida, after religious exemptions increased nearly fourfold last year, from about 6,500 in 2011 to 25,000, efforts to disallow such exemptions have stalled.[32]

Connecticut lawmakers dropped proposed legislation that would have prohibited unvaccinated students from enrolling in the state's public schools. The legislators could not agree on how to address unvaccinated children who were already in school.[33] "They let the perfect become the enemy of the good," says the American College of Physicians' McLean.

Public health officials acknowledge that countering online misinformation is an uphill battle. "It's impossible to respond to everything on social media and the internet," says Fauci of the National Institute of Allergy and Infectious Diseases. "Instead of responding tit-for-tat, we tend to give statements regarding the broad issues of what the evidence and facts are."

Dr. Mobeen Rathore, a pediatric infectious disease specialist and spokesperson for the American Academy of Pediatrics says he believes the anti-vaccine tide has slowed. "Fortunately, there is no push for expanding exemptions," he says. "People have realized that we

cannot continue with this trend, and there is increased interest in protecting us from disease. It is a slow process and a lot of damage has already been done."

OUTLOOK
Reducing Vaccine Avoidance

If declining vaccination rates continue to result in an uptick in the number of measles cases, the disease may no longer be considered eliminated in the United States.

The American Medical Association, the American Pediatric Association and the American College of Physicians support eliminating all religious and philosophical vaccine exemptions for the MMR as the first step to get measles under control.

Governors have declared states of emergency where outbreaks have occurred in Brooklyn and Rockland County, N.Y., as well as in Washington state. "There has been a 99 percent increase in vaccinations in various areas of Williamsburg, Brooklyn, compared to the same time last year," says Fauci.

In addition, new cases appear to be declining, with 54 in June and July of 2019 compared to 177 in April and 166 in March of the same year, according to Fauci. And infectious disease experts say taking an anti-vaccine stance has become increasingly unpopular this year as the nation has grappled with the measles outbreak.

But health experts worry that unless vaccine avoidance rates are reduced, even worse things are on the horizon.

"Measles is the most contagious of all the vaccine-preventable diseases, so this is the canary in the coal mine," says Blumberg, at UC Davis Children's Hospital. "If we can't get our hands on this, we will see outbreaks of rubella or mumps or meningitis. We may even see the return of something like diphtheria," which was eradicated in the 1920s.

NOTES

1. Julia Belluz, "New York's Orthodox Jewish community is battling measles outbreaks. Vaccine deniers are to blame," *Vox*, April 10, 2019, https://tinyurl.com/y8znlarg.

2. Kirk Johnson, "'A Match Into a Can of Gasoline'": Measles Outbreak Now an Emergency in Washington State," *The New York Times*, Feb. 6, 2019, https://tinyurl.com/y7trcubd; "Measles 2019: Measles in Washington State," Washington State Department of Health, undated, https://tinyurl.com/y438vmo9.

3. "What are the immunization rates for children in Clark County?" Clark County Washington Public Health, Dec. 31, 2018, https://tinyurl.com/y3dwrwgu; Asia Fields and Paige Cornwell, "Trips to Sea-Tac Airport may link cases in new measles outbreak in Seattle area; Issaquah, Bothell schools affected," *The Seattle Times*, May 16, 2019, https://tinyurl.com/yxo9lmwp.

4. Peter M. Strebel and Walter A. Orenstein, "Measles," *The New England Journal of Medicine*, July 25, 2019, https://tinyurl.com/y6dc4lbm.

5. YL Ge *et al.*, "Measles outbreak in pediatric hematology and oncology patients in Shanghai, 2015," *Chinese Medical Journal* (English), 2017, https://tinyurl.com/y3762tax.

6. "Measles Cases and Outbreaks," U.S. Centers for Disease Control and Prevention, Sept. 9, 2019, https://tinyurl.com/y39perlm.

7. *Ibid.*; "Mayor de Blasio, Health Officials Declare End of Measles Outbreak in New York City," press release, City of New York, Sept. 3, 2019, https://tinyurl.com/yxj8fgml.

8. "New measles surveillance data for 2019," World Health Organization, Aug. 15, 2019, https://tinyurl.com/y4w42atw.

9. Morgan Krakow, "A flight attendant who contracted measles has died amid a global rise in outbreaks," *The Washington Post*, Aug. 13, 2019, https://tinyurl.com/y33fdeub; "El Al flight attendant dies 4 months after contracting measles on a plane from NY," *The Times of Israel*, Aug. 13, 2019, https://tinyurl.com/yy4yr72f.

10. "Vaxxed: From Cover-Up to Catastrophe," IMDB.com, 2016, https://tinyurl.com/y5r4kf9l.

11. Rep. Adam Schiff, letter, March 1, 2019, https://tinyurl.com/y636vrnp; Hilary Brueck, "Amazon just took down a controversial documentary that links vaccines to autism," *Business Insider*, March 4, 2019, https://tinyurl.com/y6jc7uhu.

12. "Ten Threats to Global Health in 2019," World Health Organization, accessed Sept. 6, 2019, https://tinyurl.com/y66mn4sx.

13. Barbara Loe Fisher, "Freedom to Dissent and the New Black List in America," National Vaccine Information Center, July 1, 2019, https://tinyurl.com/yxor2g9b.

14. "Data and Statistics," Health Resources & Services Administration, updated Aug. 1, 2019, https://tinyurl.com/y5l4mktx.

15. Jennifer Reich, "What's wrong with these anti-vaxxers? They're just like the rest of us," *The Conversation*, May 22, 2019, https://tinyurl.com/y4mdagw4.

16. Karin Roberts, "When it comes to vaccines, celebrities often call the shots," *NBC News*, Oct. 28, 2018, https://tinyurl.com/y43u8smq.

17. Donald Trump, Twitter post, March 28, 2014, https://tinyurl.com/pzyue8h.

18. Sheila Kaplan and Dylan Scott, "Vaccine critic Robert F. Kennedy Jr. says he will chair Trump's vaccine safety panel," *Stat*, Jan. 10, 2017, https://tinyurl.com/jtyj2rm.

19. Dartunorro Clark, "Trump on measles vaccine: 'They have to get the shot,'" *NBC News*, April 26, 2019, https://tinyurl.com/y4enwgow.

20. John Aloysius Cogan, Jr., "Vaccinations will take a hit if Trump administration topples the Affordable Care Act," *Stat*, May 22, 2019, https://tinyurl.com/y5ym8kr6.

21. Lecia Bushak, "A Brief History Of Vaccines: From Medieval Chinese 'Variolation' To Modern Vaccination," *Medical Daily*, March 21, 2016, https://tinyurl.com/y426l4f.

22. "Immunizations Policy Issues Overview," National Conference of State Legislatures, May 22, 2019, https://tinyurl.com/zuyztg5; and Aleksandra

Sandstrom, "Amid measles outbreak, New York closes religious exemption for vaccinations—but most states retain it," Pew Research Center, June 28, 2019, https://tinyurl.com/yy38r8wa.

23. "Data and Statistics," *op. cit.*

24. Alexandra Minna Stern and Howard Markel, "The History Of Vaccines And Immunization: Familiar Patterns, New Challenges," *Health Affairs*, May/June 2005, https://tinyurl.com/y6lgzgzq.

25. Laura Eggertson, "Lancet retracts 12-year-old article linking autism to MMR vaccines," *Canadian Medical Association Journal*, March 9, 2010, https://tinyurl.com/z6q85j5; Alice Park, "Doctor behind vaccine-autism link loses license," *Time*, May 24, 2010, https://tinyurl.com/pb6pdgq.

26. Ashley Welch, "GOP debate fact check: Claims about vaccines and autism," *CBS News*, Sept. 17, 2015, https://tinyurl.com/y52ecxj5.

27. "Immunizations Policy Issues Overview," *op. cit.*

28. "Inslee declares local public health emergency after identifying outbreak of measles," news release, Washington Governor Jay Inslee, Jan. 25, 2019, https://tinyurl.com/y6oconjd; "MMR Vaccine Exemption Law Change 2019," Washington State Department of Health, undated, https://tinyurl.com/y3nlyve8.

29. "Senate ends non-medical exemption for vaccines amidst historic measles outbreak," news release, New York State Senator Brad Hoylman, June 13, 2019, https://tinyurl.com/yytgbvv2.

30. David Siders, Alexei Koseff and Jeremy B. White, "Jerry Brown signs California vaccine bill," *The Sacramento Bee*, July 1, 2015, https://tinyurl.com/y4ygf45c.

31. "Dr. Richard Pan Introduces SB 276 to Combat Fake Medical Exemptions that Put Children and Communities at Risk," news release, Dr. Richard Pan, California State Senator, March 26, 2019, https://tinyurl.com/yysfce8b.

32. Kirby Wilson, "Anti-vaxxers blamed as record 25,000 Florida students claim religious objections to vaccines," *Tampa Bay Times*, April 9, 2019, https://tinyurl.com/y6k4j6o2.

33. Jenna Carlesso, "No vote to end religious vaccine exemptions this year," *The CT Mirror*, May 16, 2019, https://tinyurl.com/yyjlswnt.

BIBLIOGRAPHY

Books

Fentiman, Linda, *Blaming Mothers: American Law and the Risks to Children's Health*, NYU Press, 2017.
A law professor evaluates the focus on mothers as the primary source of health risks—including making decisions about vaccinations—for their children.

Moskovitz, Richard, *Vaccines, A Reappraisal*, Skyhorse Publishing, 2017.
A family physician examines the risk posed by vaccines and argues that the current public health policy mandating vaccines for schoolchildren is unnecessary and dangerous.

Articles

Belluz, Julia, "New York's Orthodox Jewish community is battling measles outbreaks. Vaccine deniers are to blame," *Vox*, April 10, 2019, https://tinyurl.com/y8znlarg.
A journalist covers what led to the measles outbreak in Brooklyn's ultra-Orthodox Jewish community.

Branswell, Helen, "'They have to get the shots': Trump, once a vaccine skeptic, changes his tune against measles outbreak," *Stat*, April 26, 2019, https://tinyurl.com/yyv8f24s.
A medical news outlet reports that Trump now advises parents to vaccinate their children.

Carlesso, Jenna, "No vote to end religious vaccine exemptions this year," *The CT Mirror*, May 16, 2019, https://tinyurl.com/yyjlswnt.
The Connecticut state legislature failed to limit vaccine exemptions because of questions about how it would affect unvaccinated children already in school.

Cogan, John Aloysius, Jr., "Vaccinations will take a hit if the Trump administration topples the Affordable Care Act," *Stat*, May 22, 2019, https://tinyurl.com/y5ym8kr6.
A law professor lays out how vaccination coverage would change if the Affordable Care Act is repealed.

Johnson, Kirk, "'A Match Into a Can of Gasoline': Measles Outbreak Now an Emergency in Washington State," *The New York Times*, Feb. 6, 2019, https://tinyurl.com/y7trcubd.
A journalist traces the cause of the measles outbreak in the state of Washington.

Otterman, Sharon, "New York Confronts Its Worst Measles Outbreak in Decades," *The New York Times*, Jan. 17, 2019, https://tinyurl.com/y7pm4sgr.
A journalist reports on efforts to control the state of New York's measles outbreak.

Roberts, Karin, "When it comes to vaccines, celebrities often call the shots," *NBC News*, Oct. 28, 2018, https://tinyurl.com/y43u8smq.
A reporter analyzes the influence celebrities have on the vaccine debate.

Reports and Studies

"Decline in Measles Vaccination Is Causing a Preventable Global Resurgence of the Disease," National Institute of Allergy and Infectious Diseases, April 18, 2019, https://tinyurl.com/y5qfh6qq.
A federal health agency examines the link between lower vaccination rates and the return of measles.

"Immunizations Policy Issues Overview," National Conference of State Legislatures, May 22, 2019, https://tinyurl.com/zuyztg5.
An information clearinghouse on state laws tracks the status of vaccine legislation by state.

"Measles Cases and Outbreaks," Centers for Disease Control and Prevention, Aug. 18, 2019, https://tinyurl.com/y39perlm.
The federal health agency compiles the latest statistics on measles cases in the United States.

"New measles surveillance data for 2019," World Health Organization, Aug. 15, 2019, https://tinyurl.com/y4w42atw.
The United Nations' global health organization provides data about measles cases worldwide.

Cantor, Julie D., "Mandatory Measles Vaccination in New York City—Reflections on a Bold Experiment," *The New England Journal of Medicine*, July 11, 2019, https://tinyurl.com/y259o8lk.
A law professor argues for mandatory measles vaccinations.

Ge, YL, et al., "Measles Outbreak in Pediatric Hematology and Oncology Patients in Shanghai, 2015," *Chinese Medical Journal*, June 5, 2017, https://tinyurl.com/y3762tax.
Chinese doctors recount the rapid spread and deadly effect of measles on children with cancer.

Paules, Catharine I., Hilary D. Marston and Anthony S. Fauci, "Measles in 2019—Going Backward," *The New England Journal of Medicine*, June 6, 2019, https://tinyurl.com/y4qygecg.
Health experts describe the danger of the global measles resurgence.

Strebel, Peter M., and Walter A. Orenstein, "Measles," *The New England Journal of Medicine*, July 25, 2019, https://tinyurl.com/y6dc4lbm.
Doctors discuss steps for coping with measles.

Documentary

"Vaxxed: From Cover-Up to Catastrophe," IMDB.com, 2016, https://tinyurl.com/y5prvcyc.
A controversial film alleging that the government hid a link between vaccines and autism that was pulled from the Amazon streaming service after complaints that it included erroneous information about vaccines.

THE NEXT STEP

Anti-Vaccine Movement

Allen, Arthur, "How the anti-vaccine movement crept into the GOP mainstream," *Politico*, May 27, 2019, https://tinyurl.com/y5mvlaks.
While anti-vaccine sentiment had historically been relegated to the far left and far right, elected Republican officials have begun to take up the position as a matter of freedom and personal liberty.

Hall, Ellie, "Jessica Biel Says She's Not Anti-Vax Despite Lobbying With A Prominent Anti-Vaxxer," *Buzzfeed News*, June 13, 2019, https://tinyurl.com/y3okxkv7.

Actress Jessica Biel says she supports vaccines generally even though she lobbied California lawmakers earlier this year alongside Robert F. Kennedy Jr. to reject a bill that would limit medical exemptions from vaccine mandates.

Reich, Jennifer, "I've talked to dozens of parents about why they don't vaccinate. Here's what they told me," *Vox*, June 13, 2019, https://tinyurl.com/y4lbouvg.

Parents who decide not to vaccinate their children often practice a hyper-vigilant parenting style and put the interests of their own children ahead of the good of the community, writes a sociologist who has studied parental decision-making.

Recent Outbreaks

Cohen, Elizabeth, "The US eliminated measles in 2000. The current outbreak could change that," *CNN*, Sept. 3, 2019, https://tinyurl.com/yxft74zs.

According to medical experts, there is a chance the World Health Organization could withdraw the United States' designation as a country where measles has been eliminated.

Karlamangla, Soumya, "Where did the measles outbreak in LA start? Officials are looking abroad," *Los Angeles Times*, April 29, 2019, https://tinyurl.com/y3mxn8l4.

Officials and medical experts suspect that a recent measles outbreak in Los Angeles County started with travelers who contracted the virus overseas.

Weber, Jared, "Measles outbreak: As students head back to school, US and world officials warn about risk," *USA Today*, Aug. 14, 2019, https://tinyurl.com/y4hlq3dh.

This year's worldwide total of measles cases is at a 13-year high, according to the World Health Organization, and international travel is worsening the situation.

Responding to Vaccine Hesitancy

Chodosh, Sara, "We're finally studying how to combat the anti-vax movement, but the methods may surprise you," *Popular Science*, May 20, 2019, https://tinyurl.com/y2h44w64.

Researchers studying how doctors should approach parents who are hesitant about vaccines say that acknowledging their concerns before encouraging them to vaccinate is the most effective method.

Kirka, Danica, "UK to pressure social media companies to fight anti-vax info," The Associated Press, Aug. 19, 2019, https://tinyurl.com/y2fxjx7e.

The British government will hold a summit with social media companies to discuss how to fight online misinformation about vaccines, as the number of measles cases rises in the country.

Liao, Shannon, "GoFundMe pledges to remove anti-vax campaigns," *The Verge*, March 22, 2019, https://tinyurl.com/yxpq5agv.

The crowdfunding website removed anti-vaccine fundraisers from their platform a few weeks after Amazon removed the documentary *Vaxxed* from its streaming service.

Vaccine Legislation

Ho, Vivian, "The California senator fighting for the strictest vaccination laws in the US," *The Guardian*, Aug. 29, 2019, https://tinyurl.com/y4fdug9e.

A California state senator and pediatrician is leading the charge to limit exceptions to vaccine mandates for schoolchildren in the state.

Roy, Yancey, "Judge upholds law eliminating vaccine religious exemption," *Newsday*, Aug. 27, 2019, https://tinyurl.com/yy3v3vam.

A judge on the New York Supreme Court upheld a new state law that eliminated a religious exemption from mandatory vaccines for children in schools or daycare programs.

Smith, Kelsie, "New vaccine law impacting student enrollment," WHAM, Aug. 15, 2019, https://tinyurl.com/yy36a4gt.

A New York state law eliminating religious exemptions from vaccine mandates is leading to lower student enrollment in upstate New York, particularly in private schools.

For More Information

American Academy of Pediatrics, 141 Northwest Point Blvd., Elk Grove Village, IL 60007; 847-434-4000; www.aap.org. Association of physicians concerned with the health of children, adolescents and young adults.

American College of Physicians, 190 North Independence Mall West, Philadelphia, PA 9106-1572; 800-ACP-1915; www.acponline.org. National organization of internists, internal medicine subspecialists, medical students, residents and fellows.

American Medical Association, 330 N. Wabash Ave., Suite 3930, Chicago, IL 60611-5885; 312-464-4782; www.ama-assn.org. Organization that promotes the science of medicine and the improvement of public health.

California Immunization Coalition, 1331 Garden Highway, Sacramento, CA 95833; 916-414-9016; www.ImmunizeCa.org. Advocacy group that promotes full immunization in the state.

Centers for Disease Control and Prevention, 1600 Clifton Road, Atlanta, GA 30333; 404-639-3311; www.cdc.gov. Federal agency responsible for tracking and preventing disease, injury and disability.

National Institutes of Allergy and Infectious Disease, 5601 Fishers Lane, Bethesda, MD 20892-9806; 866-284-4107; www.niaid.nih.gov. Federal institute that researches infectious diseases, among other things.

National Vaccine Information Center, 204 Mill St., Suite B1, Vienna, VA 22180; 703-938-0342; www.nvic.org. An organization that lobbies for vaccine safety reforms and informed consent protections for parents.

World Health Organization, Ave. Appia 20m 1211, Geneva, 27, Switzerland; +41-22-791-2111; www.who.int/en/. United Nations organization that coordinates global public health efforts.

Intercontinental nuclear missiles are displayed during a military parade in Beijing in October 2019 to celebrate the founding of the People's Republic of China. Nonproliferation advocates say China is racing to catch up to Russia and the United States in a global arms race.

3

The New Arms Race

Are new treaties needed to control modern nuclear weapons?

By Jonathan Broder

THE ISSUES

Russia recently announced the deployment of its Avangard boost-glide vehicle, which rides a powerful rocket into orbit just above Earth's atmosphere. From there, the vehicle, armed with a nuclear warhead, can strike anywhere on the planet within 15 minutes, moving toward its target at more than 20 times the speed of sound, according to Russian military officials.[1]

With its ability to steer around air and missile defenses at hypersonic speeds, the Avangard is "practically invulnerable," Russian President Vladimir Putin has said.[2] And it is just one of half a dozen new nuclear weapons delivery systems being developed by Moscow. Meanwhile, China has deployed its own hypersonic delivery vehicle.

The United States is years behind Moscow and Beijing in developing nuclear-capable hypersonic missiles but is working hard to modernize its nuclear arsenal, including the missiles, bombers and submarines that deliver the weapons, senior defense officials say. The modernization could cost up to $1.2 trillion over the next three decades, according to a Congressional Budget Office study.[3]

"We have lost our technical advantage in hypersonics," said Gen. Paul Selva, then-vice chairman of the Joint Chiefs of Staff. But, he added: "We haven't lost the hypersonics fight."[4]

Arms control advocates say the competition to develop more advanced nuclear weapons and faster delivery systems signals a

From *CQ Researcher,*
February 14, 2020

U.S., Russia Have Most of the World's Nuclear Weapons

Although the world's nuclear arsenals have declined significantly since the 1980s, about 90 percent of the nearly 14,000 strategic nuclear weapons that still exist are controlled by Russia and the United States. The two countries have 6,500 and 6,035 weapons, respectively, far more than any of the other seven nuclear-armed nations. About a third of the U.S. and Russian weapons are retired and awaiting dismantlement; the rest are either deployed or available for use.

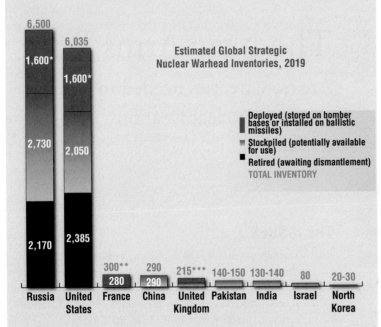

Estimated Global Strategic Nuclear Warhead Inventories, 2019

- Deployed (stored on bomber bases or installed on ballistic missiles)
- Stockpiled (potentially available for use)
- Retired (awaiting dismantlement)

TOTAL INVENTORY

* These figures exceed the 1,550 allowed in New START because they include bombs stored on bomber bases, which the START cap does not cover.

** France has 280 warheads deployed and 20 stockpiled.

*** The U.K. has 120 warheads deployed and 95 stockpiled.

Source: Hans M. Kristensen and Matt Korda, "Status of World Nuclear Forces," Federation of American Scientists, May 2019, https://tinyurl.com/junbna7

The crumbling of the international arms control architecture also comes as two new strategic competitors—Iran and North Korea—are asserting themselves in ways that further heighten nuclear risks, experts say. With denuclearization talks between the Trump administration and North Korea stalled, the North's leader, Kim Jong Un, recently declared he no longer feels bound by his self-imposed moratorium on nuclear and long-range missile testing. Analysts say that while his message has left the door open for diplomacy, it also could set the stage for another angry confrontation with President Trump, who threatened North Korea with "fire and fury" in previous face-offs.[5]

In addition, after a U.S. drone in January killed Iran's top military commander, Tehran announced it was resuming its enriched uranium production, signaling what many analysts regard as the death knell of a landmark 2015 international agreement to curb Iran's nuclear weapons program.[6]

"The risk that the world will stumble its way into nuclear war is higher today than it's been since the end of the Cold War," says Thomas Countryman, a former assistant secretary of State for international security and nonproliferation.

dangerous, new three-way arms race among the United States, Russia and China, sparked after Washington and Moscow withdrew from several key arms control treaties in recent years. (*See Box.*) In this new age of hypersonic nuclear weapons, cyber warfare and the growing militarization of space, U.S. defense hawks argue such accords are outdated and no longer serve the nation's interest. And amid the new, great-power contest, they insist the best way to deter an apocalyptic nuclear war is to be fully ready and willing to fight one, unconstrained by obsolete treaties. Some now even contend that a limited nuclear war can be won.

Such nuclear alarm bells represent a sharp turnabout from a few years ago, when the threat of nuclear war was successfully managed through a matrix of arms control agreements between the United States and Russia, which together hold more than 90 percent of the world's nearly 14,000 nuclear weapons, according to the Arms Control Association, a Washington-based advocacy organization.[7] (*See Graphic.*)

By imposing transparency, predictability and limits on each side's nuclear forces, those agreements created what officials have called a state of "strategic stability"

Mourners accompany the coffin of Iran's top military commander, Gen. Qassem Soleimani, killed by a U.S. drone strike in January 2020. Iran responded by vowing to resume enriching uranium, taking another step back from a landmark 2015 international agreement to curb its nuclear program.

between the superpower rivals that minimized the chances of a nuclear war. The treaties also helped to whittle down the U.S. and Soviet (later Russian) nuclear arsenals from their Cold War highs of tens of thousands of weapons each to their current levels of no more than 6,500 nuclear warheads each.[8]

However, in the wake of new threats, mutual allegations of cheating and a deep antipathy toward arms control in hawkish U.S. and Russian defense circles, Washington and Moscow in recent decades have withdrawn from two landmark arms control treaties, and Russia has ended a third:

• **The 1972 Anti-Ballistic Missile Treaty**, which reduced the number of anti-missile batteries each side could maintain against incoming nuclear missiles. In 2002, President George W. Bush withdrew from the treaty, concerned it prevented the United States from fielding adequate defenses in Europe against a missile attack by rogue actors such as Iraq's Saddam Hussein.

• **The 1987 Intermediate-Range Nuclear Forces Treaty**, which banned all nuclear-capable U.S. and Soviet missiles with ranges between 300 and 3,400 miles. Trump abandoned the treaty in August 2019, accusing Russia of covertly violating the pact, a charge Russia denied.

• **The 2000 Plutonium Management and Disposition Agreement**, which required the two countries to destroy their surplus military stockpiles of plutonium to prevent terrorists from acquiring the material used to make the explosive core in a hydrogen bomb. The treaty collapsed in 2016 when Russia pulled out, charging U.S. violations, which Washington denied.

In addition, in May 2018 Trump withdrew the United States from the 2015 nuclear agreement between Iran and six world powers, under which the Islamic Republic curtailed its nuclear program in return for relief from nuclear-related sanctions. Trump then imposed harsh economic sanctions that he said would force Iran to accept a more stringent accord, but Tehran has pushed back by resuming uranium enrichment.

Analysts warn that Tehran could produce bomb-grade nuclear fuel, triggering a U.S. or Israeli attack to destroy Iran's nuclear infrastructure. To prevent that, says Jeffrey Lewis, a nuclear nonproliferation expert at the Middlebury Institute of International Studies at Monterey, Calif., Trump might try to destroy Iran's underground facilities using a tactical, or low-yield, nuclear weapon with about a third of the explosive power of the atomic bomb the United States dropped on Hiroshima, Japan, in 1945.

That leaves only one major bilateral strategic arms control agreement still in force: the Obama-era New START. It allows the United States and Russia each to deploy, or install in the field, no more than 1,550 so-called strategic warheads—large, high-yield weapons that can destroy entire cities—on 700 missiles or other delivery systems. The treaty does not include weapons stored at bomber bases as part of the cap.

New START expires in February 2021 unless the two sides agree to extend it for up to five years. Putin has agreed to the extension, which he says would cover the Avangard and a new, heavy intercontinental ballistic missile (ICBM) Russia is developing.[9] (An ICBM is a guided missile with a range of at least 3,400 miles.)

A chorus of U.S. lawmakers, former military commanders and arms control experts have urged Trump to follow suit. But Trump says he prefers to pursue a broader arms control treaty that would cover small tactical nuclear weapons, which are designed for battlefield use, as well as China's growing nuclear arsenal. Administration officials say they will soon open nuclear arms control talks with Moscow.[10]

Arms control advocates have applauded Trump's ambitions but say there is not enough time to negotiate a full-fledged replacement treaty before New START expires. And Beijing, whose nuclear arsenal is far smaller than U.S. and Russian stockpiles, says it wants no part of any treaty that would limit its nuclear forces.

"It is critical to conduct a strategic stability dialogue with China, pursue transparency and confidence-building measures, and lay the groundwork for future arms control measures," retired Adm. Michael Mullen, a former chairman of the Joint Chiefs of Staff, told the House Foreign Affairs Committee in December. "But it would be an unconscionable mistake to sacrifice [New START's] . . . mutual restraints with Russia to the pursuit of an unlikely near-term arms control agreement with China."

The Trump administration also has indicated it wants to pull out of the 1992 Open Skies Treaty, which allows its 34 signatories to conduct short-notice, unarmed, reconnaissance flights over the territories of partner countries to collect data on military forces and activities. Arms control proponents say the treaty provides an important layer of verification regarding Russian military activities, but some administration officials and Republican lawmakers say it facilitates Russian spying, costs millions of dollars and does not serve U.S. interests.

Nuclear weapons experts say the demise of so many foundational arms control treaties has stoked ongoing nuclear buildups by smaller nuclear powers, such as China, North Korea, India, Pakistan and Israel, an undeclared nuclear power. In addition, aspiring powers such as Turkey and Saudi Arabia now openly declare their intentions to join the nuclear weapons club.

"If the U.S. and Russia are reinvesting in their strategic arsenals and re-emphasizing nuclear weapons in their national security strategies, they're telegraphing to the rest of the world that this is where they think security lies," says Alexandra Bell, a former senior State Department arms control adviser. "Then you have smaller powers saying they need nuclear weapons too."

Amid these developments, here are several key questions that experts, military leaders and security officials are asking as they ponder the future of arms control:

Should the United States allow New START to expire?

Not long after his 2016 election, Donald Trump raised questions about his commitment to New START, tweeting that the United States "must greatly strengthen and expand its nuclear capability until such time as the world comes to its senses regarding nukes." Asked if that meant a new arms race with Russia, Trump reportedly responded: "Let it be an arms race. We will outmatch them at every pass and outlast them all."[11]

Since then, Trump has called New START a bad deal negotiated by Obama, noting that it failed to cover the thousands of tactical nuclear weapons Russia has amassed over the years, dwarfing the much smaller U.S. arsenal of such weapons. Nor, Trump said, does it include China, which is expanding its conventional and nuclear forces—including hypersonic delivery missiles—unbound by any arms control treaties.

Though Putin has said he's ready to extend the treaty without preconditions or negotiations, Trump has made no such commitment. Last March, he ordered the State Department to draft negotiating positions for a new, tripartite arms control treaty with Moscow and Beijing, according to senior U.S. officials. In February, the White House said it would soon begin bilateral nuclear arms control negotiations with Moscow.[12]

"We have not ruled out an extension of New START, but our priority is to promote arms control that goes beyond the confines of a narrow, bilateral approach by incorporating other countries—including China—and a broader range of weapons," Undersecretary of State for Political Affairs David Hale told the Senate Foreign Relations Committee in December.[13]

In theory, say independent arms control experts, Trump is right to seek controls over tactical nuclear weapons. Under orders from President George H.W. Bush, the Pentagon eliminated many of its tactical nuclear weapons after the Soviet Union collapsed in 1991, leaving the United States with around 1,000 tactical weapons today compared to Russia's 2,000, according to Hans Kristensen, director of the Nuclear Information Project at the Federation of American Scientists, which tracks nuclear arsenals worldwide.

These experts also agree Trump is right to be concerned about China's unrestrained nuclear weapons program.

The Pentagon's top two experts on China's military say the Asian giant is on track to double its roughly 300 strategic warheads in the next 10 years, fueled by a stockpile of enriched uranium and plutonium that exceeds the country's civilian nuclear power needs.

In addition, say these officials, China is also developing its own hypersonic missiles as well as new intermediate- and long-range missiles with higher accuracy than older versions, stealthy long-range bombers and advanced missile-firing submarines. As a result, they estimate, China could attain nuclear parity with the United States and Russia within one or two decades.

But with China unwilling to consider a three-way treaty with Washington and Moscow, Trump administration aides are struggling to attract Beijing to a treaty that Moscow and domestic critics would approve, says Countryman, the former State Department arms control chief. So far, Trump's aides have suggested three possible approaches, none of which is acceptable to all parties, says Countryman, who is currently board chair of the Washington-based Arms Control Association advocacy group.

In one, China would increase its deployed nuclear arsenal fivefold to 1,550 warheads—the same as the United States and Russia—but this is a nonstarter for Washington and Moscow, Countryman says. Another approach would require the United States and Russia to reduce their nuclear arsenals fivefold to the size of China's, which neither the Pentagon nor the Kremlin is prepared to do. Under a third option, the United States and Russia would agree to freeze their nuclear arsenals at the New START ceiling of 1,550 warheads while China would agree to keep its arsenal at 300 warheads, a proposal China rejects.

Glossary of Nuclear Weapons Terminology

Nuclear weapon—A bomb that releases enormous amounts of explosive energy as a result of either nuclear fission, a reaction that occurs when the nucleus of an atom is split into two or more fragments, or nuclear fusion, which occurs when two or more atomic nuclei fuse to form a heavier nucleus.

Atomic bomb—A type of nuclear weapon that draws its explosive power from the sudden release of large amounts of atomic energy through fission. The United States is the only country to have detonated atomic bombs in wartime, in Hiroshima and Nagasaki, Japan, in 1945.

Hydrogen (thermonuclear) bomb—About 1,000 times more powerful than an atomic bomb; draws its explosive force from a fusion reaction.

Strategic nuclear weapon or warhead—Large, high-yield weapons that can destroy entire cities.

Tactical nuclear weapons—Low-yield devices with about a third of the explosive power of the atomic bomb used in Hiroshima; designed for battlefield use; can take the form of artillery shells, bombs or short-range missiles.

Deployed—Mounted on a missile or ready to be loaded onto a long-range bomber.

Ballistic missiles—Rocket-powered delivery vehicles that travel in a ballistic (free fall) trajectory.

Intercontinental ballistic missile (ICBM)—A ballistic missile that can travel more than 3,400 miles.

Delivery vehicle—A land-based or submarine-launched ballistic or cruise missile or long-range bomber that can deliver one or more warheads to a target.

Hypersonic—Many times faster than the speed of sound.

Sources: "Glossary," Nuclear Threat Initiative, https://tinyurl.com/ukzwvml; "Glossary of Terms," Nuclear Reduction/Disarmament Initiative, https://tinyurl.com/vu6oe9s; "How does stealth technology work?" HowStuffWorks, April 1, 2000, https://tinyurl.com/ybnglspb; and "NATO/Russia Unclassified," North Atlantic Treaty Organization, 2007, https://tinyurl.com/tuvoj72

"If there's a more creative idea, it has escaped me," Countryman says. "And it has escaped the administration officials who have been discussing how to realize the president's strategy for nine months now, when in fact, no such strategy is possible."

Some critics suspect Trump's tripartite treaty strategy is a ploy, designed to distract arms control advocates while New START expires, which would appease defense hawks who never liked the treaty in the first place.

"Trump and the hawks don't want to have limits on the United States' ability to increase its nuclear force," says Joseph Cirincione, president of the Ploughshares Fund, a foundation dedicated to nuclear nonproliferation, arms control and disarmament. "It's mostly about their belief that China could rapidly expand its arsenal, so they feel we have to be in a position to match it. Their view is that they protect American national security through American military might, not by pieces of paper like the New START treaty. They see that treaty as an arms control trap and its expiration next year as an opportunity to get out of it. And if that means an arms race, fine."

Defense hawks say China's rise as a military power with advanced hypersonic nuclear weapons has rendered New START obsolete. "Technology has moved," said Secretary of State Mike Pompeo.[14]

"If you want to pursue arms control, you can't do it an in old-fashioned, outmoded, Cold War-era style," said then-National Security Adviser John Bolton in June 2019. "So to extend [New START] for five years and not take these new delivery system threats into account would be malpractice," he said, referring to hypersonic missile systems. He also cited the absence of limits on tactical nuclear weapons as another flaw in New START.[15]

Although Bolton left the administration last September, the president still agrees with Bolton's criticism of New START, White House officials say.

Arms control experts argue that the need to address the threats from Chinese and Russian tactical nuclear weapons should not blind Trump to the benefits that an extended New START would bring to U.S. national security.

Rose Gottemoeller, the chief U.S. negotiator for New START, told lawmakers in December that since the treaty entered into force in 2011, it has established strategic weapons parity between the United States and Russia, providing Americans with a stable and predictable security environment. Extending the treaty for another five years, she argued, would preserve that predictability while the Pentagon modernizes its nuclear forces. It would also give the United States time to negotiate a new treaty that includes China, she said.

"Without the treaty, things could change drastically and quickly," Gottemoeller told the House Foreign Affairs Committee in December, 2019. "There is no faster way for the Russians to outrun us than to deploy more nuclear warheads on their missiles."[16]

Is a limited nuclear war a viable option?

In a striking illustration of the return to Cold War thinking, Russian and U.S. military planners now believe it is possible to wage limited nuclear war without it escalating into a nuclear apocalypse.

In such a war, each side would use low-yield, or tactical, weapons on the battlefield. Depending on its size and radiation yield, a single tactical nuclear weapon could kill thousands of troops and contaminate its blast radius for decades.

Since the start of the Cold War in the 1940s, U.S. and Soviet military leaders envisioned using smaller nuclear weapons to halt a major armored thrust by the other side in Europe, or to block the enemy's advance through a strategic mountain pass. Nowadays, they are regarded as effective weapons against military or nuclear installations buried deep underground, or to save one's forces from a conventional defeat while discouraging the enemy from waging further hostilities.

Moreover, say U.S. military experts, Russia has adopted an "escalate-to-de-escalate" strategy, believing that using such tactical nuclear weapons on the battlefield would quickly de-escalate a military confrontation with U.S. and NATO forces, because Washington would balk at a full-scale nuclear response that would lead to global annihilation.

In response, the United States has begun producing more tactical nuclear warheads for its cruise missiles and submarine-launched ballistic missiles so it can deter the threat of any tactical nuclear strike and retaliate proportionally should one be used against U.S. or allied forces. The Pentagon refers to such deterrence as "escalation dominance."

The National Nuclear Security Administration, the federal agency responsible for the effectiveness of the U.S. nuclear weapons stockpile, said new tactical warheads have been rolling off a production line in Texas since this past January. And in February, the Pentagon announced it has equipped the Navy's Trident ballistic missiles with a new tactical warhead, the W76-2, which has less than a third of the destructive power of other U.S. nuclear weapons.[17]

The Pentagon's 100-page "2018 Nuclear Posture Review" outlined the buildup of tactical nuclear weapons as a key element of the Trump administration's nuclear policy: "Expanding flexible U.S. nuclear options now, to include low-yield options, is important for the preservation of credible deterrence against regional aggression. It will . . . help ensure that potential adversaries perceive no possible advantage in limited nuclear escalation, making nuclear employment less likely."[18]

But the Trump nuclear doctrine is controversial. The Ploughshares Fund's Cirincione warns that it would blur the line between the use of conventional and nuclear weapons and expand the circumstances in which the U.S. military would go nuclear. For example, the administration's nuclear review says the United States could use nuclear weapons in response to "significant non-nuclear strategic attacks," such as a crippling cyberstrike on the nation's power grid or other essential infrastructure.[19]

Another Pentagon document, titled simply "Nuclear Operations," outlined a broad range of additional scenarios in which the U.S. military might use nuclear weapons.

The document said integrating nuclear weapons with conventional and special operations "is essential to the success of any mission or operation." Furthermore, it said, "The spectrum of nuclear warfare may range from tactical application, to limited regional use, to global employment by friendly forces and/or enemies. . . . Employment of nuclear weapons can radically alter or accelerate the course of a campaign. A nuclear weapon could be brought into the campaign as a result of perceived failure in a conventional campaign, potential loss of control or regime, or to escalate the conflict to sue for peace on more favorable terms."[20]

Further expanding the potential use of nuclear weapons in conventional combat, the Pentagon document said field commanders "can nominate potential targets to consider for nuclear options that would support [the commander's] objectives in ongoing operations."[21]

Arms control advocates, including former senior Defense officials, said the U.S. and Russian embrace of a limited nuclear war doctrine represents a highly dangerous throwback to the Cold War years.

"Anybody that thinks you can use a tactical weapon and not have a profound risk of escalation all the way to an all-out nuclear war is risking the world on a pretty naive assumption," says Sam Nunn, a former chairman of the Senate Armed Services Committee and co-founder of the Nuclear Threat Initiative, a research organization that educates policymakers on the dangers of nuclear weapons. "It's very high risk," he says.

But Elbridge Colby, a former senior Defense Department official, cautioned that with the return of great-power competition, Russia and China have developed strategies to defeat the United States in a military confrontation and that tactical nuclear weapons are a key part of their strategies.[22] He supports the U.S. production of tactical nuclear weapons, which could help defeat a Russian or Chinese attack "without provoking a nuclear apocalypse," he said, adding that demonstrating such a capability to U.S. adversaries "is the best way to avoid ever having to put it into practice."[23]

Another proponent of the limited nuclear war doctrine, Keir Lieber, a nuclear arms expert at Georgetown University, says if deterrence fails and the use of a nuclear weapon is required, a tactical weapon diminishes the chances of a full-scale nuclear exchange in certain cases. He paints a possible scenario in which Russia overruns the former Soviet republic of Estonia and explodes a low-yield nuclear weapon to get NATO forces to sue for peace. That would prompt the Western alliance to retaliate with its own tactical nuclear weapon, he says.

"Is it going to stop there?" he asks. "I don't know why one would assume that it will continue to escalate from there."

In response to the emerging doctrine of limited nuclear war, researchers at The Lab—part of Princeton University's Program on Science and Global Security, which studies nuclear arms control, nonproliferation and disarmament—recently used extensive data on U.S. and Russian nuclear forces, war plans and targets to produce a four-minute video showing how the limited use of nuclear weapons could quickly escalate into a full-scale nuclear war, killing or wounding more than 90 million people in a few hours.[24]

Underscoring the difficulty of limiting a nuclear exchange to tactical weapons, Nunn and other skeptics note that U.S. and Russian leaders would not know whether an incoming missile is carrying a tactical nuclear warhead or a city-destroying strategic weapon, raising the chances of a full-blown nuclear exchange.

"Hey all you nuclear powers out there. We're just going to trust that you recognize this is just a little nuclear weapon and won't retaliate with all you've got," tweeted Melissa Hanham, an expert on nuclear weapons at One Earth Future, a Washington-based foundation that advocates arms control. "Remember! The U.S. only intends to nuke you 'a little bit.'"[25]

Is a denuclearization agreement with North Korea possible?

In June 2017, Trump upended decades of American policy and diplomatic norms by meeting with North

Japanese schoolchildren take cover under their desks during a drill in 2017 to prepare for a possible North Korean missile attack. Even though President Trump became the first sitting U.S. president to meet with a North Korean leader in 2017, progress between the United States and North Korea on a denuclearization agreement has stalled.

Korean dictator Kim Jong Un in Singapore to discuss the denuclearization of the communist country in return for sanctions relief and U.S. economic aid.

Until then, successive administrations had held low-level negotiations with North Korean officials, offering food and other forms of assistance in a bid to get Pyongyang to curtail its fledgling nuclear program. Several times the talks produced agreements, but eventually they all collapsed amid mutual misunderstandings, charges of cheating and deep distrust left over from the 1950-53 Korean War.

To his credit, many arms control advocates say, Trump shattered that diplomatic model. In Singapore, he became the first sitting U.S. president to meet with a North Korean leader, convinced that their personal rapport could pave the way for an historic denuclearization agreement. "We fell in love," Trump said of his new relationship with Kim.[26]

At the end of that summit, the two leaders pledged to "work toward the complete denuclearization of the Korean Peninsula."[27] As a confidence-building measure, Trump scaled back joint military exercises with South Korea, and Kim reciprocated by declaring a moratorium on North Korea's nuclear and ballistic missile tests. Commentators noted that after a year in which the two leaders had publicly hurled insults and threats at each other, the simple act of talking had changed perceptions on both sides and made conflict less likely.

But the Singapore talks, and subsequent summits in 2018—in Hanoi in February and in the Demilitarized Zone (DMZ) between North and South Korea in June 2019—failed to translate their personal rapport into any meaningful progress. The biggest hurdle, arms control experts say, has been the inability of U.S. and North Korean officials to agree on how the denuclearization process should proceed.

The Trump administration says North Korea must first abandon its nuclear weapons program before Washington provides any sanctions relief, while Pyongyang insists on a gradual process, in which Washington lifts some sanctions in return for each concrete step Pyongyang takes toward denuclearization.

John D. Maurer, an expert in nuclear weapons and geopolitics at the conservative American Enterprise Institute think tank, says the failure of the Hanoi and DMZ meetings publicly embarrassed Kim, who had raised hopes at home that his diplomacy with Trump would result in economic relief. Meanwhile, Trump continued to tout his summit diplomacy with Kim as one of his signature foreign policy achievements.

Kim's loss of face prompted North Korea's warning on Dec. 1, 2019, that unless Washington made further concessions by year's end, Pyongyang would adopt a more confrontational posture.

Trump ignored the deadline. And on New Year's Day, Kim told his ruling Workers Party Central Committee that he no longer felt constrained by the testing moratorium, he would not surrender North Korea's nuclear weapons and North Korea would achieve economic prosperity on its own.

Despite Kim's tough tone, analysts say his speech left the door open for further negotiations by not declaring an end to diplomacy or the resumption of nuclear and long-range missile tests. Going forward, several experts said, Pyongyang's next moves would be based on Trump's ability to win a second presidential term in the November election.

"Donald Trump happens to be the first sitting U.S. president to view North Korea as a source of political victory, for domestic purposes," said Go Myong-Hyun, a research fellow and expert on North Korea at the Seoul-based Asan Institute for Policy Studies think tank. As the election approaches, Go said, North Korea likely will view Trump's habit of boasting to his base about his accomplishments as a source of leverage in future negotiations.[28]

But "if they calculate that President Trump won't be re-elected next year, then their approach is going to fundamentally change," Go said. North Korea could test another nuclear bomb, he said, resume missile tests or take other provocative steps that would effectively end the diplomatic dialogue that Trump and Kim began.[29]

Some Democrats say a deal with Pyongyang is still possible, but only if Trump agrees to embrace a step-by-step approach to North Korea's denuclearization. In a letter to Trump in late December, eight senior Democrats on the Senate Foreign Relations Committee urged him to consider an interim agreement under which North Korea would freeze and roll back some of its nuclear weapons programs in return for some sanctions relief as a first step in executing a "serious diplomatic plan before it is too late."[30]

"While such an interim agreement would of course only be a first step in a longer process, it would nonetheless be an important effort to create the sort of real and durable diplomatic process that is necessary to achieve the complete denuclearization of North Korea," the senators wrote.[31]

Some analysts believe the prospects are dim for a North Korean denuclearization agreement with any U.S. administration, in part because of Pyongyang's deep ideological antipathy toward, and distrust of, the United States. But perhaps the biggest obstacle to North Korea's denuclearization, says Maurer, is Washington's record of eliminating troublesome foreign leaders, such as Iraq's Saddam Hussein and Libyan leader Moammar Gadhafi.

"The North Korean leadership has to look at anything the U.S. government says about cooperation with extreme skepticism," Maurer says. "From their perspective, the United States goes around the world, killing off all the people on its naughty list. And who's at the top of that list today? Kim Jong Un."

Thus, he argues, Kim's nuclear weapons are not just a tool to win sanctions relief from the United States, they are his insurance that he will not end up like Saddam or Gadhafi.

BACKGROUND

Nuclear Age Dawns

The nuclear age dawned with a blinding flash on Aug. 6, 1945, when an American B-29 Superfortress dropped an atomic bomb on the Japanese port city of Hiroshima.

The explosion leveled the entire city, instantly killing 80,000 people. Three days later, the United States dropped a second nuclear bomb on Nagasaki, another port city, killing another 40,000 people. Tens of

Galerie Bilderwelt/Getty Images

The atomic bomb dropped by the United States on Hiroshima in 1945 leveled the Japanese port city. Today's hydrogen weapons are about 1,000 times more powerful than the atomic bomb.

thousands of wounded would die later from severe burns and radiation poisoning. On Aug. 15, Japanese Emperor Hirohito, citing the immense power of "a new and most cruel bomb," surrendered unconditionally, ending World War II.[32]

After years of bloody fighting in Europe and the Pacific, the war's end unleashed scenes of jubilation across the United States. But the bomb's enormous destructive power also forced a moral reckoning among some of the physicists who created it. One of them, J. Robert Oppenheimer, said that as he watched the fiery mushroom cloud rise over the New Mexico desert during the bomb's first test, he remembered a sentence from the Hindu scripture, the Bhagavad-Gita: "I am become death, the destroyer of worlds."[33]

Such moral qualms drove the earliest debates in Washington over controlling the spread of nuclear weapons know-how. One group in the Truman administration worried that America's monopoly over nuclear weapons would spark a dangerous arms race with the Soviet Union, which was competing with the United States in a budding Cold War for global influence. This group proposed sharing the nation's nuclear secrets with Moscow to establish a parity that would stabilize relations. Another group opposed giving up America's strategic advantage over the Soviets.[34]

In 1946, the United States proposed that the newly formed United Nations establish an international agency to control the proliferation of nuclear weapons, but preserve Washington's status as the world's only nuclear power. The Soviets, already on their way to developing

CHRONOLOGY

1939-1949 *The nuclear age dawns, and the U.S.-Soviet arms race ensues.*

1939 With Nazi Germany's discovery of nuclear fission, physicist Albert Einstein warns President Franklin D. Roosevelt of the potential for a new type of "extremely powerful bombs"; Roosevelt institutes the Manhattan Project to explore the feasibility of atomic weapons.

1945 The United States drops atomic bombs on the Japanese cities of Hiroshima and Nagasaki, ending World War II.

1949 The Soviet Union explodes an atomic bomb, marking the beginning of the U.S.-Soviet nuclear arms race.

1950-1963 *Cold War competition eventually leads to arms control efforts.*

1952-53 The United States detonates the world's first hydrogen bomb, far more powerful than the atomic bomb used at Hiroshima. . . . Britain becomes a nuclear power.

1957 The arms race moves into space after the Soviets launch the satellite *Sputnik*.

1960 France tests an atomic bomb.

1962 The Cuban missile crisis brings the U.S. and the Soviet Union to the brink of nuclear war.

1963 Washington and Moscow establish a hotline and sign the Limited Test Ban Treaty, banning nuclear weapons testing in the atmosphere, underwater and outer space but allowing underground tests.

1964-1979 *Major arms control agreements advance despite Cold War tensions.*

1964 China becomes the fifth nuclear-armed nation.

1968 The United Nations adopts the Treaty on the Non-Proliferation of Nuclear Weapons, which recognizes the five nuclear-armed countries; all other signatories commit to use nuclear power only for peaceful purposes.

1972 The United States and the Soviet Union sign SALT I agreement, freezing the number of long-range ballistic missiles at 1972 levels, and the Anti-Ballistic Missile (ABM) Treaty, which limits each side to a single anti-missile battery with 100 missiles and launchers.

1979 U.S. and Soviet leaders sign SALT II, limiting each country to 1,320 long-range missiles with multiple nuclear warheads, but the Senate fails to ratify it after the Soviets invade Afghanistan; both countries honor the treaty's limits anyway.

1980-1993 *Arms control progresses; the Soviet Union collapses.*

1987 President Ronald Reagan and Soviet leader Mikhail Gorbachev sign the Intermediate-Range Nuclear Forces (INF) Treaty, eliminating all ballistic missiles with a range of 300 to 3,400 miles.

1991 Gorbachev and President George H.W. Bush sign START I, capping each country's arsenal at 6,000 deployed nuclear warheads and 1,600 deployed long-range delivery systems. . . . After the Soviet Union collapses, the Cooperative Threat Reduction Program secures Soviet nuclear weapons and fissile material held in former satellite states.

1993 U.S. and Russia sign START II, limiting each side to 3,500 deployed strategic nuclear warheads.

2000-2015 *Cracks appear in arms control, but other agreements follow.*

2002 President George W. Bush withdraws from ABM Treaty, citing alleged threats from rogue nations such as Iraq; in response, Russia withdraws from START II. . . . Iraq is later found not to be building nuclear weapons.

2010 Obama and Russian President Dmitry Medvedev sign New START, further reducing their respective deployed nuclear arsenals to 1,550 warheads and 700 delivery systems.

2015 Iran signs agreement with six world powers, promising to curtail its nuclear program in exchange for relief from U.N. economic sanctions.

2016-Present *Trump administration begins abandoning arms control agreements.*

2016 Donald Trump wins the presidency, calls Iran nuclear agreement and New START "bad deals."

2018 Russian President Vladimir Putin unveils nuclear weapons delivery systems that can travel more than 20 times the speed of sound; Trump withdraws from Iran nuclear deal, imposes unilateral sanctions on Tehran. . . . Trump says he prefers a new arms reduction treaty that

includes China instead of a five-year extension of New START. . . . Trump meets North Korean President Kim Jong Un in Singapore; they agree to work toward denuclearization of the Korean Peninsula; Kim voluntarily freezes nuclear and missile testing.

2019 Trump and Kim fail to agree on how negotiations should proceed. . . . Trump withdraws from INF Treaty, citing alleged Russian violations. . . . Iran restarts part of its nuclear program.

2020 In a New Year's Day speech, Kim declares he is no longer bound by his freeze on nuclear and missile testing. . . . After U.S. drone kills Iran's top military commander, Tehran announces it will fully resume uranium enrichment, signaling the de facto collapse of the Iran nuclear deal (January).

their own atomic bomb, rejected the proposal, and the United States spurned a Soviet counterproposal to ban all nuclear weapons.[35]

The Soviets successfully tested a nuclear bomb in September 1949, sparking the arms race some had feared. Oppenheimer spoke out publicly against U.S. efforts to develop a hydrogen bomb, which would be far more destructive than the atomic bombs used in Japan, angering many in the administration.

Coming at the height of the so-called Red Scare stirred up by Sen. Joseph McCarthy, R-Wisc., Oppenheimer's objections led to an FBI investigation that revealed the physicist had sympathized with communism when he was a young professor at the University of California, Berkeley. At a hearing to rule on the revocation of Oppenheimer's security clearance, Edward Teller, another prominent nuclear physicist, portrayed him as a security risk. Stripped of his clearance, Oppenheimer continued to lecture widely on the dangers of nuclear weapons, but he had no impact on the burgeoning arms race.[36]

Over the next two decades, the Americans and Soviets developed immensely destructive hydrogen bombs, along with neutron bombs, which leave structures standing but kill people with high levels of radiation; intercontinental ballistic missiles capable of carrying multiple nuclear warheads; and a vast arsenal of small, tactical nuclear weapons for battlefield use,

such as nuclear landmines, artillery shells and torpedoes. With the Soviet's successful 1957 launch of *Sputnik*, the first artificial Earth satellite, the two countries extended their rivalry into outer space. During that period, Britain, France and China also became nuclear weapons states.

In 1962, the Cold War rivalry between the superpowers reached a crisis when U.S. intelligence discovered the Soviets had deployed nuclear-armed missiles in Cuba, 90 miles from the U.S. mainland. In response, President John F. Kennedy deployed a naval blockade around Cuba to prevent additional Soviet missiles from reaching the island. He also demanded that Moscow remove the existing missiles, warning he was prepared to use military force to neutralize the Soviet threat. [37]

Over the next 13 days, a tense standoff ensued that brought the two countries to the brink of nuclear war. "I thought it was the last Saturday I would ever see," Robert McNamara, Kennedy's Defense secretary, later told Cold War historian Martin Walker.[38]

Eventually, Kennedy and Soviet leader Nikita Khrushchev resolved the crisis peacefully. Kennedy agreed to Khrushchev's proposal to remove the missiles in return for a U.S. pledge not to invade Cuba. Privately, Kennedy also agreed to remove U.S. missiles from Turkey, which the Soviets saw as a threat.[39]

Experts Say Nuclear Terrorism Threat Is Overstated

"Countries won't give nuclear weapons to terrorists."

Ever since the 9/11 terrorist attacks in the United States in 2001, Western leaders, lawmakers and national security officials have feared that terrorists would obtain a nuclear weapon, or the fissile material to make one, and use it to attack Western capitals or regional rivals.

After 9/11, President George W. Bush explained the need to invade Iraq by lumping it with Iran and North Korea in his 2002 State of the Union speech, calling them "an axis of evil" that threatened world peace. "By seeking weapons of mass destruction, these regimes pose a grave and growing danger," he said. "They could provide these arms to terrorists, giving them the means to match their hatred."[1]

President Barack Obama echoed Bush's concerns when he told a 2016 White House summit on nuclear security: "There is no doubt that if these madmen ever got their hands on a nuclear bomb or nuclear material, they most certainly would use it to kill as many innocent people as possible."[2]

And former CIA Director R. James Woolsey (1993-95) famously said in 1994, "Terrorists don't want a seat at the table, they want to destroy the table and everyone sitting at it."[3]

But some terrorism experts say those assumptions are based on cartoonish perceptions of anti-American regimes and terrorists as single-minded, suicidal fanatics. Counterterrorism officials could better avoid catastrophe by approaching such threats with an eye toward terrorists' strategic priorities, they say, and not simplistic assumptions that detonation is their primary goal.

Moreover, they note, citing detailed studies and empirical data, the likelihood of a government providing a nuclear bomb or fissile material to a terrorist group is vastly overstated.

"Countries won't give nuclear weapons to terrorists," says Keir Lieber, an expert on nuclear weapons and geopolitics at Georgetown University. And "it is implausible that terrorists could develop a nuclear weapon on their own."

Even a state sponsor of terrorism would avoid giving a nuclear weapon to a proxy terrorist group, according to Lieber and Daryl G. Press, an associate professor of government at Dartmouth College and an expert on nuclear deterrence. "Nuclear weapons are the most powerful weapons a state can acquire," the two wrote in a 2013 article in the journal *International Security*. "Handing that power to an actor over which the state has less than complete control would be an enormous, epochal decision—one unlikely to be taken by regimes that are typically obsessed with power and their own survival."[4]

In addition, they argued, forensic examination of the radioactive isotopes that remain after a nuclear blast would reveal the uranium mines, reactors and enrichment facilities where the bomb originated, exposing the state sponsor to

---

Decades later, former advisers to Khrushchev disclosed that 43,000 Soviet soldiers had secretly amassed on the island to defend the missiles against a U.S. invasion, according to a new history of nuclear warfare by *Slate* defense reporter Fred Kaplan. In his review of the book for *The Washington Post*, author Evan Thomas noted that those troops were armed with tactical nuclear weapons.[40]

Arms Control Treaties

Shaken by the missile crisis, Washington and Moscow agreed the following year to establish a communications hotline between their leaders to mitigate the risk of accidental nuclear warfare. The two countries also signed the Limited Test Ban Treaty, which forbade most nuclear test explosions.[41]

Another major arms control effort occurred in 1968 with the signing of the U.N.-sponsored Nuclear Non-Proliferation Treaty. It recognized the five existing nuclear-weapons states—the United States, the Soviet Union, Britain, France and China—and required their pledge to work toward nuclear disarmament. The treaty also obligated non-nuclear states not to acquire nuclear

retaliation. Plus, they added, a state sponsor would worry that terrorists might use such a weapon in an unexpected way or provoke a response that would end the sponsor's regime.[5]

However, there is still some cause for concern, experts say. If a terrorist group obtained a nuclear weapon, its leaders would more likely be guided by strategic considerations, such as potential rewards, rather than sheer rage. Knowing the impact a nuclear blast and the ensuing retaliation would have on public opinion, the group's leaders would seriously consider other options than detonation, they say. But that could still create some painful dilemmas for the terrorists' targets.

For instance, a group could engage in nuclear blackmail, declaring that it has a nuclear weapon and threatening to use it unless the group's conditions were met.

Joseph Cirincione, president of the Ploughshares Fund, a foundation that advocates for nuclear disarmament, paints a frightening nuclear blackmail scenario in which a terrorist group somehow obtains two nuclear bombs, places one in Washington and one in New York City and threatens to destroy the nation's capital unless the United States withdraws its forces from the Middle East. Then, to prove the group's capability, it could detonate the bomb in New York or off the coast.

"What does a U.S. president do" in such a situation? Cirincione asks. "There is no good response."

Christopher McIntosh and Ian Storey, terrorism experts at Bard College, say a nuclear-armed terrorist group also could announce that it has a nuclear weapon but present no demands, instilling fear among its enemies, "without committing the organization to a definite strategic path," they wrote.[6]

Or a terrorist group could simply suggest—but not confirm—that it has a nuclear weapon, a strategic posture used by Israel for 50 years, according to Avner Cohen, author of the 1999 book *Israel and the Bomb*.

McIntosh and Storey say a terrorist group also could keep its nuclear capability a secret until it decides conditions are right to unveil it and issue demands.

But numerous studies have shown that terrorist groups try to avoid stepping over a line that will draw catastrophic damage to their organizations and communities. For example, after a border attack in 2006 by the Iranian-backed military group Hezbollah that killed several Israeli soldiers, Israel launched a full-scale war that killed or wounded some 5,600 people, displaced another million and destroyed much of Lebanon's civilian infrastructure.

Many Lebanese blamed Hezbollah for their suffering, causing Hassan Nasrallah, the group's leader, to declare that, had he known Israel's response would be so devastating, he would never have ordered the attack.

—Jonathan Broder

[1] "Text of President Bush's 2002 State of the Union Address," *The Washington Post*, Jan. 29, 2002, https://tinyurl.com/rq8zyq4.

[2] David Smith, "Barack Obama at nuclear summit: 'madmen' threaten global security," *The Guardian*, April 1, 2016, https://tinyurl.com/t4o9r3e.

[3] Nicholas Lemann, "What Terrorists Want," *The New Yorker*, Oct. 22, 2001, https://tinyurl.com/qmgejrz.

[4] Keir A. Lieber and Daryl G. Press, "Why States Won't Give Nuclear Weapons to Terrorists," *International Security*, Vol. 38, No. 1, Summer 2013, https://tinyurl.com/uwua7p8.

[5] *Ibid.*

[6] Christopher McIntosh and Ian Storey, "Would terrorists set off a nuclear weapon if they had one? We shouldn't assume so," *Bulletin of the Atomic Scientists*, Nov. 20, 2019, https://tinyurl.com/s3h69no.

weapons but guaranteed them the right to civilian nuclear power, subject to certain safeguards. Eventually, 187 countries signed on, making the treaty one of the pillars of a global arms control architecture. (Israel, India and Pakistan refused to sign and later became nuclear weapons states. Cuba and South Sudan have refused to join the treaty but do not have nuclear weapons.)[42]

In 1972, President Richard M. Nixon, long an anti-communist hawk, traveled to China, fostering a rapprochement that upended the balance of power between Washington and Moscow. Worried about a new Sino-American alliance, Moscow quickly reached two major arms control agreements with Washington that same year.

The first, the Strategic Arms Limitation Treaty, or SALT I, froze the number of each country's long-range ballistic missile launchers and submarine-launched ballistic missiles at existing levels. The second accord, the Anti-Ballistic Missile (ABM) Treaty restricted the number of anti-missile batteries each side could deploy.[43]

The Erosion of Arms Control Will Extend to Outer Space

China and Russia are developing missiles that can destroy satellites.

If the United States and Russia allow the New START arms control pact to expire next year, the subsequent end of all remaining limits on their nuclear arsenals will affect not only strategic stability on Earth but also in outer space, experts say.

The expiration will eliminate prohibitions on interfering with each other's intelligence satellites and other methods for verifying treaty compliance, warns a new study by Aerospace Corp.'s Center for Space Policy and Strategy, a research center that analyzes space programs for the U.S. military.[1]

"This will mark a significant change in the strategic context within which U.S. national security space forces operate," the study said. "U.S. space forces' resources will be taxed, and the stability of the space domain will face new risks."[2]

The study came out weeks after President Trump, authorized by Congress, announced creation of the U.S. Space Force, the military's sixth branch, which aims to defend the United States and its satellites and spacecraft from hostile forces. With New START due to expire in February 2021 and no sign from Trump that he will activate the treaty's five-year extension provision, the study details some of the challenges the Space Force and intelligence agencies will face in a post-New START world.

Michael Gleason, a senior strategic space analyst and co-author of the study, told reporters at a Jan. 15 news conference that on-site inspections conducted by U.S. and Russian officials as part of the treaty's verification provisions will end. Thus, he said, there will be greater demand—and costs—for U.S. satellite surveillance of Russia's nuclear forces.

Gleason also warned that after decades during which the United States and Russia left each other's reconnaissance and military satellites alone, the Pentagon should be prepared for the possibility that Russia may try to challenge U.S. satellite overflights of its territory by interfering with them.

According to a U.S. intelligence analysis of open-source documents, Russia is developing a satellite system called Burevestnik, believed to be designed to disrupt and destroy other countries' satellites. The documents suggest the Burevestnik will be a co-orbital satellite, or one that is deployed in an orbit similar to its target, capable of assessing the functions of Russian satellites as well as inspecting or killing an adversary's satellites.[3]

U.S. intelligence officials also have cited Russia's extensive testing of its PL-19 Nudol anti-satellite missile, which is fired from a mobile launcher and targets enemy satellites in low-Earth orbit, 250 miles above the planet.[4] The Pentagon's "2019 Missile Defense Review" cited such anti-satellite missiles as one of several Russian threats, including laser weapons.

Russia is developing a diverse suite of anti-satellite capabilities, including ground-launched missiles and laser weapons, "and continues to launch 'experimental' satellites that conduct sophisticated on-orbit activities to advance counterspace capabilities," the report said.[5]

U.S. officials acknowledge the Pentagon is developing anti-satellite capabilities, but details remain classified.

Meanwhile, studies published last April focus on counterspace activities by China, which in 2007 stunned the U.S. defense community by firing a missile that destroyed one of its own defunct weather satellites, creating a large field of space debris that continues to pose risks to the International Space Station and other satellites.[6] China demonstrated further technological advances in space last

But the budding detente quickly dissipated after Washington and Moscow lined up on opposing sides of the 1973 Arab-Israeli War. After two weeks of fierce fighting, Israeli forces had blunted a Syrian attack on the Golan Heights and advanced to within artillery range of Damascus while Israeli tanks had crossed the Suez Canal and surrounded Egypt's Third Army. With Moscow threatening to intervene with nuclear weapons to save its beleaguered Arab clients, Nixon placed U.S. nuclear forces on a midlevel alert, once again bringing the two superpowers to the precipice of nuclear war. Eventually, a battlefield ceasefire defused the crisis.

year when it became the first country to land a probe on the dark side of the moon.[7]

The April studies—one conducted by the Center for Strategic and International Studies (CSIS), an independent Washington think tank, and the other by the Secure World Foundation, a research organization that promotes the peaceful uses of space—noted that China continues to test the ability of its SJ-17 satellite to maneuver close to another to inspect, repair or monitor its functions. China also appears to have deployed mobile jammers on Mischief Reef in the South China Sea's Spratly Islands that can disrupt other countries' ground-to-space communications, according to the CSIS study.[8]

Both studies say China is developing at least three types of missiles capable of hitting satellites orbiting between 250 miles and 22,236 miles above Earth. The Secure World Foundation study says one of the three anti-satellite missiles is probably operational and may already have been deployed on mobile Chinese launchers.[9]

"China is clearly investing in its counter-space capabilities," the CSIS study says. "Evidence confirms that in 2018 alone, China tested technologies in three of the four counter-space weapon categories."[10]

The four categories include kinetic weapons, such as missiles and killer satellites, designed to smash into or explode next to a satellite; nonkinetic weapons, such as lasers, high-powered microwaves or electromagnetic pulses that can blind or disable satellites; electronic weapons that can jam satellite communications or trick them with fake signals; and cyber-weapons that target the data from satellites.[11]

"The big changes to Chinese doctrine and space organization happened a few years ago when they created their Strategic Support Force," said Brian Weeden, director of program planning at the Secure World Foundation and co-editor of its study. "This is a new military organization that combines space, electronic warfare and cyber capabilities."[12]

Military technology experts say China probably began building up its counterspace capabilities when the U.S. military started relying heavily on its constellation of communications, surveillance and intelligence-gathering satellites at the outset of its wars in Afghanistan and Iraq.

But with New START's expiration looming, Russia is the most immediate concern, the Aerospace study stressed. Urging the Trump administration to begin planning for the day after the treaty expires, the study suggested either a negotiated understanding or a formal agreement with Moscow not to interfere with one another's satellites.

"No alternative future foresees the existing status quo surviving after New START expires," the study said.

—Jonathan Broder

[1] Michael P. Gleason and Luc H. Riesbeck, "Noninterference With National Technical Means: The Status Quo Will Not Survive," Center for Space Policy and Strategy, Aerospace Corp., January 2020, https://tinyurl.com/uqgs2v9.

[2] *Ibid.*

[3] "Russia develops co-orbital anti-satellite capability," *Jane's Intelligence Review*, 2018, https://tinyurl.com/uycd8mo.

[4] "Russian Space Wars: U.S. Intelligence Claims Kremlin Made Seventh Test of Nudol ASAT Missile," Spacewatch.global, 2019, https://tinyurl.com/s7pwx7b.

[5] "2019 Missile Defense Review," Office of the Secretary of Defense, Department of Defense, January 2019, https://tinyurl.com/y9hkqfnj.

[6] Michael Safi and Hannah Devlin, "'A terrible thing': India's destruction of satellite threatens ISS, says NASA," *The Guardian*, April 2, 2019, https://tinyurl.com/yyuezl8l.

[7] Trefor Moss, "China Lands Probe on the 'Dark Side' of the Moon," *The Wall Street Journal*, Jan. 3, 2019, https://tinyurl.com/yborl7kj.

[8] Todd Harrison *et al.*, "Space Threat Assessment 2019," Center for Strategic and International Studies, April 2019, https://tinyurl.com/vwo77oh.

[9] Brian Weeden and Victoria Samson, "Global Counterspace Capabilities: An Open Source Assessment," Secure World Foundation, April 2019, https://tinyurl.com/qmnndgj.

[10] Harrison *et al.*, *op. cit.*

[11] *Ibid.*

[12] Kelsey D. Atherton, "The chicken-and-egg debate about new threats in space," C4ISRNET, April 8, 2019, https://tinyurl.com/t9m5wjq.

A year later, Nixon resigned over the Watergate scandal. U.S.-Soviet Arms control talks resumed, and in June 1979, President Jimmy Carter and Soviet General Secretary Leonid Brezhnev signed the SALT II accords, further limiting the number of each side's nuclear warheads and ICBMs. But six months later, the Soviets invaded Afghanistan, prompting Carter to ask the Senate to delay consideration of the treaty. Although the Senate never ratified SALT II, both sides honored it, underscoring the value each placed on its controls.[44]

President Ronald Reagan made arms control a priority with his bold 1981 "zero-option" proposal, which called for the removal of all U.S. and Soviet intermediate-range nuclear missiles from Europe. He followed up the following year with a proposal to reduce the number of each side's strategic nuclear warheads.[45]

In 1983, Reagan introduced a plan for a space-based missile shield against Soviet nuclear attack. Some experts questioned the effectiveness of the initiative, which they nicknamed "Star Wars." But the program alarmed the Soviets, who feared they were falling behind the Americans in both defense technology and spending.[46]

That same year, Mikhail Gorbachev became the Soviet Communist Party's general secretary and introduced greater openness along with economic and political reforms, transformative policies that set the stage for more cooperation on arms control.

In 1986, Reagan and Gorbachev met in Reykjavík, Iceland, for what arms control experts have called one of the most extraordinary U.S.-Soviet summits ever held. The two leaders nearly agreed to complete nuclear disarmament within 10 years. Gorbachev's demand to limit tests for Reagan's space missiles killed the deal, but experts say their talks paved the way for later arms control agreements.[47]

One was the Intermediate-Range Nuclear Forces, or INF, Treaty, which Reagan and Gorbachev signed in December 1987. It banned all intermediate-range nuclear missiles, an arms control milestone, experts say, because it was the first agreement to abolish an entire class of nuclear arms, as opposed to limiting their number.[48]

On Nov. 9, 1989, the Berlin Wall fell, marking the beginning of the end of the Cold War and greater progress on arms control. In July 1991, Gorbachev and President George H.W. Bush signed the Strategic Arms Reduction Treaty (START I), which limited the United States and the Soviet Union each to deploy 6,000 warheads and 1,600 delivery vehicles.[49]

After the Soviet Union collapsed in late 1991, Bush signed bipartisan legislation creating the Cooperative Threat Reduction Program. The brainchild of Democratic Sen. Nunn of Georgia and Republican Sen. Richard Lugar of Indiana, the legislation provided financial and technical assistance to former Soviet republics to dismantle thousands of nuclear weapons, remove their stockpiles of

plutonium and highly enriched uranium needed to make such weapons, and provide their nuclear scientists with civilian jobs.[50]

In 1993, Russia and the United States signed START II, banning the use of multiple nuclear warheads deployed on ICBMs. Although the U.S. Senate and the Russian Duma, or parliament, ratified the agreement, it never went into effect because of unresolved differences in other areas of arms control.[51]

Cracks Appear

Those differences opened the first cracks in the arms control edifice. In June 2002, President George W. Bush, the son of the former president, withdrew from the Anti-Ballistic Missile Treaty Nixon had signed 30 years earlier, arguing that it limited U.S. ability to deploy missile defenses against rogue states. Russia's new president, Vladimir Putin, strongly opposed the move, and in response, he also pulled out of the treaty, preventing it from taking effect.[52]

Tensions between Washington and Moscow escalated in 2007 when Bush announced plans to base anti-missile batteries in Poland and the Czech Republic, former Soviet-controlled Warsaw Pact countries that joined NATO after the Soviet Union's demise. Bush maintained the missiles were needed to defend NATO allies against Iran's missiles. But Putin saw them as anti-missile systems that could potentially be turned against Russia, blunting its nuclear arsenal.

U.S.-Russia relations improved after President Barack Obama took office in 2009. Eager to enhance cooperation, Obama announced he would scrap Bush's plan for the Eastern European anti-missile sites and rely instead on the anti-missile systems aboard U.S. Navy warships.

The following year, Obama and Russian President Dmitry Medvedev signed New START, capping each country's deployed nuclear warheads at 1,550 and its long-range delivery systems at 700. Like the previous U.S.-Russia treaties, New START included extensive verification procedures, providing transparency for both sides.[53]

In 2012, in another major nonproliferation effort, the United States and five other world powers began negotiating with Iran to halt its nuclear program, which many experts suspected was close to developing a nuclear bomb. In 2015, Tehran agreed to curtail its nuclear program in return for relief from international sanctions that had hobbled Iran's economy.

Israel and its supporters in Congress condemned the deal, arguing that once key provisions expired after 10 years, Iran would be free to resume its weapons development. In his 2016 campaign for the presidency, Republican nominee Trump echoed those allegations, vowing if elected to withdraw from the Iran deal and negotiate a tougher accord permanently halting Iran's nuclear and ballistic missile programs and ending its support for proxy military forces across the Middle East.

After winning the 2016 election, Trump turned his attention to North Korea, which was testing its nuclear weapons and long-range ballistic missiles capable of reaching the United States. Trump and North Korean leader Kim taunted each other with personal insults and threats.

In early 2018, the Pentagon released its updated "Nuclear Posture Review," detailing the administration's plans to modernize the nation's nuclear arsenal and presenting limited tactical nuclear war as a viable battlefield strategy.[54]

On May 8, that year, Trump made good on his promise to withdraw from the Iran deal. Six months later, he reimposed crippling sanctions on the Islamic Republic and gave its leaders a stark choice: sign a tougher accord or watch Iran's economy collapse. A defiant Iran refused and slowly reactivated its nuclear program.

In June of that year, Trump stunned arms control advocates and defense hawks by becoming the first sitting U.S. president to meet with a North Korean leader. Gambling that their personal diplomacy could sweep away decades of hostility and distrust, Trump and Kim held talks in Singapore and agreed to begin negotiations toward denuclearization of the Korean Peninsula.[55]

Meeting Kim for a second time in Hanoi in February 2019, Trump abruptly walked out of their summit after rejecting what U.S. officials said was the North Korean leader's demand for relief from all U.S. sanctions in return for dismantling his main nuclear facility at Yongbyon. North Korea said it had asked for a partial lifting of sanctions.[56]

Last August, the two leaders met a third time, in the Demilitarized Zone between the two Koreas, and Trump even stepped briefly into North Korean territory—another first for a U.S. president. But their differences remained over how negotiations should proceed. North Korea experts say Kim wanted a step-by-step process in which the United States would reward North Korea's gradual denuclearization with gradual sanctions relief and the removal of U.S. nuclear forces from the region. On the advice of his hawkish advisers, Trump insisted North Korea first surrender all of its nuclear and ballistic missile programs before the United States would provide any sanctions relief.

Arms control withered further last August when Trump withdrew from the Intermediate-Range Nuclear Forces Treaty with Russia. Like Obama before him, he accused Russia of covertly developing and deploying a banned intermediate-range cruise missile that could threaten both Europe and Asia, a charge Russia denied. Congress later authorized $10 million for tactical nuclear warheads to be mounted on intermediate-range ballistic missiles capable of reaching Russia after being launched from submarines in the region.[57]

The Defense and Energy appropriations bills signed into law in December provided the Trump administration with $30.8 billion to maintain and modernize the military's nuclear arsenal and to pay for new nuclear-armed missiles, missile-launching submarines and long-range bombers.[58]

In what arms control advocates considered a hopeful sign, Putin announced late last year that he was ready to extend New START until 2026. Trump, however, refused to commit to its extension, citing his preference for a treaty that would include China.

In the end, 2019 came to a close with the future of New START, North Korea's denuclearization and Iran's nuclear program under clouds of uncertainty.

CURRENT SITUATION
Korean Diplomacy Fizzles

Many analysts believe North Korean leader Kim is embarking upon a defiant path for 2020 with his year-end policy speech announcing he no longer feels bound by his self-imposed moratorium on missile tests. Kim cited

President Trump's failure to reciprocate with any relief from sanctions that have hobbled North Korea's economy.

"If the U.S. persists in its hostile policy toward the DPRK, there will never be the denuclearization on the Korean Peninsula, and the DPRK will steadily develop necessary and prerequisite strategic weapons for the security of the state until the U.S. rolls back its hostile policy," Kim said, using the initials of his country's official name, the Democratic People's Republic of Korea.[59]

Nevertheless, Trump continues to believe his personal rapport with Kim holds the promise for an historic agreement that would see the communist nation give up its nuclear weapons.

"Look, he likes me, I like him, we get along," Trump said about his relationship with Kim while speaking to reporters on New Year's Eve at his Mar-a-Lago resort. "But he did sign a contract, he did sign an agreement talking about denuclearization. . . . I think he's a man of his word, so we're going to find out."[60]

In his speech, Kim appeared to leave the door open to further diplomacy by saying the nuclear tests would resume if Washington refused to drop its demands that North Korea first fully denuclearize. Further complicating any future negotiations is North Korea's definition of denuclearization, which includes the removal of all U.S. nuclear forces from South Korea.

Since then, there has been no sign that Trump has softened his position. But Trump sent Kim birthday

JOE KLAMAR/AFP via Getty Images

U.S. President Barack Obama and Russian President Dmitry Medvedev shake hands after signing the New Strategic Arms Reduction Treaty (New START) in 2010 in Prague. The pact committed the two nations to major nuclear arms cuts.

greetings in early January in a gesture that analysts said was aimed at defusing tensions and preparing the ground for another summit. In a response, carried by the official Korean Central News Agency, North Korean Foreign Ministry adviser Kim Kye Gwan said it would be "stupid" to expect that Kim's personal relationship with Trump would be enough to restart negotiations.[61]

Talks will resume, he said, when Washington agrees to the proposal Kim put forward at his Hanoi summit with Trump last June: That North Korea would dismantle its principal nuclear facility at Yongbyon in exchange for the partial lifting of U.N. sanctions on North Korea. "There is no need for us to be present in such talks, in which there is only unilateral pressure," Kim Kye Gwan said, "and we have no desire to barter something for other things at the talks, like traders."[62]

On Capitol Hill, the eight Democratic senators who wrote to Trump in December urged him to come up with a comprehensive strategy to advance denuclearization talks, including a "phased process to verifiably dismantle the Yongbyon nuclear complex and other nuclear facilities."[63]

But Kori Schake, who has served in senior policy positions at the Pentagon, State Department and National Security Council in both Democratic and Republican administrations, says the prospects for any progress toward North Korea's denuclearization appear slim. "The Trump administration doesn't appear to think that agreements require any compromise from them," says Schake. "Most negotiations work better when your position isn't 'Give me everything first, and then I'll give you something.' They're not invested in a process that builds confidence as it builds momentum."

According to several independent experts who closely follow North Korean issues, the administration's position has thwarted Stephen Biegun, Trump's top North Korea negotiator, who has been unable to persuade Trump and Secretary of State Mike Pompeo to adopt a step-by-step negotiating process.

In an appearance on ABC's "This Week" just before the new year, Robert O'Brien, Trump's fourth national security adviser, echoed the president's hard line, warning the United States will respond if North Korea resumes nuclear weapons and long-range ballistic missile tests.

Is limited nuclear war a viable battlefield option?

YES
John D. Maurer
Jeane Kirkpatrick Fellow, American Enterprise Institute

Written for *CQ Researcher*, February 2020

The most viable way to prevent a limited nuclear war is to be ready to fight one. As such, the United States must modernize its arsenal of tactical or so-called low-yield nuclear weapons, whose explosive power can range from the equivalent of 20 tons of TNT to as high as a Hiroshima-sized bomb, which was 16,000 tons. Fielding such weapons will ensure that U.S. leaders have options short of all-out war to respond to nuclear provocation and will signal to adversaries that they cannot hope to escalate their way out of a losing conventional battle. By closing off options for escalation, low-yield U.S. weapons will help deter adversaries from embarking on militarized crises in the first place. Furthermore, improving and expanding U.S. low-yield capabilities will create an incentive for rivals to take seriously proposals to eliminate such weapons.

Those who oppose the United States developing tactical nuclear weapons argue that they are destabilizing because the collateral damage they cause is small enough that decision-makers might be tempted to use them in a crisis. But nuclear war is only likely to occur against the backdrop of a major conventional war between the great powers. If one of those powers fears defeat on the conventional battlefield, it will face strong pressures to use nuclear weapons to stave off that loss.

The escalatory pressure emerges not from the character of the nuclear weapons themselves, but from the looming threat of conventional military humiliation. If the losing great power has low-yield weapons that it can use without fear of reprisal, nuclear war is all but assured. Only the threat of a proportional nuclear response would deter adversaries from using such weapons to stave off defeat.

Modernizing the U.S. low-yield nuclear arsenal also provides the clearest path to eliminating tactical nuclear weapons entirely. Rivals such as Russia and China already maintain large numbers of these weapons and have no incentive to dismantle them if the United States does not have a similar capability to trade away in negotiations. Critics of low-yield nuclear weapons who are serious about eliminating their escalatory potential should support U.S. nuclear modernization as a first step toward bringing adversaries to the bargaining table.

The United States cannot abide a world in which adversaries such as Russia and China have low-yield weapons, while the United States does not. As our adversaries engage in increasingly threatening behavior toward U.S. allies, the United States needs a nuclear arsenal that will ensure deterrence—not just on good days, but also on the worst days.

NO
Joseph Cirincione
President, Ploughshares Fund

Written for *CQ Researcher*, February 2020

We refuse to learn from history. Almost 40 years ago, Defense Secretary Robert McNamara wrote: "It is inconceivable to me, as it has been to others who have studied the matter, that 'limited' nuclear wars would remain limited—any decision to use nuclear weapons would imply a high probability of the same cataclysmic consequences as a total nuclear exchange." McNamara concluded, along with his British colleagues, that "under no circumstances" would they have recommended "that NATO initiate the use of nuclear weapons."

But that is precisely what a new generation of Dr. Strangeloves recommends today. They have embraced the Cold War theory of "escalation dominance" and favor new, more usable nuclear weapons to fight even conventional conflicts. They argue that if the United States has greater military force on every rung of the "escalatory ladder," it can convince an enemy to surrender early in a conflict.

But that attractive theoretical concept has little relationship to any conceivable conflict scenario, in which even a militarily inferior adversary has multiple ways of escalating a conflict. For example, the United States is militarily superior to Iran, but with a few mines and speedy patrol boats, Tehran could close the Strait of Hormuz, crippling oil flows and plunging the world economy into recession.

Yet, Iran is precisely where some in Washington favor using nuclear weapons. A 2017 Pentagon war game used U.S.-based bombers to drop a low-yield nuclear weapon on Iran. But because it would take a 10-hour flight to deliver this weapon, the Trump administration has just deployed—with congressional approval—a low-yield nuclear warhead that can be launched from submarines off Iran's coast. This Hiroshima-sized bomb could explode within 15 minutes of launch.

Supporters justify this scenario by arguing it offers "multiple options" and "maximum flexibility," providing military solutions to even the most difficult political problems. Most serious analysts recognized long ago that this strategy leads to disaster.

"A nuclear weapon is a nuclear weapon," warned former Secretary of State George Shultz. "You use a small one, then you go to a bigger one."

Iran does not have nuclear weapons, but Russia and China do. The first use of nuclear weapons against those countries would not be the last. Commanders can have no confidence that they can control or contain a limited nuclear war. Rather than being a strategy for victory, it guarantees defeat for all sides.

"We will take action, as we do in these situations," O'Brien said. "If Kim Jong Un takes that approach, we will be extraordinarily disappointed, and we will demonstrate that disappointment." He declined to provide any specifics but said the administration has many "tools in its tool kit" to respond to any such tests.[64]

Other White House officials say Trump is not looking for another confrontation with Kim in an election year. If the tests resume, they say, Trump is likely to press the United Nations to tighten sanctions against North Korea—a strategy that previous administrations have used to little effect.

Nuclear weapons experts say in the year and a half since the Singapore summit, Kim has built up his missile stores and produced enough bomb-grade nuclear fuel for about 38 warheads—double an earlier estimate issued by U.S. intelligence analysts.

Pressure for New START

Meanwhile, lawmakers are stepping up pressure on the Trump administration to extend New START, introducing bipartisan legislation in both chambers that would strengthen a requirement to assess the costs and implications of allowing the treaty to expire next February.

With Trump still unwilling to commit to the pact's extension in order to explore including China, the House and Senate bills would require the administration to provide intelligence estimates on how much Russian and Chinese nuclear forces could expand if New START expires. Lawmakers also want to know how much it would cost for U.S. intelligence to ascertain such developments without an extension of New START's verification provisions.

The bills echo a provision in the new fiscal 2020 National Defense Authorization Act, which requires the administration to estimate how large Russia's tactical nuclear arsenal and China's nuclear modernization program will grow if New START is allowed to lapse.[65]

Congressional aides say the legislation reflects serious concerns on Capitol Hill that the administration has not sufficiently analyzed the strategic implications of allowing New START to expire. Moreover, lawmakers from both parties and arms control experts say they are unaware of any concerted administration effort to formulate a negotiating strategy for China.

Countryman, the former assistant secretary of State for international security and nonproliferation, notes that while Trump announced his plan for a tripartite arms control treaty last May, the State Department only invited China to begin what it called a bilateral "strategic security dialogue" in December. "After saying they wanted to negotiate with China, it took them nine months to officially communicate that," he says.

State Department officials will not say whether China has responded to its invitation, but Beijing repeatedly has said it has no interest in three-way nuclear arms reduction talks, because the Russian and U.S. arsenals are already 20 times the size of China's.

In February 2020, national security adviser Robert O'Brien said the Trump administration would soon open nuclear arms control negotiations with Russia. His remarks came 10 months after Secretary of State Mike Pompeo told lawmakers the administration was at the "very beginning of conversations about renewing" New START, indicating it had made no serious diplomatic efforts in the interim.[66]

With the administration struggling to deal with North Korea and Iran, some arms control experts suggest it may not have the bandwidth to focus on Trump's trilateral treaty proposal. The State Department's Office of Strategic Stability and Deterrence Affairs, responsible for negotiating arms control treaties, reportedly has gone from having 14 staffers when Trump took office in 2017 to four. The State Department's top two arms control officials were among those who left, says Bell, the former State Department arms control adviser, and neither has been replaced. The State Department has not commented on the report.

"We simply don't have enough people doing this," says Bell, now the senior policy director at the Council for a Livable World, a Washington-based organization that advocates for nuclear disarmament. "To create these kinds of agreements, you need patience and high-level, disciplined attention paid to those goals. It's hard to see that forthcoming from this administration."

And without the robust verification procedures allowed by New START, it would cost billions of dollars to create new intelligence programs to determine the disposition of Russia's nuclear arsenal, with no guarantees that such programs would succeed, say former arms control officials. The treaty's expiration also would remove any restrictions on the numbers of new hypersonic nuclear weapons Russia could deploy, experts say.

"It is hard to overstate, from my perspective as a senior military leader, how much we benefit from the knowledge and predictability the treaty provides about Russia's nuclear forces and operational practices," Mullen, the former Joint Chiefs chairman, told the House Foreign Affairs Committee in December 2019. "Without the treaty and its verification provisions, we'd be flying blind."[67]

OUTLOOK
Grim Future

The Ploughshares Fund's Cirincione says the future of arms control looks grim. "It's on life support," he says, citing the steady erosion of treaties that once formed the pillars of the arms control architecture.

The United Nations will conduct its five-year review of the nuclear Non-Proliferation Treaty in April and May of 2020, providing a comprehensive assessment of arms control, nonproliferation efforts and progress toward disarmament. Arms control experts expect poor report cards for the United States, Russia and China regarding their commitments to nuclear disarmament.

Arms control experts predict that the review will cite the development of new hypersonic nuclear weapons, cyberwarfare capabilities and the militarization of space as troubling technological advances that will only make nuclear disarmament more difficult. The review is also expected to raise concerns over the collapse of the Intermediate Nuclear Forces Treaty, the stalemate in U.S.-North Korean negotiations, President Trump's withdrawal from the Iran nuclear deal and the possible lapse of the New START and Open Skies treaties.

Meanwhile, the Council for a Livable World's Bell says U.S. investments in both new missiles and missile defenses and the Pentagon's buildup of tactical nuclear weapons are foreboding signs. "This looks like a recommitment to the concept of nuclear war fighting," she says.

Nunn, of the Nuclear Threat Initiative, says a key factor for the future of arms control is sustained communication between the United States and Russia over maintaining strategic stability. Although Putin and Trump have agreed to hold such talks, few meetings between their military representatives have taken place. "When we're not having a military-to-military dialogue, arms control is eroded," Nunn says.

The American Enterprise Institute's Maurer believes arms control will probably remain dormant for the next 10 to 30 years—the time it will take for the United States to fully modernize its nuclear weapons and delivery systems. At that point, he predicts, Russia and China will make arms control a priority because the technical superiority of America's arsenal will leave them vulnerable.

"Once our capabilities mature, that's when we'll see the Russians and the Chinese become interested in arms control negotiations," Maurer said. "We saw this during the Cold War. The Russians were always the most eager for arms control talks when we had a big military program coming down the pipeline, whether it was our missile defense system in the 1970s that resulted in the ABM Treaty, or our Pershing II and Trident missiles in the 1980s that led to the INF and START treaties."

But Nunn fears that kind of thinking is an enormous gamble.

"We've gone 75 years without a nuclear explosion," he says. "To think we're going to go another 50 years without an awful lot of cooperation between the nuclear powers is pretty naive. We've become accustomed to thinking that because it hasn't happened, it won't happen. But that defies both the odds and history."

NOTES

1. "Russia deploys new hypersonic nuclear-capable missiles that can travel 27 times the speed of sound," *The Associated Press*, *The Straits Times*, Dec. 28, 2019, https://tinyurl.com/wb7k59q; R. Jeffrey Smith, "Hypersonic Missiles Are Unstoppable. And They're Starting a New Global Arms Race," *The New York Times*, June 19, 2019, https://tinyurl.com/y2nberq2.

2. Brad Lendon, "Russia's 'invulnerable' nuclear missile ready to deploy, Putin says," *CNN*, Dec. 27, 2018, https://tinyurl.com/y7b674l9.

3. David E. Sanger and William J. Broad, "To Counter Russia, U.S. Signals Nuclear Arms Are Back in a Big Way," *The New York Times*, Feb. 4, 2018, https://tinyurl.com/ybufvz59.

4. Aaron Mehta, "Hypersonics 'highest technical priority' for Pentagon R&D head," *Defense News*, March 6, 2018, https://tinyurl.com/y8ckzk27.

5. Choe Sang-Hun, "North Korea Is No Longer Bound by Nuclear Test Moratorium, Kim Says," *The New York Times*, Dec. 31, 2019, https://tinyurl.com/uefzf3f.

6. Max Burman and The Associated Press, "Iran pulling out of nuclear deal commitment following U.S. strike that killed Soleimani," *NBC News*, Jan. 5, 2020, https://tinyurl.com/r42hksc.

7. "Nuclear Weapons: Who Has What at a Glance," Arms Control Association, July 2019, https://tinyurl.com/6ovpr2v.

8. *Ibid.*

9. Vladimir Isachenkov, "Putin offers US an immediate extension to key nuclear pact," *The Associated Press*, Dec. 5, 2019, https://tinyurl.com/vgxb884.

10. Nicole Gaouette, "US to start negotiating with Russia on nuclear arms control soon," *CNN*, Feb. 5, 2020, https://tinyurl.com/rlf6kwl.

11. Ed Pilkington and Martin Pengelly, "'Let it be an arms race': Donald Trump appears to double down on nuclear expansion," *The Guardian*, Dec. 24, 2016, https://tinyurl.com/zyz4elr.

12. Gaouette, *op. cit.*

13. David Hale, testimony before the Committee on Foreign Relations, U.S. Senate, Dec. 3, 2019, https://tinyurl.com/tdkxcbp.

14. Rebecca Kheel, "Pompeo: Russia complying with nuclear treaty that's up for renewal," *The Hill*, April 10, 2019, https://tinyurl.com/y2gjqe5v.

15. Bill Gertz, "Bolton: China Continuing Cyberattacks on Government, Private Networks," *The Washington Free Beacon*, June 18, 2019, https://tinyurl.com/y674ua97.

16. Rose Gottemoeller, testimony before the Committee on Foreign Affairs, U.S. House of Representatives, Dec. 4, 2019, https://tinyurl.com/vv6drv3.

17. Gordon Lubold, "U.S. Deploys New, Less Destructive Nuclear Warhead," *The Wall Street Journal*, Feb. 5, 2020, https://tinyurl.com/ufqrg9j.

18. "2018 Nuclear Posture Review," Office of the Secretary of Defense, February 2018, https://tinyurl.com/yc7lu944.

19. *Ibid.*

20. "Nuclear Operations," Joint Chiefs of Staff, June 11, 2019, https://tinyurl.com/y4khdm2r.

21. *Ibid.*

22. Elbridge Colby, "If You Want Peace, Prepare for Nuclear War," *Foreign Affairs*, November/December 2018, https://tinyurl.com/vkruuy3.

23. *Ibid.*

24. Matthew Gault, "Even 'Limited' Nuclear War Could Cause 90 Million Casualties in a Few Hours," *Vice News*, Sept. 16, 2019, https://tinyurl.com/y3egjc4y.

25. Melissa Hanham, Twitter post, Jan. 27, 2019, https://tinyurl.com/rglk8g2.

26. Roberta Rampton, "'We fell in love:' Trump swoons over letters from North Korea's Kim," *Reuters*, Sept. 30, 2018, https://tinyurl.com/ybpomjgc.

27. Simon Denyer, "Confusion over North Korea's definition of denuclearization clouds talks," *The Washington Post*, Jan, 16, 2019, https://tinyurl.com/y7jfz33w.

28. Anthony Kuhn, "Why North Korea's Kim Jong Un May Be Leaving The Door Open To Nuclear Talks," *NPR*, Jan. 1, 2020, https://tinyurl.com/yxxghmsq.

29. *Ibid.*

30. "Letter from Senior Democratic senators to President Donald Trump on the administration's North Korea policy," Senate Foreign Relations Committee, Dec. 18, 2019, https://tinyurl.com/vngdnv5.

31. *Ibid.*

32. "Truman's Legacy: Breakout Box Activity," Harry S. Truman Library and Museum, https://tinyurl.com/s6vqelg; Emperor Hirohito, "Accepting the Potsdam

Declaration, Radio Broadcast," Federal Communications Commission, Aug. 14, 1945, https://tinyurl.com/ycvld9t8.

33. James A. Hijiya, "The Gita of J. Robert Oppenheimer," *Proceedings of the American Philosophical Society*, Vol. 144, No. 2, June 2000, https://tinyurl.com/yx7m5nkx.

34. "The United States presents the Baruch Plan," History.com, July 17, 2019, https://tinyurl.com/up34tul.

35. *Ibid.*

36. "J. Robert Oppenheimer Biography," Biography .com, July 26, 2019, https://tinyurl.com/st34k9h.

37. "Cuban Missile Crisis," Encyclopaedia Britannica, Feb. 4, 2020, https://tinyurl.com/ybyumlfj.

38. "Cuban Missile Crisis," History.com, June 10, 2019, https://tinyurl.com/yb83yomu.

39. *Ibid.*

40. Evan Thomas, "America's history of preparing for, and trying to avoid, nuclear war," *The Washington Post*, Jan. 30, 2020, https://tinyurl.com/wc6vqcn.

41. "Hot Line Agreement (1963)," Atomicarchive.com, https://tinyurl.com/ru9yt95; "Limited Test Ban Treaty (1963)" Atomicarchive.com, https://tinyurl .com/tymckbf.

42. "Nuclear Non-Proliferation Treaty (1968)," Atomicarchive.com, https://tinyurl.com/ wm2azag.

43. "Strategic Arms Limitation Treaty I," Atomicarchive. com, https://tinyurl.com/vngomxq; "Anti-Ballistic Missile Treaty (1972)," Atomicarchive.com, https:// tinyurl.com/yx6u676m.

44. "Strategic Arms Limitation Treaty II (1979)," Atomicarchive.com, https://tinyurl.com/smqmmly.

45. "The zero option," *The Christian Science Monitor*, Nov. 19, 1981, https://tinyurl.com/wldt6ho; Daryl G. Kimball, "Looking Back: The Nuclear Arms Control Legacy of Ronald Reagan," Arms Control Association, https://tinyurl.com/7gskwlm.

46. *Ibid.*

47. *Ibid.*

48. *Ibid.*

49. "Strategic Arms Reduction Treaty (1991)," Atomicarchive.com, https://tinyurl.com/2dd9sc.

50. Justin Bresolin and Brenna Gautam, "Fact Sheet: The Nunn-Lugar Cooperative Threat Reduction Program," Center for Arms Control and Non-Proliferation, June 1, 2014, https://tinyurl.com/wfbk47l.

51. "Strategic Arms Reduction Treaty (START II)," Federation of American Scientists, https://tinyurl .com/vd39j3x.

52. *Ibid.*

53. "New Strategic Arms Reduction Treaty (New START) (2010)," Atomicarchive.com, https:// tinyurl.com/rsn3m34.

54. Sanger and Broad, *op. cit.*

55. Mark Landler, "Trump and Kim See New Chapter for Nations After Summit," *The New York Times*, June 11, 2018, https://tinyurl.com/y8d3ptod.

56. Kevin Liptak and Jeremy Diamond, "'Sometimes you have to walk': Trump leaves Hanoi with no deal," *CNN*, Feb. 28, 2019, https://tinyurl.com/ yxr5oulm.

57. David E. Sanger and William J. Broad, "U.S. Suspends Nuclear Arms Control Treaty With Russia," *The New York Times*, Feb. 1, 2019, https:// tinyurl.com/y8oakt5y; "Summary: House-Senate Conference Agreement on FY2020 National Defense Authorization Bill (S.1790)," Center for Arms Control and Non-Proliferation, Dec. 11, 2019, https://tinyurl.com/tl7qpek.

58. Kingston Reif, "Congress OKs Trump Nuclear Priorities," Arms Control Association, January/ February 2020, https://tinyurl.com/uuasmf7.

59. Kim Tong-Hyung, "North Korea's Kim touts strategic weapon amid stall in talks," *The Christian Science Monitor*, Jan. 1, 2020, https://tinyurl .com/qnx35wl.

60. Adam Forrest, "Trump insists Kim is a 'man of his word' despite North Korea ramping up nuclear programme," *The Independent*, Jan. 1, 2020, https:// tinyurl.com/yx7ozrcl.

61. Kanga Kong, "North Korea Says Won't Trade Nuclear Weapons for Sanctions Lift," *Bloomberg*, Jan. 11, 2020, https://tinyurl.com/v6y6t6v.

62. *Ibid.*

63. "Democratic senators' letter to Trump regarding North Korea talks," *op. cit.*

64. "'This Week' Transcript 12-29-19: Amb. Robert O'Brien, Sen. Chris Van Hollen, Andrew Yang," *ABC News*, Dec. 29, 2019, https://tinyurl.com/s9fbyew.

65. "Summary: House-Senate Conference Agreement on FY2020 National Defense Authorization Bill (S.1790)," *op. cit.*

66. Gaouette, *op. cit.*

67. Michael G. Mullen, testimony before the Committee on Foreign Affairs, U.S. House of Representatives, Dec. 5, 2019, https://tinyurl.com/vw6r7of.

BIBLIOGRAPHY

Books

Hersey, John, *Hiroshima*, Vintage Press, 1989.
In the 49th printing of a 1946 book, a journalist interviews six survivors shortly after the atomic bomb fell on Hiroshima.

Kaplan, Fred, *The Bomb: Presidents, Generals and the Secret History of Nuclear War*, Simon & Schuster, 2020.
A veteran defense reporter uses recently declassified documents and interviews with former presidents and generals to recount how they considered using nuclear weapons in war.

Perry, William J., *My Journey at the Nuclear Brink*, Stanford University Press, 2015.
The former U.S. Secretary of Defense (1994-97) recounts how he changed from a nuclear weapons hawk to an advocate for disarmament.

Roberts, Brad, *The Case for Nuclear Weapons in the 21st Century*, Stanford University Press, 2015.
A senior Pentagon official in the Obama administration argues the United States needs a strong nuclear arsenal to deter other nuclear powers.

Sherman, Wendy R., *Not For The Faint At Heart: Lessons in Courage, Power and Persistence*, Public Affairs, 2018.
A former senior U.S. diplomat recounts her experiences negotiating the Iran nuclear agreement and past accords with North Korea.

Articles

Borger, Julian, "US nuclear weapons: first low-yield warheads roll off production line," *The Guardian*, Jan. 28, 2019, https://tinyurl.com/y7x3mzjs.
A veteran British national security journalist reports on the U.S. buildup of smaller tactical nuclear weapons.

Choe, Sang-Hun, "North Korea Is No Longer Bound by Nuclear Test Moratorium, Kim Says," *The New York Times*, Dec. 31, 2019, https://tinyurl.com/uefzf3f.
The North Korean leader says U.S. concessions will determine whether he resumes nuclear and missile testing.

Gault, Matthew, "Even 'Limited' Nuclear War Could Cause 90 Million Casualties in a Few Hours," *Vice News*, Sept. 16, 2019, https://tinyurl.com/y3egjc4y.
A journalist details a Princeton University study showing a limited nuclear war would quickly become unlimited, with catastrophic results.

Gould, Joe, "Trump upbeat on nuclear talks with Russia and China, but lawmakers warn of 'blow up,'" *Defense News*, Dec. 4, 2019, https://tinyurl.com/qsqk6lf.
The president is optimistic China and Russia will join in three-way negotiations for a new arms reduction treaty despite Beijing's stated refusal to take part.

Kong, Kanga, "North Korea Says Won't Trade Nuclear Weapons for Sanctions Lift," *Bloomberg*, Jan. 11, 2020, https://tinyurl.com/v6y6t6v.
Pyongyang hardens its negotiating position on denuclearization in response to Trump's tough line.

Kristensen, Hans, "The New START Treaty Keeps Nuclear Arsenals In Check and President Trump Must Act To Preserve It," *Forbes*, Dec. 10, 2019, https://tinyurl.com/vwd86rp.
A nuclear weapons expert discusses why the New START Treaty should be extended for another five years.

Mohammed, Arshad, and Jonathan Landay, "U.S. Congress pressures Trump to renew arms control pact," *Reuters*, Dec. 17, 2019, https://tinyurl.com/wen3v52.

Two reporters detail lawmakers' concerns that President Trump may let the New START Treaty expire next year.

Moniz, Ernest J., and Sam Nunn, "The Return of Doomsday," *Foreign Affairs*, September/October 2019, https://tinyurl.com/yyxqquhl.

Former Energy secretary and a former Democratic senator who is a nuclear nonproliferation advocate detail how the arms control regime constructed over 50 years has unraveled.

Sanger, David E., and William J. Broad, "To Counter Russia, U.S. Signals Nuclear Arms Are Back in a Big Way," *The New York Times*, Feb. 4, 2018, https://tinyurl.com/ybufvz59.

Two reporters detail the Trump administration's nuclear weapons policies.

Tannenwald, Nina, "The Vanishing Nuclear Taboo? How Disarmament Fell Apart," *Foreign Affairs*, Oct. 15, 2018, https://tinyurl.com/wj679gl.

A Brown University expert on nuclear policy examines how arms control has withered during the Trump administration.

Reports

"2018 Nuclear Posture Review," Office of the Secretary of Defense, 2018, https://tinyurl.com/yc7lu944.

The Trump administration lays out its nuclear weapons policy, which includes waging limited nuclear war with tactical nuclear weapons.

Gleason, Michael P., and Luc H. Riesbeck, "Noninterference with National Technical Means: The Status Quo Will Not Survive," Center for Space Policy and Strategy, Aerospace Corporation, April 2019, https://tinyurl.com/uqgs2v9.

Two experts in the military uses of space explain the challenges facing U.S. satellite surveillance of Russia's nuclear arsenal if the New START treaty expires in 2021.

Harrison, Todd, *et al.*, "Space Threat Assessment 2019," Center for Strategic and International Studies, April 2019, https://tinyurl.com/qulgrwm.

Space war experts detail the weapons other countries have or are developing to counter U.S. military dominance in space.

Hruby, Jill, "Russia's New Nuclear Weapon Delivery Systems," Nuclear Threat Initiative, November 2019, https://tinyurl.com/rn7ux3k.

A nuclear weapons expert describes Russia's new lines of hypersonic boost-glide vehicles, nuclear-powered torpedoes and other systems to deliver nuclear warheads.

THE NEXT STEP

China's Weapons

"China displays new hypersonic nuclear missile on 70th anniversary," *Al Jazeera*, Oct. 1, 2019, https://tinyurl.com/y5s958ew.

China unveiled a new weapon believed to be capable of breaching all existing U.S. anti-missile shields.

Chan, Minnie, "China nuclear missile development steps up a gear with test of weapon capable of hitting US mainland," *South China Morning Post*, Jan. 4, 2020, https://tinyurl.com/t93cf64.

China tested a new submarine-launched nuclear missile capable of hitting the continental United States.

Wainer, David, "Chinese nuclear plans cloud prospects for new U.S.-Russia missile deal," *Bloomberg*, Oct. 18, 2019, https://tinyurl.com/svlbdfn.

China plans on rapidly expanding its nuclear arsenal and seems unlikely to join Russia and the United States in an extension of New START, the arms control accord that is due to expire in early 2021.

New START

Arkhipov, Ilya, "Russia Says U.S. Silence on Last Nuclear Treaty May Be 'Fatal,'" *Bloomberg*, Aug. 26, 2019, https://tinyurl.com/y3pxf9hx.

A Kremlin spokesman raised concerns about the lack of controls on nuclear weapons if New START, the arms reduction treaty signed by the United States and Russia in 2010, is allowed to expire.

Brennan, David, "America is Risking a Nuclear 'Free-For-All' By Delaying New START Extension With Russia: Former National Security Official," *Newsweek*, **Jan. 16, 2020, https://tinyurl.com/uy6wpzu.**
A White House National Security Council staffer during the Obama administration is concerned that delaying, even for a short time, the extension of New START will create long-term security risks for the United States.

Zengerle, Patricia, "Senior U.S. official: Russia in compliance with New START weapons treaty," *Reuters*, **Dec. 3, 2019, https://tinyurl.com/vc3tmgt.**
A top U.S. State Department official said Russia remains in compliance with New START, even as it fails to comply with most other arms control obligations.

Space

Erwin, Sandra, "Pentagon report: DoD needs to test how satellites would perform under attack," *Space News*, **Feb. 1, 2020, https://tinyurl.com/svf8zaw.**
In a new report the Pentagon warns that the U.S. military currently cannot assess the durability of its satellites if they came under attack.

Kiang, Charlotte, "What Exactly Is The Space Force?" *Forbes*, **Jan. 27, 2020, https://tinyurl.com/wf69cw4.**
The recently established U.S. Space Force's work includes procuring and operating space vehicles and satellites and rockets to launch them into orbit.

Strout, Nathan, "What we know about Iran's counterspace weapons," **C4ISRNET, Jan. 8, 2020, https://tinyurl.com/rfxlvc4.**
While it is unlikely that Iran has strong anti-satellite weaponry, defense experts believe the Islamic Republic can jam U.S. satellite communications and GPS.

Tactical Weapons

Brumfiel, Geoff, "U.S. Has Deployed New, Small Nukes on Submarine, According to Group," *NPR*, **Jan. 29, 2020, https://tinyurl.com/vb4xctn.**
A U.S. submarine has begun carrying one or two low-yield nuclear warheads, according to the Federation of American Scientists.

Ioanes, Ellen, and Dave Mosher, "A terrifying new animation shows how 1 'tactical' nuclear weapon could trigger a US-Russia war that kills 34 million people in 5 hours," *Business Insider*, **Jan. 23, 2020, https://tinyurl.com/yyrqpfta.**
A simulation from Princeton University shows how the use of one tactical nuclear weapon could lead to a worldwide nuclear conflict.

Meier, Lauren, "Putin to develop new 'tactical' nuclear missiles after Trump spikes weapons treaty," *The Washington Times*, **Sept. 5, 2019, https://tinyurl.com/vwxhy7m.**
After the United States abandoned the Intermediate-Range Nuclear Forces (INF) Treaty in August 2019, Russia said it planned to develop short-range tactical nuclear weapons.

For More Information

American Enterprise Institute, 1789 Massachusetts Ave., N.W., Washington, DC 20036; 202-862-7177; aei.org. Conservative think tank that analyzes U.S. nuclear policy and takes generally hawkish positions.

Arms Control Association, 1200 18th St., N.W., Suite 1175, Washington, DC 20036; 202-463-8270; armscontrol.org. Nonpartisan organization that advocates for arms control through briefings, seminars and its magazine, *Arms Control Today.*

Carnegie Endowment for International Peace, 1779 Massachusetts Ave., N.W., Washington, DC 20036; 202-483-7600; ceip.org. Centrist think tank with experts on strategic nuclear weapons and nonproliferation.

Council for a Livable World, 820 First St., N.E., Suite LL-180, Washington, DC 20002; 202-543-4100; Livableworld.org. Advocacy organization that promotes peace through arms control, nonproliferation and disarmament.

European Council on Foreign Relations, 4th Floor, Tennyson House, 159-165 Great Portland St., Marylebone, London W1W 5PA, UK; +44 20 7227 6860; ecfr.eu. Centrist think tank that provides the European perspective on U.S. and Russian nuclear arms policy, arms control and national security issues.

International Institute for Strategic Studies, 2121 K St., N.W., Suite 801, Washington, DC 20037; 202-659-1490; iiss.org. Nonpartisan think tank that produces papers and briefings and holds conferences on nonproliferation and nuclear policy.

Nuclear Threat Initiative, 1776 I St., N.W., Suite 600, Washington, DC 20006; 202-296-4810; nti.org. Nonpartisan research organization whose staff includes former senior government officials and nuclear weapons experts who provide studies and other materials aimed at reducing the threat of nuclear, chemical and biological weapons.

Ploughshares Fund, 1100 Vermont Ave., N.W., Suite 300, Washington, DC 20005; 202-783-4401; ploughshares.org. A public grantmaking foundation that supports initiatives aimed at preventing the spread and use of nuclear weapons.

New Hampshire residents prepare to vote in Manchester during the state's presidential primary in February 2020. A Senate Intelligence Committee report found that Russia attempted to penetrate voting systems in all 50 states during the 2016 election, and intelligence officials say it is trying again.

4

Cyberwarfare

Can the U.S. and other democracies develop an effective defense?

By Reed Karaim

THE ISSUES

When a U.S. drone strike ordered by President Trump killed Iranian Gen. Qassem Soleimani early in January, Iran vowed to retaliate. A few days later Iran fired missiles at two U.S. military bases in Iraq, injuring scores of service members.[1]

But current and former defense officials warned that retaliation was likely to take place not only through traditional military action, but also in the evolving arena of cyberwarfare, which encompasses the use of computer worms, viruses, hacking and even online social media misinformation campaigns to damage or demoralize an enemy.

"The most immediate threat here at home is from Iranian cyberforces who have targeted our financial sector and energy infrastructure," said Lisa Monaco, former Homeland Security and counterterrorism adviser to President Barack Obama.[2]

Although the Department of Homeland Security said it knew of no new credible Iranian threats, Christopher Krebs, director of the department's Cybersecurity and Infrastructure Security Agency, warned private companies and government agencies to be on guard against Iranian hackers. "Pay close attention to your critical systems," he tweeted.[3]

Cyberwarfare, unknown before the internet connected the world's computers and billions of other devices, has emerged as a critical battleground in the struggles between nations and conflicting global ideologies. Defense and information technology experts

From *CQ Researcher,*
February 28, 2020

say cyberattacks now rank as one of the most serious threats facing the United States and other Western nations. Yet, analysts note, the United States and other nations are still struggling with how to defend against or limit the scope of cyber conflict.

"The central issue is, can we protect the way we live, our ability to share information, our ability to [maintain an open society] in an arena in which all these things are under attack?" says Simon Clark, chair of Foreign Policy for America, a nonpartisan group that advocates for maintaining U.S. engagement in the world.

The challenge, Clark and other analysts note, comes in part from the wide-ranging scope of the arena where cyber conflict is waged. The battleground extends from highly protected military command-and-control systems to corporate computer networks and even to popular social media platforms such as Facebook and Twitter.

Incursions are possible from nearly anywhere. In a critical difference from traditional warfare, the diffuse nature of the internet can make it difficult to determine where an attack comes from and who is responsible.

Cyberattacks can bring down systems through "denial-of-service attacks" in which computer servers are overwhelmed by a flood of bogus requests generated by automated "bots" that prevent legitimate requests from getting through. Malicious software can take control of operating systems for power plants, dams or other essential facilities, causing them to shut down or malfunction. Sophisticated viruses or worms could even be used to damage another nation's defense capabilities. Other cyberweapons are designed to capture data, anything from personnel records to industrial and government secrets.

But some attacks require little technological expertise, such as online campaigns that use fake accounts on social media to spread false information intended to sow divisions within a society or influence a nation's politics.

Russia's campaign to influence the 2016 U.S. presidential election through an extensive social media disinformation campaign, along with its probing of online American voting systems, has received the most attention in the United States. A heavily redacted Senate Intelligence Committee report released last July concluded that the Russians targeted election systems in all 50 states. "In 2016, the U.S. was unprepared at all levels of government for a concerted attack from a determined foreign adversary on our election infrastructure," wrote committee Chairman Richard M. Burr, a Republican from North Carolina.[4]

Anatomy of Russia's 2016 Cyber Effort to Elect Trump

U.S. intelligence agencies and special counsel Robert Mueller's investigation concluded that Russia conducted a sophisticated cyber campaign to interfere with the 2016 presidential election to help elect Republican nominee Donald Trump and hurt Democratic candidate Hillary Clinton. This effort consisted of a disinformation campaign on social media, hacks into the Democratic National Committee computer system and attempts to penetrate the voting systems of every state. The Justice Department indicted 25 Russian nationals, some of them members of the Russian intelligence agency GRU, for hacking emails and computer networks or for trying to defraud the United States.

The Russian Cyberattack and Disinformation Campaign in the 2016 U.S. Election

- Successful phishing attacks enabled access to Democratic campaign emails.
- Emails obtained through hacks were published by WikiLeaks, damaging the Clinton campaign.
- At least one employee of a U.S. voting machine company had email account compromised.
- More than 3,000 ads posted on Facebook were later identified as Russian disinformation.
- Some ads on Facebook were aimed at voters in the swing states of Michigan and Wisconsin.
- Russian online trolls posed as Black Lives Matter activists to depress black support for Clinton.
- Russians sought to penetrate voting systems in all 50 states, but investigators found no evidence votes were changed.
- Hackers obtained the ability to delete or change voter data in Illinois, but did not do so.

Sources: Robert S. Mueller III, "Report on the Investigation into Russian Interference in the 2016 Presidential Election Pursuant to 28 C.F.R. 600.8(c)," U.S. Department of Justice, March 2019, https://tinyurl.com/v42ym4e; "2016 Presidential Campaign Hacking Fast Facts," CNN, Oct. 31, 2019, https://tinyurl.com/ycqdxyhz; and David E. Sanger and Catie Edmondson, "Russia Targeted Election Systems in All 50 States, Report Finds," *The New York Times*, July 25, 2019, https://tinyurl.com/y2nlsrz2

A separate report by Robert Mueller, the special counsel appointed to investigate Russian interference in the election, found that Moscow undertook an extensive effort to influence the election for Republican nominee Trump through an online social media campaign targeting voters. "The Russian government interfered in the 2016 presidential election in sweeping and systematic fashion," the report concluded. Intelligence officials also said Russia is interfering in the 2020 campaign.[5]

Russia is hardly alone in its efforts. A study by researchers at Oxford University in England concluded that 70 countries mounted online disinformation campaigns in 2019 to discredit internal political opponents or interfere in the affairs of other nations. Authoritarian regimes are increasingly using social media to drown out dissenting opinions, the study found.[6]

Other types of cyberattacks can have more immediate and dramatic impact. In 2010, the Stuxnet computer worm, which experts believe was deployed by the United States and Israel, partially crippled Iran's efforts to enrich uranium that could be used to create a nuclear weapon by infecting critical control systems. In 2015 and 2016 Russia used malware to bring down elements of Ukraine's power grid as part of an undeclared war designed to intimidate Ukraine.

Both Russia and the United States reportedly have digitally probed the other nation's power grid and other critical infrastructure such as oil pipelines and water systems and may have already inserted malware that could be triggered in the event of a confrontation.[7]

In addition, China and Iran are believed to have mounted cyberattacks on U.S. utility companies. U.S. financial institutions are facing more frequent cyberattacks from other countries, including North Korea, Russia, Iran and China, according to a recent study.[8]

Federal, state and local governments in the United States have suffered attempted and successful incursions. Between 2006 and 2016, cyber incidents reported by federal agencies increased by more than 600 percent, from 5,503 to 33,632.[9]

Although most incidents are minor, two breaches of government records in 2014 and 2015 resulted in the theft of personal data from more than 25 million people. Another may have allowed China to obtain data on the design of the Air Force's F-35 stealth fighter, helping Chinese develop their own version of the warplane.[10]

Yichuan Cao/NurPhoto via Getty Images

Hackers reportedly working for China's military stole plans for the U.S. F-35 stealth fighter, shown here flying over San Francisco Bay in October 2019. Analysts believe the 2008 theft helped China build its own version of the plane, known as the J-20.

Analysts note that the United States, as one of the most connected nations in the world, is highly vulnerable to cyberattacks. Some believe the extent of the ongoing attacks means the conflict has already reached the threshold of a new kind of war.

"We're already engaged in a cyberwar. We're engaged [with antagonists] in a weekly, if not daily basis in this domain," says James Lewis, senior vice president at the Center for Strategic and International Studies, a Washington-based research institution. "We're engaged in a military conflict that tries to stay below the threshold of [open military] force. It's low-level conflict. It's a kind of guerrilla warfare."

Critics of the U.S. government say it has been slow to recognize the size of the threat and its response has been fragmented, with authority spread across several departments and agencies, including Homeland Security, Defense and the National Security Administration. Some analysts have called for the creation of an intelligence and law enforcement agency focused on fighting cyberattacks.[11]

The difficulty of defending against cyberattacks in a world with billions of internet connections is expected to only get worse as 5G (fifth generation), the superfast wireless technology, boosts internet traffic and as artificial intelligence (AI) enables malicious software to penetrate systems. The situation has led some experts to conclude that the best defense is a strong offense. The threat of retaliation is the best deterrent, they argue.[12]

The U.S. Defense Department's 2018 Cyber Strategy adopts a more assertive approach, a "defend forward" strategy that recognizes the need to sometimes take proactive steps to prevent attacks. Speaking at a cybersecurity summit last September, Defense Secretary Mark Esper said winning cyber conflicts requires an offensive strategy. "We need to do more than just play goal-line defense," he said.[13]

But other experts believe that approach risks an overreaction. They argue that most cyberattacks have had limited impact on the targeted countries and have been generally unsuccessful in forcing them to change their policies.

Two military analysts at the Cato Institute, a libertarian think tank in Washington, who compiled a database of all major cyber operations by nations intended to pressure a rival state found that of the 272 such operations that occurred between 2000 and 2016, "only 11 operations (4 percent) appear to have produced even a temporary political concession."[14]

Benjamin Jensen, an associate professor at the Marine Corps University in Quantico, Va., and one of the Cato analysts, says the evidence argues for a policy of restraint and building effective cyberdefenses. "The focus should be on reducing your vulnerabilities," he says. "A boxer always keeps their guard up. You don't just come into the ring throwing haymakers."

As defense and foreign policy experts focus more attention on cyber conflict, here are some of the questions they are debating:

Are cyberattacks a serious threat to U.S. security?

Since then-Defense Secretary Leon Panetta warned in 2012 of the possibility of a "cyber Pearl Harbor," U.S. officials and defense analysts have regularly raised the possibility of a devastating cyberattack on U.S. infrastructure.[15]

The scenario has not changed significantly since Panetta first described it. Using cyberweapons to shut down or take control of computerized control systems, he warned, enemies "could derail passenger trains, or even more dangerous, derail passenger trains loaded with lethal chemicals. They could contaminate the water supply in major cities or shut down the power grid across large parts of the country."[16]

More recently, Tarah Wheeler, a cybersecurity fellow at New America, a policy research organization in Washington, said that U.S. health care and transportation infrastructure remain largely unprotected and inviting targets.

Speaking at a public forum in 2018, Wheeler said many cybersecurity experts believe a big cyberattack, similar to the surprise Japanese bombing attack on Pearl Harbor in 1941 or the 9/11 terrorist attacks in 2001, lies ahead. "The most horrifying cybersecurity attack is going to have its own name, and I think it's going to involve something more terrifying than we've thought of yet," she said.[17]

But other analysts believe the threat of a massive cyberattack that throws the country into chaos is overstated. Lewis, of the Center for Strategic and International Studies, says cyberweaponry is a serious threat, but not in the way some experts and others often portray it.

America's opponents recognize that a Pearl Harbor-scale cyberattack would likely lead to a larger, traditional conflict, he says, one in which the United States would hold a significant military advantage.

"The problem is, we're kind of infected with nuclear imagery—this apocalyptic event," Lewis says. "But the threshold here is that the countries want to avoid [traditional] warfare, if at all possible. With cyberattacks, Russia and China can stay below the threshold that will provoke a conventional military or even nuclear response."

For that reason, Lewis says, it is wrong to think of a cyberattack as a weapon of mass destruction.

But the United States' antagonists, he continues, are operating in the cyber arena in ways that can cause significant economic harm. "Economic espionage from China is damaging to the American economy, and probably costs us hundreds of billions a year," Lewis says. "The Chinese have built their technology base largely on stolen technology."

Also damaging is Russia's "growing ability to manipulate public U.S. opinion," he adds. "That's a Russian specialty. They call it cognitive warfare. The chief of the Russian army has basically said that information operations are more effective than conventional weapons."

In 2016, Russians created false accounts on Facebook and other social media platforms and bought online ads that appeared to come from Americans to bolster Trump and spread often-false stories about Democratic presidential nominee Hillary Clinton, including messaging designed to anger specific groups such as veterans or minority voters. They even organized rallies around hot-button issues, such as gun control, to energize pro-Trump voters.[18]

But other analysts see a growing risk to critical U.S. infrastructure and the possibility of widespread physical disruption. Anthony Ferrante, a former director for cyber incident response at the White House's National Security Council, said attempts to infiltrate the control systems in crucial infrastructure such as nuclear power plants, telecommunications and health care will increase as "hackers seek to lay the groundwork for a future attack."[19]

Adam Levin, chairman and founder of CyberScout, a cybersecurity firm that works in the public and private sectors, says the poor state of U.S. cybersecurity invites attacks from other nations and nonstate actors such as terrorist groups. "Cybersecurity is an existential threat," he says. "There are two absolute realities in this world. One is that cyberwar has replaced the Cold War in the struggle between nations, and the second is that security breaches have become a certainty."

Jacquelyn Schneider, who studies cybersecurity at Stanford University's Hoover Institution, believes the biggest threat is more insidious: the work of nations such as Russia and Iran to undermine faith in our basic institutions through online disinformation or interruptions in service.

"The long-term threat is that we no longer believe in data," she says. "There are institutions such as elections or finance where everything is based on people believing that the information they have is the correct information and means something."

If Americans stop believing they can trust election results or the numbers in their bank account, Schneider says, faith in the basic underpinnings of society will be undermined. "I'm really afraid, especially in open, democratic countries like the United States, we will no longer believe in the data we use to make decisions," she says.

Other analysts wonder how long cyber battles can remain below the threshold of more open conflict. "Cyber conflict remains in the gray area between war and peace, an uneasy equilibrium that often seems on the brink of spinning out of control," said David Sanger, author of *The Perfect Weapon*, a 2018 book about cyberwar, and a veteran national security journalist. "As the pace of attacks rises, our vulnerability becomes more apparent each day."[20]

Is the United States falling behind its adversaries in cyberwar capability?

Last March, the Navy released a scathing internal assessment of its cybersecurity efforts. "Competitors and potential adversaries have exploited [Navy] information systems, penetrated its defenses, and stolen massive amounts of national security [intellectual property]. This has lessened our capabilities and lethality, while strengthening their offensive and defensive capabilities," the report stated.[21]

The assessment described the failure of the Navy and Marine Corps to protect their information systems as "an existential threat to their existence." The services, the report said, remain too focused on traditional warfare while failing to recognize the shifting nature of global conflict. "We find the [Navy] preparing to win some future kinetic battle, while it is losing the current global . . . cyberwar," the report said.

That cyber battlefield includes "many bad actors," the assessment said, "but China and Russia in particular have focused their efforts in strategic ways and are executing at scale to achieve their objectives, while the U.S. remains relatively flat-footed, and is too often incapable of defending itself."[22]

Michael Bayer, a Pentagon adviser who led the cybersecurity review, was blunt in his final assessment. "I believe we are in a declared cyberwar," said Bayer. "It is aimed at the whole of society and the state. I believe we are losing that war."[23]

Investigations by the Defense Department's Inspector General's (IG) Office and the Government Accountability Office, Congress' investigative arm, back the Navy's conclusions. A 2019 IG report found that U.S. weapon systems such as ballistic missiles and front-line computers share basic weaknesses: Their passwords are generally poorly protected, and the systems are easily hackable with basic tools.[24]

But other security analysts say the problems are not necessarily traced to U.S. cyberwar resources. The United States, they note, leads the world in information and computing technology, and they point to the Stuxnet worm used to disable Iran's nuclear fuel processing capability (which the United States has never acknowledged it was behind) as evidence of America's sophisticated capabilities.

In addition, they point out, last year the U.S. military used a cyberweapon to shut down the computers of the Internet Research Agency, a Russian troll farm that was spreading online political disinformation aimed at U.S. citizens.[25]

"I find it hard to believe that China or Russia have better cyber capabilities than the U.S. government," says Cato's Jensen. The problem, he says, is that other nations have been more willing to use their capability. "Those actors are much more brazen and have a higher acceptance of risk than the United States has had. Sometimes it's not your capability; it's your willingness to use what you have and the way you use it that comes into play."

Richard Hartnett, a political science professor and cybersecurity expert at the University of Cincinnati, says the United States must be willing to take offensive cyber actions to gain the upper hand. "If you're not trying to gain and sustain the initiative, you will lose. You will come out on the losing end because there's somebody out there who has the will to exploit the vulnerability in your system to shift relative power," he says. "If you do not contest that, you will suffer the consequence."

The U.S. Cyber Command's revised 2018 strategy, which includes a focus on taking the cyber battle onto an opponent's terrain, as was done with the attack on the Internet Research Agency, should help the United States gain the initiative, Hartnett says.

But Clark, the chair of Foreign Policy for America, makes a sharp distinction between offensive and defensive cyber capabilities. "It seems clear that U.S. offensive capabilities in the cyber arena remain pre-eminent. . . . However, the U.S. is also clearly the most vulnerable to further attacks because it is one of [the], probably the most, connected societies," he says. "And in recent years, it's hard to draw the conclusion that the U.S. has its defenses in order."

CyberScout head Levin says that is partly because many U.S. targets, such as utilities and financial information, are in private hands, and the government has not collaborated with private industry on cybersecurity as closely as necessary.

The United States, he says, also needs a significantly greater investment in another area. "You need to be investing in people whose work is to do nothing but find cyber vulnerabilities in their systems," Levin says, "and we have a massive shortage of cybersecurity professionals in this country."

The United States faced an overall shortage of 314,000 cybersecurity personnel at the start of 2019, a shortfall of roughly 30 percent, according to the Center for Strategic and International Studies.[26] Analysts further note that higher-paying private sector jobs lure cybersecurity experts away from the Defense Department or other government jobs.

The United States will remain highly vulnerable, Levin says, unless it recognizes the scale of the challenge, increases public-private cybersecurity partnership and invests in the technology and the people needed.

"No one is ever going to achieve perfect cybersecurity," he says. "But at the same time, it still requires an effort, and we really haven't seen that effort."

Can democracies prevent cyber disinformation campaigns while protecting free speech?

The protection of free speech, enshrined in the First Amendment to the U.S. Constitution, is a bedrock principle of democratic government, not just in the United States but in many free nations. Yet Russia and other countries have found ways to weaponize that principle through carefully orchestrated cyber campaigns on social media and other channels intended to weaken their perceived enemies, both internally and externally.

Russia's effort in the United States, where it has used fake accounts on Facebook and other platforms to spread false or divisive information, is only one of several such operations. According to the study by Oxford University researchers, at least six other nations—China, India, Iran, Pakistan, Saudi Arabia and Venezuela—have mounted online campaigns intended to influence views outside their borders.[27]

These efforts often use phony social media accounts. The information they spread is sometimes false, but at other times simply expresses an inflammatory opinion intended to influence others. Posts of either kind are amplified as they are spread by legitimate members of Facebook and other platforms.

The blend of false information and opinion that goes viral through sharing presents a challenge to societies

More Countries Turn to Social Media Campaigns

Seventy countries engaged in social media manipulation either domestically or in a foreign nation in 2019, up 150 percent since 2017, when only 28 countries practiced this cyberwarfare technique. The goals of these campaigns can range from suppressing human rights to discrediting political opposition, drowning out political dissent or manipulating opinion in another country, according to a report from the University of Oxford in England.

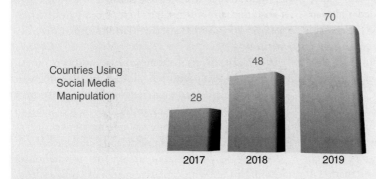

Countries Using Social Media Manipulation

28 — 2017
48 — 2018
70 — 2019

Source: Samantha Bradshaw and Philip N. Howard, "The Global Disinformation Order," Oxford Internet Institute, University of Oxford, Sept. 26, 2019, https://tinyurl.com/y4yxoz7f

that value free speech, leading to the question of whether disinformation can be effectively controlled.

"That's the 64,000-dollar question," says William Banks, a law professor at Syracuse University whose specialties include cybersecurity. "I think the answer is no. It just can't be done. We're a victim of our own ideals in that respect."

Banks says effective efforts to suppress disinformation online would inevitably end up restricting the freedom of Americans who were sharing that information to express their own views.

The solution, he continues, is the one the Founders had in mind when they made freedom of speech part of the Constitution. "It's the traditional First Amendment idea: You fight bad speech with good speech," Banks says. "I think that's true in this era as well, as hard as it might be."

But at least one Western democracy, Germany, has taken legislative action to control the spread of misinformation on social platforms such as Facebook. The country's Network Enforcement Act requires platforms to take down false information or hate speech within 24 hours or face a fine that could reach 50 million euros (about $55 million). Other European nations have considered similar laws.[28]

However, Jessica Brandt, head of research and policy at the Alliance for Securing Democracy, a Washington-based advocacy group founded to defend democracy, says focusing simply on the accuracy of online information ignores how these campaigns work. "Most disinformation is not demonstrably true or false," she says. "It's about lifting up the most polarizing views that exist in a society and making them more prevalent."

The United States so far has not imposed greater regulation on social media platforms, although lawmakers have raised the possibility.[29] Facing mounting criticism, the major platforms have taken steps to police themselves. After China mounted an online campaign last summer to discredit Hong Kong's pro-democracy protesters, for example, Twitter took down 1,000 accounts it said were part of the effort and suspended another 200,000 it felt were connected to the operation but had not yet become active.[30]

"The platforms are aware of the problem," says Kathleen Hall Jamieson, director of the Annenberg Public Policy Center at the University of Pennsylvania and author of the 2018 book *Cyber-War: How Russian Hackers and Trolls Helped Elect a President.* "They're now policing their systems in a way that they weren't. It doesn't mean they're not going to have intrusions and inauthentic accounts, but it does mean we're going to be more likely to check them."

Still, most analysts believe disinformation on social media will continue to be a problem as the 2020 presidential campaign intensifies. Nina Jankowicz, a fellow at the Wilson Center, a Washington think tank, says just trying to suppress inauthentic accounts run by foreign agents cannot solve the problem.

"I don't think the answer is playing 'whack a troll,'" she says. "You'll never win the battle, because it's so cheap and easy to create those inauthentic accounts."

Jankowicz, author of the upcoming book *How to Lose the Information War,* says countries that have had the best success fending off cyber disinformation have turned to education. Finland, Estonia and Ukraine, among others, have programs to build critical thinking skills for the digital age. (*See Short Feature.*)

In Ukraine, for example, she says, a nongovernmental agency trained 15,000 people in how to evaluate sourcing and spot emotional manipulation. It found a 29 percent increase in participants double-checking news sources.

"The societies that have mounted what I consider partially successful responses have all included a human element. You're never going to stop this stuff, it's always existed . . . the question is, how do we combat it?" Jankowicz says. "The answer is, giving people the tools they need to identify [disinformation] and make a rational choice based on their own beliefs."

But other experts doubt that the United States can address the problem while honoring its fundamental beliefs. "The Russians did a careful analysis of our laws and realized this was a vulnerability we cannot really fix," says Lewis of the Center for Strategic and International Studies. "They don't have this problem; the Chinese don't have this problem. They just squelch; they censor, and they realized we do not. It's an opportunity for them."

"If they persuade some wacko American to say the Ukrainians were responsible for 2016 [election hacking], is that protected speech? I think so," Lewis says. "It's kind of like arguing that the Brazilians were responsible for the Pearl Harbor attack, but it's protected. . . . They've actually got the Americans fighting among themselves and [voicing] Russian propaganda. It's a triumph for Russia."

BACKGROUND

Cyberwar Predecessors

Cyberwarfare may take place in a digital battleground and involve some of the latest technology, but security experts note that its aims—planting false information and using covert means to hit an opponent at home—are as old as warfare itself.

Slandering enemies with "fake news" goes back at least as far as ancient Rome, when military leader Octavian used short slogans—one historian calls them the tweets of their day—etched on coins to paint his political rival, Mark Antony, as a womanizer and a drunk. The campaign helped Octavian ascend to the emperor's throne.[31]

Many centuries later, the KGB, the Soviet Union's intelligence agency, successfully spread the false story

that the AIDS virus was developed at a secret U.S. military facility. The KGB planted the story in an obscure Indian journal in 1983. After a pause, Soviet publications then reprinted the story, which they could claim originated elsewhere. The story spread around the globe and still has online believers.[32]

Disinformation campaigns have "been part of espionage forever," says Jensen, the Marine Corps University professor.

Clandestine efforts to sabotage key industries or critical infrastructure also have a long history. In 1916, the year before the United States entered World War I, German agents were secretly working inside the United States to damage plants and warehouses containing supplies such as ammunition being shipped to England and France.[33]

On July 30, 1916, saboteurs set fire to warehouses and ships loaded with explosive materials on Black Tom Island in New York Harbor. The resulting blast was powerful enough to shatter windows in Manhattan and caused damages estimated at more than $400 million in today's dollars. With the United States still officially neutral in the conflict, authorities initially downplayed the incident, but it later played a role in the U.S. decision to join the war on the side of Britain and France.[34]

But if disinformation and sabotage are well-established practices in times of conflict, security experts acknowledge that the emergence of the cyber battlefield has dramatically changed how those tools can be used. Sabotage no longer requires the physical presence of

Massive explosions at the Black Tom Island munitions plant in New York Harbor in 1916 killed more than 50 people and leveled the facility. Authorities blamed German agents for the incident—a form of sabotage that predated cyberwarfare.

human agents on enemy territory, and disinformation campaigns have gained much more power to shape public opinion.

"It's the tools of amplification," says Jankowicz, the Wilson Center fellow, about the key change. "Because of social media, you can reach people at a very minute level with a message tailored for them; you can share content very quickly, share content across the globe. It's the speed at which information now travels and the reach that's different."

Internet's Birth

Cyberwarfare would be largely impossible without the internet, where billions of computers and other devices are tied together in a vast communications web that offers nearly unlimited points of entry.

The concept behind the internet emerged in 1962 when most computers were still room-sized devices. J.C.R. Licklider, a computer scientist at the Massachusetts Institute of Technology (MIT) in Cambridge, proposed his "Galactic Network," an interconnected set of computers through which people around the world would be able to quickly access data and programs.[35]

Licklider soon became the first head of computer research at the Pentagon's Defense Advanced Research Projects Agency (DARPA), responsible for the development of advanced technology for the military. The agency funded the first, limited computer network, known as ARPANET.

ARPANET went online in 1969, connecting four computers from the University of California at Los Angeles, Stanford University, the University of California at Santa Barbara and the University of Utah. The network expanded slowly to other universities and research institutions, eventually reaching Europe.

The online computing network, which would evolve into the internet, at first was largely the tool of computer scientists and other researchers. That changed dramatically in 1989, when Tim Berners-Lee, a European computer scientist, created the Web, which made documents widely accessible across the internet by standardizing the identification system and linking them together in a vast digital library.[36]

Since the 1990s, the internet has grown exponentially. In 1995, about 16 million people worldwide had online access. By late 2019, that number had risen to more than 4.5 billion, or about 58 percent of the world's population.[37] An estimated 4 billion mobile devices are connected to the internet, according to Statista, the online statistics database, and analysts say their use should increase dramatically as 5G high-speed networks spread.[38]

But concern about how enemy nations or even individual hackers might use the internet to compromise national security had emerged long before going online became commonplace.

Cyberwar Threat

In the summer of 1983, President Ronald Reagan finished a day at the Camp David presidential retreat in Maryland by watching *WarGames*. The movie was a techno-thriller in which a teenager accidently hacks into the computers at the Pentagon's North American Aerospace Defense Command (NORAD) and nearly triggers World War III by sending off a barrage of missiles.[39]

The next week, during a meeting at the White House focused on national defense, Reagan asked the assembled generals, Cabinet members, staffers and lawmakers if such a thing was possible. Several reportedly reacted with suppressed amusement. But Reagan persisted, asking the chairman of the Joint Chiefs of Staff, Army Gen. John Vessey Jr., about the possibility. Vessey said he would look into it.[40]

A week later, Vessey reported back: The concern was real. Reagan's query set in motion the first U.S. effort to prepare for cyber conflict. A directive placed the National Security Agency (NSA), the nation's most secretive intelligence agency, in charge of securing government computers from hacking.[41]

But skepticism about the severity of the threat remained high in government, and there was little follow-through. The nation's vulnerability to cyberattack remained a low priority for nearly 25 years. In 2007, when John Negroponte, then director of national intelligence, presented Congress with his annual worldwide threat assessment ranking the dangers facing the nation, cyberattacks did not even appear.[42]

Yet global events were conspiring to bump cyber conflict up higher on the list. In the spring of 2007, Russia launched a series of cyberattacks on Estonia that included both misinformation on early online message boards and an orchestrated effort to knock out the computers of

CHRONOLOGY

1969-1974 *Researchers funded by the U.S. Defense Department create the precursor to the internet.*

1969 ARPANET, the first version of a modern computer network, connects four computers at universities in California and Utah.

1971 Computer scientist Ray Tomlinson invents an email program to send messages across a computer network.

1974 Computer networking pioneers Vinton Cerf and Robert Kahn coin the term "internet."

1983-2002 *As the internet grows, the first attacks on online computer systems begin.*

1983 President Ronald Reagan, after watching the movie *WarGames*, in which a teenage hacker penetrates U.S. missile-control systems, directs the government to protect computer systems.

1988 Cornell University graduate student Robert Tappan Morris develops the first computer worm—software that can replicate itself—to conduct research, but it ends up crashing computers across the internet.

1989 English computer scientist Tim Berners-Lee creates the Web, which links pages of online information, greatly expanding the internet's reach and capability.

1993 The Mosaic browser helps popularize the Web with the public by making it easily accessible.

1998 As the U.S military prepares for a possible conflict with Iraq, hackers penetrate Defense Department computers in a cyberattack dubbed "Solar Sunrise." Iraq is suspected, but the culprits turn out to be three teenage boys from California and Israel.

2002 Computer servers critical to the internet's operation come under attack in the first direct assault on the internet's infrastructure itself. The perpetrators are never identified.

2003-2015 *Cyberattacks become more sophisticated.*

2003 Titan Rain, a multiyear series of computer attacks on U.S. and British government computer systems,

begins. Analysts believe the Chinese government is behind the intrusions.

2007 Estonia is the victim of what some analysts term the first cyberwar when Russia sows social unrest through online sites and takes down Estonian government and private computer systems.

2008 U.S. Defense Department computers are hacked in a broad attack that takes 14 months to eradicate. U.S. officials believe the source is an infected flash drive planted by Russian operatives.

2009 The Pentagon creates the U.S. Cyber Command, a unified command to handle cyber operations.

2010 Stuxnet, a computer worm believed to be developed by the United States and Israel, causes Iranian centrifuges, which could be used to enrich uranium to fuel nuclear weapons, to spin out of control.

2014 North Korea launches a cyberattack on Sony Pictures in retaliation for *The Interview*, a movie that includes the fictional assassination of North Korean leader Kim Jong Un.

2015 Russian hackers take down part of the Ukrainian power grid, leaving roughly a quarter of a million people without electricity.

2016-Present *Concern grows about Russian hacking and disinformation campaigns in U.S. elections.*

2016 Russia mounts a wide-ranging cyber campaign to influence the 2016 presidential election in favor of Republican nominee Donald Trump, according to U.S. intelligence agencies.

2018 U.S. Cyber Command adopts a more offensive strategy, in which it will take the initiative when necessary to take on cyber opponents on their home ground.

2019 Russian hackers target several European government agencies ahead of European Union elections. . . . A U.S. cyber operation disables some Iranian computer systems after a drone attack on Saudi Arabian oil facilities that is blamed on Iran. . . . Russia's main military intelligence agency conducts a broad cyberattack against the republic of Georgia that interferes with government operations and disrupts TV broadcasts and more than 2,000 websites, according to U.S. officials and key allies.

2020 Following a U.S. drone attack that kills an Iranian military leader, U.S. officials warn Iran may retaliate with cyberattacks (January). . . . U.S. intelligence officials tell House members that Russia is interfering in the presidential campaign, including the Democratic primaries (February).

both the government and key private businesses by overwhelming them with traffic. (*See Short Feature.*)

Only a year later, a pair of hacks into the U.S. Defense Department's computer systems rocked the Pentagon. Hackers reportedly working for China's People's Liberation Army got inside defense contractor Lockheed-Martin's systems and stole plans for the advanced F-35 stealth fighter. China denied responsibility, but a Chinese national in the United States eventually was convicted of stealing the data and confessed to working with others in China. Defense analysts later noted that China's J-20 stealth fighter shared several features with the F-35.[43]

The same year, in what some analysts describe as the most significant penetration of U.S. military systems, Defense Department computers were infected with malware, probably Russian in origin, designed to steal classified and unclassified information.[44]

Investigators determined the software, known as Agent.btz, likely entered the department's network when an infected flash drive was inserted into a military laptop in the Middle East. The malware spread quickly through the Pentagon's computers. It took 14 months to eradicate and led to a temporary ban on the use of flash drives by military personnel.[45]

In 2009, Defense Secretary Robert Gates created a dedicated Cyber Command, which grew dramatically in its first three years. The budget rose from $2.7 billion to $7 billion, while the number of personnel grew from 900 to 4,000. At the same time, the Army, Navy, Coast Guard and Air Force were collectively spending an additional $7 billion on cyberwarfare capabilities.[46]

The United States was not alone in its focus on cyberweapons and cyberdefenses.

By 2012, more than 20 nations had created military cyberwarfare units. Countries, including the United States, began regularly probing the online vulnerabilities of other nations' military systems, banks, electric power utilities and key industries, facilities that if disrupted could damage an opponent.[47]

In 2015 and 2016, the potential of cyberweapons was illustrated when Russia hacked its way into control systems and brought down parts of Ukraine's power grid during an ongoing military conflict between the two countries.

In the United States, cyberattacks had also become a major concern in the worldwide threat assessment. "As late as 2009 cyberthreats were so far down the list they were right near the bottom, just after drug trafficking in West Africa," Amy Zegart, co-director of Stanford University's Center for International Security and Cooperation, said in a 2015 TED Talk. "Not anymore.

Then-Iranian President Mahmoud Ahmadinejad (center) visits a uranium enrichment facility outside Tehran in 2008. In separate cyberattacks in 2010 and 2012 reportedly orchestrated by the United States and Israel, a computer worm known as Stuxnet penetrated the control systems of the facility's centrifuges, which are used to refine uranium to nuclear weapons grade level.

Estonia Works to Fend Off the Russian Bear

Baltic nation has become a leader in cyberdefense.

In the spring of 2007, the small Baltic nation of Estonia suddenly found itself under assault from Russia in what many experts consider the first cyberwar.[1]

In the aftermath, Estonia emerged as a global leader in cyberdefense, applying lessons it learned that analysts say are valuable to the United States and other nations that have been recent targets of cyber campaigns by Russia and other countries.

Estonia, a nation of about 1.2 million and a NATO member since 2004, takes a two-pronged approach to cyberdefense that includes technology and public education, says Nina Jankowicz, a scholar specializing in disinformation campaigns at the Wilson Center, a Washington think tank.

"They are a good example of a whole-of-society solution," says Jankowicz. "It's not just about [social] media, not just about technology. It also involves investing in people. Education is key."

Estonia, part of the Soviet Union from 1940 until it gained independence in 1991, angered Russia in 2007 by planning to move a World War II memorial honoring Soviet soldiers out of the center of its capital, Tallinn, to a cemetery on the city's outskirts. To ethnic Estonians, the statue, which was eventually relocated, represented the Soviet occupation; to Russia, it symbolized Soviet sacrifices during the war.[2]

In response to plans to move the statue, the online message boards and the comments sections of Estonian news sites were filled with inflammatory false information, claiming, among other things, that Estonia planned to cut up the statue, and calling on ethnic Russians living in Estonia to defend it. Two nights of rioting followed, as angry Russians took to the streets of Tallinn. One person was killed and 156 were injured. About 1,000 were detained before the authorities restored order. Western security analysts believe Russia was behind the disinformation campaign, although Russian officials have never acknowledged involvement.[3]

Much like Russia's effort in the 2016 U.S. presidential election, Jankowicz notes, the disinformation was aimed at amplifying divisions in Estonian society, whose ethnic makeup is 69 percent Estonian and 25 percent Russian.[4] "There was a campaign by Russians to exacerbate ethnic fissures between Russians and native Estonians," she says.

Russia is also believed to be behind a series of 2007 cyberattacks knocking out Estonian government, banking and newspaper websites. Computer servers were swamped with massive waves of spam and automated online requests that overwhelmed and crashed the systems.[5]

At the cyberattacks' peak, 58 websites were down, disrupting daily life and leaving the government and the Estonian press crippled in its efforts to counter Russian disinformation.[6]

But rather than establish limits on internet access or otherwise try to control its citizens' online activity, Estonia decided to embrace and master digital technology. The country has become one of the most connected in Central and Eastern Europe, and proclaims itself e-Estonia.[7]

The year after Russia's cyberassault, the country took the lead in establishing NATO's Cooperative Cyber Defence Centre of Excellence in Tallinn. The mission of the center, which now has 25 member nations, including the United States, is to promote cyberdefense research and training. It regularly conducts training exercises in which military personnel and intelligence technology experts participate in cyber war games to prepare for potential attacks.[8]

The country has established a central system for monitoring, reporting and responding to cyber intrusions and has created new intrusion detection and protection systems. "There is a common understanding that cybersecurity can only be ensured through cooperation and that a joint contribution is required at all levels—state, private sector and individuals," said Klaid Mägi, head of the Incident Response Department at the Estonian Information System Authority, which is responsible for protecting the nation's cyber infrastructure.[9] One step was to create a volunteer force, the Estonian Defense League's Cyber Defense Unit, made up of citizens who work in information technology or other fields such as law and who give their own time to help protect Estonian cyberspace.

The Cyber Defense Unit's responsibilities include promoting the sharing of cybersecurity information in the private sector and providing expertise and personnel to back up full-time cyberdefense units when needed.[10]

In the United States, the Cyberspace Solarium Commission, a 14-member panel created by Congress, is putting together a comprehensive U.S. cyberdefense strategy that similarly engages both the public and private sphere.

The U.S. Defense Department and Estonia's Ministry of Defence also recently announced they will be collaborating to build a joint platform to share cyberthreat intelligence.[11] In addition, some analysts have suggested the United States should consider building its own volunteer cyberdefense force.[12]

Estonia's approach is not limited to building up cyber expertise and technology. The country has worked to integrate its Russian population into the broader culture, Jankowicz says, investing in Russian-language media and opening a Russian-language campus for its most prestigious university. The goal is to remove the sense of alienation that allowed Russian disinformation to flourish—a challenge considering the bitterness that remains from the Soviet occupation.

After independence, many Estonians viewed ethnic Russians as interlopers, and the nation granted citizenship only to those Russians who could pass a tough Estonian language and history exam. Today, about one-third of ethnic Russians are citizens, while nearly another third have kept their citizenship in the Russian Federation and the rest are noncitizens.[13]

Estonia also has mounted a wide-ranging media literacy effort, offering classes and programs to help citizens distinguish between factual news and false information, and between suspect and reliable online sources. "Education is key, and not just among school students," Jankowicz says. "They are educating fully fledged adults, and they're finding it's working."

A 2018 study by the Open Society Institute, a policy organization in Sofia, Bulgaria, dedicated to promoting open societies, found Estonia the most media literate country among Eastern European nations. Overall, it ranked

fifth among 35 European countries, topping Germany and the United Kingdom, and trailing only four Scandinavian nations.[14]

Jessica Brandt, head of research and policy at the Alliance for Security Democracy, a trans-Atlantic advocacy group formed to counter Russian efforts to undermine democracy, notes that nations with high levels of media literacy generally have proven resistant to cyber disinformation intended to create discord.

"I think there's a lot we can learn from what countries like Estonia have done," she says.

— *Reed Karaim*

[1] Elizabeth Schulze, "When this country faced a suspected Russian attack—it took some big steps to stop another," *CNBC*, Sept. 21, 2018, https://tinyurl.com/y6vf59lk.

[2] "Russia's Playbook for Disrupting Democracy," *The Weekly, The New York Times*, Sept. 6, 2019, https://tinyurl.com/y256lh2g.

[3] Damien McGuinness, "How a cyber attack transformed Estonia," *BBC*, April 27, 2017, https://tinyurl.com/y556truv.

[4] "Europe: Estonia," *CIA World Factbook,* https://tinyurl.com/24sbeb.

[5] McGuinness, *op. cit.*

[6] "How Estonia became a global heavyweight in cybersecurity," e-Estonia, June 2017, https://tinyurl.com/wgt254m.

[7] Nathan Heller, "Estonia, the Digital Republic," *The New Yorker*, Dec. 11, 2017, https://tinyurl.com/y4cs3p6b.

[8] "About Us," NATO Cooperative Cyber Defence Centre of Excellence, https://tinyurl.com/ruwf8zc; "Exercises," NATO Cooperative Cyber Defence Centre of Excellence, https://tinyurl.com/wltzyzn.

[9] "How Estonia became a global heavyweight in cybersecurity," *op. cit.*

[10] Bruce Sterling, "Estonian Cyber Security," *Wired*, Jan. 9, 2018, https://tinyurl.com/t3qle89.

[11] "Estonia and the United States to build a joint cyber threat intelligence platform," e-Estonia, January 2020, https://tinyurl.com/vx2ggmn.

[12] Monica M. Ruiz, "Is Estonia's Approach to Cyber Defense Feasible in the United States?" *War on the Rocks*, Jan. 9, 2018, https://tinyurl.com/w4r38fl.

[13] Lee Hockstader, "Baltic Independence Left Ethnic Russians Stateless," *The Washington Post*, March 28, 1996, https://tinyurl.com/slc77kf; Paul Goble, "Experts: Estonia has successfully integrated nearly 90% of its ethnic Russians," *Estonian World*, March 1, 2018, https://tinyurl.com/yxxh4qeg.

[14] Craig Turp, "Estonia is Emerging Europe's Most Media Literate Country," *Emerging Europe*, April 3, 2018, https://tinyurl.com/u5gesop.

After 2016 Hacks, Illinois Moves to Improve Its Voting Security

"They are in a much, much better position going into this election."

In the 2016 election, Russian hackers probed the election systems of all 50 states, according to a Senate investigation, but gained significant access in only one: Illinois.[1]

"We notified 76,000 voters individually that their information may have been viewed in the intrusion," says Matt Dietrich, public information officer for the Illinois State Board of Elections. "The basis for that notification was that we believed enough of their data had been viewed to constitute a violation of the Illinois Personal Information Protection Act."

The information the Russian hackers obtained was mostly fragmentary. "They may have gotten a ZIP code here, a first name there," Dietrich says, and there is no evidence they tampered with the voting rolls or that the hack had any impact on the state vote. Democratic presidential nominee Hillary Clinton won Illinois' 20 electoral votes, receiving 55.2 percent of votes cast to 38.4 percent for Republican nominee Donald Trump.[2]

But Illinois has taken a series of steps to increase voting security, a move that reflects increased attention to protecting U.S. elections in all states, according to a study by the Center for American Progress, a liberal policy research and advocacy organization based in Washington.

A center report found that every state has taken at least some steps to increase election security since the 2016 election.[3] "What we saw in 2016 frightened a lot of people, and for good reason," says Danielle Root, the report's lead author. "After the 2016 election, we saw a lot of concrete action by governors, mayors, election officials and at the federal level."

Following the Russian hack, Illinois passed an election security law to bolster the system's security through training and increased oversight. The state also announced it would spend nearly $14 million on a five-year program to improve the cybersecurity of the state's election system.[4]

Most of the money came from a federal grant of $13.2 million under the Help America Vote Act, a 2002 law enacted after the 2000 presidential election fiasco in Florida. This law finances election system upgrades, Dietrich says, with the state providing an additional 5 percent in matching funds.

Still, state officials have acknowledged that it would take significantly more money to completely upgrade security. To replace the state's voting machines, most of which are 15 years old, with newer, more secure systems would cost $175 million.[5]

"We're in an unusual time, and yes, there is concern about whether we have enough to go into 2020 totally prepared for what the Chinese, Russians or North Koreans, or any enemy of the United States, may do to influence our elections," said Illinois Gov. J.B. Pritzker, a Democrat.[6]

Matthew Masterson, senior adviser on election security at the Homeland Security Department, said smaller and rural counties throughout the nation often lack adequate security measures, such as two-step verification for

Cyberthreats in the past two years have vaulted to the top of the threat list."[48]

But even though the United States was concerned about its vulnerabilities, it had already made use of its own cyberweapons. In 2010 and again in 2012, the United States and Israel reportedly used the Stuxnet computer worm to significantly hobble Iran's nuclear enrichment efforts. The worm penetrated the control systems of the centrifuges used to refine uranium to weapons grade level, causing many of them to spin out of control.[49]

In response, the Iranians launched their own cyberattacks on the United States. They penetrated the control systems of a small dam in upstate New York without doing any damage. They also mounted denial-of-service attacks on the servers of at least 46 banks and financial firms, including Chase, American Express and Wells Fargo, crowding out legitimate clients and costing the banks millions of dollars in lost business.[50]

As cyber conflict grew more common, worries grew that attacks could disable the military or other key infrastructure.

accessing internal election databases. "They think, 'Who would want to bother us?'" he said.[7]

The cyber navigator program in the Illinois election security law is the heart of the state's effort to secure its voting system. "That is probably the biggest thing that we've done both in the wake of 2016 and also in preparation for 2020," Dietrich says. "The goal of the program is to make sure that none of our 108 local election authorities ever experience what we experienced here in 2016. We want to make sure that all of those county clerks and boards of elections have the same training, resources and best cybersecurity resources we have here at the state level."

The state hired 10 cyber navigators—essentially information technology and cybersecurity specialists situated across the state—to conduct training in safe data handling practices, perform risk assessments and identify equipment or software that needs to be updated. Local officials can then apply to the state board for grants from the $14 million available to make the upgrades.

The state also is moving data transmission between local election boards and the state authority to a secure network, the Illinois Century Network. "It's an intranet [private network] for state government, so you can't break into it from the public internet," says Dietrich. "That work is underway and should be done by the time the state primary rolls around" on March 17, 2020.

Illinois has what Dietrich described as an "extensive, pre-election testing regime" for ballot tabulating machines that all jurisdictions will participate in to make sure they are operating properly.

He emphasized that the voting machines are not hooked up to the internet but are programmed individually, which means machines at multiple locations would have to be tampered with to significantly alter a vote outcome. "People need to understand that we have such a decentralized election system in the U.S. that it would be next to impossible to throw an election through that kind of hacking," he says.

Still, he says, election officials have partnered with the Illinois National Guard and will have the guard's cybersecurity team standing by and ready to travel to voting sites in case an attack on a local system occurs on Election Day.

Finally, Illinois is one of many states that conducts a postelection audit of results. "We do a random 5 percent retabulation," Dietrich says, "and those have to come out with 100 percent accuracy."

The Center for American Progress believes even stronger postelection ballot checking would be best, but it gave Illinois a passing grade overall on election security for the steps the state has taken since 2016.

"I think they are in a much, much better position going into this election," says Root.

— *Reed Karaim*

[1] Rick Pearson, "3 years after Russian hackers tapped Illinois voter database, officials spending millions to safeguard 2020 election," *Chicago Tribune*, Aug. 5, 2019, https://tinyurl.com/r8xvwwc.

[2] "Presidential Election Results: Donald J. Trump Wins," *The New York Times*, Aug. 9, 2017, https://tinyurl.com/y56dyslf.

[3] Danielle Root *et al.*, "Election Security in All 50 States, Defending America's Elections," Center for American Progress, February 2018, https://tinyurl.com/y26r4dd8.

[4] Pearson, *op. cit.*

[5] *Ibid.*

[6] Kartikay Mehrotra and Alyza Sebenius, "Election Security in 2020 Comes Down to Money, and States Aren't Ready," *Bloomberg Businessweek*, Aug. 16, 2019, https://tinyurl.com/y39r585x.

[7] *Ibid.*

Some analysts warned that the theft of intellectual property, particularly by China, could undermine U.S. economic strength. But the largest and most brazen cyberattack on the United States would come from a different direction.

The 2016 Election

Russian interference in the 2016 U.S. presidential election remains a hot-button issue in American politics, particularly with the recent impeachment of President Trump inflaming an already intense partisan divide.

But repeated studies—including by the Senate Intelligence Committee, special counsel Mueller and academic experts—have established that Russia tried to influence the election through several different online efforts.

The Russians hacked into the Democratic National Committee's computer network to steal confidential emails that were then released to embarrass the campaign of Democratic presidential nominee Clinton.[51] They also set up the Internet Research Agency (IRA) to flood social media platforms with disinformation.

Facebook later estimated that over a two-year period, 126 million people may have received content from the Russian troll farm.

Testifying before a Senate subcommittee, Facebook General Counsel Colin Stretch emphasized that the IRA's 80,000 posts amounted to a tiny fraction of the total content on Facebook's news feed during that period.[52]

Still, Stretch said, "many of the ads and posts we've seen so far are deeply disturbing—seemingly intended to amplify societal divisions and pit groups of people against each other." For example, the Russians encouraged secessionist movements in California and Texas and urged right-wing voters to be more confrontational.[53] "They would be controversial even if they came from authentic accounts in the United States," Stretch said. "But coming from foreign actors using fake accounts they are simply unacceptable."[54]

Author Jamieson says much of Russia's online disinformation was focused on undermining Clinton's support among African Americans, a critical Democratic voting bloc. "The Russian strategy in social media was to depress the black vote, and the black vote reached a 20-year low in the last election," she says.

The Russians also probed the election systems of all 50 states. It appears they significantly penetrated only one, the voter registration data of Illinois. (*See Short Feature.*) But Brandt of the Alliance for Securing Democracy says the Russians may still have accomplished their goal.

"They have been trying to undermine confidence in the [U.S. election] system," she says. "You don't have to actually change a vote to undermine confidence in the system. You just have to make people think it's possible."

Political analysts differ on the impact the Russian cyber campaign had on the election. Some dismiss its significance, particularly the social media disinformation effort, claiming the direct influence on voters cannot be quantified.[55] But others believe it may have influenced the outcome.

Jamieson notes that if the combined effect of all of Russia's effort shifted the vote by only 1 percent, that would have been enough to change the outcome in key states such as Pennsylvania, Michigan and Wisconsin. She considers it probable that Russia's efforts made the difference in electing Trump, who lost the popular vote by nearly 3 million but won the Electoral College 306-232.[56]

CURRENT SITUATION
2020 Election

U.S. intelligence officials believe Russia is working to get President Trump re-elected in 2020, according to a report in *The New York Times*. The officials also told House members in a mid-February briefing that Russia is interfering in the Democratic presidential primaries. White House National Security Adviser Robert C. O'Brien disputed the conclusion that Russia is aiding Trump, saying he had not seen any intelligence to support it.[57]

A recent hack by Russia on a Ukrainian company is further raising suspicions about Russian intentions in the U.S. presidential election. Russian military agents late last year successfully penetrated Burisma Holdings, a Ukrainian natural gas company that once employed Hunter Biden, the son of Democratic presidential contender and former Vice President Joe Biden.[58]

The reasons for the hack, which came to light this mid-January, are unclear—but Trump was impeached over allegations that he improperly pressured Ukraine's president to investigate the Bidens' ties to Burisma. Trump's defenders say there were legitimate reasons to be concerned about the connection, and he behaved properly.

Democratic congressional leaders say the hack shows the Russians will again actively work to support Trump in this year's election. House Intelligence Committee Chairman Adam Schiff, D-Calif., who also headed the House impeachment investigation, said it appears the

This building in Kiev reportedly houses a subsidiary of Burisma Holdings, the Ukrainian gas company that was a victim of a recent Russian hacking attack. Burisma once employed the son of Democratic presidential candidate Joe Biden.

Russians "are at it again with an eye toward helping this president"—an assertion Trump and other Republicans vigorously deny.[59]

Sen. Mike Rounds, R-S.D., chairman of the Senate Armed Services Committee's Cybersecurity Subcommittee, discounted the finding's significance. "They are constantly probing and to find that they have been involved with a Ukrainian business or something like that simply is not a surprise," he said.[60]

But in November 2019, virtually all the federal government agencies involved in cyberdefense and law enforcement—including the departments of Justice, Defense and Homeland Security, along with the FBI and the NSA—issued a joint statement saying that cyberattacks on the election process were coming.

"Our adversaries want to undermine our democratic institutions," the statement said. "Russia, China, Iran and other foreign malicious actors all will seek to interfere in the voting process or influence voter perceptions."[61]

Analysts warn that the methods Russia and other adversaries use this time around likely will be more sophisticated than in 2016. For example, security experts pointed to a recent effort by a Russian intelligence agency to bore into an Iranian hacking unit, which, the experts said, they could then use as a cover for their own operations.[62]

In addition, one Russian cyber intelligence unit, known as "Fancy Bear," reportedly has shifted some of its work to computer servers in the United States to make it harder to tie Russia to the unit's actions. The Russians also are reportedly working around Facebook's ban on foreigners buying U.S. political advertisements by paying Americans to set them up.[63]

Lewis, of the Center for Strategic and International Studies, says the Russians and others are likely emboldened by the lack of a strong U.S. response following the last presidential election. "I had a Russian friend tell me a couple of years ago [that] they did what they did in 2016

and then they waited to see what the Americans would do back," Lewis says. "They were sure we would punish them, and then we never did anything, and they took that as a green light."

Election Security

Cybersecurity is a priority among state election officials following reports that Russia probed the voting systems of all 50 states in 2016.[64]

But 41 percent of Americans believe the United States is not very prepared or not at all prepared to safeguard the next national election from interference, according to a new poll by *NPR*, the *PBS NewsHour* and the Marist Institute for Public Opinion.[65]

A majority of those polled, 51 percent, also felt Trump, who has regularly cast doubt on Russian interference in 2016, has actually encouraged foreign intervention in the U.S. election. Not surprisingly, Democrats were much more likely to believe Trump welcomed interference than were Republicans.[66]

U.S. elections are administered at the state and local level and, despite the public's skepticism, all 50 states

Six States Replace Paperless Voting Machines

In preparation for the 2020 presidential election, six states have replaced, or are on track to replace, their paperless voting machines, but eight others still plan to use some machines that do not have paper backups. Paper-based systems are considered more secure than paperless ones because they are less susceptible to cyberattack and because election officials can audit the returns for accuracy.

Paperless Voting Machine Replacement Since 2016

Source: Andrea Córdova McCadney, Elizabeth Howard and Lawrence Norden, "Voting Machine Security: Where We Stand Six Months Before the New Hampshire Primary," Brennan Center for Justice, New York University, Aug. 13, 2019, https://tinyurl.com/twktcpr

Should the United States respond to Russian interference in U.S. elections with cyberattacks of its own?

YES

James Andrew Lewis
Senior Vice President and Director, Technology Policy Program, Center for Strategic and International Studies

Written for *CQ Researcher*, February 2020

Few unclassified networks can be defended against an advanced cyberattack. Thus, a cyber strategy based on defense will fail.

The United States cannot deter cyberattacks. In peacetime, opponents will avoid actions that justify the use of conventional force in response. Perception is crucial. Opponents such as Russia, China or Iran believe they can take cyber action against the United States without facing retaliation. Some even believe they have overestimated the risk of retaliation.

A Russian interlocutor with ties to the government said, "After the [2016] election, we waited for the U.S. response. We were surprised when nothing happened." If opponents assume that cyber actions will not produce retaliation, they will test the limits of how much they can get away with.

The question is how to force opponents to recalculate the risk of cyberattack. Possessing overwhelming conventional and nuclear forces does not do this. The Kabuki of Cold War deterrence is ineffective in this opaque environment.

Nuclear strategists assumed that nuclear weapons would never be used. In contrast, cyber "weapons" are used daily. But our opponents use coercive acts that fall just below the threshold for retaliation, inhabiting a gray area that is neither peace nor war, where the United States has been stymied in designing an effective reply. Possessing a powerful cyberforce and having it glower at opponents from the sidelines does not deter.

Defining what is unacceptable requires pushback—confronting opponents in ways that mirror their own tactics, using cyberattacks that punish, but not enough to provoke war. This kind of engagement does not come without risk, but the days when the United States faced no strategic risks are over. Being cautious and lawyerly cedes the initiative to others.

The goal here is not to conquer or defeat opponents. They are not going away. Naming and shaming them does not work. The goal is to get them to reduce their attacks, and to do this, they must believe that the risk of attacking the United States using "gray zone" tactics is too great. Countermeasures could include disrupting opponents' own cyberattack infrastructure, exposing corruption and putting personal financial assets at risk. Actions that are painful, but temporary and reversible, send the right message.

If the United States is uncomfortable pushing back, it should not expect the Russians to pass up the opportunity in 2020.

NO

Benjamin Jensen
Professor of Strategic Studies, Marine Corps University, and Scholar-in-Residence, School of International Service, American University

Written for *CQ Researcher*, February 2020

To counter Russian cyber operations the United States should use all instruments of government power and also collaborate with the private sector.

First, cyber operations do not work in isolation. For example, studies such as *Cyber Strategy: The Evolving Character of Power and Coercion* find that offensive cyber operations are unlikely to generate political concessions. Cyber operations are ambiguous signals—digital covert action—and only work when combined with other instruments of power, such as diplomatic pressure, economic sanctions and military threats. The Iranians did not stop enriching uranium because of the Stuxnet computer worm that damaged their nuclear program. They stopped because of the looming threat of military attack, crippling economic sanctions and the promise of new diplomatic ties that would pull the country out of isolation.

This insight matches key findings from the broader literature on competition short of armed conflict. Combining multiple instruments of power produces costly signals and dilemmas for rival states.

Second, cyber operations are more espionage than war fighting. U.S. cyber operators—the best in the world—can gain access to Russian systems, but then what? Once you attack, you sacrifice these digital spies. Cyber operations are use-and-lose weapons that produce effects difficult to quantify in advance. Once the target knows you are in its networks, it can shut down access. Why lose access for an indefinite gain? It is better to keep an eye on Kremlin networks and use economic sanctions, diplomatic pressure and legal indictments to deter Russian cyber operations.

Third, and most important, there are better ways to deter Russian aggression than relying exclusively on cyber operations. The fact is, the private sector owns 85 percent of the networks in cyberspace, according to the U.S. Chamber of Commerce. Cyber conflict takes place in these networks, essentially on private property. Therefore, the United States cannot secure its interest in cyberspace without promoting public- and private-sector coordination. Better to deny Russian access to networks than threaten cyber punishment.

Using a combination of government reform, market incentives and smart regulation would better thwart Russian cyber operations than dropping logic bombs on the Kremlin.

In cyberspace, deterrence-by-denial requires a holistic approach.

The world is at an inflection point. With increasing connectivity in cyberspace comes increasing vulnerability. Declining powers such as Russia will take advantage of these vulnerabilities if we let them. Contemporary strategy must start with building security into the cyber ecosystem and making it harder for the Russian bear to byte.

have taken at least some steps to improve the security of their election systems since 2016, according to a study by the Center for American Progress, a liberal public policy group in Washington.[67]

The study found that 36 states are now coordinating with the Department of Homeland Security or their state National Guard's cybersecurity unit on "assessing and identifying potential threats to voter registration systems."

Several states are instituting postelection audits that recount a mathematically determined percentage of the vote to ensure the results are accurate. States also are training local election officials on how to spot and report signs of cyber intrusions into voting machines or reporting systems.[68]

"We've seen much better coordination between officials at all levels attacking election security and cybersecurity concerns," says Danielle Root, associate director of voting rights at the center. "We've seen election officials around the country open their eyes to their vulnerabilities."

Still, she says, problems remain. Root notes that as of 2018, 33 states had not instituted rigorous postelection audit procedures to check results. At the start of this year, eight states were still using electronic voting machines in some precincts without a paper backup, which provides a way to check results if tallies seem suspect. (*See Graphic.*)[69]

Root also says voter registration databases could be a potential weak point. "I continue to be concerned by the threat posed to voter registration systems because if there was some kind of breach—changes in a person's first or last name, date of birth—these are things that wouldn't necessarily set off a major alarm but could keep people from voting," she says.

After initial resistance from Senate Majority Leader Mitch McConnell, R-Ky., who said he feared a Washington takeover of elections, Congress passed and Trump signed a spending bill last December that includes $425 million in federal aid to bolster voting systems and security.[70]

But a Democratic-backed House version of the bill would have authorized $1 billion, and some analysts say the final legislation remains far short of what is needed to replace outdated voting machines and make other improvements. Larry Norden, director of election reform at the Brennan Center for Justice, a liberal law and public policy institute based in New York City, dismissed the $425 million as a Band-Aid on a problem that requires significantly more money and federal attention. McConnell disagreed, saying "the Trump administration has made enormous strides to help states secure their elections without giving Washington new power to push the states around."[71]

McConnell previously refused to consider bipartisan legislation that specifically targeted foreign interference in U.S. elections, such as the Defending Elections from Threats by Establishing Redlines (DETER) Act, which would impose sanctions on a country that was found to be interfering in U.S. elections.

Republicans also blocked three different election security measures from coming before the Senate this February. Sen. Marsha Blackburn, R-Tenn., said the bills would take control of elections from the states and place it in "the hands of Washington, D.C., bureaucrats." Democrats lampooned McConnell as "Moscow Mitch" and accused him of turning the Senate into a legislative graveyard for election reform.[72]

Senate Minority Leader Charles Schumer, D-N.Y., called action essential. "If there is anything we can say for certain about our elections at this point, it's that foreign entities—Putin, China, perhaps others—are already implementing their schemes to undermine the public confidence in the integrity of those elections," Schumer said.[73]

Top election officials from all 50 states met the last week in January in Washington to prepare for the 2020 election. Noting the changes they have made to address the security of their systems, officials said their principal worry is not about significant tampering, but that someone will be able to create enough confusion to raise doubts among already skeptical voters.

"My biggest concern in 2020 is that regardless of outcome, we will be faced with somewhere around the end of the first week in November, this concern by half of the country that they lost the election illegitimately," said Judd Choate, Colorado's election director.[74]

Developing a Cyber Strategy

A special commission created by Congress to develop a national strategy on how to deal with cybersecurity is scheduled to present its recommendations this spring.

The Cyberspace Solarium Commission is modeled after a commission that President Dwight Eisenhower convened in the 1950s to develop a coherent approach to dealing with the Soviet Union during the Cold War.

The commission's co-chairs—Sen. Angus King, I-Maine, and Rep. Mike Gallagher, R-Wisc.—said the panel's creation is a recognition that the country has yet to come up with a consensus approach on how to defend U.S. interests and promote U.S. values in cyberspace.[75]

The commission's 14 members include representatives from Congress, the executive branch and the private sector, and are supported by technology and defense experts. "It's clear to us that the cyberthreat is significant," says retired Adm. Mike Montgomery, the executive director. "It's a mix of adversary capability that improved greatly over the last two decades combined with our own vulnerabilities, which are a product of the increasing connectivity of our economy, government and our daily lives."

The commission is looking at a range of issues, including defensive and offensive cyber strategy and how the United States could work with other Western democracies to establish norms of behavior in cyberspace concerning transparency and the rule of law.

He declined to preview the commission's expected recommendations. But Montgomery says developing a closer working relationship on cybersecurity between government and industry is a priority, noting that up to 85 percent of "the defended area, our critical national security infrastructure," is owned by the private sector.

"The private-public collaboration is the thing that needs to move the most and the fastest over the next five years," he says. "Other recommendations about offensive capabilities, government organizations, the norms, I think are all critical, but secondary to development of the robust public-private collaboration."

OUTLOOK
New Threats

Superfast 5G technology is expected to transform cellular communications over the next few years, putting high-speed internet connections and data transfer into the pockets of millions, eventually billions, of mobile users.

As more people go online directly through cellular connections rather than wireless links to routers, "it will greatly increase the attackable surface," providing a tempting target for cyber warriors, says Levin of CyberScout. He predicts a new focus on cellular security with devices requiring strong passwords to operate and automatic security updates no longer optional but built in.

The number of other devices—everything from security cameras to refrigerators—being tied together online in the Internet of Things also means cybersecurity will move beyond primarily a government and corporate concern to one that touches most everyone, he adds. "Vulnerability management is going to become an even more critical part of our lives in the future," Levin says.

The growing sophistication of artificial intelligence is expected to complicate cyberdefense as "smart bots," or AI-enabled programs, increasingly are able to mimic human speech and behavior online and AI-powered computer viruses and worms will be able to mutate and adapt to their environment, making them far more difficult to detect and defeat.[76]

The University of Pennsylvania's Jamieson says cyberwarfare's destructive capability is large enough—particularly when it comes to upending the internal politics of any nation—that the global community will eventually agree it needs to be brought under control. "I think we're going to have a cyber treaty on elections at some point in which the nations of the world agree to stand down and agree that an attack on one is an attack on all," she says. "I actually believe you could get that and get it to work."

Lewis, of the Center for Strategic and International Studies, is less optimistic about the outlook for the next five to 10 years.

"Right now, things are going to get worse because the advantage lies with the attacker," he says. "It's just so easy to break into most networks, especially for the high-end opponents. There's probably only a handful of networks Russia or China can't get into. What happens after that depends on what we do—if we make them afraid of us, if we come up with a standard approach to protecting infrastructure, if we do the political things we need to do to deal with Russian misinformation—things could get better."

Dealing with misinformation campaigns, he says, is going to require holding social media companies more accountable for the material they allow to spread on their platforms, an active effort to call out clear falsehoods, and a willingness to send a clear message to other nations that they will pay a price for interfering in the U.S. political process.

Brandt at the Alliance for Securing Democracy sees the ability of cyber campaigns to sow confusion and threaten security as growing. "Some of the concerns will only accelerate," she says. "New technologies will lower barriers of entry and enable more actors to get into the game. . . . One of the things I worry the most about is the popularity of manipulated media—deep fakes [doctored photos or videos that appear highly realistic]— where you can no longer trust your own eyes."

Clark, of Foreign Policy for America, says that governments, particularly authoritarian regimes, could attempt to wall off their countries from the broader internet, both to protect from cyberattack and to control their citizens' access to information.

The other option, he says, would be that nations recognize they need to adopt norms to safely manage an open internet and build tools to increase its resilience. But, he says, "it's much more likely you end up with fragmented networks where you lose the dream of a single global network. You end up with regional networks with walls around them, and that would be sad."

NOTES

1. Deirdre Shesgreen and Tom Vanden Brook, "US launched Baghdad airstrike that killed Iranian military leader Qasem Soleimani," *USA Today*, Jan. 3, 2020, https://tinyurl.com/tftov4a; Rebecca Kheel, "Additional US service member diagnosed with brain injury from Iran attack," *The Hill*, Feb. 21, 2020, https://tinyurl.com/seyalqa.

2. Lisa Monaco, "We are in uncharted territory now. Are we prepared for that?" *The Washington Post*, Jan. 6, 2020, https://tinyurl.com/s7y7yjf.

3. Frank Bajak, "Iranian cyberattacks feared after killing of top general," *The Associated Press*, Jan. 4, 2020, https://tinyurl.com/vm87pkt.

4. David E. Sanger and Catie Edmondson, "Russia Targeted Election Systems in All 50 States, Report Finds," *The New York Times*, July 25, 2019, https://tinyurl.com/y2nlsrz2.

5. Robert S. Mueller III, "The Mueller Report," Melville House, Kindle edition, location 12; Adam Goldman *et al.*, "Lawmakers Are Warned That Russia Is Meddling to Re-elect Trump," *The New York Times*, Feb. 20, 2020, https://tinyurl.com/uh9vnxx.

6. Samantha Bradshaw and Philip N. Howard, "The Global Disinformation Order: 2019 Global Inventory of Organised Social Media Manipulation," University of Oxford, 2019, https://tinyurl.com/y4yxoz7f.

7. David E. Sanger and Nicole Perlroth, "U.S. Escalates Online Attacks on Russia's Power Grid," *The New York Times*, June 15, 2019, https://tinyurl.com/yytd88b3.

8. Zak Doffman, "Chinese State Hackers Suspected Of Malicious Cyber Attack On U.S. Utilities," *Forbes*, Aug. 3, 2019, https://tinyurl.com/vffowpw; Mark Thompson, "Iranian Cyber Attack on New York Dam Shows Future of War," *Time*, March 24, 2016, https://tinyurl.com/wjeymtp; and Angela Moon, "State-sponsored cyberattacks on banks on the rise: report," *Reuters*, March 22, 2019, https://tinyurl.com/t8bqp29.

9. "The Cost of Malicious Cyber Activity to the United States," Council of Economic Advisers, The White House, February 2018, p. 35, https://tinyurl.com/ycogtpds.

10. *Ibid.*

11. Andrew Burt and James C. Trainor, "Our Government's Approach to Cybersecurity Is a Costly Mess. Here's What Would Fix the Problem," *Time*, Jan. 2, 2020, https://tinyurl.com/v3ghbze.

12. Michael Sulmeyer, "How the U.S. Can Play Cyber-Offense," *Foreign Affairs*, March 22, 2018, https://tinyurl.com/y3424w26.

13. C. Todd Lopez, "DOD More Assertive, Proactive in Cyber Domain," U.S. Department of Defense, June 28, 2019, https://tinyurl.com/tp7ddrs; Jim Garamone, "Esper describes DOD's Increased Cyber Offensive Strategy," U.S. Department of Defense, Sept. 20, 2019, https://tinyurl.com/yx4q5avy.

14. Brandon Valeriano and Benjamin Jensen, "The Myth of the Cyber Offense: The Case for Restraint," Cato Institute, Jan. 15, 2019, https://tinyurl.com/w88c24k.

15. Elisabeth Bumiller and Thom Shanker, "Panetta Warns of Dire Threat of Cyberattack on U.S.," *The New York Times*, Oct. 11, 2012, https://tinyurl.com/97yv9ee.

16. *Ibid.*

17. Natasha Turak, "The next 9/11 will be a cyberattack, security expert warns," *CNBC*, June 1, 2018, https://tinyurl.com/y8uhyb2u.

18. Alicia Parlapiano and Jasmine C. Lee, "The Propaganda Tools Used by Russians to Influence the 2016 Election," *The New York Times*, Feb. 16, 2018, https://tinyurl.com/y776zjs2.

19. Anthony Ferrante, "2020 cybersecurity predictions: Evolving vulnerabilities on the horizon," *The Hill*, Jan. 22, 2020, https://tinyurl.com/vcxcdgq.

20. David E. Sanger, *The Perfect Weapon: War, Sabotage, and Fear in the Cyber Age* (2018), p. xv.

21. Michael J. Bayer *et al.*, "Secretary of the Navy, Cybersecurity Readiness Review," U.S. Navy, March 2019, https://tinyurl.com/reecqqv. Also see Dustin Volz and Gordon Lubold, "Navy, Beset by Aging Tech, Pushes for Rapid Modernization," *The Wall Street Journal*, Feb. 19, 2020, https://tinyurl.com/tcfljom.

22. Bayer *et al.*, *ibid.*

23. Gopal Ratnam and John M. Donnelly, "America is woefully unprepared for cyber-warfare," *Roll Call*, July 11, 2019, https://tinyurl.com/yxqmqwjs.

24. Wes O'Donnell, "New IG Report Says U.S. Military Lags in Cybersecurity," *InCyberDefense*, March 25, 2019, https://tinyurl.com/qv7vzfe.

25. Ellen Nakashima, "U.S. Cyber Command operation disrupted Internet access of Russian troll factory on day of 2018 midterms," *The Washington Post*, Feb. 27, 2019, https://tinyurl.com/yxs8twyv.

26. William Crumpler and James Andrew Lewis, "The Cybersecurity Workforce Gap," Center for Strategic and International Studies, Jan. 29, 2019, https://tinyurl.com/ycty7khb.

27. Davey Alba and Adam Satariano, "At Least 70 Countries Have Had Disinformation Campaigns, Study Finds," *The New York Times*, Sept. 26, 2019, https://tinyurl.com/y3jy7xmh.

28. Mathew Ingram, "Faceplant: a tech giant's culpability to the international community," *Columbia Journalism Review*, Summer 2019, https://tinyurl.com/uoz9ss5.

29. *Ibid.*

30. Raymond Zhong, Steven Lee Myers and Jin Wu, "How China Unleashed Twitter Trolls to Discredit Hong Kong's Protestors," *The New York Times*, Sept. 18, 2019, https://tinyurl.com/yxur664s.

31. Julie Posetti and Alice Matthews, "A short guide to the history of 'fake news' and disinformation," International Center for Journalists, July 2018, https://tinyurl.com/y2n6em5t.

32. Gordon Corera, "Cold War fake news: Why Russia lied over Aids and JFK," *BBC*, April 1, 2017, https://tinyurl.com/t24j3to.

33. Michael S. Neiberg, "World War I Intrigue: German Spies in New York!" History.net, https://tinyurl.com/swv2gp8.

34. *Ibid.*

35. Barry M. Leiner *et al.*, "Brief History of the Internet," Internet Society, 1997, https://tinyurl.com/y7kfqkf8.

36. *Ibid.*

37. "History and Growth of the Internet from 1995 till Today," Internet World Stats, 2019, https://tinyurl.com/vjnqe4p.

38. J. Clement, "Mobile internet usage worldwide," Statista, Sept. 11, 2019, https://tinyurl.com/ycdqdkkr.

39. Fred Kaplan, *Dark Territory: The Secret History of Cyber War* (2016), pp. 1-2.

40. *Ibid.*

41. *Ibid.*, p. 3.

42. Sanger, *The Perfect Weapon, op. cit.*, p. 18.

43. KG Chan, "PLA's J-20 fighters use stolen U.S. tech: report," *Asia Times*, Oct. 21, 2019, https://tinyurl.com/u8dbo3l.

44. "Agent.btz," Cyber Operations Tracker, Council on Foreign Relations, November 2008, https://tinyurl.com/vp7yvfw.

45. *Ibid.*

46. Kaplan, *op. cit.*, p. 4.

47. *Ibid.*

48. Amy Zegart, "Cyberwar," TED Talk, YouTube, June 29, 2015, https://tinyurl.com/szx4mas.

49. David E. Sanger, "Obama Order Sped Up Wave of Cyberattacks Against Iran," *The New York Times*, June 1, 2012, https://tinyurl.com/85kk6sn.

50. Dustin Volz and Jim Finkle, "U.S. indicts Iranians for hacking dozens of banks, New York dam," *Reuters*, March 24, 2016, https://tinyurl.com/rgsmmj8.

51. Ellen Nakashima and Shane Harris, "How the Russians hacked the DNC and passed its emails to WikiLeaks," *The Washington Post*, July 13, 2018, https://tinyurl.com/yapaoywd.

52. Colin Stretch, testimony before the U.S. Senate Committee on the Judiciary, Subcommittee on Crime and Terrorism, Oct. 31, 2017, https://tinyurl.com/uzfotn3.

53. Mark Hosenball, "Russia used social media for widespread meddling in U.S. politics: reports," *Reuters*, Dec. 17, 2018, https://tinyurl.com/u5fugyd.

54. Stretch, *op. cit.*

55. Aaron Maté, "New Studies Show Pundits Are Wrong About Russian Social-Media Involvement in US Politics," *The Nation*, Dec. 28, 2018, https://tinyurl.com/wtcc7zw.

56. "Presidential Election Results: Donald J. Trump Wins," *The New York Times*, Aug. 9, 2017, https://tinyurl.com/y56dyslf.

57. Goldman *et al.*, *op. cit.*; David E. Sanger, "Dueling Narratives Emerge From Muddied Account of Russia's 2020 Interference," *The New York Times*, Feb. 23, 2020, https://tinyurl.com/sk7s8ns.

58. Martin Matishak, "Democrats press for details on alleged Burisma hack," *Politico*, Jan. 14, 2020, https://tinyurl.com/uzxms75.

59. *Ibid.*

60. *Ibid.*

61. "Joint Statement from DOJ, DOD, DHS, DNI, FBI, NSA, and CISA on Ensuring Security of 2020 Elections," news release, FBI, Nov. 5, 2019, https://tinyurl.com/qoykyeo.

62. Matthew Rosenberg, Nicole Perlroth and David E. Sanger, "Chaos Is the Point: Russian Hackers and Trolls Grow Stealthier in 2020," *The New York Times*, Jan. 10, 2020, https://tinyurl.com/w49jcyy.

63. *Ibid.*

64. Pam Fessler, "Election Officials to Convene Among Historic Focus on Voting and Interference," *NPR*, Jan. 27, 2020, https://tinyurl.com/tjw9pj9.

65. Brett Neely, "NPR Poll: Majority of Americans Believe Trump Encourages Election Interference," *NPR*, Jan. 21, 2020, https://tinyurl.com/udxz7aw.

66. *Ibid.*

67. Danielle Root *et al.*, "Election Security in All 50 States, Defending America's Elections," Center for American Progress, Feb. 12, 2018, https://tinyurl.com/y26r4dd8.

68. *Ibid.*

69. Andrea Córdova McCadney, Elizabeth Howard and Lawrence Norden, "Voting Machine Security: Where We Stand Six Months Before the New Hampshire Primary," Brennan Center for Justice,

New York University, Aug. 13, 2019, https://tinyurl.com/twktcpr.

70. "EAC Commissioners Welcome Deal To Make Available $425 Million In New Help America Vote Act Funds For Elections," U.S. Election Assistance Commission, https://tinyurl.com/u6alvcw.

71. Kevin Collier, "Congress to Approve $425 million for election security upgrades," *CNN*, Dec. 16, 2019, https://tinyurl.com/ttf5sln; Philip Ewing, "McConnell, Decried as 'Moscow Mitch,' Approves Election Security Money," *NPR*, Sept. 20, 2019, https://tinyurl.com/y44jvqb6.

72. Igor Derysh, "Senate GOP blocks election security bills as intel report warns of Russian meddling in 2020," *Salon*, Feb. 13, 2020, https://tinyurl.com/tahcne5.

73. *Ibid.*

74. Fessler, *op. cit.*

75. Angus King and Mike Gallagher, "Announcing the Cyberspace Solarium Commission," *Lawfare*, Aug. 19, 2019, https://tinyurl.com/qunwn7y.

76. William Dixon and Nicole Egan, "3 ways AI will change the nature of cyber attacks," World Economic Forum, June 19, 2019, https://tinyurl.com/uemorj6.

BIBLIOGRAPHY

Books

Jamieson, Kathleen Hall, *Cyber-War: How Russian Hackers and Trolls Helped Elect a President*, Oxford University Press, 2018.
The director of the Annenberg School for Communication at the University of Pennsylvania analyzes Russia's cyber campaign in the 2016 election and polling data to argue that the Russians most likely played a significant role in electing President Trump.

Sanger, David E., *The Perfect Weapon: War, Sabotage, and Fear in the Cyber Age*, Crown, 2018.
A *New York Times* national security correspondent reviews the development of cyberweapons and how their capabilities are transforming the political and defense landscape.

Valeriano, Brandon, and Ryan C. Maness, *Cyber War versus Cyber Realities, Cyber Conflict in the International System*, Oxford University Press, 2015.
Cybersecurity experts at the Marine Corps University (Valeriano) and the Naval Postgraduate School (Maness) argue the cyberwar threat has been overstated and responses to cyber incursions should be restrained and proportional.

Articles

Coppins, McKay, "The Billion-Dollar Disinformation Campaign to Reelect the President," *The Atlantic*, March 2020, https://tinyurl.com/uvwucv8.
A journalist argues the Trump re-election campaign is adopting cyber disinformation tactics pioneered by the Russians and other authoritarian regimes as it seeks to defend the president against charges of illegal or improper behavior.

Gambacorta, David, "Iran's next move: A cyberattack on the U.S.?" *Philadelphia Inquirer*, Jan. 10, 2020, https://tinyurl.com/sdydayc.
Cyberwarfare and intelligence experts are concerned Iran could launch cyberattacks on U.S. infrastructure and private companies in response to President Trump's decision to assassinate Iranian military leader Qassem Soleimani.

Goldman, Adam, *et al.*, "Lawmakers Are Warned That Russia Is Meddling to Re-elect Trump," *The New York Times*, Feb. 20, 2020, https://tinyurl.com/uh9vnxx.
In a House briefing, U.S. intelligence officials said Russia is already interfering in the 2020 presidential campaign, including the Democratic primaries.

Greenberg, Andy, "The WIRED Guide to Cyberwar," *Wired*, Aug. 23, 2019, https://tinyurl.com/w8ahrss.
The idea of cyberwar has evolved with the growth of the internet and social media from a concept focused on disrupting a nation's military command and control systems to one that includes damaging public infrastructure and sowing misinformation and political discord.

Perlroth, Nicole, David E. Sanger and Scott Shane, "How Chinese Spies Got the N.S.A.'s Hacking Tools and Used Them for Attacks," *The New York Times*, May 6, 2019, https://tinyurl.com/s4llhmt.

Cyberwarfare's risks are illustrated by how China was able to capture a hacking tool used by the U.S. National Security Agency and use it to attack governments and private companies in Europe.

Reports and Studies

Bodine-Baron, Elizabeth, *et al.*, "Countering Russian Social Media Influence," RAND Corp., 2018, https:// tinyurl.com/y754hblq.
Researchers at a global policy think tank find that efforts to counter Russian cyber campaigns designed to sow political division and influence U.S. elections remain fragmented and incomplete.

Bradshaw, Samantha, and Philip N. Howard, "The Global Disinformation Order: 2019 Global Inventory of Organized Social Media Manipulation," Oxford Internet Institute, University of Oxford, 2019, https://tinyurl.com/y4yxoz7f.
At least 70 countries engaged in online campaigns in 2019 to spread propaganda and disinformation, manipulate social media and harass political opponents, according to a comprehensive study by Oxford researchers.

Mueller, Robert S. III, "Report on the Investigation into Russian Interference in the 2016 Presidential Election Pursuant to 28 C.F.R. 600.8(c)," U.S. Department of Justice, March 2019, https://tinyurl .com/v42ym4e.
Commonly known as "The Mueller Report," the published results of an investigation led by former FBI Director Robert Mueller conclude there was a widespread Russian cyber campaign to influence the 2016 presidential election on behalf of Donald Trump, but the report reaches no conclusion on whether the president colluded with Russian operatives.

Root, Danielle, "Election Security in All 50 States, Defending America's Elections," Center for American Progress, February 2018, https://tinyurl.com/ y6y9z937.
All U.S. states have taken at least some steps to improve election security following Russian hacking during the 2016 election, according to a liberal public interest group, but significant vulnerabilities remain.

THE NEXT STEP

Election Security

Asokan, Ashkaya, "Cybersecurity Plan for 2020 US Election Unveiled," *Bank Info Security*, Feb. 17, 2020, https://tinyurl.com/s6437s2.
A U.S. cybersecurity agency released a plan to help federal, state and local agencies protect voting machines and other election infrastructure.

Carney, Jordain, "Senate GOP blocks three election security bills," *The Hill*, Feb. 11, 2020, https:// tinyurl.com/rbtb6vr.
A Democratic effort to pass by unanimous consent three bills that would require campaigns to alert the FBI and Federal Election Commission about foreign offers of assistance, provide more election funding and ban voting machines from being connected to the internet failed in the Senate after Sen. Marsha Blackburn, R-Tenn., raised objections.

Wallace, Gregory, "Watchdog says Homeland Security 'not well-positioned' on election security," *CNN*, Feb. 6, 2020, https://tinyurl.com/qvb6waq.
A report from the Government Accountability Office says the Department of Homeland Security lacks plans and a nationwide strategy to safeguard elections against cyberattacks.

Foreign Cyberattacks

Doffman, Zak, "Russia Unleashes New Weapons In Its 'Cyber Attack Testing Ground': Report," *Forbes*, Feb. 5, 2020, https://tinyurl.com/t58o9v4.
Russia is testing new malware as it conducts cyberattacks on strategic Ukrainian targets.

Keshner, Andrew, "If China did hack Equifax, these Americans may have more reasons to be concerned," *MarketWatch*, Feb. 12, 2020, https://tinyurl.com/ wsfsqev.
Federal prosecutors charged four members of China's army with carrying out a 2017 hack of consumer credit agency Equifax and stealing the personal information of nearly 150 million Americans.

Tucker, Eric, "FBI director warns of ongoing Russian 'information warfare,'" *The Associated Press*, Feb. 5, 2020, https://tinyurl.com/s4hp93o.

Russia is spreading disinformation ahead of the 2020 presidential election but has not targeted election infrastructure, FBI Director Chris Wray told Congress.

Private Companies' Cybersecurity

Fingas, Jon, "Facebook says it will tighten account security following 2018 hack," *Engadget*, Feb. 8, 2020, https://tinyurl.com/tfp8q8v.
Facebook has promised to bolster its security and check more often for suspicious activity as part of a settlement in a lawsuit over a 2018 hack that exposed data for 29 million users.

Lyons, Kim, "Google will provide political campaigns free access to Titan security keys for better 2FA," *The Verge*, Feb. 11, 2020, https://tinyurl.com/t4bzazk.
Google plans to give qualifying political groups another level of security to protect their Google accounts.

Myre, Greg, "Tech Companies Take a Leading Role Warning of Foreign Cyber Threats," *NPR*, Jan. 23, 2020, https://tinyurl.com/vddbg3n.
Private cybersecurity firms often are the first to sound the alarm on foreign cyberattacks and are selling their services to the U.S. intelligence community.

U.S. Cybersecurity

Coble, Sarah, "Report Finds Cybersecurity Issues with 2020 Census," *InfoSecurity*, Feb. 13, 2020, https://tinyurl.com/t8cu9mx.
The Government Accountability Office questions whether personal data collected during the decennial census can be kept private.

Vavra, Shannon, "Pentagon, FBI, DHS jointly expose a North Korean hacking effort," *CyberScoop*, Feb. 14, 2020, https://tinyurl.com/ukahk58.
U.S. officials warned the private sector of a North Korean hacking effort meant to steal data and create and delete files.

Wolfgang, Ben, "Defense industry 'report card' finds that U.S. lags on cybersecurity," *The Washington Times*, Feb. 5, 2020, https://tinyurl.com/u8as8vr.
Defense leaders said the United States was falling behind China on cybersecurity after data breaches by state and nonstate actors involving leading defense and technology firms.

For More Information

American Press Institute, 4401 N. Fairfax Drive, Suite 300, Arlington, VA 22203; 571-366-1200; americanpressinstitute. org. A news industry group that researches the growth of misinformation in the internet age and how it can be countered.

Cato Institute, 1000 Massachusetts Ave., N.W., Washington, DC 20001; 202-842 0200; cato.org. A conservative-leaning public policy research organization that has a "cyberskeptics" webpage with links to research and articles by experts who argue the cyberwar threat has been overstated.

Center for Internet Security, 31 Tech Valley Drive, #2, East Greenbush, NY 12061; 518-266-3460; cisecurity.org. A nonprofit group of corporations, government agencies and academic researchers dedicated to safeguarding private and public organizations from cyberthreats.

Center for Strategic and International Studies, 1616 Rhode Island Ave., N.W., Washington, DC 20036; 202-887-0200; csis.org. A defense and international relations think tank whose experts conduct research on cybersecurity.

The Computational Propaganda Project, Oxford Internet Institute, 1 St Giles, Oxford, OX1 3JS, UK; +44 (0)1865 287210; https://comprop.oii.ox.ac.uk. A part of Oxford University's Internet Institute that examines how algorithms, computer "bots" and other automated systems are used to manipulate public opinion.

National Security Agency, Fort George G. Meade, 9800 Savage Road, Suite 6272, Fort Meade, MD 20755-6000; 301-688-6311; nsa.gov. A code-breaking and electronic intelligence agency that also plays a lead role in U.S. cybersecurity operations.

NATO Cooperative Cyber Defence Centre of Excellence, Filtri tee 12, 10132 Tallinn, Estonia; +372-7176-800; https:// ccdcoe.org. A research center that brings together NATO experts to train in cyberdefense.

U.S. Cyber Command, Fort George G. Meade, 4409 Llewellyn Ave., Fort Meade, MD 20755; 301-677-2300; cybercom.mil. The U.S. military force that is tasked with coordinating and directing cyberspace planning and operations to defend the nation from cyberattacks.

5

Getty Images/NurPhoto/John Lamparski

A COVID-19 patient is transported by ambulance to Mt. Sinai Morningside hospital in New York City on May 18, 2020. The virus is only the most recent example of a disease that originated in animals and then spread widely and lethally among humans.

From *CQ Researcher,*
June 26, 2020

Zoonotic Diseases

Can future pandemics be prevented?

By Sarah Glazer

THE ISSUES

In the second week of January 2020, a 61-year-old man died from a mysterious pneumonia that was causing a spate of illnesses from an unknown virus in Wuhan, China. The man was a regular customer at Wuhan's giant seafood market, which also sold exotic animals, some live, for meat. Of the first 41 cases of pneumonia tied to the viral infection that first arose in December 2019, two-thirds had either been workers or customers at the market.[1]

According to a widely circulated menu and to reports from vendors and observers, offerings at the market included snakes, dogs, baby crocodiles, arctic foxes, raccoon dogs, bamboo rats and civet cats, sometimes butchered on site.[2]

At such Asian markets, exotic animals are often stacked in cages on top of animals they would never encounter in nature. Exchanging excretion and saliva under stressful conditions makes animals prone to contagion and creates a petri dish for viruses to jump from one species to another, scientists say.

Speculation was rampant that the Wuhan market was the source of the virus that causes COVID-19, which erupted into a pandemic that has killed hundreds of thousands of people across the globe. But in recent months, scientists have cast doubt on the theory. They instead fear that the virus jumped earlier from an animal to a human, perhaps in the wild, and that the market's crowded conditions simply helped to spread the virus from one infected human to many others.[3]

Regardless of what exactly happened, COVID-19 is just the most recent example of a growing threat to human health—zoonotic diseases, which leap from animals to humans and which, if the virus mutates successfully in humans, can also be transmitted from human to human. Researchers believe COVID-19 spilled over from a horseshoe bat in China, possibly to another intermediate animal, such as an endangered pangolin, considered a culinary luxury in China, and then to humans.[4]

Scientists have long warned of a new epidemic of zoonotic diseases, but it is only recently that the environmental roots, such as human encroachment on wild habitats, are gaining the kind of public and media attention given to climate change.

Some of the most well-known epidemics originated with animals, including HIV (from chimpanzees), severe acute respiratory syndrome or SARS (from bats) and Middle East respiratory syndrome or MERS (from camels). An epidemic is a disease that affects a large number of people within a community or region, as opposed to a pandemic, which affects most of the globe.

Scientists say the frequency of such outbreaks has been increasing in recent years. According to estimates, 60 to 75 percent of newly emerging infectious diseases can be traced to animals and more than 70 percent of those come from wildlife.[5]

In fact, scientists have been predicting a zoonotic epidemic similar to COVID-19 for more than a decade, and some even targeted coronaviruses from bats, which likely produced both SARS and COVID-19. For example, in 2007, a Hong Kong scientists' study of SARS said the presence of SARS-like coronaviruses in horseshoe bats, "together with the culture of eating exotic mammals in southern China, is a time bomb."[6]

Andrew Cunningham, a professor of wildlife epidemiology at the Institute of Zoology, London, said in March, "The emergence and spread of COVID-19 was not only predictable, it was predicted [in the sense that] there would be another viral emergence from wildlife that would be a public health threat."[7]

Some scientists and advocacy groups say the spread of both new and existing zoonotic diseases can be attributed to declining biodiversity in natural animal habitats, as humans slash forests for agriculture, mining, roads or housing. Other studies pinpoint increasing human contact with wild animals as the root of growing risks.

With the human population growing and global trade and travel expanding, the human activities that trigger outbreaks "are accelerating and magnifying globally, which is why we're seeing more and more outbreaks happening and will continue to," says Jonathan Epstein, one of the researchers who discovered that horseshoe bats were the likely origin of the SARS virus, and who is vice president for science and outreach at EcoHealth Alliance, an environmental health research group in New York. "The single biggest cause of these epidemics is people. . . . We're encroaching on natural systems and disrupting them, and it's leading to epidemics and pandemics."

Yet traditional public health approaches to disease outbreaks have ignored the role played by environmental destruction, says Samuel S. Myers, an environmental health scientist at Harvard University's School of Public Health, who is promoting a new discipline, planetary health, to unite environmental health and medicine.[8]

"The way we're transforming our natural systems is a dominant driver of the global burden of disease," he says, but "we're completely unequipped to confront these [environmental] problems as a public health community."

That problem extends to the approach to pandemics such as COVID-19 by the U.S. Centers for Disease Control and Prevention (CDC), says Howard Frumkin, a former director of the CDC's National Center for Environmental Health and professor emeritus at the University of Washington School of Public Health. "If you focus on vaccines and public health strategies like contact tracing and isolation, you may overlook some of the root causes of diseases that lie outside the biomedical world," he says.

Along similar lines, several bills in Congress aim to promote greater collaboration among environmental experts, veterinarians and human health experts to anticipate and tackle future pandemic threats in an approach known as One Health.[9]

Some scientists are trying to raise money to create a comprehensive library of zoonotic viruses, saying such a repository could predict and prevent pandemics. But critics point out that similar efforts along those lines, including one funded by the U.S. Agency for International Development (USAID), failed to find COVID-19.[10]

"It's hard to claim success in searching the world over for the virus that will cause the next pandemic when this virus eluded all that tremendous effort," says Richard S. Ostfeld,

Amazon Deforestation Accelerated in Past Decade

The Amazon rainforest continues to lose tree cover in general and primary forest—forest that has existed undisturbed for a long period of time—in particular. During 2010–19, the average annual number of hectares of forest lost increased from the previous decade. (One hectare equals 2.47 acres.)

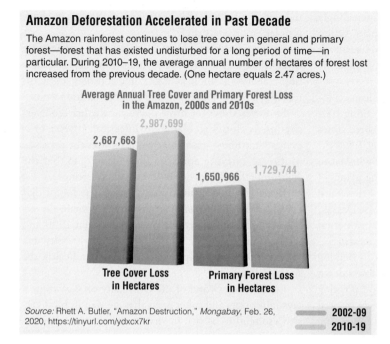

Average Annual Tree Cover and Primary Forest Loss in the Amazon, 2000s and 2010s

Source: Rhett A. Butler, "Amazon Destruction," *Mongabay*, Feb. 26, 2020, https://tinyurl.com/ydxcx7kr

2002-09
2010-19

a disease ecologist at the Cary Institute of Ecosystem Studies, a private research center in Millbrook, N.Y.

Many scientists agree that the dramatic changes humans have imposed on the planet as a result of world population growth is one major reason for the increase in new zoonotic diseases. "The 21st century is paying the price for what happened in the 20th century," when the world population grew from 1.6 billion to more than 6 billion and humans pushed deeper into virgin forests, says Dennis Carroll a former USAID official who oversaw efforts to forecast zoonotic disease outbreaks.[11] "As we're accommodating this increasing population, we're seeing the increasing frequency and intensity of these spillover events" when diseases leap from animals to humans, he says.

As the world's population heads toward a projected 11 billion people in 2100, developing countries are increasing their wealth and their appetite for meat, with an accompanying demand for more agricultural land in the vast tropical rain forests of the Amazon and Congo River basins.[12]

The loss of biodiversity that results is a major cause of zoonotic disease, according to Ostfeld. As humans cut down and transform virgin forests, coming into extended contact with displaced wild animals and their viruses for the first time, "we've made [these regions] increasingly dangerous by disturbing them and fragmenting the natural habitats," he says. But other scientists question Ostfeld's biodiversity theory, arguing that urbanization and growing wealth helped reduce infectious disease rates between 1990 and 2010.[13]

"Cities bring people into close contact with doctors, make it efficient for public health to do mosquito spraying, vaccinations, offer drugs to infected people. Cities are good for people's health," says Chelsea L. Wood, assistant professor at the University of Washington School of Aquatic and Fishery Sciences. "When you stack up biodiversity against all these other drivers, biodiversity is totally inconsequential."

Experts also disagree on whether governments should ban the trade in exotic animals for human consumption.

"We're creating the perfect storm. If you're a virus whose goal is to spread, you couldn't design a better system to aid and abet a pandemic than these wildlife markets" in Wuhan and across Asia, said Steven Osofsky, professor of wildlife health and health policy at the Cornell University College of Veterinary Medicine. "A lot of these pathogens are meeting species they've never met before, and that's when we have these viral jumps—and create the situation we're in now."[14]

Some researchers and environmentalists argue that certain kinds of well-regulated legal wildlife trade pose little danger of transmitting disease, but other environmental groups dispute that.

As scientists, conservationists and members of government in the United States and around the world debate the threat of zoonotic disease, here are some of the issues they are considering:

Is loss of biodiversity increasing the spread of diseases from animals to humans?

Environmental advocacy groups and some scientists say human incursion into natural habitats is causing viruses that circulate harmlessly in animals to jump increasingly to humans, with sometimes fatal consequences. Other scientists, however, argue that the loss of biodiversity is not necessarily a bad thing because it can reduce the populations of disease-carrying animals.

A widely cited study by British and American ecologists estimated that outbreaks of newly emerging zoonotic diseases are occurring about two to three times more frequently per decade than in the 1940s.[15]

That increasing frequency is "pretty clearly linked to our human footprint and what we do on the planet—building roads, cutting down forests, global trade and travel—all increasing exponentially," says Peter Daszak, president of EcoHealth Alliance, a nongovernmental research organization, and a co-author of the study.

"In some areas where there is a high risk of emerging zoonotic disease, maybe we shouldn't cut the forest down and have people move in and eat wildlife," he says, pointing to his group's research finding that cutting down tropical forests in Asia for palm oil is leading to workers contracting malaria and occasionally a new zoonotic disease.

Two New York-based researchers argue that the reduced diversity of animals that results from such human activity is leading to an increase in zoonotic disease and that conserving biodiversity can protect against such new diseases emerging and spreading.

The researchers, Ostfeld of the Cary Institute and Felicia Keesing, professor of science, mathematics and computing at Bard College in Annandale-on-Hudson, N.Y., say they have demonstrated this theory in their study of Lyme disease in the U.S. Northeast. (*See Short Feature.*)

The number of ticks carrying the disease is lower in undisturbed forests—areas with more animal diversity—than in the fragmented forests typical of suburban sprawl, their research finds. They theorize that is because expansive forests can support more large predators of the mice that are the hosts of Lyme disease, and can also support opossums, which typically remove the ticks through grooming and also transmit Lyme to far fewer ticks than mice do.[16]

"The species we lose in the Northeast when we lose biodiversity are foxes and bobcats, and those species actually protect us because they keep mouse numbers low," says Keesing. "We should be protecting biodiversity far more than we're doing now; because the best way

to keep [the animals that host] these pathogens in check is to let biodiversity do it."

Keesing and Ostfeld say this conclusion—that more diversity equals less disease, which they call the "dilution" theory—is applicable globally, and they argue for resisting land development that cuts up natural forests.

However, other scientists question whether biodiversity loss is always to blame for infectious disease or is even a bad thing—particularly if it reduces the presence of disease-carrying animals. They also argue that the "dilution effect" does not hold true in all settings.

In one study of 60 countries, researchers found that urbanization and growing wealth were the main drivers behind reducing infectious diseases between 1990 and 2010. Contrary to the dilution theory, biodiversity was not correlated with improvements in human health, the study found.[17]

Lead author Wood of the University of Washington says rainforests and other areas that are rich in biodiversity also tend to be rich in viruses and parasites that circulate in animals, so in some cases, when humans preserve those areas or reforest them, "we're also potentially facilitating other diseases."

Both sides in the debate agree that the more contact people have with wild animals, the greater the possibility of animal diseases jumping to people, especially as humans enter natural habitats. But the solution proposed by some environmentalists—to turn those habitats into national parks—"doesn't necessarily recognize the reality of people's lives; lots of people who live near biodiverse forests depend on those forests for their livelihoods, so saying they can't live there is akin to taking away their livelihoods," Wood says.

Some researchers have found that it is often degraded areas on the edge of pristine habitats, rather than the undisturbed core, where humans are most likely to come in contact with animals in ways that could lead to a spillover—when a virus or other disease pathogen jumps from an animal to a human.

In a recent study of farmers living next to Kibale National Park in Uganda, Stanford University researchers found that fragments of residual forest, not larger expanses of habitat, were most likely to be the site of human contacts with primates because they shared borders with farms. For example, a monkey bit a boy digging in his garden, according to lead author Laura Bloomfield.[18]

"We humans go to these animals," said study co-author Eric Lambin, professor of earth system science at Stanford. "We are forcing the interaction through transformation of the land."[19]

In such situations, where humans are chopping up a natural habitat into a mosaic of forest and human dwellings, the loss of diversity may be the "visible result," but the real driver of zoonotic disease is the man-made environment, says Roger Frutos, an infectious disease specialist at CIRAD, a French government research center working in developing countries.

A study from the University of California, Davis, finds the more abundant a species, the more likely it is to carry a disease that jumps to humans. Domestic animals such as cattle have been the most frequent carriers of a zoonotic disease. But among wild mammals, most zoonotic diseases can be found in three groups—rodents, bats and primates.[20]

"They're super-adaptable" animals, explains Christine Johnson, lead author of the study, and professor of epidemiology and wildlife health at the University of California, Davis, School of Veterinary Medicine. She points to rats and mice that feed on human garbage and white-faced monkeys that steal tourists' food in Costa Rica. Once people clear land for farming and housing, she says, these animals "move right in, they shelter with us, they depend on our food."

Ostfeld says Johnson's research is consistent with his findings about Lyme disease—that such diseases thrive best in ecosystems that have been highly disturbed by humans. "It's the little weedy species [like mice] that are often the best reservoirs for zoonotic pathogens; they're the ones that benefit when we muck things up," he says.

Since 1940, agricultural drivers such as clearing land for farms have been linked to about half of emerging zoonotic diseases, according to a study co-authored by Jason R. Rohr, a professor of biological sciences at Notre Dame University.[21]

Growing demand for meat among developing nations means agricultural production will need to double or triple to feed the planet's population by 2100, Rohr projects, posing the threat of more land clearance and more zoonotic disease. At the same time, he says, more food and meat protein equate to better health. "We shouldn't be thinking of biodiversity and disease in a bubble. We have to think about the cost and benefits," he says. "In some cases, the land may be better used for agriculture."

Should selling wildlife for human consumption be banned?

Many critics point to markets in China and other parts of Asia where wild animals in cages are often stacked on top of chickens and in close proximity with humans, making it more likely that they will get sick and transmit viruses to other animals and people.

Species that are endangered because of hunting, wildlife trade and habitat loss have twice the number of zoonotic diseases as other threatened species, according to a recent study by University of California, Davis, researchers.[22]

The stress that wild animals experience in being transported to markets is akin to the "shipping fever" contracted by cows that get sick after being crowded into a trailer for the slaughterhouse, says Johnson, the study's lead author. "Basically, we've given these viruses a unique evolutionary pathway," she says.

The Wildlife Conservation Society, together with other environmental groups, has formed an "End the Trade" coalition, urging governments around the world to enact legislation to "permanently end commercial trade and sale of terrestrial wild animals" for human consumption.[23]

Susan Lieberman, vice president for international policy at the Wildlife Conservation Society, says there is clear evidence that wildlife markets have contributed to zoonotic disease epidemics such as SARS. "Do we spend years investigating which might be the next one? Or do we say we can't accept any risk of this happening again? . . . If we stop the commercial markets where people eat wildlife, the chances of this happening again are infinitesimal."

But some experts say some kinds of legal wildlife trade pose little danger of transmitting disease. For example, kudu and springbok, two species of antelope, are raised in South Africa in settings "almost like farmed systems, controlled and traceable—that's a really important food source there," says Catherine Machalaba, policy adviser at the EcoHealth Alliance. She argues that any ban should be limited to the species experts know are most likely to put humans at risk of disease, such as rodents, bats and primates.

EcoHealth is supporting a more restrictive proposal to ban high-risk wildlife, an approach taken in a

Nurse's aide Benetha Coleman, herself an Ebola survivor, comforts an infant girl with symptoms of the disease in Paynesville, Liberia, in 2015. Following the Ebola outbreak in West Africa in 2014-16, governments imposed a ban on hunting wild animals and eating their meat in an effort to halt the spread of zoonotic diseases.

bipartisan bill introduced by Sens. Lindsey Graham, R-S.C., and Chris Coons, D-Del., and supported by the World Wildlife Fund.[24]

In that proposed ban, "we're not including farmed wildlife, livestock that has appropriate veterinary management and that is well regulated," says Jan Vertefeuille, senior adviser for wildlife conservation advocacy at the World Wildlife Fund.

In a recent opinion piece, economists at the University of Oxford in England wrote that "banning all wildlife trade is a knee-jerk and potentially self-defeating measure." Bans, especially those that remove currently legal supplies of farmed wildlife, could "drive up black market prices and increase incentives for poaching," they wrote.[25]

In China, the wildlife breeding farms and the associated trade are estimated to involve 14 million people and be worth $74 billion, so the impact of a ban on that economy would be "uncertain," the economists said. In January, China imposed a temporary ban on the wildlife trade in the wake of the Wuhan outbreak, and in May 2020, China's legislature began consideration of a permanent ban.[26]

A previous Chinese effort to ban wildlife trade in southern China in the wake of the SARS outbreak in 2002-03, which was traced to a market, was a failure, critics say. Wildlife markets in Guangdong closed down, but reopened a few months later. Black market activity ramped up, and after the outbreak ended the ban was abandoned under a combination of cultural and economic pressures.[27]

Following the 2013-16 Ebola outbreak in West Africa, governments across the region imposed a ban on hunting and eating meat from wild animals.[28]

But those bans led to illegal markets and sometimes a boomerang effect, where consumption of bush meat actually increased, perhaps because the meat became more desirable after the ban took effect, says Diogo Verissimo, an economist and research fellow at Oxford. "We also saw unequal impacts," he says, where communities dependent on bush meat suffered nutritionally.

Harvard's Myers points to research he has overseen in Madagascar villages where people eat wild lemurs and tenrecs (a mammal resembling a hedgehog). "If people in those villages stopped giving bush meat to their children, you would see a 30 percent increase in anemia rates in those kids," he says. "It means a blanket policy [banning wildlife] could cause a lot of hardship and suffering."

Verissimo says that although cattle have often been the source of outbreaks of illnesses such as mad cow disease, "our response to those pandemics was not to ban that industry, because we understand that millions of people rely on that for nutrition, and lots of livelihoods depend on it. What we did was to say, we need to improve regulation."

Many experts say a ban alone will not change traditional food habits. Verissimo has been studying a different strategy—using advertisements with celebrities to shift consumer preferences away from eating pangolin, an anteater-like animal that is the most highly trafficked mammal in the world, prized for the supposed medicinal properties of its scales and its meat. Some scientists think the pangolin may have been the intermediate animal that passed the COVID-19 virus from bats to people.[29]

In one such ad, Miss Universe Vietnam looks horrified and stalks away when her host ceremoniously presents her with a pangolin dish at a restaurant.[30]

Finally, wildlife markets are not the biggest cause of zoonotic epidemics. Research shows that land use changes, such as farmers cutting into forests and moving closer to bat habitats, are a much bigger factor—and the leading cause of new diseases.[31]

"If you blocked the wildlife trade completely in China you would still get lots of people infected every year by bat coronaviruses," says Daszak of EcoHealth Alliance.

Is it possible to predict the next pandemic?

In the wake of the 2003-06 H5N1 bird flu that provoked fears of a global pandemic, USAID in 2009 created a program called PREDICT, charged with strengthening "global capacity for detection and discovery of zoonotic viruses with pandemic potential."

From 2009 to 2019, PREDICT funded research to find viruses among animals in the wild, trained about 5,000 people around the world to identify new diseases and helped develop 60 research labs.[32]

The program found about 1,000 viruses, including bat coronaviruses similar to the ones that caused SARS and COVID-19, but it did not discover the virus causing the current pandemic. Critics say hunting for the next pandemic virus in nature is like looking for a needle in a haystack, because thousands of zoonotic viruses are present and are frequently mutating in ways that could change their potential to infect and thrive in humans.

"The difficulty with that approach is that there are so many viruses, and the vast majority of them are undescribed and harmless," says Barbara Han, disease ecologist at the Cary Institute of Ecosystem Studies. She uses a different strategy, one of constructing computer models based on the distinctive traits of animals that have given humans viruses in the past to forecast which animals are most likely to host new zoonotic diseases.

Some prominent scientists have called for reorienting the government's approach.

"Although PREDICT almost certainly discovered hundreds of potential zoonoses [zoonotic diseases], their true zoonotic potential is almost impossible to assess," wrote Colin J. Carlson, a biologist at Georgetown University who studies newly emerging infectious diseases. "For now, the only real way" to distinguish potentially zoonotic viruses from their low-risk counterparts is to observe a human infection caused by a virus that has spilled over from animals, he said. The government's approach "oversells basic science" and detracts from funding for primary health care, diagnosis and other efforts to catch clusters of human infection early, according to critiques cited by Carlson.[33]

Daszak's group EcoHealth Alliance is one of the most prominent funded by PREDICT to perform virus-hunting research in the wild. After the SARS outbreak, the group's hunting led it to a group of bat coronaviruses that it concluded were the likely source.[34] After 20 years of studying animals that cause zoonotic outbreaks, Daszak says, "it's clear to me there are patterns to disease emergence that are predictable. It doesn't mean that we can predict the next one." But much like an earthquake forecaster, he says, his research can point to the hotspots where clusters of animal viruses are likely to jump to humans, then take steps to limit people's contact with the host animals.

In 2015, Daszak's group, together with Chinese researchers, found 3 percent of people living near bat caves in Yunnan province, China, where hunting and eating bats is common, had antibodies to a SARS-like coronavirus found in bats. That finding suggested bats could directly infect people, the researchers said.[35] (See Short Feature.)

As for the argument that it would be better to focus on early clusters of people infected with a new disease, Daszak says that is essentially what countries are doing now with their public health approach: "We wait for pandemics to emerge and hope we'll get a vaccine. It's not a strategy at all."

Daszak wants to raise private and public funds for a $1.2 billion project to discover and catalog the majority of the 1.5 million zoonotic viruses—mostly unknown—in mammals, humans and waterfowl. "To prevent the few that could cause a pandemic, we have to discover all of the potential ones," Daszak says. This proposed atlas of viruses, dubbed the Global Virome Project, would be a logical successor to PREDICT, supporters say.

"The Global Virome Project will begin lowering risk of spillover because we'll have greater granularity about where and what needs to be done," says Dennis Carroll, the project's chair, who founded PREDICT when he led USAID's emerging pandemic threats program. The new project would expand the kind of research done in Yunnan province that discovered antibodies in people to animal viruses, Carroll says, then use that knowledge as an early-alarm system to work closely with communities and national governments to prevent an epidemic.

But some scientists say the government should shift away from this biomedical approach. "Rather than emphasizing virological research in places where people

CHRONOLOGY

1300s-1800s *Bubonic plague and influenza cause worldwide pandemics.*

1346 Bubonic plague arrives in Europe from China, killing 30 to 60 percent of Europeans.

1688 Influenza strikes England, Ireland and Virginia.

1889 Influenza pandemic spreads from Britain to continental Europe and the U.S., infecting 40 percent of Boston.

1900s-1960s *The world suffers three flu pandemics, and scientists isolate the flu virus.*

1918-19 The Spanish flu kills 40 million to 100 million, including an estimated 675,000 Americans.

1939 Invention of the electron microscope permits scientists to see a virus for the first time.

1942 Studies begin on first flu vaccine after scientists isolate two strains of influenza.

1953 DNA is discovered, permitting scientists to identify the building blocks of a virus.

1957 Hong Kong flu (H2N2) becomes a worldwide pandemic but kills relatively few compared to 1918— 116,000 in the U.S.

1968 Asian flu (H3N2) pandemic causes 100,000 U.S. deaths.

1970s-1990s *Animal-origin viruses spur outbreaks of AIDS, Ebola and Nipah viruses.*

1976 Ebola cases erupt in South Sudan and the Democratic Republic of Congo with fatality rates of more than 80 percent. The likely origin was fruit bats, with primates as intermediate animals.

1981 AIDS epidemic is first recognized in the United States. Similar viruses long existed in primates.

1995 Gabon and Zaire (now Democratic Republic of the Congo) report clusters of Ebola virus, linked to gorilla and chimpanzee carcasses in nearby forests.

1999 Nipah breaks out among pig farmers in Malaysia; researchers later trace the virus to bats. Fatality rate is 40 to 75 percent.

2000s-Present *Three major coronavirus outbreaks erupt, and COVID-19 pandemic shuts down the globe.*

2001 Nipah breaks out in Bangladesh, linked to sap from date palms contaminated by bats, that is then consumed by people.

2002 First death from severe acute respiratory syndrome (SARS) is recorded in China's southern Guangdong province. More than 8,000 people are infected, with a fatality rate of about 10 percent.

2003 After a tourist returns to Toronto from Hong Kong in February, SARS spreads from Asia to North and South America and Europe. The World Health Organization (WHO) declares the pandemic contained in July.

2004 WHO reports first case of human-to-human transmission, in Thailand, of bird flu (H5N1). Fears of a worldwide pandemic fail to be realized.

2005 In response to the bird flu threat, President George W. Bush requests and Congress approves $3.8 billion to develop vaccines and stockpile anti-flu medications.

2007 Ebola outbreak in Gabon is linked to hunters eating bats during massive bat migration.

2009 WHO declares the swine flu (H1N1), which scientists trace to pig and poultry farming and to human contact with waterfowl, a pandemic; the flu eventually infects millions and kills thousands.

2010 WHO declares an end to the swine flu pandemic.

2012 In Saudi Arabia, the first death from Middle East respiratory syndrome (MERS) is recorded. The fatality rate is about 35 percent, and the disease kills 866 people.

2014-16 Largest outbreak of Ebola occurs in West Africa since the virus was discovered, with more cases and deaths in this outbreak than all others combined.

2019 In December, WHO receives first report of COVID-19 cases in Wuhan, China; most are linked to a live-animal market.

2020 China closes the Wuhan market and announces temporary ban on wildlife trade (January). . . . Chinese government proposes limiting types of wildlife sold for meat (April). . . . Chinese legislature begins drafting permanent ban on wildlife sale and consumption (May). . . . U.S. House passes recovery act, which includes a ban on imports of high-risk wildlife (May). . . . A bipartisan bill authorizing presidential sanctions against nations that sell high-risk wildlife, supported by environmental groups, is introduced in the Senate (May).

and wildlife come into dangerously close contact, investments should be dramatically shifted to focus on making such human-wildlife contact much less likely in the first place," wrote Cornell's Osofsky. The focus, he said, should be on preventing the risky behaviors likely to cause future outbreaks—eating and trading the body parts of wild animals, mixing species in markets and human incursions into wild areas that increase contact with wildlife.[36]

Governments should focus on catching the disease in animals before it even gets to humans and then act quickly, according to Larry Brilliant, a leading epidemiologist who helped the World Health Organization (WHO) eradicate smallpox and is now board chair of Ending Pandemics, a group that advises governments on the early discovery and containment of pandemics.

He pointed to a Cambodian program where a farmer "can call the government and say, 'I have 20 dead chickens,' and they'll come and bring you 30 live ones and clean up your place. That's a phenomenal bi-direction system that cleans up the virus for you, puts you back into business, and the epidemic is aborted. Being able to survey bats, pigs, birds . . . that's what we're going to have to do in the age of pandemics."[37]

The main reason a zoonotic disease emerges "is not biology, it's sociology; it's human," says Frutos, a molecular microbiologist at CIRAD. "It's not possible," he says, to predict which virus will cause the next pandemic because that requires a chain of largely accidental events triggered by humans, from destroying wild places to successful spillover to the mutation into a human disease. "We should put the filter at the bottleneck" of human activity, he says. "Whatever the virus, it has to go through the bottleneck."

Getty Images/Bettmann

An artist depicted an outbreak of plague in Florence in the 14th century based on the description of writer Giovanni Boccaccio. A bubonic plague pandemic in that century, which killed between 30 percent and 60 percent of Europe's population, originated from fleas on black rats.

BACKGROUND
Rodents and Plagues

One of the most notorious early zoonotic diseases was the Black Death, the name given to bubonic plague carried by rodents that devastated Europe in successive waves starting in the 14th century. The plague first reached Europe in 1346, most likely carried by fleas on black rats that inhabited merchant ships. The disease wiped out as much as 30 to 60 percent of Europe's population.[38]

Recent genomic research has revealed that the plague originated in China, then traveled through Asia, Europe and Africa from 1346 to 1351.[39]

Bats Can Harbor and Transmit Many Viruses

"It's just a matter of probability for disease to happen."

In 1998, people started getting sick in northern Malaysia with fever, headache, drowsiness and convulsions. All of them were pig farmers or involved in the pork industry. By the end of the outbreak, at least 283 people had been infected and almost 40 percent had died.

Scientists would later trace the illness—Nipah virus—to bats that had roosted in fruit trees above the pig sties, dropping chewed mango and water apple into the sties. The pigs ate the droppings, contracted the virus and passed it on to the rest of the herd, infecting their human handlers.[1]

Bats have also been linked to coronaviruses, including severe acute respiratory syndrome (SARS), Middle East respiratory syndrome (MERS), two coronaviruses that cause the common cold and the virus behind COVID-19. In a new study, researchers from the EcoHealth Alliance, a New York City-based environmental research group, and China's Wuhan Institute of Virology identified more than 780 new coronaviruses in bats and traced the likely origin of the viruses behind both SARS and COVID-19 to horseshoe bats.[2]

Why have bats been linked to so many outbreaks of human disease? They are highly social animals, roosting in packed groups as large as millions. The authors of the new study point out that horseshoe bats in southern China often share their roost with other bat species, which may make it easier for coronaviruses to leap to different species.[3]

The lineage of bats can be traced back about 50 million years, and scientists believe they may have co-evolved with viruses in a way that permits them to carry viruses without being affected by them—a trait that is perhaps related to their ability to fly.[4]

"They have an interesting immune system," says Peter Daszak, EcoHealth Alliance president and a co-author of the recent paper. "There's pretty good evidence that bats reduce their natural immune response to viruses. Maybe it's part of the [evolutionary] cost of flight, which is energetic; they have to reduce stress."

Bats "seem to be able to recover from infection from a pathogen but not completely clear it from their system, which they do by suppressing their immune system," said Kate Jones, professor of ecology and biodiversity at University College London. "[An] over-responsive immune system is sometimes what actually kills you—from organ failure."[5]

Bats are attracted to human habitation and farms, especially if the bats have been disturbed from their natural habitat. That is one reason they showed up in such large numbers on pig farms in Malaysia. Booming pork demand contributed to slash-and-burn deforestation as farmers cut into the forests where bats lived to create industrialized pig operations, while vast tracts were logged.[6]

Light from houses attracts insects, which in turn attract the bats that eat them, says Roger Frutos, a microbiologist with the French government research agency CIRAD, who focuses on infectious diseases. EcoHealth researchers expect as many as 10,000 to 15,000 bat coronaviruses have yet to be discovered in addition to the 781 they recently discovered and the 509 previously known bat coronaviruses.[7]

"Since we attract bats to human environments, we therefore attract a very large reservoir of viruses," Frutos says. "After that, it's just a matter of probability for disease to happen: The more contact you have, the higher the presence of bats, the higher the probability to get emergence [of disease]—and contamination of humans."

The first step to prevention, he says, is to fortify barns and pig sheds against bats—the United Nations recommends applying wire screens to open-sided pig sheds, installing roofing and placing netting over ventilation openings.[8] Such

The bacterium that causes the plague, *Yersinia pestis*, still resides in rodents indigenous to North and South America, Africa and Central Asia.[40] Plague is now treatable with antibiotics. Human plague infections continue to occur in rural areas in the western United States, but significantly more cases occur in Africa and Asia, according to the CDC.[41]

Zoonotic diseases predated the plague. Today, they account for more than 60 percent of human infectious diseases.[42] Zoonoses include diseases that cross routinely from animals to humans, such as rabies, or have recently crossed and now pass from human to human, such as HIV, which originated in a chimpanzee.[43]

Many diseases that people now consider human-to-human—including smallpox and measles—are believed to have originated with animals in the distant past.[44] For example, researchers believe influenza jumped from

steps, along with the Malaysian government's ban on pig farming in high-risk areas following the Nipah outbreak, helped to eradicate the disease from Malaysia, according to Dennis Carroll, who oversaw the pandemics prevention program at the U.S. Agency for International Development.[9]

The area where southern China converges with Laos, Myanmar and Vietnam is likely to be a future hot spot for emerging disease, EcoHealth researchers predict, because a growing human population, urbanization and intense poultry and livestock farming all provide opportunities for a virus to jump from animals to people.[10]

One study by Daszak's group found about 3 percent of a human community in southern China living near bat caves had antibodies to SARS-like bat coronaviruses, despite recalling no SARS symptoms.[11] He says his organization wants to conduct more such studies to anticipate viruses likely to cause epidemics.

However, EcoHealth's funding for this work was abruptly terminated in April by the U.S. National Institutes of Health (NIH) after EcoHealth's grant got caught up in a political controversy over the Wuhan lab. The $3.7 million grant was canceled a few days after President Trump responded to a question at a press conference from a reporter who erroneously claimed that millions of dollars in grants were going to the Wuhan Institute. Trump told the reporter the grant would be ended immediately, amid mounting but unproven theories targeting the Wuhan lab as the source of the coronavirus.[12]

In fact, only about 10 percent of that grant was slated for the Wuhan Institute for collecting and analyzing samples, according to EcoHealth's Daszak.[13]

Thirty-one U.S. scientific societies and 77 Nobel laureates wrote to the NIH calling for an investigation into the grant's cancellation. The Nobel laureates said the termination of the grant "sets a dangerous precedent by interfering in the conduct of science."[14]

"Our future plans were to sequence whole genomes" of viruses, EcoHealth said in a statement accompanying the recent study, "particularly . . . to see if any of these viruses are likely able to infect humans. That work will not happen without the funding from NIH."[15]

— Sarah Glazer

[1] David Quammen, *Spillover: Animal Infections and the Next Human Pandemic* (2012), pp. 314-328.

[2] Alice Latinne *et al.*, "Origin and cross-species transmission of bat coronaviruses in China," bioRxiv, posted June 1, 2020, https://tinyurl.com/y85f63fc.

[3] *Ibid.*

[4] Quammen, *op. cit.*

[5] Kate Jones *et al.*, "FAQs—Relationship between habitat loss, biodiversity, bats and live wildlife markets," 2020, https://tinyurl.com/yaz2csh9.

[6] Tom Evans *et al.*, "Links between ecological integrity, emerging infectious diseases originating from wildlife, and other aspects of human health—an overview of the literature," Wildlife Conservation Society, April 2020, https://tinyurl.com/y8dd4ac4.

[7] "Talking points from Latinne *et al.*, Origin and cross transmission of bat CoVs in China," EcoHealth Alliance, June 1, 2020.

[8] "Nipah Virus Frequently Asked Questions," Food and Agriculture Organization of the United Nations, https://tinyurl.com/ybhp37p8.

[9] Ferris Jabr, "How Humanity Unleashed a Flood of New Diseases," *The New York Times Magazine*, June 17, 2020, https://tinyurl.com/yc26pngc.

[10] Latinne *et al.*, *op. cit.*

[11] Nin Wang *et al.*, "Serological Evidence of Bat SARS-Related Coronavirus Infections in Humans, China," Virologica Sinica, March 2, 2018, https://tinyurl.com/ycqze63h.

[12] James Gorman, "Prominent Scientists Denounce End to Coronavirus Grant," *The New York Times*, May 21, 2020, https://tinyurl.com/y9vl62de.

[13] Nurith Aizenman, "Why The U.S. Government Stopped Funding A Research Project On Bats And Coronaviruses," *NPR*, April 29, 2020, https://tinyurl.com/yc47l3po.

[14] Gorman, *op. cit.*

[15] "Talking points from Latinne *et al.*, Origin and cross transmission of bat CoVs in China," *op. cit.*

horses to humans soon after horses were domesticated and then made additional jumps to humans from other domesticated animals, such as poultry and swine.[45]

The moment when a pathogen leaps from a member of one species into members of another is known as a spillover. Spillover leads to the emergence of a new disease only when the alien pathogen thrives in a new species and spreads among its members.[46]

Spillovers are actually "fairly common events," says the Global Virome Project's Carroll: In studies, 10 to 15 percent of communities that have routine exposure to wildlife test positive for antibodies to wildlife viruses. But many animal pathogens that make the jump to humans "fizzle out," says the Cary Institute's Han, either failing to transmit to another human or infecting only a limited number of people.

As Deer Population Explodes, Lyme Disease Spreads

"We're placing homes, dogs and kids right in the hot zone we've created."

The first thing many summer visitors see on the ferry to Martha's Vineyard is the pamphlet warning them to beware of Lyme disease.

Martha's Vineyard, an island off Cape Cod in Massachusetts that is famed for its beaches, has consistently ranked among the top 10 counties in the country for Lyme disease rates.[1]

But old-timers who grew up on the island in the 1950s or earlier "say they never saw a tick here" of the Lyme variety, the blacklegged or deer tick, says Richard Johnson, director of the Martha's Vineyard Tick Program, a county effort that educates the public about Lyme.[2]

Many people think of Lyme as a recent invader, because it was first identified in Lyme, Conn., in 1976. Cases have risen steadily from just under 10,000 in 1991 to more than 300,000 a year, according to the U.S. Centers for Disease Control and Prevention (CDC). Initial symptoms include skin rash, headache, fever and fatigue. Lyme can be treated with antibiotics, but if not caught early, the infection can spread to joints, the heart and the nervous system.[3]

It turns out the Lyme bacterium has been in North America for at least 60,000 years, circulating unnoticed in forests, according to recent genomic analysis by Yale University researchers. The researchers concluded that the suburban explosion of the deer population—without predators—allowed the tick population to soar in New England and the Midwest.[4]

Like many parts of the Northeast, the Vineyard was originally covered by virgin forest, then turned into treeless pastureland for sheep by European colonists starting in the 18th century. With the collapse of the sheep industry in the early 1900s, the trees started growing back.

They provided cover for deer, which carry the adult ticks, and for white-footed mice, which carry the poppy seed-sized tick nymphs, the stage when ticks bite people. Deer ticks reappeared in the 1960s or '70s, Johnson estimates, when second-growth forest blanketed the island's pastures.

While it is true that some forest seems to be a prerequisite for ticks and their hosts, humans have made it worse by cutting up the forest into small fragments, where large predators of mice and deer can no longer survive, says Richard S. Ostfeld, a disease ecologist at the Cary Institute of Ecosystem Studies, a research center in Millbrook, N.Y.

Ostfeld's research finds more infected ticks in small patches of woods than in undisturbed forest, where predators of mice such as foxes live, as do opossums, which eat most of the ticks on them.[5]

In suburban developments, "we're placing homes, dogs and kids right in the hot zone we've created," Ostfeld says. "If you're right next to a bit of forest, that's more dangerous than living next to a big continuous forest." One solution he proposes is building houses together in clusters.

Yet on the Vineyard, as in much of the Northeast, it would be hard to change the longstanding suburban and

Carroll says, "What is less common is a virus that is able to spread human to human after the initial spillover."

One characteristic that makes zoonotic pathogens so problematic is that they can hide in "reservoir hosts," animals that carry the pathogen while suffering little or no illness, such as the white-footed mice that carry Lyme disease.[47]

By contrast, eradicating smallpox worldwide, as the WHO announced had been accomplished in 1980, was

feasible because it lacked the ability to live anywhere but in the human body, according to science writer David Quammen in his 2013 book, *Spillover*. The virus could not hide in animals.

It would be far more difficult to eradicate yellow fever, a zoonotic disease that is infectious to both monkeys and people and is passed by mosquitoes. It will continue to occur in humans unless the WHO "kills every mosquito vector or every susceptible

rural patterns, where houses abut small patches of woods, observes Johnson.

Traditional approaches to controlling Lyme disease have been to clear vegetation and cull the animals hosting the ticks, says Chelsea L. Wood, an assistant professor at the University of Washington's School of Aquatic and Fishery Sciences in Seattle. "The unfortunate reality is that is the only strategy that's ever worked for us in the past," she says.

For example, Monhegan Island off Maine employed sharpshooters to kill the entire herd of 100 deer on its four-and-a-half square miles between 1996 and 1999. [6] By 2004, no ticks could be found on the island. [7]

If an adult tick can no longer feed on a deer, she can no longer reproduce, so killing one fed adult female tick is the equivalent of killing 2,000 larvae or several hundred nymphs. [8]

Looking to Monhegan, Martha's Vineyard has been encouraging more deer hunting, offering bow hunters a bounty of $100 for taking their third doe. It also has been encouraging homeowners to allow hunting on their property. [9] Last year, hunters took almost twice as many deer as in 2015, according to Johnson.

But simply reducing the deer population will not necessarily eliminate ticks, cautions Ostfeld. Ticks are constantly seeking a host, he says, noting one case where halving the deer population led to twice as many ticks living on each deer. However, other studies find that reducing the deer population dramatically resulted in a significant reduction in Lyme cases. [10]

"I don't think there's any doubt that reducing deer will eventually reduce ticks," says Johnson, explaining his strategy for the Vineyard. "The question is how low do you have to get the numbers."

Reducing density to eight or fewer deer per square mile might break the cycle of ubiquitous Lyme disease, according to one estimate Johnson cites. That would be an ambitious goal for the Vineyard, which averages 30 to 50 deer per square mile on its approximately 100 square miles.

"No one has tried it on the scale we're doing it on the Vineyard," Johnson says. As an island, the Vineyard has an advantage: Deer cannot walk over a land border from a neighboring county to replace those that have been killed.

Success, for Johnson, would be to return the island to "the way it used to be 60 years ago"—before the ticks arrived.

— *Sarah Glazer*

[1] Noah Asimow, "Funding for Tick Program Runs Out; Tick Spread Marches On," *Vineyard Gazette*, June 27, 2019, https://tinyurl.com/y6w5hace; Matt Rocheleau, "Mass. counties have some of the highest rates of Lyme disease in the U.S.," *The Boston Globe*, May 10, 2018, https://tinyurl.com/y9l8o4s2.

[2] "MV Tick Program," Dukes County, https://tinyurl.com/ycfk7tol.

[3] "Lyme Disease," U.S. Centers for Disease Control and Prevention, https://tinyurl.com/yx9fq6n2.

[4] "Ancient History of Lyme Disease in North America Revealed with Bacterial Genomes," Yale School of Medicine, Aug. 28, 2017, https://tinyurl.com/yakh9mxz.

[5] Felicia Keesing *et al.*, "Hosts as ecological traps for the vector of Lyme disease," *Proceedings, Biological Sciences*, Aug. 19, 2009, https://tinyurl.com/ycqkl4a3.

[6] George Smith, "Monhegan killed all its deer and eliminated Lyme disease," *George's Outdoor News*, Oct. 28, 2016, https://tinyurl.com/yb5r6bs8.

[7] Joseph Piesman, "Strategies for Reducing the Risk of Lyme Borreliosis in North America," *International Journal of Medical Microbiology*, May 2006, https://tinyurl.com/y6vsqbn3.

[8] "Could Reducing Deer Populations Reduce Lyme Disease?" *Entomology Today*, Sept. 28, 2017, https://tinyurl.com/ycl7y4jw.

[9] Julia Wells, "Bow Hunters Offered Financial Incentive to Take More Deer," *Vineyard Gazette*, Sept. 30, 2019, https://tinyurl.com/yakwamw2.

[10] Howard J. Kilpatrick *et al.*, "The Relationship between Deer Density, Tick Abundance, and Human Cases of Lyme in a Residential Community," *Journal of Medical Entomology*, July 1, 2014, https://tinyurl.com/y9ym5k25.

monkey in tropical Africa and South America," Quammen wrote. [48]

Zoonotic diseases include several diseases better known in the United States, including Lyme disease (from mice), West Nile virus (mosquitoes), hantavirus pulmonary syndrome (rodents) and monkeypox (monkeys). [49]

COVID-19 is the third coronavirus (so-called because of its crown-like structure) to cause an outbreak of serious illness in the past 20 years. All three—SARS, MERS and COVID-19—have been linked to animal origins. Many of the most serious recent zoonotic outbreaks can be traced to environmental causes, often to human contact with animals disturbed from their natural habitats, according to the Wildlife Conservation Society. [50]

Influenza Outbreaks

Influenza pandemics were first documented about 300 years ago. The 20th century alone saw three such

Red Cross medical personnel transport a victim of the 1918 influenza pandemic in St. Louis. The disease killed 675,000 Americans and at least 40 million people worldwide.

pandemics: Two were comparatively mild, but the 1918-19 "Spanish flu" pandemic infected an estimated 25 to 30 percent of the world's population. About 675,000 Americans died from the flu in 1918—nearly half of all U.S. deaths that year. Worldwide, 40 million to 100 million people died.[51]

The two milder 20th-century pandemics, in 1957 and 1968, were probably caused by the exchange of genes between human and avian flu viruses. The 1957 and 1968 outbreaks caused about 116,000 and 100,000 U.S. deaths, respectively.[52]

The 1918 flu was a novel, or new, virus that originated in birds and then spent some time in another host, perhaps pigs or horses, before it emerged as a human disease. Striking during World War I, it was able to spread quickly among soldiers in cramped army barracks and steerage-like transports. The majority of deaths probably resulted from secondary infections, such as bacterial pneumonia, which were deadly before the discovery of antibiotics. The death rate in the 1918 flu was 20 times greater than that for today's influenza, which kills fewer than 0.1 percent of those who catch it.[53]

In 1939, the newly invented electron microscope took a picture of a virus—the first time in history it could be seen. By the 1940s, scientists had isolated two strains of influenza and had begun to test vaccines. After the discovery of DNA in 1953, scientists were able to identify the building blocks of a virus.[54]

Ebola, Nipah and AIDS

The Ebola virus causes a hemorrhagic fever that is among the most virulent known diseases.[55]

It first appeared in two separate outbreaks in 1976 in the African countries of South Sudan and the Democratic Republic of the Congo (formerly Zaire) near the Ebola River with fatality rates of more than 80 percent. Researchers suspect fruit bats are the natural hosts of Ebola virus.[56]

Although the exact origin of Ebola is unknown, the virus is introduced to humans through contact with the blood, organ or secretions of bats or from chimpanzees, gorillas, monkeys, antelopes or porcupines found ill in the forest.[57]

Beginning around 1995, Gabon and the Democratic Republic of the Congo reported clusters of the disease—in each case linked to gorilla and chimpanzee carcasses in nearby forests that were sometimes eaten by villagers. As researchers searched for the cause between 2001 and 2005, they discovered that bats, which carried the virus, came into contact with apes during the dry season when fruits become less plentiful and they compete for the same food. A 2007 outbreak in Gabon was linked to hunters eating bats during a massive migration when fruits were plentiful.[58]

Although the AIDS epidemic was first recognized in 1981 in the United States, researchers say it originated far earlier, as similar immunodeficiency viruses long existed in primates. The first spillover to humans likely occurred in the course of hunting, butchering and eating primates carrying viruses. One of these events likely occurred in Africa between 1910 and 1930, some researchers believe, giving rise to the HIV strain behind AIDS.[59]

Nipah virus, which can cause severe respiratory infection and encephalitis, broke out among pig farmers in Malaysia in 1999, followed by Bangladesh in 2001. Nipah virus has a fatality rate of 40 to 75 percent, and it has no cure or vaccine.[60]

Since 2001, Bangladesh has had nearly yearly outbreaks and India has had several. In Malaysia, the virus has been traced to fruit bats that roost above pig sties, with pigs passing the disease via direct contact with people who work in the pork industry.[61]

Slash-and-burn deforestation, together with drought, initially drove bats into fruit orchards adjoining pig farms that had recently expanded into forests.[62]

The 2014-16 Ebola outbreak in West Africa was the largest since the virus was discovered in 1976, with more cases and deaths in this outbreak than all others combined. A total of 11,310 deaths were reported in Guinea, Liberia and Sierra Leone.[63] Vaccines are under development and have been used to control outbreaks in Guinea and the Democratic Republic of the Congo, according to the WHO.[64]

Ebola reappeared in the Democratic Republic of the Congo in August 2018, causing more than 2,000 deaths by November 2019 at a 67 percent mortality rate, the second-largest Ebola outbreak in history.[65]

21st-Century Outbreaks

The first pandemic of the 21st century started in China's southern Guangdong province in 2002 after a patient died from an unusual pneumonia, later identified as SARS.[66]

SARS has infected at least 8,000 people and killed about 10 percent of them.[67]

Early cases were linked to wildlife markets and restaurants in Guangdong, where coronaviruses were found in masked palm civets, a cat-like mammal considered a culinary delicacy in China. Chinese authorities responded by imposing a temporary ban on the hunting, sale, transportation and export of all wild animals in southern Chinese provinces. They also culled and quarantined civets in the region's many civet farms.[68]

Horseshoe bats have been identified as the likely origin of the virus, while farmed civets probably served as an intermediary, passing the disease to humans. The disease spread to four continents (Asia, North and South America and Europe) after a tourist returned to Toronto in February 2003 from a Hong Kong hotel, spurring a planetary public health panic. The WHO declared the outbreak contained on July 5, 2003.[69]

Bird flu, a highly contagious disease among chickens in Asia, Africa and Europe, raised fears of a worldwide pandemic after the WHO reported the first case of human-to-human transmission in Thailand on Sept. 28, 2004, from the H5N1 flu strain.

In December 2005, in response to an emergency request from President George W. Bush, Congress approved $3.8 billion to develop vaccines and stockpile anti-flu medications.[70]

Dozens of human cases and some deaths were reported in Turkey in January 2006.[71] But the outbreak failed to turn into a transmissible disease between humans. Most of the 648 cases since 2003 have occurred in people who had close contact with poultry.

Currently, human infection is rare, and there is no ongoing transmission in humans, according to the CDC, but the bird flu can be fatal, with a 60 percent mortality rate. The first case in North America occurred almost a decade after the first outbreak, in Canada in 2014, when a person who had recently returned from China died.[72]

Swine flu (H1N1), meanwhile, killed thousands and infected millions in 2009, when it was declared a pandemic by the WHO in June of that year, the last declared pandemic before COVID. The WHO declared an end to the pandemic on Aug. 10, 2010. The WHO said H1N1 had become much like any other flu strain, no longer causing the majority of flu outbreaks or triggering outbreaks during the summer.[73] Globally, an estimated 151,700 to 575,400 people died from swine flu in the first year of the pandemic.[74] It has been traced to pig and poultry farming and contact with wild waterfowl.[75]

MERS, a severe respiratory disease caused by a coronavirus, was first reported after a 60-year-old man died of a novel virus in Saudi Arabia in 2012. Across the globe, 27 countries have reported cases of MERS, but about 80 percent occurred in Saudi Arabia. The disease, which has a fatality rate of about 35 percent, has killed 866 people. There is no specific treatment and no vaccine.[76]

Although the disease emerged from dromedary camels in Saudi Arabia, some researchers view them as an intermediary, since the virus is found in bats and African dromedaries.[77]

COVID-19's Emergence

On Dec. 31, 2019, the WHO received a report from China of a cluster of cases in Wuhan with a pneumonia of unknown cause, later identified as COVID-19.[78] Of the first 44 patients hospitalized, 27 had been exposed to the local seafood market in December 2019, where live wildlife was also sold.[79]

Authorities closed the Wuhan market in January 2020. They also reported finding environmental samples of COVID-19 virus (on sewage and surfaces) in the area where wild game was sold.[80]

Since then, however, cases of COVID-19 have been traced back to November 2019, and some scientists began questioning in early 2020 if the market was the source.[81]

In late May 2020, George Gao Fu, the director of the Chinese Center for Disease Control and Prevention, said the center had been unable to trace the virus to an animal in the market. "At first, we assumed the seafood market might have the virus, but now the market is more like a victim," Gao Fu told the state-owned *Global Times*.[82]

It remains unclear how the virus was transmitted to humans. Many scientists believe the virus probably came from a horseshoe bat, where a virus whose genome is 96 percent similar to COVID-19's has been identified. One scientist at the Sorbonne University in Paris has suggested that the virus may be the result of a recombination of two different viruses—one closer to the horseshoe bat's and the other closer to a pangolin virus.[83]

CURRENT SITUATION

International Developments

Moving toward its first permanent national ban on the trade in wildlife food, China's legislature is considering changes to the nation's wildlife law that would outlaw the sale and human consumption of some wild animals; the drafting of new legislation is likely to take at least until the end of the year.[84] That change would replace the temporary wildlife ban issued in January 2020 in the wake of the coronavirus outbreak in Wuhan, which was to stay in effect until the pandemic ended.[85]

In April 2020, the Chinese government issued a proposed list of animals that could be sold for meat, drastically curtailed from the species that are currently legal. Notably, the approved list left out some of the animals of most concern for zoonotic disease, such as pangolins, civet cats and bamboo rats—a large rodent that lives in bamboo thickets—as well as dogs, which Chinese markets have long sold for food.[86]

Some provinces have begun to offer farmers cash to end the practice of rearing civets and other wild animals.[87]

In May 2020, Guangdong province, a prime center for wildlife gastronomy where SARS originated, started imposing tough fines for ordering restaurant dishes, such as bat soup, a positive sign that the provinces are prepared to enforce a stronger national law, according to Aili Kang, executive director of the Wildlife Conservation Society's Asia program. But she says some of the biggest

A pangolin, an endangered species that is the most highly trafficked mammal in the world, was rescued from poachers in Uganda in April 2020. Pangolins are prized in China as a culinary delicacy and for alleged medicinal purposes, and may have been part of the transmission chain of the COVID-19 virus.

industries, such as breeders of bamboo rats, are seeking exemptions from the ban.

Wildlife advocates say the proposed law still has big loopholes—permitting wildlife trade for traditional Chinese medicine, for fur and for exotic pets. Pets such as "rare reptiles or turtles may not be as risky as primates or rodents, but they still have risky pathogens," says Kang.

China's wildlife ban will have limited effect if nearby countries continue the exotic animal trade, experts say. In March, Vietnamese Prime Minister Nguyen Xuân Phúc requested draft legislation by April 1, 2020, to restrict the trade and consumption of wildlife, but no information about a ban has been made public, raising concerns among conservation groups as to the government's seriousness.[88]

In May 2020, the WHO said it was not recommending a ban on live animal markets globally, despite urging from some environmental groups and members of the U.S. Congress.[89] WHO food safety and animal diseases expert Peter Ben Embarek said live animal markets—which exist in many countries, including in Africa—are essential to providing food and livelihoods to millions around the world and that governments should focus on improving the markets' hygiene and food safety standards.[90]

The Wildlife Conservation Society and other conservation groups are calling on national governments to issue bans on all wildlife for human consumption, with narrow exceptions for indigenous communities that rely on wildlife for subsistence.[91]

Should the trade in wildlife for human consumption be banned?

YES
Susan Lieberman
Vice President, International Policy, Wildlife Conservation Society

Written for *CQ Researcher*, June 2020

NO
Amy Hinsley
Senior Research Fellow, Wildlife Conservation Research Unit, Department of Zoology, University of Oxford

Stephanie Brittain
Postdoctoral Researcher, Interdisciplinary Centre for Conservation Science, Department of Zoology, University of Oxford

Written for *CQ Researcher*, June 2020

In only four months, people everywhere have awakened to the massive global tragedy that can result from zoonotic pandemics, when animals pass on pathogens to humans. If we want to avoid the next COVID, we need to accept that tweaks to current policies or targeted closures of some risky wildlife markets will be irresponsibly insufficient. Business as usual and mere improvements to existing policies will not prevent the next zoonotic pandemic.

Global public opinion is moving rapidly to a place where decision-makers can adopt policies that once would have been considered radical but seem sensible now as people experience the impact of this pandemic on their economies, well-being and lives. If governments view the challenges of avoiding a future pandemic through this newly shifted Overton Window, they will see how bold policies that reorder our relationship with wildlife will allow for solutions that reflect local realities. Nuanced changes to current policies or targeted closures of only today's problem markets will not prevent future zoonotic pandemics.

This shift in public opinion means we need lawmakers and decision-makers to know that now is the time to make wholesale changes to our fractured relationship with wildlife. For example, we need to stop relentlessly destroying wildlife habitat for logging, mining and agriculture, which increases the possibility of spillover of deadly pathogens from wildlife to humans. Protecting ecological integrity should be a priority within any comprehensive plan to avoid future zoonotic outbreaks.

With large-scale reform of the global wildlife trade, we can then support local solutions that will preserve wildlife for those who depend on it for food security or sustainable income-generating enterprises such as wildlife-based tourism. Indeed, under this new framework, locally and socially accepted solutions will be stronger and more sustainable. Globally, the commercial trade in wildlife for human consumption, particularly birds and mammals, poses an enormous risk to humans. This trade for urban consumers is especially unnecessary, because they do not need to eat wildlife; it is neither a dietary nor a cultural necessity for them, as it still is for some rural communities.

With bold action for an overarching change in our relationship to wildlife, we can significantly reduce the risk of zoonotic pandemics; help address the world's biodiversity crisis; support local economies through nonconsumptive industries such as ecotourism; and preserve wildlife for those who depend on it for their well-being and cultural identity. It is only through recognizing that we are at a global inflection point with our relationship with wildlife that we will make progress.

With the highly publicized links between the coronavirus that caused COVID-19 and wild animal meat, banning wildlife trade and consumption has been widely suggested as the only way to stop future pandemics. This is a simple and powerful message, but this very simplicity means this approach is unlikely to work.

Proposed bans ignore the complexity of the wildlife trade and the diversity of both its consumers and of the plant, animal and fungal species being consumed. Wild meat is not just threatened high-disease-risk animal species being traded illegally in the tropics, but also pigs, deer, birds, antelope and rodents hunted globally. Further, while wild meat may be consumed as a luxury in high-income areas, it contributes to the food security and livelihoods of millions of people globally, especially those in rural communities.

Banning wildlife consumption presents the real risk of unintended consequences and perverse outcomes. Markets can be driven underground where monitoring and regulation are impossible, potentially increasing zoonotic disease transmission by reducing the potential and incentives for applying food hygiene standards. Where bans are successful, wild-meat traders, who are often women, lose valuable employment. Further, viable alternative sources of food and income are rarely available or provided, which could result in increased malnutrition and poverty.

Alternatives such as livestock or poultry are often named but, in the Congo Basin, an estimated additional 4.5 million tons of pigs or chickens would be needed to replace wild meat, requiring millions of hectares of forest clearance. Deforestation would destroy globally important habitats. Further, disease emergence from domestic animals is also a real risk, and agricultural intensification and land use change, particularly in tropical regions where wildlife biodiversity is high, are root causes of disease emergence. It is time to learn from past mistakes, not repeat them.

This is not to say that nothing should change following the COVID-19 pandemic. We must dramatically re-evaluate our relationship with animals and with nature more broadly. A priority should be better regulation rather than outright bans, focused on addressing illegal, unsustainable and high-disease-risk trade, whether this involves wild or domestic animals. We should also carefully consider the impact of regulation on food security, and focus efforts on areas where wild meat is a luxury. While a blanket ban may sound good on paper, in reality, long-term policy changes need to be designed with enough nuance to be feasible, to be effective, and to not cause further harm.

Some environmentalists are seeking an international ban on all live wildlife trade, including pets, working through existing treaties. The Convention on International Trade in Endangered Species of Wild Fauna and Flora (CITES), a legally binding accord agreed to by 183 countries, is one possible avenue, according to Elly Pepper, deputy director of the International Wildlife Conservation Initiative at the Natural Resources Defense Council, a New York-based environmental group.[92]

The treaty prohibits international commercial trade in about 670 animal species threatened with extinction and regulates trade in more than 5,000 species that could become threatened. But most wildlife species traded for food are not covered.[93]

"The purpose of CITES is to address unsustainable trade, and this pandemic has made us realize that the wildlife trade has a component we haven't thought about—human health," says Pepper. She wrote in a blog that the leadership of CITES should be "scouring" the treaty's text to bring changes in that direction and not "shrugging its shoulders."[94]

However, the CITES secretariat said recently that "matters regarding zoonotic diseases are outside of CITES's mandate," and other experts agree that the treaty would have to be amended to make public health a reason for prohibiting trade in a designated species.[95]

"Amending treaties is really complicated—it would not happen quickly," says Lieberman of the Wildlife Conservation Society, noting that the last time the treaty was amended it took 30 years, requiring a two-thirds majority.[96]

Pepper says another possible international forum is the United Nations Convention on Biological Diversity, signed by 150 government leaders at the 1992 Rio Earth Summit, which calls for commitments by nations to prevent the long-term decline of biodiversity. The United States is not a party to that treaty.

The next meeting of the diversity convention in 2021 should pledge to meet the Natural Resources Defense Council's goal of protecting 30 percent of the Earth's land and water by 2030, according to Pepper. "When thousands of acres of the Amazon are destroyed for agriculture, for example, the risk to humans from contact with wildlife increases," she said.[97]

But the convention, while filled with commendable recommendations, has "no teeth" to enforce any actions by governments, according to Machalaba, the policy adviser at the EcoHealth Alliance. Machalaba says she wants zoonotic risk made part of risk assessments for new development projects, much like environmental impact statements used by governments, corporations and international agencies such as the World Bank.

U.S. Efforts

To prevent another zoonotic epidemic, leading members of Congress are pushing for more funding to enforce laws against illegal wildlife trafficking and legislation to encourage a ban on overseas markets that sell live and exotic animals.

Sen. Tom Udall, D-N.M., said in April that congressional members were pushing for a "substantial increase" in funding for the U.S. Fish and Wildlife Service to stop illegal wildlife from other countries. Udall is the ranking Democrat on the Senate Appropriations subcommittee that oversees the Fish and Wildlife Service. Subcommittee Chairman Lisa Murkowski, R-Alaska, said she was also concerned about the link between the illegal wildlife trade and public health.[98]

In early February 2020, in its fiscal 2021 budget request, the Trump administration proposed a 16 percent cut in the Fish and Wildlife Service, the agency charged with enforcing wildlife anti-trafficking laws.[99] However, Congress rejected many of Trump's proposed cuts in environmental agencies when it passed the 2020 appropriations package, so it is questionable whether Trump's cuts will make it into the final bill for 2021 intact.[100]

Several bills seek to prohibit zoonotically dangerous imports from wildlife markets overseas and offer incentives to other countries to ban these markets. Buried in the $3 trillion act passed by the House to deal with the pandemic-caused economic downturn is a section making it illegal to import species designated by Fish and Wildlife as a "biohazard to human health." It authorizes $111 million to help foreign countries end the trade in animals that pose a disease risk to human health and to strengthen early detection of zoonotic diseases.[101]

However, the Democratic-controlled House passed the bill in a party line vote, and Senate Majority Leader Mitch McConnell, R-Ky., has said it has "no chance of becoming law" and will not pass in the Republican-controlled Senate.[102] Some environmental groups think a bipartisan measure dealing with wildlife may have more chance of success than the Democrats' bill—perhaps as part of a future economic stimulus measure.

In one such effort in the Senate, Republican Graham and Democrat Coons have introduced a measure aimed at banning the sale of "high-risk" wildlife in live animal markets for human consumption. The more than $1 billion bill requires federal agencies to identify which species have a high risk of spreading a zoonotic disease and authorizes the president to use sanctions against nations that continue to permit markets selling those animals, along with aid to help communities that depend on wildlife for subsistence.[103]

"How can we prevent this from happening again?" Graham asked in a statement referring to the COVID-19 pandemic. "Governments in Asia and elsewhere should immediately shut down markets that sell high-risk wildlife for human consumption and fully enforce laws already on the books to end the global illegal trade in wildlife."[104]

Several mainstream conservation groups, including the World Wildlife Fund and the Nature Conservancy, have endorsed the bill.

However, two environmental groups say it does not go far enough. The trade in all live wildlife should be banned, not just those designated "high-risk," say the Natural Resources Defense Council and the Center for Biological Diversity, based in Tucson, Ariz.

The bill's approach—directing federal agencies to predict a species' risk before banning its import—is "like playing Russian roulette," considering some 5,000 species are traded internationally, says Brett Hartl, the Center for Biological Diversity's government affairs director: "Every single species on the planet has viruses and bacteria. So the notion that somehow we could ever determine what species and combination of events are likely to cause a disease is extremely low."

Moreover, he says, the bill ignores the United States' own role in the trade; it is the No. 1 importer of exotic animals for pets and the site of markets selling live reptiles and amphibians for food in large American cities.

The bill also encourages the federal government to use a so-called One Health approach to detection and response to pandemic threats, uniting expertise from animal health, human health and environmental health experts.[105]

Earlier this year, the Trump administration had planned to shut down USAID's 10-year PREDICT program, which trains science and lab workers in developing countries to identify potential zoonotic diseases. Sens. Elizabeth Warren,

D-Mass., and Angus King, I-Maine, protested the shutdown in late January, saying COVID-19 "heightens the need for a robust, coordinated, and proactive response to emerging pandemics—one of the roles that PREDICT played."[106]

In an about-face effective April 1, the administration extended the program's funding for six months. With the $2.26 million extension, PREDICT will continue to provide technical expertise to support detection of cases of COVID-19 in Africa, Asia and the Middle East to support the public health response.[107]

OUTLOOK
Growing Pressures

Pressure to clear land for agriculture and hunt bush meat for food is expected to increase with an expanding world population, raising worries about increasing spillovers of zoonotic diseases in degraded landscapes.

"The intensity and frequency of outbreaks will continue in China, but we will see parallel events beginning with much greater intensity in areas that were remote and isolated," predicts the Global Virome Project's Carroll, pointing to Africa, where the population is expected to boom along with a growing middle class. "If they assume the dietary patterns that are prevalent in the U.S., then we will have a huge problem in land use, because they will demand cattle protein."

Sharing similar concerns, Harvard's Myers says habitat destruction in Africa and the Amazon basin for agriculture could be stemmed by innovations in food production, including artificial milk and eggs, plant-based meat substitutes along the lines of the Impossible Burger, insect-based foods and new crop varieties. "It's not too late, but we absolutely can't continue on our current trajectory without paying enormous human health costs," he says.

Some scientists hope that advances in interpreting the genome of viruses will help predict and prevent zoonotic pandemics.

"Ultimately, one of our big goals—the holy grail—is to look at the genome of a virus before it's caused even a single human infection and understand whether it will cause disease," says EcoHealth scientist Epstein, who sees the Global Virome Project's proposed virus library as one step in that direction. Each experience of studying these viruses in animals and people "brings us closer" to that goal, he says.

For bat coronaviruses, which EcoHealth has studied extensively, "we're five to 10 years from being able to break down the risk of them emerging and disrupt them from emerging," says EcoHealth President Daszak. "In a few decades, we'll be able to prevent many pandemics."

Daszak adds, "Fifty years from now, people will look back on this time and say, 'That was the pandemic era and thank goodness they got to grips with that.'"

In the meantime, COVID-19 has been a reminder of how much faster a disease can spread in the modern world via planes and global trade than in earlier centuries. "The rate of spread of the [bubonic] plague from Central Europe took years; now it's hours," says Stanford's Lambin, who calls COVID-19's "double whammy" of zoonotic disease plus globalization "a very dangerous cocktail."

One of the biggest obstacles to attacking the environmental roots of zoonotic epidemics, scientists and advocates agree, is getting the world to listen. Many of them hope that will change because of the current pandemic.

"The issue of high-risk wildlife trade has been around forever," says the World Wildlife Fund's Vertefeuille. "What's new and different right now is the entire world and the global economy is bearing the costs of that risky wildlife trade. So we really have a moment in time to address this issue—that if we act quickly and aggressively we can try to stop the next pandemic."

The current pandemic is just one of many signals, along with a changing climate, that our planet is in trouble, says Myers.

"I'm hoping COVID-19 will be the loudest and most immediate of these warning bells that we've been hearing, that it will be a wake-up call," he says. "We need to pause and address this relationship we have with our natural systems."

NOTES

1. Andrew Joseph, "First death from Wuhan pneumonia outbreak reported as scientists release DNA sequence of virus," *STAT*, Jan. 11, 2020, https://tinyurl.com/s4wx3nk; Derrick Bryson Taylor, "How the Coronavirus Pandemic Unfolded: a Timeline," *The New York Times*, June 9, 2020, https://tinyurl.com/wb48cut; and Chaolin Huang *et al.*, "Clinical features of patients infected with 2019 novel coronavirus in Wuhan, China," *The Lancet*, Jan. 24, 2020, https://tinyurl.com/w5qfs4w.

2. Jeremy Page and Natasha Khan, "On the ground in Wuhan, Signs of China Stalling Probe of Coronavirus Origins," *The Wall Street Journal*, May 12, 2020, https://tinyurl.com/ycqtmqkp.

3. James T. Areddy, "China Rules out Animal Market and Lab as Coronavirus Origin," *The Wall Street Journal*, May 26, 2020, https://tinyurl.com/yb7jyb78.

4. David Cyranoski, "The biggest mystery: what it will take to trace the coronavirus source," *Nature*, June 5, 2020, https://tinyurl.com/yd7ooc6a; Alexandre Hassanin, "Coronavirus origins," *The Conversation*, March 24, 2020, https://tinyurl.com/rynx542.

5. Kate E. Jones, "Global trends in emerging infectious diseases," *Nature*, Feb. 21, 2008, https://tinyurl.com/y8676bqx; "One Health, Zoonotic Diseases," Centers for Disease Control and Prevention, last reviewed July 14, 2017, https://tinyurl.com/yaxup36m.

6. Vincent C.C. Cheng *et al.*, "Severe Acute Respiratory Syndrome Coronavirus in an Agent of Emerging and Reemerging Infection," *Clinical Microbiology Review*, October 2007, https://tinyurl.com/w2yjfj6.

7. Damian Carrington, "Coronavirus: 'Nature is sending us a message,' says UN environment chief," *The Guardian*, March 25, 2020, https://tinyurl.com/ycvgc7lt.

8. "Our health depends on our environment," Planetary Health Alliance, https://tinyurl.com/yaospq78.

9. "Global Wildlife Health and Pandemic Prevention Act," Sen. Chris Coons and Sen. Lindsey Graham, https://tinyurl.com/ya72mg34; "Bi-Partisan One Health Congressional Bills introduced in U.S. Senate and House," One Health Commission, 2020, https://tinyurl.com/yyn8b8vj.

10. "Reducing Pandemic Risk, Promoting Global Health," USAID, accessed June 17, 2020, https://tinyurl.com/yad4gotw.

11. "World Population by Year," worldometer, https://tinyurl.com/y2nw28sa.

12. Anthony Cilluffo and Neil G. Ruiz, "World's population is projected to nearly stop growing by end of the century," Pew Research Center, June 17, 2019, https://tinyurl.com/yd2kw8j2.

13. Chelsea L. Wood *et al.*, "Human infectious disease burdens decrease with urbanization but not with biodiversity," *Philosophical Transactions of the Royal Society B*, April 24, 2017, https://tinyurl.com/ya89fgmg.

14. "The Wildlife Origins of SARS-COV2 and Employing a One Health Approach," podcast interview with Dr. Steve Osofsky, Excellsior, April 3, 2020, https://tinyurl.com/yacvagop.

15. Kate E. Jones *et al.*, *op. cit.*

16. "Forest ecology shapes Lyme disease risk in the eastern US," *Science Daily*, July 9, 2018, https://tinyurl.com/y7h82kja; Richard S. Ostfeld *et al.*, "Tick-borne disease risk in a forest web," *Ecology*, May 8, 2018, https://tinyurl.com/ybskbxce.

17. Wood *et al.*, *op. cit.*

18. Laura S.P. Bloomfield *et al.*, "Habitat fragmentation, livelihood behaviors, and contact between people and nonhuman primates in Africa," *Landscape Ecology*, April 1, 2020, https://tinyurl.com/y8uxnems.

19. "How forest loss leads to spread of disease," Stanford University, April 8, 2020, https://tinyurl.com/yahrzsuu.

20. Christine K. Johnson *et al.*, "Global shifts in mammalian population trends reveal key predictors of virus spillover risk," *Proceedings of the Royal Society B*, April 8, 2020, https://tinyurl.com/rcjgms2.

21. Jason R. Rohr *et al.*, "Emerging human infectious diseases and the links to global food production," *Nature Sustainability*, June 11, 2019, https://tinyurl.com/y9uuc5y9.

22. Johnson, *op. cit.*

23. "End the Trade: Coalition Invites Global Community to Take a Stand Against Future Pandemics," WildAid, April 20, 2020, https://tinyurl.com/y7amshwc.

24. "A Global Call to Action on Covid-19 and Wildlife Trade," preventpandemics.org, https://tinyurl.com/ybhcdpb7.

25. Dan Challender *et al.*, "Coronavirus: Why a blanket ban on wildlife trade would not be the right response," *The Conversation*, April 8, 2020, https://tinyurl.com/y8exr4sf.

26. "China Suspends Wildlife Trade to Curb Novel Coronavirus," Xinhuanet, Jan. 26, 2020, https://tinyurl.com/yag4e22g.

27. George Wittemyer, "The new coronavirus emerged from the global wildlife trade and may be devastating enough to end it," *The Conversation*, March 31, 2020, https://tinyurl.com/spztlfm.

28. Jesse Bonwitt *et al.*, "Unintended Consequences of the 'Bushmeat Ban' in West Africa during 2013-2016 Ebola Virus Disease Epidemic," *Social Science & Medicine*, March 2018, https://tinyurl.com/yc4p9bq9.

29. "Wildlife Crime: Pangolin Scales," United Nations Office on Drugs and Crime, 2020, https://tinyurl.com/yablpa5e.

30. Candace Famiglietti and Maria Ivanova, "We must address exotic wildlife consumption to avoid the Next Global Pandemic," *New Security Beat*, April 20, 2020, https://tinyurl.com/ybgucocn.

31. "One Health," World Bank Group, 2018, p. 15, https://tinyurl.com/t6gbr7e.

32. "Shutdown of PREDICT Infectious Disease Program Challenged by Senators Warren and King," *Global Biodefense*, Feb. 4, 2020, https://tinyurl.com/y8pzml9p.

33. Colin J. Carlson, "From PREDICT to prevention, one pandemic later," *The Lancet Microbe*, March 21, 2020, https://tinyurl.com/yaw424hr.

34. Cyranoski, *op. cit.*

35. Nina Wang *et al.*, "Serological Evidence of Bat SARS-related Coronavirus Infection in Humans, China," *Virological Sinica*, March 2, 2018, https://tinyurl.com/y8e4j53b.

36. Steve Osofsky, "Emerging 'dis-ease': US foreign assistance needs to focus on the root causes of pandemics," *The Hill*, May 24, 2020, https://tinyurl.com/ycds8yoa.

37. Steven Johnson, "How Data Became One of the Most Powerful Tools to Fight an Epidemic," *The New York Times Magazine*, June 10, 2020, https://tinyurl.com/y9mk9vt8.

38. Christian Nordqvist, "Origins of the Black Death Traced Back to China, Gene Sequencing Has Revealed," *Medical News Today*, Nov. 1, 2010, https://tinyurl.com/yd27waez.

39. *Ibid.*

40. "The History of Plague—Part 1. The Three Great Pandemics," *Journal of Military and Veterans Health*, https://tinyurl.com/yckb75kl.

41. "Plague," Centers for Disease Control and Prevention, https://tinyurl.com/saz8w86.

42. "One Health, Zoonotic Diseases," *op. cit.*

43. David Quammen, *Spillover* (2013), p. 427.

44. *Ibid.*, p. 137.

45. Jason R. Rohr, *op. cit.*

46. Quammen, *op. cit.*, p. 43.

47. *Ibid.*

48. *Ibid.*, pp. 22-23.

49. *Ibid.*, p. 31; "Monkeypox," Centers for Disease Control and Prevention, https://tinyurl.com/y726qbrh.

50. Tom Evans *et al.*, "Links between ecological integrity, emerging infectious disease originating from wildlife, and other aspects of human health," Wildlife Conservation Society, April 2020, https://tinyurl.com/y8dd4ac4.

51. Sarah Glazer, "Avian Flu Threat," *CQ Researcher*, Jan. 13, 2006, https://tinyurl.com/ycb53he2.

52. "Influenza; 1957-1958 Pandemic (H2N2 Virus)," Centers for Disease Control and Prevention, Jan. 2, 2019, https://tinyurl.com/ycqqgbqb; "Influenza; 1968 Pandemic (H3N2 virus)," Jan. 2, 2019, https://tinyurl.com/ybxo853d.

53. Jeremy Brown, *Influenza: The Hundred-Year Hunt to Cure the Deadliest Disease in History* (2018), p. 60.

54. *Ibid.*, p. 65.

55. "Hot Spots for Emerging Diseases," *The New York Times*, July 15, 2012, https://tinyurl.com/y5kl5vhu.

56. Warren Andiman, *Animal Viruses and Humans, a Narrow Divide* (2018), p. 165, p. 167.

57. "Ebola Virus Disease," World Health Organization, Feb. 10, 2020, https://tinyurl.com/y24gcxvg.

58. Andiman, *op. cit.*, pp. 170-173.

59. Evans *et al.*, *op. cit.*

60. "Nipah virus," World Health Organization, May 30, 2018, https://tinyurl.com/y8hudome; Paul M. Sharp and Beatrice H. Hahn, "Origins of HIV and the AIDS Pandemic," *Cold Spring Harbor Perspectives in Medicine*, September 2011, https://tinyurl.com/y5pftt2w.

61. "Hot Spots for Emerging Diseases," *op. cit.*

62. Evans *et al.*, *op. cit.*

63. "2014-2016 Ebola Outbreak in West Africa," Centers for Disease Control and Prevention, March 8, 2019, https://tinyurl.com/y7aqqxp2.

64. "Ebola virus disease," *op. cit.*

65. "Top 9 Infectious Disease Outbreaks of 2018," Contagion Live, Dec. 31, 2018, https://tinyurl.com/y8los7fp; Grant M. Gallagher, "The Ebola Outbreak Response So Far," Contagion Live, Jan. 2, 2020, https://tinyurl.com/y8ryuglp; and "Ebola Virus Disease," *op. cit.*

66. "CDC SARS Response Timeline," Centers for Disease Control and Prevention, April 26, 2013, https://tinyurl.com/vsp9qng.

67. Brown, *op. cit.*, p. 6.

68. Diana Bell, "Coronavirus: We still haven't learned the lessons from Sars," *The Conversation*, Jan. 24, 2020, https://tinyurl.com/yc5u86el.

69. "SARS (Severe Acute Respiratory Syndrome)," World Health Organization, 2020, https://tinyurl.com/vnwflw4; "Update 95—SARS: Chronology of a Serial Killer," World Health Organization, Nov. 16, 2002, https://tinyurl.com/y8p2uuxy.

70. Glazer, *op. cit.*

71. *Ibid.*

72. "Influenza (Flu)," Centers for Disease Control and Prevention, Jan. 8, 2014, https://tinyurl.com/u4jjgh5.

73. Martin Enserink, "WHO Declares Official End to H1N1 'Swine Flu' Epidemic," *Science*, Aug. 10, 2010, https://tinyurl.com/ybxkojbb.

74. Mackenzie Bean, "A look back at swine flu," *Becker's Hospital Review*, March 12, 2020, https://tinyurl.com/t5n5jpk.

75. "Hot Spots for Emerging Diseases," *op. cit.*; Jim Robbins, "The Ecology of Disease," *The New York Times*, July 14, 2012, https://tinyurl.com/qpmwpry.

76. Yella Hewings-Martin, "How do SARS and MERS Compare with COVID-19?" *Medical News Today*, April 10, 2020, https://tinyurl.com/y77vpj7t.

77. Roger Frutos *et al.*, "COVID-19, The Conjunction of Events Leading to the Coronavirus Pandemic and Lessons to Learn for Future Threats," *Frontiers in Medicine*, May 12, 2020, https://tinyurl.com/yd388hkr.

78. "Pneumonia of Unknown Cause-China," World Health Organization, Jan. 5, 2020, https://tinyurl.com/qwxenbk.

79. Chaolin Huang *et al.*, "Clinical features of patients infected with 2019 novel coronavirus in Wuhan, China," *The Lancet*, Jan. 24, 2020, https://tinyurl.com/w5qfs4w.

80. Hassanin, *op. cit.*

81. Daniel Lucey, "Recent Data and Maps to help find origin of COVID-19," *Science Speaks: Global ID News*, March 15, 2020, https://tinyurl.com/szykfa2; Frutos, *op. cit.*; Josephine Ma, "Coronavirus: China's first confirmed COVID-19 case traced back to November 17," *South China Morning Post*, March 13, 2020, https://tinyurl.com/sdajymy; and Page and Khan, *op. cit.*

82. Jackie Salo, "Wuhan market is the 'victim' of coronavirus outbreak," *New York Post*, May 27, 2020, https://tinyurl.com/y89u8g3m.

83. Hassanin, *op. cit.*

84. Steven Lee Meyers, "China Vowed to Keep Wildlife off the Menu, a Tough Promise to Keep," *The New York Times*, June 7, 2020, https://tinyurl.com/y9havdyf.

85. David Stanway, "China legislators take on wildlife trade, but traditional medicine likely to be exempt," *Reuters*, May 20, 2020, https://tinyurl.com/y8pmgfnj.

86. Ben Westcott, "Chinese government reveals draft list of animals which can be farmed for meat," *CNN*, April 10, 2020, https://tinyurl.com/s9fpupq.

87. "China offers farmers cash to give up wildlife trade," *AFP, Bangkok Post*, May 19, 2020, https://tinyurl.com/ydcwt343.

88. Michael Tatarski, "Vietnam wildlife trade ban appears to flounder amid coronavirus success," *Mongabay*, May 25, 2020, https://tinyurl.com/ya7k2uqy.

89. Jackie Northam, "Calls to Ban Wildlife Markets Worldwide Gain Steam Amid Pandemic," *NPR*, April 19, 2020, https://tinyurl.com/yceea6rd; Helen Briggs, "Coronavirus: WHO developing guidance on wet markets," *BBC News*, April 21, 2020, https://tinyurl.com/y7rx5j6x.

90. "UN: Live Animal Markets Shouldn't Be Closed Despite Virus," *The Associated Press/U.S. News & World Report*, May 8, 2020, https://tinyurl.com/y9sjswby.

91. "End the Trade: New Coalition Invites Global Community to Take a Stand Against Future Pandemics," *WSCNewsroom*, April 21, 2020, https://tinyurl.com/yajo6ys8.

92. "What is CITES?" CITES, https://tinyurl.com/zrccyqb.

93. Susan Lieberman, "CITES, the Treaty that Regulates Trade in International Wildlife, Is Not the Answer to Preventing Another Zoonotic Pandemic," *National Geographic*, May 22, 2020, https://tinyurl.com/y8d5qzk6.

94. Elly Pepper, "We must prevent future viruses by ending the wildlife trade," NRDC, April 14, 2020, https://tinyurl.com/ya6gdy99.

95. "CITES Secretariat's statement in relation to COVID-19," CITES, https://tinyurl.com/ydgudnxy.

96. Lieberman, *op. cit.*

97. Pepper, *op. cit.*

98. Stephen Lee and Dean Scott, "As Lawmakers Push Global Wildlife Market Ban, U.S. Issues Remain,"

Bloomberg Law, April 28, 2020, https://tinyurl .com/ybjungch.

99. "U.S. Fish and Wildlife Service: FY2021 Appropriations," Congressional Research Service, March 20, 2020, https://tinyurl.com/yclp53wu.

100. John R. Platt, "Trump's Budget Plan: A Push for Even Greater Environmental Regression," *EcoWatch*, Feb. 12, 2020, https://tinyurl.com/y79sor5s.

101. Rebecca Beitsch, "Two green groups call for end to wildlife trade to prevent next pandemic," *The Hill*, May 18, 2020, https://tinyurl.com/yasezlar.

102. Lauren Frias, "House passes $3 trillion coronavirus relief bill dubbed HEROES Act," *Business Insider*, May 15, 2020, https://tinyurl.com/yaccyogl.

103. "Discussion Draft," coons.senate.gov, accessed June 17, 2020, https://tinyurl.com/y7wxw5mu.

104. "Sens. Coons, Graham introduce legislation to shut down high-risk wildlife markets that could ignite another global disease outbreak," press release, Sen. Chris Coons, May 19, 2020, https:// tinyurl.com/y77otomf.

105. "Global Wildlife Health and Pandemic Prevention Act," *op. cit.*

106. "Senators Warren, King Question USAID on Decision to Shutter Global Infectious Disease Prevention Program," press release, Elizabeth Warren, Jan. 31, 2020, https://tinyurl.com/ y8u6nw7m.

107. Kristin Burns, "PREDICT Receives Extension for COVID-19 Pandemic Emergency Response," UCDavis, March 31, 2020, https://tinyurl.com/ ybcw8p35.

BIBLIOGRAPHY

Books

Andiman, Warren A., *Animal Viruses and Humans, A Narrow Divide: How Lethal Zoonotic Viruses Spill Over and Threaten Us*, **Paul Dry Books, 2018.**
A professor emeritus of pediatrics and epidemiology at the Yale University Schools of Medicine and Public Health explains the science behind some of the biggest zoonotic outbreaks in recent years, including MERS, SARS and Ebola.

Brown, Jeremy, *Influenza: The Hundred-Year Hunt to Cure the Deadliest Disease in History*, **Touchstone, 2018.**
The director of the Office of Emergency Care Research at the National Institutes of Health provides a readable history of flu epidemics, including the 1918 Spanish flu, and traces scientific and governmental efforts to cure the disease.

Quammen, David, *Spillover: Animal Infections and the Next Human Pandemic*, **W.W. Norton, 2012.**
A science writer accompanies prominent virus hunters into the wild to illustrate how scientists have tried to trace zoonotic diseases such as SARS, Ebola and AIDS back to their animal origins and how animal diseases spill over to humans.

Articles

Areddy, James T., "China Rules Out Animal Market and Lab as Coronavirus Origin," *The Wall Street Journal*, **May 26, 2020, https://tinyurl.com/yb7jyb78.**
In an interview with Chinese state media, the head of China's Center for Disease Control and Prevention said his scientists were unable to trace the virus that caused COVID-19 to an animal at the Wuhan seafood market, originally suspected as a source.

Beitsch, Rebecca, "Two green groups call for end to wildlife trade to prevent next pandemic," *The Hill*, **May 18, 2020, https://tinyurl.com/yasezlar.**
Two environmental groups urged Congress to ban the trade in all live wildlife, saying the recent House-passed Heroes Act does not go far enough.

Bell, Diana, "Coronavirus: We still haven't learned the lessons from Sars," *The Conversation*, **Jan. 24, 2020, https://tinyurl.com/yc5u86el.**
A professor of conservation biology at the University of East Anglia in England argues that the world should learn the lesson from the 2002-03 SARS outbreak—that the wildlife trade is a "threat to human health."

Meyers, Steven Lee, "China Vowed to Keep Wildlife Off the Menu, a Tough Promise to Keep," *The New York Times*, **June 7, 2020, https://tinyurl.com/ y9havdyf.**
A journalist discusses the economic pressures to narrow China's wildlife ban as the government considers permanent legal changes.

Osofsky, Steve, "Emerging 'dis-ease': US foreign assistance needs to focus on the root causes of pandemics," *The Hill*, May 24, 2020, https://tinyurl.com/ycds8yoa.
A wildlife veterinarian at Cornell University argues that the government should reorient its efforts away from hunting for the viruses that could cause the next pandemic and toward stopping root causes such as wildlife trade and deforestation.

Watts, Jonathan, " 'Promiscuous treatment of nature' will lead to more pandemics—scientists," *The Guardian*, May 7, 2020, https://tinyurl.com/yaf3l4gr.
A journalist quotes scientists who say human beings' destruction of nature, such as habitat occupied by bats in Asia, will lead to more pandemics of diseases jumping from animals.

Reports and Studies

Evans, Tom, *et al.*, "Links between ecological integrity, emerging infectious diseases originating from wildlife, and other aspects of human health—an overview of the literature," Wildlife Conservation Society, April 2020, https://tinyurl.com/y8dd4ac4.
A global conservation group that also runs the Bronx Zoo summarizes research showing links between human incursions into the environment and outbreaks of infectious diseases.

Keesing, Felicia, *et al.*, "Impacts of biodiversity on the emergence and transmission of infectious diseases," *Nature*, Dec. 2, 2010, https://tinyurl.com/yaja4q8j.
A Bard College professor and other environmental health researchers conclude that preserving ecosystems "should generally reduce the prevalence of infectious diseases."

Magnusson, Magnus, *et al.*, "Effect of spatial scale and latitude on diversity-disease relationships," *Ecology*, December 2019, https://tinyurl.com/yab8tbbg.
This meta-analysis by Swedish and American ecology experts found that high biodiversity was linked to reduced risk of infectious disease in large regions in the temperate zone.

Wood, Chelsea L., *et al.*, "Human infectious disease burdens decrease with urbanization but not with biodiversity," *Philosophical Transactions of the Royal Society B*, April 24, 2017, https://tinyurl.com/ya89fgmg.
In this study of 60 countries, researchers from universities in Washington, California and Maryland find that urbanization and growing wealth have been the main drivers in reducing infectious diseases, while biodiversity has had a minimal to negative effect.

THE NEXT STEP

Biodiversity

Hall, Louise, "World Bee Day: Are we ignoring biodiversity risks in the same way we ignored the pandemic?" *The Independent*, May 20, 2020, https://tinyurl.com/y85s2j6s.
Experts warn that losses of biodiversity, especially bees, constitute a crisis that people are unprepared for, much the way many were caught off guard by the coronavirus pandemic.

Rankin, Jennifer, "EU plan for 3bn trees in 10 years to tackle biodiversity crisis," *The Guardian*, May 19, 2020, https://tinyurl.com/ybku3t9q.
A European Union initiative calls for one-third of the continent to become protected zones, but some scientists say the strategy is not specific enough.

Win, Thin Lei, "Will pandemic push humans into a healthier relationship with nature?" *Reuters*, May 21, 2020, https://tinyurl.com/yagvjtf8.
The coronavirus pandemic has hampered ongoing efforts to preserve biodiversity, according to environmentalists.

Coronavirus and the Environment

Beitsch, Rebecca, "Efforts to rescue recycling complicated by coronavirus," *The Hill*, June 17, 2020, https://tinyurl.com/ybnznbzo.
Municipalities facing budget shortfalls due to the coronavirus pandemic might be forced to recycle less material, and the recycling industry has turned to Congress for help.

Harvey, Fiona, "Covid-19 pandemic is 'fire drill' for effects of climate crisis, says UN official," *The Guardian*, June 15, 2020, https://tinyurl.com/ycu6ww4c.
A United Nations business chief warns that crises like the coronavirus pandemic will multiply until humans adopt more environmentally sustainable practices.

Miller, Ryan W., " 'More masks than jellyfish': Environmental groups worry about coronavirus waste in oceans," *USA Today*, June 9, 2020, https://tinyurl.com/ydfe6rlw.
Environmentalists warn that masks, gloves and other pandemic-related waste are polluting the ocean.

Regulations

Challender, Dan, *et al.*, "Coronavirus: why a blanket ban on wildlife trade would not be the right response," *The Conversation*, April 8, 2020, https://tinyurl.com/y8exr4sf.
Environmental researchers argue blanket bans on wildlife consumption would encourage illegal sales, but that targeted regulations would make wildlife trade safer.

Khadka, Navin Singh, "Coronavirus: China wildlife trade ban 'should be permanent,'" *BBC*, Feb. 4, 2020, https://tinyurl.com/ybve9hom.
Conservationists called on China to make its temporary wildlife trade ban permanent, and state-run media in the country denounced the lack of regulations in the wildlife market.

Londoño, Ernesto, Manuela Andreoni and Letícia Casado, "Amazon Deforestation Soars as Pandemic Hobbles Enforcement," *The New York Times*, June 6, 2020, https://tinyurl.com/y9tqce7v.
Illegal loggers and miners in the Amazon see little chance of punishment because deforestation regulations are going unenforced during the pandemic.

Wildlife Consumption

Alden, Chris, and Ross Harvey, "A South African proposal to allow the breeding of wildlife for slaughter could end in disaster," *Quartz Africa*, June 15, 2020, https://tinyurl.com/y9rbc2q9.
South Africa is considering expanding the number of species that can be bred for slaughter, raising the risk of humans contracting zoonotic diseases, according to the authors.

Kays, Roland, "Can Asia end its uncontrolled consumption of wildlife? Here's how North America did it a century ago," *The Conversation*, June 17, 2020, https://tinyurl.com/yazbkl3d.
North America limited wildlife consumption in the early 1900s, after many species were driven nearly extinct, and China could pursue a similar conservation plan, according to a scientist.

Stanway, David, "China legislators take on wildlife trade, but traditional medicine likely to be exempt," *Reuters*, May 20, 2020, https://tinyurl.com/y9h6skc4.
Wildlife continues to be used in medicine and in the fur trade in China, because those practices are exempt from the country's ban on consumption.

For More Information

Center for Biological Diversity, PO Box 710, Tucson, AZ 85702-0710; 520-623-5252; biologicaldiversity.org. Advocacy group working to protect endangered species.

Centers for Disease Control and Prevention, 1600 Clifton Road, Atlanta, GA 30329; 800-232-4636; cdc.gov. Federal government's lead public health agency.

EcoHealth Alliance, 520 Eighth Ave., Suite 1200, New York, NY 10018; 212-380-4460; ecohealthalliance.org. Research group developing science-based solutions to prevent pandemics and promote conservation.

One Health Commission, PO Box 972, Apex, NC 27502; 984-500-8093; onehealthcommission.org. Nonprofit advocating "One Health" approaches, which

join experts in animal, plant and human health with ecosystem professionals.

Wildlife Conservation Society, 2300 Southern Blvd., Bronx, NY 10460; 718-220-5100; wcs.org. Global advocacy and research group dedicated to protecting wildlife and wild places.

World Health Organization, 1 Dag Hammarskjold Plaza, 885 Second Ave., 26th floor, New York, NY 10017; 646-626-6060; who.int. United Nations agency that is responsible for international public health.

World Wildlife Fund, 1250 24th St., N.W., Washington, DC 20037; 202-293-4800; worldwildlife.org. Global conservation group dedicated to protecting wildlife and natural habitats.

6

European Union at a Crossroads

Will political divisions tear the EU apart?

By Jonathan Broder

Signs outside the British Parliament denounce the 2016 decision by U.K. voters to leave the European Union. Some analysts say the Brexit debacle has increased public support for the EU throughout Europe.

From *CQ Researcher,*
April 5, 2019

The European Union (EU) was founded in 1993 in a burst of hope and unity, the culmination of a decades-long quest for greater European integration. But today, a resurgence of nationalist and populist fervor is threatening the core values, and future, of the 28-nation federation.

In France, violent fuel tax protests by an amorphous group called the *gilets jaunes*, or yellow vests, have metastasized into a potent populist movement that demands greater social justice for low-skilled workers left behind by Europe's economic integration. Those populists now imperil the pro-EU presidency of Emmanuel Macron.[1]

In Germany, a far-right party hostile to the EU scored major gains in regional elections in October at the expense of the ruling coalition. In response, German Chancellor Angela Merkel, who has long been regarded as Europe's de facto leader, announced she would step down as head of her party, the Christian Democratic Union (CDU), and retire from politics when her term as chancellor ends in 2021.[2]

In the United Kingdom, chaos is engulfing the government as Prime Minister Theresa May struggles with a mutinous Cabinet and a fractured Parliament over how to implement the island nation's 2016 Brexit vote to leave the EU—a decision favored by nationalists who say they want Britons, not EU officials in Brussels, to chart their trade, immigration and fiscal paths.[3]

Until now, Germany, the U.K. and France, with their strong economies and pro-European governments, were regarded as the EU's primary engines. But many political analysts say their difficulties are stark reminders that even Europe's most stable governments may not be strong enough to withstand the populist wave that spread across the Continent in the wake of two crises: the 2009 European debt crisis and the 2014-16 refugee crisis that saw more than a million African and Mideast migrants flee to European shores.

"For the first time in my professional career, I'm afraid—existentially—for Europe," says Charles Kupchan, the top National Security Council adviser on European affairs under former President Barack Obama and now a senior fellow at the Council on Foreign Relations.

A major test looms in May, when elections are scheduled for the European Parliament, the EU's legislative branch. Polls show that populist parties seeking to return more sovereignty to member states pose a major challenge to the European integrationists who have dominated the rule-making body.[4]

"Never, since World War II, has Europe been as essential," Macron wrote in a newspaper column urging voters to support the EU. "Yet never has Europe been in so much danger."[5]

In addition to populism and the political troubles of Merkel, May and Macron, the EU is facing numerous other challenges:

- Splits between its wealthier, creditor northern members and poorer, debtor members in the south, as well as between traditionally democratic Western European nations and more authoritarian Eastern European members, such as Hungary and Poland.

- Slowing economic growth throughout the Union. Italy already is in recession, and the EU as a whole is likely to fall into recession later this year or in 2020, according to economists. The European Central Bank in mid-March cut its forecast for economic growth in the eurozone, the 19 countries that use the euro currency, from 1.7 percent to 1.1 percent.[6]

- German-French tensions over the EU's direction. Macron is pushing for a common EU fiscal policy, but Merkel has resisted because she wants Germany to keep control over its own financial affairs.

- Worsening relations with the Union's erstwhile closest ally, the United States.

Unlike his predecessors, President Trump has called the EU a "foe" on trade, portraying it as "a vehicle for Germany" to "beat the United States when it comes to making money."[7]

Hoping to weaken the EU's collective bargaining power, Trump praised Brexit, imposed tariffs on European steel and aluminum and threatened additional levies on European cars—a move that would spur retaliation and a trade war, says David O'Sullivan, the outgoing EU ambassador to the United States.[8]

Meanwhile, U.S. Secretary of State Mike Pompeo urged European nations in December to reassert their sovereignty over the EU to protect their national interests.[9]

Ivo Daalder, a former U.S. ambassador to NATO, says the Trump White House is the first administration that does not support the EU and the principle of shared economic and political sovereignty that underpins the federation.

"In the European Union, sovereignty is explicitly shared," says Daalder, citing the EU's single market as the most powerful manifestation of continental integration. Pompeo's "calling for the end of shared sovereignty is calling for the end of the European Union," he says.

For all its challenges, however, the EU still has much going for it, many analysts say. The common market has removed border controls between member nations, allowing the free flow of people, goods and services, capital and labor. The EU's economic integration has created the world's second-largest market after the United States.[10] And in recent years, the EU has begun speaking as a single voice on political issues ranging from human rights to support of the Iran nuclear deal.

"People have anticipated the demise of the EU every year since its founding, but at the end of each year, the EU is somehow still around," says Bart Oosterveld, an expert on Europe at the Atlantic Council, a Washington think tank that focuses on trans-Atlantic issues. The federation's economic and political integration, he says, has benefited millions of Europeans.

Europeans' support for the EU is generally strong, according to a September 2018 Eurobarometer poll by the European Parliament: More than two-thirds of respondents said their country has benefited from EU membership.[11]

Populist parties in France, Germany and Italy, inspired by Britain's Brexit vote, were calling for their own referendums on leaving the EU. But after watching how chaotic and costly the U.K.'s exit has become, they have tempered their political objectives. Rather than leave the EU, they now say they want to overhaul it from the inside by running for seats in the European Parliament.

"Brexiteers have done Europe no end of good," said Denis MacShane, a writer and former minister for Europe in the government of former British Prime Minister Tony Blair. "Frexit and Grexit and Italexit and all the rest of it are gone."[12]

Populism, however, remains a potentially serious threat to the EU mission. When Merkel opened Germany's borders to refugees in 2015 and provided billions of euros for their resettlement, her humanitarian gesture and an EU-imposed quota system designed to resettle migrants across member states backfired because of the hostility these policies generated. In the 2017 national elections, the far-right Alternative for Germany party (AfD) became the third-largest party in the Bundestag, Germany's parliament, effectively forming the main opposition.[13]

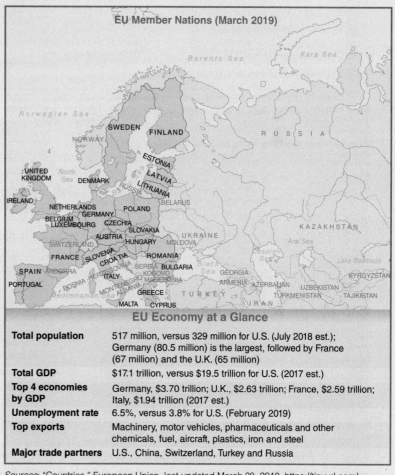

EU Economy Under Pressure

The European Union (EU) remains a global economic powerhouse, with a gross domestic product (GDP) second only to that of the United States. But the EU economy is slowing, and the United Kingdom—with the EU's second-largest economy behind Germany's—could leave the 28-nation federation as early as this spring. Founded in 1993, the EU encompasses a single market with free movement of goods, services and people.

EU Member Nations (March 2019)

EU Economy at a Glance

Total population	517 million, versus 329 million for U.S. (July 2018 est.); Germany (80.5 million) is the largest, followed by France (67 million) and the U.K. (65 million)
Total GDP	$17.1 trillion, versus $19.5 trillion for U.S. (2017 est.)
Top 4 economies by GDP	Germany, $3.70 trillion; U.K., $2.63 trillion; France, $2.59 trillion; Italy, $1.94 trillion (2017 est.)
Unemployment rate	6.5%, versus 3.8% for U.S. (February 2019)
Top exports	Machinery, motor vehicles, pharmaceuticals and other chemicals, fuel, aircraft, plastics, iron and steel
Major trade partners	U.S., China, Switzerland, Turkey and Russia

Sources: "Countries," European Union, last updated March 28, 2019, https://tinyurl.com/h887qhw; "Europe: European Union," *CIA World Factbook*, Central Intelligence Agency, last updated March 15, 2019, https://tinyurl.com/y2efwtxl and https://tinyurl.com/27j377; and "European Union Unemployment Rate," Trading Economics, undated, https://tinyurl.com/y9rtfx8f

In Britain, the refugee issue helped fuel populist demands for the Brexit referendum. In France, the far-right Nationalist Front of Marine Le Pen called for a similar vote. Meanwhile, southern European countries, some still struggling under the EU's austerity dictates that followed the 2009 debt crisis, saw the EU's refugee resettlement mandate as an added burden.[14] And in central Europe, defiant member states simply refused to take any refugees, says Rachel Ellehuus, the deputy director of the Europe program

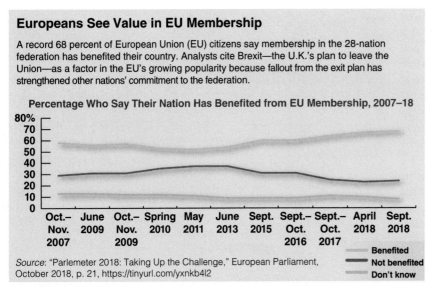

Europeans See Value in EU Membership

A record 68 percent of European Union (EU) citizens say membership in the 28-nation federation has benefited their country. Analysts cite Brexit—the U.K.'s plan to leave the Union—as a factor in the EU's growing popularity because fallout from the exit plan has strengthened other nations' commitment to the federation.

Percentage Who Say Their Nation Has Benefited from EU Membership, 2007–18

Benefited
Not benefited
Don't know

Source: "Parlemeter 2018: Taking Up the Challenge," European Parliament, October 2018, p. 21, https://tinyurl.com/yxnkb4l2

With Merkel, May and Macron all preoccupied with their domestic political challenges, Europe's three major leaders no longer are focused on an EU agenda in any meaningful, consistent way, says Ellehuus, a former principal director for European policy at the Pentagon.

"The people who are normally the engines of Europe are not there to drive it," she says. As a result, she says, "the EU is in a state of flux."

Amid such challenges, here are some of the key questions that policymakers, political analysts and others are asking about the European Union:

at the Center for Strategic and International Studies (CSIS), a centrist Washington think tank.

Macron's victory over Le Pen in France's 2017 presidential election brought temporary relief to European allies who had feared another populist upheaval following Brexit, says Quentin Lopinot, a senior French Foreign Ministry official. He notes that Macron, a European integrationist, won Merkel's support for his proposal to create a European army and began talks with her on additional steps toward integration.

But today, Macron is fighting for his political life, and Le Pen is urging the yellow vests to support National Front candidates for the European Parliament elections. The new movement's calls for Macron's resignation, along with direct democracy and greater national sovereignty, echo many of Le Pen's demands.[15]

Meanwhile, political experts say Russia is trying to weaken the EU by supporting the Continent's nationalist-populists. Over the past decade, they note, Russia has provided populist parties with financial, political and propaganda support as part of its long-standing effort to exploit Europe's divisions and undercut its liberal institutions. "They're very good at figuring out the vulnerabilities in these countries," says Lopinot.

Is the EU in danger of unraveling?

As the U.K. prepares to leave the EU and member countries gear up for European parliamentary elections, bitter differences over immigration, budgets and democratic values have raised the specter of a vote that could produce a paralyzed Parliament, possibly leading to the EU's eventual collapse.

Unless Britain's Parliament can agree on a plan for a smooth exit, the country is in danger of crashing out of the EU under a "hard Brexit" that some analysts have called the geopolitical equivalent of a major amputation without anesthesia. But hard or soft, they say, the result will be an EU that is weaker economically because of the trade barriers that will go up between Britain and the Continent, disrupting labor flows, supply chains and financial services.

In a December 2017 study, a group of Dutch and British economists determined that Brexit's economic impact would fall heaviest on nations geographically closest to Britain—Ireland, the Netherlands and Belgium—as well as those with the highest volumes of trade with Britain, such as France, Germany and Sweden. The study said these countries faced losses ranging from 5 percent to 10 percent of their GDP from Britain's exit from the EU. The remaining EU member states faced 1 percent to 4 percent losses to their GDPs.[16]

"There will be a shock," says William Reinsch, a CSIS expert on the European economy. "It will cost a lot of money" for businesses on both sides of the English Channel to adapt to the new rules governing trade, customs and border inspections, "and the new equilibrium will be far less efficient than the old equilibrium."

The parliamentary elections also pose a major challenge. The EU Parliament, once a mere consultative body, has matured into a formidable check on the European Commission, the executive arm of the EU, and the national governments of member states on issues ranging from trade and environmental standards to the democratic rule of law. Until now, older lawmakers from centrist parties who favor European economic and political integration have dominated it.

This year's new class of legislators, however, is likely to be younger and contain many members from populist parties that are hostile to the EU and want their nations to claw back sovereignty from Brussels, particularly on immigration, fiscal policy and judicial affairs, analysts say.

Many will come from populist movements that have sprung up in nearly every EU member state, mostly since the 2009 debt crisis. Their political targets: Middle Eastern and African migrants; the liberal, cosmopolitan elite; and EU bureaucrats, whom the populists deeply resent over the immigration mandates and other requirements they have imposed, such as legalizing gay marriage, implementing smoking bans and passing strict limits on budget deficits.

"The other parties—the Social Democrats, the Christian Democrats, the Left and the Greens—they don't talk about these issues," said Hugh Bronson, an Alternative for Germany politician. "There has never been a discussion about security. There was never a big discussion in Parliament [over such questions as,] Shall we open the borders? Can we do this? . . . Now a party like the AfD comes along and says, 'OK, now we are going to address this.'"[17]

Populist parties are strongest in Hungary, Italy and Sweden, where they serve in the national governments.

A girl runs near a refugee camp on Lesbos, a Greek island in the Mediterranean Sea, in August 2018. An influx of refugees and migrants from the Middle East and Africa beginning in 2014 has fueled a rise in anti-immigrant sentiment and boosted populist movements across Europe.

ARIS MESSINIS/AFP/Getty Images

Populist parties also are a growing presence in Austria, Denmark, Finland, Spain and Slovakia. In France and Germany, these parties form the principal opposition.

According to a January study by the *Politico Europe* news organization, euroskeptics—those who are critical of the EU—from nearly a half dozen far-right and far-left parties are expected to win more than a third of the European Parliament's 705 seats.[18] That is enough to block policy initiatives on financial matters, social welfare and migration, effectively halting European integration, says Daalder, now president of the Chicago Council on Global Affairs, a think tank that focuses on international issues.

"If the Parliament can't get anything done, that will have a major impact on the ability of the European Union to function," Daalder says. "Ultimately, as countries increasingly focus on their own narrow national interests and they become much more resistant to share sovereignty and make compromises, there would be [a political] collapse."

O'Sullivan, the outgoing EU ambassador to the United States, cautions against dire scenarios. "Support for the European Union across all our member states is at an all-time high in terms of public opinion," he says. "So there are conflicting trends across the body politic."

Sixty-one percent of European Union citizens said EU membership is "a good thing," according to the May 2018

Eurobarometer poll, an increase of 4 percentage points from 2017. But the 2018 poll also showed that half of EU citizens believe things "are going in the wrong direction," an 8 percentage-point increase over poll results six months earlier.[19]

Despite such stresses, Daalder reckons Europe's center will hold. A major reason, he says, is Trump's antipathy toward the EU, which is making many Europeans appreciate the Union's value.

"There's a real understanding that maintaining the European Union is vitally important because the member states can't necessarily count on the United States for their security," Daalder says. "And if the EU wants to compete economically in a world with China and the United States as competitors, they've got to remain united; otherwise, they'll be eaten up. So the strategic rationale for the Union is only becoming stronger."

Other political experts warn that populism's allure should not be underestimated. Pointing to Italy, the Council on Foreign Relations' Kupchan calls its election of a populist government last year "as concerning as any development" on the Continent.

"Italy is a founding member of the EU. It's a large economy, and yet the center has not held there," he says. "If it can happen in Italy, it can probably happen anywhere."

Can the crucial Franco–German alliance survive?

On Jan. 22, 2019, French President Macron and German Chancellor Merkel met in the cavernous 14th-century town hall in the German city of Aachen to sign the Franco–German Treaty of Cooperation and Integration.[20]

The ceremony was laden with historical significance. Aachen was the home of Charlemagne, the Frankish king who united much of Western Europe during the early Middle Ages. The signing also echoed a foundational event 56 years earlier, when French President Charles de Gaulle and West German Chancellor Konrad Adenauer signed the first Franco–German friendship pact in Paris after centuries of enmity.[21]

The earlier pact, known as the Élysée Treaty, institutionalized the post-World War II Franco–German partnership, placing it at the center of efforts to integrate Europe economically and politically ever since. But now, a half century later, with the U.K. preparing to leave the EU and populism and nationalism threatening to weaken it, Merkel and Macron felt the need to reassure other integrationists that France and Germany would continue to guide the European project.

"We reaffirm that we want to tackle the great challenges of our time hand-in-hand," Merkel said after signing the document, which pledges Franco–German cooperation on European political and economic issues, defense projects and common foreign and security policies.[22]

Political experts say the treaty builds on a foundation of close Franco–German cooperation during some of the EU's most challenging moments. They point out that during the debt crisis, senior aides to Merkel and then-French President Nicolas Sarkozy conferred daily as they successfully created the European Stability Mechanism, a bailout fund for struggling economies in the eurozone.

And when British officials tried to divide European countries as they negotiated the United Kingdom's exit from the EU, France and Germany led the resistance to those attempts, says the Atlantic Council's Oosterveld. "The fact that Europe maintained a unified front in those negotiations couldn't have happened without close coordination between the French and the Germans," he says.

Oosterveld says the Franco–German partnership remains strong. "I don't currently see anyone in political circles in either France or Germany who would actively work to loosen that alliance," he says.

French President Emmanuel Macron (left) and German Chancellor Angela Merkel sign a treaty of friendship in Aachen, Germany, on Jan. 22, 2019. With the EU facing numerous challenges, the leaders of the federation's two most powerful member nations reaffirmed their support for the Union.

Sascha Schuermann/Getty Images

But other political experts say the Aachen treaty papers over deep differences between the two countries that threaten to weaken their alliance.

Since entering office in 2017, Macron has pushed for greater European economic integration by proposing a common budget for the eurozone. He also proposed a banking union and a large pool of funds for bailouts in the event of another debt crisis. But Merkel has refused to go along.

"Merkel and Macron fundamentally disagree about what the next big steps are in terms of European economic integration," says Daalder of the Chicago Council on Global Affairs. "Macron argues that if you have a single monetary policy—the euro—you need to have a single fiscal policy, which makes perfect sense. But Merkel, as the leader of Europe's strongest economy, wants to maintain German control over [her nation's] fiscal policy and not surrender it to European control. Germany's economic hegemony is simply not something she's willing to give up in order to advance European integration."

Merkel also has resisted Macron's pleas to boost German spending, which economists say would stimulate more demand across the EU. Now Italy has fallen into recession, Germany is close to it, and the rest of Europe is facing a cyclical downturn with growth in China slowing, says Reinsch, CSIS's European economy expert.

Most recently, Macron and Merkel have been locked in a dispute over European arms exports to Saudi Arabia. Germany's arms embargo on Saudi Arabia over last October's killing of Saudi journalist Jamal Khashoggi may jeopardize a joint Franco–German program to develop a fighter jet, as well as a large Eurofighter warplane order from Riyadh that includes parts made in Germany. France has imposed no such embargo, and Macron has slammed the German sanctions as "pure demagoguery."[23]

"As long as we don't have unified European rules for arms exports, we will always have this problem," said Tim Stuchtey, executive director of the Brandenburg Institute

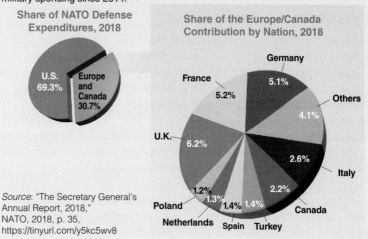

U.S. Pays Bulk of NATO Bill

The United States supplied 69 percent of NATO's defense budget in 2018, more than double the share that Canada and the military alliance's 27 European members collectively provided. Most nations have been slowly increasing their military spending since 2014.

Share of NATO Defense Expenditures, 2018

- U.S. 69.3%
- Europe and Canada 30.7%

Share of the Europe/Canada Contribution by Nation, 2018

- Germany 5.1%
- France 5.2%
- Others 4.1%
- U.K. 6.2%
- Italy 2.6%
- Canada 2.2%
- Turkey 1.4%
- Spain 1.4%
- Netherlands 1.3%
- Poland 1.2%

Source: "The Secretary General's Annual Report, 2018," NATO, 2018, p. 35, https://tinyurl.com/y5kc5wv8

for Society and Security, a think tank in Potsdam, Germany, that focuses on European security issues. "It will be difficult to square French and British attitudes about arms exports with German moral imperatives."[24]

Perhaps the most debilitating threat to the Franco–German partnership, experts say, is Merkel and Macron's political difficulties at home, which have limited their ability to support each other's initiatives or compromise on their differences. In the face of anti-immigrant sentiment in France, Macron has done nothing to advance Merkel's efforts to formulate an EU-wide immigration policy. And in an attempt to appease the yellow vest protesters, Macron lifted his fuel tax, which would have added the equivalent of 29 cents to the $10.13 per gallon the French pay for gasoline or diesel—half of which already goes to taxes. Macron's capitulation to the protesters damaged his credibility with the fiscally conservative Merkel.[25]

But the Atlantic Council's Oosterveld says that the yellow vests have been losing support in France lately, improving Macron's chances for survival, while Merkel's likely successor, CDU leader Annegret Kramp-Karrenbauer, is a strong advocate of Franco–German cooperation. Still, he cautions against any assumptions that the Aachen treaty signals a reinvigoration of the alliance.

"You can argue that in France and Germany, the center is holding for now," Oosterveld says. "But these days, you have to watch and worry. It's not a very reassuring situation."

Is a European army a realistic prospect?

In November 2018, French President Macron jolted the trans-Atlantic alliance by calling for the mobilization of a "true European army." Speaking in advance of ceremonies marking the end of World War I, he said the time had come for Europe to defend itself without depending on the United States. A week later, German Chancellor Merkel echoed Macron's call.[26]

Political analysts say Macron and Merkel's support for a collective European force is a direct result of their doubts about President Trump's willingness to defend the Continent against Russia. Trump first shook European confidence in long-standing U.S. security guarantees during his presidential campaign by calling NATO "obsolete" and by refusing to endorse its charter's mutual defense commitment when he attended his first NATO summit as president in May 2017. A month later, he reversed himself on the defense commitment, but his announcement in February that the United States would withdraw from a Cold War-era nuclear arms treaty with Russia has added fresh urgency for the call to create a European force.[27]

Under that treaty, Russia and the United States eliminated their medium- and short-range ballistic missiles, which had primarily targeted each side's European allies. Without the treaty, Europe will once again find itself within range of these missiles.

"When I see President Trump announcing that he's quitting a major disarmament treaty, who is the main victim? Europe and its security," Macron said. Because of Trump's policies, he said, Europe needs to defend itself.

But defense experts say, at best, a European force is a long-term prospect. Most European nations, they say, are spending a paltry amount on defense. European members of NATO pledged to devote 2 percent of GDP to military spending by 2024, but only six nations—Estonia, Greece, Latvia, Lithuania, Poland and the United Kingdom—have met that target, according to a NATO report published in March.[28]

One of the smallest defense spenders is Germany, whose military has become a shell since the end of the Cold War in 1991. The German Defense Ministry acknowledged late last year that the majority of the military's newly acquired weapons systems—tanks, fighter jets, helicopters, transport planes and warships—are not operational.[29]

The German government is likely to break Merkel's pledge to increase military spending. Under a new budget plan, defense spending, now at 1.2 percent of GDP, would rise to 1.37 percent in 2020, but then gradually decrease to 1.25 percent by 2023.[30]

Moreover, Paris and Berlin disagree over the shape and mission of a European army and whether it should compete with or complement NATO, security experts say. Merkel views a continental army as a way to improve Germany's defense capabilities, raise the level of professionalism in its armed forces and strengthen its defense industries. Significantly, says the Council on Foreign Relations' Kupchan, Merkel has scaled back her views regarding the independence of such a force and now regards it as a complement to NATO.

By contrast, says the Chicago Council on Global Affairs' Daalder, Macron views the army as a new reserve of soldiers that France can call upon to help protect its interests in places such as North Africa.

"Macron wants a coalition of capable and willing nations to provide troops and equipment to help out in Mali," Daalder says, referring to the former French colony in North Africa where French and European troops are backing the government's fight against Islamist militants. "So it's two very different views."

Eastern and central European capitals, meanwhile, worry that a European force would alienate the United States, whose military is still seen as the only credible guarantor of their survival against a Russian attack.[31]

"We believe that the United States is indispensable in European security," said Bartosz Cichocki, Poland's deputy foreign minister for security affairs.[32]

With Russia on their borders, NATO countries in Eastern and central Europe worry Trump could use a European army as a pretext to end U.S. participation in the rotation of NATO forces across the region. Poland has even told the Pentagon it is ready to spend $2 billion to build a U.S. military base on its soil and call it Fort Trump if the president agrees to permanently station a brigade-size—1,500 to 3,200 troops—contingent of American soldiers there.[33]

Because of all these political and economic obstacles, some defense experts doubt a European army will happen.

But German Defense Minister Ursula von der Leyen maintains that "Europe's army is already taking shape" with the launch of several defense cooperation initiatives. One is the $15 billion European Defense Fund, which aims to boost Europe's defense industries so they can better compete with U.S. arms makers. Another is the Permanent Structured Cooperation initiative, or PESCO, a collection of some three dozen defense projects that is working to standardize the weapons and equipment used by different European armies. A third is the European Intervention Initiative, which envisions an EU rapid deployment force.[34]

Supporters of a European army reject the argument that it would undermine the Trump administration's support for NATO. "This is just a red herring," says Kupchan, who points out the Pentagon quietly backs the idea. "The more capable Europe is," he says, "the more the United States will value the partnership because they will bring more to the table."

Most importantly, say other advocates, such a force would go a long way toward bolstering the EU's self-confidence in its defense capabilities.

"We Europeans have talked ourselves into believing that we cannot achieve a degree of strategic autonomy," says Bastian Giegerich, director of defense analysis at London's International Institute of Strategic Studies. "That's wrong. Yes, it would take a lot of money; yes, it would take a lot of time. But collectively, there's enough potential, and there's enough political will, to actually try and achieve this."

With initiatives such as the European Defense Fund, "we've done more in the past three years to strengthen our security and defense capabilities than we've probably done in the previous 30 years," says O'Sullivan, the outgoing EU ambassador to the United States.

BACKGROUND
A United States of Europe

After World War II, fears that a rebuilt Germany or renewed European rivalries might lead to new wars prompted Europeans to find ways to keep the peace.

Some historians credit former British Prime Minister Winston Churchill with providing the solution in a speech he delivered in 1946.

"We must build a kind of United States of Europe," Churchill said, arguing that a democratic federal union of European nations would bind Germany and other countries to its institutions.[35]

Belgium, France, Germany, Holland, Italy and Luxembourg took the first step toward union when they created the European Coal and Steel Community, a free trade zone for those key industrial resources. The idea behind its formation was to rebuild Europe's heavy industry and to control Germany, which was eager to restore its manufacturing base.[36]

Britain was invited to join, but the Labour government decided against membership out of a desire to maintain economic independence.[37]

To manage the new industrial community, the founding treaty created a governing body that included an executive authority with a common assembly to formulate policy, a legislative council of ministers and a court of justice to interpret the treaty and resolve disputes. These would grow into the EU's key governing bodies.[38]

The six states making up the industrial community hit their first bump in the mid-1950s, when they proposed expanding their union to include a European

Allied bombing during World War II left Dresden, Germany, in ruins. Efforts to ensure a peaceful—and unified—Western Europe eventually led to the creation of the European Union in 1993.

ullstein bild/ullstein bild via Getty Images

defense community. The proposal envisioned a joint European army overseen by new supranational defense minister. But in 1954, France rejected the initiative, and it was scrapped.[39]

In 1957 the same six nations signed two treaties in Rome that bound them closer together. One accord established the European Atomic Energy Community, which facilitated cooperation on research and development of nuclear energy. The second created the European Economic Community (EEC), which established a common market that required the six nations to overhaul their respective trade laws.[40]

The changes included the abolition of all internal tariffs to allow the free movement of goods, services, capital and labor. In addition, the treaty required the six governments to eliminate protectionist regulations that favored domestic industries and to fall in line behind a common international trade policy.[41]

Meanwhile, the rivalry between France and the United States complicated membership. The U.K., which saw its economic growth lag the EEC's, reconsidered its earlier decision to remain outside the EEC and asked to join in 1963. But French President de Gaulle torpedoed its bid, concerned Britain would act as a proxy for the United States.[42]

Membership in the EEC expanded in the 1970s and 1980s. Replacing de Gaulle in 1969, Georges Pompidou reversed the veto on Britain, which was admitted in 1973, as were Denmark and Ireland. Greece joined in 1981, followed by Spain and Portugal in 1986.[43]

EU's Debut

On Feb. 7, 1992, the leaders of EEC member countries gathered in the Dutch city of Maastricht to sign the treaty that officially created the European Union. The treaty then went to each member state for ratification. It met with resistance in Britain, Denmark and France, where voters feared their countries would lose control over their affairs. An amended version won approval from all member states and went into effect in November 1993.[44]

Under the Maastricht Treaty, the EU consisted of three main elements. The first gave the European Community broad powers as the central component of the new European Union. The treaty also established common EU citizenship, which gave a citizen of one EU country the right to vote in the elections in another EU nation.

The treaty paved the way for replacing national currencies with a euro currency and created new monetary institutions, including the European Central Bank. The accord laid out the conditions member countries had to meet to join the monetary union. These included annual budget deficits below 3 percent of GDP, low inflation and stable exchange rates.[45]

The second element required EU members to implement a common foreign policy and, where possible, a common defense policy. Any joint military action required unanimity. The third element mandated enhanced cooperation in domestic and judicial affairs, including immigration, asylum and residency policies.[46]

In 1995, the EU expanded to include Austria, Finland and Sweden, leaving Iceland, Norway and Switzerland as the only major Western European nations outside the bloc.

In 1999, 11 countries—Austria, Belgium, Finland, France, Germany, Ireland, Italy, Luxembourg, the Netherlands, Portugal and Spain—adopted the euro, handing over control of their exchange rates to the European Union. Greece, which initially failed to qualify, was admitted in 2001. During that period, internal borders between EU member states came down.[47]

Limited Membership

With the Cold War's end, many countries in central and Eastern Europe, along with Turkey and Cyprus, asked to join the EU. But because of their underdeveloped economies, these countries did not quality for full membership. So the EU came up with a limited membership category, which allowed these countries to join some of the EU's integrated areas, such as the free trade zone, but restricted their membership in others, such as the eurozone.[48]

Some Western European members feared that opening the door even partially to these countries would further dilute consensus on issues ranging from foreign policy and security to rule of law and cultural issues. This was particularly the case with Turkey, which had strained relations with EU member Greece and a poor human rights record.

In addition to the controversy over a multitiered membership system, the EU faced other unresolved issues. These

CHRONOLOGY

1940s *The vision of a united Europe is born.*

1945 World War II ends, leaving Europe in ruins.

1946 Former British Prime Minister Winston Churchill calls for a "United States of Europe" to avoid another continental war.

1948 Belgium, Luxembourg and the Netherlands form the Benelux customs union, a precursor to pan-European organizations . . . . U.S. undertakes the Marshall Plan to reconstruct Western Europe.

1949 NATO is formed, creating a U.S.-led defense alliance in Western Europe.

1950s-1960s *Europe takes halting steps toward union.*

1951 Benelux countries, plus Germany, France and Italy, form the European Coal and Steel Community, a free trade zone for those key resources.

1954 France rejects a proposal to form a European Defense Community.

1957-58 Treaties of Rome create the European Economic Community (EEC), a common market that requires member nations to overhaul their trade laws, and the European Atomic Energy Community to facilitate the development of nuclear energy.

1961 France rejects Britain's bid to join the EEC, because of the U.K.'s close ties to the United States; France rejects a second British bid in 1967.

1968 The EEC establishes a full customs union.

1970s-1980s *More countries join the European Economic Community.*

1973 France relents and allows Britain, along with Denmark and Ireland, to join the EEC.

1979 First direct elections to European Parliament are held. . . . European Monetary System is created, linking EEC members' currencies.

1981 Greece joins the EEC; Portugal and Spain follow five years later.

1990s-2007 *The European Union (EU) replaces the EEC.*

1992 Maastricht Treaty creates the EU and takes effect a year later after the 13 member nations approve an amended treaty.

1995 Austria, Finland and Sweden join the EU.

1999–2002 A common euro currency is introduced in 11 countries, creating a eurozone. . . . Convention on the Future of Europe convenes to draft an EU constitution.

2004 Draft constitution is signed. . . . Cyprus, Malta and eight Eastern European nations, including Hungary and Poland, join the EU.

2005 France and the Netherlands reject draft constitution.

2007 Treaty of Lisbon is signed, modifying the constitution. It takes effect in 2009 after ratification by all EU members. . . . Bulgaria and Romania join the EU.

2009-Present *Debt crisis and populism threaten EU.*

2009-12 A debt crisis begins in Greece and spreads to Italy and other European nations, threatening the euro's survival. The crisis leads to EU bailouts and severe austerity measures for Greece, Spain, Portugal, Cyprus and Ireland; populist movements opposing the EU grow in response.

2013 Croatia joins the EU, bringing membership to 28 countries.

2014-16 Large numbers of Middle Eastern and African refugees arrive on the Continent, intensifying the populist backlash against the EU.

2016 British voters, citing a need to control their borders and economy, vote to leave the EU.

2017 Pro-EU politician Emmanuel Macron is elected French president. . . . Far-right Alternative for Germany party becomes the third-largest party in Germany's parliament.

2018 German Chancellor Angela Merkel, considered the de facto EU leader, announces she will retire when her current term ends in 2021. . . . Number of migrants illegally entering Europe falls to 150,000, down from 1.5 million in 2015.

2019 EU agrees to a Brexit delay (March). . . . European Parliament is scheduled to hold elections, in which populists are predicted to make substantial gains (May).

EU Seeks to Restrict Flow of African Migrants

Critics say the policies are fueling a humanitarian crisis in Libya.

For the past several years, the Libyan coast guard has been operating a fleet of swift patrol boats, courtesy of the European Union (EU) and Italy, to intercept African migrants and refugees headed for the Italian coast. Since the operation began in 2017, the Italian-trained Libyans have apprehended thousands at sea and sent them to detention centers in Libya.[1]

The EU also is providing hundreds of millions of euros to Niger and Sudan to intercept migrants and asylum-seekers as smugglers guide them across the Sahara to the Libyan coast. Once in custody, the Africans are then taken to one of a half-dozen EU-funded transit centers in Niger, where those seeking European asylum remain until their applications are processed. The others are returned to their home countries, says Kathleen Newland, a migration expert at the Migration Policy Institute, a Washington think tank.

The Libyan patrol boats, the Niger transit centers and the partnerships with African countries are some of the measures that make up the European Agenda on Migration, the EU's official policy to control the flow of migrants into the Continent.

A principal aim of the EU is "to push the [migration] crisis as far away from its borders as possible," said the Center for Strategic and International Studies (CSIS), a centrist Washington think tank, in a report on the crisis.[2]

EU officials consider the strategy largely a success. The number of illegal arrivals in Europe dropped to 150,000 in 2018, according to a March EU report—the fewest since 2015, when 1.5 million people fleeing war-ravaged Syria and other Middle Eastern countries came ashore in the world's worst refugee crisis since World War II.[3]

But human rights groups say the EU is complicit in the tragedy unfolding at Libya's government detention centers. Migrants intercepted at sea are held against their will under horrific conditions, according to a January report by Human Rights Watch. The advocacy group said that as many as 10,000 detainees suffer from "severe overcrowding, unsanitary conditions, malnutrition and lack of adequate health care." In addition, the report said, the detainees, including children, are regularly subjected to beatings, rape, extortion and forced labor.[4]

The report also said the EU has done little to pressure Libya to improve detainees' treatment.

"Fig-leaf efforts to improve conditions do not absolve the EU of responsibility for enabling the barbaric detention system in the first place," said Judith Sunderland, associate director of Human Rights Watch's Europe and Central Asia division.[5]

The EU's March report acknowledged "appalling conditions" in the detention centers, but said the EU has joined a task force with United Nations and African Union officials to help the detainees. So far, the EU said,

Migrants wait inside the Ganzour shelter in Libya on Sept. 5, 2018. With support from the EU, the Libyan coast guard has intercepted refugees and migrants crossing the Mediterranean and placed them in Libyan detention centers. Human rights groups have called conditions in the centers horrific.

MAHMUD TURKIA/AFP/Getty Images

the task force has facilitated the return of 37,000 migrants to their home countries and evacuated another 2,500 of the most vulnerable to the EU-funded transit centers in Niger.[6]

The transit centers provide migrants with food, water and shelter, as well as medical, psychological and social assistance, according to Newland. "Stay [at the transit centers] is voluntary," she says, adding that migrants who choose to go home receive travel documents, transportation and money.

Since 2016, when the EU struck a deal with Turkey that sharply reduced migrant flows from the Middle East, the bulk of Europe-bound migrants and asylum-seekers have come from Africa, primarily Sudan, Nigeria and Eritrea. Until 2017, Libya's loosely controlled Mediterranean coast, teeming with human traffickers, was the principal departure point for Europe.

In response, Italy and the EU teamed up that year with Libya's government to block the migrant trail. Together, Rome and Brussels spent more than 90 million euros (about $101 million) to provide the Libyan coast guard with patrol boats and training. It also provided 230 million euros to Niger, 100 million to Sudan and an unspecified amount to tribes along Libya's southern border, for their help in interdicting migration traffic.[7]

A total of 23,000 migrants and refugees arrived in Italy from Libya in 2018, down from nearly 119,000 in 2017, according to the International Organization for Migration.[8]

The EU's report said the bloc has made far more progress in preventing migrants from reaching Europe through its partnerships with African countries than it has in integrating those who already have landed in Europe.[9]

Rachel Ellehuus, deputy director of the Europe program at CSIS, says the EU's 28 member states have been unable to agree on a one-size-fits-all immigration policy.

"The policies, in terms of who you accept, how they're processed, that's all still happening at a national level," Ellehuus says.

Germany, France and the Scandinavian countries are Europe's leaders in granting asylum to refugees whose claims of fleeing political persecution have been vetted, according to Ellehuus. They also provide skilled migrants with work permits but deport those who do not meet their requirements. Those who do not qualify as political refugees are deported as well. By contrast, many people who successfully crossed the Mediterranean still languish in overcrowded camps in Italy and Greece, their bids for asylum or work permits unaddressed. Hungary refuses to take in any migrants.

"There is a fundamental need for an EU-wide approach," the EU report said. "It must be based on strong guarantees that each Member State will deal with the asylum applications it is responsible for."[10]

But in a bid to mollify Italy, which has refused to take in any more refugees rescued at sea, Brussels announced in late March that it will suspend EU maritime patrols that have been conducting such rescue operations and provide only aerial surveillance and continued support for the Libyan coast guard.[11]

— *Jonathan Broder*

[1] Giovanni Legorano and Jared Malsin, "Migration from Libya to Italy, Once Europe's Gateway, Dwindles After Clampdown," *The Wall Street Journal*, March 10, 2019, https://tinyurl.com/y3dzgcg3; Judith Sunderland and Hanan Salah, "No Escape from Hell: EU Policies Contribute to Abuse of Migrants in Libya," Human Rights Watch, Jan. 21, 2019, https://tinyurl.com/yyh4b7pg.

[2] Heather A. Conley and Donatienne Ruy, "Crossing Borders: How the Migration Crisis Transformed Europe's External Policy," Center for Strategic and International Studies, August 2018, p. 11, https://tinyurl.com/y64eywxo.

[3] "Progress Report on the Implementation of the European Agenda on Migration," European Commission, March 6, 2019, https://tinyurl.com/y2pk2yzd.

[4] Sunderland and Salah, *op. cit.*

[5] "Libya: Nightmarish Detention for Migrants, Asylum-Seekers," Human Rights Watch, Jan. 21, 2019, https://tinyurl.com/y5hafoqg.

[6] "Progress Report on the Implementation of the European Agenda on Migration," *op. cit.*

[7] Legorano and Malsin, *op. cit.*

[8] "Mediterranean Migrant Arrivals Reach 113,145 in 2018; Deaths Reach 2,242," International Organization for Migration, Dec. 21, 2018, https://tinyurl.com/y4y43kls.

[9] "Progress Report on the Implementation of the European Agenda on Migration," *op. cit.*

[10] *Ibid.*

[11] "EU recalls ships helping in Mediterranean refugee rescues," Al Jazeera, March 27, 2019, http://tinyurl.com/y423x5ap.

Europe Defies U.S. on Iran Nuclear Deal

Administration threatens "severe consequences" if Continent circumvents sanctions.

Of all the disputes roiling the U.S.-European relationship, no issue has divided the two sides as starkly—or as politically dangerously—as their quarrel over the Iran nuclear deal, experts say.

With the United Kingdom, Germany and France's recent creation of a special financial mechanism to allow continued trade with Iran in defiance of renewed U.S. sanctions, the increasingly acrimonious disagreement risks sparking a diplomatic war between European Union (EU) members and the United States, these experts warn. Such a battle, they say, could result in a serious European challenge to the United States' long-standing dominance over the global banking system and weaken the U.S. position in global affairs.

"The dirty little secret of U.S. financial hegemony is that it rests on far more shallow foundations than its most enthusiastic proponents realize," said Henry Farrell, an associate professor of political science and international relations at George Washington University.[1]

The dispute centers on the 2015 deal in which Iran agreed to scale back its nuclear program in exchange for relief from crippling international economic sanctions. Signatories to the pact were the Obama administration, the other four permanent members of the United Nations Security Council—the United Kingdom, France, Russia and China—Germany and the EU.

As a candidate, President Trump denounced the deal as shortsighted, saying it failed to address Iran's missile program, its support for terrorism and its military activity in the Middle East. Last May, Trump pulled the United States out of the accord and reinstated U.S. sanctions on Tehran.[2]

The administration imposed what are known as secondary sanctions, which stipulate that any company or country that trades with Iran will be barred from doing business with all public or private U.S. entities. Because the U.S. dollar is the preferred international reserve currency and the United States controls the New York-based SWIFT bank wire system used to move dollars around the world, the Treasury Department can easily discover who is doing business with Iran.

Faced with the choice of trading with Iran or losing access to the huge U.S. market, dozens of foreign companies such as France's Total SA oil company already have severed their business ties with Tehran. As a result, Iran's oil exports have been reduced by half, its rial currency has lost more than half its value and its inflation rate has soared to 47.5 percent.[3]

Although the Trump administration has tried to rally international support for its "maximum pressure" campaign against Iran, the International Atomic Energy Agency, U.N. Secretary-General António Guterres and, most recently, U.S. Director of National Intelligence Dan Coats have all said that Iran has upheld its end of the nuclear deal. Therefore, other signatories say they are bound to do so as well.

Like Trump, the Europeans condemn Iran's missile program, assassination plots and what they call its Middle East meddling. But they say it will be much harder to contain Iran if President Hassan Rouhani withdraws from the nuclear accord.

To help keep the accord alive, Britain, Germany and France in January introduced a "special purpose vehicle" to enable Tehran to continue doing business with the rest of

included determining the authorities of large and small member nations and balancing the EU's drive to achieve deeper European integration against the need to maintain the national character of member states. To resolve these issues, EU leaders decided they needed a constitution.[49]

Inspired by the 1787 convention in Philadelphia that wrote the U.S. Constitution, the Convention on the Future of Europe, consisting of 105 members representing national governments and EU bodies, met in Brussels in 2002 to draft the document.

"After 50 years devoted to economic integration culminating in the crowning achievement of the single currency, we are now at the start of a second phase which might also last for 50 years," said former French President Valéry Giscard d'Estaing, the convention chairman.[50]

the world. The new company allows foreign companies and Iran to conduct trade through barter, thereby avoiding use of the dollar and the American banking system. The company is called INSTEX, for Instrument in Support of Trade Exchanges, and has the EU's support.[4]

Vice President Mike Pence has demanded the Europeans abandon the Iran accord. "The time has come for our European partners to withdraw from the disastrous Iran nuclear deal and join with us as we bring the economic and diplomatic pressure," he told the annual Munich conference on international security in February.[5]

The question now, experts say, is what the administration will do to enforce its demand. The threat of a harsh American response to INSTEX came from Treasury Undersecretary Sigal Mandelker. "Those that engage in activities that run afoul of U.S. sanctions risk severe consequences, including losing access to the U.S. financial system and the ability to do business with the United States," she warned in an op-ed.[6]

So far, however, the Europeans have refused to back down. "Iran is one of those issues where there is a strong divergence of views between the European side and the U.S.," says David O'Sullivan, the outgoing EU ambassador to the United States. "We are firmly committed to the [pact], and we will remain committed."

INSTEX's utility in resisting U.S. sanctions policy does not stop with Iran, former officials said. Europe and the United States also have clashed over American sanctions against Russia, whose natural gas supplies have made European leaders less willing to punish Moscow for its bad international behavior.

The Trump administration and Congress have threatened additional sanctions against European nations if they move ahead with the Nord Stream 2 natural gas pipeline, a project that will increase the flow of Russian gas to Europe. Trump worries Europe, especially Germany, is becoming overly reliant on energy supplied by an ideological enemy. He also wants Europe to buy U.S. gas.[7]

If the dispute over U.S.-Russia sanctions comes to a head, European governments and companies will be able to utilize INSTEX, said Jarrett Blanc, a former U.S. State Department official who is now a senior fellow with the Carnegie Endowment for International Peace, a Washington think tank.

"This is the nightmare scenario of the U.S. pushing its financial power so far that our allies and partners feel compelled to build financial alternatives to New York and the dollar, with profound political and economic effects," Blanc said. "In the worst case, the U.S. could lose the capacity to sanction transactions that threaten our interests and the profit centers that accrue from providing global services for simple banking."[8]

— Jonathan Broder

---

[1] Henry Farrell, "Trump may be about to call Europe's bluff on Iran. Europe isn't bluffing," *The Washington Post*, Feb. 25, 2019, https://tinyurl.com/y3jvcc9r.

[2] Mark Landler, "Trump Abandons Nuclear Deal He Long Scorned," *The New York Times*, May 8, 2018, https://tinyurl.com/y7u4oy5s.

[3] Alex Lawler, "Despite sanctions, Iran's oil exports rise in early 2019: sources," Reuters, Feb. 19, 2019, https://tinyurl.com/y2kuz5as; Thomas Erdbrink, "Iran's Economic Crisis Drags Down the Middle Class Almost Overnight," *The New York Times*, Dec. 26, 2018, https://tinyurl.com/ybbjghj4; and "Iran Inflation Rate," Trading Economics, https://tinyurl.com/y9rrrg27.

[4] Ellie Geranmayeh and Esfandyar Batmanghelidj, "Trading with Iran via the special purpose vehicle: How it can work," European Council on Foreign Relations, Feb. 7, 2019, https://tinyurl.com/yyf2fqou.

[5] Linda Givetash, "Pence renews criticism of U.S. allies, urging action on Iran and Venezuela in Munich speech," NBC News, Feb. 16, 2019, https://tinyurl.com/y23kckau.

[6] Sigal Mandelker, "Europe's trust in Iranian promises is severely misplaced," *The Hill*, Feb. 22, 2019, https://tinyurl.com/y636l7mx.

[7] "US threatens sanctions over Russia-Germany gas pipeline," Agence France-Presse, *The Straits Times*, Jan. 13, 2019, https://tinyurl.com/y39gajg8.

[8] Jarrett Blanc, "Trump Risking Financial Disaster for America," *Politico*, Jan. 13, 2019, https://tinyurl.com/y7b3tw87.

In 2003, the convention produced a draft constitution that greatly expanded the EU's powers. One provision gave the EU sole authority to negotiate most treaties on members' behalf. The draft was then sent to member states, all of whom had to agree on ratification for the constitution to take effect.[51]

Meanwhile, the EU the following year admitted eight former communist countries: the Czech Republic, Estonia, Hungary, Latvia, Lithuania, Poland, Slovakia and Slovenia, along with Cyprus and Malta.

In 2005, France and the Netherlands rejected the draft constitution, scuttling its chances. The EU then declared a two-year "period of reflection" before it considered any further constitutional efforts.[52]

In 2007, Bulgaria and Romania came on board, bringing the EU's membership to 27. By this time, the

EU had achieved an unprecedented level of economic and political integration, with its executive, legislative and judicial institutions operating as a democratic, federal system at a supranational level. But the business of the constitution remained unfinished, and in June of that year, EU officials decided to draft a treaty that would replace the failed constitution. By October 2018, they had finished. The treaty was signed in December and later ratified by all member states.[53]

For the first time, the treaty clarified the EU's powers. Under its exclusive authority, the EU alone could legislate; under shared authority, member states could write and adopt legally binding measures if the EU had not done so; and with its supporting authority, the EU could adopt measures that support or complement the policies of member states.[54]

The accord retained some provisions from the draft constitution, including the power to sign international treaties. And for the first time, it created a formal procedure for member states to withdraw from the EU.[55]

2009 Debt Crisis

Amid a global economic downturn, several EU members were unable to repay or refinance their government debts in 2009. Starting in Greece, the debt crisis spread to Portugal, Ireland, Italy and Spain, threatening the survival of the euro and, according to some analysts, the EU itself.

At first, the EU and the International Monetary Fund implemented stopgap measures to prevent the crisis from spreading, but it became clear that a much larger response was needed. In 2010, German Chancellor Merkel and French President Sarkozy, representing the eurozone's two largest economies, put together a bailout package for Greece. Similar rescues for Ireland, Spain, Portugal and Cyprus followed. The terms, however, were harsh, requiring these countries to drastically cut government spending and public services and raise taxes.[56]

The debt crisis also exposed weaknesses in enforcement provisions of the Maastricht Treaty governing the eurozone. In 2012, EU leaders drew up tougher regulations in which member states that failed to limit government deficits to 3 percent of GDP would face automatic penalties.[57]

The measures calmed markets, and the financial threats facing the eurozone receded. But the austerity measures turned many Europeans against the EU and stoked a wave of populism that took a high political toll. By 2012, more than half of the governments in the eurozone's 17 member states either collapsed or changed hands.

In 2013, Croatia joined the EU, becoming its 28th member.

In 2014, the populists who had changed the political complexion of so many eurozone governments turned their sights on the EU itself. In the elections for the European Parliament that year, euroskeptics won up to 25 percent of the chamber's seats. EU leaders were suddenly confronted by a bloc of euroskeptics who were calling for less economic and political integration and a return of sovereignty to member states.[58]

Populist sentiment intensified in 2015 as a result of the migrant crisis, during which hundreds of thousands of refugees and migrants from the Middle East and Africa came ashore on the Greek islands and Italy, all seeking asylum in the EU. Populist leaders such as the Netherlands' Geert Wilders and France's Le Pen stoked anti-immigrant fears, blaming them for terrorist attacks in Brussels and Paris.[59]

Under pressure from the anti-immigrant U.K. Independence Party and euroskeptics in his own Conservative Party, former British Prime Minister David Cameron agreed to hold a referendum on the country's continued membership in the EU. On June 23, 2016, a narrow majority of British voters chose to leave the EU. The following day, Cameron announced he would resign as prime minister, and in July, he was succeeded by his former home secretary, Theresa May.[60]

Even though May had voted to remain in the EU, she said she felt obligated to implement the Brexit vote. She invoked Article 50, the provision in the EU charter under which a member can withdraw from the Union. The declaration began a two-year countdown in which Britain was to depart the EU by March 29, 2019.[61]

During that period, May met with EU leaders in an effort to negotiate what many called a "soft Brexit"—arrangements that would cause the least amount of dislocation for the U.K. The biggest sticking point was how to deal with the border between Northern Ireland, which also would withdraw as part of the U.K., and the Republic of Ireland, which would remain in the EU.

Neither side wanted a return of checkpoints and customs posts at the border for fear they could disrupt the unimpeded flow of people and trade and reignite the sectarian conflict between Protestant and Catholic Irish.

Unable to find a solution, May and the EU agreed to a "backstop"—an agreement that whatever the outcome of trade talks between Britain and the EU, no hard Irish border would result. The agreement also stipulated that the U.K. would remain in the EU customs union and the backstop would continue indefinitely, ending only when Britain and the EU reached a final deal.[62]

British euroskeptics denounced the plan, fearing it could leave Britain tied to the EU indefinitely with no say over its rules and no freedom to negotiate trade deals with other countries. May said it was the best deal she could get.[63]

May had planned to ask Parliament to ratify the deal in December 2018, but facing certain defeat, she canceled the vote and appealed for more support. On Jan. 15, 2019, May did put the plan to a vote and suffered a 202-432 loss, the biggest defeat for a prime minister in modern British history. A revote in March 2019 produced a similar result.[64]

CURRENT SITUATION

Brexit Chaos

The Brexit drama continues to dominate the EU agenda.

On March 21, 2019, EU leaders agreed to extend the deadline for the U.K.'s departure to May 22 of the same year if British Prime Minister May could persuade Parliament to accept her plan for leaving the bloc. But if May could not do so, the EU said it would make the deadline April 12, 2019.[65]

With little prospect for the passage of May's plan, Parliament voted on March 25, 2019, to take control of the Brexit process from the prime minister and explore alternative policy proposals, including one to hold a second Brexit referendum. But after a series of nonbinding "indicative votes," no proposal garnered a majority.[66]

Then, in an extraordinary last-gasp bid to win over opponents of her plan, May offered to resign if Parliament approved it—a move that would have handed the plan's implementation to her successor. But when the plan came up for a vote on March 29, 2019, Parliament decisively rejected it for a third time.

As things now stand, Britain will leave the EU on April 12, 2019, without any agreement. But members of

Parliament believe it is more likely that the government will ask the EU for another deadline extension. May also has hinted she may call for a general election over the issue.[67]

May is now trying a different approach. On April 2, 2019, after a seven-hour Cabinet meeting, the embattled prime minister announced she would seek a May 22, 2019, deadline extension to allow her time to work out a Brexit compromise with the opposition Labour Party. May's hope is that a combination of votes from Labour and less doctrinaire members of her Conservative Party will produce a new Brexit deal that can win parliamentary approval. "It requires national unity to deliver the national interest," May said.[68]

Analysts say her approach is politically risky because Labour supports keeping the U.K. inside the European Union's customs union. That means a deal with Labour likely would leave Britain more closely tied to the EU, angering hard-line conservatives and weakening support for her government within her own party. As of April 3, 2019, no agreement had been reached between May and Labour.

The other ongoing drama is the European Parliament election scheduled for May 2019. As campaigning begins in the EU member states, a major battle is shaping up between the supporters of continued European integration and the euroskeptics.

In France, President Macron is urging voters to reject nationalism and Brexit-style proposals. "The trap is not being part of Europe," he warned.[69]

The French leader proposed a far-reaching agenda for the EU, including a defense treaty that would increase the bloc's military spending. He also said he wants Europe to take the lead in fighting climate change, proposing a target of zero emission of carbon dioxide by 2050.

Macron called for the establishment of an EU agency with responsibility to protect each member state's voting machinery from cyberattack. In a direct swipe at Russia, he urged the EU to ban foreign powers from financing European political parties. And in a nod to rising anti-immigrant sentiment across the Continent, Macron called for stricter border controls.[70]

But Macron's ambitious plans for the EU stand in sharp contrast to his political troubles at home.

As the yellow vest demonstrations continue, Macron scrapped the fuel tax and announced a package of measures worth about 10 billion euros (about $11.4 billion) to boost workers' and retirees' benefits. He also undertook a two-month "grand debate," in which he held town hall meetings across the country to listen to the public's views on France's economic and democratic issues and to explain the rationale for his economic policies.[71]

Polls show Macron's popularity is rising, up to 31 percent from a low of 23 percent in December 2018. But the yellow vests have announced they will field a dozen candidates for the European Parliament elections, opening another populist front against the French leader's pro-European agenda.[72]

Le Pen, leader of France's populist National Rally party, is campaigning for Europe's populist parties in the European Parliament. Confident of a strong showing, she has portrayed these far-right parties as the future of the European Union—one that will include eliminating policies that she says sacrifice national sovereignty, borders and identity for a globalized world that leaves many Europeans behind.

"Today Europe has taken a turn," Le Pen told a political rally in Nanterre, a suburb of Paris, in February 2019. "We can legitimately envision today changing Europe from the inside, modifying the very nature of the European Union, because we consider ourselves powerful enough."[73]

Merkel Speaks Out

In Germany, the customarily reserved Merkel no longer feels compelled to hold back when speaking publicly about another major European concern: President Trump's treatment of the EU as an adversary.

In a speech at the Munich Security Conference in February, Merkel delivered a scathing critique of Trump's policies, accusing him of strengthening Russia and Iran with his plan to withdraw U.S. troops from Syria. She rejected U.S. demands that European allies pull out of the Iran nuclear deal and castigated Trump for withdrawing from the Intermediate-Range Nuclear Forces (INF) Treaty—a move that she said would put European states in the crosshairs of rival U.S. and Russian missile forces.[74]

Merkel also alleged that under Trump, the U.S.-led global order "has collapsed into many tiny parts."[75]

"The relationship between Europe and the United States is as bad as it has ever been," says Daalder, who attended the security conference.

Republican and Democratic lawmakers have supported Trump's decision to withdraw from the nuclear treaty, citing U.S. intelligence reports that Russia's deployment of a medium-range cruise missile has violated the accord. "The Russian Federation brazenly violated the INF treaty and has been unwilling to take the steps necessary to come back into compliance," said Sen. Robert Menendez of New Jersey, ranking Democrat on the Senate Foreign Relations Committee.[76]

The specter of automobile tariffs is the most urgent issue between the EU and the United States, trans-Atlantic analysts say. Many analysts believe Trump will impose tariffs, primarily to punish Germany, the largest European exporter of cars to the United States and one of the principal targets of Trump's anger over the ballooning U.S. trade deficit.

European carmakers exported 1.2 million automobiles worth 37.3 billion euros to the United States in 2018, according to the European Automobile Manufacturers Association. But the trade group added that the European and U.S. auto industries have been integrated for decades. In 2018, the U.S. plants of European carmakers produced 3 million cars, accounting for 27 percent of total U.S. car production. More than half of those cars were exported to third countries, the trade group said, helping to improve the U.S. trade balance, the association said.[77]

"Automobiles are the largest manufactured item that Europe exports," says Reinsch, the European economist at CSIS. The European auto industry "employs thousands of workers. A 25 percent tariff would have an enormous impact on the EU economy."

The Council on Foreign Relations' Kupchan says Germany and France have experienced slower growth in the past few quarters and could join Italy in a recession. With the slowdown in China, analysts say, the EU is likely to fall into a recession by 2020. But a U.S. auto tariff, which would affect France, Sweden, Italy and the U.K. as well as Germany, would push it there that much faster, with unwelcome political repercussions.

"It's a problem, because if you were to point to the two main causes of the populism and discontent, number one would be immigration, and the second would be economic insecurity," Kupchan says. "It's particularly troubling for France, where Macron really needs to deliver and get the economy jump-started."

Is the European Union in danger of unraveling?

YES

Charles A. Kupchan
Senior Fellow, Council on Foreign Relations;
Professor of International Affairs,
Georgetown University

Written for *CQ Researcher*, April 2019

The project of European integration is passing through a perilous moment. Is the European Union (EU) likely to unravel? No. Is the EU at risk of unraveling? Most certainly yes.

A combination of economic insecurity and immigration is fueling a populist revolt against Brussels and political establishments across the EU. Britain is already in the process of quitting the EU—and making a hash of it. Poland, Hungary and Italy all have populist, euroskeptic governments determined to roll back power from Brussels. Although Italy has not (yet) gone down the illiberal path followed by Poland and Hungary, it is in some ways the bigger story. Italy is a founding member of the EU, with one of the Union's largest economies. That the political center has not held in Italy suggests that centrist, pro-EU parties are vulnerable everywhere.

So far, the center has held in most other EU member states. Although they are weakening as populist parties on the left and right gain market share, center-left and center-right parties still call the shots in most countries. The same goes for elections to the European Parliament scheduled for May. Populist parties are poised to make significant gains, but centrist, pro-EU parties are likely to do well enough to form a stable governing coalition.

The key question is what lies ahead. Will disaffection deepen, drawing more voters to the populist extremes, or will the center hold, if not rebound? The most likely scenario is that centrist parties will maintain power in France, Germany and most other member states. But uncertainties abound. Will French President Emmanuel Macron prove adept at jump-starting the country's economy and facing down unemployment? German Chancellor Angela Merkel, who has anchored European politics for more than a decade, is preparing to step aside. What comes next?

Europe's fate rides on its ability to tackle many of the same challenges facing the United States. As automation advances, the Atlantic democracies need to ensure that workers earn a living wage. Immigration continues to roil politics, requiring new policies that enjoy popular support. Addressing inequality and communal fragmentation are key to sustaining pluralism, multiethnic tolerance and social cohesion.

Europeans should not be complacent about the fate of their Union. The EU needs to demonstrate that it can deliver prosperity and security to its citizens. In so doing, it can re-legitimate the project of integration among European publics.

NO

Ivo Daalder
President, Chicago Council on Global Affairs

Written for *CQ Researcher*, April 2019

Following the end of the world's most devastating war, which had left the Continent destroyed and destitute, Europe after 1945 set out to build a new order in which differences between nations would be settled by peaceful means rather than by force of arms.

The result was the European project—ever-growing cooperation among European nations that culminated in the creation of the European Union, uniting 28 diverse countries into a single economic market, governed by executive and legislative bodies that derive their legitimacy from the voters and individual member states. It has proven to be an extraordinary experiment of international cooperation, one that effectively eliminated war from a continent whose history was forged by centuries of armed conflict.

That Union is now under severe stress, mainly as a result of the domestic politics and divisions among its member states, including in each of the six largest members. Growing populist and nationalist movements have ascended to power in Italy and Poland and shown increased strength in France, Germany and Spain. In Britain, such sentiment expressed itself in a nationwide vote in favor of leaving the Union altogether.

To many observers, these political developments bode ill for Europe's future—that after a steady march of ever closer European integration, the Union will now disintegrate into its constituent parts. There are at least three reasons why these fears are misplaced.

First, the international environment is making the case for European cooperation and unity stronger with each passing day. Recognition is growing among Europeans that unity is the best, if not the only, way to thwart the ambitions of a rising China (now seen by the EU not just as a large market but also as a "strategic rival"). And growing fissures across the Atlantic enhance the imperative of European cooperation as continued reliance on the United States becomes increasingly questionable.

Second, the fallout from Brexit, including its inordinate costs for Britain's politics and economy, has markedly increased support for the EU in all European countries (including, paradoxically, in Britain itself). Indeed, two out of three European adults now have a favorable view of the Union.

Finally, for the vast majority of Europeans, the project has worked. European cooperation has brought more prosperity, greater freedom and lasting peace for more than 500 million people. These successes are not something anyone is prepared to give up.

Italy recently defied both the Trump administration and Brussels by signing on to China's Belt and Road Initiative, a trillion-dollar infrastructure program designed to link markets in Europe, Asia and Africa to China. Concerned over Beijing's growing influence, Washington and Brussels have urged EU countries not to join the initiative. But Rome, still deeply in debt from the 2009 debt crisis, found China's offers of investment in Italy's ports, energy and telecommunications sectors too attractive to resist, analysts said.[78]

Meanwhile, Reinsch says, Trump's tariff threats have insulted Germany. "The biggest car exporter from the U.S. right now is BMW, the second is Daimler-Benz. They ship to Europe tens of thousands of cars from their factories in Alabama and South Carolina," he says. "They have more employees in the U.S. than lots of American companies. They're totally exercised about this."

O'Sullivan, the outgoing EU ambassador to the United States, says if Trump moves ahead with automobile tariffs, the EU will retaliate by imposing $24 billion in tariffs on U.S. exports. He calls the administration's national security rationale for U.S. tariffs "patently absurd."

Administration officials defend the use of tariffs, saying they are driven by Trump's belief that EU members routinely take advantage of the United States. "We have wonderful relationships with a lot of people. But nobody treats us much worse than the European Union," Trump said last year, noting on another occasion that the United States had a $15 billion trade deficit with the EU. "The European Union was formed in order to take advantage of us on trade, and that's what they've done."[79]

Security Threats

On the security front, defense experts say the EU faces an ongoing terrorism threat from North Africa and the Middle East, as well as Russian interference in the form of loans and other political assistance to populist and nationalist parties across the Continent. They say Russia routinely wages sophisticated online disinformation campaigns aimed at weakening Western institutions.

Last September, the European Parliament approved a report that said democracy, the rule of law and fundamental rights are under "systematic threat" in Hungary and recommended sanctions against the government of Prime Minister Viktor Orbán. The report cited Orbán's efforts to curtail judicial independence, press freedom and the rights of Roma (also known as Gypsies), Jews, migrants and refugees. The report also accused Orbán of corruption.[80]

Hungary could temporarily lose its EU voting rights, and Orbán's government could be required to repay 43 million euros in what investigators say were misappropriated EU development funds.[81]

Orbán has denounced the threatened EU sanctions, challenging Brussels' authority over EU member states. "European policy is distorted," he said. "The essence of Europe is not in Brussels but in the member states, and if the institutions don't respect the member states, that is depressing."[82]

The report has gone to the EU Council, the body's highest executive authority, for a final ruling.

OUTLOOK
Populism's Impact

Many analysts say populism could decide the EU's future.

Determined to return greater sovereignty to their nations, populists could in May establish a bloc of parties in the European Parliament strong enough to thwart initiatives meant to advance the Continent's integration.

"Just how large will the populist representation be—under 20 percent, more than 30 percent?" asks Daalder, of the Chicago Council on Global Affairs. "The future health of the European project will be judged in some large measure by that."

At the moment, the populist movement appears ascendant, with polls showing EU voters are poised to send more populists from both the left and right than ever before. Europe traditionally has had coalition governments made up of parties from both sides of the political spectrum.

But some experts doubt the populists will be able to influence key policies and appointments, saying right-wing and left-wing populists may be too divided to form a cohesive political force.

Still, "it would be a mistake to assume that means their impact will be minimal," Mujtaba Rahman, director of European analysis for the Eurasia Group, a political and economic consultancy, wrote in a recent commentary for *Politico*'s European edition. "If populists perform well in the May 2019 election, it will be much harder than it was in 2014 [after the last European Parliament elections] for the pro-European establishment to simply dust itself off and carry on."[83]

Since 2014, Hungary, Italy and Poland have elected populist governments, enabling them to make appointments to the European Commission. Coalition governments in several other member states include populist parties, giving them a say in their country's commission choices.

Against that backdrop, Daalder predicts three possible scenarios over the next five years. The first envisions a weak populist showing in the elections and broad agreement among European centrists that the EU must make a major leap forward in economic integration if it is to compete successfully with China and the United States.

"That means getting Germany to agree with Macron's proposals for integrating the eurozone's monetary and fiscal policies, as well as his vision for a European army," Daalder says. "And that's not very likely."

The second scenario is one in which European integration moves forward at different speeds. The wealthier northern countries—Belgium, France, Germany, Luxembourg, the Netherlands and the Scandinavian members—accelerate their economic and security cooperation while the other member states integrate more slowly. Depending on the election outcome, Daalder says, such a compromise is possible.

In the third scenario, he says, the EU stumbles into a dystopian future.

"The EU becomes more contentious, and there are more differences that make policymaking more difficult," he says. "There's a sense of stalemate in the Union, with not much happening and everyone increasingly focusing on their own narrow national interests."

The Council on Foreign Relations' Kupchan warns that if the member states go down that road, the EU's eventual collapse is not out of the question. "Then all bets are off," he says. "Europe returns to its old ways."

NOTES

1. David A. Andelman, "Can Macron survive France's 'yellow vest' revolution?" bdnews24.com, Dec. 8, 2018, https://tinyurl.com/yy4quccs.

2. Griff Witte, "Germany's Angela Merkel says she won't run again for party leader or chancellor," *The Washington Post*, Oct. 29, 2018, https://tinyurl.com/y3awhrf9.

3. Tom McTague, "British politics goes over a cliff," *Politico Europe*, March 28, 2019, https://tinyurl.com/ycn5vmbp.

4. Ryan Heath *et al.*, "Europe in pieces: Where voters disagree," *Politico Europe*, Jan. 23, 2019, https://tinyurl.com/ycwvlf5d.

5. Sylvie Corbet, "France's Macron makes pro-European plea before EU elections," The Associated Press, *Star Tribune*, March 4, 2019, https://tinyurl.com/y2xydj59.

6. David McHugh, "European Central Bank joins global push to help economy," The Associated Press, March 7, 2019, http://tinyurl.com/y6hw5csd.

7. Maegan Vazquez, "Trump calls the EU a 'foe' of the United States," CNN, July 16, 2018, https://tinyurl.com/y6wbp7wq; Ben Jacobs, "Donald Trump: EU was formed 'to beat the US at making money,'" *The Guardian*, July 23, 2016, https://tinyurl.com/jm4qbu3; and "Donald Trump takes swipe at EU as 'vehicle for Germany,'" *Financial Times*, Jan. 15, 2017, https://tinyurl.com/y3laar64.

8. Emily Tamkin, "Outgoing E.U. ambassador on Trump tactics: 'This is not maybe the best way to build an alliance,'" *The Washington Post*, Feb. 22, 2019, https://tinyurl.com/y2dqt5as; "Donald Trump and the New World Order," *Der Spiegel*, Jan. 20, 2017, https://tinyurl.com/hqnnuww.

9. Michael R. Pompeo, "Restoring the Role of the Nation-State in the Liberal International Order," U.S. Department of State, Dec. 4, 2018, https://tinyurl.com/y4hbbh5g.

10. "Gross domestic product at market prices," Eurostat, European Commission, 2019, https://tinyurl.com/yyul2tq4.

11. "Parlemeter 2018: Taking Up the Challenge," European Parliament, October 2018, p. 21, https://tinyurl.com/yxnkb4l2.

12. Steven Erlanger, "The Messier Brexit Gets, the Better Europe Looks," *The New York Times*, Jan. 30, 2019, https://tinyurl.com/yc2zgghg.

13. Matthew Goodwin, David Cutts and Thomas Raines, "What Do Europeans Think of Muslim Immigration?" Chatham House, Feb. 7, 2017, https://tinyurl.com/h7jbpjl; Amanda Taub, "What the Far Right's Rise May Mean for Germany's Future," *The New York Times*, Sept. 26, 2017, https://tinyurl.com/y98vcdfn.

14. Ian Dunt, "It's a Brexit World: Tide of anti-immigrant sentiment sweeps globe," politics.co.uk, Aug. 11, 2016, https://tinyurl.com/y27o6d6n.

15. Geert de Clercq, "France's Le Pen launches EU campaign with appeal to 'yellow vests,'" Reuters, Jan. 13, 2019, https://tinyurl.com/y48kl9ns.

16. Wen Chen *et al.*, "The continental divide? Economic exposure to Brexit in regions and countries on both sides of The Channel," *Regional Science*, March 2018, https://tinyurl.com/y9977uev.

17. "German elections: How right-wing is nationalist AfD?" BBC, Oct. 13, 2017, https://tinyurl.com/yxujlhsu.

18. Heath *et al.*, *op. cit.*

19. "Democracy on the Move: European Elections—One Year To Go," European Parliament, May 2018, https://tinyurl.com/y3gj9nay; "Parlemeter 2017: A Stronger Voice—Citizens' Views on Parliament and the EU," European Parliament, Nov. 10, 2017, https://tinyurl.com/yxenat6v.

20. Guy Chazan, "Macron and Merkel sign Aachen treaty to deepen Franco–German ties," *Financial Times*, Jan. 22, 2019, https://tinyurl.com/yxuf7lfp.

21. *Ibid.*

22. "Merkel and Macron seal friendship pact," *Der Spiegel*, Jan. 22, 2019, https://tinyurl.com/yaax8s9w.

23. "Germany's moral qualms about arms sales infuriate its allies," *The Economist*, March 2, 2019, https://tinyurl.com/y2duezdn.

24. Andrea Shalal and Sabine Siebold, "German halt to Saudi arms sales could put squeeze on Eurofighter," Reuters, Oct. 23, 2018, https://tinyurl.com/y4vdzoj4.

25. Stephen Pope, "Long Live Gilets Jaunes As Macron's Makes A Fuel Tax U-Turn," *Forbes*, Dec. 6, 2018, https://tinyurl.com/y6n2b5nb.

26. Katrin Bennhold and Steven Erlanger, "Merkel Joins Macron in Calling for a European Army 'One Day,'" *The New York Times*, Nov. 13, 2018, https://tinyurl.com/ydhry8eh.

27. Rosie Gray, "Trump Declines to Affirm NATO's Article 5," *The Atlantic*, May 25, 2017, https://tinyurl.com/mmlqrho.

28. "The Secretary General's Annual Report: 2018," NATO, 2018, https://tinyurl.com/y5kc5wv8; Michael-Ross Fiorentino, "NATO Pledge: Which European countries spend over 2% of GDP on defence?" euronews, March 14, 2019, https://tinyurl.com/y6c8gypd.

29. "German Army to be fully equipped for combat . . . in 13 years—Defense Chief," RT, Jan. 5, 2019, https://tinyurl.com/y55fz6ck.

30. Bojan Pancevski and Laurence Norman, "Germany Plans to Renege on Pledge to Raise Military Spending, Defying Trump," *The Wall Street Journal*, March 18, 2019, https://tinyurl.com/yykr5pbo.

31. Yaroslav Trofimov, "Is Europe Ready to Defend Itself?" *The Wall Street Journal*, Jan. 4, 2019, https://tinyurl.com/y7ke5z7q.

32. *Ibid.*

33. Trofimov, *op. cit.*; Rod Powers, "How The U.S. Army Is Organized," The Balance Careers, Dec. 18, 2018, https://tinyurl.com/y6xtm7op.

34. "The Paper Euro-army," *The Economist*, Jan. 31, 2019, https://tinyurl.com/y5r8dyj8.

35. "Winston Churchill, speech delivered at the University of Zurich," Sept. 19, 1946, https://tinyurl.com/y3y355zu.

36. Ina Sokolska, "The First Treaties," Fact Sheets on the European Union, European Parliament, 2019, https://tinyurl.com/y4b2mqjt.

37. Matthew J. Gabel, "European Union," *Encyclopeadia Britannica*, Jan. 24, 2019, https://tinyurl.com/y5yxzakr.

38. Sokolska, *op. cit.*

39. "The failure of the European Defense Community (EDC)," CVCE.eu, 2019, https://tinyurl.com/y42rbulz.

40. Sokolska, *op. cit.*

41. *Ibid.*

42. Gabel, *op. cit.*; "Common Market Founded," History.com, Feb. 9, 2010, https://tinyurl.com/y2amm9mq.

43. "Common Market Founded," *ibid.*

44. Morgane Griveaud, "Why is the Maastricht Treaty considered to be so significant?" E-International Relations Students, May 29, 2011, https://tinyurl.com/yxbksmp7.

45. *Ibid.*

46. *Ibid.*

47. Cynthia Kroet, "A timeline of the eurozone's growth," *Politico Europe*, Dec. 26, 2014, https://tinyurl.com/y5xrc2fk.

48. Gabel, *op. cit.*

49. *Ibid.*

50. "Interview with Valéry Giscard d'Estaing from Le Figaro," CVCE.eu, Jan. 22, 2003, https://tinyurl.com/yyr8m2e7.

51. "EU draft constitution agreed," BBC, June 13, 2003, https://tinyurl.com/y5ff4bq5.

52. "Dutch say 'devastating no' to EU constitution," *The Guardian*, June 2, 2005, https://tinyurl.com/yyvuh2gg.

53. Gabel, *op. cit.*

54. Roberta Panizza, "The Treaty of Lisbon," Fact Sheets on the European Union, European Parliament, October 2018, https://tinyurl.com/yyxoamh7.

55. *Ibid.*

56. Michael Ray, "Euro-zone debt crisis," *Encyclopaedia Britannica,* Sept. 3, 2017, https://tinyurl.com/yyuzsj2f.

57. *Ibid.*

58. Kristin Archick, "The 2014 European Parliament Elections: Outcomes and Implications," CRS Insights, July 24, 2014, https://tinyurl.com/y2lydlnx; Andrew Grice and Nigel Morris, "European election results 2014: Farage and UKIP top poll as Europe swings to the right," *The Independent*, May 26, 2014, https://tinyurl.com/y4v9qob8.

59. Charlotte McDonald-Gibson, "Europe's Anti-Immigrant Parties Make Hay From Paris Terrorist Attack," *Time*, Jan. 8, 2015, https://tinyurl.com/yyyc3c6e.

60. Paul Dallison, "Theresa May takes over as British prime minister," *Politico Europe*, July 13, 2016, https://tinyurl.com/yxznoaeo.

61. Curt Mills, "Brexit Officially Begins," *U.S. News & World Report*, March 29, 2017, https://tinyurl.com/yyeoa95z.

62. Kevin Doyle and Shona Murray, "Brexit deal reached: No hard border for Ireland as 'sufficient progress' made on talks," *The Independent*, Dec. 8, 2017, https://tinyurl.com/y63tufwu.

63. Ylenia Gostoli, "Brexit: the backstop and why some oppose it," Al Jazeera, Feb. 5, 2019, https://tinyurl.com/yawprelx.

64. Jonathan Broder, "Can Theresa May and Angela Merkel Resist the Forces They Helped Create?" *Newsweek*, Jan. 24, 2019, https://tinyurl.com/ycm9tm2y; "The Brexit Plan Failed Again: What Happened, and What's Next?" *The New York Times*, March 12, 2019, https://tinyurl.com/y25eelaf.

65. Stephen Castle and Steven Erlanger, "E.U. Approves Brexit Extension, but Chaotic Departure Still Looms," *The New York Times*, March 21, 2019, https://tinyurl.com/y2xo869w.

66. Danica Kirka and Jill Lawless, "UK lawmakers prepare to vote on alternatives to Brexit deal," The Associated Press, *The Washington Post*, March 27, 2019, https://tinyurl.com/y6kmovph.

67. Max Colchester and Jason Douglas, "May's Brexit Deal Is Rejected for a Third Time by Lawmakers," *The Wall Street Journal*, March 29, 2019, https://tinyurl.com/y6yua4ak.

68. "Brexit: Theresa May meets Jeremy Corbyn to tackle deadlock," BBC, April 3, 2019, http://tinyurl.com/y2qegkel.

69. Corbet, *op. cit.*

70. *Ibid.*

71. Sophie Law, "Yellow Vest activists set bins ablaze while police pelt mobs with tear gas," *Daily Mail*,

March 2, 2019, https://tinyurl.com/yxbrrfej; James McAuley, "Macron hoped a 'grand debate' would curb the yellow vests. It may or may not have worked," *The Washington Post*, March 17, 2019, http://tinyurl.com/y6exdbcp.

72. "L'Observatoire politique," Les Echos/Radio Classique, March 7, 2019, https://tinyurl.com/yygx6jjk; Nicholas Vinocur, "Why the Yellow Jacket movement is a gift to Macron," *Politico Europe*, Jan. 28, 2019, https://tinyurl.com/y92uo55m; and McAuley, *ibid.*

73. Elaine Ganley, "France's Le Pen Boasts Far-Right Power for EU Elections," *U.S. News & World Report*, Feb. 15, 2019, https://tinyurl.com/y284znpy.

74. Steven Erlanger and Katrin Bennhold, "Rift Between Trump and Europe Is Now Open and Angry," *The New York Times*, Feb. 17, 2019, https://tinyurl.com/yxwno378.

75. Griff Witte and Michael Birnbaum, "Trump foreign policy under attack from all sides at European security conference," *The Washington Post*, Feb. 16, 2019, https://tinyurl.com/y446bc57.

76. "Menendez Statement on Trump Administration's Withdrawal from Nuclear Treaty," Office of Sen. Bob Menendez, Feb. 1, 2019, https://tinyurl.com/yyfbhoyc.

77. "EU-US Automobile Trade: Facts and Figures," European Automobile Manufacturers Association, March 2019, https://tinyurl.com/y43fu4ru.

78. Jason Horowitz, "Defying Allies, Italy Signs On to New Silk Road With China," *The New York Times*, March 23, 2019, https://tinyurl.com/y4pha7jv.

79. Lesley Stahl, "President Trump on Christine Blasey Ford, His Relationships With Vladimir Putin and Kim Jong Un and More," "60 Minutes," Oct. 15, 2018, https://tinyurl.com/y7dddnmw; Gabriela Galindo, "Trump: EU was 'set up' to take advantage of U.S.," *Politico*, June 28, 2018, https://tinyurl.com/y9grdxjv.

80. Keno Verseck, "Hungary's Viktor Orban challenges EU over Article 7 sanctions," Deutsche Welle, Sept. 25, 2018, https://tinyurl.com/y4dk4gcc.

81. Bernd Riegert, "EU wants to hit Viktor Orban where it hurts: the wallet," Deutsche Welle, April 7, 2018, https://tinyurl.com/y2dt7efy.

82. "Hungary PM Orban criticizes EU sanctions threat," *Daily Sabah*, May 19, 2017, https://tinyurl.com/y5la74ld.

83. Mujtaba Rahman, "Populism's rising tide," *Politico Europe*, Jan. 28, 2019, https://tinyurl.com/yaevc8sq.

BIBLIOGRAPHY
Books

Clarke, Harold D., Matthew Goodwin and Paul Whiteley, *Brexit: Why Britain Voted to Leave the European Union*, Cambridge University Press, 2017.
Three political scientists explore the social and political forces that led to the United Kingdom's vote in 2016 to quit the European Union (EU).

Drozdiak, William, *Fractured Continent: Europe's Crises and the Fate of the West*, W.W. Norton & Co., 2017.
A former chief European correspondent for *The Washington Post* examines the political, economic and ethnic fractures that the author says could pull Europe apart.

McCormick, John, *Understanding the European Union: A Concise Introduction*, Red Globe Press, 2017.
An Indiana University political science professor reviews the history and structure of the EU and its current challenges.

Verhofstadt, Guy, *Europe's Last Chance: Why the European States Must Form a More Perfect Union*, Basic Books, 2017.
A former Belgian prime minister argues for an overhaul of the EU to ensure it more closely resembles the federal system in the United States.

Articles

Crawford, Alan, "Trump's Foreign Policy Discord Drives Wedge Between Vital Allies," Bloomberg, Feb. 14, 2019, https://tinyurl.com/y3wtlt8n.

A journalist writes that President Trump's policies on Iran, trade and global security have alienated Washington's European allies.

Erlanger, Steven, "The Messier Brexit Gets, the Better Europe Looks," *The New York Times*, Jan. 30, 2019, https://tinyurl.com/yc2zgghg.
The Times' chief European correspondent reports on how political chaos in Britain over Brexit has dampened enthusiasm among EU skeptics for similar votes in other European countries.

Trofimov, Yaroslav, "Is Europe Ready to Defend Itself?" *The Wall Street Journal*, Jan. 4, 2019, https://tinyurl.com/y7ke5z7q.
A journalist describes the EU's efforts to form a European army and the political divisions that stand in the way.

Reports and Studies

Conley, Heather A., and Donatienne Ruy, "Crossing Borders: How the Migration Crisis Transformed Europe's External Policy," Center for Strategic and International Studies, Oct. 18, 2018, https://tinyurl.com/y4dldp32.
The EU decided in the wake of the 2014-16 refugee crisis to focus on blocking migration routes in Africa and the Middle East to Europe, according to experts at a centrist Washington think tank.

Dennison, Susi, and Pawel Zerka, "The 2019 European Election: How Anti-Europeans Plan to Wreck Europe and What Can Be Done to Stop It," European Council on Foreign Relations, February 2019, https://tinyurl.com/y6hrgsr8.
Researchers at a European think tank present various strategies to blunt the nationalist influence of euroskeptics, critics of the EU who are expected to control more than one-third of the seats in the European Parliament after May elections.

Goodwin, Matthew, David Cutts and Thomas Raines, "What Do Europeans Think of Muslim Immigration?" Chatham House, Feb. 7, 2017, https://tinyurl.com/h7jbpjl.
Three political scientists present research that points to widespread public anxiety over migration to Europe from mainly Muslim countries.

Grevi, Giovanni, "Shaping Power: A Strategic Imperative for Europe," European Policy Center, Feb. 22, 2019, https://tinyurl.com/yxdb9v3e.

A senior fellow at a pro-EU think tank in Brussels analyzes how updating the EU's industrial, social and fiscal policies can strengthen Europe's ability to compete with the United States and China.

Heath, Ryan, *et al.*, "Europe in pieces: Where voters disagree," *Politico Europe*, Jan. 23, 2019, https://tinyurl.com/ycwvlf5d.
Journalists examine the issues dividing Europeans today and assess their impact on this spring's European Parliament elections.

Megerisi, Tarek, "Order From Chaos: Stabilising Libya the Local Way," European Council on Foreign Relations, July 19, 2018, https://tinyurl.com/y3r55l3h.
A visiting fellow at a think tank focusing on European security explores how a partnership between European governments and nongovernmental organizations and local authorities in Libya can restore order to that country and help stem the flow of refugees to Europe.

THE NEXT STEP
Brexit

Chrisafis, Angelique, and Jennifer Rankin, "EU must learn from Brexit and reform, says Emmanuel Macron," *The Guardian*, March 4, 2019, https://tinyurl.com/yydcz6eh.
French President Emmanuel Macron has called for a major overhaul of the European Union (EU) in response to Brexit, proposing protections against internet threats, a higher minimum wage and a new defense treaty, among other things.

McCann, Allison, *et al.*, "Where Europe Would Be Hurt Most by a No-Deal Brexit," *The New York Times*, Feb. 7, 2019, https://tinyurl.com/yd5hshhw.
If the United Kingdom departs from the European Union under a worst case scenario—with no official withdrawal agreement with the EU—Northern Europe's economy would suffer the most because of tariffs, labor shortages and banking complications, according to a *New York Times* analysis.

Meredith, Sam, "'Last chance': EU leaders issue ultimatum to Britain over no-deal Brexit," CNBC, March 22, 2019, https://tinyurl.com/y3th2gc2.

The European Union will grant a two-month Brexit delay if the British Parliament passes the current withdrawal agreement. If lawmakers don't act, the EU will force Britain to leave on April 12 with no deal in place and greater harm to the U.K.

Migration

"Operation Sophia: EU to scale back Mediterranean rescue mission," euronews, March 27, 2019, http://tinyurl.com/y69zy3vd.
The EU plans to end its naval patrols that intercept African migrants who are crossing the Mediterranean Sea to Europe, but it said it will extend its air patrols.

Roth, Clare, "EU Commission strikes back at Hungarian migration campaign 'fiction,'" Reuters, Feb. 28, 2019, https://tinyurl.com/y655rxv7.
The EU accused Hungarian Prime Minister Viktor Orbán of spreading misinformation by claiming that the European Commission and American billionaire George Soros conspired to encourage mass immigration to Europe.

Smith-Spark, Laura, "Illegal migration to EU falls to lowest level in 5 years—but spikes in Spain," CNN, Jan. 5, 2019, https://tinyurl.com/y9xj3p45.
The number of migrants crossing the western Mediterranean Sea from Morocco to Spain jumped in the past two years after Italy cut off access to the central Mediterranean crossing.

Populist Threat

Mason, Josephine, "As worries about populism in Europe rise, investors bet on stock market volatility," Reuters, March 21, 2019, https://tinyurl.com/y4452lhs.
International investors say populists' expected strong showing in the upcoming European Parliament elections could lead to big swings in European stock markets.

Tomek, Radoslav, and Peter Luca, "Populists Slapped as Slovaks Poised to Elect Pro-EU President," Bloomberg, updated March 18, 2019, https://tinyurl.com/y68z6zn2.
Slovakia's presidential runoff election features two candidates who favor European integration, a stark contrast to its populist neighbors.

Wilkes, William, "Europe's Populist Right Threatens to Erode Climate Consensus," Bloomberg, Feb. 25, 2019, https://tinyurl.com/yyxdvw9r.
Several right-wing populist parties that cast doubt on climate change or deny that humans contribute to it could jeopardize the EU's environmental policies, says a Bloomberg reporter.

Tariffs

Byrd, Haley, "Trump eyes auto tariffs in EU standoff," CNN, March 20, 2019, https://tinyurl.com/y4eoprwj.
President Trump has threatened to enact auto tariffs if trade negotiations with the EU do not succeed in opening the European market to U.S. agriculture products.

Pandey, Ashutosh, "Malaysia threatens to raise stakes in EU palm oil spat," Deutsche Welle, March 27, 2019, https://tinyurl.com/yyf57kxy.
A proposed EU free trade pact in Asia is in jeopardy after Malaysia challenged the Union's plan to phase out palm oil, the country's main agricultural export, due to environmental concerns.

Wishart, Ian, and Emma Ross-Thomas, "How a 'Customs Union' Could Define Post-Brexit Trade," *The Washington Post*, March 27, 2019, https://tinyurl.com/y5m9sew3.
The United Kingdom might form a customs union—an agreement allowing the free flow of goods—with other nations to avoid EU tariffs.

For More Information

Atlantic Council, 1030 15th St., N.W., 12th Floor, Washington, DC 20005; 202-778-4952; www.atlanticcouncil .org. Think tank that promotes the trans-Atlantic alliance through policy papers and briefing seminars.

Center for Strategic and International Studies, 1616 Rhode Island Ave., N.W., Washington, DC 20036; 202-887-0200; www.csis.org. Think tank that focuses on defense and security, regional studies and transnational challenges, including those involving the European Union (EU).

Confrontations Europe, 227 Boulevard Saint-Germain, 75007 Paris, France; +33 (0) 1 43 17 32 83; http:// confrontations.org. Think tank that seeks to foster economic growth and influence European policy through papers, seminars and conferences.

European Council on Foreign Relations, 159-165 Great Portland St., London W1W 5PA; +44 (0) 20 7227 6860; https://www.ecfr.eu. Think tank that researches European foreign and security policy.

European Parliament Think Tank, 60 Rue Wiertz / Wiertzstraat 60, B-1047, Brussels, Belgium; +32 (0) 2 28 42111; www.europarl.europa.eu. Research department of the European Parliament that assists members in their parliamentary work.

European Policy Centre, 14-16 Rue du Trône/Troonstraat, B-1000, Brussels, Belgium; +32 (0) 2 231 03 40; www.epc .eu. Think tank that promotes European integration through issue papers, policy briefs and commentaries, as well as the journal *Challenge Europe.*

Migration Policy Institute Europe, 155 Rue de la Loi, 1040 Brussels, Belgium; +32 (0) 2235 2113; www .migrationpolicy.org. Think tank that provides research and policy proposals to European governments and nongovernmental organizations on immigration.

Notre Europe-Institut Delors, 18, Rue de Londres 75009 Paris, France; +33 1 44 58 97 97; http://institutdelors.eu. Think tank that contributes to the debate on the EU through political, economic and social analyses and proposals.

AP Photo/Jim Mone

Michael Petefish stands inside a soybean bin at his farm near Claremont, Minn., in July 2018. When President Trump imposed $250 billion in tariffs on Chinese exports, China responded with its own tariffs. The trade war, which has cooled, has hurt some U.S. farmers. China is the largest buyer of American soybeans.

From *CQ Researcher,*
March 29, 2019

7

U.S. Foreign Policy in Transition

Is the United States relinquishing its global supremacy?

By Bill Wanlund

At an annual security conference of the United States' European allies in February 2019, a gathering that normally celebrates trans-Atlantic unity, German Chancellor Angela Merkel delivered a harsh assessment of U.S. foreign policy.

Merkel criticized the Trump administration's unilateral approach to international affairs, specifically questioning U.S. plans to pull troops out of Syria and Afghanistan and a decision to abandon the 31-year-old intermediate-range nuclear weapons treaty with Russia. Both actions, she said, would endanger Europe while strengthening Moscow's position.

The liberal world order—the U.S.-led system of institutions and alliances created after World War II and credited with establishing postwar global peace and prosperity—"has collapsed into many tiny parts," Merkel said.[1]

Attendees gave the German leader a standing ovation, in contrast to the cool reception that met Vice President Mike Pence hours later when he extended greetings from Trump. In that speech, Pence defended the administration's foreign policy, saying that under President Trump, "America is leading the free world once again." Pence also urged Europeans to "do more" in their own defense and "stop undermining" U.S. sanctions against Iran by joining the U.S.

Global Approval of U.S. Leadership Plunges

After falling to a new low of 30 percent in the first year of Donald Trump's presidency, median global approval of U.S. leadership remained largely unchanged in 2018, according to surveys of adults across more than 130 countries and areas of the world. The 2018 rating was down 17 percentage points from 2016, the final year of Barack Obama's administration, and 3 points less than the previous low of 34 percent in the final year of the George W. Bush presidency.

Median Global Assessment of U.S. Leadership, 2007–18

— Median approval rate
— Median disapproval rate

Source: Julie Ray, "Image of U.S. Leadership Now Poorer Than China's," Gallup, Feb. 28, 2019, http://tinyurl.com/y67ozzpf

withdrawal from a 2015 agreement to halt Iran's development of nuclear weapons.[2]

Trump is changing the U.S. role on the global stage. Unlike his postwar predecessors, who tended to promote U.S.-style democracy and other values overseas through multinational alliances and agreements, Trump prefers fewer international commitments and a foreign policy focused on protecting U.S. jobs and interests.

The president's supporters say America's largesse has reached its limit and that the United States should use its economic and political might to its advantage. Trump's critics say the United States is withdrawing from global leadership, which they argue means a decline of democracy, a return to cutthroat international economic competition and a heightened threat of conflict. The debate has led to a re-evaluation of U.S. priorities and the nation's place in the world.

Trump has vowed to extract the United States from what he views as economically harmful international agreements and limits on U.S. sovereignty. "From this moment on, it's going to be America First," he said in his inaugural address. "We will seek friendship and goodwill with the nations of the world—but it is the right of all nations to put their own interests first."[3]

Henry Nau, a professor of political science and international affairs at George Washington University,

agrees that U.S. foreign policy has needed adjusting. "Trump clearly was elected to pull back our responsibilities around the world," he says. "The country has been in that mood for the last 10 years at least."

A recent survey by the Eurasia Group Foundation, a New York City research organization, supports Nau's view, identifying a "public desire for a more restrained U.S. foreign policy." Only 18 percent of respondents agreed that "promoting and defending democracy around the world" is the best way to help sustain global peace, while 34 percent said the path to peace means focusing on "domestic needs and the health of American democracy."[4]

Trump's worldview appears to coincide with the 34 percent, according to Thomas Shannon, who retired in 2018 as undersecretary of State for political affairs, the State Department's highest position for a career diplomat. "Trump believes we live in a dangerous, complicated world in which America has carried a huge security burden, and a large economic burden in managing the world trading system," says Shannon, now senior international policy adviser for the Washington law firm Arnold & Porter. "He thinks that over time this has disadvantaged the U.S., and that even allies and partners have taken advantage of this relationship for their own benefit."

To correct that perceived imbalance, Trump has, among other things:

- Pulled out of three international agreements signed by President Barack Obama: the Paris climate agreement aimed at limiting planet-warming carbon emissions; the 2015 treaty to limit Iran's nuclear weapons; and the Trans-Pacific Partnership (TPP), a free-trade agreement, which had covered 12 Pacific region nations.
- Questioned how fairly the United States has been treated by international organizations such as the 70-year-old North Atlantic Treaty Organization (NATO) military alliance.

- Initiated a series of trade disputes with China.
- Renegotiated a trade agreement among the United States, Canada and Mexico.
- Aggressively tried to limit U.S. immigration, both legal and illegal.
- Withdrawn from the agreement to ban land-based intermediate-range missiles, originally signed in 1987 by President Ronald Reagan and Soviet leader Mikhail Gorbachev.

Critics of the administration worry about the long-term impact of Trump's embrace of anti-immigrant populist leaders in Eastern Europe and Italy who question the value of the European Union and his praise for autocrats with questionable human rights records—such as Russian President Vladimir Putin and the leaders of Egypt, Brazil, the Philippines and Saudi Arabia.

For instance, shortly after his inauguration President Trump traveled to Saudi Arabia—his first overseas trip as president—and a year later welcomed Saudi Crown Prince Mohammed bin Salman to the White House. In both instances, Trump hailed

U.S. Abandons Key International Agreements

President Trump has begun or concluded withdrawal from five major treaties and agreements, involving climate change, trade and nuclear arms. In addition, Trump, who during his presidential campaign threatened to withdraw from the North American Free Trade Agreement (NAFTA), negotiated a revised version of the pact, now called the U.S.-Mexico-Canada Agreement (USMCA), which awaits congressional approval.

Top International Agreements the U.S. Has Abandoned or Altered, as of 2019

Agreement/ Treaty	Description	Status
Intermediate-Range Nuclear Forces (INF) Treaty	Established 1987; required the U.S. and Soviet Union to destroy all land-based missiles with ranges between 300 and 3,400 miles. U.S. obligations suspended in February, with formal withdrawal in six months. The U.S. and Russia have accused each other of violating the treaty.	Withdrawing
North American Free Trade Agreement (NAFTA)	Established 1994 among the U.S., Canada and Mexico; eliminated tariffs and other restrictions among the three countries. The Trump administration has negotiated a new version, the USMCA, which the White House says provides more advantages for the U.S. workforce and economy.	Renegotiated; awaiting congressional approval
Joint Comprehensive Plan of Action (Iran nuclear deal)	Agreement reached July 2015 among Iran, the U.S., the U.K., France, China, Russia and Germany; limited Iran's nuclear program development and allowed international inspections in exchange for the lifting of economic sanctions. In May 2018 Trump announced that the U.S. was withdrawing from the deal and reinstated U.S. sanctions against Iran.	Withdrawn
Paris Agreement on Climate Change	Adopted December 2015 by 195 countries; set universal goals on limiting climate-warming emissions. Trump said the agreement put the U.S. at a disadvantage. The agreement prevents official withdrawal until 2020.	Withdrawing
Trans-Pacific Partnership (TPP)	Established 2016 by 12 countries bordering the Pacific Ocean; designed to reduce tariffs and foster free trade and economic growth among members. Trump said the agreement is unfair to U.S. workers. The remaining 11 countries have moved forward with the deal, renaming it the Comprehensive and Progressive Agreement for Trans-Pacific Partnership.	Withdrawn

Sources: Zachary B. Wolf and JoElla Carman, "Here are all the treaties and agreements Trump has abandoned," CNN, Feb. 1, 2019, https://tinyurl.com/yau3v64d; "The Intermediate-Range Nuclear Forces (INF) Treaty at a Glance," Arms Control Association, https://tinyurl.com/6oxqkas; "Paris Agreement," European Commission, https://tinyurl.com/zxwwpa2; Colin Dwyer, "The TPP Is Dead. Long Live the Trans-Pacific Trade Deal," NPR, March 8, 2018, https://tinyurl.com/yy23bs6u; "North American Free Trade Agreement (NAFTA)," Office of the U.S. Trade Representative, https://tinyurl.com/yy2grr44; F. Brinley Bruton, "What is the Iran nuclear deal?" NBC News, May 10, 2018, https://tinyurl.com/ya3cshut

the kingdom's help in fighting terrorism and the thousands of American jobs that would be created by Saudi Arabia's large purchases of U.S. military

A U.S. Marine gets ready for a NATO-led training exercise in Norway in November 2018. More than 30 NATO partner countries participated in the joint exercise. President Trump caused a stir last year when he told a NATO summit that the United States was prepared to "go our own way" if other members did not pay more toward the alliance.

equipment, but did not mention the kingdom's poor human rights record.

"Saudi Arabia is a very wealthy nation, and they're going to give the United States some of that wealth, hopefully, in the form of jobs, in the form of the purchase of the finest military equipment anywhere in the world," he told reporters during Salman's White House visit.[5]

Trump's actions and policies could spell the end of the economic and social progress enjoyed by most of the world since 1945, says Robert Kagan, a senior fellow at the centrist Brookings Institution think tank, who has served as a foreign policy adviser in Republican administrations. "I fear we will find ourselves where we were between the world wars, where no one is keeping the order and everything fell apart," says Kagan, author of *The Jungle Grows Back: America and Our Imperiled World.*

Others disagree. "The [U.S.] economy is booming, the military is rapidly recovering from 15 years of over-extension, and the Trump administration is concluding trade deals in record time," wrote Salvatore Babones, an American associate professor of sociology and social policy at the University of Sydney in Australia.[6]

Meanwhile, foreign public approval of the United States has "plummeted" since Trump's election, according to the Pew Research Center's 2018 Global Attitudes Survey. It found "widespread opposition to [Trump's] policies and a widely shared lack of confidence in his

leadership." Seventy percent of respondents in 25 countries said they had "no confidence" in Trump's leadership, compared to 27 percent who said they did.[7]

"People generally aren't interested in seeing the U.S. disengage, or wall itself off from the rest of the world," says Richard Wike, Pew's director of global attitudes research.

James Poulos, executive editor of *The American Mind,* an online publication of the conservative Claremont Institute think tank in Upland, Calif., says a poor global image "is obviously not what you want to achieve in your foreign policy, but you do have to put the prosperity and security of America at the top of your priorities list."

The ranks of professional diplomats have thinned under Trump, who says he prefers to rely on his own instincts and one-on-one rapport rather than experts when dealing with foreign leaders. "I talk to a lot of people . . . but my primary [foreign policy] consultant is myself, and I have a good instinct for this stuff," Trump said during the 2016 campaign.[8]

The State Department lost 60 percent of its career ambassadors during the first 11 months of the Trump administration, and 59 of the nation's 188 ambassadorships remained unfilled as of March, according to the American Foreign Service Association, a professional organization representing diplomats. In comparison, in February 2011, two years into the Obama administration, 14 of 173 ambassadorships were vacant.[9]

"No national security institution can withstand the unprecedented loss of highly skilled senior officers . . . without weakening America's capacity to lead globally," says the association's president, Barbara Stephenson. She blamed Trump's first secretary of State, former ExxonMobil CEO Rex Tillerson, who slashed the department's budget, eliminated many positions and halved promotion rates.[10]

Besides diminishing U.S. influence, the administration has "hollowed out American diplomacy and only deepened the divisions among Americans about our global role" at a time when the international landscape is shifting, wrote former Deputy Secretary of State William J. Burns in his new book, *The Back Channel: A Memoir of American Diplomacy and the Case for its Renewal.*

"The United States is no longer the only big kid on the geopolitical block," Burns, now president of the Carnegie Endowment for International Peace, said on CBS News' "Face the Nation." "It's a moment when diplomacy, when our alliances, our capacity for building coalitions—what sets us apart from lonelier powers like China or Russia—is more important than ever. And my concern is that we are squandering those assets right now."[11]

But Randall Schweller, director of the Program for the Study of Realist Foreign Policy at Ohio State University, said, "Trump is merely shedding shibboleths and seeing international politics for what it is: . . . a highly competitive realm populated by self-interested states concerned with their own security and economic welfare."[12]

Trump's foreign policy, he said, "seeks to promote the interests of the United States above all [and] has given the lie to the notion that many of the institutions of the postwar order actually bind the United States, and he has walked away from them accordingly."[13]

As Trump pursues his "America First" approach to foreign policy and U.S. citizens sort out their views on the direction of that policy, here are some of the questions being asked:

Is the United States relinquishing its global supremacy?

Since the dissolution of the Soviet Union and the end of the Cold War in 1991, the United States has enjoyed pre-eminence as the world's superpower—"the indispensable nation," as former Secretary of State Madeleine Albright described it.[14]

But some historians and foreign policy experts say the Trump administration has undercut U.S. global supremacy by withdrawing from the nation's leadership role in multilateral organizations and agreements, opening a power vacuum that authoritarian countries such as China and Russia will fill.

The president has been "demolishing," one by one, "the essential pillars of U.S. global power that have sustained Washington's hegemony for the past 70 years," said Alfred McCoy, a history professor at the University of Wisconsin-Madison and author of *In the Shadows of the American Century:*

The Rise and Decline of U.S. Global Power. Trump has done that, McCoy said, by weakening post-World War II alliances such as NATO and "withdrawing the United States, almost willfully, from its international leadership, most spectacularly with the Paris climate accord but also very importantly with the Trans-Pacific Partnership."[15]

In 2018, McCoy said that by relying on his "strikingly inept version of one-man diplomacy" and favoring "narrow national interest over international leadership," Trump had undercut the U.S. strategic position at a time when China was pushing relentlessly to dominate the vast Eurasian continent.[16]

But Babones, at the University of Sydney, praised Trump's foreign policy moves. "Trump has [delivered] an as-yet-uninterrupted string of foreign-policy successes," he wrote. North Korea "hasn't launched a rocket in 10 months; America's NATO allies are finally starting to . . . increase defense spending; . . . and the U.S. embassy in Israel moved to Jerusalem in May without sparking the Third Intifada predicted by Trump's opponents."[17]

Other scholars say the days of U.S. dominance were waning long before Trump was elected. Canadian political scientist Robert Muggah, for instance,

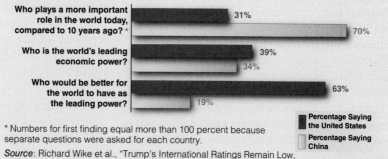

China Seen as Growing U.S. Rival

More than two-thirds of respondents say China plays a more important role in the world than it did a decade ago, according to a 2018 survey conducted across 25 countries. But a plurality still calls the United States the world's leading economic power, and a substantial majority prefers U.S. leadership.

Median Global Opinion on Balance of Power Between the U.S. and China, 2018

Who plays a more important role in the world today, compared to 10 years ago? *	31%	70%
Who is the world's leading economic power?	39%	34%
Who would be better for the world to have as the leading power?	63%	19%

■ Percentage Saying the United States
▢ Percentage Saying China

* Numbers for first finding equal more than 100 percent because separate questions were asked for each country.

Source: Richard Wike et al., "Trump's International Ratings Remain Low, Especially Among Key Allies," Pew Research Center, Oct. 1, 2018, https://tinyurl.com/y95dqags

predicted in 2016 that by 2030 there would be "no single hegemonic force" overseeing international peace, but rather a handful of countries—such as the United States, Russia, China, Germany, India and Japan— exhibiting "semi-imperial tendencies." This broadening of global power has been caused in part by "a vicious backlash against globalization" triggered by the 2008 worldwide financial crisis, said Muggah, co-founder of the Igarape Institute, a nonpartisan research organization in Rio de Janeiro.[18]

This redistribution of power is "profoundly disrupting the global order," Muggah said. The United States and the European Union are ceding influence to China and India, whose economies are growing more rapidly, and postwar alliances are yielding to new regional coalitions, he wrote. Muggah added, "While these reconfigurations reflect regional political, economic and demographic shifts, they also increase the risk of volatility, including war."[19]

Brookings' Kagan says that if the United States withdraws from its role as an indispensable nation, conflicts will result thousands of miles away. "We will find ourselves, as we did in the world wars, economically affected by these conflicts and then sucked into them."

Gordon Adams, a professor emeritus at the American University School of International Service, said the United States is not relinquishing its global supremacy; rather, the world is undergoing an inevitable post-World War II and post-Cold War rebalancing of power.

"The power of other countries has grown, giving them both the ability and the desire to [affect] global affairs independently of U.S. desires," Adams wrote in June 2018. "This global trend spells the end of the 'exceptional nation' Americans imagined they were since the nation was founded and the end of the American era of global domination that began 70 years ago."[20]

But in an interview Adams says the fears of a U.S. decline are exaggerated. "Everybody focuses on China and says the U.S. is declining, but it isn't about declining," he says. "It's about a shift in the power balance."

Tufts University assistant professor of political science Michael Beckley believes the United States is not about to be pushed off its perch. In his 2018 book, *Unrivaled: Why America Will Remain the World's Sole Superpower*, Beckley wrote that the United States "will remain the world's only superpower for many decades,

and probably throughout this century," because of its economic and military advantages.[21]

China, America's most powerful economic competitor for global pre-eminence, he said, has an inefficient economy that "is barely keeping pace" as its wealth is eroded by "the burden of propping up loss-making companies and feeding, policing, protecting and cleaning up" after its 1.4 billion people. By contrast, the United States "is big and efficient, producing high output at relatively low costs" with much lower welfare and security costs but five to 10 times the military capabilities of China, Beckley wrote.[22]

Russia, meanwhile, wants to expand its influence beyond Eastern Europe but is likely to remain only a regional power, Beckley says in an interview, because its military and economic strength is much weaker than that of the United States. "The U.S. holds all the high cards, [with] the best fundamentals for being able to amass wealth and military power in the decades ahead," he says.

Is President Trump playing into Vladimir Putin's hands?

Since the collapse of the Soviet Union in 1991, every U.S. president has vowed to ease tensions between Russia and the United States.[23]

"The post-Cold War era has been punctuated by high-profile attempts to reset the relationship," says Alexander Cooley, director of the Harriman Institute for the Study of Russia, Eurasia and Eastern Europe at Columbia University. But those efforts have tended to fail, he says, "because they don't get at the structural sources of U.S.-Russian discord"—Russia's desire to control the former Soviet states and satellites of Central and Eastern Europe where the United States has been promoting democratic reforms.

President Trump has said that he and Russian President Vladimir Putin would "end up having an extraordinary relationship. Getting along with Russia is a good thing, not a bad thing."[24]

But Trump's critics say he has a puzzling history of soft-pedaling criticism of Putin, despite a string of apparent provocations, including Russia's interference in the 2016 U.S. presidential elections, its 2014 incursion into Ukraine and its support for Syrian President Bashar al-Assad, whom the United States opposes in that country's civil war.

The CIA, FBI and National Security Agency unanimously concluded with "high confidence" that the Russians interfered in the 2016 presidential election to aid Trump's candidacy. But after a private, two-hour meeting with Putin in Helsinki in 2018, Trump stunned U.S. intelligence officials by saying he didn't see "any reason" that Russia would have meddled in the elections and was inclined to believe Putin's "extremely strong and powerful . . . denial" of such activity.[25]

Many Republican and Democratic leaders were astounded. "No prior president has ever abased himself more abjectly before a tyrant," said the late Republican Sen. John McCain of Arizona.[26] (Trump later said he "misspoke" and that he had meant to say he saw no reason Russia "wouldn't" have interfered in the elections.[27])

Trump also has likened America's conduct to Russia's with regard to political assassinations. In February 2017, for instance, he appeared to excuse allegations that Putin has had political opponents and journalists assassinated, saying, "There are a lot of killers. You think our country's so innocent?"[28]

Vladimir Frolov, a Russian foreign affairs analyst, has called Trump "God's gift that keeps on giving." He added: "Trump implements Russia's negative agenda by default, undermining the U.S.-led world order, U.S. alliances, U.S. credibility as a partner and an ally. . . . Russia can just relax and watch and root for Trump, which Putin does at every TV appearance."[29]

But George Washington University's Nau says that despite Trump's friendly words about Putin, the administration's actions toward Russia have been tough, such as endorsing the placement of NATO forces, including U.S. troops, in Poland and the Baltic states, on Russia's borders. "How's that coddling Russia?" Nau asks. "And he's given lethal weapons to the Kiev government in Ukraine, a big step Obama never would have taken."

Trump supporters also point out that the administration continues to enforce sanctions against Russia for its 2014 invasion of Ukraine and its cybercrime-related activities, human rights violations, weapons proliferation, support for Syria, trade with North Korea and terrorism-related activities.[30]

"Trump is dealing with Russia in the right way," says James Carafano, director of the Douglas and Sarah Allison Center for Foreign Policy Studies at the Heritage Foundation,

a conservative think tank. "Trump is consistently saying to Putin, 'I'm here to safeguard American interests.'"

But critics point out that Trump did not stand up to Russia until March 2018, after Congress pressured him to use the Countering America's Adversaries Through Sanctions Act, which Congress had passed in August 2017. Trump had signed the legislation reluctantly, complaining that it "improperly encroaches on executive power."[31]

Some of Trump's critics have asked whether the president's business interests in Russia—including a proposal to build a Trump Tower in Moscow—have affected his approach to Putin, something the president has repeatedly denied.[32] But Trump's former attorney, Michael Cohen, told the House Oversight Committee Feb. 27, 2019, that Trump "knew of and directed the Trump Moscow negotiations throughout the campaign, and lied about it . . . because he stood to make hundreds of millions of dollars" on the project.[33]

Stephen Sestanovich, a professor of international diplomacy at Columbia University and a former State Department official, said, "We can't rule out the more sinister and sordid explanations of [the Trump-Putin] 'bromance.'" But some explanations for the mutual attraction are not mysterious, he said. "Putin's got this record as a bad-boy statesman that puts him outside the bounds of polite society in Europe and America. Trump admires that."[34]

Are post-World War II alliances and structures suited for today's foreign policy challenges?

Some foreign policy experts say that, with notable exceptions, the world has enjoyed 70 years of relative peace and prosperity, due largely to international political, economic and military structures and alliances established after World War II by U.S. and other Western leaders. The goal of the liberal international order was to prevent the Soviet Union from expanding communism into other countries and to promote democracy, human rights and free-market economies.

The international order was defended by NATO—a military alliance established in 1949 that now has 29 member countries—and was implemented through economic rules and standards of behavior established by the United Nations (U.N.), World Bank, International Monetary Fund and General Agreement on Tariffs and

Trade (GATT)—the predecessor of the World Trade Organization (WTO).

Many historians say the U.S. architects of those institutions felt it was in the nation's long-term interest to surrender some sovereignty to advance global harmony. Without such institutions, they say, the world would revert to the chaotic political rivalries and unregulated trade practices that twice led to global war.

The institutions enable national leaders "to better manage the kind of conflicts that would otherwise have spun up into wars," says E. Anthony Wayne, former assistant secretary of State for economic and business affairs. Abandoning them, he says, means "the world becomes more like a jungle."

But since the fall of the Soviet Union, some foreign policy experts have questioned whether these institutions should be scrapped, or at least retooled, to deal with modern problems such as terrorism, climate change, religious and ethnic conflicts and migration.

"The world has changed in profound ways over the last several decades, and . . . our alliance structures were built for another time," says former diplomat Shannon. "Although they're still useful, we are rethinking the world and America's purpose in it, a discussion which the president, in his own way, is driving by his behavior."

Indeed, Trump's skepticism about NATO has led some Europeans to wonder whether Europe should start looking after its own security needs. French President Emmanuel Macron and German Chancellor Merkel have called for consideration of a military force run by the 28-member European Union. "The days where we can unconditionally rely on others are gone," Merkel said.[35]

Trump caused a stir last July when he told a NATO summit meeting that the United States was prepared to "go our own way" if other member states did not pay more to fund the organization. Trump said he told the gathered leaders, "The United States is paying close to 90 percent of the costs of protecting Europe. . . . You got to pay your bill." (The United States paid nearly $7 billion of NATO's costs in 2017.)[36]

His threats got results. NATO renewed a 2014 pledge that every member would spend at least 2 percent of its gross domestic product on national defense, as is required under the NATO charter, by 2024. Since 2014, annual defense spending by non-U.S. members has increased by $14.6 billion, an average of 1.47 percent of members' GDP. The U.S. spends 3.5 percent of its GDP on defense.[37]

In January, NATO Secretary-General Jens Stoltenberg said members had agreed to increase their defense spending by $100 billion. "There is no doubt that [Trump's] very clear message is having an impact," Stoltenberg said. "And the message was that . . . President Trump [is] committed to NATO, but we need fair burden sharing."[38]

Trump also has criticized the WTO, which sets rules and adjudicates international trade disputes. In October 2017 he complained that the organization "was set up for the benefit of everybody but us. . . . [W]e lose . . . almost all of the lawsuits."[39] He threatened to withdraw the United States from the 164-member body "if they don't shape up."[40]

But Dan Ikenson, director of the libertarian Cato Institute's Herbert A. Stiefel Center for Trade Policy Studies, has studied WTO trade disputes in which the United States was either the complainant or the defendant. "There is no anti-American bias" in the WTO's Dispute Settlement Body, he said. The United States won 91 percent of the 114 complaints it filed with the WTO from 1995 to March 2017, a higher success rate than of any other country, he found, and lost in 89 percent of the 129 cases filed against it.[41]

Dennis Shea, U.S. ambassador to the WTO, has said certain outdated WTO procedures should be reformed, including rules that allow China to protect its domestic industries while "creating disadvantages for foreign companies."

In addition, two-thirds of WTO members—including China, Saudi Arabia, Brunei and Qatar—are allowed to claim special privileges because they classify themselves as developing countries. On Feb. 15, 2019, Shea proposed that the WTO withhold special treatment from countries classified as "high income" by the World Bank or other institutions, including any state accounting for 0.5 percent or more of world trade.[42]

The WTO is unlikely to undertake serious reform because all member states must approve any rule changes, "a formidable roadblock," according to the Center for Strategic and International Studies, a Washington think tank. Yet, a failure to enact major reform proposals "could lead to the disintegration of key pillars of the organization," the center concluded.[43]

BACKGROUND

Isolationism

As George Washington left the presidency in 1796, he counseled fellow citizens about the risks of foreign entanglements. "Steer clear of permanent alliances with any portion of the foreign world," he advised. Take a neutral path, he said, by avoiding both "permanent, inveterate antipathies against particular nations, and passionate attachments for others."[44]

In its early years, the United States generally clung to an isolationist policy, except with regard to the 1823 Monroe Doctrine, which declared that the Western Hemisphere was America's sphere of influence. In 1898, the United States used that doctrine to justify going to war against Spain, siding with Cuban revolutionaries seeking independence from the colonial power. The Spanish-American War ended with Cuba nominally independent and Spain ceding Puerto Rico, the Philippines and Guam to the United States as territories.[45]

In the early 20th century, the United States reverted to isolationism but was thrust into global pre-eminence by its involvement in two world wars, despite early efforts to remain neutral. In 1914, when World War I broke out in Europe, President Woodrow Wilson declared that the United States would remain neutral. But after German submarine attacks on U.S. vessels, Wilson abruptly reversed direction in 1917.[46]

Even before the war ended, Wilson—in his 1918 "Fourteen Points" speech—called for diplomatic transparency, freer trade, arms reduction and "a general association of nations [to provide] mutual guarantees of political independence and territorial integrity," the founding principles of the League of Nations, championed by Wilson. Isolationist sentiment returned after the war ended, however, and the Senate refused to ratify the treaty. In fact, Congress passed four Neutrality Acts in the 1930s, aiming to keep the United States neutral by avoiding financial dealings with belligerents.[47]

Isolationism still reigned in the late 1930s and early '40s, when President Franklin D. Roosevelt was forced to heed public sentiment against entering World War II until Dec. 7, 1941, when Japan bombed the U.S. naval base at Pearl Harbor. Public opinion changed overnight, and Congress declared war on Japan the next day. Germany declared war against the United States four days later.

In 1944, before World War II ended, Roosevelt led a move to establish an array of major international institutions designed to prevent future wars and promote economic stability. Among those were two largely U.S.-financed international lending institutions: the World Bank, which provides aid to less developed nations, and the International Monetary Fund, which lends funds to help countries out of short-term currency crises. Roosevelt also pushed for establishment of the U.N., an international organization to promote global peace, which was created on Oct. 24, 1945, with the United States as a permanent and powerful member of its enforcement arm, the Security Council.[48]

Containment

After the war, Roosevelt's successor, President Harry S. Truman, began to identify U.S. interests as global and espoused the Truman Doctrine—vowing "to support free peoples who are resisting attempted subjugation by armed minorities or outside pressures."[49] As the Cold War emerged between the United States and the Soviet Union, the doctrine morphed into one of containment—using whatever diplomatic, economic and military means were necessary to contain the spread of Soviet communism. Often, the United States ended up siding with anti-communist dictators, such as when it helped the authoritarian Greek government put down an insurgency during a civil war in the late 1940s.

The Truman Doctrine also led to the Marshall Plan in 1948, and the Korean War in the early 1950s.

The Marshall Plan, named for its architect, Secretary of State George C. Marshall, provided $13 billion between 1948 and 1951 to help rebuild war-torn Europe. Besides jump-starting Western Europe's economic recovery, the aid program required recipient countries to exclude communists from their governments and to purchase supplies from U.S. manufacturers whenever possible. The total gross national product among recipient nations increased by 32 percent during the four years the plan was in effect.[50]

Also under Truman, the United States in 1949 joined Canada and 10 European countries to form NATO. In response, in 1955 the Soviet Union created the Warsaw Pact, an alliance with its Eastern European satellite states, several of which would join NATO after the Soviet Union's collapse in 1991.

CHRONOLOGY

1700s-1800s *Early America adopts an isolationist foreign policy.*

1796 George Washington warns against "permanent alliances."

1823 Monroe Doctrine establishes principle that Western Hemisphere is U.S. sphere of influence.

1898 Spanish-American War ends with Cuba nominally independent and the U.S. with three territories: Puerto Rico, Guam and the Philippines.

1900-1945 *U.S. participates in two world wars, beginning its ascent as a superpower.*

1917-18 U.S. enters World War I; President Woodrow Wilson pushes for a League of Nations to foster international cooperation and prevent future wars.

1919 Isolationist Congress refuses to join new League of Nations.

1935-1939 Congress passes four Neutrality Acts aimed at keeping the U.S. out of foreign conflicts.

1941 Japanese bomb Pearl Harbor; U.S. declares war on Japan, and Germany in turn declares war on U.S.

1944 Bretton Woods conference lays plans for postwar world economic system, including the World Bank and International Monetary Fund.

1945 World War II ends; United Nations is established to promote world peace.

1946-1980s *In Cold War, U.S. foreign policy focuses on multilateralism and containment of communism.*

1947-50 President Harry S. Truman adopts a containment policy to limit Soviet expansion by aiding Greece and Turkey, introducing Marshall Plan to rebuild Europe and guaranteeing the security of Western Europe by joining the North Atlantic Treaty Organization (NATO).

1950-53 North Korea, aided by the Soviet Union, attacks South Korea. U.S.-led coalition intervenes on behalf of the South; truce leaves Korea divided.

1962 Cuban missile crisis leads the U.S. and the Soviet Union to brink of nuclear war.

1965 U.S. support for South Vietnam against communist North Vietnam leads to a major escalation of American forces. Protracted war results in domestic calls for retrenchment.

1972 President Richard M. Nixon promotes opening to China and détente with the Soviet Union while maintaining containment strategy.

1978 President Jimmy Carter makes support for human rights a major foreign policy objective.

1982 President Ronald Reagan adopts hawkish foreign policies by increasing military spending, calling the Soviet Union an "evil empire" and vowing to support democracy in communist countries.

1983 U.S. invades Grenada, claiming it is enabling "Soviet-Cuban militarization" in the Caribbean.

1986-87 Investigations reveal the Reagan administration illegally sold weapons to Iran and supported anti-communist insurgents in Nicaragua.

1987 U.S. and Soviet Union sign Intermediate-Range Nuclear Forces (INF) Treaty, agreeing to destroy all land-based missiles with ranges between 300 to 3,400 miles.

1990s-2000s *Cold War ends, leaving U.S. as sole superpower; rise of jihadist terrorism forces U.S. foreign policy to focus on the Middle East.*

1991 Iraq invades Kuwait; U.S.-led, U.N.-sanctioned coalition ousts Iraqis. Soviet Union collapses.

1994 U.S., Mexico and Canada sign landmark North America Free Trade Agreement (NAFTA).

2001 Sept. 11 terrorist attacks prompt President George W. Bush to launch NATO-backed attack on Afghanistan, which is protecting Osama bin Laden, the architect of the attacks and leader of al Qaeda, a jihadist group.

2002 Bush widens the conflict by declaring the right to "prevent or forestall" attacks by terrorists or others.

2003 Bush invades Iraq in search for weapons of mass destruction (none are found) and ousts President Saddam Hussein. Years of U.S. occupation, chaos and ethnic violence ensue.

2006 Iran enriches uranium, triggering U.N. sanctions amid fears it will develop nuclear weapons; North Korea announces it has carried out its first nuclear test.

2009 Barack Obama begins presidency; calls for "new beginning" in U.S. relations with Muslim world.

2010-Present *Pro-democracy movement sweeps Middle East.*

2011-12 U.S. troops withdraw from Iraq; Arab Spring protests depose dictators in Tunisia, Libya and Egypt but spark prolonged civil war in Syria.

2015 Obama signs international agreement to curb Iran's nuclear weapons development and the Paris climate accord to limit carbon emissions.

2016 Obama signs Trans-Pacific Partnership (TPP) to lower trade barriers in 12 Pacific countries. Donald Trump is elected president, vowing to follow an "America First" foreign policy.

2017 Trump withdraws U.S. from TPP; announces intention to leave climate accord and demands that NATO allies pay their share for maintaining the alliance.

2018 Trump withdraws U.S. from Iran nuclear deal, renegotiates NAFTA, meets North Korean leader Kim Jong Un to discuss removing nuclear weapons from Korean peninsula and embarks on trade war with China.

2019 Second Trump-Kim meeting ends without denuclearization agreement; U.S. and Russia announce they are pulling out of INF agreement.

In 1950, the West's fears of aggressive communist expansion seemed to be realized when North Korea, backed by the Soviet Union (and later communist China), attacked South Korea. The United States, backed by U.N. troops, joined South Korea in the conflict. An inconclusive truce ended the fighting in 1953.

During most of the Cold War, the United States avoided direct military confrontations with the Soviet Union or China but often backed anti-communist governments or insurgents in proxy wars. But in October 1962, during President John F. Kennedy's administration, Soviet bombers and launch sites for medium-range missiles capable of reaching the United States were discovered in Cuba. A tense two-week standoff raised the specter of nuclear war between the two superpowers. Eventually, Soviet Premier Nikita Khrushchev agreed to remove the Soviet launchers and bombers in exchange for a U.S. pledge that it would not invade Cuba; the United States also removed its Turkey-based nuclear missiles targeting the Soviet Union.

Realpolitik

In the 1960s, Presidents Kennedy and Lyndon B. Johnson viewed the conflict in Vietnam between the communist North and pro-Western South as a critical test of U.S. containment policy. The so-called domino theory, first articulated by President Dwight D. Eisenhower in 1954, held that if Vietnam fell to the communists, nearby countries would follow.[51]

A small U.S. military presence in South Vietnam in the 1950s grew to 16,000 by 1963 and continued to increase. During U.S. involvement in the war, which officially ended in 1973, more than 2.7 million U.S. troops had served in Vietnam. Richard M. Nixon, elected president in 1968, initially expanded the war but eventually worked to end U.S. involvement. By the time the United States pulled out, the war had cost more than 58,000 American lives and an estimated $168 billion in military operations and economic aid.

There were other costs as well. The U.S. role in the war prompted sometimes-violent street protests at home and abroad and diminished world confidence in U.S. superiority. America turned inward, and the term "Vietnam syndrome" described the ensuing U.S. reluctance to intervene abroad.

The Nixon administration, under the direction of National Security Adviser and later Secretary of State Henry Kissinger, adopted Realpolitik—the theory that practical considerations rather than ideology should govern foreign relations. This approach enabled the

Populist Governments Are Up Fivefold

"The economic approach in Brussels and in Washington is failing."

Populist politicians—who practice a brand of nationalistic politics that claims to represent "the people" instead of society's "elites"—are on a global roll.

Twenty governments, including the United States, now have populists either in charge of, or as part of, a governing coalition—a fivefold increase since 1990, according to the Tony Blair Institute for Global Change, an international affairs research center in London. "Whereas populism was once found primarily in emerging democracies, populists are increasingly gaining power in systemically important countries," the institute's researchers said.[1]

Some experts say that while President Trump, a populist, did not cause the global rise in populism, his friendliness toward and praise for populist leaders are fueling it. "There's a lot of speculation about Trump's effect on populist movements and leaders," says Leslie Vinjamuri, head of the U.S. and the Americas Program at Chatham House, a London-based international affairs think tank.

Newly elected Brazilian President Jair Bolsonaro presents President Trump with a national soccer team jersey during a meeting at the White House on March 19, 2019. Critics say Trump's embrace of Bolsonaro and other populist leaders is helping to fuel a rise in nationalistic politics.

One of Trump's first foreign visitors to the White House was Nigel Farage, the right-wing British populist who helped engineer Brexit, the successful referendum calling for the United Kingdom to withdraw from the European Union (EU).[2] Anti-EU sentiment is a major tenet of today's European populists, and Trump has said EU trade policies have made the European Union a "foe" of the United States.[3]

Brazil's far-right populist president, Jair Bolsonaro, sometimes called "the Trump of the Tropics," endeared himself to the American president with a Trump-like attack on "fake news" and a campaign vow to "make Brazil great." Trump said he intended to designate Brazil a "major non-NATO ally," which would give it preferential treatment in buying U.S. military equipment and receiving other security assistance.[4]

Trump also has established warm relations with Viktor Orbán, the prime minister of Hungary, and Polish President Andrzej Duda, populists who have been critical of the EU. Orbán, who has cracked down on the press, the judiciary and nonprofit groups to create what he calls an "illiberal" state, was the first world leader to endorse Trump's election.[5] Duda, who has overseen efforts to put Poland's judicial system under the control of the ruling party, reportedly has offered the United States $2 billion toward construction of a U.S. military base in Poland that he proposed calling Fort Trump.[6]

Vinjamuri says populist leaders like Orbán and Duda "serve to drive a wedge through Europe's internal coherence in the post-Cold War period." Max Bergmann, a policy analyst at the Center for American Progress, a liberal think tank in Washington, says that could "allow countries like Russia and China to build ties within Europe," serving as beachheads for them to weaken U.S. alliances there.

Chris Kleponis-Pool/Getty Images

Some say Trump's rhetoric encourages populists abroad. So too, they say, does his association with right-wing political strategist Steve Bannon and senior policy adviser Stephen Miller, known for his hardline views on immigration.[7]

Bannon, a controversial former adviser to Trump with ties to extreme right-wing U.S. groups, has established a populist think tank in Brussels called The Movement to promote anti-EU populist politicians. In March 2018, Bannon told supporters of France's extreme right-wing National Front Party, led by populist politician Marine Le Pen, "Let them call you racist, let them call you xenophobes, let them call you nativist. Wear it as a badge of honor."[8]

Bergmann has attributed the current wave of populism to the 2008 financial crisis, which he called "the biggest economic calamity since the Great Depression." Even 10 years later, he says, there is "general angst in parts of the U.S. as well as Europe [and] a steeper divide between economic winners and losers. That angst is the sense that the economic approach in Brussels [the EU headquarters] and in Washington is failing," particularly on behalf of industrial workers.

Bergmann says right-wing populists do not usually have an economic plan but that they do have scapegoats—typically immigrants. Politicians on both sides of the Atlantic, he says, can say, "'Hey—you know why things are bad? It's because the elites favor these open borders and cultural dilution.'" Populists in the United States and Europe are appealing to a day when their countries were more ethnically and culturally homogeneous, he says.

But others see expanding populism as a sign of citizen participation in a healthy democracy. James Miller, professor of liberal studies and politics at The New School, a university in New York City, said, "Popular insurrections and revolts in the name of democracy have become a recurrent feature of global politics [and] form the heart and soul of modern democracy as a living reality."

At various times and "in virtually every country," he continued, "crowds of ordinary people unite to demand a fairer share of the common wealth [and more truly] democratic institutions." Such revolts "against remote elites are essential to the vitality, and viability, of modern democracy."[9]

Yves Leterme, former prime minister of Belgium and secretary-general of the International Institute for Democracy and Electoral Assistance, a democracy-promotion think tank in Stockholm, and Sam van der Staak, head of the institute's Europe program, also find some positive features in populism. Populist parties have "made reforming the political system a key part of their agenda," they wrote, and have championed policies that give citizens "who feel alienated by their government a sense of control."

Mainstream parties that "embrace populism's better ideas will be the ones who survive to shape the political future," they said.[10]

— Bill Wanlund

[1] Jordan Kyle and Limor Gultchin, "Populists in Power Around the World," Tony Blair Institute for Global Change, Nov. 7, 2018, https://tinyurl.com/yyu3gl55.

[2] Simon Shuster, "The Populists," *Time*, Dec. 24-31, 2018, https://tinyurl.com/ydyrtad2.

[3] Erin Corbett, "Donald Trump Calls the European Union a 'Foe' of the U.S.," *Fortune*, July 15, 2018, https://tinyurl.com/y23qnwqy.

[4] Rebecca Ballhaus and Samantha Pearson, "Trump, Meeting With Bolsonaro, Backs Stronger Ties With Brazil," *The Wall Street Journal*, March 25, 2019, https://tinyurl.com/yyrgxr64.

[5] Ishaan Tharoor, "Hungary's right-wing leader hopes Trump will bring him in from the cold," *The Washington Post*, Nov. 30, 2016, https://tinyurl.com/y64cmjzw. John Shattuck, "How Viktor Orbán degraded Hungary's weak democracy," The Conversation, Jan. 11, 2019, https://tinyurl.com/y97g8obm.

[6] Jeremy Diamond, "'Fort Trump'? Polish President urges US to consider opening base," CNN, Sept. 19, 2018, https://tinyurl.com/ycbt76ll. Marc Santora and Joanna Berendt, "Poland Overhauls Courts, and Critics See Retreat from Democracy," *The New York Times*, Dec. 20, 2017, https://tinyurl.com/yctccpfu.

[7] Dan Merica, "Stephen Miller is crucially important to the immigration debate—or maybe not," CNN, Jan. 22, 2018, https://tinyurl.com/y5d7qp7u.

[8] Daniel Politi, "Bannon: 'Let Them Call You Racist . . . Wear It as a Badge of Honor,'" *Slate*, March 10, 2018, https://tinyurl.com/y3gx494d. Joshua Green and Richard Bravo, "Europe's Crisis of Confidence Opens Door to Bannon-Style Chaos," Bloomberg, Jan. 13, 2019, https://tinyurl.com/ydy83br2.

[9] James Miller, "Could populism actually be good for democracy?" *The Guardian*, Oct. 11, 2018, https://tinyurl.com/ydc7qlgs.

[10] Yves Leterme and Sam van der Staak, "What populists get right," *Politico*, June 26, 2018, https://tinyurl.com/y4wpvakn.

Economic Sanctions Can Be Double-Edged

"There's a danger in overusing" them.

Countries commonly use economic sanctions—restrictions on commerce imposed on countries, companies or individuals—as a nonmilitary method of inducing them to change their behavior.

The United States is by far the world's leader in applying sanctions. As of Feb. 1, it was enforcing sanctions on 20 countries and some 6,300 individuals, according to the U.S. Treasury Department.[1]

Sanctions typically target certain commercial activities with an entire country or certain industries or companies in a country, or they block the financial assets of individuals such as terrorists, drug traffickers or corrupt government officials. An embargo—or a complete ban on all commercial activity with one or more countries—is another type of sanction. Sanctions usually are designed to enhance the sanctioning country's security or to punish another country's behavior, such as human rights violations or aggression against another nation.

"Sanctions often are used if diplomacy and words alone are insufficient but use of military force is too costly or extreme to effect the changes they want against a government that is behaving badly," says Bryan Early, an associate professor of political science at the University at Albany, State University of New York, who researches sanctions.

Nigel Gould-Davies, a lecturer in international relations at Bangkok's Mahidol University, cites the international sanctions imposed on Russia in 2014 for its incursions into Ukraine as having proved "more effective, more quickly, than their advocates expected."[2]

Russia has not returned Crimea or withdrawn from Ukraine, he said, but the sanctions, imposed by the United States, the European Union and others, had three goals: to deter further Russian military aggression; to reaffirm international norms and condemn their violation; and to encourage Russia to reach a political settlement with Ukraine. "Judged against those goals, sanctions have largely worked," Gould-Davies said.[3]

But sanctions achieve their goals only about one-quarter to one-third of the time, studies show.[4]

Sanctions fail, Early says, when the sanctioned countries "find other states willing to support them for geopolitical reasons." For instance, he says, communist Cuba has survived a U.S. embargo since 1960 with support from the Soviet Union during the Cold War and later from China and Venezuela.

Former State Department economics official E. Anthony Wayne agrees that sanctions can fail. "There's a danger in overusing sanctions," he says. "Eventually, the people you're sanctioning will just find other ways to get around the U.S. economy."

And unilateral sanctions—those imposed by only one country—in particular often do not work, he says. "It takes pressure from all different angles to make a country change," he says. "Unilateral sanctions can harm individuals, so the sanctions that target specific companies and individuals do have an impact, but it's rare that they can bring a whole country to change its ways."

Wayne argues that the Trump administration may be over-relying on unilateral sanctions and neglecting diplomatic efforts needed to get other countries to join in. The United States has imposed unilateral sanctions on several countries, including those already under multilateral sanctions, such as Russia and North Korea. When President Trump pulled the United States out of the 2015 Iran nuclear deal last year, he announced that he was reinstating the tough U.S. sanctions suspended by the agreement. Under the renewed sanctions, U.S. companies could no longer trade with Iran, and neither could any foreign company wanting to continue doing business with the United States.[5]

---

staunchly conservative Nixon in 1972 to be the first U.S. president to visit the People's Republic of China, a communist nation since 1949. The normalization of U.S.-China relations helped widen a rift between China and Russia that strengthened the U.S. position in the Cold War. Also in 1972, Nixon went to the Soviet Union, initiating a series of arms control measures and a period of détente between the two rivals.[52]

During his administration, President Jimmy Carter sought to make protecting human rights a major foreign policy objective, and Congress ordered the State Department to produce an annual report evaluating

Trump's unilateral move did not sit well with the European signatories to the nuclear agreement. To avoid the renewed U.S. sanctions, Britain, Germany and France in late January created a complicated workaround mechanism called the Instrument in Support of Trade Exchanges (INSTEX). It would allow Iran to continue doing business with other countries by paying for goods through a barter system, avoiding use of the dollar and the U.S. banking system.[6] It is unclear how successful INSTEX will be.

In the meantime, the renewed sanctions have hurt Iran's economy: Oil exports, Iran's main source of income, have dropped 60 percent since Trump reinstated sanctions, and Iran's economy is expected to shrink by 3.6 percent this year.[7]

Despite the U.S. withdrawal from the nuclear deal, Iran so far has continued to abide by the terms of the agreement, according to CIA Director Gina Haspel and the International Atomic Energy Agency, which monitors nuclear weapons activity worldwide.[8]

Early says sanctions can have unintended consequences: Authoritarian regimes often are willing to allow their populations to suffer the negative economic consequences created by sanctions in order to advance their objectives. "Broad-based sanctions are . . . good at inflicting broad-scale harms against their targets, but they're not very good at actually forcing the regimes to change their behavior," he says.

Sanctions also have been associated with a range of social and political harms, says Early, such as making governments more repressive when leaders "use the restrictions imposed on them as an excuse for consolidating their authoritative regimes. So, even if the sanctions don't force the government to change their policies, they can, inadvertently but effectively, do harm to the country."

— *Bill Wanlund*

An Iranian man burns a dollar bill in November 2018 outside the former U.S. embassy in Tehran during a demonstration marking the anniversary of the 1979 Iran hostage crisis. President Trump pulled the United States out of the 2015 Iran nuclear deal, and the administration has imposed unilateral economic sanctions on Iran.

ATTA KENARE/AFP/Getty Images

[1] "Sanctions Programs and Country Information," Research Center, U.S. Department of the Treasury, https://tinyurl.com/ybsocltu.

[2] Nigel Gould-Davies, "Sanctions on Russia Are Working," *Foreign Affairs*, Aug. 22, 2018, https://tinyurl.com/y77eyswz.

[3] *Ibid.*

[4] Bryan Early, *Busted Sanctions: Explaining Why Economic Sanctions Fail* (2015), p. 5.

[5] "Remarks by President Trump on the Joint Comprehensive Plan of Action," The White House, May 8, 2018, https://tinyurl.com/y3t2xsg3.

[6] Ellie Geranmayeh and Esfandyar Batmanghelidj, "Trading with Iran via the special purpose vehicle: How it can work," European Council on Foreign Relations, Feb. 7, 2019, https://tinyurl.com/yyf2fqou.

[7] Doyle McManus, "Trump's sanctions are hurting Iran's economy, but that doesn't mean they're working," *Los Angeles Times*, Feb. 13, 2019, https://tinyurl.com/y6aegdhl.

[8] "IAEA says Iran adhering to terms of nuclear deal," Agence France-Press, Feb. 22, 2019, https://tinyurl.com/y343kmp4.

countries' human rights practices. Carter enjoyed some success in the troublesome Middle East by brokering the Camp David Accords, a peace agreement that ended hostilities between Israel and Egypt. However, his presidency never recovered from the humiliation of the seizure of 52 U.S. diplomats and citizens in Tehran, Iran, by Islamic fundamentalists in 1979. The hostages were held for 444 days and then released on Jan. 20, 1981—the day Carter's successor, Ronald Reagan, was inaugurated.[53]

In his two terms, Reagan maintained a hawkish foreign policy, increasing military spending, branding the Soviet Union an "evil empire" and vowing to support democracy

A man with a pickax swings at the Berlin Wall separating communist East Berlin from democratic West Berlin on Nov. 9, 1989. The wall's demise helped usher in the end of the Cold War and a rebalancing of global power.

in communist countries. In 1983, he sent troops to Grenada to oust a Marxist military junta. His administration also illegally sold weapons to Iran and used the proceeds to support anti-communist insurgents in Nicaragua.[54]

Meanwhile, reform-minded Soviet Premier Gorbachev had begun to restructure the hidebound Soviet system. In 1987, he and Reagan signed the Intermediate-Range Nuclear Forces (INF) Treaty, representing the first time the superpowers had agreed to eliminate an entire category of nuclear weapons.[55]

Also in 1987, speaking near the Berlin Wall separating democratic West Berlin from Soviet-controlled East Berlin, Reagan challenged Gorbachev to "tear down this wall."[56]

Two years later, East German citizens themselves began to dismantle the wall, and the authorities did not intervene. That year, the nominally independent Eastern European countries that were part of the Warsaw Pact, such as Poland and Hungary, began to distance themselves from the Soviet Union. Two years later, Soviet republics such as the Baltic states and Ukraine would be moving toward independence.

In January 1991, the United States, under President George H. W. Bush, led a U.N.-authorized coalition to expel the Iraqis from Kuwait, which they had invaded the previous August to seize its oil fields. After a six-week campaign, the coalition had routed the Iraqis, but Bush decided not to remove Iraqi dictator Saddam Hussein from power,

believing it would be too costly and could have fractured the coalition, created solely to oust Iraq from Kuwait.

On Christmas Day that year, the Union of Soviet Socialist Republics was officially dissolved, ending the Cold War.

War on Terror

Bill Clinton's presidency opened in 1993 amid a changed world. The Soviet Union's collapse left the United States without its archenemy. International problems arose, but they lacked the clear-and-present-danger character that would rally public support for intervention.

For instance, in Bosnia in 1993 Orthodox Christian Serb fighters conducted a brutal ethnic cleansing program against Muslims. Faced with conflicting advice and sketchy intelligence, Clinton waited until 1995 to initiate a U.S.-led NATO bombing campaign against Bosnian Serb targets, finally bringing the Serbs to the negotiating table. The resulting Dayton Accords brought peace, backed by a 60,000-member NATO force. An estimated 100,000 people had died in the civil war, about 80 percent of them Muslims.[57]

During the Clinton administration, al Qaeda jihadist leader Osama bin Laden demanded that U.S. military forces leave Saudi Arabia and issued a "Fatwa" against the United States in 1998, declaring that killing "Americans and their allies—civilians and military—is an individual duty for every Muslim who can do it in any country."[58] About six months later, Qaeda suicide truck-bombers struck U.S. embassies in Kenya and Tanzania, killing 224. Clinton responded by bombing suspected Qaeda targets in Afghanistan and Sudan. Two years later, Qaeda operatives rammed an explosives-filled boat into the USS *Cole*, a Navy destroyer refueling in Yemen, killing 17 sailors.[59]

Qaeda bombers again struck the United States, in devastating fashion, early in the administration of Clinton's successor, George W. Bush. To root out those responsible for the Sept. 11, 2001, terrorist attacks, the United States, with NATO support, invaded Afghanistan, where bin Laden and al Qaeda were based.[60] Bush also declared a worldwide war on terror and instituted several fundamental changes in U.S. foreign policy, notably opting for unilateral action instead of multilateral initiatives and espousing a doctrine of preventive or pre-emptive war.

In March 2003, the United States led a 30-nation coalition of mostly European countries, recruited by Bush and Secretary of State Colin Powell, to invade Iraq over what later proved to be unfounded claims that Iraq was stockpiling weapons of mass destruction. Hussein was deposed (and later executed by Iraqis), but no such weapons were found. The invasion damaged America's global standing.

By the time the United States left Iraq in 2010, more than 4,400 Americans and tens of thousands of Iraqi civilians had died. Years of conflict followed, fed by political and ethnic rivalries and jihadist terrorist attacks, creating fertile ground for the Islamic State to establish a caliphate there in 2014.[61]

Shortly after his inauguration in 2009, President Obama tried to repair damaged relations with the Middle East, proposing in a speech in Cairo "a new beginning between the United States and Muslims around the world, one based on mutual interest and mutual respect."[62] His foreign policy aimed to use diplomacy rather than force, and he maintained a cool relationship with Putin and other authoritarian leaders.

Despite his noninterventionist stance, Obama ordered an 18-month "surge" of 30,000 troops to Afghanistan to train the Afghan military in their fight against al Qaeda and the Taliban, domestic religious militants who had controlled most of the country before the U.S.-led invasion in 2001. He also authorized a special operations raid in Abbottabad, Pakistan, on May 2, 2011, that found and killed bin Laden.

Although al Qaeda's influence has diminished, the Islamic State and other terrorist groups have filled the void—many based in Afghanistan, where the United States has been fighting for more than 17 years.[63]

Obama also had to respond to pro-democracy demonstrations that churned the Middle East, especially Egypt, during the Arab Spring of 2011-12. Eventually, dictators in Tunisia, Libya and Egypt were deposed, but protests in Syria sparked a prolonged civil war.

After weeks of massive public demonstrations in Egypt, Obama called for Egyptian President Hosni Mubarak to step down, which he eventually did. But Obama offered only a tepid response to government crackdowns on protesters in Bahrain, home to two U.S. Navy facilities. He helped the opposition in Libya depose dictator Moammar Gadhafi, but later said he regretted not foreseeing the chaos that followed Gadhafi's overthrow.[64]

Obama also promoted the downfall of President Bashar al-Assad in Syria, and warned him in August 2012 that the United States would respond if he crossed "a red line" by using chemical weapons against Syrian civilians. A year later, Assad did use such weapons, killing hundreds of people in two sarin gas attacks in the Damascus suburbs. Obama sought congressional authorization for a retaliatory missile strike, but Congress refused to vote on the request, and Obama in the end did not act. That decision was "a serious mistake" that "impacted American credibility," Obama's Secretary of Defense Robert Gates later said.

Instead, the United States and Russia negotiated a deal in which Assad agreed to give up his chemical weapons, which he did, but he later used similar weapons.[65]

Obama's signature foreign policy achievements both occurred in 2015: signing the international agreement under which Iran agreed to limit its nuclear weapons development in return for the lifting of economic sanctions and the completion of the Paris climate accord, in which 195 countries agreed to limit carbon emissions that are warming the planet.[66]

During Obama's last year in office, the United States signed the Trans-Pacific Partnership (TPP), an agreement to lower trade barriers among 12 countries in the Pacific region.[67]

"America First"

President Trump came into office with vastly different ideas about multilateral agreements, vowing to scrap or amend those that he felt did not protect American interests and workers. He also differs in how he treats and negotiates with dictators such as Putin and North Korea's Kim Jong Un, both of whom he has praised as being strong.

Right away Trump made it a point to distinguish his administration from that of his predecessor. He immediately pulled out of the TPP and later the Iran nuclear deal and the Paris climate accord. Trump also renegotiated the 24-year-old North American Free Trade Agreement (NAFTA) among the United States, Mexico and Canada, which he called "a bad joke." Congress has yet to ratify the new United States-Mexico-Canada Agreement.[68]

And, in a Cairo speech laying out the administration's Middle East policy, Secretary of State Mike Pompeo criticized Obama for "willful blindness" to "the danger of the [Iran] regime" when he signed the 2015 nuclear agreement, and for criticizing Israel.[69]

A longtime critic of what he sees as China's discriminatory trade barriers, theft of intellectual property and economic espionage, Trump imposed $250 billion worth of tariffs on Chinese imports, demanding that China mend its ways. China retaliated with $110 billion in import tariffs on U.S. products.[70]

On Dec. 1, 2018, Trump and Chinese President Xi Jinping agreed to a 90-day "truce," since extended, while the two countries negotiated a range of economic irritants. Without an agreement, Trump threatened to raise tariffs on another $200 billion of Chinese products, and China said it would respond with punitive measures.[71]

Trump has also made removing North Korea's nuclear threat a top foreign policy goal. His relationship with Kim had a rocky start: Trump threatened "fire and fury" if Kim continued provocative missile tests and belittled Kim as "Rocket Man"; Kim called Trump a "mentally deranged U.S. dotard."[72]

Then the two met in Singapore in June 2018 to discuss removing nuclear weapons from the Korean Peninsula, the first-ever meeting between leaders of the two countries. Although no concrete steps toward denuclearization took place, both sides made concessions: North Korea paused its nuclear weapons-testing program and dismantled some weapons-making facilities, and the United States cancelled scheduled joint military exercises with South Korea.

As the Trump-Kim relationship grew warmer, Trump told a campaign audience in West Virginia that Kim had sent him "beautiful letters" and "we fell in love."[73]

CURRENT SITUATION

North Korea and China

Expectations for an agreement with North Korea were high in February, when Trump and Kim met again in Hanoi, Vietnam. Trump had scheduled a signing ceremony before the talks had even started. But the summit ended early after Kim reportedly insisted that the United States lift nearly all U.S. economic sanctions on his country before he would start incrementally dismantling his nuclear weapons program.[74]

However, North Korean Foreign Minister Ri Yong Ho disputed this account, saying his country had only demanded partial relief from the sanctions in exchange for closing its main nuclear complex, and that the talks ended when the United States demanded further disarmament steps. An unidentified State Department official said Ri was only "parsing words" and that the North Koreans had asked for the lifting of all sanctions except those on weapons.[75]

After walking out of the summit, Trump told a press conference that lifting sanctions before Pyongyang has dismantled its nuclear program would allow Kim to continue producing weapons of mass destruction, and "we couldn't do that."[76]

White House National Security Adviser John Bolton said Trump had simply rejected "a bad deal."[77] Even some of Trump's critics agreed. "The president did the right thing by walking away," said Obama's vice president, Joe Biden.[78]

Days after the summit collapsed, South Korean and U.S. intelligence officials said satellite imagery showed that North Korea appeared to have rebuilt a satellite rocket launching facility it had dismantled as a confidence-building measure after the first summit, and that the work had begun even before the Feb. 27-28 Hanoi meeting.[79]

Two weeks later North Korean Vice Foreign Minister Choe Son Hui told reporters in Pyongyang that the United States, with its "gangster-like stand," had thrown away "a golden opportunity." In addition, she said, "we understood very clearly that the United States has a very different calculation to ours."[80]

John Delury, an expert on East Asia at Seoul's Yonsei University, said Choe's comments did not necessarily mean further negotiations would be abandoned, noting that there was no name-calling or insults and that Choe praised Kim's relationship with Trump. "A lot of this is rhetoric or posturing, but both sides have been careful not to fling mud," he said. "This is each side reminding each other what's at stake."[81]

On March 22, 2019, Trump tweeted that he was rolling back new sanctions his administration planned to impose on North Korea.[82] The decision apparently surprised the president's foreign policy advisers, and White House spokesperson Sarah Sanders said only, "President Trump likes Chairman Kim, and he doesn't think these sanctions will be necessary."

On March 25, 2019, Sanders told reporters: "The sanctions that were in place before are certainly still on.

Should the United States continue promoting democracy abroad?

YES
Thomas Carothers
Senior Vice President for Studies, Carnegie Endowment for International Peace

Written for *CQ Researcher*, March 2019

NO
Henry R. Nau
Professor of Political Science and International Affairs, Elliott School of International Affairs, George Washington University; Author, Conservative Internationalism: Armed Diplomacy Under Jefferson, Polk, Truman and Reagan

Written for *CQ Researcher*, March 2019

Analyses of the role of democracy promotion in U.S. foreign policy often emphasize the tension between American ideals and interests abroad. Ideals may be nice, the argument typically goes, but hard interests, above all security, need to take priority.

This is not a useful framing. Supporting democracy abroad is not just about living up to U.S. ideals. Just as importantly, it is about advancing hard U.S. interests. Most of America's closest security relationships are with democracies. Most of our geopolitical rivals are non-democracies. Of course, there are exceptions. Certain nondemocracies are useful security partners. But when our security partners are repressive and corrupt, we have to be significantly concerned about the destabilizing anger and radicalism they generate internally.

A more democratic world is one in which the United States has more allies and fewer adversaries. Regions dominated by democracies, such as Europe, South Asia and Latin America, are places where the United States has stable, productive partnerships. Regions dominated by autocracies, such as the Middle East, the former Soviet Union and parts of Asia, are sources of geopolitical conflict and competition.

Thus, for example, supporting democratic reform in Ukraine is not just a good thing to do for the Ukrainian people; it increases the chances that the Ukrainian government will productively balance the country's ties with Russia and friendly relations with the West. Stabilizing the democratic experiment in Tunisia is not just some idealistic venture; it is crucial to helping head off potentially dangerous radicalization or civil conflict. A more democratic Venezuela is less likely to ally itself with Russia and China, shelter drug trafficking or precipitate a regional humanitarian crisis, as Venezuela's authoritarian regime has done in recent years.

Making support for democracy an integral part of U.S. foreign policy does not mean full-bore democracy promotion everywhere all the time, pushing our political model on others and going it alone. Nor does it mean intervening militarily at great cost as in Afghanistan and Iraq—those interventions were primarily motivated by security concerns and were not representative cases of democracy promotion. Instead, it means—or it should mean—modulating U.S. pro-democracy diplomacy and assistance to take account of local political conditions and the overall balance of U.S. interests. It also means supporting homegrown efforts to advance democracy and working closely with other governments engaged in democracy support, as well as with relevant international organizations and nongovernmental organizations, on a broad positive-sum approach.

Under current circumstances the United States should defend, not promote, democracy. And that defense should be targeted on Eastern Europe and the Korean Peninsula, not everywhere across the globe.

The United States pursued a more aggressive policy after World War II when it confronted an existential threat from an anti-democratic power, the Soviet Union. Germany and Japan became enduringly democratic for the first time in their history. And the United States did so again when it emerged from the Cold War as the world's sole superpower. More than 60 countries became democratic, some durably (South Korea), others still struggling (Poland).

The United States paid a disproportionate price for these gains. U.S. soldiers manned the ramparts of freedom around the world and died or were wounded too frequently in long wars in Vietnam, Iraq and Afghanistan. U.S. workers moved relentlessly from one job to another to accommodate exports and create jobs for other countries. And U.S. society heaved under the disruption of immigrant flows that totaled more than 59 million from 1965 to 2015. In the end, the United States benefitted from this liberal world order. It defeated communism, grew wealthier and became a less racist and more diverse society.

But enough is enough. Circumstances have changed. Today the United States neither faces an existential threat nor enjoys unchallenged pre-eminence. Terrorism is not the equivalent of a new Cold War, democratic allies are now equal in wealth and technology, and authoritarian powers—China and Russia—challenge the United States regionally rather than globally.

In these circumstances, defending, not expanding, democracy is the strategic imperative. While Europe is whole and free for the first time ever, Russia strikes to weaken it. Moscow seizes territory in Ukraine and menaces struggling democracies in Poland, Hungary and the Baltic states. China extinguishes freedom at home and bulldozes peaceful aspirations in the South China Sea and on the Korean Peninsula. If Ukraine succumbs to Russian thuggery and Korea stabilizes or unites under the authoritarian talons of China, all the postwar gains of democracy may be lost.

Thus, holding out the prospects of freedom in Ukraine and Korea far outweigh the loss or gain of freedom anywhere else in the world. In the Middle East and elsewhere, the United States should counter threats but not deploy large numbers of U.S. forces and resources to build democratic nations. Circumstances allow the United States to take a break. The American people have earned it.

They are very tough sanctions. The president just doesn't feel it's necessary to add additional sanctions at this time. . . . The president likes him [Kim]. They want to continue to negotiate and see what happens."[83]

Harry Kazianis, director of Korean studies at the conservative think tank Center for the National Interest, said Trump might be trying to reduce tensions between Washington and Pyongyang and keep North Korea from pulling out of the negotiations.[84]

But an unnamed administration official quoted in *The New York Times* denied Trump made the decision in order to speed progress toward an agreement, telling reporters, "It would be a mistake to interpret the policy as being one . . . where we release some sanctions in return for piecemeal steps toward denuclearization. That is not a winning formula and it is not the president's strategy."[85]

The Trump administration has tried to get China, which accounts for 90 percent of North Korea's trade, to pressure Kim to dismantle its nuclear arsenal.[86] However, U.S. relations with China have been complicated by the ongoing trade dispute.

Negotiations during the trade-war truce reportedly have shown signs of progress, and Trump extended the original March 1, 2019, deadline. Trump and Xi are expected to meet in late spring or early summer at Trump's Mar-a-Lago resort in Florida.

Both sides have suffered during the trade war. American farmers and manufacturers have lost sales due to increased tariffs on their exports to China. But some economists say that China, with its slowing economy and greater reliance on exports, has been hurt more than the United States.[87]

Trans-Atlantic Relations

Trump has said he is not worried about his low popularity in Europe. "I shouldn't be popular in Europe," he said in January 2019. "I'm not elected by Europeans; I'm elected by Americans."[88]

Doug Bandow, a senior fellow specializing in foreign policy at the libertarian Cato Institute in Washington, agrees that it doesn't matter if Trump is unpopular abroad. "If another country is irritated because the U.S. says 'You should be capable of defending yourself,' that doesn't strike me as a major problem," he says.

But Leslie Vinjamuri, head of the U.S. and the Americas Program at Chatham House, a nonpartisan think tank in London, says Trump's skepticism toward NATO could alter trans-Atlantic diplomacy "for a long time," because "reliability and predictability are at issue."

In March 2019, former Vice President Richard B. Cheney, who served under Republican President George W. Bush, sharply criticized Trump's foreign policy at a private retreat sponsored by the American Enterprise Institute, a conservative think tank. Cheney told Vice President Pence that Trump's policies feed "this notion on the part of our allies overseas, especially in NATO, that we're not long for that continued relationship," according to *The Washington Post*.[89]

Cheney also complained about reports that Trump plans to demand that Germany, Japan, South Korea and other countries that host U.S. troops pay the full cost for such deployments—plus 50 percent. Noting that NATO countries are fighting alongside U.S. soldiers in Afghanistan, Cheney said that foreign relations are "a lot more complicated than just: 'Here's the bottom line. Write the check.'"[90]

Pence defended the administration's policies. "I think there is a tendency by critics of the president and our administration to conflate the demand that our allies live up to their . . . commitments and an erosion in our commitment to the post-World War II order," Pence said. "This president is skeptical of foreign deployments and only wants American forces where they need to be."[91]

Two days later, signaling bipartisan support for the alliance, congressional leaders said they were inviting NATO chief Stoltenberg to address a joint session of Congress in April to celebrate the 70th anniversary of the organization.[92]

Not all European countries are dissatisfied with Trump. He gets favorable ratings in Poland and Hungary, where anti-immigrant, nationalist leaders have emerged. Hungarian-American writer Boris Kálnoky explained Eastern Europeans' affinity for Trump: "We like plainspoken men who have the [guts] to say what they're thinking. If they're vulgar, so much the better." The president also "represents the idea that the United States is, and should remain, the most powerful country in the world," which is a "powerful guarantee of our security," he said.[93]

Western European allies were disappointed on Feb. 1, 2019, when Trump announced the United States was withdrawing from the INF Treaty on midrange nuclear weapons with Russia. German Chancellor Merkel said it was "unavoidable" after "years of violations of the terms of the treaty by Russia." However, she lamented, the pact "directly affects our security . . . and we are left sitting there."[94]

Trump and Putin say each other's country has repeatedly violated the treaty. Trump also has noted that China, which is not a signatory, is developing intermediate-range missiles. "If Russia's [building its arsenal] and if China's doing it, and we're adhering to the agreement, that's unacceptable," he said.[95]

Terrorism and Iran

Secretary of State Pompeo's Jan. 10, 2019, Middle East policy speech in Cairo stressed concern for Israel and a desire to strengthen relations with Saudi Arabia, Egypt and other countries friendly to the United States. He promised to reduce the threat to Israel from Lebanon-based Hezbollah militants and to stifle Iran's "deadly ambitions."[96]

A month later, Pompeo told a Middle East summit in Warsaw, Poland: "You can't achieve stability in the Middle East without confronting Iran." Israeli Prime Minister Benjamin Netanyahu echoed those sentiments, but he also called the summit a group of nations "sitting down together with Israel in order to advance the common interest of war with Iran."[97]

Democratic Sens. Tom Udall of New Mexico and Richard Durbin of Illinois worry about just such a scenario. Trump is "barreling toward war with Iran," they said, using "false narratives that Iran is not meeting its obligations under the nuclear deal." The senators said Trump is being egged on by Pompeo and Bolton, whom they called "committed advocates of virtually unchecked interventionism."[98]

In a March 5, 2019, *Washington Post* op-ed, Udall and Durbin said Trump's breach of the Iran nuclear deal had left the United States isolated and that Congress must "end the growing threat of a national security calamity, return our country to diplomacy and rebuild international trust in U.S. foreign policy." The two are preparing to introduce bipartisan legislation to restrict U.S. funds from being used to attack Iran.[99]

Carnegie president Burns said pulling out of the Iran deal "added to the fissures between us and our closest European allies, [and] in a way it's done Vladimir Putin's work for him" by sowing discord among the allies.[100]

Meanwhile, on Dec. 19, 2018, Trump unexpectedly announced the "full and rapid" withdrawal of the 2,200 U.S. troops from Syria, declaring that ISIS had been defeated—and prompting the resignation of Defense Secretary Jim Mattis, who disagreed with the decision. On Jan. 6, 2019, Trump backtracked, saying "we won't be finally pulled out until ISIS is gone."[101]

Such actions exemplify Trump's shoot-from-the-hip approach to diplomacy and its negative consequences, critics say.[102]

"Careless talk about the fight against ISIS being over is counterproductive [and] undermines our counterterrorism efforts and undermines our partners" in the region, says Daniel Benjamin, former State Department coordinator for counterterrorism and now director of Dartmouth College's John Sloan Dickey Center for International Understanding.

On March 23, 2019, U.S.-backed forces announced they had driven ISIS fighters out of the last territory they had been occupying in Syria. However, U.S. intelligence officials say ISIS is far from finished as a fighting force. According to Russ Travers, deputy director of the National Counterterrorism Center, about 14,000 armed and active ISIS fighters remain in Syria and Iraq.[103]

"A lot of ISIS has gone to ground and obviously there needs to be more engagement there" before it is no longer a threat, Benjamin says.

Venezuela

Trump told the U.N. General Assembly last year, "The United States will not tell you how to live or work or worship."[104] But events in Venezuela have put that pledge to the test.

On Jan. 23, 2019, Trump pronounced the regime of Venezuelan President Nicolas Maduro, re-elected last May in a vote widely regarded as rigged, "illegitimate." Trump said he considered Juan Guaidó, president of the legislative National Assembly, the lawful interim president. Some 50 other Latin American and European countries also support Guaidó.[105]

On Jan. 29, 2019, the administration announced sanctions effectively blocking imports of oil from

Venezuela's state-owned oil company, the country's biggest revenue source. Venezuela, with the world's largest proven oil reserves, shipped 500,000 barrels of crude a day to the United States in 2018, representing about 75 percent of the cash it received for its crude exports.[106]

"Trump said the United States wouldn't interfere in other countries' business," says Thomas Carothers, a senior vice president at the Carnegie Endowment, "but when it comes to countries we can't get along with, he points to their internal values and says that's a problem. There's an inconsistency."

OUTLOOK
End of 'Unipower'

Foreign policy experts tend to agree that Trump's presidency has coincided with a disruption in the international order that prevailed during much of the postwar period. They are far less united, however, on what will replace that order or on Trump's ultimate impact on the world.

American University's Adams, who calls himself a foreign policy "realist," says the United States' days as a "unipower" are over, but through no fault of its own. "Power is rebalancing. We couldn't have prevented the rebalancing of global power after the Cold War," he says. "It's not something brought on by Donald Trump," but his role has been "that of accelerant."

Ohio State's Schweller, who also calls himself a foreign policy realist, says, "For the U.S., there really are very few threats right now," although China is a looming competitor. Terrorism, meanwhile, is "a side show, a minor discomfort [but] not something we should spend too much time focusing on in our foreign policy. We're currently in a threat trough, so the U.S. should act accordingly and retrench."

It is unclear whether Trump's nationalism has left an indelible stamp on how the United States conducts diplomacy. For Thomas Wright, director of the Center on the United States and Europe at Brookings, the next presidential election is key.

If Trump is defeated in 2020, he predicts, "a lot of U.S. foreign policy would revert to some version of internationalism." But if Trump is re-elected, "over time he will be able to get his agenda through, and a lot of people will say America has fundamentally changed, and we will have to adjust accordingly."

But Carnegie's Burns is optimistic that American diplomacy will return to a place of legitimacy "over the medium term," regardless of how much it is "belittled and disdained today."[107]

Salman Ahmed, a senior fellow at the Carnegie Endowment, has some advice for U.S. leaders: "The strategic and economic rationale for the U.S. acting abroad is less clear than in the past. Those with responsibility for clarifying it would be wise to step back and try to understand what Americans think about it."

Ahmed is overseeing a series of state-level case studies to record how middle-class Americans view foreign policy and its impact on their economic well-being. He says those views are more nuanced than the country's political polarization would suggest.

"People get it," he says. "They know the 1960s aren't coming back. They have legitimate questions, though. What's going to happen to their town if it was dependent on a labor-intensive, heavy manufacturing practice which has gone away? Whatever caused it—trade and economic policies or something else—something has radically changed for them."

Former diplomat Shannon says, "In many ways, we're experiencing the end of a certain structure of the world order . . . driven by social and economic changes.

"We're kind of at a moment of re-founding, where the American people want a larger conversation with our collective leadership about what we're doing in the world," Shannon says. "And whether you like him or not, the president is the catalyst of that discussion."

NOTES

1. Griff Witte and Michael Birnbaum, "Trump foreign policy under attack from all sides at European security conference," *The Washington Post*, Feb. 16, 2019, https://tinyurl.com/y36tgvxs.

2. "Remarks by Vice President Pence at the 2019 Munich Security Conference, Munich, Germany," The White House, Feb. 16, 2019, https://tinyurl.com/y2qz66up; Katrin Bennhold and Steven Erlanger, "Merkel Rejects U.S. Demands That Europe Pull Out of Iran Nuclear Deal," *The New York Times*, Feb 16, 2019, https://tinyurl.com/yx8skap6.

3. Donald J. Trump, "Inaugural Address," The White House, Jan. 20, 2017, https://tinyurl.com/yxo997ez.

4. Mark Hannah, "Worlds Apart: U.S. Foreign Policy and American Public Opinion," Eurasia Group Foundation survey, February 2019, https://tinyurl.com/y58w7mbs.

5. Steve Holland and Yara Bayoumy, "Trump praises U.S. military sales to Saudi as he welcomes crown prince," Reuters, March 20, 2018, http://tinyurl.com/y5x7jxwz.

6. Salvatore Babones, "Trump's Foreign Policy Successes Show Principled Realism in Action," *The National Interest*, Sept. 26, 2018, https://tinyurl.com/y6ebcr38.

7. Richard Wike *et al.*, "Trump's International Ratings Remain Low, Especially Among Key Allies," Pew Research Center, Oct. 1, 2018, https://tinyurl.com/y95dqags.

8. Eliza Collins, "Trump: I consult myself on foreign policy," *Politico*, March 16, 2016, https://tinyurl.com/yax7xahb.

9. "Tracker: Current U.S. Ambassadors," American Foreign Service Association, March 13, 2019, https://tinyurl.com/gppkm54; Twenty-nine of the 59 unfilled positions have nominees awaiting Senate confirmation; another six are in countries with which the U.S. currently does not exchange ambassadors: Belarus, Bolivia, Eritrea, Sudan, Syria and Venezuela; "Lists of Chiefs of Mission as of February 2011," U.S. State Department, https://tinyurl.com/yx9axkmk.

10. Barbara Stephenson, "Time to Ask Why," *The Foreign Service Journal*, December 2017, https://tinyurl.com/y53ctxvy.

11. "Face the Nation," CBS News, March 10, 2019, https://tinyurl.com/y2kevn5z.

12. Randall Schweller, "Three Cheers for Trump's Foreign Policy," *Foreign Affairs*, Sept./Oct. 2018, https://tinyurl.com/y44ncnfx.

13. *Ibid.*

14. "Interview with Secretary of State Madeleine Albright," "Today Show," NBC News, Feb. 19, 1998, https://tinyurl.com/y2248a2l.

15. Jeremy Scahill, "Donald Trump and the Coming Fall of American Empire," The Intercept, July 22 2017, https://tinyurl.com/ydyp3qut.

16. Alfred W. McCoy, "The World According to Trump Or How to Build a Wall and Lose an Empire," Tikkun, Jan. 16, 2018, https://tinyurl.com/y4v6bf95.

17. Babones, *op. cit.*

18. Robert Muggah, "America's dominance is over. By 2030, we'll have a handful of global powers," World Economic Forum, Nov. 11, 2016, https://tinyurl.com/y4amv59w.

19. *Ibid.*

20. Gordon Adams, "A new world is dawning, and the US will no longer lead it," The Conversation, June 26, 2018, https://tinyurl.com/yynaao49.

21. Michael Beckley, *Unrivaled: Why America Will Remain the World's Sole Superpower* (2018), p. 1.

22. *Ibid.*, p. 5.

23. Robert E. Hamilton, "The Reset that Wasn't: The Permanent Crisis of U.S.-Russia Relations," Foreign Policy Research Institute, Dec. 14, 2018, https://tinyurl.com/y5nxwkp8.

24. Jordan Fabian, "Trump: 'Getting along with Russia is a good thing,'" *The Hill*, July 16, 2018, https://tinyurl.com/yczb87re.

25. Jeremy Diamond, "Trump sides with Putin over US intelligence," CNN, July 16, 2018, https://tinyurl.com/y84yl3nn.

26. Jessica Taylor, "'Disgraceful,' 'Pushover,' 'Deeply Troubled': Reaction To The Trump-Putin Summit," NPR, July 16, 2018, https://tinyurl.com/y7z96jk4.

27. Brian Naylor, "Trump Walks Back Controversial Comments on Russian Election Interference," NPR, July 17, 2018, https://tinyurl.com/yay5mwsh.

28. Sophie Tatum, "Trump defends Putin: 'You think our country's so innocent?'" CNN, Feb. 6, 2017, https://tinyurl.com/yxara4ff.

29. Neil MacFarquhar, "Glee in Russia Over Trump's Foreign Policy Largess," *The New York Times*, Dec. 21, 2018, https://tinyurl.com/y7rcafwq.

30. "U.S. Sanctions on Russia, Updated January 11, 2019," Congressional Research Service, https://tinyurl.com/y33m9u3b.

31. Kevin Liptak, "Trump administration finally announces Russia sanctions over election meddling," CNN, March 15, 2018, https://tinyurl.com/yaf93q4k; "Statement by President Donald J. Trump on Signing the 'Countering America's Adversaries Through Sanctions Act,'" The White House, Aug. 2, 2017, https://tinyurl.com/y2uv2prs.

32. John Haltiwanger and Sonam Sheth, "Here's a glimpse at Trump's decades-long history of business ties to Russia," Business Insider, Dec. 15, 2018, https://tinyurl.com/y6s6d9zy; Donald J. Trump, Twitter post, Jan. 11, 2017, https://tinyurl.com/y37ewy4k.

33. "Testimony of Michael D. Cohen, Committee on Oversight and Reform, U.S. House of Representatives, Feb. 27, 2019," CNN, https://tinyurl.com/y2mjpflp.

34. "5 Questions with Foreign Policy Expert Steve Sestanovich on the Trump-Putin Summit," Columbia News, July 13, 2017, http://tinyurl.com/y4klsrdw.

35. Katrin Bennhold and Steven Erlanger, "Merkel Joins Macron in Calling for a European Army 'One Day,'" The New York Times, Nov. 13, 2018, https://tinyurl.com/ydhry8eh.

36. David M. Herszenhorn and Lili Bayer, "Trump's whiplash NATO summit," Politico, July 12, 2018, https://tinyurl.com/yayp9evp; Donald Trump (transcript), "Trump Confirms He Threatened to Withdraw from NATO," CSPAN, Aug. 22, 2018, https://tinyurl.com/ybbswx69; Lucie Béraud-Sudreau, "The US and its NATO allies: costs and value," Military Balance Blog, International Institute of Security Studies, July 9, 2018, https://tinyurl.com/y4detsz7.

37. "Defence Expenditure of NATO Countries (2011-2018)," NATO, July 10, 2018, https://tinyurl.com/y65x4j5a.

38. Julie Allen, "Nato members increase defence spending by $100 billion after Donald Trump called them 'delinquents,'" Telegraph, Jan. 27, 2019, https://tinyurl.com/y89vgrfn; Brent D. Griffiths, "NATO head: Trump 'committed' to the alliance," Politico, Jan. 27, 2019, https://tinyurl.com/yaf42wzg.

39. Ian Schwartz, "Full Lou Dobbs Interview: Trump Asks What Could Be More Fake Than CBS, NBC, ABC and CNN?" Real Clear Politics, Oct. 25, 2017, https://tinyurl.com/yyjvhscl.

40. John Micklethwait, Margaret Talev and Jennifer Jacobs, "Trump Threatens to Pull U.S. Out of WTO If It Doesn't 'Shape Up,'" Bloomberg, Aug. 31, 2018, https://tinyurl.com/y6tqxctb.

41. Dan Ikenson, "US Trade Laws And The Sovereignty Canard," Forbes, March 9, 2017, https://tinyurl.com/y3kebsbq.

42. "Statement of the United States by Ambassador Dennis Shea at the 14th WTO Trade Policy Review of the United States of America," Office of the U.S. Trade Representative, Dec. 17, 2018, https://tinyurl.com/y9k4tmkp; Tom Miles, "U.S. drafts WTO reform to halt handouts for big and rich states," Reuters, Feb. 15, 2019, https://tinyurl.com/y4vsb8uy.

43. Jack Caporal and Dylan Gerstel, "WTO Reform: The Beginning of the End or the End of the Beginning?" Center for Strategic and International Studies, Oct. 23, 2018, https://tinyurl.com/yxpkjppv.

44. "Transcript of President George Washington's Farewell Address (1796)," Ourdocuments.gov, https://tinyurl.com/y8ufm2e6.

45. "1898: The Birth of a Superpower," Office of the Historian, U.S. Department of State, https://tinyurl.com/y669brmx.

46. "Wilson's War Message to Congress, April 2, 1917," Brigham Young University document archive, https://tinyurl.com/ybmbkn9n.

47. "President Wilson's Fourteen Points, Address to Congress," Jan. 8, 1918, Yale Law School—Lillian Goldman Law Library, https://tinyurl.com/y6s8gkw3. "The Neutrality Acts, 1930s," Office of the Historian, U.S. Department of State, https://tinyurl.com/ych68pxj.

48. Sandra Kollen Ghizoni, "Creation of the Bretton Woods System," Federal Reserve History, https://tinyurl.com/yxocydeh; "The United Nations," The Eleanor Roosevelt Papers Project, The George

Washington University, https://tinyurl.com/y7t983va.

49. "President Harry S. Truman's address before a joint session of Congress, March 12, 1947," Yale Law School—Lillian Goldman Law Library, https://tinyurl.com/678rja.

50. "Marshall Plan: Reconstructing Europe," BBC News, Jan. 6, 2005, https://tinyurl.com/yxo6ob5b.

51. "Domino Theory," The Vietnam War, May 4, 2016, https://tinyurl.com/yxvcn2uf.

52. Laura Deal, "Nixon Goes to China," The Wilson Center, Feb. 21, 2017, https://tinyurl.com/y3mkl5ph; "Nixon's Foreign Policy," Office of the Historian, U.S. Department of State, https://tinyurl.com/y2alhk65.

53. "1977-1981: The Presidency of Jimmy Carter," Office of the Historian, U.S. Department of State, https://tinyurl.com/yxutb9ld.

54. "The Iran-Contra Affair," PBS, https://tinyurl.com/y4jznprt.

55. Daryl Kimball, "The Intermediate-Range Nuclear Forces (INF) Treaty at a Glance," Arms Control Association, Feb. 2, 2019, https://tinyurl.com/6oxqkas.

56. Peter Robinson, "Tear Down This Wall," Prologue, U.S. National Archives, Vol. 39, No. 2, Summer 2007, https://tinyurl.com/y783bcrr.

57. Ivo Daalder, "Decision to Intervene: How the War in Bosnia Ended," The Brookings Institution, Dec. 1, 1998, https://tinyurl.com/jxqcn7w.

58. Marc Sageman, *Understanding Terror Networks* (2004), p. 19.

59. Steve Coll, *Ghost Wars: The Secret History of the CIA, Afghanistan, and Bin Laden, From the Soviet Invasion to September 10, 2001* (2004), pp. 405-409, 466-468, 534-537.

60. Jens Stoltenberg, "NATO's Vital Role in the War on Terror" *The Wall Street Journal*, May 24, 2017, https://tinyurl.com/y5os7cv6.

61. "Iraq War Timeline," Council on Foreign Relations, https://tinyurl.com/y295tqqg.

62. "Remarks by the President at Cairo University, 6-04-09," The White House, June 4, 2009, https://tinyurl.com/yxbkk64k.

63. Brian Michael Jenkins, "Five Years After the Death of Osama bin Laden, Is the World Safer?" Rand, May 1, 2016, https://tinyurl.com/yyp9szjd; "Remarks by the President in Address to the Nation on the Way Forward in Afghanistan and Pakistan," The White House, Dec. 1, 2009, https://tinyurl.com/y3gvkwnk.

64. Helene Cooper and Robert F. Worth, "In Arab Spring, Obama Finds a Sharp Test," *The New York Times*, Sept. 24, 2012, https://tinyurl.com/yxjr5nat.

65. Pamela Engel, "Former US defense secretary: Obama hurt US credibility when he backed down from his red line on Syria," *Business Insider*, Jan. 26, 2016, https://tinyurl.com/y68h7j8g.

66. Kelsey Davenport, "The Joint Comprehensive Plan of Action (JCPOA) at a Glance," Arms Control Association, May 2018, https://tinyurl.com/y9mvd9qd; "Statement by the President on the Paris Climate Agreement," The White House, Dec. 12, 2012, https://tinyurl.com/y8c36tqb.

67. Barack Obama, "President Obama: The TPP would let America, not China, lead the way on global trade," *The Washington Post*, May 2, 2016, https://tinyurl.com/y5a98rh5.

68. Mark Landler, "Trump Abandons Iran Nuclear Deal He Long Scorned," *The New York Times*, May 8, 2018, https://tinyurl.com/y7u4oy5s; "United States-Mexico-Canada Agreement," Office of the U.S. Trade Representative, https://tinyurl.com/y3vfe8qx.

69. "A Force for Good: America Reinvigorated in the Middle East," Secretary of State Michael Pompeo in Cairo, Egypt, Jan. 10, 2019, U.S. Department of State, https://tinyurl.com/y9w5qafw.

70. Dorcas Wong and Alexander Chipman Koty, "The US-China Trade War: A Timeline," China Briefing, Feb. 7, 2019, https://tinyurl.com/y2suzjkc.

71. Zhou Xin and Orange Wang, "Donald Trump can outgun China on trade tariffs but Beijing has other ways to fight back," *South China Morning Post*, June 19, 2018, https://tinyurl.com/y6gqel2s.

72. Matt Stevens, "Trump and Kim Jong-un, and the Names They've Called Each Other," *The New York Times*, March 9, 2018, https://tinyurl.com/ybt8koxr.

73. Chris Mills Rodrigo, "Trump: Kim Jong Un and I 'fell in love,'" *The Hill*, Sept. 29, 2018, https://tinyurl.com/ybkf52yl.

74. Carmin Chappell, "Trump schedules joint agreement signing ceremony with North Korean dictator Kim Jong Un at end of Vietnam summit," CNBC, Feb. 27, 2019, https://tinyurl.com/yxw5hoe5; Kim Tong-Hyung, "North Korea says it will never give up nukes unless US removes threat," The Associated Press, *Military Times*, Dec. 20, 2018, https://tinyurl.com/y4qft3v5.

75. Deirdre Shesgreen and John Fritze, "North Korea contradicts Trump's account of negotiations. State Dept. official says NK is 'parsing words,'" *USA Today*, Feb. 28, 2019, https://tinyurl.com/yybnsec8.

76. Alex Ward, "Transcript of Trump's North Korea summit press conference in Vietnam," *Vox*, Feb. 28, 2019, https://tinyurl.com/yyh9m5vs.

77. Felicia Sonmez, "John Bolton: North Korea summit was not a failure," *The Washington Post*, March 3, 2019, https://tinyurl.com/yyqjq2cr.

78. Laura Litvan, Daniel Flatley, Anna Edgerton and Bloomberg, "Trump Gets Bipartisan Praise for Walking Out of Summit With Kim," *Fortune*, Feb. 28, 2019, https://tinyurl.com/y4ox34zs; Sara Gray, "Biden praises Trump for 'walking away' from the North Korea summit with no nuclear deal," *Business Insider*, March 1, 2019, https://tinyurl.com/y2t7ppub.

79. Simon Denyer and Carol Morello, "North Korea Threatens to Suspend Denuclearization Talks with the United States," *The Washington Post*, March 15, 2019, http://tinyurl.com/y5qh5wn5.

80. *Ibid.*

81. *Ibid.*

82. Donald J. Trump, Twitter post, March 22, 2019, https://tinyurl.com/y5l7y843.

83. "Sarah Sanders on the Mueller Report," C-Span, March 25, 2019, http://tinyurl.com/y2sdkp6j.

84. Roberta Rampton, "Trump decides against more North Korea sanctions at this time: source," Reuters, March 22, 2019, https://tinyurl.com/y36axjbw.

85. Alan Rappeport, "Trump Overrules Own Experts on Sanctions, in Favor to North Korea," *The New York Times*, March 22, 2019, https://tinyurl.com/y63v947l.

86. Randy Kluver, Robert Hinck and Skye Cooley, "China more friend than foe to U.S. in North Korea denuclearization," UPI, Nov. 14, 2018, https://tinyurl.com/yarmpwy6; Atsuhito Isozaki, "Why Kim Jong Un Has Turned to 'Tributary Diplomacy,'" *The Diplomat*, Jan. 23, 2019, https://tinyurl.com/y9u87wte.

87. Will Martin, "Lost jobs, shrinking growth, and rotting crops—here are the ways Trump's trade war is hurting America," *Business Insider*, Nov. 28, 2018, https://tinyurl.com/yxgt4s3y; Milton Ezrati, "Trade War from the Chinese Side," *Forbes*, Oct. 3, 2018, https://tinyurl.com/y5ch36w6.

88. "Remarks by President Trump in Cabinet Meeting," The White House, Jan. 2, 2019, https://tinyurl.com/yyl8rkaq.

89. Robert Costa and Ashley Parker, "Former vice president Cheney challenges Pence at private retreat, compares Trump's foreign policy to Obama's approach," *The Washington Post*, March 12, 2019, https://tinyurl.com/y5yoljbx; Nick Wadhams and Jennifer Jacobs, "Trump Seeks Huge Premium From Allies Hosting U.S. Troops," Bloomberg, March 8, 2019, https://tinyurl.com/y4puqg39.

90. Costa and Parker, *ibid.*

91. *Ibid.*

92. Jake Sherman, "Pelosi, McConnell to invite NATO's secretary-general to address Congress," *Politico*, March 11, 2019, https://tinyurl.com/y3d4j5lg.

93. Boris Kálnoky, "My Europe: Why Eastern Europeans like Donald Trump," Deutsche Welle, Nov. 12, 2018, https://tinyurl.com/y6qhkk4k.

94. Shervin Taheran, "Select Reactions to the INF Treaty Crisis," Arms Control Now, Feb. 1, 2019, https://tinyurl.com/y4lj9qmc.

95. "US has violated INF Treaty since 1999, Lavrov tells Putin," TASS, Feb. 2, 2019, https://tinyurl.com/

y43to72c; Amy F. Woolf, "Russian Compliance with the Intermediate Range Nuclear Forces (INF) Treaty: Background and Issues for Congress, Updated Feb. 8, 2019," Congressional Research Service, https://tinyurl.com/hwkzn8y; Zeke Miller and Michael Balsamo, "Moscow says U.S. nuke treaty pullout would be 'very dangerous step,'" The Associated Press, Oct. 21, 2018, https://tinyurl.com/y5pgnau4.

96. "A Force for Good: America Reinvigorated in the Middle East," *op. cit.*

97. Tom Udall and Richard J. Durbin, "Trump is barreling toward war with Iran. Congress must act to stop him," *The Washington Post*, March 5, 2019, https://tinyurl.com/y2u6lvf8.

98. *Ibid.*

99. *Ibid.*

100. "Face the Nation," *op. cit.*

101. Kathy Gilsinan, "Trump Is Rushing the Syria Withdrawal—And That Could Backfire," *The Atlantic*, Jan. 11, 2019, https://tinyurl.com/ycfoy2zp; Francesca Paris, "Trump Adviser Bolton Says U.S. Withdrawal From Syria Is Conditional on Defeat of ISIS," NPR, Jan. 6, 2019, https://tinyurl.com/ybwf52fh.

102. Stephen Collinson, "Shocking Syria withdrawal plan is pure Trump," CNN, Dec. 21, 2018, https://tinyurl.com/yadpavy7.

103. Mark Katkov and Larry Kaplow, "Analysis: The End Of The 'Caliphate' Doesn't Mean The End Of ISIS," NPR, March 22, 2019, https://tinyurl.com/y299grlt.

104. "Remarks by President Trump to the 73rd Session of the United Nations General Assembly, New York, NY," The White House, Sept. 25, 2018, https://tinyurl.com/yc3xfnrr.

105. William Neuman and Nicholas Casey, "Venezuela Election Won by Maduro Amid Widespread Disillusionment," *The New York Times*, May 20, 1918, https://tinyurl.com/yban46hs; "Statement from President Donald J. Trump Recognizing Venezuelan National Assembly President Juan Guaidó as the Interim President of Venezuela,"

The White House, Jan. 23, 2019, https://tinyurl.com/ycrz8ejv; Amy Mackinnon, "Maduro vs. Guaidó: A Global Scorecard," *Foreign Policy*, Feb. 6, 2019, https://tinyurl.com/yxzay7yc.

106. Jeremy Diamond and Allie Malloy, "Trump approves sanctions on Venezuelan oil company," CNN, Jan. 29, 2019, https://tinyurl.com/yafcnrse; Devika Krishna Kumar and Collin Eaton, "Venezuelan oil exports to U.S. still a primary source of cash" Reuters, Jan. 25, 2019, https://tinyurl.com/ydzyzxpm.

107. From interview on "The 11th Hour with Brian Williams," MSNBC, March 12, 2019, https://tinyurl.com/y67bwkne.

BIBLIOGRAPHY

Books

Beckley, Michael, *Unrivaled: Why America Will Remain the World's Sole Superpower*, Cornell University Press, 2018.
A Tufts University political scientist says the United States' overwhelming wealth and military might, if used wisely, will assure its continued international dominance.

Daalder, Ivo H., and James M. Lindsay, *The Empty Throne: America's Abdication of Global Leadership*, Public Affairs, 2018.
The president of the Chicago Council on Global Affairs (Daalder) and senior vice president at the Council on Foreign Relations (Lindsay) argue that the United States has abandoned its commitment to alliances, free trade, democracy and human rights.

Kagan, Robert, *The Jungle Grows Back: America and Our Imperiled World*, Knopf, 2018.
A senior fellow at the Brookings Institution warns that rising nationalism threatens the relative peace, prosperity and progressive character of the post-World War II years.

Simms, Brendan, and Charlie Laderman, *Donald Trump: The Making of a World View*, I. B. Tauris, 2017.
Two British historians explain that President Trump's foreign policy views, far from being impulsive and improvised, were formed in the 1980s and are deeply rooted in American history.

Articles

Allison, Graham, "The Myth of the Liberal Order," *Foreign Affairs*, **July/August 2018, https://tinyurl .com/ybk6nu8p.**
A professor at the John F. Kennedy School of Government at Harvard University says as the U.S. share of global power shrinks, it must coexist with China, Russia and other emerging powers with their own ideas of how the world should be run.

Cox, Michael, "Understanding the Global Rise of Populism," LSE Ideas, Feb. 12. 2018, https://tinyurl .com/y4jjw4r8.
A professor of international relations at the London School of Economics dissects various theories on why populism is on the rise and on its possible consequences.

Nau, Henry R., "Trump's Conservative Internationalism," *National Review*, **Aug. 28, 2017, https://tinyurl.com/ yytv6zsw.**
A professor of international affairs at George Washington University writes that the president's unilateral foreign policy, based on national sovereignty rather than international institutions, is what the United States needs now.

Nye, Joseph S., "A Time for Positive-Sum Power," *The Wilson Quarterly*, **Fall, 2018, https://tinyurl. com/y4rgqnb6.**
The former dean of Harvard's Kennedy School of Government and a former Defense Department official urges a return to multilateralism in U.S. dealings with China and in other foreign policy challenges.

Plattner, Marc F., "Illiberal Democracy and the Struggle on the Right," *Journal of Democracy*, **Vol. 30, No. 1, January 2019, https://tinyurl.com/ y6qt7er4.**
The founding co-editor of the *Journal of Democracy* and co-chair of the Research Council of the International Forum for Democratic Studies writes that the rise of right-wing populist parties in Europe and Latin America threatens liberal democracy.

Reports and Studies

"National Security Strategy of the United States of America," The White House, December 2017, https:// tinyurl.com/y6rtr789.
The Trump administration outlines its plans to defend the homeland from economic, military and diplomatic threats, both foreign and domestic.

"Summary of the 2018 National Defense Strategy of The United States of America," U.S. Department of Defense, Jan. 19, 2018, https://tinyurl.com/y8a3laof.
The Pentagon analyzes defense challenges facing the United States and the military's response.

Cimino-Isaacs, Cathleen D., Rachel F. Fefer and Ian F. Fergusson, "World Trade Organization: Overview and Future Direction," Congressional Research Service, updated Feb. 15, 2019, https://tinyurl.com/ y64vvn7b.
Analysts from the research arm of Congress examine the history of the World Trade Organization and the challenges it faces in today's economic and political environment, emphasizing the role of the United States.

Kyle, Jordan, and Limor Gultchin, "Populists in Power Around the World," Tony Blair Institute for Global Change, Nov. 7, 2018, https://tinyurl.com/ yyu3gl55.
Two researchers at the nonpartisan institute define populism, evaluate its impact and track its growth in a global database.

Mazarr, Michael J., et al., "Understanding the Emerging Era of International Competition: Theoretical and Historical Perspectives," RAND Corp., 2018, https://tinyurl.com/y2vkb476.
Researchers examine the Trump administration's national security strategy in the context of the new military, economic and political competition facing the United States.

THE NEXT STEP

North Korea

Denyer, Simon, "North Korea denounces scaled-back U.S.-South Korea military exercises," *The Washington Post*, **March 7, 2019, https://tinyurl.com/y4faokx8.**
In the latest indication of increased tension between the United States and North Korea, Pyongyang condemned a U.S.-South Korean military exercise, even though it was reduced in scope.

Perez, Evan, and David Shortell, "North Korean-backed bank hacking on the rise, US officials say," CNN, March 1, 2019, https://tinyurl.com/y43nq9ze.
The bite of U.S. economic sanctions has driven North Korea to resort to digital bank heists, according to U.S. officials.

Shin, Hyonhee, " 'All-or-nothing' U.S. approach toward North Korea won't work: Moon adviser," Reuters, March 12, 2019, https://tinyurl.com/yxvcw9tx.
While both sides bear responsibility for the failed North Korea-U.S. summit, the United States "made excessive demands" by abruptly toughening its stance to demand complete North Korean denuclearization, says a South Korean national security adviser.

Russia

Pancevski, Bojan, "How a Russian Gas Pipeline Is Driving a Wedge Between the U.S. and Its Allies," *The Wall Street Journal*, March 10, 2019, https://tinyurl.com/y4ufknps.
The Trump administration plans to impose sanctions on companies and investors involved in a natural gas pipeline project that would increase German consumption of Russian gas.

Sonne, Paul, "U.S. military to test missiles banned under faltering nuclear pact with Russia," *The Washington Post*, March 13, 2019, https://tinyurl.com/yylu8mvx.
The United States is preparing to test a ground-launched cruise missile previously banned by the Intermediate-Range Nuclear Forces Treaty shortly after the U.S. withdrawal from the accord takes effect this summer.

Zengerle, Patricia, "U.S. senators to try again to pass Russia sanctions bill," Reuters, Feb. 13, 2019, https://tinyurl.com/y2afa74h.
A bipartisan group of senators has proposed legislation that would impose new sanctions on Russia's banks, cyber sector and energy industry.

Sanctions

Domm, Patti, and Tom DiChristopher, "US sees room to be more aggressive on sanctions and take Iran oil exports to zero," CNBC, March 13, 2019, https://tinyurl.com/y2clyoc9.

Market projections that show global oil supply exceeding demand may enable the United States to increase its pressure on Iranian energy exports, a State Department official said.

Weissenstein, Michael, and Matthew Lee, "Trump symbolically tightens embargo on Cuba," The Associated Press, March 4, 2019, https://tinyurl.com/y2b4lkh6.
The Trump administration is allowing lawsuits against some Cuban businesses and government agencies, but the effect is likely to be largely symbolic because most of the targeted entities are not connected to the U.S. legal or financial systems.

Wyss, Jim, "As U.S. sanctions against Venezuela mount, what's the human toll?" *Miami Herald*, updated March 12, 2019, https://tinyurl.com/y3ekuonv.
The United States is increasing its economic pressure on the regime of Venezuelan leader Nicolás Maduro, but there is debate about whether the strategy is appropriate given the increased suffering it is causing.

Trade War

Wei, Lingling, and Bob Davis, "U.S., China Close In on Trade Deal," *The Wall Street Journal*, March 3, 2019, https://tinyurl.com/y66l647v.
China is prepared to ease tariffs and other restrictions on U.S. goods if the United States lifts most of the trade sanctions it imposed last year, say a Beijing-based finance reporter and a *Wall Street Journal* senior editor.

Weinraub, Mark, "Why U.S. growers are betting the farm on soybeans amid China trade war," Reuters, March 14, 2019, https://tinyurl.com/y649y6wn.
U.S. farmers are still planting soybeans, despite losing their biggest market because of the U.S.-China trade dispute, because of a lack of good alternatives.

Wu, Wendy, "Casualties of trade war: Chinese in US denied licences to work with sensitive technologies," *South China Morning Post*, March 12, 2019, https://tinyurl.com/yxdoxdxv.
Heightened U.S. concerns over technology security may be preventing Chinese-born workers from getting technology access work permits, says a Beijing-based reporter.

For More Information

Brookings Institution, 1775 Massachusetts Ave., N.W., Washington, DC 20036; 202-797-6000; www.brookings.edu. Bipartisan think tank concerned with issues of national and international policy.

Carnegie Endowment for International Peace, 1779 Massachusetts Ave., N.W., Washington, DC 20036-2103; 202-483-7600; https://carnegieendowment.org. U.S. think tank analyzing global policy issues.

Center for American Progress, 1333 H St., N.W., 10th Floor, Washington, DC, 20005; 202-682-1611; www.americanprogress.org. Think tank providing liberal perspective on global and domestic policy issues.

Center for Security and International Studies, 1616 Rhode Island Ave., N.W., Washington, DC 20036; 202-887-0200; www.csis.org. Bipartisan think tank that researches and highlights U.S. and international strategic topics.

Council on Foreign Relations, 58 East 68th St., New York, NY 10065; 212-434-9400; www.cfr.org. Nonpartisan foreign affairs membership organization, publisher and think tank.

Heritage Foundation, 214 Massachusetts Ave., N.E., Washington DC 20002-4999; 202-546-4400; www.heritage.org. Conservative public-policy think tank that promotes public policies, including foreign policies, based on the principles of free enterprise, limited government, traditional American values and a strong national defense.

National Security Archive Gelman Library, Suite 701, The George Washington University, 2130 H St., N.W., Washington, DC, 20037; 202-994-7000; https://nsarchive.gwu.edu. An independent nongovernmental research institute and library that collects and publishes declassified government documents, including those on U.S. foreign policy, acquired through the Freedom of Information Act.

Peterson Institute for International Economics, 1750 Massachusetts Ave., N.W., Washington, DC 20036; 202-328-9000; https://piie.com. Independent nonprofit think tank researching and analyzing global trade and economic issues.

Royal Institute of International Affairs, Chatham House, 10 St James' Square, London SW1Y 4LE; +44 (0)20 7957 5700; www.chathamhouse.org. Nongovernmental, nonpartisan British institute that analyzes major international issues from a European perspective.

U.S. Institute of Peace, 2301 Constitution Ave., N.W., Washington, DC 20037; 202-457-1700; www.usip.org. Congressionally funded, nonpartisan think tank researching and promoting nonviolent solutions to global challenges.

Woodrow Wilson International Center for Scholars, Ronald Reagan Building and International Trade Center, One Woodrow Wilson Plaza, 1300 Pennsylvania Ave., N.W., Washington, DC 20004-3027; 202-691-4000; www.wilsoncenter.org. Nonpartisan think tank that researches and presents programs on international issues.

Xinhua/Pan Xu/Getty Images

A freight train from Chengdu, China, arrives in
Vienna, Austria, one of 15 European countries
connected by rail to Chinese cities. Chinese goods
now reach European markets in as little as 12 days,
half the time they would take by sea.

From *CQ Researcher,*
January 25, 2019

8

China's Belt and Road Initiative

Does it pose a threat to the West?

By Jonathan Broder

THE ISSUES

Once a week, a China Rail freight train carrying clothing and
household goods pulls into London's Barking Station, the final
stop on a 7,500-mile journey from the Chinese city of Yiwu.

Another rail line connects Shanghai with Lisbon, and a third
links Chengdu, the capital of China's Sichuan province, to
Nuremberg, Germany. Rolling across the vast Eurasian supercon-
tinent on new tracks financed by Beijing's state-run banks,
Chinese goods now reach their markets in as little as 12 days,
European officials say—half the time they would take by sea.[1]

Meanwhile in Africa, China is financing a new railway linking
Tanzania's Indian Ocean port of Dar es Salaam to Africa's landlocked
interior. In South America, plans for China to fund a transcontinental
railroad from Brazil to the Pacific Ocean are on track. And on the
Asian subcontinent, Chinese workers are building a railway, several
power plants and fiber-optic lines that will connect western China
with the Indian Ocean, via Pakistan's Arabian Sea coast.[2]

These projects are just some of the thousands of ventures across
Asia, Africa, Europe and Latin America that make up China's
sprawling international infrastructure program known as the Belt
and Road Initiative (BRI). President Xi Jinping has celebrated his
signature initiative as the recreation of the Silk Road, the ancient
network of Eurasian trading routes that merchants crisscrossed
with camel caravans, hauling goods between China and Europe.

China Investing Heavily in Asia

Asia accounts for seven of the 10 countries drawing the most investment under China's infrastructure program known as the Belt and Road Initiative (BRI).

Top 10 Countries by BRI Investment, in Billions of Dollars, 2014–18

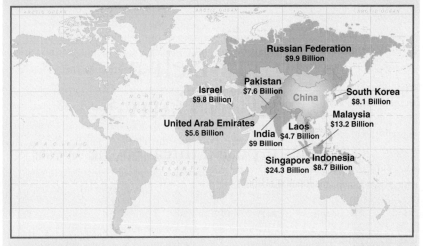

Russian Federation
$9.9 Billion

Pakistan
$7.6 Billion

Israel
$9.8 Billion

South Korea
$8.1 Billion

Malaysia
$13.2 Billion

United Arab Emirates
$5.6 Billion

India
$9 Billion

Laos $4.7 Billion

Singapore
$24.3 Billion

Indonesia
$8.7 Billion

* Investment includes the acquisition of companies and other assets.

Source: Cecilia Joy-Pérez and Derek Scissors, "Be Wary of Spending on the Belt and Road," American Enterprise Institute, November 2018, https://tinyurl.com/y83akbrz

Xi's 21st-century version is harnessing China's industrial know-how, the world's largest foreign exchange reserves and the lending power of the country's state-run banks to construct vast transportation, energy and telecommunications networks that will link China to markets and crucial resources from the Arctic Circle to the Indian, Atlantic and Pacific oceans.

China specialists say the BRI lies at the heart of Xi's grand strategy to transform China into a global power by 2050, a goal originally set in the 1950s by Mao Zedong, Communist China's first leader, and embraced by his successors. With the participation of more than 100 countries, all eager for a slice of the $1 trillion in infrastructure loans and investments that China intends to spend on the program, the BRI is reshaping longstanding global alliances and drawing some Western allies closer to Beijing.[3]

And at a time when critics say the United States is retreating from the world stage as President Trump pursues his "America First" policies, many experts say the BRI could help lead to a new economic and political order based on China's standards.

"The BRI is a grand strategy," says Nadège Rolland, a former adviser on China to the French Defense Ministry who is now a senior fellow at the National Bureau of Asian Research, a Washington think tank. "It's not just about building bridges or railways. It's much more profound. It's about reshaping the world according to Beijing's norms."

Others, however, say that China is likely exaggerating the size of the initiative and thus its potential to reshape its relations with other countries. "For now, Chinese officials can enjoy watching the estimates [of BRI spending] rise and could even reap some political benefits. They have conjured up a massive carrot that has caught the world's attention," wrote Jonathan Hillman, an Asia expert at Washington's Center for Strategic and International Studies, a centrist think tank. "But China also faces downsides to unrealistic BRI estimates. . . . For China, perhaps the biggest risk is unmet expectations. With the world watching, China now faces pressure to deliver on its promises."[4]

The process by which China undertakes Belt and Road infrastructure projects or invests in overseas commercial ventures is highly fluid and murky, according to Martin Chorzempa, a China expert at the Peterson Institute for International Economics, a Washington think tank.

Generally, he says, governments interested in participating in the BRI sign a memorandum of understanding (MOU) with Beijing. Officials from both sides then negotiate what infrastructure projects will be built; how much the member government must borrow from China's state-owned banks; and the terms of the loan. In some cases, he adds, the two sides forgo a MOU and proceed directly to negotiations, the details of which are often shrouded in secrecy.

Development experts point out that unlike the World Bank and other multilateral lending institutions in the West, China does not require borrower governments to abide by free-market principles and democratic norms. Beijing only requires that the borrower hire state-owned Chinese construction companies to perform the work.

"So even though the money is officially loaned to a country, much of it winds up back in China," Chorzempa says.

In the five years since the BRI's official launch in late 2013, China has provided $404 billion in loans and investments to developing countries, according to the China Global Investment Tracker, a program run by two conservative Washington think tanks, the American Enterprise Institute and the Heritage Foundation.[5]

The money has made the BRI the largest development endeavor in history, dwarfing the United States' $13.2 billion Marshall Plan—$135 billion in today's dollars—that helped reconstruct Western Europe after World War II. The amount also tops the World Bank, which lent $289.4 billion worldwide between fiscal 2013 and 2017, according to David Theis, the bank's press secretary.[6]

For China, the BRI is paying significant economic dividends. Beijing now controls 10 percent of European port capacity, according to the Organisation for Economic Co-operation and Development, a Paris-based economic research institution composed of 36 industrialized member countries.[7] The initiative also has opened new markets for Chinese exports and is giving China access to untapped sources of raw materials. And the program is soaking up some of China's excess industrial capacity that built up during Beijing's massive stimulus spending following the 2007-09 global financial crisis.

The initiative, however, holds a dangerous downside for China, says Allen Carlson, director of Cornell University's China and Asia Pacific studies program. With Beijing approving hefty loans to developing

Belt and Road Spending Is Slowing

Total annual spending under China's Belt and Road Initiative (BRI) peaked at nearly $106 billion in 2016. Funding for construction projects, in which China builds infrastructure within a country, also crested in 2016. Spending on investment projects, in which China takes an ownership stake in a country's assets, rose to about $44 billion in 2015 but has fallen since.

BRI Spending on Investment and Construction Projects, in Billions of Dollars, 2014–18

	2014	2015	2016	2017	2018*
Total	$73.80	$91	$105.80	$94.90	$38.20
Investment**	$24.10	$43.90	$33.70	$32.90	$13.60
Construction	$49.70	$47.10	$72.10	$62	$24.60

* 2018 figures are for six months and are preliminary.

** Investment includes the acquisition of companies and other assets in BRI countries.

Source: Cecilia Joy-Pérez and Derek Scissors, "Be Wary of Spending on the Belt and Road," American Enterprise Institute, November 2018, https://tinyurl.com/y83akbrz

countries with poor credit ratings and few other sources of capital, Carlson says China's state-run banks could be left holding billions of dollars in bad foreign loans at a time when the nation already is saddled with significant domestic debt. China, for example, has lost $20 billion of the $62.2 billion it lent to Venezuela, according to the American Enterprise Institute.[8]

"That's the kind of situation that definitely adds to systemwide financial risks in China," says Johan van de Ven, a China analyst at the RWR Advisory Group, a Washington-based business consultancy that specializes in political risk.

Strategically, many analysts say, BRI infrastructure projects are fostering closer security ties with authoritarian Central Asian governments such as Kazakhstan on China's western periphery, providing Beijing with allies in the struggle against the region's growing Islamist threat.

BRI pipelines running from the Caspian Sea oil fields to western China guarantee a secure overland energy supply route if a conflict were to close off maritime routes. The BRI also is exporting Chinese standards for everything from development loans to security measures. All these pieces make up the scaffolding for a new world order in which Xi envisions all roads leading to Beijing.

The Belt and Road Initiative has translated into greater Chinese geopolitical influence in member countries, a development that has unsettled U.S., African and Western officials, according to China-watchers. Senior Trump administration officials and African critics warn of poor countries falling victim to what they call China's "debt-trap diplomacy," an alleged strategy in which Beijing deliberately saddles BRI governments with more debt than they can pay and then forces them to surrender strategic assets, such as ports, gold mines or oil reserves.

"When China comes calling, it's not always to the good of your citizens," Secretary of State Mike Pompeo warned Latin American governments in October, shortly after Xi said China would invest $250 billion in Latin America over the next decade. "When they show up with deals that seem to be too good to be true, it's often the case that they, in fact, are."[9]

Xi denies the BRI is a debt trap or a power grab. "It is not designed to serve any hidden geopolitical agenda," he told a gathering of Asian leaders in November 2018. "It is not targeted against anyone, and it does not exclude anyone."[10]

Many independent analysts say, however, that China appears to have employed debt-trap diplomacy in a handful of countries, such as Sri Lanka, where Beijing took control of the Chinese-built Hambantota port in 2017 after the Sri Lankan government could not pay off its loans. But other experts say the vast majority of BRI projects are economically viable for the host governments.

"China has a comparative advantage in providing affordable infrastructure, and there are many cases where China is filling a legitimate need," says Jeff M. Smith, an Asia expert at the Heritage Foundation.

Still, U.S. officials worry about the BRI's strategic dimensions, warning that the seaports China is building throughout the Indo-Pacific region could accommodate China's growing navy. Xi's ultimate aim, they say, is for China to supplant the United States as the principal economic and military power across huge stretches of the globe.

"That's clearly the goal—pushing the U.S. and the Western influence back to the margins while China exerts its own power over the vast region that is covered by the Belt and Road," Rolland says.

To compete with the BRI, the Trump administration has announced a $60 billion loan program for infrastructure projects in the Indo-Pacific region.[11]

The new U.S. development program forms part of a broader policy of pushing back against Beijing after what Trump and some independent analysts say were previous administrations' halfhearted responses to China's unfair trade practices and questionable territorial claims in the South China Sea. Trump points to his tariff war with China, steps to halt China's theft of U.S. intellectual property and the U.S. Navy's stepped-up challenges to Beijing's military presence in the South China Sea as evidence of his hard-nosed approach.[12]

But even as Trump flexes American muscles on trade and territorial issues, both conservative and left-leaning experts say Trump's aversion to multilateral agreements has set back Washington's ability to constrain Beijing as it seeks to challenge the U.S.-dominated world order.

Trump's hostility toward alliances "plays to China's interest," van de Ven says.

To illustrate, many experts point to Trump's decision in early 2017 to withdraw the United States from the Trans-Pacific Partnership (TPP), a 12-nation free-trade agreement that formed the centerpiece of former President Barack Obama's "pivot to Asia."[13] With the United States at its center, the TPP could have leveraged the power of free trade to draw Pacific nations away from China, these experts say.

But the United States' withdrawal "has left a vacuum that allows for China to assume a larger role within regional trade networks," says van de Ven.

Amid such challenges, here are some key questions being asked about China's Belt and Road Initiative:

Is the BRI a good deal for participating countries?

Trump administration officials, as well as some independent analysts, charge Beijing uses predatory loan practices to finance "white elephant" infrastructure projects that provide few local jobs, offer little training to those residents it does employ and bury poor countries under mountains of debt that force them to surrender strategic assets to China as payment. In the end, these critics charge, BRI projects produce little economic growth for participating countries.

"The benefits flow overwhelmingly to Beijing," Vice President Mike Pence said in an October speech that accused China of abusing its economic power and bullying its neighbors.[14]

But researchers who have studied thousands of Belt and Road projects say the accusation does not hold up under scrutiny.

"Looking at the entire range of countries in the initiative, the risk of debt distress is not widespread," concluded a 2018 study by the Center for Global Development, a Washington think tank that works to reduce global poverty and inequality. "The majority of BRI countries will likely avoid [debt] problems . . . due to BRI projects."[15]

Other analysts agree with that assessment. "There are many countries that have accepted BRI investments where those investments have been productive, economically viable and . . . have contributed to the GDP and welfare of the country," says the Heritage Foundation's Smith.

Smith and other analysts cite Greece as a success story. After struggling for years under austerity measures imposed by its European partners following the 2008 global financial meltdown, the country is finally emerging from its economic doldrums, thanks in part to major Chinese investments.

In 2016, the state-owned China Ocean Shipping Co. (Cosco) purchased a majority stake in the port of Piraeus, the seaport that serves Athens, for $312 million.[16] Since then, Cosco has invested nearly a half billion euros in new cranes, an ultramodern floating dock and a new passenger terminal, transforming Piraeus into the Mediterranean's busiest port and a principal entry point to Europe. Greek officials say Cosco has created 1,000 permanent jobs, as well as short-term contracts for some 1,500 workers.

State-backed Chinese companies also have invested billions of euros to build an upscale resort outside Athens as part of plan to bring more than 1.5 million Chinese tourists to Greece over the next few years.[17]

"The Greek economy is thirsty for investments, and the presence of Chinese companies is important, and we welcome it," said Prime Minister Alexis Tsipras.[18]

In August, Xi said that over the past five years, the BRI has created more than 200,000 jobs in member countries.[19] Western analysts say they do not have the data to verify Xi's claim, but a 2015 study of 400 BRI projects in Africa by the Institute for Emerging Market Studies at Hong Kong University of Science and Technology found that 87 percent of their workforces consisted of African workers.[20]

"One of the key benefits of these development projects is the skills and experience and training that get transferred to local staff," says the Peterson Institute's Chorzempa.

Meanwhile, researchers at Johns Hopkins University and Boston University have constructed a database of China's development loans since 2000 that challenges U.S. critics who allege that BRI projects do not provide economic benefits to developing countries. According to Deborah Bräutigam, a political economist and director of Johns Hopkins' China Africa Research Initiative, researchers found that most of nearly $100 billion that China lent to African nations between 2000 and 2015 financed projects to address the continent's yawning infrastructure gap.

"On a continent where over 600 million Africans have no access to electricity, 40 percent of the Chinese loans paid for power generation and transmission," Bräutigam said. "Another 30 percent went to modernizing Africa's crumbling transport infrastructure."[21]

A September 2018 study by AidData, a development finance research organization based at the College of William & Mary in Williamsburg, Va., found that China's ability to quickly finance and build so-called connective infrastructure—railways, highways, bridges and ports—has spread economic growth to rural areas faster and more effectively than Western development programs, which often take years to complete.[22]

But skeptics say the BRI has built little-utilized vanity projects for corrupt politicians, adding that more than a half-dozen recipient nations have taken on significant debt. Last August, the new Malaysia government suspended construction on two pipelines, a railway and other projects worth $22 billion out of concerns the previous government had taken on too many liabilities for projects that were not necessary.[23]

In early January, a *Wall Street Journal* investigation revealed the previous Malaysian government of then-Prime Minister Najib Razak had offered to give China lucrative stakes in the $2.5 billion pipeline project and the $16 billion railway in return for Beijing's offer to bail out a Malaysian government fund at the center of a multibillion-dollar graft scandal.[24]

Critics routinely point to Sri Lanka as an example of how the BRI can hurt a nation. In addition to its surrender of Hambantota port to China, Sri Lanka has a new Chinese-built airport that virtually no one uses.[25] "It is literally the world's emptiest airport," says Hillman of the Center for Strategic and International Studies.

Environmentalists warn that many BRI projects could damage biodiverse areas.

Energy Sector Leads Spending

Energy projects dominate China's Belt and Road Initiative (BRI), followed by transportation and real estate construction and investment. Eleven percent of the $404 billion in BRI spending so far is classified as "troubled," meaning those loans are in or near default or the investments have failed.

BRI Spending by Sector, in Billions of Dollars, 2014–18*

Sector	Construction	Investment**	Troubled
Energy (alternative, coal, gas, hydro, nuclear, oil)	$111.00	$56.40	$26.00
Transportation (autos, aviation, rail, shipping)	$74.50	$18.50	$8.00
Real Estate (construction, property)	$30.20	$12.10	$0.70
Utilities	$8.70	$1.80	$0.20
Chemicals (potash, phosphates, methanol)	$8.40	-	$1.90
Metals (iron, bauxite, copper, gold)	$7.90	$6.90	$3.60
Agriculture	$4.80	$5.20	$0.10
Other (education, textiles, etc.)	$7.20	$16.20	$0.40
Technology	$1.20	$6.30	$1.10
Entertainment	$0.90	$6.70	-
Logistics	$0.70	$11.40	-
Finance (banking, investment)	-	$6.60	$3.40
Total	**$255.50**	**$148.00**	**$45.20**

* 2018 data are for six months and are preliminary.
** Investment includes the acquisition of companies and other assets in BRI countries.

Source: Cecilia Joy-Pérez and Derek Scissors, "Be Wary of Spending on the Belt and Road," American Enterprise Institute, November 2018, https://tinyurl.com/y83akbrz

For instance, conservationists say, a massive Chinese-financed dam project in Indonesia threatens the only known habitat of the Tapanuli orangutan, the world's rarest great ape. Indonesia also shelved plans for China to build a high-speed rail line, citing a lack of environmental impact studies. And critics have raised concerns about environmental damage in Laos, Cambodia and Vietnam from Chinese-funded hydroelectric power projects along the Mekong River.[26]

In November, Pence mocked Chinese construction on BRI projects as low quality. In Kenya, for example, a $12 million bridge collapsed in 2017.[27] Pence also accused China of bullying its BRI trading partners, portraying the program as a Trojan horse for extending China's geopolitical clout.

"Know that the United States offers a better option," Pence told leaders attending the Asia-Pacific Economic Cooperation summit in Papua New Guinea. "We don't drown our partners in a sea of debt; we don't coerce, compromise your independence. We do not offer a constricting belt or a one-way road."[28]

Is the BRI fulfilling China's economic and strategic goals?

When President Xi unveiled his Belt and Road Initiative in 2013, he envisioned an impressive set of economic and strategic benefits that would flow from the hard and soft networks linking China to the rest of Asia, Africa and Europe. The Chinese-financed infrastructure projects would strengthen trade and financial integration with BRI countries, he said, and facilitate greater policy coordination with their governments. And the soft components of the initiative, such as student scholarships and a new Chinese international finance payment system, would advance Chinese models for business and governance.

Analysts say the program has achieved remarkable growth in membership and produced impressive economic and strategic results for China in a short period.

"Lots of countries have joined, and it's taking root in the international discourse," says the National Bureau of Asian Research's Rolland. "So I'd say from China's perspective, things are pretty positive so far."

But the BRI also is encountering pushback from partner governments and others. In China, a rare wave of criticism of the BRI surfaced last September when critics took to social media to complain that the government was financing projects overseas instead of at home. Government censors quickly removed the posts.[29]

For now, however, the BRI continues to add countries to its roster. Since its launch with 64 partner countries at the end of 2013, the BRI has nearly doubled in size to 117 countries in 2018, according to the China Global Investment Tracker. Analysts who monitor the program say China is now funding thousands of BRI projects on every continent but Antarctica.

China's ambitions for the BRI appear boundless. Beijing has called upon the nations bordering the Arctic

Circle to cooperate in developing a "Polar Silk Road" that would exploit energy sources in the region and link China and Europe through the Arctic Ocean.

The initiative even has reached outer space, with Beijing aiming to provide BRI countries priority access to China's new Beidou satellite-navigation system. At its current rate of growth, the BRI could meet its $1 trillion pledge in combined investment and construction activity in roughly four years, says China scholar Derek Scissors, who created the China Global Investment Tracker.

Economically, China says the BRI has boosted its foreign trade. According to China's Ministry of Commerce, the imports and exports to and from BRI countries from January to October 2018 accounted for 27.3 percent of China's total foreign trade volume of $3.84 trillion for the same period, up nearly 15 percent over the same period in 2017.[30]

The BRI also is helping China fulfill another economic goal: greater use of its renminbi currency in international trade. Until 2015, all international trade transactions were conducted in dollars through the SWIFT interbank payment system. But as part of the BRI, Beijing established the China International Payment System to facilitate cross-border renminbi transactions.

According to Eswar Prasad, a former head of the China division of the International Monetary Fund (IMF) and now a trade policy expert at Cornell University, the payment system will likely reduce transaction costs and increase the international use of the renminbi, diminishing the dollar's dominant role.[31]

The BRI has provided China with a raft of strategic rewards. For example, Beijing's investments in Djibouti, a tiny African country that serves as a gateway to the Red Sea and the Suez Canal, have resulted in China establishing its first overseas military base there.

Under several BRI projects, Pakistan, a key U.S. ally until President Trump cut off its security aid last year, is planning to expand its manufacture of Chinese warplanes, weaponry and other military hardware, according to *The New York Times*. Beijing also has granted Pakistan access to the military function of China's Beidou satellite-navigation system, which provides guidance for missiles, aircraft and ships. Their cooperation is meant to pave the way for other BRI countries to use Beidou, ending their reliance on the United States' GPS network and drawing them closer to China.[32]

Chinese troops and tanks parade at the opening ceremony of China's first overseas military base, in Djibouti, in August 2017. China's investments in the tiny African country are giving the Asian nation military access to the strategically important Red Sea and Suez Canal.

Finally, the BRI has helped China advance a long-standing strategic goal: the diplomatic isolation of Taiwan, which Beijing considers a renegade Chinese province. Over the past two years, Beijing has persuaded five BRI countries—the African island nation of São Tomé and Príncipe, Panama, Dominican Republic, Burkino Faso and El Salvador—to break relations with Taipei.[33]

But the BRI has some serious downsides for China. A significant portion of the $404 billion in loans and investments that China's state-run policy banks have provided for infrastructure projects in poor countries since late 2013 are already "nonperforming"—in default or near default—adding to China's staggering public and private debt, last clocked at $34 trillion, or 266 percent of GDP.[34]

And of the $1 trillion in loans that China made to developing countries between 2005 and 2017, according to the American Enterprise Institute's Scissors, more than a third—$370 billion—are "troubled investments," which include nonperforming loans and investments in deals that either have failed altogether or have not produced any profits.

Van de Ven says China's state-owned development banks are at high risk of having large numbers of nonperforming loans on their balance sheets at a time when China's domestic banks already have high numbers because of the nation's economic slowdown.

Some economists say the grumbling over the BRI that erupted on social media indicates the loans to developing countries are stoking domestic tensions. The criticism appeared after Xi pledged $60 billion in new loans to Africa. One blogger said that money could fund China's struggling Education Ministry for three years. "China is a poor country," the blogger wrote. "Is there any country that can provide China with $60bn in aid?"[35]

Several economists who track the BRI say that officials at China's development banks recognize the risk of their growing debt exposure and are trying to walk a fine line between reining in their BRI loans and following Xi's orders to fund his signature policy. As a result, BRI lending has continued but at a reduced pace. According to figures compiled by the RWR Advisory Group, combined overseas lending by Beijing's two principal policy banks, the China Development Bank and the Export-Import Bank of China, fell from $221 billion in the 2013-16 period to $66 bn in 2017-18.

"There's concern about lending to risky countries because China wants to reduce its debt," says the Peterson Institute's Chorzempa. "But that domestic imperative is hitting up against the continued drive to be involved in the BRI. And that's something they have to balance. It's extremely politically sensitive."

Does the BRI increase the chances for military conflict between the United States and China?

Graham Allison, a professor at Harvard University's Kennedy School of Government, predicted that if the animosity between the United States and China continues unchecked, the two nations are more likely to go to war than many people realize.

Allison's prediction was the sobering takeaway from his 2015 book, *Destined for War: Can America and China Escape Thucydides's Trap?* The book takes its title from the ancient Greek general and historian who concluded that the Peloponnesian War in the 5th century B.C. stemmed from the threat that a rising Athens posed to the established power of Sparta.

Allison argued the same power dynamic has held true throughout history. In 12 of 16 past cases where a rising power confronted a ruling power—most notably, a rising Germany versus Britain in the early 1900s and a rising Japan versus the United States in the 1940s—the result has been bloodshed, Allison said. And if China

and the United States don't change course, he warned, the same dynamic could entrap them too.[36]

While Allison cited mounting tensions over China's claims to the South China Sea as a trigger for a U.S.-China conflict, some analysts point to Xi's Belt and Road Initiative—and the U.S. response to it.

China says it built up and militarized several reefs that it claims in the South China Sea to defend the sea lanes that make up the eastern reaches of the Maritime Silk Road, an essential component of the BRI. In response, the United States has stepped up its naval patrols in the disputed waters, prompting China to do the same.

Such moves, said Michael T. Klare, a senior visiting fellow at the Arms Control Association in Washington, raise the chances for a miscalculation or a collision between U.S. and Chinese warships that could spark a wider conflict. An October encounter in the South China Sea in which a Chinese warship deliberately came within 45 yards of a U.S. destroyer has underscored that danger.[37]

In its 2018 annual report to Congress on China-related security issues, the Pentagon said "some BRI investments could create potential military advantages for China, should China require access to selected foreign ports" to protect its interests. The report cites the Chinese-built ports in Hambantota, Sri Lanka, and in Gwadar, Pakistan, as potential Chinese military assets on the Indian Ocean.[38]

The threat the BRI poses to U.S. interests in the region has prompted American military planners to re-evaluate their strategy, Klare said. The Pentagon's move at the end of May to change the name of the U.S. Pacific Command to the U.S. Indo-Pacific Command and strengthen military ties with India and other friendly countries on China's periphery represent what Klare called a concerted U.S. drive to "encircle China with pro-American, anti-Chinese alliance systems."[39]

"China remains our biggest long-term challenge," said the outgoing commander, Adm. Harry Harris Jr. "Without focused involvement and engagement by the U.S. and our allies and partners, China will realize its dream of hegemony in Asia. We should cooperate with Beijing where we can . . . but stand ready to confront them where we must."[40]

Allison also cited festering differences over trade as another possible path to war between the United States and China. While Trump and Xi reached a temporary truce over their tariff war at the December 2018 G-20 summit in Buenos Aires, many analysts say the major irritants—China's nontariff trade barriers, its theft of trade secrets and its coercive use of licensing to gain U.S. technology—remain unresolved.

Trump has threatened to impose stiff tariffs on all Chinese goods unless Xi agrees to make major concessions on these issues—an outcome many analysts regard as unlikely. "Trump's problem is that he has demanded the structural transformation of the Chinese economy into something that works more like the U.S. economy," said William Overholt, an expert on U.S.-Asia relations and a senior fellow at Harvard's Kennedy School. "The demand is non-negotiable, and everyone in both the U.S. and China knows it."[41]

Meanwhile, the tensions over the BRI and trade have highlighted the important role that the two leaders' personalities play in the larger U.S.-China rivalry and the chances for a military clash.

Clay Chandler, a veteran Asia hand, said Allison drew laughs during an April gathering of Hong Kong's Asia Society chapter when he remarked that if Hollywood ever produced a movie about a war between the United States and China, the casting director could not come up with two more archetypal antagonists than Trump and Xi. Both leaders, Chandler said, "have seemed to be reading almost line-for-line from the Thucydides script."[42]

Xi won changes to China's constitution last year that effectively have made him president for life. Emboldened by the United States' retreat into isolationism, he appears determined to press ahead with the BRI.

"There is little room for the two leaders to get along for any extended period of time," says Cornell University's Carlson.

For now, however, some analysts say that a shared fear of a war will prevent them from falling into the Thucydides trap.

"Both men have cast themselves as 'maximum leaders,' strong men defending the interests and honor of their nations," said Aaron Friedberg, a former foreign policy adviser to Vice President Dick Cheney and now a China expert at Princeton University. But "neither wants to be blamed for a complete breakdown in relations."[43]

The National Bureau of Asian Research's Rolland says Xi and his aides designed the Belt and Road

GREG BAKER/AFP via Getty Images

Chinese President Xi Jinping, left, walks with Zimbabwe President Emmerson Mnangagwa, in Beijing in April 2018. Xi is pushing the Belt and Road Initiative as a way to harness China's industrial know-how, the world's largest foreign exchange reserves and the lending power of the country's state-run banks. African nations, including Zimbabwe, have been major recipients of Chinese investment.

Initiative as a way to boost China's regional influence to the detriment of the United States without provoking an American military response.

"It is the archetypical illustration of how to win without fighting," she says. "If the Belt and Road generates military conflict, it will mean, from Beijing's perspective, that it has failed." Nonetheless, she acknowledges the BRI "could increase the risk that China and the U.S. could bump up against each other in various places and that China might get drawn into conflicts that draw in the U.S. too."

Dean Cheng, an expert on China's military doctrine and foreign policy at the Heritage Foundation, rejects Allison's prediction of an armed clash between China and the United States.

"It's a very Western-centric view," Cheng says. The Chinese, he explains, don't look at the world through a Thucydidean lens of rising powers challenging established powers, which form coalitions to balance the rising powers. They instead view the world through the lens of their own 5,000-year history, which has no record of Asian states aligning to balance China's power. "China's historical model is one in which China was the single, dominant hegemon for thousands of years, and all the others in Asia behaved as tributary states," he says.

With that historical framework in mind, Cheng sees increased political, economic and strategic rivalry between the United States and China, but not necessarily armed conflict.

"We're not shooting at each other, but it's very clear we're competing intensely," he says.

BACKGROUND
The Silk Road

In ancient times, the Silk Road functioned as China's economic, cultural and intellectual highway to the rest of the world. Its traffic included not only the delicate woven cloth that gave the Silk Road its name but also ancient China's most significant inventions. Some, such as the compass and paper-making, fueled the rise of empires; others, such as gunpowder and the crossbow, would hasten their fall.

The traffic along the Silk Road also spread ideas and philosophies that changed people's lives. In the first century, Buddhist monks from India brought their beliefs via the Silk Road to China and the Far East. Islam's warriors thundered out of Arabia in the seventh century to spread their faith to Central Asia. European travelers returning from the Far East in the 18th century brought back Confucianism, a set of ancient Chinese beliefs that became popular among Western philosophers.

The Venetian adventurer Marco Polo traveled to China along the Silk Road in the 13th century, and his descriptions of China's spices inspired European merchants to break the Arab monopoly on the lucrative spice trade by developing their own sources for the spices.[44]

Various Chinese dynasties welcomed goods carried over the Silk Road, such as the large horses from Central Asia that strengthened China's imperial armies. Chinese elites also prized Roman glass and rugs.[45]

But sometimes China's imperial overlords regarded anything foreign as barbaric and corrupting, prompting various attempts to shut down the Silk Road.

By the time the Qing dynasty came to power in 1644, British and French appetites for Chinese tea and porcelain had made China's economy the largest in the world.[46] But the emperor had no interest in European goods and closed off China's ports to Western trade except the one in Guangzhou. Meanwhile, the emperor required China's trading partners to pay in silver, leading to massive trade imbalances between those countries and China.

In the late 18th century, however, Britain finally hit upon a product that ordinary Chinese wanted: opium. Grown in British-controlled India, the opium was shipped to smugglers in China, who paid for it with silver. Despite imperial decrees banning the drug's sale, other Western countries, including the United States, joined in the lucrative opium trade.[47]

With addiction spreading, opium threatened Qing rule. In 1839, the emperor seized more than 1,000 tons of opium from British dealers in Guangzhou. The dealers demanded payment for their losses; the emperor refused and British warships shelled several coastal cities in what became known as the Opium Wars. The outcome was a series of unequal treaties that severely weakened the Qing dynasty.[48]

The treaty ending the first Opium War (1839-42) forced China to surrender Hong Kong to Britain in perpetuity and to give British merchants access to five other "treaty ports" where foreign goods could be traded. Agreements after the second Opium War (1856-1860), which Britain launched to force China's legalization of the opium trade, required China to open as many as 80 treaty ports to foreign trade.[49]

In the final years of the 19th century, the eruption of the so-called Boxer Rebellion again threatened European interests in China. Led by a group of martial arts students who gave the movement its name, the Boxers sought to restore Chinese sovereignty over the treaty ports. With the support of Qing rulers, they called for the death or expulsion of all foreigners from the country. But when a mob closed in on foreign nationals huddled in Beijing's Legation Quarter, 50,000 troops from eight Western nations intervened and defeated the Boxers. The coalition nations, which included the United States, required China to pay them the equivalent of $10 billion in reparations over the next 39 years.[50]

Meanwhile, word of the Qing dynasty's weakness reached Japan, once a tributary state of China. Now a rising Asian power with a modernized army, Japan seized Manchuria in northeast China and Taiwan in 1895.

Between the Europeans and the Japanese, the Silk Road had become a conduit for foreign conquest.

In 1911, as civil disorder spread, Sun Yat-sen, a revolutionary inspired by Western democratic thought, led an uprising that would prove decisive. A year later, the Qing dynasty collapsed, marking an end to 4,000 years of imperial rule and the birth of the nationalist Republic of China.[51]

CHRONOLOGY

130 B.C.-A.D. **1860** *Silk Road enables China to trade with the West.*

130 B.C. Silk Road, which grows into a network of overland trade routes connecting China with Eurasia and Europe, opens.

618-907 Silk Road expands to include maritime routes to the Middle East and East Africa, creating one of China's greatest periods of prosperity.

1275 Venetian adventurer Marco Polo arrives in China; his descriptions inspire a boom in European trade with China.

1368-1644 Ming dynasty expands trade along the maritime Silk Road.

1839-1860 Britain's Opium Wars force China to allow foreign trade after Qing dynasty rulers try to stop the British sale of opium to the Chinese.

1912-1949 *Silk Road trade dwindles as the Republic of China faces economic chaos, Japanese invasion and civil war.*

1912 Republic of China is established.

1921 Chinese Communist Party is founded amid anti-government protests.

1926-1937 Chiang Kai-shek, commander of nationalist Kuomintang forces, launches a military campaign with the Communists to overthrow the government but later attacks the Communists, forcing their "Long March" retreat in 1934.

1937-1945 Japan seizes Chinese province of Manchuria, then occupies the entire country during World War II.

1945-1949 After Japan's World War II defeat, civil war erupts between Kuomintang and Communist forces, resulting in a Communist victory, the establishment of the People's Republic of China and the Kuomintang's flight to Taiwan.

1949-1999 *Reformers cause upheaval and, eventually, dramatic growth.*

1958-1962 Mao Zedong's Great Leap Forward, a program designed to communize all farming, devastates agriculture, bringing China's economy to the brink of collapse.

1966-1976 Mao's Cultural Revolution delivers another economic blow as professionals are forced to perform manual labor and Red Guards assume management of factories and mines.

1978 Under reformer Deng Xiaoping, China embraces limited market economy principles and allows foreign trade to resume.

1979 U.S. and China establish full diplomatic relations.

1979-1984 Deng creates four special economic zones giving foreign investors tax breaks and other preferential treatment.

1993 China's economy continues to expand, fueled by the establishment of 2,000 more special economic zones.

1996 China's economy grows 9.5 percent.

2000-Present *China revives the Silk Road.*

2000-2008 China's economy grows at an average 10 percent annually, the highest in the world.

2009 In response to the global financial crisis, China invests $586 billion in domestic infrastructure, fueling an industrial surge at home and a global commodities boom abroad to meet China's demand for raw materials.

2011 President Barack Obama outlines his "pivot to Asia," an integrated diplomatic, military, and economic strategy to confront China's rise.

2013 With China's economy slowing, President Xi Jinping announces his Belt and Road Initiative to build transportation, energy and telecommunications networks connecting China to Europe, Africa and the rest of Asia.

2017 President Trump withdraws the United States from the Trans-Pacific Partnership, a 12-nation trade agreement designed to pull Pacific nations closer to the United States.

2018 After several countries cancel or scale back Belt and Road projects over debt concerns, President Xi announces the program will focus on smaller projects.

To Counter China, Trump Reverses Course on Foreign Aid

New agency to compete with the Belt and Road Initiative.

As a presidential candidate, Donald Trump proposed drastic cuts in foreign aid as part of his "America First" platform, saying he would "stop sending aid to countries that hate us."

Since becoming president, Trump has kept his word. He has ended aid to the United Nations agency that helps support Palestinian refugees, citing disagreements with how the agency spends its money. He has suspended nearly all security assistance to Pakistan, accusing the country of harboring terrorists. And his fiscal 2018 and 2019 budgets called for cutting billions in foreign aid, at least partly to encourage "self-reliance" among developing nations. Congress rejected those cuts.[1]

In October 2018, however, Trump reversed course, signing a bill to create a foreign aid agency—the U.S. International Development Finance Corp.—with authority to provide $60 billion in loans and other assistance for one year to firms conducting business in developing countries. The new agency will begin operating Oct. 1, 2019.[2]

Why the turnaround? Administration officials and independent experts say Trump understands the need to counter China's Belt and Road Initiative (BRI) in the fight for political and economic influence in the developing world.

"This is very much meant to be a new tool that allows the U.S. to compete with China in development finance," says Scott Morris, a former Treasury Department official who is a senior fellow at the Center for Global Development, a liberal think tank in Washington that focuses on international development issues.

A few days before Trump signed the bill creating the agency, Vice President Mike Pence said the administration would focus on development financing to give "foreign nations a just and transparent alternative to China's debt-trap diplomacy," a reference to the administration's view that the BRI's true purpose is to saddle poor countries with debt so China can take control of important infrastructure.[3]

The new agency is "a good thing for these small countries," says Nadège Rolland, a senior fellow at the National Bureau of Asian Research, a centrist Washington think tank. "It's better to have competition in the choices they can have."

Riley Walters, an Asia expert at the conservative Heritage Foundation think tank in Washington, says the focus of the U.S. loan program will be on developing countries in Asia and Africa where government leaders have either rejected China's loan offers or voiced concerns over the costs of Belt and Road projects. "The idea is to drive private investment toward countries where there's a strategic competition with China," he says.

Experts add that the appetite for U.S. involvement in development projects is especially strong in sub-Saharan countries, such as Kenya and Tanzania, where leaders have complained about shoddy Chinese workmanship on BRI projects and Beijing's preference for Chinese labor over local workers.

"Some African countries don't want to deal with China," says Heritage Foundation Africa expert Joshua Meservey. "American companies still have a good reputation on the continent for delivering quality work, and that has an enormous appeal for a lot of African countries."

Communist Control

For all practical purposes, the Silk Road ceased functioning for the next six decades, a turbulent period marked by Japan's occupation of China before and during World War II, economic chaos and a civil war that ended in a communist victory and the 1949 establishment of the People's Republic of China.

With the exception of purchases from the Soviet Union, China's international trade effectively ended as

Communist Party Chairman Mao Zedong and his successors implemented a succession of economic plans that focused on developing self-sufficiency and the importance of Marxist-Leninist political orthodoxy.

Mao's Great Leap Forward of 1958-60 sought to communize all agriculture, but it decimated farm production and brought China's economy to the brink of collapse. During the three years the policy was in force, as many as 45 million Chinese died of starvation.[52]

The new U.S. agency combines the Overseas Private Investment Corp. (OPIC), the federal agency that provides loans and risk insurance to U.S. corporations for overseas investments, and the Development Credit Authority, which guarantees loans made by overseas banks to local businesses and entrepreneurs.[4]

The credit authority is part of the U.S. Agency for International Development (USAID), the State Department office that distributes roughly $23 billion in foreign aid each year. Previously, Trump had proposed sharply reducing money for USAID and had called for eliminating OPIC.[5]

The $60 billion that the new agency plans to invest in less developed countries is double OPIC's annual budget. And unlike OPIC, which extended loans only to U.S. companies operating in developing countries, the U.S. International Development Finance Corp. can lend money to foreign companies. It also can purchase equity stakes in new projects, make loans in local currencies and guarantee the bond issues of foreign governments—all in the interest of sharpening competition with China, administration officials say.

OPIC Vice President David Bohigian says the new agency "puts us in a position where we can be the world's leading development force."

But some foreign policy experts say the agency is not equipped to compete directly with China in development finance.

For one thing, the agency's $60 billion is a fraction of the $1 trillion that China has earmarked for the BRI. Beijing already has made $404 billion in development loans and investments since late 2013, when the initiative begun.

"There's a large discrepancy between what the U.S. is going to bring to the table in terms of public resources and what China is bringing," says Jonathan Hillman, a China expert at the Center for Strategic and International Studies, a centrist foreign policy think tank in Washington.

In addition, China's state-owned banks provide loans to governments in developing nations, which normally finance most major infrastructure improvements in those nations, such as road, bridge, water and sanitation projects. The U.S. International Development Finance Corp., by contrast, will lend only to private businesses. Experts question whether that market-driven approach can address the developing world's big need for infrastructure funding.

"Those public dollars are supposed to be used to attract more dollars from the private sector," says Hillman. "The assumption is there are longer-term investors who would love to invest in more infrastructure assets if they think they can get a safe return. But many of these environments don't meet that criteria. Meanwhile, the Chinese are willing to take that chance, for better or worse."

—Jonathan Broder

[1] Karen DeYoung and Ruth Eglash, "Trump administration to end U.S. funding to U.N. program for Palestinian refugees," *The Washington Post*, Aug. 30, 2018, https://tinyurl.com/y79sk6yq; Mark Landler and Gardiner Harris, "Trump, Citing Pakistan as a 'Safe Haven' for Terrorists, Freezes Aid," *The New York Times*, Jan. 4, 2018, https://tinyurl.com/y8eu567r; Justin Sink, "Trump's $4.4 Trillion Budget Boosts Defense With More Red Ink," Bloomberg, Feb. 12, 2018, https://tinyurl.com/ydzemtje; and John Campbell, "President Trump Embraces Foreign Aid After Trying to Gut It," blog, Council on Foreign Relations, Oct. 16, 2018, https://tinyurl.com/y9ovg944.

[2] Glenn Thrush, "Trump Embraces Foreign Aid to Counter China's Global Influence," *The New York Times*, Oct. 14, 2018, https://tinyurl.com/y8jdh4ty.

[3] "Vice President Mike Pence's Remarks on the Administration's Policy Towards China: October 4 Event," Hudson Institute, Oct. 4, 2018, https://tinyurl.com/y72mstcn; Niharika Mandhana, "U.S. Fights China for Influence, One Project at a Time," *The Wall Street Journal*, Nov. 13, 2018, https://tinyurl.com/yb6kf84y.

[4] Adva Saldinger, "A new US development finance agency takes flight," Devex, Oct. 4, 2018, https://tinyurl.com/yaxwxo4r.

[5] "USAID.gov FY 2017 Development and Humanitarian Assistance Budget," USAID, undated, https://tinyurl.com/ya693xar; Gregory Korte, "The 62 agencies and programs Trump wants to eliminate," *USA Today*, March 16, 2017, https://tinyurl.com/y9h5lxzr.

During Mao's Cultural Revolution of 1966 to 1976, which attempted to purge capitalist elements from society, China's agricultural production stagnated and industrial output fell due to radical policies that sent virtually all professional personnel to the countryside to perform manual labor while inexperienced Red Guards were put in charge of the country's mines, factories and farms.[53]

It was not until 1978, when China's reformist party leaders under the leadership of Deng Xiaoping embraced free-market principles and revived foreign trade, that the Silk Road figuratively came back to life.

Deng loosened restrictions against private ownership, relaxed procedures for foreign trade and allowed individual businesses and government offices to negotiate directly with foreign companies. These contacts produced a wide range of commercial arrangements that accelerated China's return to international trade.

U.S. Firms Profit from Chinese Infrastructure Program

"The Belt and Road Initiative can bring huge opportunities."

The Trump administration views China's Belt and Road Initiative (BRI)—a massive program to build infrastructure in Africa, Asia and Europe—as a threat to American interests, but several U.S.-based multinational companies are happily participating in the program.

The companies are earning billions of dollars supplying software and construction equipment—from generators to earthmovers—for projects that are part of China's BRI infrastructure investments. Analysts say additional opportunities are available in Belt and Road countries for U.S. banks, financial services companies and law firms.

"The Belt and Road Initiative can bring huge opportunities to Honeywell," said Shane Tedjarati, president and CEO for global growth at the multinational industrial conglomerate. The initiative, he said, "has really increased significantly . . . our presence" in the former Soviet states of Turkmenistan, Kazakhstan and Azerbaijan, where Honeywell is providing equipment for BRI oil and gas pipeline and energy installation projects.[1]

In 2017, Honeywell's sales to China increased 17 percent from 2016 and accounted for $2.9 billion of the company's $40.5 billion in revenue that year, says Honeywell spokeswoman Victoria Ann Streitfeld.

General Electric, another U.S.-based multinational conglomerate, signed on as a subcontractor in 2015 with a state-owned Chinese company to provide up to 60 wind-driven generators, machine parts, technical support and training for a BRI clean-energy project in sub-Saharan Africa.[2]

Since then, the company has subcontracted to supply technical equipment to Chinese construction companies working on infrastructure in more than 70 BRI countries, including more than 10 power projects in Pakistan.[3]

"We are well-equipped in being a great partner participating in the Belt and Road Initiative, and we can also benefit from that," GE Vice Chairman John Rice said when he accompanied President Trump on a visit to China in November.[4]

GE's engineering, procurement and construction sales to China increased from $400 million in 2010 to $2.5 billion in 2017, says a company spokeswoman who declined to be named. She says most of the growth occurred since 2014, when the BRI began to gain momentum.

GE's ability to win BRI contracts stems from the company's long relationship with China, the spokeswoman says. GE has been operating there for more than a century and was one of the first U.S. multinationals to return to China after it and the United States restored diplomatic relations in 1979. According to the spokeswoman, some 40 percent of the hardware GE sells to China is manufactured at GE plants there.

Meanwhile, global construction equipment manufacturer Caterpillar, based in Deerfield, Ill., has established more than two dozen dealerships across China to sell its line

Unlike Mao who shunned foreign trade as an admission of China's dependence on the outside world, Deng recast foreign trade as a vital source of investment funds and modern technology that would help China become self-sufficient. Deng also created some 2,000 economic zones, where foreign companies received tax breaks and other incentives in return for sharing their advanced technology with Chinese companies.

Over the ensuing years, as Deng's successors opened China's doors wider to foreign trade, foreign direct investment in Chinese businesses grew. By 2005, companies in China with foreign investment produced 58.3 percent of Chinese exports and 59.7 percent of imports.[54]

In 2008, with a GDP of $4.6 trillion, China began a massive economic stimulus program in response to the global financial crisis. The government earmarked $586 billion to build railways, subways, airports and housing in China, fueling an industrial boom as scores of state-owned factories arose to supply cement, steel and other materials for the infrastructure projects. According to historian Vaclav Smil, China used more cement between 2011 and 2013 than the United States used in the entire 20th century.[55]

of huge excavators, earthmovers and road-making machinery to Chinese companies working on BRI construction and mining projects in Central Asia and Africa.

"Belt and Road is becoming a very important driver for Caterpillar's development," said Chen Qihua, the company's chief in China. Industry analysts say Caterpillar's 22 percent increase in Asia-Pacific sales in 2017 reflects growing demand for heavy machinery used in BRI projects.[5]

Waters Corp., a Massachusetts company that makes and sells laboratory instruments and software, provides BRI projects with mass spectrometry and chromatography systems, which identify and analyze the components of various substances. In 2017, the company's China sales accounted for 17 percent—$387 million—of its worldwide revenues of $2.3 billion, a 10 percent increase over 2016, according to Waters' 2017 annual report.[6]

Chinese President Xi Jinping has stressed that the BRI is open to all countries and companies, but analysts say U.S. firms that have secured contracts linked to the initiative have done so only because they can provide technology and machinery that the Chinese do not have.

But big U.S. construction companies such as the Bechtel Group in San Francisco and Fluor Corp. in Texas have been effectively frozen out of the initiative. That is because the developing nations that borrow money from China's state-owned banks to finance BRI infrastructure projects are required to hire state-owned Chinese construction firms.

"This is all about helping Chinese [construction] firms, not helping American firms," says Johan van de Ven, senior analyst at RWR Advisory Group, a consulting firm in Washington. He notes that U.S. law similarly requires domestic development banks to lend only to U.S. construction companies.

Market analysts say U.S. banking, financial services and legal consultancy companies have greater potential to benefit from the Belt and Road Initiative if they already have a presence in BRI countries and know their laws. Earlier this year, Citigroup investment bank in New York, which does business in 160 countries, agreed to help Chinese companies explore overseas markets. Since then, Citigroup has served as a global coordinator for the Bank of China on BRI-linked bonds.[7]

"There's a significant amount of opportunity going on in western China," said Gerry Keefe, Citigroup's head of corporate banking in the Asia Pacific region. "I think the Belt and Road will actually open up a lot of economic activity in these countries for global competition that will not necessarily be won by one set of companies from one country."[8]

— *Jonathan Broder*

[1] "What is the Belt and Road Initiative?" Honeywell, Sept. 8, 2017, https://tinyurl.com/y842z7wq; Evelyn Chang, "Honeywell, other US companies hope to benefit from China's gigantic 'Belt and Road' initiative," CNBC, March 12, 2018, https://tinyurl.com/yawltz45.

[2] Yang Ziman, "Sinomach links with GE in clean-energy initiative," *China Daily*, Sept. 18, 2015, https://tinyurl.com/yahyu6lc.

[3] Zheng Xin, "Foreign firms, too, gain from Belt & Road," *China Daily*, Jan. 15, 2018, https://tinyurl.com/y8ehco2k.

[4] *Ibid.*

[5] Rajesh Kumar Singh and Brenda Goh, "Caterpillar drives sales on China's new Silk Road," Reuters, March 4, 2018, https://tinyurl.com/y8omuruk.

[6] "2017 Waters Annual Report," Waters Corp., 2017, https://tinyurl.com/ybbgwhkm.

[7] Thomas Hale, "Western banks gather to catch the Chinese investment crumbs," *Financial Times*, Sept. 25, 2018, https://tinyurl.com/y6vzn2vz.

[8] *Ibid.*

Birth of the BRI

By 2013, the domestic infrastructure projects had largely been completed, which left the government with a slowing economy and an excess of industrial capacity. Later that year, President Xi unveiled what he then called the Silk Road Economic Belt and the 21st-Century Maritime Silk Road, his policy of financing trade and infrastructure networks spanning East Asia, Western Europe and Africa. The government later shortened the name to the Belt and Road Initiative.

Pledging $1 trillion to finance BRI infrastructure projects, Xi directed the state-owned China Development Bank, the Export-Import Bank of China and the Asian Infrastructure Investment Bank to make the loans and investments.

The strategy behind the BRI evolved from China's success in weathering the 2008 financial crisis, says the National Bureau of Asian Research's Rolland. The crisis discredited the American capitalist model in the eyes of many developing nations and even some Western countries, such as Greece, that suffered the most from the economic downturn.

Communist leader Mao Zedong reviews army troops in November 1967. Mao's social programs and economic plans of the late 1950s and '60s decimated China's agricultural and industrial sectors and effectively ended the nation's international trade.

A Pakistani man mourns the death of a relative killed in an attack at the Chinese consulate in Karachi in November 2018. Anti-Chinese sentiment has been growing in Pakistan, one of a number of Belt and Road partner countries re-evaluating their loan agreements with China.

These developments, Rolland says, opened what China called its "strategic opportunity" to extend both its state controlled economic model and political influence globally.

In 2014, Chinese construction companies began work on the China-Pakistan Economic Corridor, initially a $46 billion project that included construction of a railway, power stations, an upgraded highway and a fiber-optic network, all connecting China's westernmost city of Kashgar to Pakistan's port city of Gwadar, some 2,000 miles away on the Arabian Sea. The cost of the project, which included a major expansion of the port and hotels and other tourist facilities, ballooned to $64 billion.[56]

At the same time, work began on several other economic corridors to connect China with BRI partner countries near and far. Chinese engineers began construction on a $7 billion railway from southern China through Laos, Thailand and Malaysia to Singapore. For a second corridor running from southern China to Myanmar, Beijing agreed to finance several hydroelectric dams. China signed on for rail and power projects for a third corridor running from northern China through Mongolia to Russia's Far East.[57]

Meanwhile, the BRI financed major infrastructure projects in Africa. In 2017 a Chinese company completed construction of a $3.2 billion, 290-mile railway from Kenya's Indian Ocean port of Mombasa to the capital, Nairobi. The project was completed last year, 18 months ahead of schedule.[58]

But Xi emphasized the Belt and Road Initiative was far more than simply a program for infrastructure investment and expanded trade. The BRI, he said, was building a more peaceful world through exchange programs that promoted cooperation in scientific research, education and health. To jump-start such exchanges, Xi said China would provide 10,000 scholarships annually for BRI-country students to learn in Chinese schools.[59]

"When it comes to different civilizations, exchange will replace estrangement, mutual learning will replace clashes, and coexistence will replace a sense of superiority," Xi told 130 world leaders and senior ministers attending the 2017 Belt and Road Forum in Beijing.[60]

Some in the West were skeptical, saying Beijing's definition of the BRI was so broad that it was difficult to determine what actually qualified as a BRI project. For example, they said that Beijing included among its BRI projects Chinese concert performances in Europe and hundreds of foreign aid projects that China began in Africa long before the BRI was announced.

"Almost anything now can be counted as Belt and Road," Tom Miller, author of *China's Asian Dream: Empire Building Along the New Silk Road*, said in 2017.[61]

CURRENT SITUATION
Debt Risks and Backlash

Xi's Belt and Road Initiative faces new headwinds as additional countries scrap their plans for China-financed infrastructure projects and he grapples with an economic slowdown at home.

At the same time, however, China added 42 countries to the BRI between June 30 and October 2018, according to a report by the American Enterprise Institute.[62] Their enrollment, analysts say, shows China's money remains a powerful draw, even as some countries reassess their participation in the program.

The BRI's setbacks, these analysts say, reflect the growing acceptance of the narrative, advanced by the United States, the European Union, Japan, India and Australia, that depicts the initiative as a risky venture that could leave developing countries so heavily indebted to Beijing that they might have to forfeit strategic assets in the event of a default.

"The blessing of the BRI is, yes, you get roads, you get jobs," says Shailesh Kumar, a former adviser on South Asia at the U.S. Treasury Department. "But the curse is you are now beholden to China in a way that you would never, ever dreamt of being beholden to the IMF or World Bank."

For now, the BRI is helping soften China's economic slowdown by exporting the country's excess industrial capacity to participating countries, analysts say. But the slowdown also has heightened concerns over the BRI's contribution to China's enormous debt—a burden that will make it harder for Xi to stimulate the economy in the event of another major downturn, analysts add.[63]

The slowdown is breeding resentment among some Chinese who want Xi to spend more money to improve conditions at home rather than loan it to other countries. "Why is China, a country with over 100 million people who are still living below the poverty line, playing at being the flashy big-spender?" wrote Xu Zhangrun, a Tsinghua University law professor. "How can such wanton generosity be allowed?"[64]

"If the economy continues to slow down, there will be less to go around for everyone," says the Center for Strategic and International Studies' Hillman. "But fortunately for Xi, he has more political insulation, unlike in Western democracies. As president for life, he's not up for election."

Meanwhile, Pakistan, which has taken out billions in BRI loans to finance the China-Pakistan economic corridor, faces an $18 billion balance of payments deficit, aggravated by its purchase of expensive Chinese machinery needed for BRI construction projects.

Last September, Islamabad took several steps to shore up its finances that angered the Chinese. Pakistani officials said they would scale back some BRI projects while newly elected Prime Minister Imran Khan announced Saudi Arabia had offered to provide financial relief by investing in Pakistan's BRI projects. Islamabad also approached the IMF for a $12 billion bailout.[65]

But when IMF officials demanded Pakistan provide full details of its Chinese loans, pledge not to use the bailout to repay Beijing and give IMF officials a place at the table in any future BRI negotiations, Beijing pushed back. Chinese officials insisted the terms of its BRI loans remain secret, promising Islamabad additional funds for a bailout. The result: Pakistan will not scale back its BRI projects. It also rejected the Saudi investment and pulled out of talks with the IMF.[66]

The BRI, however, is stoking anti-China sentiment in Pakistan's southwest Balochistan province, where the economic corridor is being built. In November three militants attacked the Chinese consulate in Karachi. Two police officers and two civilians were killed before security forces shot the attackers dead. No Chinese were hurt.[67]

In August, a suicide car bomber wounded six people when he detonated his vehicle beside a bus carrying Chinese mining engineers in western Pakistan. And in February, militants killed a Chinese shipping agent in Karachi. The Pakistani government has stationed 15,000 troops in the economic corridor to protect Chinese workers.[68]

Yet despite some countries' second thoughts about the BRI, including Sierra Leone, which in October 2018 canceled a new airport project, other countries are eagerly climbing aboard.[69]

The latest country to join the BRI is Portugal, which signed a memorandum of understanding with China during Xi's visit to Lisbon in December 2018. The memorandum names Sines, Portugal's largest Atlantic port, as a candidate for Chinese-financed redevelopment. Sines would join dozens of other European ports where China has invested heavily.[70]

Analysts said Beijing was likely to see the Lisbon accord as an important victory because European Union officials, wary of China's growing geopolitical influence on the continent, had urged Portugal not to join the BRI.

"For Brussels, this is a bit of a diplomatic defeat," said Jan Weidenfeld, head of the European China Policy Unit at the Mercator Institute for China Studies in

Is China lending money in ways that exploit its Belt and Road partners?

YES Scott Morris
Senior Fellow, Center for Global Development

Written for *CQ Researcher*, January 2019

China has shown itself to be an irresponsible lender in some cases, but for the most part, its finance program for developing countries does not carry major debt risks. In a recent study for the Center for Global Development, we found that most of the 68 countries identified under China's Belt and Road Initiative have sustainable debt levels, and loans from China do not threaten to change this outlook much.

Eight Belt and Road countries *do* have rising debt levels that have raised red flags, and Chinese lending in these cases seems to be proceeding with indifference to these risks. This includes Djibouti, which has made an export industry of its strategic locale by hosting commercial ports and military bases for countries like the United States and now China. But even in this extreme case, where loans from China threaten to cause Djibouti's debt to spike to an alarming 90 percent of the country's GDP, it is hard to determine whether Chinese policymakers are deliberately seeking to drive Djibouti's government into a debt crisis.

But more often, China does not seem to be exploiting those countries' debt problems for other gains. Over the past decade, there have been nearly 100 cases of China rescheduling or forgiving debt in order to avoid defaults. Sometimes these concessions appear to come with strings attached, as in the case of Sri Lanka's Hambantota port, where an inability to pay back a loan to China caused Sri Lanka's government to turn over ownership of the port to the Chinese.

Most Chinese debt rescheduling appears to reflect genuine efforts to extend terms in order to ensure repayment. In short, like any other lender, China expects to get paid back when it offers a loan.

China's lending practices clearly lack important constraints, resulting in many instances of irresponsible lending. For example, while China is one of many creditors to developing countries in general, it is now the *dominant* creditor to the riskiest of these countries—those that have been through massive rounds of debt relief from global creditors and once again find themselves in debt distress.

In these situations, large-scale lending on China's part is not good for the distressed countries and, ultimately, is not good for China. After all, how long can a lending operation stay afloat if it is indifferent to borrower risk?

NO Cecilia Joy-Pérez
Research Associate, American Enterprise Institute

Written for *CQ Researcher*, January 2019

China does not want to set "debt traps," in which it saddles governments with more debt than they can service and then forces them to surrender assets, such as ports.

China cannot afford debt traps along the Belt and Road, nor does it need to. Some argue that in order to gain influence, China baits poor countries with cheap financing offers that they cannot repay. But China gains influence in most Belt and Road countries simply by being the only partner that is willing to provide construction services or loans in difficult environments. Losing additional money via debt traps is thus unnecessary.

As far as affordability, debt traps would pressure China's now-vulnerable foreign exchange reserves. The Belt and Road Initiative consists primarily of construction projects, not investment. These projects are typically accompanied by cheap Chinese financing, funded by foreign reserves.

While China's foreign exchange reserves, at $3.1 trillion, remain considerable, they have dropped nearly $1 trillion from their 2014 peak and remain at risk due to trade tensions with the United States. Granted, China can win collateral in countries that default on payments. But it is rare that these assets generate foreign exchange.

A small number of high-profile cases feed hype surrounding debt traps. Most notorious is the Sri Lankan port at Hambantota, acquired by China Merchants Shipping as collateral. However, Hambantota is one case in roughly 500 large construction projects in the Belt and Road Initiative.

A more reflective example of a debt trap is Venezuela, a newly inducted country in the Belt and Road. From 2005 to 2017, China lent Venezuela $62 billion against oil purchases. Venezuela's economy has deteriorated, leaving an outstanding balance of nearly $20 billion in loans.

But even now, China is still pouring money into Venezuela's state oil company in the hopes of recovering lost foreign exchange—good money after bad. Replicating this on a smaller scale with other Belt and Road countries is indeed a trap, one that China does not want to be caught in.

Providing cheap financing produces enough of a strain on China's foreign exchange reserves as it is. With influence already won with this financing, and with giant state-owned construction firms willing to take on unprofitable projects, China has no need to go further. Winning collateral while losing dollars is almost always going to be a bad trade for Beijing.

Berlin. "EU ambassadors in Beijing had agreed on clear guidelines that caution member states when it comes to signing [memorandums of understanding] on the Belt and Road plan, effectively suggesting they should not."

He said China could leverage Portugal's BRI endorsement to persuade other European countries to join. "China can use this to approach other [EU] member states and say, 'Look, another EU member state signed up to the initiative. Why aren't you signing [a memorandum]?'"[71]

Despite a hard sell by Xi during a visit in November, Spain so far has resisted joining the BRI.[72] But that same month, Xi visited the Philippines, where President Rodrigo Duterte signed agreements calling for negotiations over future BRI infrastructure projects as well as joint oil and gas exploration in the South China Sea, despite an ongoing territorial dispute between the two countries over several island clusters in the sea.[73]

The peripatetic Xi followed up in December 2018 with a visit to Panama, where he secured a $1.4 billion contract for a Chinese company to build a bridge over the Panama Canal.[74] The deal would extend Beijing's economic and political influence to the Western Hemisphere's most vital choke point for shipping.

Australia's Fears

In June 2018, the tiny South Pacific country of Vanuatu pushed back against Australian officials who had grown alarmed about the strategic implications of a new wharf that China had financed and built for the island nation in 2014 under the BRI. The Australian officials warned that in the event of a default, China could seize the wharf as payment—just as it took over Sri Lanka's Hambantota port—and then use it as a military base within striking distance of Australia's east coast.[75]

But Vanuatu's leaders dismissed Australia's concerns, publicizing details of the wharf contract to prove it contained no provisions for a Chinese takeover in case of a default. They also insisted they could pay China back and make their own decisions about working with Beijing.

"The loan was considered economically viable for such infrastructure as the main gateway for international trade between the northern part of the country and the rest of the world," said Vanuatu Foreign Minister Ralph Regenvanu.

Australian officials remain uneasy, however, pointing out that in the event of a default, the contract allows China's Export-Import Bank to call in the entire debt at once. They also said Vanuatu has taken out several Chinese loans for other building projects, including roads, airport runway extensions, government buildings and stadiums.[76]

Australia has had better luck heading off a plan by the Chinese telecommunications firm Huawei to install an undersea fiber-optic cable linking the South Pacific's Solomon Islands to Sydney. Concerned that Huawei, which has links to the Chinese government, could use the cable project to spy on Australia's internet communications, the Australian government in April took over financial responsibility for the $70 million project and gave it to an Australian telecom.[77]

The cable deal will "deliver a message, first to China but also in the region, that Australia is much more receptive than it used to be" to assuming a leadership role in cybersecurity, said Jonathan Bogais, a senior associate at the Center for Strategic and International Studies.[78]

Yet Australia in October 2018 could not stop the Victoria state government from becoming the first in the country to sign on to the initiative.[79] Australian law gives its states wide latitude in pursuing international trade agreements.

"This new Australian-first agreement sums up everything we have achieved with China over the past four years," said Victoria Premier Daniel Andrews. "It means more trade and more Victorian jobs and an even stronger relationship with China."[80]

OUTLOOK
Slowdown Predicted

Many analysts predict the Belt and Road Initiative will slow down in the coming years as President Xi shifts the focus to smaller infrastructure projects that can provide rapid results for participating countries.

Meantime, rival infrastructure initiatives undertaken by the United States and its allies are expected to sharpen competition with China for influence in the developing world.

But China, with far more money to offer than its rivals and under intense pressure from Xi to make the BRI a success, will not be pushed aside easily, experts say.

"President Xi has very much tied his name and legacy to the Belt and Road Initiative," says the Heritage Foundation's Smith. "As long as Xi is in power, China has no choice other than for the BRI to succeed."

Experts expect trade disputes between Washington and Beijing to spill over into other areas, raising the stakes for their competing infrastructure loan initiatives. And as the developing world watches the U.S.-China rivalry play out, China can expect some of its BRI partners to demand more-favorable terms on their loans. Other nations will play China and the West against each other for the best loan deals.

"We'll see a lot more pushback over the next few years," says Riley Walters, a China economist at the Heritage Foundation. "Countries will question what infrastructure contracts have to say about using local labor and the impact on the environment."

There will be ample room for competition over infrastructure financing, says Hillman, of the Center for Strategic and International Studies. Last year, the Asian Development Bank, a regional multilateral bank based in Manila that provides loans to developing countries in Asia, estimated that Asian countries alone will need to invest $26 trillion in infrastructure by 2030 to maintain growth, cut poverty and deal with climate change.[81]

"The BRI alone can't fulfill Asia's needs," Hillman says. "So others will need to be involved."

Despite Beijing's efforts to improve its international image, some analysts predict China may employ more debt-trap financing to take possession of strategic assets in cash-strapped BRI countries. They also suspect China will install facilities at BRI port projects, such as Pakistan's Gwadar, to accommodate China's warships.

"Hambantota won't be the only one," says Hillman. "There will be a handful of other projects that underscore China's strategic aims. It won't be speculative anymore. And there will be Chinese naval ships at Gwadar."

The coming years also are likely to see delays or the failure of some BRI projects because of construction difficulties, contract disputes and political unrest.

But analysts agree that as long as Xi remains at the helm, he won't stop trying to resolve such challenges in his determination to make the BRI a pillar of China's power and influence.

"They're learning, they're adapting, and they're not going to just give up," the National Bureau of Asian Research's Rolland says. "This is the direction they've set for themselves. They're very serious about it, and so we should be taking it seriously, too."

NOTES

1. Benjamin Kentish, "First direct train service from China to the UK arrives in London," *The Independent*, Jan. 18, 2017, https://tinyurl.com/yabz376a; "Shanghai to Lisbon by train," Railcc, Sept. 12, 2018, https://tinyurl.com/yad292k9; and "Silk Road Chengdu-Europe Express Rail—Connecting the World," Realogistics, undated, https://tinyurl.com/ycqn2k3b.

2. Fumbuka Ng'wanakilala, "Tanzania signs $1.2 bln deal for new railway line," Reuters, Feb. 3, 2017, https://tinyurl.com/yanfb6vy; "Railway project connecting Pacific, Atlantic still on track: Chinese embassy in Brazil," *Global Times*, Feb. 15, 2018, https://tinyurl.com/y7r7uwfb; and Daniel S. Markey and James West, "Behind China's Gambit in Pakistan," Council on Foreign Relations, May 12, 2016, https://tinyurl.com/y8b999vk.

3. Sulmaan Wasif Khan, "Grand Strategy in China From Mao to Xi: 'Haunted by Chaos,'" Wilson Center, Sept. 27, 2018, https://tinyurl.com/y784gv7o.

4. Jonathan E. Hillman, "How Big Is China's Belt and Road?" Center for Strategic and International Studies, April 3, 2018, https://tinyurl.com/yao7wceu.

5. China Global Investment Tracker, American Enterprise Institute and the Heritage Foundation, 2018, https://tinyurl.com/pefswye; Cecilia Joy-Pérez and Derek Scissors, "Be wary of spending on the Belt and Road," American Enterprise Institute, Nov. 14, 2018, https://tinyurl.com/yapksfo7.

6. "Marshall Plan," *Encyclopedia Britannica*, Dec. 6, 2018, https://tinyurl.com/kjalo4t. The World Bank total is compiled from the annual reports for fiscal years 2013-2017: https://tinyurl.com/k9doypk; https://tinyurl.com/lhs5m67; https://tinyurl.com/y7aossbl; and https://tinyurl.com/ybu9rjwy.

7. Keith Johnson, "Why Is China Buying Up Europe's Ports?" *Foreign Policy*, Feb. 2, 2018, https://tinyurl.com/y6u6alss.

8. Joy-Pérez and Scissors, *op. cit.*, p. 5.

9. Secretary of State Michael R. Pompeo, "Remarks to Traveling Press," U.S. Department of State, Oct. 18, 2018, https://tinyurl.com/yaad9s2p.

10. "Full text of Chinese President Xi's speech at APEC CEO summit," Xinhua, Nov. 17, 2018, https://tinyurl.com/y8lo5qjk.

11. Josh Zumbrun and Siobhan Hughes, "To counter China, U.S. Looks to Invest Billions More Overseas," *The Wall Street Journal*, Aug. 31, 2018, https://tinyurl.com/yc6grs8x.

12. Mark Landler, "The Road to Confrontation," *The New York Times*, Nov. 25, 2018, https://tinyurl.com/ybywwdlj.

13. Mireya Solís, "Trump withdrawing from the Trans-Pacific Partnership," Brookings Institution, March 24, 2017, https://tinyurl.com/yb4p6898.

14. Vice President Mike Pence, "Remarks on the Administration's Policy Towards China," Hudson Institute, Oct. 4, 2018, https://tinyurl.com/y72mstcn.

15. John Hurley, Scott Morris and Gailyn Portelance, "Will China's Belt and Road Initiative Push Vulnerable Countries Into a Debt Crisis?" Center for Global Development, March 5, 2018, https://tinyurl.com/ycjxp225.

16. George Georgiopoulos, "China's Cosco acquires 51 pct stake in Greece's Piraeus Port," Reuters, Aug. 10, 2016, https://tinyurl.com/yat8gdg5.

17. Jason Horowitz and Liz Alderman, "Chastised by E.U., a Resentful Greece Embraces China's Cash and Interests," *The New York Times*, Aug. 26, 2017, https://tinyurl.com/y94d5u2g.

18. Nikolia Apostolu, "China's economic lifeline for Greece tangles political relations with EU," *The Washington Times*, March 5, 2018, https://tinyurl.com/y7xu7e52.

19. Catherine Wong, "Xi Jinping says belt and road plan isn't about creating a 'China Club,'" *South China Morning Post*, Aug. 27, 2018, https://tinyurl.com/ybze74c9.

20. Barry Sautman and Yan Hairong, "Localizing Chinese Enterprises in Africa: from Myths to Policies," Hong Kong University of Science & Technology, Institute for Emerging Market Studies, Feb. 2015, https://tinyurl.com/ycmqzw7c.

21. Deborah Bräutigam, "U.S. politicians get China in Africa all wrong," *The Washington Post*, April 12, 2018, https://tinyurl.com/yaflyhna.

22. Richard Bluhm, "Connective Financing: Chinese Infrastructure Projects and the Diffusion of Economic Activity in Developing Countries," AidData, September 2018, p. 12, https://tinyurl.com/yc28jfer.

23. Hannah Beech, "'We cannot Afford This': Malaysia Pushes Back Against China's Vision," *The New York Times*, Aug. 20, 2018, https://tinyurl.com/ycfz224m.

24. Tom Wright and Bradley Hope, "WSJ Investigation: China Offered to Bail Out Troubled Malaysian Fund in Return for Deals," *The Wall Street Journal*, Jan. 7, 2019, https://tinyurl.com/y9ous69n.

25. Brook Larmer, "What the World's Emptiest International Airport Says About China's Influence," *The New York Times*, Sept. 13, 2017, https://tinyurl.com/ydck6oqs; Kai Schultz, "Sri Lanka, Struggling With Debt, Hands a Major Port to China," *The New York Times*, Dec. 12, 2017, https://tinyurl.com/yc42gv6x.

26. Basten Gokkon, "Environmentalists are raising concerns over China's Belt and Road Initiative," *Pacific Standard*, July 18, 2018, https://tinyurl.com/yc88wzxj.

27. Briana Duggan, "How did a $12 million bridge collapse in Kenya?" CNN, July 4, 2017, https://tinyurl.com/y97uvte9.

28. Gerry Shih, "Pence and Xi deliver dueling speeches despite signs of trade detente," *The Washington Post*, Nov. 17, 2018, https://tinyurl.com/y9prju2h.

29. Lucy Hornby and Tom Hancock, "China pledge of $60bn to Africa sparks anger at home," *Financial Times*, Sept. 4, 2018, https://tinyurl.com/y7otxm5k.

30. "MOFCOM Department of Foreign Trade Comments on China's Foreign Trade Operation in January-October, 2018," Ministry of Commerce,

People's Republic of China, Nov. 14, 2018, https://tinyurl.com/y76mlmc7; Wong, op. cit.

31. Eswar S. Prasad, "China's Efforts to Expand the International Use of the Renminbi," Brookings Institution, Feb. 4, 2016, https://tinyurl.com/yctupc7e.

32. Maria Abi-Habib, "China's 'Belt and Road' Plan in Pakistan Takes a Military Turn," *The New York Times*, Dec. 19, 2018, https://tinyurl.com/ybyajo6q.

33. "China Resumes Ties with São Tomé, Which Turned Away from Taiwan," The Associated Press, *The New York Times*, Dec. 26, 2016, https://tinyurl.com/yd7hlg3k; Carrie Khan, "China Lures Taiwan's Latin American Allies," NPR, Oct. 13, 2018, https://tinyurl.com/ya5cx79g; and Chris Horton, "Burkino Faso Cuts Ties With Taiwan, Dealing It Another Blow," *The New York Times*, May 24, 2018, https://tinyurl.com/ybeuylaa.

34. Enda Curran, "China's Debt Bomb," Bloomberg, Sept. 17, 2018, https://tinyurl.com/j7ht8vo.

35. Hornby and Hancock, *op. cit.*

36. Graham Allison, "The Thucydides Trap: Are the U.S. and China headed for War?" *The Atlantic*, Sept. 24, 2015, https://tinyurl.com/jh9qbef.

37. Michael T. Klare, "The United States Is Pushing Toward War With China," *The Nation*, June 19, 2018, https://tinyurl.com/yd4xje2v.

38. "Annual Report to Congress: Military and Security Developments Involving the People's Republic of China 2018," Department of Defense, May 16, 2018, pp. i, 112, https://tinyurl.com/y9znykvr.

39. Klare, *op. cit.*

40. Adm. Harry Harris Jr., "U.S. Indo-Pacific Command Change of Command Ceremony," U.S. Indo-Pacific Command, May 30, 2018, https://tinyurl.com/y7vsbzs6.

41. David J. Lynch, "Despite pause in trade war, U.S. and China's economic relationship is forever changed," *The Washington Post*, Dec. 2, 2018, https://tinyurl.com/yaxt9ve4.

42. Clay Chandler, "Are the U.S. and China 'Destined for War'?" *Fortune*, June 2, 2018, https://tinyurl.com/ydh6rqmz.

43. David J. Lynch, "U.S. and China agree to new talks as Trump pulls back on tariffs," *The Washington Post*, Dec. 1, 2018, https://tinyurl.com/y8mv7one.

44. Edward Peters and Fosco Maraini, "Marco Polo, Italian Explorer," *Encyclopedia Britannica*, Nov. 5, 2018, https://tinyurl.com/yad6a7ol.

45. Timothy B. Lee, "40 Maps that Explain the Roman Empire," *Vox*, Aug. 19, 2014, https://tinyurl.com/ybfw44cd.

46. Angus Maddison, "Statistics on World Population, GDP, and Per Capita GDP, 1-2008 AD," Global Health Data Exchange, Nov. 6, 2018, https://tinyurl.com/y8gbnu9w.

47. "Opium Trade: British and Chinese History," *Encyclopedia Britannica*, Jan. 3 2018, https://tinyurl.com/lysqynr.

48. Ian Morris, "The Opium War and the Humiliation of China," *The New York Times*, July 2, 2018, https://tinyurl.com/ydxldnxr.

49. Kenneth Pletcher, "Opium Wars: Chinese History," *Encyclopedia Britannica*, Nov. 2, 2018, https://tinyurl.com/jxw9hus.

50. Immanuel C.Y. Hsu, "Late Ch'ing Foreign Relations, 1866-1905," in John King Fairbank, ed., *The Cambridge History of China* (1978), p. 481.

51. Chusei Suzuki and Albert Feuerwerker, "Late Qing: Reformist and revolutionist movements at the end of the dynasty," *Encyclopedia Britannica*, https://tinyurl.com/ybdcxhzq.

52. Frank Dikötter, "Mao's Great Leap to Famine," *The New York Times*, Dec. 15, 2010, https://tinyurl.com/y9k4g8dr.

53. *Ibid.*

54. Wayne M. Morrison, "China's Economic Rise: History, Trends, Challenges, and Implications for the United States," Congressional Research Service, Feb. 5, 2018, https://tinyurl.com/y952ra8q.

55. "Data, China," World Bank, Oct. 23, 2018, https://tinyurl.com/y9334uuz; David Barboza, "China Unveils Sweeping Plan for Economy," *The New York Times*, Nov. 9, 2008, https://tinyurl.com/y79gnmf5; Jonathan Broder, "Commodities Supercycles," *SAGE Business Researcher*, Feb. 12, 2018, https://tinyurl

.com/ycsu7gh9; and Ana Swanson, "How China used more cement in 3 years than the U.S. did in the entire 20th Century," *The Washington Post*, March 24, 2015, https://tinyurl.com/ybwnm86r.

56. Markey and West, *op. cit.*

57. Nadège Rolland, "China's Eurasian Century? Political and Strategic Implications of the Belt and Road Initiative," National Bureau of Asian Research, May 23, 2017, https://tinyurl.com/y8gekm7a.

58. *Ibid.*

59. Xi Jinping, "Work Together to Build the Silk Road Economic Belt and the 21st Century Maritime Silk Road," Xinhua, May 14, 2017, https://tinyurl.com/y8sot3t8.

60. *Ibid.*

61. Charlie Campbell, "China Says It's Building the New Silk Road: Here Are Five Things to Know Ahead of a Key Summit," *Time*, May 12, 2017, https://tinyurl.com/mvvojck.

62. Joy-Pérez and Scissors, *op. cit.*, p. 4.

63. Hornby and Hancock, *op. cit.*

64. Robyn Dixon, "China has spent billions in Africa, but some critics at home question why," *Los Angeles Times*, Sept. 3, 2018, https://tinyurl.com/ydzyhyjs.

65. Maria Abi-Habib, "China's Belt and Road' Plan in Pakistan Takes a Military Turn," *The New York Times*, Dec. 19, 2018, https://tinyurl.com/ybyajo6q.

66. *Ibid.*

67. Adnan Aamir, "Pakistan struggles to contain rise of anti-China sentiment," *Nikkei Asian Review*, Nov. 26, 2018, https://tinyurl.com/y9e2lwjw.

68. Ayaz Gul, "Suicide Bomber Attacks Chinese Engineers in Pakistan," VOA News, Aug. 11, 2018, https://tinyurl.com/yc2ka2jw.

69. "Mamamah Airport: Sierra Leone cancels China-funded project," BBC, Oct. 10, 2018, https://tinyurl.com/yddk6ngx.

70. Liu Zhen, "Portugal's support for China's belt and road plans sets alarm bells ringing in Brussels," *South China Morning Post*, Dec. 6, 2018, https://tinyurl.com/y6u3b654; Johnson, *op. cit.*

71. *Ibid.*

72. "Spain rejects China's Silk Road Plan," *Business Times*, Nov. 28, 2018, https://tinyurl.com/ycsnub9a.

73. Li Jianwei and Ramses Amer, "Xi's Visit to the Philippines: Implications for China-Philippine Relations," China-U.S. Focus, Institute for Security & Development Policy, December 2018, https://tinyurl.com/ycqv4scg.

74. "Chinese consortium to build fourth Panama Canal bridge," Reuters, July 29, 2018, https://tinyurl.com/ybmlbrra.

75. Ben Bohane, "South Pacific Nation Shrugs Off Worries on China's Influence," *The New York Times*, July 13, 2018, https://tinyurl.com/y8pbtjk3.

76. *Ibid.*

77. Mike Cherney, "No Way, Huawei: Australia Looks to Cut China's Line Into South Pacific," *The Wall Street Journal*, April 20, 2018, https://tinyurl.com/yck39z9s.

78. *Ibid.*

79. "One Belt, One Road: Victoria signs MOU to join China's controversial global trade initiative," Australian Broadcasting Corp., Oct. 26, 2018, https://tinyurl.com/ycbzjycz.

80. *Ibid.*

81. Michael Peel and Tom Mitchell, "Asia's $26tn infrastructure gap threatens growth, ADB warns," *Financial Times*, Feb. 27, 2017, https://tinyurl.com/y7fcbn3q.

BIBLIOGRAPHY

Books

Allison, Graham, *Destined for War: Can America and China Escape Thucydides's Trap?*, Houghton Mifflin Harcourt, 2017.
A former senior Pentagon official says rising powers like China historically have gone to war with dominant powers like the United States but that prudent policies can avoid such a fate.

Economy, Elizabeth C., *The Third Revolution: Xi Jinping and the New Chinese State*, Oxford University Press, 2018.
A China scholar identifies the successes, shortcomings and tensions of the domestic and foreign policies of Chinese President Xi Jinping.

Miller, Tom, *China's Asian Dream: Empire Building Along the New Silk Road*, Zed Books, 2017.
A British journalist says the Belt and Road Initiative is enhancing China's global clout at the expense of the United States.

Rolland, Nadège, *China's Eurasian Century? Political and Strategic Implications of the Belt and Road Initiative*, National Bureau of Asian Research, 2017.
A former Asia adviser to the French defense ministry analyzes the origins, drivers and components of China's Belt and Road Initiative.

Articles

Bräutigam, Deborah, "U.S. politicians get China in Africa all wrong," *The Washington Post*, April 12, 2018, https://tinyurl.com/y9k75uqw.
A political economist presents research that contradicts U.S. officials who say China's infrastructure projects in Africa are funded by predatory loans, create few jobs and grab land from local residents.

Cordesman, Anthony H., "China and the U.S.," Center for Strategic and International Studies, Oct. 3, 2018, https://tinyurl.com/yd9hpn46.
A foreign policy and defense analyst cautions that the Trump administration should not view the U.S. relationship with China as a zero-sum game.

Li, Xue, and Liu Tianyi, "How Will the Indo-Pacific Strategy Impact the Belt and Road Initiative?" Hong Kong Trade and Development Council, June 19, 2018, https://tinyurl.com/yd8tzexf.
Two Chinese foreign policy experts say the Trump administration's Indo-Pacific strategy poses little threat to China's Belt and Road Initiative.

Majendie, Adam, *et al.*, "Trade and Debt: How China is building an empire across new Silk Road," Bloomberg, Aug. 3, 2018, https://tinyurl.com/y9whttfu.
Bloomberg correspondents report from Yiwu, China; the Sri Lankan port of Hambantota; Gwadar, Pakistan; Mombasa, Kenya; and Piraeus, Greece, on the impact of China's Belt and Road Initiative on these critical locations.

Marston, Hunter, "The US Needs a Reality Check on China's Belt and Road," *The Diplomat*, May 31, 2018, https://tinyurl.com/y95zw2yu.
An analyst argues that Washington must offer a credible alternative to the Belt and Road Initiative if it is going to compete successfully with China in Asia.

Sharma, Mihir, "China's Silk Road Isn't So Smooth," Bloomberg, July 10, 2018, https://tinyurl.com/y8hprqdd.
A Bloomberg columnist says recent decisions by several Asian countries to scrap or scale back their Belt and Road projects have stalled President Xi Jinping's signature foreign policy initiative.

Reports and Studies

"Meeting Asia's Infrastructure Needs," Asia Development Bank, February 2017, https://tinyurl.com/y9zw24u2.
The Manila-based development bank says Asia must invest $26 trillion in infrastructure by 2030 to maintain economic growth, reduce poverty and deal with climate change.

Prasad, Eswar, "China's Efforts to Expand the International Use of the Renminbi," U.S.-China Economic and Security Review Commission, Feb. 4, 2016, https://tinyurl.com/yctupc7e.
A Cornell University trade policy professor says some of China's steps to promote its renminbi currency are gaining traction in global trade and finance.

Sautman, Barry, and Yan Hairong, "Localizing Chinese Enterprises in Africa: from Myths to Policies," Hong Kong University of Science & Technology, Institute for Emerging Market Studies, February 2015, https://tinyurl.com/ycmqzw7c.
Data from more than 400 Chinese enterprises and projects in Africa show that 87 percent of their workforces are African laborers, contradicting Western critics who say Chinese projects create few local jobs.

Smith, Jeff, "China's Belt and Road Initiative: Strategic Implications and International Opposition," Heritage Foundation, Aug. 9, 2018, https://tinyurl.com/y72r4so5.
An expert at a conservative Washington think tank analyzes the strategic advantages China has gained through its Belt and Road Initiative and the growing pushback to the policy.

THE NEXT STEP

Africa

Chaudhury, Dipanjan Roy, "Africa cancels a Belt and Road Initiative project for the first time," *Economic Times*, Oct. 25, 2018, https://tinyurl.com/ya7pkq5u.
Sierra Leone President Julius Maada Bio pulled out of a deal made by his predecessor for China to construct a $318 million airport outside the country's capital.

Dixon, Robin, "China has spent billions in Africa, but some critics at home question why," *Los Angeles Times*, Sept. 3, 2018, https://tinyurl.com/ydzyhyjs.
China's massive Belt and Road spending in Africa is drawing increasing domestic criticism, with some Chinese academics and citizens arguing the money would be better spent internally.

Tiezzi, Shannon, "China's Belt and Road Makes Inroads in Africa," *The Diplomat*, July 31, 2018, https://tinyurl.com/ycjy4e2d.
Senegal and Rwanda signed on to Belt and Road infrastructure plans last year, including the construction of a roadway and participation in an ongoing railway project.

Debt

"Fearing debt trap, Pakistan rethinks China's Belt and Road projects," *The Straits Times*, Sept. 30, 2018, https://tinyurl.com/yb48pax7.
Pakistan's new government has been attempting to renegotiate all Belt and Road deals that appear to favor China financially.

Anwar, Anu, "How BRI poses risks to 21st-century geopolitical landscape," *Asia Times*, Jan. 15, 2019, https://tinyurl.com/yamg439y.
Overly ambitious projects and the likelihood of some countries defaulting on their loans mean China is overextended financially because of the Belt and Road Initiative, says a geopolitical analyst.

Griffiths, James, "Are the wheels coming off China's Belt and Road megaproject?" CNN, Dec. 31, 2018, https://tinyurl.com/ya2dthus.
Some countries, such as Kenya and Indonesia, have begun struggling to meet their loan obligations under the Belt and Road Initiative.

Environmental Concerns

Alkon, Meir, "Water is getting scarcer. Is foreign investment making the problem worse?" *The Washington Post*, Dec. 21, 2018, https://tinyurl.com/y9kv83vr.
South Asia's limited fresh-water resources will become further strained as China builds power plants and other infrastructure under its Belt and Road Initiative, says a Princeton University Ph.D. candidate.

Gokkon, Basten, "Environmentalists Are Raising Concerns Over China's Belt and Road Initiative," *Pacific Standard*, July 18, 2018, https://tinyurl.com/yc88wzxj.
China's Belt and Road Initiative could harm at least 265 threatened species, according to a 2017 World Wide Fund for Nature analysis.

Hilton, Isabel, "How China's Big Overseas Initiative Threatens Global Climate Progress," *Yale Environment 360*, Jan. 3, 2019, https://tinyurl.com/ycntpesu.
The Belt and Road Initiative will lead to greater industrialization and coal-burning, raising greenhouse gas emissions, says a London-based climate change editor.

Military Presence

"China expanding access to strategic foreign ports: Pentagon," Press Trust of India, *Business Standard*, last updated Jan. 16, 2019, https://tinyurl.com/y6wvogqq.
China's army is a growing presence at strategic ports near the Indian Ocean in Pakistan and Sri Lanka, according to a recently released Pentagon report.

Abi-Habib, Maria, "China's 'Belt and Road' Plan in Pakistan Takes a Military Turn," *The New York Times*, Dec. 19, 2018, https://tinyurl.com/ybyajo6q.
The Belt and Road partnership has paved the way for further military collaboration between China and Pakistan, with Pakistan agreeing to manufacture weapons and military aircraft for China.

Parameswaran, Prashanth, "What's in the China-Cambodia Military Base Hype?" *The Diplomat*, Nov. 24, 2018, https://tinyurl.com/y9mrvv8y.
China has cemented Cambodia's growing participation commercially and militarily in its Belt and Road Initiative by establishing a naval base in the country, says a senior editor at *The Diplomat*.

For More Information

American Enterprise Institute, 1789 Massachusetts Ave., N.W., Washington, DC 20036; 202-862-5800; www.aei .org. Conservative think tank that created and regularly updates the China Global Investment Tracker, the only U.S. database that monitors China's Belt and Road activities.

Australian Institute of International Affairs, Stephen House, 32 Thesiger Court, Deakin ACT, Canberra 2600, Australia; (02) 6282-2133; www.internationalaffairs.org.au. Leading Australian think tank for China policy and regional security issues; produces papers and holds briefings.

Center for Global Development, 2055 L St., N.W., 5th Floor, Washington, DC 20036; 202-416-4000; www.cgdev.org. Liberal think tank that conducts research and produces policy papers aimed at reducing poverty in the developing world.

Center for Strategic and International Studies, 1616 Rhode Island Ave., N.W., Washington, DC 20036; 202-887-0200; www.csis.org. Nonpartisan research institute with strong China and Asia-related programs; publishes papers and reports and holds symposia featuring senior current and former officials.

China Foreign Affairs University, 24 Zhanlanguan Road, Xicheng District, Beijing 100037, People's Republic of China; http://en.cfau.edu.cn/. China's top school for diplomats, administered by Ministry of Foreign Affairs; website takes questions from researchers.

Heritage Foundation, 214 Massachusetts Ave., N.E., Washington, DC 20002; 202-546-4400; www.heritage.org. Conservative think tank that provides analytical papers, reports and books on Asia and China-related issues; experts provide commentary on Asian developments.

Hong Kong University of Science and Technology, Clear Water Bay, Kowloon, Hong Kong; 852-2358-8888; www .ust.hk. The university's political science faculty provides a China-centric view of global affairs.

National Bureau of Asian Research, 1819 L St., N.W., Ninth Floor, Washington, DC 20036; 202-347-9767; www .nbr.org. Centrist think tank that offers papers, books and reports on Asian regional and national security issues, as well as expert briefings.

Elijah Nouvelage/Getty Images

Democratic presidential candidate Elizabeth Warren holds up two fingers to represent her 2 percent "wealth tax" at a campaign event at Clark Atlanta University in Atlanta on Nov. 21, 2019. A Reuters/Ipsos poll in January found strong support among Americans for additional taxes on the rich, who critics say are not paying their fair share.

From *CQ Researcher,*
February 07, 2020

9

Hidden Money

Can governments rein in tax evaders?

By Charles P. Wallace

THE ISSUES

Low Taek Jho, a Malaysian financier who liked to party with Paris Hilton and other celebrities, had a penchant for acquiring extravagant real estate in the United States. Low did not buy the properties in his own name, however, but instead employed anonymous companies with vague titles such as 80 Columbus Circle (NYC) LLC, which bought the penthouse at New York's landmark Time Warner Center for $30 million in cash.[1]

After a long investigation, U.S. authorities indicted Low in 2018 on charges of money laundering and foreign bribery. The Justice Department alleged that Low was the leader of a ring that diverted up to $4.5 billion from a Malaysian government investment fund into U.S.-based shell companies, which financed his lavish lifestyle—and helped bankroll actor Leonardo DiCaprio's movie about financial corruption, *The Wolf of Wall Street.* Low remains a fugitive, but has said that "the idea that I am some kind of 'mastermind' is just wrong."[2]

Unlike other companies that have employees who make products or provide services, shell companies are often nothing more than legal identities that mask their owners' identities. While the majority of these firms have been created for legitimate reasons, shell companies are also used to hide money—part of a global shadow economy estimated at $10 trillion.[3]

"One of the consistent elements of any illicit financial activity, whether it's related to human trafficking, gun-running or sanctions-busting, is that the chances are you find an anonymous shell

Switzerland Is Home to the Most Offshore Wealth

In Switzerland, foreigners' total holdings in local banks — known as offshore accounts — were $2.3 trillion in 2017, more than double that of the runner-up, Hong Kong. Except for the United States, all the jurisdictions that make up the top 10 holders of foreign wealth were in Europe or Asia.

Jurisdictions With Largest Offshore Holdings, 2017

Switzerland	$2.3 trillion
Hong Kong	$1.1 trillion
Singapore	$900 billion
United States	$700 billion
Channel Islands and Isle of Man*	$500 billion
United Arab Emirates	$500 billion
Luxembourg	$300 billion
United Kingdom mainland	$300 billion
Bahrain	$200 billion
Monaco	$200 billion

* British crown dependencies

Source: Anna Zakrzewski et al., "Global Wealth 2018: Seizing the Analytics Advantage," Boston Consulting Group, June 2018, p. 13, https://tinyurl.com/tg3po94

company involved," says Mark Hays, anti-money laundering campaign leader for Global Witness, a Washington-based human rights group. "You're looking for access to financial markets, distance from the scene of the crime, legitimacy for your operation, a place to actually invest that money and have it appreciate in value."

The shadow economy is known by many names, such as the black market or the hidden economy, and it encompasses all the money and jobs generated outside the official economy, whether legally or illegally.[4]

Hidden money runs the gamut from money laundering by drug cartels to tax evasion by wealthy investors. In its accounting of "the hidden corners of the global economy," the International Monetary Fund (IMF) now includes profits that multinational companies transfer to tax havens.[5]

Despite international efforts to curtail the shadow economy, it remains a serious problem that is costing governments billions in lost tax revenue and is helping to finance criminal activity.

"The secrecy world creates a criminogenic hothouse for multiple evils including fraud, tax cheating, escape from financial regulations, embezzlement, insider dealing, bribery, money laundering and plenty more," said the Tax Justice Network, a London-based organization that campaigns to eliminate tax havens. "It provides multiple ways for insiders to extract wealth at the expense of societies."[6]

The U.S. record in combating the shadow economy is mixed: In 2019, the United States levied more money laundering fines than any other nation; Congress approved legislation in 2017 to tax foreign profits; and the Trump administration supports a 2019 House-passed measure requiring shell companies to disclose their ownership. Yet the United States has itself become a leading tax haven, and the administration has resisted other nations' efforts to tax multinational internet companies.

While no one has precise data on the hidden economy, experts agree the sums are large:

- At least $7 trillion, according to various studies, is stashed in offshore bank accounts in places such as Switzerland, the largest offshore financial center with over $2 trillion in assets from foreigners.[7]
- The amount of money laundered worldwide annually is between $800 billion and $2 trillion, or 2 to 5 percent of global gross domestic product (GDP), the United Nations says; in the United States, the figure is $300 billion a year, or about 1.5 percent of GDP. (Laundering involves taking "dirty" money obtained illegally and making it appear "clean" by concealing it in foreign banks or legitimate businesses.)[8]
- Governments, according to the IMF, lose $700 billion to $800 billion a year in tax revenue from corporations and individuals that use tax havens, which are financial centers that have no or low taxes, no effective policy of exchanging financial information with other countries, lack transparency and do not require a company based there to engage in substantial local activity.[9]

"Money laundering is tax evasion in progress," says John Cassara, a former investigator for the U.S. Treasury who specializes in money laundering cases. "If tax evasion here and abroad is included in the list of offenses that result in money laundering—such as drug trafficking, child pornography and illegal weapons sales—the magnitude of international money laundering is truly staggering."

Cassara says there is a distinction between tax avoidance, which is legal, and tax evasion, which is not. Tax avoidance means taking legal deductions and using approved strategies to limit tax liability, while tax evasion involves hiding assets or not reporting income to avoid paying taxes. Many multinational companies including Apple, Google and Microsoft have used legal tax structures in low-tax countries such as Ireland and Luxembourg to reduce their overall tax bill. The IMF says profit-shifting into tax havens by U.S. multinationals has risen from an estimated 5 to 10 percent of profits in the 1990s to about 25 to 30 percent in 2019.[10]

The use of tax havens by U.S. multinationals has become an issue in the 2020 presidential campaign, with Democratic candidates vowing to increase taxes that companies are required to pay on offshore earnings.

"We can . . . stop giant multinational corporations from calling themselves American companies while sheltering their profits in foreign tax havens to avoid paying their share for American investments," said Sen. Elizabeth Warren, D-Mass.[11]

At the same time, Democratic proposals to place a "wealth tax" on the assets of the richest Americans have raised warnings that the wealthy might respond by shifting their assets into tax havens or adopting other tax avoidance schemes.[12]

"Will the wealthy do things that wealthy people can do to avoid paying the tax?" said Mark Zandi, chief economist of Moody's Analytics, an economic research firm. "A lot of other countries have tried [wealth taxes] and backtracked because of tax avoidance issues."[13]

In the United States, the 2017 Tax Cuts and Jobs Act slashed the maximum corporate tax rate from 35 percent to 21 percent, but it also contained a provision designed to force multinationals to pay more taxes on their overseas profits. Under previous rules, these profits were not taxed until brought back to the United States.[14]

After the 2017 legislation was passed, Apple announced it would pay $38 billion in taxes on its

Skyscrapers dominate New York City's so-called Billionaire's Row near Central Park. Investing in urban real estate, including condos, is a popular way to launder money, according to authorities.

Gary Hershorn/Getty Images

offshore profits, while Google said it was bringing its intellectual property back to the United States from low-tax Ireland. However, some businesses complained the higher taxes on overseas profits were too burdensome, and a concerted lobbying campaign by big U.S. companies prompted the U.S. Treasury to grant several major exceptions that benefited the companies. Treasury rule writers allowed firms with overseas subsidiaries a 50 percent exemption for certain types of expenses, increasing their foreign tax credits.[15]

Multinationals' tax strategies are the focus of a dispute between the United States and France over internet companies that have no physical presence in many countries but earn profits in those countries, such as Google, which sells ads in France but does not pay taxes there. In July 2019, France imposed a 3 percent tax on the revenues earned by Google, Apple, Facebook, Amazon and others in France. An angry President Trump accused France of unfairly targeting U.S. companies and proposed 100 percent tariffs on $2.4 billion worth of French exports, such as cheese and wine. After a meeting in Switzerland in January 2020, France agreed to suspend the tax until the end of the year while negotiations on a comprehensive global tax deal take place.[16]

France's action is part of a campaign, led primarily by European countries, to gain acceptance for taxing multinational companies where they have employees and sales, rather than in the jurisdiction they are registered and often pay low taxes.[17]

But critics dismiss the effort as grandstanding. "All of this really is being done for political reasons, not for economic or really tax reasons," says Scott Hodge, president of the Tax Foundation, a conservative Washington think tank. "Countries are trying to grab more tax revenue and politicians are trying to prove to taxpayers that they're gouging the big guys."

Alex Cobham, chief executive of the Tax Justice Network, disagrees: "Apportioning profit according to where multinationals' real activity takes place wouldn't fix everything. But those estimates of corporate taxes being avoided would end up an order of magnitude smaller."

In recent months, meanwhile, the use of shell companies in the United States to evade taxes and launder money has come under greater scrutiny. Both U.S. law enforcement officials and international agencies focused on combating money laundering have warned that the ease of setting up a shell company in states such as Delaware, Nevada and Wyoming has attracted international criminals to the United States and made it harder for officials to track crimes.[18]

"America is the largest dirty-money haven in the world," said Edward Luce, a columnist for the *Financial Times.* "Its illicit-money flows dwarf that of any other territory, unless you treat Britain and its offshore tax havens as one."[19]

For example, when the U.S. government began tracking shell company purchases of luxury real estate in New York and Miami, it found that almost 30 percent of the companies involved had been reported to authorities by their banks for suspicious activities.[20]

"Criminals thrive when they have somewhere to hide," said Kenneth A. Blanco, director of the Treasury Department's Financial Crimes Enforcement Network (FinCEN). "And the secrecy behind shell companies— businesses that exist only on paper—is a clear and present danger."[21]

President Trump supports legislation pending in Congress that would require shell companies to disclose to the Treasury details of their "beneficial ownership"— the actual person who owns or controls 25 percent or more of a company. The White House said one bill, the Corporate Transparency Act, which passed the House in September 2019, "represents important progress in strengthening national security, supporting law enforcement and clarifying regulatory requirements."[22]

In contrast to the United States, the European Union (EU) already requires members to collect beneficial ownership information about company ownership and make the data publicly available on central registries.[23]

The Internal Revenue Service (IRS), facing what it terms a "tax gap" of $458 billion a year in unpaid taxes, is under pressure to increase collection of data about financial accounts belonging to Americans in offshore banks. The United States is one of only two countries that taxes its people based on citizenship instead of residence.[24] (*See Short Feature.*)

As governments struggle to combat money laundering and rein in tax evasion, here are some of the questions that politicians, tax experts and others are asking:

Switzerland, U.S. Are Top Countries for Financial Secrecy

Switzerland and the United States top an index ranking places by the scale of their usefulness to those who want to keep their financial activities secret. The index — compiled by the Tax Justice Network, a London-based organization that is campaigning to eliminate tax havens — defines a secrecy jurisdiction as a place that "provides facilities that enable people or entities [to] escape or undermine the laws, rules and regulations of other jurisdictions elsewhere, using secrecy as a prime tool."

Secrecy Ranking by Jurisdiction, 2018		
	1	Switzerland
	2	United States
	3	Cayman Islands*
	4	Hong Kong
	5	Singapore
	6	Luxembourg
	7	Germany
	8	Taiwan
	9	United Arab Emirates
	10	Guernsey*

* British overseas territory or crown dependency

Source: "Financial Secrecy Index — 2018 Results," Tax Justice Network, accessed Oct. 4, 2019, https://tinyurl.com/vsc3ej3

Does the international community need to do more to control hidden or illicit money?

In October 2019, a 74-year-old man from Spokane, Wash., pleaded guilty to filing a false tax return that omitted mentioning he had more than $5 million in an account in Switzerland. Unlike other tax evasion cases involving offshore accounts, however, the money was hidden not in a bank but in what has become known as an "insurance wrapper."[25]

An insurance wrapper is a life insurance policy that is "wrapped" around a client's investment portfolio containing stocks, bonds and other securities. Investors can place some of their financial assets in the wrapper. What is unique about wrappers is that they are held in the name of the insurance company, not the individual investor. As a result, people use insurance wrappers as a new way to avoid taxes because financial institutions are not required to report the policies to the IRS or other nations' tax authorities.[26]

"Insurance wrappers have become a big problem for tax authorities in the U.S. and other countries," says Cobham of the Tax Justice Network. "It's not a company or a bank account, or anything else that you own; it is an insurance contract. Therefore, it's not reportable."

Despite a decade of progress in government efforts to clamp down on tax avoidance and money laundering, some experts say, the development of insurance wrappers and other new tactics shows that governments need to do much more to eliminate illicit financial flows. These experts maintain that progress can be achieved only when authorities coordinate at the international level to increase transparency in financial transactions, making it harder to hide money.

"There already are international standards for anti-money laundering obligations, but they are not really fully implemented," says Maíra Martini, a money laundering specialist at Transparency International, an anti-corruption organization in Berlin.

One proposal would create a global asset registry, where all stocks and bonds worldwide would be listed along with their actual human owners. Because securities trading is computerized and no longer uses paper certificates, asset registers already exist, such as the Depository Trust Co. in the United States and Clearstream in Europe, but they are private and do not share their information with governments.[27] Under the global registry proposal, data would be pooled to track asset ownership.

"A registry would . . . prove a vital tool against illicit financial flows by ending impunity for hiding and using the proceeds of crime, and for removing legitimate income and profits from the economy in which they arise for tax purposes," said the Independent Commission for the Reform of International Corporate Taxation, a coalition of civic groups.[28]

But the proposal has raised both technical and policy concerns. Most stocks are held in mutual funds, so identifying a stock's individual owners could be problematic. In addition, the securities industry opposes a global financial registry on the grounds that collecting the information would create expensive inefficiencies and increase costs for small investors while also compromising data privacy.[29]

"A 'global asset registry' would end financial privacy," said Mark Nestmann, a free-market financial newsletter publisher in Phoenix.[30]

To reduce tax evasion, reformers also want to strengthen rules for the exchange of foreign financial account information. Sen. Warren has said that, if elected president, she would toughen the Foreign Account Tax Compliance Act (FATCA), which requires overseas banks to report on accounts held by U.S. citizens.

"Automatically matching FATCA reports to tax returns and instituting sanctions for noncompliant foreign financial institutions would help narrow the tax gap," Warren said, referring to the gap between the taxes owed and taxes collected.[31]

But conservatives oppose even FATCA's existing requirements for U.S. citizens to report to the IRS all overseas financial accounts that have over $5,000 in assets. "Congress should reform FATCA's heavy-handed approach to tax enforcement now to lessen the burden it is imposing on Americans living abroad," said the Heritage Foundation, a conservative think tank in Washington.[32]

At the same time, a number of Europeans campaigning against tax evasion have urged the United States to become part of the global financial data-sharing agreement known as the Common Reporting Standard, in which more than 100 jurisdictions share bank information, to ensure that U.S. banks are not used to hide

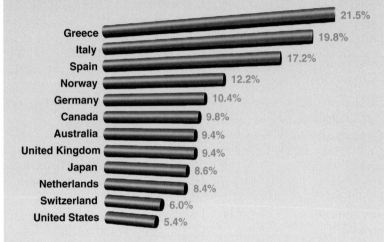

Mediterranean Countries Have Large Shadow Economies

Greece's shadow economy is equal to more than 20 percent of its official gross domestic product (GDP), far more than in the United States, where these transactions amount to 5.4 percent of GDP. A shadow economy refers to goods and services that are paid for in cash, without paying taxes, and therefore are not part of the GDP.

Shadow Economies as a Percentage of GDP in Select Countries, 2017

Country	Percentage
Greece	21.5%
Italy	19.8%
Spain	17.2%
Norway	12.2%
Germany	10.4%
Canada	9.8%
Australia	9.4%
United Kingdom	9.4%
Japan	8.6%
Netherlands	8.4%
Switzerland	6.0%
United States	5.4%

Source: Friedrich Schneider and Bernhard Boockmann, "Persistently positive employment and tax relief lead to a further decline in the shadow economy," Table 4.2, Institute for Applied Economic Research, University of Tübingen, Germany, Feb. 7, 2017, p. 23, https://tinyurl.com/tfddxau

assets. The United States, however, prefers relying on FATCA.[33]

Tax-evasion critics such as Cobham also are calling for the creation of registries relating to beneficial ownership of shell companies, trusts and foundations. Critics have long maintained that tax evasion and money laundering are increasingly hidden behind the veil of shell companies, trusts and foundations that do not disclose their real owners.[34]

"We have been advocating for a public beneficial ownership register as one of the measures that we believe would bring more transparency and make it more difficult for the corrupt to abuse legal entities," says Transparency International's Martini.

The EU enacted legislation requiring the creation of public registries of beneficial ownership information for investments by shell companies, trusts and foundations in 2019. Legislation requiring a federal register of the beneficial owners of shell companies was passed by

the U.S. House of Representatives last year, and the Senate is considering a similar version.[35]

Law enforcement groups support such disclosures, but small-business groups oppose them, saying the reporting requirements would be burdensome.[36]

Another emerging concern is the use of fraudulent invoices in international trade as a way of moving illegally obtained money between countries. Global Financial Integrity, a Washington-based organization that studies illicit financial flows, estimated in a 2019 report that fraudulent trade-based invoicing totaled $1.7 trillion from 2006 to 2015, representing almost 20 percent of all trade between developing and developed nations.

The fraudulent invoices, employed in both imports and exports, are used to disguise illicit financial transfers from drug dealers, terrorists and other criminals, it said.

"Governments should adopt laws making trade misinvoicing illegal," the report said.[37]

Should Congress pass legislation to reveal the beneficial owners of shell companies?

While the United States has led international efforts to stamp out tax evasion and terrorist financing, it is now paradoxically regarded as one of the best places in which to set up an anonymous company for tax evasion or other criminal purposes, with no requirement to identify the person who actually owns or controls it. Delaware, Nevada, Wyoming and other states welcome the creation of shell companies that guarantee the owners' privacy and make it difficult for law enforcement to pierce the ownership veil.

"The United States is one of the easiest places in the world to set up a shell company," says Lakshmi Kumar, who studies shell companies at Global Financial

Integrity. She says that all 50 states have "glaring weaknesses" in their company-formation requirements.

The reason for the lax regulations is simple: States want to attract businesses to increase their tax base. In the absence of a federal rule on shell companies, states compete by offering the fewest requirements for disclosure of ownership and other business-friendly laws. Delaware, a tiny state with a 2019 population of about 975,000, is home to 1 million corporations whose tax payments account for 17 percent of the state budget.[38]

One widely quoted study concluded that it is harder to obtain a library card in most states than it is to open an anonymous shell company. While the Bank Secrecy Act nominally requires financial institutions to conduct due diligence on the beneficial owners of shell companies that open bank accounts in the United States, a loophole allows people to open U.S. shell companies and fund them with foreign bank accounts not subject to scrutiny.[39]

"The pervasive use of shell companies, front companies, nominees, or other means to conceal the true beneficial owners of assets is a significant loophole in this country's anti-money laundering regime," Steven M. D'Antuono, acting deputy assistant director of the FBI's criminal investigative division, told a Senate hearing in May 2019. "The FBI has countless investigations, spanning criminal and national security threats, in which illicit actors, operating both domestically and internationally, use shell and front companies to conceal their nefarious activities and true identities."[40]

The Corporate Transparency Act, which passed the House in October 2019, would require people wanting to open shell companies to provide detailed information about the beneficial owners to the U.S. Treasury's Financial Crimes Enforcement Network. The legislation does not include trusts or foundations.[41]

"It is absurd that the U.S. allows criminals to launder their money here," said Rep. Carolyn Maloney, D-N.Y., one of the bill's sponsors. "We're the only advanced country in the world that doesn't already require disclosure of beneficial ownership information, and my Corporate Transparency Act will change that."[42]

The Maloney bill requires applicants wanting to open a shell company to provide FinCEN with the name, address and birth date of the beneficial owners of the company, as well as providing a passport or other identification. The bill exempts public companies and businesses with more than 20 employees and gross receipts of more than $5 million a year, which are presumed not to be a shell company.

Opposition to the legislation has come mostly from business groups, which argue that the reporting requirements would burden small companies that do not have in-house legal teams, and from privacy advocates concerned that ownership information could be obtained by criminals who might target owners for kidnapping or other crimes.

"Many small-business owners will be forced to decide between the risk of possible criminal prosecution and the expense of counsel," said the American Civil Liberties Union, which opposes the measure.[43]

Similar legislation, the Illicit Cash Act, was introduced in the Senate in September 2019 by a bipartisan group of eight senators and was the subject of hearings in the Senate Banking Committee in December 2019. Like the House bill, the act would apply to corporations and limited liability companies, but also includes "other similar" entities without defining them. A difference with the House bill is that in the Senate version exemptions for churches and charities would be automatic.

"Right now, criminals and terrorists are exploiting our financial system using shell companies that hide their identities," said Sen. Tom Cotton, R-Ark., one of the sponsors. "This legislation will allow law enforcement to track ill-gotten gains while at the same time protecting small businesses from unnecessary regulation.[44]

Privacy advocates disagree. "Both bills are easily and lawfully avoided by the sophisticated, and would do virtually nothing to achieve their stated aim of protecting society from illicit finance," said David Burton, a senior fellow in economic policy at the Heritage Foundation.[45]

Many state and federal officials have endorsed the bills. "If beneficial ownership information were required at company formation, it would be harder and more costly for criminals, kleptocrats and terrorists to hide their bad acts, and for foreign states to avoid detection and scrutiny," said FinCEN Director Kenneth A. Blanco.[46]

Jeffrey W. Bullock, secretary of state for Delaware, supports the House legislation on beneficial ownership, saying "I believe FinCEN possesses the expertise required to responsibly implement an effective and sustainable framework that safeguards privacy."[47]

But business coalitions are working to defeat the legislation. A group of 48 small-business associations said the reporting requirements in Warner's bill would be duplicative and burdensome for small companies and raise "significant privacy concerns."[48]

Jeffrey Brabant, manager of federal government relations for the National Federation of Independent Businesses, says the bills are seeking to transfer a compliance burden from banks to small businesses, which can ill afford the extra paperwork.

"The majority of our members have never heard of FinCEN and they are going to have an entire new reporting burden, which is going to be quite difficult to comply with over the long term, under penalty of potential jail time and large fines," Brabant says.

Should authorities try to restrict the use of cryptocurrency?

In April 2019, German police arrested three people in connection with a website called Wall Street Market. According to court documents, the website was the Amazon of crime, with more than 5,400 vendors selling everything from drugs and guns to stolen identifications. Some 1.1 million registered customers paid for their purchases using cybercurrencies such as bitcoin and monero.[49]

The Wall Street Market was only the latest site on the so-called Dark Web to be revealed. The Dark Web is accessible only on special networks like Tor, which are designed to conceal users' internet addresses. Wall Street Market was a successor to earlier Dark Web marketplaces, such as the Silk Road and Hansa, which were closed by authorities.[50] All used cybercurrencies—a Web-based medium of exchange outside government channels—as the method of payment.

While the users of bitcoin and other cybercurrencies are anonymous in most cases, the technology underlying cybercurrencies uses a digital ledger called blockchain, which is often open to public scrutiny. A study by three Australia-based scholars of bitcoin's blockchain concluded that 46 percent of all bitcoin transactions were for illegal activity, such as arms smuggling and human trafficking. The study, published in 2019, calculated that the illegal transactions using bitcoin reached $76 billion a year.[51]

By combining the anonymity of cash with digitization and enabling online and cross-border commerce to take place efficiently but anonymously, cryptocurrencies have the potential to cause "an important structural shift in how the black market operates," the study's authors warned.

These concerns are prompting calls for the U.S. government to tighten regulation of cryptocurrencies. "There is a gap in the regulation of crypto-assets that Congress needs to fix," said Timothy G. Massad, a senior fellow at the John F. Kennedy School of Government at Harvard University. "Crypto-assets are used increasingly to avoid government-sponsored sanctions and for illicit payments—including ransomware for cyberattacks and transactions in narcotics, firearms or other dark market goods."[52]

The issue was brought to a head by Facebook, which was considering issuing libra, a type of digital money called a stable coin that seeks to limit its volatility by tying its value to existing currencies such as the dollar. In response to the Facebook move, two House members from Texas proposed a bill to regulate stable coins as securities similar to stocks.

"This is a national security risk," said Rep. Sylvia Garcia, D-Texas. "We cannot afford to have money laundering made easier by the app you have or the Libra network that would make it much easier for them to access."[53]

Another bill, the Keep Big Tech Out of Finance Act, seeks to keep companies like Facebook from

Jakub Porzycki/NurPhoto via Getty Images

Passersby can get bitcoins from an ATM in Sopot, Poland. Criminals often use cybercurrencies, which can be used anonymously, to buy drugs and weapons on the black market.

issuing cryptocurrencies. Under the bill, technology companies with $25 billion or more in annual revenue "may not establish, maintain, or operate a digital asset that is intended to be widely used as medium of exchange, unit of account, store of value, or any other similar function."[54]

Elsewhere, Australia, Canada and the Isle of Man in the Irish Sea—formerly a tax haven—passed legislation that made cryptocurrency transactions and institutions that handle them part of their money laundering and counterterrorist financing laws.[55]

The Financial Action Task Force, a 39-member international body based in Paris, is recommending that governments adopt a "travel rule" that would require member governments to pass information to other members when its citizens transfer more than $1,000 worth of cybercurrency assets.[56]

But obtaining the information could prove difficult given the decentralized nature of cryptocurrency transactions.

"Cryptocurrency exchanges and other virtual asset businesses are struggling with the meaning and impact of this new guidance, which, once adopted by [task force] member countries, will require them to pass customer information to each other when transferring crypto-assets," said CipherTrace, a cybercurrency security firm.[57]

The U.S. House has passed three bills to fund studies of the use of cryptocurrencies in money laundering. Another measure would give FinCEN authority to coordinate with foreign intelligence officials about the use of cryptocurrencies in money laundering investigations.[58]

But even as concern grows about the use of bitcoin and other cryptocurrencies in illegal transactions, lawmakers acknowledge it would be hard to ban them. "If the United States were to decide we don't want cryptocurrency to happen in the United States and tried to ban it, I'm pretty confident we couldn't succeed in doing that because this is a global innovation," said Sen. Mike Crapo, R-Idaho, chairman of the Senate Banking Committee.[59]

Critics of government efforts to regulate cryptocurrency also argue that the technology underlying the currencies means that they cannot really be reined in by enacting laws. "It would be ridiculous to think any government could regulate the entire network," said John Martindale, a columnist for the website *Digital Trends*. "Trying to ban bitcoin or regulate it in a manner that allows actual oversight would be . . . impossible on a technical level."[60]

Cryptocurrency proponents argue that governments shouldn't try to inhibit progress. "I don't know whether bitcoin, blockchain or other cryptocurrencies are going to be big in the future," said Dan Smith, a blogger on a libertarian website. "But . . . our politicians shouldn't be trying to thwart those of us trying to find a more prosperous future through innovation."[61]

Nonetheless, regulations aimed at restricting cryptocurrencies appear to be gaining momentum.

FinCEN issued guidelines in May that made transmission of cybercurrencies valued at more than $3,000 subject to the Bank Secrecy Act provisions requiring identification of the people sending or receiving funds.[62]

In October 2019, the IRS issued guidelines on how the digital currencies will be taxed. "We want to help taxpayers understand the reporting requirements as well as take steps to ensure fair enforcement of the tax laws for those who don't follow the rules," said IRS Commissioner Chuck Rettig.[63]

"Cybercrimes and cybercriminals who commit them don't have any borders, and it's imperative that we work together to protect the global financial system and the integrity of each nation's tax system," says Ryan Corner, special agent in charge of the IRS' criminal investigation field office in Los Angeles.

Corner says his unit consists of experts trained in "identifying criminals who are using cryptocurrency and the Dark Web to thwart their tax-paying responsibilities and hide illicit proceeds from narcotics trafficking and other illegal activities." It is part of an international effort called the J5—the Joint Chiefs of Global Tax Enforcement—involving the United States, Canada, Britain, Australia and the Netherlands, which was formed in 2018 to fight crime using cybercurrencies.

BACKGROUND
Recessionary Pressures

The global crackdown on tax evasion had its roots in the deep recession of 2007-09. Before the downturn, the United States and other governments had begun to relax pressure on financial centers that offered secrecy to their

CHRONOLOGY

1890s-1990s *As governments raise income taxes, tax havens proliferate.*

1899 To attract more businesses to the state, Delaware enacts a law with easy incorporation requirements.

1908 France and Britain sign the first treaty calling for the two countries to automatically exchange tax information about each others' citizens. Britain agrees to provide France with information on money inherited in Britain by French taxpayers.

1912 Switzerland's central bank becomes a lender of last resort, guaranteeing the safety of deposits in times of crisis.

1920-1929 After World War I, European public debt skyrockets, followed by huge increases in tax rates. By 1924, France's top income tax rate has risen from 5 percent to 72 percent; assets in Swiss banks then grow at a yearly average of 14 percent.

1934 Swiss Banking Act provides for up to five years in prison for disclosing bank customer information. . . . Deposits in Swiss banks increase from $10 billion to $125 billion.

1941 U.S. freezes Swiss bank customer assets in the United States because of Switzerland's collaboration with Axis powers.

1945 France demands that Switzerland identify French citizens with assets in Swiss banks. . . . U.S. demands that Swiss banks identify owners of frozen Swiss assets in the United States; Switzerland responds that Swiss citizens or Panamanian companies own the assets.

1965 The Bahamas becomes the first Caribbean nation to enact bank secrecy laws similar to Switzerland's forbidding the disclosure of customer account information.

1970 U.S. Bank Secrecy Act requires American banks to report daily cash transactions over $10,000 and to identify Americans with foreign bank accounts containing $10,000 in assets.

1994 Caribbean island of Nevis passes a law creating an offshore financial center.

1998 Swiss National Bank begins reporting statistics on foreign wealth in Swiss banks.

2000-Present *Crackdowns on tax evasion and money laundering gain momentum.*

2000 Internal Revenue Service (IRS) requires foreign banks to report accounts held by U.S. citizens.

2001 USA Patriot Act, passed in the wake of the Sept. 11 terrorist attacks, gives the federal government new powers to fight money laundering.

2008 A Senate subcommittee holds hearings on tax evasion, citing $100 billion in lost taxes. . . . IRS demands Swiss bank UBS release the names of U.S. account holders.

2009 UBS agrees to provide U.S. with the names of some 4,500 U.S. account holders and pay a fine of $780 million for helping U.S. citizens avoid paying taxes. . . . A French computer technician steals 60,000 documents from HSBC in Switzerland detailing tax evasion by French citizens, and HSBC pays a $353 million fine. . . . The Organisation for Economic Co-operation and Development (OECD) creates a global forum to increase transparency and facilitate the exchange of information for tax purposes.

2010 President Barack Obama signs the Foreign Account Tax Compliance Act requiring foreign banks to report on U.S.-owned financial accounts.

2012 UBS whistleblower Bradley Birkenfeld receives $104 million payment from the IRS but also is sentenced to 40 months in prison.

2013 Swiss private bank Wegelin pleads guilty to bank fraud in the U.S. and closes. . . . OECD proposes Common Reporting Standard that requires the automatic exchange of bank information between countries. . . . Switzerland signs pacts with Austria and Great Britain agreeing to withhold tax on deposits held by their citizens in Swiss bank accounts. . . . OECD adopts a program to combat "tax base erosion," which occurs when multinationals shift profits from high tax countries to lower tax jurisdictions.

2016 A group of investigative journalists begins publishing details of 11.5 million files from the Panamanian law firm Mossack Fonseca showing dozens of rich people set up more than 210,000 shell companies to conceal their assets from tax authorities.

2017 U.S. Tax Cuts and Jobs Act cuts taxes on companies from 35 percent to 21 percent but requires payment of tax on profits held offshore.

2018 In an effort to stop money laundering, U.S. Treasury requires banks to collect information on shell companies' bank accounts.

2019 U.S. House passes law requiring shell companies to disclose owners; a similar bill is introduced in the Senate. . . . OECD proposes global minimum tax for multinationals. . . . France adopts 3 percent tax on digital companies doing business in France, and President Trump threatens to retaliate with tariffs on French exports. . . . The IRS requires foreign financial institutions to begin collecting Social Security numbers of Americans with foreign bank accounts.

clients, but that relationship came to a halt as bankers were increasingly blamed for the collapsing global economy.

"Severe tax scandals concerning financial institutions in Liechtenstein and Switzerland made the governments of France, Germany and the U.S. very angry," said Dries Lesage, a professor at Ghent University in Belgium.[64]

The anger erupted after it was revealed that Bradley Birkenfeld, a former employee of UBS, Switzerland's largest bank, confessed to U.S. authorities that the bank was knowingly helping U.S. citizens evade taxes on millions of dollars in investments.[65] The IRS in 2008 obtained a court-issued "John Doe" summons, which did not list any taxpayers by name but required UBS to produce information on its U.S. customers.

The IRS' maneuvering was a frontal assault on Switzerland's storied bank secrecy laws, which made it a criminal offense to disclose information about a customer. Switzerland became Europe's primary tax haven after World War I, when economically ruined countries hiked income taxes on the wealthy, who then began looking for ways to avoid the levies. By 2015, foreign wealth in Swiss accounts had reached $2.3 trillion.[66]

The U.S. strategy worked. UBS entered into a deferred prosecution agreement with the Justice Department and agreed to turn over the names of 4,500 Americans who had accounts at the bank. It also agreed

to pay a $780 million fine on charges of defrauding the United States.[67]

Birkenfeld, who pleaded guilty to defrauding the U.S. government, was sentenced to 40 months in prison, but he also received a $104 million payment from the IRS as a whistleblower.[68]

The Justice Department aggressively pursued tax evasion cases involving other Swiss banks, including Credit Suisse, which paid a $2.6 billion fine, the largest on record, and Wegelin & Company, a 250-year-old Swiss private bank, which went out of business after pleading guilty to the U.S. charges.[69]

Bank Bailouts

The disclosures of widespread tax evasion resonated globally, as governments in Europe struggled with the costs of bank bailouts during the financial crisis. Meeting in the resort of L'Aquila, Italy, in July 2009, President Barack Obama and other leaders of the Group of Eight advanced economies made combating tax evasion part of their plans to repair the world economy.

"In this difficult time, the protection of our tax base and the efforts to combat tax fraud and tax evasion are all the more important," a communiqué issued after the meeting said. "We cannot continue to tolerate large amounts of capital hidden to evade taxation."[70]

'Accidental Americans' Find Themselves in IRS' Crosshairs

Complaints grow about tax penalties, reporting requirements for those living abroad.

Inge Frye was born in the United States nearly 70 years ago to an American father and a German mother, but she left when she was 1 year old and never thought of herself as an American. In recent years, however, banks in Europe began demanding that she supply information such as a Social Security number that could be sent to the U.S. Internal Revenue Service (IRS) or risk closure of her financial accounts.

"In past years I have been so harassed by the banks that I finally decided to give up my American citizenship," said Frye, who is now a Belgian citizen. "What kind of a country forces their citizens to take such a drastic step? And what angers me is how the [European Union] can kowtow to the American government and allow them to do this to us." [1]

Frye is among an estimated 300,000 to 500,000 people who have been dubbed "accidental Americans": people who are legally U.S. citizens but were not aware of their status and now face possible penalties from the IRS for not reporting income and foreign bank accounts for tax purposes. [2] Accidental Americans fall into two main groups—people born in the United States who automatically became U.S. citizens under the birthright provisions of the 14th Amendment to the Constitution, or those who are born abroad to at least one U.S. citizen parent, a process called jus sanguinis, or right of blood. [3]

The problem arises because U.S. citizens living abroad have the same tax obligations as people living in the United States—which is one of only two countries that bases its tax system on citizenship rather than residence. The other is Eritrea. [4]

"Most of the people concerned did not know that they were U.S. citizens and were therefore considered by the IRS as U.S. taxpayers," says Fabien Lehagre, the Paris-based president of L'Association des Américains Accidentels. "It is by no means obvious for someone who was only born on U.S. soil to be aware of their tax obligations to the United States. Many accidental Americans do not even speak English. Many of them were even convinced that they had lost their American citizenship when they reached the age of majority," which is usually 18.

Lehagre says most of those affected only found out about their citizenship status following passage of the 2010 Foreign Account Tax Compliance Act (FATCA). The law requires foreign financial institutions to report assets they are holding for U.S. citizens to the IRS, with citizenship usually determined by place of birth on passports when an account is opened. Banks that do not comply face a 30 percent withholding tax on all their U.S.-based income, a powerful incentive to cooperate. [5]

FATCA was adopted following claims that the United States was losing up to $100 billion a year in tax revenue to offshore tax havens. "Amid the growing concern over our budget deficit and American families' concerns about making ends meet, we can no longer afford to allow tax dodgers to hide behind this curtain, avoiding their obligations and leaving their rightful tax burden for honest taxpayers to carry," then-Sen. Carl Levin, D-Mich., said in 2010. [6]

Because foreign banks cannot enforce U.S. law, the U.S. government signed Intergovernmental Agreements on sharing tax information with 130 countries, which then adopted local regulations implementing the reporting requirements. [7]

One of the earliest accidental Americans to object to the status was Boris Johnson, who became Britain's prime minister in July 2019. The IRS asked Johnson, who was born in

A primary focus of the leaders' wrath was parts of the Caribbean, such as the Cayman Islands, Nevis and the British West Indies, that offered no-questions-asked offshore accounts to U.S. and European citizens.[71]

The revelations about tax evasion by wealthy Americans prompted Congress to include the Foreign Account Tax Compliance Act in omnibus legislation passed in 2010 to stimulate the economy. The law requires foreign financial institutions to report to the IRS all financial accounts belonging to U.S. citizens. The United States compelled foreign banks to comply beginning in 2013 by threatening to impose a 30 percent withholding tax on their U.S.-based income.[72]

New York City and lived there until he was 5, to pay capital gains tax on the 2009 sale of a London house. Johnson called the demand "absolutely outrageous," and renounced his U.S. citizenship in 2016. A spokesman for Johnson said the tax matter was settled before he renounced his citizenship, but did not give details about how much he paid. [8]

Almost as soon as FATCA became law, a number of foreign banks decided to close accounts for U.S. citizens rather than go through the expense of filing reports to the IRS. [9]

For foreign residents who have discovered they are also U.S. citizens, a new problem is that the IRS has notified foreign banks that they must begin reporting a tax identification number such as a Social Security number for all U.S. citizens starting in 2020 or they will be considered in non-compliance with the law and face the 30 percent withholding penalty. In previous years, banks have been able to satisfy the reporting requirements by providing only a date of birth. But that transition period ended in 2019. [10]

With the deadline looming, banks have been chasing their U.S. clients for the information and warning that their assets could be frozen if they do not comply. [11] But for many who left the United States as children decades ago, getting a Social Security number has proven to be a scramble. In most cases they must make an appointment with the federal benefits unit at a U.S. embassy, which can involve expensive travel for those who do not live nearby, Lehagre says.

To ease some of these concerns, especially for banks that are legally barred from closing accounts, the IRS issued new guidelines in October. It gave banks 120 days from Jan. 1, 2020, to comply with the requirement to provide tax identification numbers for U.S. citizens. If the numbers are still not obtained, the IRS said it will consider the reasons the bank cannot obtain the information before asking the local government to intervene to close accounts. [12]

Complaints from European banks about the new guidelines prompted Terhi Järvikare, chair of the European Union Council's High-Level Working Party on Tax Questions, to write to U.S. Treasury Secretary Steven Mnuchin asserting that the rules were still unclear and to ask for consultations with European tax authorities. [13]

While praising the U.S. government's recent decision to make it easier for people to renounce their U.S. citizenship if they meet certain qualifications, Järvikare said the process is still "lengthy, costly and complex."

— *Charles P. Wallace*

[1] "Accidental Americans," Facebook, https://tinyurl.com/wfok874.

[2] Kalyeena Makortoff, "EU joins fight against US tax on 'Accidental Americans,'" *The Guardian*, Dec. 12, 2019, https://tinyurl.com/yx66nc7v.

[3] "U.S. Citizenship & Naturalization Overview," Findlaw, https://tinyurl.com/vx4nye5.

[4] "Taxpayers Living Abroad," Internal Revenue Service, https://tinyurl.com/z4rpedm; "Citizenship Based Taxation—International Comparison," Taxes for Expats, https://tinyurl.com/wbgxuba.

[5] "FATCA Provisions in HIRE Act Favored On Balance," LexisNexis Legal Newsroom, March 30, 2010, https://tinyurl.com/r7tns7l.

[6] "S1636," *Congressional Record*, March 17, 2010, https://tinyurl.com/qnys6bf.

[7] "Despite Spending Nearly $380 Million, the Internal Revenue Service Is Still Not Prepared to Enforce Compliance With the Foreign Account Tax Compliance Act," Treasury Inspector General for Tax Administration, July 5, 2018, https://tinyurl.com/tp5bxua.

[8] George Parker and Vanessa Houlder, "London Mayor Bows to 'Outrageous' Demand to Pay US Tax Bill," *Financial Times*, Jan. 21, 2015, https://tinyurl.com/vp9gpy3.

[9] Geoff Williams, "U.S. expats find their money is no longer welcome at the bank," *Reuters*, June 11, 2014, https://tinyurl.com/v2v35br.

[10] "United States: New FATCA FAQ on Model 1 FFIs and Expiration of TIN Relief—KPMG United States," KPMG, Nov. 7, 2019, https://tinyurl.com/snclpyw.

[11] Kalyeena Makortoff, "British Citizens Born in US Risk Having UK Bank Accounts Frozen," *The Guardian*, Aug. 25, 2019, https://tinyurl.com/r5ltfpk.

[12] "FATCA FAQs—General," Internal Revenue Service, Dec. 18, 2019, https://tinyurl.com/s5vypc8.

[13] Terhi Järvikare, "FATCA—Exchange of Information Under Intergovernmental Agreements," Council of the European Union, Dec. 3, 2019, https://tinyurl.com/s5ey2uu.

FATCA was designed to toughen regulations about foreign bank accounts that were part of the Bank Secrecy Act, a law enacted in 1970. The Bank Secrecy Act required Americans with more than $10,000 in a foreign bank account to report the account to the U.S. Treasury separately from their income tax filings. The secrecy act's failure to solve the tax evasion problem became clear in a 2008 report by the Senate Permanent Subcommittee on Investigations, which concluded that "each year, the United States loses an estimated $100 billion in tax revenues due to offshore tax abuses."[73]

FATCA was designed to toughen regulations on foreign bank accounts. In the years after it took effect, the

Tax Expert: U.S. Companies 'the Global Grandmasters of Tax Avoidance'

Critics question effectiveness of 2017 law designed to tax foreign profits.

The Double Irish, Dutch Sandwich and Green Jersey may sound like professional wrestling moves, but they are the names of strategies used by Apple, Microsoft and other multinational corporations to reduce their taxes by setting up subsidiaries in low-tax nations. [1]

Critics have long charged that multinational companies use such strategies to avoid paying the full taxes due on their overseas earnings, both to their home country and to the countries where the sales take place. Multinationals avoid $100 billion to $240 billion in taxes each year, according to the Organisation for Economic Co-operation and Development (OECD), a Paris-based body that provides research on developed countries' economies. [2]

To avoid paying the 35 percent corporate tax rate that existed before 2018, U.S. multinationals had accumulated an estimated $2.6 trillion in assets in offshore subsidiaries. [3]

"U.S. multinational firms are the global grandmasters of tax avoidance schemes that deplete not just U.S. tax collection but the tax collection of most every large economy in the world," said Edward Kleinbard, a professor of tax law at the University of Southern California. [4]

In response, Congress in December 2017 changed how foreign profits are taxed. Besides reducing the maximum corporate tax rate to 21 percent, the Tax Cuts and Jobs Act included a tax on "global intangible low-taxed income" (GILTI). The tax is aimed primarily at internet and pharmaceutical companies that have shifted ownership of their intellectual property, such as copyrights, patents and trademarks, to subsidiaries in low-tax countries like Ireland and the Netherlands. [5] The patent on a top-selling pharmaceutical can bring in billions of dollars in revenue, while copyrights on software owned by Microsoft also earn hundreds of millions of dollars each year.

The GILTI rule requires firms to pay a repatriation tax on their accumulated offshore profits, regardless of whether they brought those earnings home, as well as future offshore income from "intangibles"—such things as those copyrights and patents.

Technology giant Apple was the company most affected by the law, because it had $252 billion stashed tax-free in overseas subsidiaries.

Apple was using several strategies to reduce its global taxes, all of which were legal, according to documents from an offshore law firm, which were leaked to journalists in a security breach known as the Paradise Papers. The strategies, given nicknames such as Double Irish and Green Jersey, involved setting up subsidiaries in the low-tax Republic of Ireland that would own Apple's intellectual property, then send those profits to another Apple-owned unit in Jersey, a tiny island in the English Channel with no corporate tax. Then the money would be returned to another Irish company tax-free, the documents showed. [6]

After the documents were published, Apple denied that its overseas subsidiaries enabled the company to avoid paying its fair share of taxes. "At Apple we follow the laws, and if the system changes we will comply," said spokesman Josh

IRS offered taxpayers an amnesty from criminal prosecution if they voluntarily came forward to disclose their foreign assets and paid their outstanding taxes, interest and penalties. In 2016, the IRS said it had collected more than $10 billion from taxpayers who took advantage of the amnesty.[74]

Despite those achievements, government auditors criticized FATCA for failing to meet all of its goals. "Despite spending nearly $380 million, the Internal Revenue Service is still not prepared to enforce compliance with the Foreign Account Tax Compliance Act," according to a 2018 report from the Treasury Department's inspector general for tax administration. It accused the IRS of taking "limited or no action" on the majority of activities required by FATCA.[75]

An April 2019 study from the Government Accountability Office, Congress' investigative arm, also criticized how FATCA was implemented, noting

Rosenstock. "We strongly support efforts from the global community toward comprehensive international tax reform and a far simpler system." [7]

After President Trump signed the tax legislation, Apple announced that it would pay $38 billion worth of taxes to the U.S. government, which it said "would likely be the largest of its kind ever made." In a filing with the Securities and Exchange Commission, the company said it would pay the tax in installments over eight years, as the law allows. [8]

Critics say the 2017 law may not work as designed. "In principle, GILTI is meant to reduce profit shifting by targeting highly mobile income, specifically income from intellectual property," says Kyle Pomerleau, a resident fellow at the American Enterprise Institute, a conservative Washington think tank. "However, the way that GILTI is structured, the effects of the provision are highly company-specific. GILTI may work in principle, but not in practice."

For one thing, because the law allows money earned from tangible assets such as factories to offset GILTI profits, multinationals might move jobs offshore or adopt other tax-saving strategies using foreign subsidiaries. [9]

Even before the U.S. tax law had been passed, the OECD had issued a 15-point program to help countries avoid erosion of their tax bases by corporate profit shifting. So far, more than 135 countries have adopted the program, which prohibits companies from using some tax havens, such as Caribbean countries that formerly offered zero corporate taxes even to firms with no local presence. [10]

An OECD proposal released in October would allow countries to tax the profits that internet companies earn in countries where they have no physical presence. But U.S. Treasury Secretary Steven Mnuchin wrote to the OECD that "the United States firmly opposes digital services taxes because they have a discriminatory impact on U.S.-based businesses and are inconsistent with the architecture of current international tax rules." Because all OECD decisions must be unanimous, U.S. opposition would kill the idea. [11]

— *Charles P. Wallace*

[1] Sumeet Swarup, "Green Jersey, Dutch Sandwich, Irish Double and Single Malt," NASSCOM Community, Feb. 14, 2019, https://tinyurl.com/r3tya35.

[2] "Base Erosion and Profit Shifting—OECD BEPS," Organisation of Economic Co-operation and Development, https://tinyurl.com/s6nl3n6.

[3] "What is global intangible low-taxed income and how is it taxed under the TCJA?" Tax Policy Center, 2018, https://tinyurl.com/tx4eq32; Rochelle Toplensky, "Multinationals Pay Lower Taxes Than a Decade Ago," *Financial Times*, March 11, 2018, https://tinyurl.com/ycubt46r.

[4] Jesse Drucker and Simon Bowers, "After a Tax Crackdown, Apple Found a New Shelter for Its Profits," *The New York Times*, Nov. 6, 2017, https://tinyurl.com/y7m2s9ob.

[5] "What is global intangible low-taxed income and how is it taxed under the TCJA?" *op. cit.*

[6] Richard Waters and Tom Braithwaite, "Apple Will See Up to $47bn Potential Benefit From Tax Reform," *Financial Times*, Dec. 6, 2017, https://tinyurl.com/y8o5vcj4; Simon Bowers, "Leaked Documents Expose Secret Tale Of Apple's Offshore Island Hop," International Consortium of Investigative Journalists, Nov. 6, 2017, https://tinyurl.com/yavxylqe.

[7] Drucker and Bowers, *op. cit.*

[8] "Apple accelerates US investment and job creation," press release, Apple, Jan. 17, 2018, https://tinyurl.com/yad2pljd; "Form 10-K Apple Inc.," Securities and Exchange Commission, Nov. 5, 2018, https://tinyurl.com/vk73vsm.

[9] Reuven Avi-Yonah, "The Tax Act Actually Promotes Off-Shore Tax Tricks," *The American Prospect*, June 28, 2018, https://tinyurl.com/yx3pdwt7.

[10] "Base Erosion and Profit Shifting—OECD BEPS," *op. cit.*

[11] "Secretariat Proposal for a 'Unified Approach' under Pillar One," Organisation of Economic Co-operation and Development, Oct. 9, 2019, https://tinyurl.com/s3u5r7a; "U.S. Treasury Secretary Sends Letter to OECD Secretary-General on Work to Address the Tax Challenges of the Digitalization of the Economy," *Orbitax News*, Dec. 3, 2019, https://tinyurl.com/r8mw2ns.

that the IRS had trouble matching the information provided by foreign banks with U.S. taxpayers because the banks' reports often lacked Social Security numbers. Foreign banks will be required to start collecting the Social Security numbers of Americans with overseas accounts in 2020 or face the withholding penalties.[76]

Despite this criticism about FATCA's implementation, some lawmakers denounced the act as government overreach. In a 2017 letter to Treasury Secretary Steven Mnuchin, Sen. Rand Paul, R-Ky., and Rep. Mark Meadows, R-N.C., called FATCA "a massive, wasteful regulatory mandate that has failed in its ostensible purpose of recovering tax revenues hidden offshore." They unsuccessfully introduced legislation to repeal the law.[77]

Just as the UBS case aroused anger in the United States, Europeans were angered by revelations from a

French computer technician named Hervé Falciani, who in 2008 handed over to French authorities 60,000 documents he had stolen from the Swiss branch of the multinational bank HSBC. These records showed how the bank helped its clients hide their money from the tax authorities. HSBC paid a $353 million fine to France to settle the case.[78]

Panama Papers

Further evidence of wrongdoing was revealed in the 2016 leak of 11.5 million files, known as the Panama Papers, from the Mossack Fonseca law firm in Panama. The files showed that 140 politicians from 50 countries—including then-Argentine President Mauricio Macri, then-President Petro Poroshenko of Ukraine and Icelandic Prime Minister Sigmundur Davíd Gunnlaugsson—had used the law firm to set up shell companies.[79]

The papers, which were published by a group of reporters called the International Consortium of Investigative Journalists, revealed that Mossack Fonseca helped clients set up 214,000 shell companies. The revelations led to police raids across Europe. Four people were indicted in the United States on a variety of charges related to tax evasion; their trial is slated to begin later this year.[80] The consortium estimated that $1.2 billion in taxes were recovered after the disclosures.

Jonathan Ernst/Bloomberg via Getty Images

HSBC bank officials (from left) David Bagley, Paul Thurston, Michael Gallagher and Christopher Lok prepare to testify at a Senate subcommittee hearing in Washington in 2012. Internal documents showed that the multinational bank helped hide client money from tax authorities. In 2017, HSBC agreed to pay a $353 million fine in the tax evasion case.

The case was made into a 2019 movie called *The Laundromat*, starring Meryl Streep and Antonio Banderas.

"Before the Panama Papers there was a public tolerance, a kind of 'good for you' attitude toward anyone who could avoid paying their fair share of tax," said Rita de la Feria, a tax law professor at the University of Leeds in England. "The Panama Papers has helped to shift this perception to one of, 'You're robbing us of public services.'"[81]

Earlier, soon after FATCA went into effect in 2013, the Organisation for Economic Co-operation and Development (OECD) proposed a similar automatic exchange of bank account information for all countries. The Common Reporting Standard, which was adopted in July 2014 and now has 108 nations participating, including several former tax havens in the Caribbean, calls on financial institutions to supply financial account data to the account holder's country of residence.[82]

The OECD estimates that money deposited in overseas bank accounts has declined by $410 billion since the adoption of the reporting standard. The United States has not adopted the standard because it prefers using FATCA. But it has signed Intergovernmental Agreements with 63 countries requiring them to provide taxpayer information about U.S. citizens, while agreeing to provide reciprocal data about foreign citizens in certain cases.[83]

Critics, however, say the Intergovernmental Agreements have not worked well.[84]

"We're increasingly aware that the U.S. is effectively increasing its market share in the holding of overseas assets," says the Tax Justice Network's Cobham. "It's the most attractive tax haven for residents elsewhere."

Several states, especially Delaware, Nevada and Wyoming, became financial centers by offering to permit the creation of shell companies without obtaining detailed information about their beneficial owners. This laxity led Sen. Sheldon Whitehouse, D-R.I., to complain that "America too often enables global corruption, by allowing the looters the shelter of our rule of law for their ill-gotten gains."[85]

The relative ease of hiding assets in the United States has increasingly made the country a center for money laundering, according to law enforcement authorities. In one case, a drug cartel used U.S. shell companies to launder more than $250 million in proceeds.[86]

The Financial Action Task Force evaluated U.S. efforts to control money laundering in 2016. It concluded that "lack of timely access to adequate, accurate and current beneficial ownership information remains one of the fundamental gaps in the U.S. context."[87]

As a result of such criticism, Treasury's FinCEN amended its regulations in 2016 to require U.S. banks to collect more information on companies when they open a bank account.[88]

The Tax Justice Network, which publishes a biannual ranking of countries by their secrecy rules and offshore financial activities, said that Switzerland remained the most secretive offshore location, but that the United States had moved from third to second in 2018.[89]

Money laundering has proven problematic even in places with a reputation for little corruption, such as Scandinavia. A scandal engulfed Nordic banks following disclosures that Russians had laundered around $230 billion through the Estonian branch of Danske Bank, Denmark's biggest lender. It was the largest money laundering case ever involving a single bank.[90]

Danske's CEO was forced to resign in 2018 and authorities later charged him with money laundering. The scandal then spread to Sweden, where the CEO of Swedbank, the country's largest mortgage lender, was fired and the chairman resigned.[91]

CURRENT SITUATION
Money Laundering Crackdown

Government efforts to stamp out money laundering are ramping up, with a record $8.14 billion in fines assessed globally in 2019.

The United States led with 25 cases involving $2.29 billion in money laundering fines, according to Encompass, a British firm that makes anti-money laundering software. The United Kingdom was second, with 12 cases in which $388 million in fines were assessed. The single largest penalty was a $5.1 billion fine handed down by a French court against UBS for helping its clients hide their assets from the French government.[92]

One of the most prominent money laundering cases involved Chinese telecom giant Huawei, which the U.S.

government accused of bank fraud and money laundering in its business with a subsidiary in Iran. (The government also accused Huawei of violating U.S. sanctions on Iran.) The company's chief financial officer, Meng Wanzhou, was also charged and is being held by Canadian authorities on an extradition request from the United States.[93]

Another major case involved a former minister of industry in Barbados, Donville Inniss, who was convicted by a U.S. federal court jury in January of taking bribes from an insurance company and laundering the money through U.S. banks.[94]

In an effort to step up its anti-money laundering efforts overseas, the Treasury Department created a global investigations division at FinCEN, which it said will "investigate and target terrorist finance and money laundering threats."[95]

At the same time, FinCEN issued guidelines bringing "money services businesses" that deal in cryptocurrencies under its regulations to reduce the risk of digital currencies being used for money laundering.[96]

In Europe, France, Germany, Italy, Latvia, the Netherlands and Spain issued a joint position paper in November calling for the creation of a central anti-money laundering supervisor with responsibility for the entire European Union. Combating money laundering is currently the responsibility of each EU member country. The proposal came after a series of embarrassing scandals involving banks in Sweden, Denmark, Germany, Cyprus, Malta, the Netherlands, Estonia and Latvia.[97]

Digital Tax Truce

France and the United States called a temporary truce in a major tax case involving internet companies. In 2019, France imposed a 3 percent tax on the revenues of Google, Facebook and other companies that earn money in France but have no physical presence there. President Trump threatened to retaliate with tariffs on $2.4 billion worth of French exports.

After a meeting with Treasury Secretary Mnuchin at the World Economic Forum in Davos, Switzerland, in January, French Finance Minister Bruno Le Maire said France would suspend imposition of the tax while an international agreement on multinational taxation is negotiated at the OECD in Paris. The French want a

A worker makes cheese at a dairy farm in the French Alps in December 2019. France agreed to put on hold a 3 percent tax on U.S.-based internet companies after President Trump threatened retaliatory tariffs on some French exports, including cheese.

compulsory tax on the revenues of multinationals in each country where they operate, while the United States believes each company should be able to decide whether to reallocate a portion of their corporate profits.

Le Maire said France seeks an agreement that is "solid, credible and fair. An optional basis would not be credible."[98]

While France agreed to put its tax on hold, Britain, which left the European Union on Jan. 31, 2020, announced that it planned to go ahead with its own digital tax in April 2020. "It is a proportionate tax, and a tax that is deliberately designed as a temporary tax," said Sajid Javid, the U.K. chancellor of the exchequer. Italy also plans to go ahead with a digital tax.[99]

Mnuchin warned Britain and Italy that they will face retaliatory tariffs if they proceed with their tax plans.[100]

Phil Hogan, the EU's new trade commissioner, called the digital taxation "a very major bone of contention" with the United States and said: "We will look at all possibilities if any tariffs or measures are imposed by the United States. The European Commission will stand together with France and all other member states who wish to have the sovereign right to impose digital taxation on companies in a fair way."[101]

While the United States is trying to contain the effort to tax multinationals, pressure to go after the firms is growing. Google parent Alphabet Inc. announced in

December that because of changes to tax laws, it was dropping a tax strategy that used an Irish subsidiary and is bringing the business home to the United States.[102]

The IMF has estimated that $12 trillion of multinationals' overseas activity "consists of financial investment passing through empty corporate shells with no real activity."[103]

France's move was part of an effort by European countries to tax multinationals where they have sales, rather than in their home countries. Some estimates say the countries are losing $100 billion to $240 billion a year in taxes because profits are shifted to low-tax nations. Companies are currently required to report their country-by-country earnings to their respective governments under an agreement reached at the 2015 summit of the Group of 20 nations. Now, countries such as France and Germany want multinationals to share their earnings data with local governments and pay taxes based on where their employees and sales are located, as well as a global minimum tax on their earnings.[104]

Campaign Debates

The taxing of multinationals is generating debate in the 2020 U.S. presidential campaign. Several Democratic candidates criticized the 2017 Tax Cuts and Jobs Act for reducing corporate tax rates from 35 percent to 21 percent and for increasing the federal budget deficit.[105]

Sen. Warren said she would crack down on the use of shell companies and coordinate with foreign governments to bring about more global financial transparency. Warren also would impose a 35 percent tax rate on U.S. companies' foreign earnings.[106]

Sen. Bernie Sanders, I-Vt., announced he would tax all corporate profits, including those earned overseas, at one unitary rate of 35 percent. "For the longest time, the one thing that has been [Sanders'] push is to go to this full worldwide tax system," said Kyle Pomerleau of the Tax Foundation.[107]

Former Vice President Joe Biden announced plans to double taxation of foreign profits. "First thing I'd do is repeal those Trump tax cuts," Biden said on a campaign stop. The corporate rate should be returned to its previous levels, he said.

Although Biden's tax proposals are more limited than those of his Democratic rivals, conservatives were quick

Should Congress pass legislation to reveal the true owners of shell companies?

YES Michael Findley
Professor of Political Science, University of Texas, Austin

Written for CQ Researcher, February 2020

A serious obstacle to stopping criminal activity and tax evasion has been the use of shell companies—firms with no substantive business purpose that can be set up online, inexpensively and in relatively short order, and that serve as legal entities that can hold bank accounts and assets.

Unless banks know the real person behind the shell company holding the account, it is de facto anonymous, and money transfers to or from it are untraceable. Corporate service providers (CSPs) and banks are required to establish the true identity of their customers and to identify and flag suspicious activity and transactions to the authorities.

Global Know Your Customer rules are established by the Financial Action Task Force (FATF), and supplemented by the Basel Committee on Banking Supervision, an international club consisting of 35 of the world's most powerful countries that is the world's anti-money laundering standard-setter and enforcer. Nine associate organizations extend the FATF standards to 180 other countries and financial jurisdictions.

While the rules are set down by international actors, countries implement them, and nations' compliance is periodically and publicly assessed by the FATF. Governments cannot simply wash their hands and say noncompliance is a private-sector problem. Several countries, including in Europe, have made important strides in implementing international rules domestically. The United States, while a driver of international standards, has lagged behind in domestic implementation. And U.S. CSPs are the world's least compliant, making domestic legislation in the United States urgent.

In October, the U.S. House of Representatives passed the Corporate Transparency Act. The Senate is now considering a similar bill, the Illicit Cash Act. Both are bipartisan bills that for the first time would put the United States in a credible position to stem this crucial channel for illicit financial flows. In a statement of administration policy, the White House endorsed legislation to end anonymous incorporation, stating "the Administration believes this legislation [H.R. 2513] represents important progress in strengthening national security, supporting law enforcement, and clarifying regulatory requirements."

Because shell companies with bank accounts have been perhaps the single most common mechanism for money laundering, transnational corruption, tax evasion and other related crimes, and because the United States ranks dead last in its implementation of international standards, some reconciled version of the Corporate Transparency Act and Illicit Cash Act is indispensable.

NO Kevin Kuhlman
Senior Director for Federal Government Relations, National Federation of Independent Business

Written for CQ Researcher, February 2020

The House-passed Corporate Transparency Act and the Senate's proposed Illicit Cash Act saddle America's smallest businesses with a substantial new paperwork requirement and threaten small-business owners with significant jail time and fines for paperwork violations. They impose these reporting mandates only on small businesses, those least equipped to handle new paperwork requirements. Additionally, these bills put the personal information of small-business owners at serious risk.

The bills require nearly every corporation and limited liability company with 20 or fewer employees to file new reports with the Treasury Department's Financial Crimes Enforcement Network (FinCEN) regarding the personally identifiable information of the business' beneficial owners and to update that information periodically. The Congressional Budget Office estimates the cost to comply would be substantial.

The National Federation of Independent Business (NFIB) estimates the mandate would initially result in more than 12 million new paperwork hours at the cost of more than $530 million. Moreover, both bills would make it a federal crime to fail to provide completed and updated reports, with civil penalties up to $10,000 and criminal penalties up to three or four years in prison.

NFIB members report that the burden of federal paperwork ranks in the top 20 percent of the problems they encounter as small-business owners. While large businesses and financial institutions have access to teams of lawyers and compliance experts to gather beneficial ownership information and report it to the government, small-business owners do not. These owners have difficulty affording legal experts to help them comply with reporting requirements, and they lack time to gather information to fill out yet more forms for the government.

Both bills also raise serious privacy concerns for small businesses. Each would allow federal, state, tribal, local and even foreign law enforcement agencies access to business owners' personally identifiable information, via the FinCEN database, without a subpoena or warrant. The potential for improper disclosure or misuse of private information grows as the number of individuals with access to the information increases.

Both proposals establish a first-of-its-kind federal registry of small-business owners. While this registry will not be publicly available initially, this legislation would be a first step toward establishing a publicly accessible registry, which can be used to name and shame small-business owners.

to criticize him. "Hiking the tax rate on American businesses will kill jobs, lower wages and reduce new investment in America," said Grover Norquist, president of Americans for Tax Reform, a conservative group that favors lower taxes.[108]

Trump said in January he will propose a middle-class tax cut in the next 90 days, which he said will be subject to his Republican Party "taking back the House and obviously keeping the Senate and keeping the White House." He gave no details of the plan.[109]

A *Reuters*/Ipsos poll of U.S. adults in January found that nearly two-thirds of respondents agreed the very rich should pay more in taxes; 64 percent strongly or somewhat strongly agreed that "the very rich should contribute an extra share of their total wealth each year to support public programs," a definition that resembles the wealth tax proposed by Sanders and Warren. Support was strongest among Democrats at 77 percent, but a majority of Republicans, 53 percent, also agreed with the idea.[110]

OUTLOOK
Enforcement Challenges

One of the truths about financial crime is that when authorities crack down in one area, criminals quickly find other areas to exploit. Experts say this reality makes it especially difficult to reduce tax evasion and money laundering, although many agree the international community is making progress.

Tax cheating is "still a big problem," says Zayda Manatta, who heads the OECD's global forum on taxation. "Whenever you close one door, they find a new one. But if we compare it to a lake, the fact is that the water is going down and down and you can see more of the big fish."

Switzerland, for example, was once the preferred destination for offshore accounts by people trying to avoid paying taxes. But pressure on Switzerland to end bank secrecy resulted in life insurance policy wrappers and other innovations that are not covered by financial reporting requirements, or by placing assets in shell companies in jurisdictions where the true owners do not have to be revealed.[111]

Former Treasury agent Cassara says governments need to turn their attention to two areas that have contributed to illicit activities: gatekeepers and invoice fraud.

Gatekeepers are the lawyers and accountants who help individuals set up bank accounts and shell companies. While most arrangements are legal, gatekeepers also have set up accounts for criminals.

Great Britain and the EU are adopting regulations to eliminate the ability of accountants and lawyers to set up anonymous shell companies. Similar proposals are gaining support in the United States.

"The U.S. has lagged far behind countries and regions like the European Union, United Kingdom and other jurisdictions in this area," said Brian Monroe of the Association of Certified Financial Crime Specialists, an anti-money laundering organization in Miami. "These areas have made commitments to eliminate the ability for attorneys, company service providers and other gatekeepers to create anonymous shell firms."[112]

But the legal community strongly opposes any government regulation of their relationship with clients. "Lawyers around the globe have emphatically argued that certain anti-money laundering obligations, particularly a mandate that lawyers report suspicious activity relating to their clients, would undermine the relationship of trust and the attorney-client privilege," said attorneys Stephanie Brooker and Joel Cohen of Gibson, Dunn & Crutcher, a California law firm.[113]

Another concern is the unchecked growth of trade invoice fraud, a method of money laundering in which goods are priced at either more or less than their actual value to facilitate the movement of illicit money from one country to another. While little known, trade-based fraud is estimated to total more than $1 trillion a year.[114]

"There are a million and one great ways to move money illegally through trade," says Channing Mavrellis, a transnational crime analyst at Global Financial Integrity. For example, Mavrellis says Latin American drug dealers recycle their cash earned in the United States through what are called peso brokers—people who buy goods with the cash and ship them back to Latin America.

Mavrellis says that trade fraud and money laundering is difficult to stop because it requires the cooperation of customs officials in both the exporting and importing nations, which rarely happens.

Cassara proposes establishing what he calls global trade transparency units to exchange "transaction-level trade data on trade between individuals or trading companies of the two countries to detect and combat wrongdoing." A transparency unit has been set up in the U.S. Department of Homeland Security, but other nations have been slow to adopt the idea.

The question of taxing multinational companies is scheduled to advance at the OECD in 2020 after France and the United States agreed to move talks on taxing internet companies to the Paris-based organization.

The talks are likely to focus on a two-pronged approach: providing detailed information on revenues earned in each country to the local government and implementing a global minimum tax to prevent multinationals from using low-tax jurisdictions to pay little or no tax on their profits.[115]

Cobham of the Tax Justice Network says he proposed a similar approach 10 years ago, but it is only now being taken seriously. Under this proposal, if 10 percent of a company's employment and sales are in, say, the United Kingdom, then 10 percent of the profits would be registered in that country for tax purposes. It is similar to the way U.S. states apportion taxes, he says.

"There's a complexity to the negotiations," Cobham says. "Governments know their own multinationals are probably playing these games in other countries. So, there's a bit of caution about how the new rules might impact their own multinationals as they try to prevent other countries' multinationals dodging their taxes."

NOTES

1. Louise Story and Stephanie Saul, "Jho Low, Well Connected in Malaysia, Has an Appetite for New York," *The New York Times*, Feb. 8, 2015, https://tinyurl.com/yxhlxapw.

2. "Malaysian Financier Low Taek Jho, Also Known As 'Jho Low,' and Former Banker Ng Chong Hwa, Also Known As 'Roger Ng,' Indicted for Conspiring to Launder Billions of Dollars in Illegal Proceeds and to Pay Hundreds of Millions of Dollars in Bribes," U.S. Justice Department, Nov. 1, 2018, https://tinyurl.com/y76clr4e; Shamim Adam, Laurence Arnold and Yudith Ho, "How Malaysia's 1MDB Scandal Shook the Financial World," *Bloomberg*, Jan. 9, 2019, https://tinyurl.com/y7r6v6aa; and Noah Manskar, "Financial fugitive Jho Low claims he wasn't 'mastermind' of 1MDB scam," *New York Post*, Jan. 6, 2020, https://tinyurl.com/szumoyj.

3. Michael Findley, Daniel Nielson and Jason Sharman, "Global Shell Games: Testing Money Launderers' and Terrorist Financiers' Access to Shell Companies," Michael-Findley.com, https://tinyurl.com/u47xoqj; Robert Neuwirth, "The Shadow Superpower," *Foreign Policy*, Oct. 28, 2011, https://tinyurl.com/s2qdffb.

4. Chris Prentice, "Shadow Economies on the Rise Around the World," *Bloomberg*, July 29, 2010, https://tinyurl.com/udmo6d2.

5. "Hidden corners of the global economy," International Monetary Fund, September 2019, https://tinyurl.com/vxwv87y.

6. "Financial Secrecy Index—2018 Results," Tax Justice Network, Oct. 4, 2019, https://tinyurl.com/s5s5j8h.

7. Annette Alstadsæter, Niels Johannesen and Gabriel Zucman, "Who owns the wealth in tax havens? Macro evidence and implications for global inequality," *Journal of Public Economics*, June 2018, https://tinyurl.com/qmqxux6.

8. "Money-Laundering and Globalization," United Nations Office on Drugs and Crime, 2019, https://tinyurl.com/yxkwa9e4.

9. "Hidden corners of the global economy," *op. cit.*; "What Is A Tax Haven?" Whistleblower Justice Network, https://tinyurl.com/urn5cfu.

10. "Hidden corners of the global economy," *op. cit.*

11. Elizabeth Warren, "Ending the Stranglehold of Health Care Costs on American Families," *Medium*, Nov. 1, 2019, https://tinyurl.com/yx8hlk8b.

12. Misyrlena Egkolfopoulou, "Warren Plans to Crack Down on U.S. Shell Companies, Tax Evasion," *Bloomberg*, Dec. 17, 2019, https://tinyurl.com/qv658w2; Tara Golshan, "Bernie Sanders's plan to reshape corporate America, explained," *Vox*, Oct. 14, 2019, https://tinyurl.com/y2hy99xv; and Allison Schrager, "Will a wealth tax change the behavior of the very rich?" *Quartz*, Nov. 8, 2019, https://tinyurl.com/wfy4hho.

13. Toluse Olorunnipa, "Warren's ambitious agenda relies on a massive wealth tax that the rich may

evade," *The Washington Post*, May 22, 2019, https://tinyurl.com/sw2r696.

14. "What is global intangible low-taxed income and how is it taxed under the TCJA?" Tax Policy Center, 2018, https://tinyurl.com/tx4eq32.

15. "Apple Accelerates US Investment and Job Creation," press release, Apple, Jan. 17, 2018, https://tinyurl.com/yad2pljd; Richard Waters, "Google to End Use of 'Double Irish' as Tax Loophole Set to Close," *Financial Times*, Jan. 1, 2020, https://tinyurl.com/vccv8qm; Jesse Drucker and Jim Tankersley, "How Big Companies Won New Tax Breaks From the Trump Administration," *The New York Times*, Dec. 30, 2019, https://tinyurl.com/tvd6aab; and "Treasury and IRS Issue Proposed and Final Guidance on Foreign Tax Credits and the Base Erosion and Anti-Abuse Tax to Continue Modernizing the US Tax System," press release, Treasury Department, Dec. 2, 2019, https://tinyurl.com/wuz9wky.

16. James Politi, "US Proposes 100% Tariffs on French Goods over Digital Tax," *Financial Times*, Dec. 2, 2019, https://tinyurl.com/wvr4bsh; Bojan Pancevski and Sam Schechner, "France's Macron Pauses Tech Tax After U.S. Pressure," *The Wall Street Journal*, Jan. 20, 2020, https://tinyurl.com/rb8wys3.

17. Chris Giles, "G20 Finance Ministers Back OECD Push to Tax Profits of Multinationals," *Financial Times*, Oct. 18, 2019, https://tinyurl.com/yxuvrml2.

18. Casey Michel, "The U.S. Is a Good Place for Bad People to Stash Their Money," *The Atlantic*, July 13, 2017, https://tinyurl.com/vywgsek.

19. Edward Luce, "How Money Laundering Is Poisoning American Democracy," *Financial Times*, Nov. 28, 2019, https://tinyurl.com/vwr6z22.

20. "FinCEN Targets Shell Companies Purchasing Luxury Properties in Seven Major Metropolitan Areas," Financial Crimes Enforcement Network, Aug. 22, 2017, https://tinyurl.com/y99gow3z.

21. "Prepared Remarks of FinCEN Director Kenneth A. Blanco, Delivered at the American Bankers Association/American Bar Association Financial Crimes Enforcement Conference," Financial Crimes Enforcement Network, Dec. 10, 2019, https://tinyurl.com/vfoe9ur.

22. "Statement of administration policy," The White House, Oct. 22, 2019, https://tinyurl.com/uff6jqv.

23. "Ultimate Beneficial Owner (UBO) Register Requirements: The Netherlands, Belgium, Luxembourg and Ireland," IQEQ.com, 2019, https://tinyurl.com/uhfgvq7.

24. "What is the tax gap?" Tax Policy Center, 2016, https://tinyurl.com/u9sdbvk; Melanie Waithe, "US IRS Begins FATCA Crackdown," *Trinidad and Tobago Newsday*, May 23, 2019, https://tinyurl.com/wk3qejs; and "Citizenship Based Taxation—International Comparison," Taxes for Expats, https://tinyurl.com/wbgxuba.

25. "Washington Resident Pleads Guilty to Filing a False Tax Return That Failed to Report Over $1 Million Held in Offshore Swiss Bank Account," U.S. Attorney for the Eastern District of Washington, Oct. 23, 2019, https://tinyurl.com/y6tvakun.

26. George Rosenberg, Ari Rosenberg and Niv Goldstein, "Using Insurance Wrappers for Asset Protection and Tax Planning," *Financier Worldwide*, April 2014, https://tinyurl.com/r46arco; "Tax Gap Estimates for Tax Years 2011-2013," Internal Revenue Service, September 2013, https://tinyurl.com/rj3g5go.

27. Reuven Avi-Yonah, "The Shame of Tax Havens," *The American Prospect*, Dec. 1, 2015, https://tinyurl.com/tghmqlb.

28. "A Roadmap For A Global Asset Registry," Independent Commission for the Reform of International Corporate Taxation, March 2019, https://tinyurl.com/ry3lb78.

29. Delphine Nougayrède, "Towards a Global Financial Register?" Columbia Law School, March 2017, https://tinyurl.com/v723f3h.

30. Mark Nestmann, "A 'Global Asset Registry' Would End Financial Privacy," Nestmann Group, July 9, 2019, https://tinyurl.com/t9plk7v.

31. Warren, *op. cit.*

32. Curtis Dubay and Anthony Kim, "FATCA Hurts Law-Abiding Americans Living Abroad," Heritage Foundation, June 10, 2014, https://tinyurl.com/r5j2qdz.

33. Joe Kirwin, "EU's Expanded Tax Haven Blacklist Could Apply to U.S.," *Bloomberg Tax*, Dec. 13, 2018, https://tinyurl.com/tyjw8un.

34. "Beneficial Ownership," Tax Justice Network, 2019, https://tinyurl.com/rkpdr6o.

35. "Directive (EU) 2015/849 of the European Parliament and of the Council of 20 May 2015," *Official Journal of the European Union*, June 6, 2015, https://tinyurl.com/sgegfg5; Maureen Heydt, "With Spate of New Bills, Congress Has Chance to Tackle Kleptocracy," Global Financial Integrity, Oct. 21, 2019, https://tinyurl.com/vwsjy8n.

36. "Best Practices on Beneficial Ownership for Legal Persons," Financial Action Task Force, October 2019, https://tinyurl.com/y4nqjvc2; Mark Schremmer, "ILLICIT CASH Act would hurt small-business owners, coalition says," *Land Line*, Nov. 13, 2019, https://tinyurl.com/vwojoa2.

37. "Illicit Financial Flows to and from 148 Developing Countries: 2006-2015," Global Financial Integrity, January 2019, https://tinyurl.com/twdbj5y.

38. Alana Semuels, "Loose Tax Laws Aren't Delaware's Fault," *The Atlantic*, Oct. 5, 2016, https://tinyurl.com/tjhvx86.

39. "The Library Card Project: The Ease of Forming Anonymous Companies in the United States," Global Financial Integrity, March 21, 2019, https://tinyurl.com/y3bgsfks.

40. "Combating Illicit Financing by Anonymous Shell Companies," FBI, May 21, 2019, https://tinyurl.com/yxc6pu7p.

41. "H.R.2513—Corporate Transparency Act of 2019," Congress.gov, Oct. 23, 2019, https://tinyurl.com/ugdswwn.

42. "Reps. Maloney, King, and Malinowski Introduce Bipartisan Corporate Transparency Act," press release, Office of Rep. Carolyn B. Maloney, May 3, 2019, https://tinyurl.com/ug38seb.

43. "Corporate Transparency Act Would Require Public Disclosure of the True Owners of Many Shell Companies," GovTrack.us, July 23, 2019, https://tinyurl.com/qugzsdb.

44. "Senators Introduce Legislation to Improve Corporate Transparency and Combat Money Laundering, Terrorist Financing," press release, Office of Sen. Mark R. Warner, Sept. 26, 2019, https://tinyurl.com/u49b9fw.

45. David R. Burton, "The Corporate Transparency Act and the ILLICIT CASH Act," Heritage Foundation, Nov. 7, 2019, https://tinyurl.com/v6ckmtm.

46. "Prepared Remarks of FinCEN Director Kenneth A. Blanco," *op. cit.*

47. Jeffrey W. Bullock, "Letter to Honorable Maxine Waters," Office of Delaware Secretary of State, April 30, 2019, https://tinyurl.com/vqfao7t.

48. "ILLICIT CASH Act Opposition Letter," Air Conditioning Contractors of America *et al.*, Nov. 13, 2019, https://tinyurl.com/sb75x5m.

49. *US v Tibo Lousee et al.*, U.S. Justice Department, May 1, 2019, https://tinyurl.com/rbyhe35.

50. Samuel Gibbs and Lois Beckett, "Dark Web Marketplaces AlphaBay and Hansa Shut Down," *The Guardian*, July 20, 2017, https://tinyurl.com/y7379u7w.

51. Sean Foley, Jonathan R. Karlsen and Talis J Putnins, "Sex, Drugs, and Bitcoin: How Much Illegal Activity Is Financed through Cryptocurrencies?" *Review of Financial Studies*, May 2019, https://tinyurl.com/sexwnhs.

52. Timothy G. Massad, "It's Time to Strengthen the Regulation of Crypto-Assets," Brookings Institution, March 18, 2019, https://tinyurl.com/wrtgmlr.

53. Jason Brett, "A Bipartisan Bill In Congress Defines 'Managed Stablecoins' As Securities," *Forbes*, Nov. 26, 2019, https://tinyurl.com/rbxodwb.

54. Rachel Wolfson, "What You Need To Know About Congress's Two Proposed Crypto Laws," *Cointelegraph*, Jan. 1, 2020, https://tinyurl.com/suo7c27.

55. "Regulation of Cryptocurrency Around the World," Law Library of Congress, June 2018, https://tinyurl.com/y5tn9qab.

56. Dave Jevans, "Cryptocurrency Exchanges Grappling with New FATF Rule Requiring Disclosure of Customer Information," *CipherTrace*, June 21, 2019, https://tinyurl.com/rfg2nde.

57. *Ibid.*

58. Jay Sykes and Nicole Vanatko, "Virtual Currencies and Money Laundering: Legal Background, Enforcement Actions, and Legislative Proposals," Congressional Research Service, April 3, 2019, https://tinyurl.com/sg856rk.

59. Kyle Torpey, "U.S. Lawmakers Are Realizing They Can't Ban Bitcoin," *Forbes*, July 30, 2019, https://tinyurl.com/y5b3h5fy.

60. Jon Martindale, "Go ahead, pass laws. They can't kill bitcoin, even if they try," *Digital Trends*, Dec. 19, 2017, https://tinyurl.com/qls6jwa.

61. Dan Smith, "New York Has Tried to Kill off Cryptocurrency—We Shouldn't Let Them," LarrySharpe.com, Feb. 19, 2018, https://tinyurl.com/ttqssp9.

62. "Application of FinCEN's Regulations to Certain Business Models Involving Convertible Virtual Currencies," Financial Crimes Enforcement Network, May 9, 2019, https://tinyurl.com/r6vxspp.

63. "Virtual Currency: IRS Issues Additional Guidance on Tax Treatment and Reminds Taxpayers of Reporting Obligations," Internal Revenue Service, Oct. 9, 2019, https://tinyurl.com/y4r4nwkn.

64. Dries Lesage, "The G20 and Tax Havens: Maintaining the Momentum?" draft proposal, University of Ghent, June 18, 2010, https://tinyurl.com/v8vo32b.

65. Niels Johannesen *et al.*, "Taxing Hidden Wealth: The Consequences of U.S. Enforcement Initiatives on Evasive Foreign Accounts," Oct. 7, 2019, https://tinyurl.com/qlmxbr3.

66. *Ibid.*; Sébastien Guex, "The Origins of the Swiss Banking Secrecy Law and Its Repercussions for Swiss Federal Policy," *Business History Review 74*, https://tinyurl.com/ryf6ut2; and Gabriel Zucman, *The Hidden Wealth of Nations* (2015).

67. Kevin McCoy, "UBS must release data on 4,500 suspected tax cheats," *ABC News*, Aug. 19, 2009, https:// tinyurl.com/qlo7axm; "UBS Enters into Deferred Prosecution Agreement," U.S. Justice Department, Feb. 18, 2009, https://tinyurl.com/qrrqujj.

68. Laura Saunders and Robin Sidel, "Whistleblower Gets $104 Million," *The Wall Street Journal*, Sept. 11, 2012, https://tinyurl.com/royj4fk; "Swiss banker Raoul Weil acquitted in tax evasion trial in Florida," *The Associated Press, The Guardian*, Nov. 3, 2014, https://tinyurl.com/tbe6wuk.

69. "Credit Suisse Pleads Guilty to Conspiracy to Aid and Assist U.S. Taxpayers in Filing False Returns," U.S. Justice Department, May 19, 2014, https://tinyurl.com/gvotfn3; Nate Raymond and Lynnley Browning, "Swiss bank Wegelin to close after guilty plea," *Reuters*, Jan. 4, 2013, https://tinyurl.com/tgh6s2c.

70. "Responsible leadership for a sustainable future," Group of 8, July 9, 2009, https://tinyurl.com/v6xbrv4.

71. "Taxation, Economic Globalisation and the Caribbean," Caribbean Council, Dec. 12, 2017, https://tinyurl.com/s7vrglc.

72. "Foreign Account Tax Compliance Act FATCA," Internal Revenue Service, July 31, 2019, https:// tinyurl.com/hvznnay.

73. "Understand How to Report Foreign Bank and Financial Accounts," Internal Revenue Service, April 2019, https://tinyurl.com/sxwgjfw; Elise J. Bean *et al.*, "Tax Haven Banks and U.S. Tax Compliance," Permanent Subcommittee on Investigations, July 17, 2008, https://tinyurl.com/vh22rr4.

74. "Offshore Voluntary Compliance Efforts Top $10 Billion; More Than 100,000 Taxpayers Come Back into Compliance," Internal Revenue Service, Oct. 21, 2016, https://tinyurl.com/v7dpn47.

75. "Despite spending nearly $380 million, the Internal Revenue Service is still not prepared to enforce compliance with the Foreign Account Tax Compliance Act," Treasury Inspector General for Tax Administration, July 5, 2018, https://tinyurl.com/tp5bxua.

76. "Foreign Asset Reporting: Actions Needed to Enhance Compliance Efforts, Eliminate Overlapping Requirements, and Mitigate Burdens on U.S. Persons

Abroad," U.S. Government Accountability Office, April 1, 2019, https://tinyurl.com/uzdlnen; "United States: New FATCA FAQ on Model 1 FFIs and Expiration of TIN Relief—KPMG United States," KPMG, Nov. 7, 2019, https://tinyurl.com/snclpyw.

77. Rand Paul and Mark Meadows, "Letter to Secretary Steven Mnuchin and White House Budget Director Mick Mulvaney," April 3, 2017, https://tinyurl.com/vx29jc5.

78. "HSBC to Pay $353 Million to Settle French Tax-Fraud Probe," *Yahoo Finance*, Nov. 15, 2017, https://tinyurl.com/whftahm.

79. "Panama Papers FAQ: All You Need to Know About The 2016 Investigation," International Consortium of Investigative Journalists, Aug. 21, 2019, https://tinyurl.com/yyfgprzv.

80. "Four Defendants Charged in Panama Papers Investigation for Their Roles in Panamanian-Based Global Law Firm's Decades-Long Scheme to Defraud the United States," press release, U.S. Justice Department, Dec. 4, 2018, https://tinyurl.com/y9okzljc.

81. Douglas Dalby and Amy Wilson-Chapman, "Panama Papers Helps Recover More Than $1.2 Billion Around the World," International Consortium of Investigative Journalists, April 3, 2019, https://tinyurl.com/r5h2c2d.

82. "Common Reporting Standard," Organisation for Economic Co-operation and Development, 2018, https://tinyurl.com/y3uuq7ds; "AEOI: status of commitments," Organisation for Economic Co-Operation and Development, January 2020, https://tinyurl.com/j7v7o9q.

83. Robert Goulder, "Should The U.S. Adopt The OECD's Common Reporting Standard?" *Forbes*, June 29, 2016, https://tinyurl.com/unsobo2; Erika K. Lunder and Carol A. Pettit, "FATCA Reporting on U.S. Accounts: Recent Legal Developments," Congressional Research Service, Sept. 7, 2016, https://tinyurl.com/rlnuorm; and Pierce O'Reilly, Kevin Parra Ramirez and Michael A. Stemmer, "Exchange of Information and Bank Deposits in International Financial Centres," *OECD Taxation Working Papers*, No. 46, 2019, https://tinyurl.com/s2xjqnc.

84. Peter A. Cotorceanu, "Hiding in plain sight: how non-US persons can legally avoid reporting under both FATCA and GATCA," *Trusts & Trustees*, Oct. 21, 2015, https://tinyurl.com/qv8cm74.

85. "Whitehouse Remarks In Judiciary On Combating Kleptocracy," Office of Sen. Sheldon Whitehouse, June 19, 2019, https://tinyurl.com/wv8hc82.

86. "Testimony of FinCEN Director Kenneth A. Blanco before the Senate Committee on Banking, Housing and Urban Affairs," Financial Crimes Enforcement Network, May 21, 2019, https://tinyurl.com/w47r62x; "Leader of International Drug Money Laundering Organization Sentenced to 30 Years in Prison," Department of Justice, Aug. 14, 2018, https://tinyurl.com/ybcd6xxy.

87. "Who we are," Financial Action Task Force, https://tinyurl.com/y6dw3w9z; "Anti-money laundering and counter-terrorist financing measures: United States," Financial Action Task Force, December 2016, https://tinyurl.com/ya6bfcxp.

88. "Information on Complying with the Customer Due Diligence (CDD) Final Rule," Financial Crimes Enforcement Network, https://tinyurl.com/u3oyluy.

89. "Financial Secrecy Index—2018 Results," *op. cit.*

90. Sue Reisinger, "Nordic Countries Top the Non-Corruption Chart in Latest Transparency International Index," Law.com, Jan. 30, 2019, https://tinyurl.com/wuu8bhe; Juliette Garside, "Is Money-Laundering Scandal at Danske Bank the Largest in History?" *The Guardian*, Sept. 21, 2018, https://tinyurl.com/ychotd39.

91. Johannes Hellstrom and Helena Sondpalm, "Ex-Danske CEO Borgen charged over money laundering case: report," *Reuters*, May 7, 2019, https://tinyurl.com/y4675hbv; "Swedbank chairman quits over money laundering scandal," *Reuters*, April 5, 2019, https://tinyurl.com/rly5dml.

92. Cheri Burns, "$8.14 billion of AML fines handed out in 2019, with USA and UK leading the charge," *Encompass*, Jan. 13, 2020, https://tinyurl.com/uf3cqbd; Hugo Miller, "UBS Hit With Record Penalty After Money-Laundering Conviction," *Bloomberg*, Feb. 20, 2019, https://tinyurl.com/v8h6fo9.

93. "Chinese Telecommunications Conglomerate Huawei and Huawei CFO Wanzhou Meng Charged With Financial Fraud," press release, U.S. Justice Department, Jan. 28, 2019, https://tinyurl.com/ybfsjnan.

94. Dylan Tokar, "Former Barbadian Official Found Guilty of Laundering Bribes," *The Wall Street Journal*, Jan. 17, 2020, https://tinyurl.com/u2cd5gx.

95. "New FinCEN Division Focuses on Identifying Primary Foreign Money Laundering Threats," press release, Financial Crimes Enforcement Network, Aug. 28, 2019, https://tinyurl.com/wdg2v97.

96. "Application of FinCEN's Regulations to Certain Business Models Involving Convertible Virtual Currencies," Financial Crimes Enforcement Network, May 9, 2019, https://tinyurl.com/r6vx-spp.

97. Nicholas Véron and Joshua Kirschenbaum, "A Major Step Toward Combating Money Laundering in Europe," Bruegel, Nov. 25. 2019, https://tinyurl.com/shl2ld8.

98. Silvia Amaro, "French finance minister says the battle over digital tax is not over yet," *CNBC*, Jan. 22, 2020, https://tinyurl.com/uphmykr.

99. Larry Elliott, "UK to press ahead with digital tax despite US pressure, Javid insists," *The Guardian*, Jan. 22, 2020, https://tinyurl.com/u4lv9no.

100. Greg Ip and Paul Hannon, "Mnuchin Warns U.K., Italy Over Digital-Tax Plans," *The Wall Street Journal*, Jan. 21, 2020, https://tinyurl.com/rxw-mqq9.

101. Victor Mallet and Kiran Stacey, "France and US seek to resolve digital tax dispute," *Financial Times*, Jan. 7, 2020, https://tinyurl.com/wmmnx38.

102. Waters, *op. cit.*

103. Jannick Damgaard, Thomas Elkjaer and Niels Johannesen, "Piercing the Veil," F&D, International Monetary Fund, June 2018, https://tinyurl.com/y5znhjym.

104. "Base Erosion and Profit Shifting," Organisation of Economic Co-operation and Development, 2018, https://tinyurl.com/s6nl3n6; "G20 Agrees to Advance International Tax Agenda," International Institute for Sustainable Development, Nov. 23, 2015, https://

tinyurl.com/tde4jla; and "Secretariat Proposal for a 'Unified Approach' under Pillar One," Organisation of Economic Co-Operation and Development, Oct. 9, 2019, https://tinyurl.com/s3u5r7a.

105. Coleen Murphy and Lydia O'Neal, "Hill Tax Briefing: 2020 Candidates Criticize Trump's Tax Cuts," *Bloomberg*, June 28, 2019, https://tinyurl.com/uu4a3gh.

106. Egkolfopoulou, *op. cit.*; Peter Cohn, "Elizabeth Warren has a plan: Here's what it would cost," *Roll Call*, Nov. 19, 2019, https://tinyurl.com/yx2d8yh4.

107. Golshan, *op. cit.*

108. Richard Rubin, "Joe Biden Proposes $1 Trillion in New Corporate Taxes," *The Wall Street Journal*, Dec. 4, 2019, https://tinyurl.com/ut7cfur; Adam Sabes, "Biden Calls for 28% Corporate Tax Rate," Americans for Tax Reform, Oct. 24, 2019, https://tinyurl.com/vgjtbaq.

109. Naomi Jagoda, "Trump says new tax cut plan to be unveiled in 90 days," *The Hill*, Jan. 21, 2020, https://tinyurl.com/wm9lkkz.

110. Howard Schneider and Chris Kahn, "Majority of Americans favor wealth tax on very rich: Reuters/Ipsos poll," *Reuters*, Jan. 10, 2020, https://tinyurl.com/rcf4oj9.

111. Alexander Weber, Boris Groendahl and Nicholas Comfort, "Swiss regulator tightens insurance wrapper rules," *Reuters*, Jan. 4, 2011, https://tinyurl.com/vzaub28; "Money to Launder? Here's How (Hint: Find a Bank)," *Bloomberg*, March 9, 2019, https://tinyurl.com/y3s778gc.

112. Brian Monroe, "Fincrime Briefing: In historic vote, House passes bill to counter shells, bolster AML, Finra fines BNP $15 million on AML, penny stocks, and more," Association of Certified Financial Crime Specialists, Oct. 24, 2019, https://tinyurl.com/s85of4q.

113. "International Comparative Legal Guide to Anti-Money Laundering 2018," Global Legal Group, 2018, https://tinyurl.com/rtqru4v.

114. "Illicit Financial Flows to and from 148 Developing Countries: 2006-2015," Global Financial Integrity, January 2019, https://tinyurl.com/ukn9mzk.

115. "Secretariat Proposal for a 'Unified Approach' under Pillar One," *op. cit.*

BIBLIOGRAPHY
Books

Bernstein, *Jake, Secrecy World: Inside the Panama Papers Investigation of Illicit Money Networks and the Global Elite*, Henry Holt and Co., 2017.
A reporter examines the scandal that involved the release of millions of documents from the Panama-based law firm Mossack Fonseca, showing how wealthy individuals used shell companies to hide their assets from tax collectors.

Saez, Emmanuel, and Gabriel Zucman, *The Triumph of Injustice: How the Rich Dodge Taxes and How to Make Them Pay*, W.W. Norton & Company, 2019.
Two professors of economics at the University of California, Berkeley, provide an overview of hidden wealth and tax havens and offer their prescriptions for solving the problem.

Shaxson, Nicholas, *Treasure Islands: Uncovering the Damage of Offshore Banking and Tax Havens*, St. Martin's Press, 2011.
A *Financial Times* reporter delves into the world of offshore banking and explains how tax havens colluded with financial institutions to hide assets and reduce tax obligations.

Articles

Dalby, Douglas, and Amy Wilson-Chapman, "Panama Papers Helps Recover More Than $1.2 Billion Around The World," *International Consortium of Investigative Journalists*, April 3, 2019, https://tinyurl.com/r5h2c2d.
Two journalists look at how the disclosure of millions of documents from a Panama law firm changed the course of regulation for tax evasion around the world.

Drucker, Jesse, and Simon Bowers, *"After a Tax Crackdown, Apple Found a New Shelter for Its Profits,"* The New York Times, Nov. 6, 2017, https://tinyurl.com/y7m2s9ob.
Two reporters describe how companies use various strategies in low-tax countries to reduce their tax bills.

Mashberg, Tom, "The Art of Money Laundering," *International Monetary Fund*, September 2019, https://tinyurl.com/wzrb3h2.
A reporter explains the ways money laundering is used to hide illicit cash.

Reports and Studies

"Anti-money laundering and counter-terrorist financing measures: United States," *Financial Action Task Force*, December 2016, https://tinyurl.com/ya6bfcxp.
The 39-member-nation task force conducted a "mutual evaluation" of U.S. anti-money laundering efforts and found several important shortcomings.

"Directive (EU) 2018/843 of the European parliament and of the Council of 30 May 2018," *Official Journal of the European Union*, 2018, https://tinyurl.com/y4be29q7.
Better known as the fifth anti-money laundering directive, this set of rules requires European countries to set up a public register of shell companies showing the names and addresses of people who own more than 25 percent of the companies.

"Foreign Asset Reporting: Actions Needed to Enhance Compliance Efforts, Eliminate Overlapping Requirements, and Mitigate Burdens on U.S. Persons Abroad," *Government Accountability Office*, April 1, 2019, https://tinyurl.com/uzdlnen.
A congressional agency examines the Foreign Account Tax Compliance Act of 2010 and finds several major issues with its implementation, including the fact that foreign banks were turning away Americans abroad.

"Secretariat Proposal for a 'Unified Approach' under Pillar One," *Secretariat, Organisation for Economic Co-operation and Development*, October 2019, https://tinyurl.com/s3u5r7a.
The multilateral organization that tracks economic activity in developed countries proposes enabling countries to tax part of the profits earned in their countries by international digital companies.

Cassara, John A., "Countering International Money Laundering," *FACT Coalition*, August 2017, https://tinyurl.com/u3hg7pc.
A former special agent for the Internal Revenue Service and U.S. Secret Service explains how money laundering is a frequently overlooked aspect of international crime. He details authorities' successes and failures in their efforts to restrict money laundering.

Johannesen, Niels, et al., "Taxing Hidden Wealth: The Consequences of U.S. Enforcement Initiatives on

Evasive Foreign Accounts," Internal Revenue Service, March 20, 2017, https://tinyurl.com/skyd4vd.
A group of international experts analyzes U.S. efforts to find overseas financial accounts belonging to American citizens and compel them to pay taxes.

Schneider, Friedrich, and Colin C. Williams, "The Shadow Economy," Institute of Economic Affairs, 2013, https://tinyurl.com/the26hp.
Economists at the Center for Economic Studies and Ifo Institute for Economic Research (Schneider) and Britain's University of Sheffield (Williams) calculate the size of the global shadow economy and discuss how it affects tax collection.

THE NEXT STEP

Cryptocurrency

Hamacher, Adriana, "New money laundering regulations threaten crypto firms in Europe," *Decrypt*, Jan. 14, 2020, https://tinyurl.com/qt78pxf.
Some cryptocurrency firms that are unable or unwilling to comply with new money laundering regulations in the United Kingdom, Austria and the Netherlands are fleeing to other countries or shutting down.

Roberts, Daniel, "H&R Block is telling its tax customers: Disclose your crypto gains," *Yahoo Finance*, Jan. 24, 2020, https://tinyurl.com/sxgyvao.
A tax preparation company is advising customers to disclose the amount of cryptocurrency they bought or sold in 2019 when filing their taxes. Some people use bitcoin and other cryptocurrencies to hide illicit purchases.

Torpey, Kyle, "New Bill in Congress Could Have Massive Impact On Bitcoin, Ethereum, And Other Cryptocurrencies," Forbes, Jan. 20, 2020, https://tinyurl.com/wdof3up.
Legislation introduced in Congress in January would exempt small cryptocurrency transactions from capital gains taxes.

Legislation

"French government to scan social media for tax cheats," *BBC News*, Dec. 27, 2019, https://tinyurl.com/sy2eqw7.
A new law in France will allow tax officials to review social media accounts for evidence of undisclosed income.

Kiel, Paula, "The IRS Decided to Get Tough Against Microsoft. Microsoft Got Tougher," *ProPublica*, Jan. 22, 2020, https://tinyurl.com/tlo4dlu.
The Internal Revenue Service conducted the largest audit by dollar amount in history after Microsoft shifted at least $39 million in profits to Puerto Rico, but the company successfully lobbied Congress to change the law and limit the tools the agency could use.

Saska, Jim, "Senators seek GOP support for bill to crack down on anonymous shell companies," *Roll Call*, Oct. 25, 2019, https://tinyurl.com/wyoufw8.
After the House passed a bill that would curb the use of anonymous shell companies, Democrats in the Senate are reaching out to Republican senators to support a similar bill.

Shell Companies

Glantz, Aaron, "American Cities Are Becoming Shell Companies for the Rich," *TruthDig*, Dec. 26, 2019, https://tinyurl.com/sx2pb39.
The proportion of residential rental properties owned by individuals and families has fallen from 92 percent in 1991 to 74 percent in 2015 as shell companies have purchased more homes and apartments, particularly in major cities.

Voreacos, David, and Neil Weinberg, "How the Pentagon Was Duped by Contractors Using Shell Companies," *Bloomberg*, Jan. 4, 2020, https://tinyurl.com/tkvp7bj.
Several defense contractors won manufacturing bids by using shell companies to fraudulently apply for contracts meant for disabled veterans or minorities and to hide that they were making U.S. military equipment abroad, risking national security.

Wollan, Malia, "How to Set Up a Shell Company," *The New York Times Magazine*, Nov. 7, 2019, https://tinyurl.com/y4e4og3k.
Researchers at the University of Cambridge in England found it easier to set up an untraceable shell company in Nevada, Delaware or Wyoming than in an offshore tax haven in a developing country.

Tax Havens

Goclowski, Marcin, "Tax avoidance, evasion costs EU 170 billion euros a year, says Poland," *Reuters*, Jan. 22, 2020, https://tinyurl.com/saw3ek3.

European Union member states lose the equivalent of $188 billion a year due to tax avoidance, according to a report from a Polish state think tank.

Kanter, Jake, "Netflix Accused Of Funnelling $430M Of International Profits Into Tax Havens," *Deadline*, **Jan. 15, 2020, https://tinyurl.com/rm9cnop.**
Netflix moved $430 million of its international profits into low-tax jurisdictions, including the Netherlands, said a report by Tax Watch, a British think tank.

Warren, Katie, "The top 15 tax havens around the world," *Business Insider*, **Nov. 19, 2019, https://tinyurl.com/tvn4e63.**
An Amsterdam-based research group ranked offshore financial centers by how much more money comes into the country or territory than would be merited given the size of its economy. The jurisdiction that placed No. 1: the British Virgin Islands.

For More Information

FACT Coalition, 1225 I St., N.W., Suite 600, Washington, DC 20005; 202-827-6401; thefactcoalition.org. Alliance of more than 100 organizations that is working to end money laundering and tax evasion.

Financial Action Task Force, 2 Rue André Pascal, 75775 Paris, France; + 33 1 45.24.90.90; fatf-gafi.org. Group of 37 countries and two regional organizations that is fighting money laundering by proposing international rules and regulations and conducting audits of nations' enforcement performance.

Financial Crimes Enforcement Network (FinCEN), PO Box 39, Vienna, VA 22183; 703-905-3591; fincen.gov. U.S. Treasury division tasked with combating money laundering.

Global Witness, 1 Mark Square, London, EC2A 4EG, UK; +44 (0)207 4925820; globalwitness.org/en/. International organization that fights corruption.

Organisation of Economic Co-operation and Development, 1776 I St., N.W., Suite 450, Washington, DC 20006; 202-785-6323; oecd.org. Global organization representing 36 developed countries that organized the Common Reporting Standard for tax reporting and is seeking a global minimum tax for multinational corporations.

Tax Justice Network, 38 Stanley Ave., Chesham, Buckinghamshire, HP5 2JG, United Kingdom; +44 300 302 0062; taxjustice.net. Private group campaigning to end tax evasion.

10

Supply Chains at Risk

Are tariffs and technology disrupting global trade routes?

By Rachel Layne

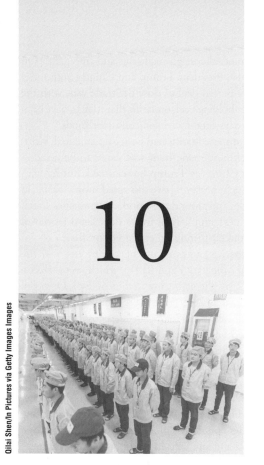

Employees line up for roll call before their shift starts at a Pegatron Corp. factory in Shanghai in 2016. Few other nations have the manufacturing scale and expertise China has developed over decades, with 100 million factory workers—equivalent to about a third of the total U.S. population.

From *CQ Researcher*,
January 3, 2020

THE ISSUES

Headquartered near Pittsburgh and founded nearly a century ago, American Textile Co. is used to weathering big economic changes.

Today, its 1,200 employees, up from about 100 in 1991, work in four finishing plants in Georgia, Pennsylvania, Utah and Texas to make bedding for retailers and hotels. But like most textile companies, American Textile Co. keeps prices down by importing fabric and other components from around the world, including China and El Salvador.

So when President Trump began imposing tariffs on Chinese imports, which are paid not by China but by importers, and then tweeted that U.S. companies should abandon Chinese suppliers altogether, CEO Lance Ruttenberg grew alarmed.[1] It takes years to develop relationships with suppliers for quality components, he says, even for something as simple as a pillow.

Ruttenberg says the tariffs will cost his firm $1 million a month, eliminating any profit. "The average American—they can't in any way appreciate the complexity of a supply chain," he says, referring to the network of suppliers who provide the components and materials that go into a finished product. "And this administration, in my estimation, has made a very oversimplified case for why they're doing what they're doing."

Making 6,000 items for 40,000 stores, sourced from around the world, involves "an infinite amount of iterations that have to be considered in order to make things show up on the right shelf at the right time for the right retailer," Ruttenberg explains. "So . . . to oversimplify that by saying 'just move it' or 'just get a better price,' . . . it's just incorrect. It's wrong."

Trump's trade policy of using tariffs and other punitive measures as negotiating tools has upended norms and disrupted the flow of goods and services developed under a postwar system championed by the United States and later governed by the World Trade Organization (WTO). As U.S. companies scramble to find alternate suppliers and brace for lower profits, they warn that the cost of the tariffs eventually will trickle down to consumers in the form of higher prices. China has retaliated by imposing its own tariffs on U.S. products and halting purchases of American corn, soy and pork, triggering fears among some experts of a prolonged "cold" trade war between the United States and China, its biggest trading partner in 2018.[2]

Trump's new tariffs on steel and aluminum, washing machines and solar panels angered traditional political and trade allies. He also renegotiated the 25-year-old North American Free Trade Agreement (NAFTA) with Mexico and Canada, exited the 12-nation Trans-Pacific Partnership (TPP) in favor of negotiating with individual countries and

Employees work on the assembly line of Volkswagen's Tiguan model at the company's plant in Puebla, Mexico, in 2018. Importing products and parts from countries with lower labor costs holds down consumer prices and facilitates the consumer spending that drives U.S. economic growth. Mexican factory wages are one-fifth the U.S. average.

threatened to tax all foreign-made cars and auto parts.[3] On Dec. 13, 2019, President Trump and Chinese authorities announced a partial deal to slow the trade war, with the United States holding back on tariffs that were to have been enacted two days later, mostly on consumer goods.[4]

If all the proposed tariffs had been implemented, virtually every Chinese-made item was slated to be taxed— paid not by China, as Trump has claimed, but by U.S. importers. Such measures have disrupted supply chains in both countries and around the world, as companies search for non-Chinese suppliers or move their factories out of China to avoid tariff-induced erosion of profits.[5]

In October, as a result of the trade tensions, the International Monetary Fund (IMF), which keeps tabs on economies across the globe, lowered its outlook for global economic growth in 2019. Some U.S. companies are cutting supply chain investments to prepare for a possible recession, just as new technologies that could further transform supply chains, such as 5G, the revolutionary fifth-generation cellular telecommunications technology, start to come online.[6]

These developments have alarmed experts who support the international system of ever-freer trade implemented worldwide after World War II. They fear a long trade war that could split global supply chains into one tied to China and another tethered to the United States.[7]

Henry Paulson, the Treasury secretary under Republican President George W. Bush during the global 2007-09 financial crisis, warned that there could be a "decoupling" of the world's two biggest economies. The stakes are much bigger than a trade war, he said, calling the potential divide an economic "iron curtain," referring to the political split that separated capitalist and communist countries from the 1940s to the late '80s.[8]

"This is a battle between two countries . . . to set the standards for the technologies of the future, the technologies which are going to bolster economic growth and competitiveness around the world," Paulson said.[9]

But some trade specialists argue Trump's approach may be working, at least in part. The U.S.-China partial deal announced Dec. 13, 2019, later earned Paulson's congratulations as a "hard fought" first step. On Dec. 23, 2019, China announced it was lowering tariffs on some 8,000 products including frozen pork, pharmaceuticals and some semiconductor products for all trading partners, starting on Jan. 1, 2020, ahead of a deal-signing with the United States.[10]

"It's important to under-stand that the president inher-ited a very difficult situation, one where we probably should have addressed some of these problems with China a lot sooner," said Stephen Vaughn, former general counsel for the U.S. trade representative under Trump. "But I think the presi-dent had great courage and wisdom to step up and realize that we really can start to make progress."[11]

The Trump administra-tion's shift to protectionist poli-cies seeks in part to rein in China, accused by U.S. officials, lawmakers and companies of stealing intellectual prop-erty—or patented inventions, designs, names and images—used in commerce and erecting other unfair trade barriers. "China is home to widespread infringing activity, including trade secret theft, rampant online piracy and counterfeit-ing," said a 2017 report from the U.S. Trade Representative's Office (USTR). Such practices are prohibited by WTO policies, and China denies the assertions.[12]

The Trump administration is not alone in leveling those charges. Several Democratic senators in February 2019 urged the administration to address such allega-tions in negotiations with China.[13]

Unfair trade practices, such as creating counterfeit goods, pirating software and trade secret theft, are esti-mated to cost the U.S. economy at least $225 billion each year and may reach $600 billion, according to a 2017 report by the Commission on the Theft of American Intellectual Property. Trade secret theft is esti-mated to cost between 1 percent and 3 percent of U.S. gross domestic product (GDP), or the total value of goods and services as measured in one year, the report said. The United States accounts for about a quarter of the world's $85.8 trillion in GDP; China accounts for about 16 percent.[14]

Trump's policies also are curbing foreign direct investment between the two countries, such as the construction of factories in the United States by Chinese companies, and vice versa. Such investment fell 60 percent in 2018, according to a report from the Rhodium Group, an economic research organization in New York City that specializes in the Chinese economy.[15]

"There's a lot of focus on production-worker jobs—where has the production gone and the assembly. And that's important," says Susan Helper, an economics pro-fessor at Case Western Reserve University and a former chief economist in the U.S. Department of Commerce during the Obama administration. "But it's also impor-tant where the design and engineering gets done. And China's policy in recent years has really focused on how they're going to get those jobs. [It's] how they're going to move up the value chain."

One way they hope to do that is by winning the race to develop and deploy 5G technology. Downloading data from the internet with 5G is expected to occur 100 times faster than with existing 4G technology, and 5G will reach more broadly and deeply into everyday life by expanding a hundredfold the use of wireless consumer products, from automobiles to drones to household appliances.[16]

Technological advances in manufacturing—includ-ing robotics, monitoring software and 3D printing of parts—are changing where and how companies procure components. Companies already use such technologies to make products ranging from rocket parts to blood vessels.[17] The speed and accuracy with which a product can be traced along the supply chain using tracking sen-sors and complex software is changing as well.

Strategies Dictate Where Manufacturing Moves

Manufacturers make decisions on where to locate their operations based on which strategic goals they are pursuing.

Where Manufacturing Is Moving and Why

Strategy	Example	Sourcing
Lowest cost	Apparel, most footwear	Most remain in China, but Vietnam/ Bangladesh increasingly popular
Low cost and closer to demand	Aerospace parts, auto parts, some footwear	Moving to Mexico, Dominican Republic
Fast, responsive supply chain for low volume/high margin	High-end consumer goods	Slowly returning to the United States
Bound by huge existing supplier base	Consumer electronics	Staying in China

Source: "CTL.SC3x — Supply Chain Dynamics," Center for Transportation & Logistics, Massachusetts Institute of Technology, 2019, p. 56, https://tinyurl.com/m8msu3e

For example, Amazon, Walmart and Best Buy are introducing free next-day delivery for consumers—unthinkable without sophisticated supply chain software that tracks goods almost instantly. Soon, consumers will be able to see exactly how their food, such as fish, traveled from ocean to dinner plate. And U.S. consumers will increasingly communicate with freestanding electronic devices to regulate heat in their homes, turn off the lights or order dinner.[18]

Thus, to make fast decisions, American Textile Co. and other companies must be able to almost instantly track goods through every step in a supply chain. That includes all kinds of goods from textiles to electronics with hundreds of parts.

Changing technology, such as 3D printing, also can play a huge role in shortening supply chains and cutting costs. "If you can . . . print parts when you need it, maybe you don't have to be outsourcing them for the economics to faraway countries," says Kamala Raman, a senior director analyst at Gartner, a research and consulting firm in Stamford, Conn.

Even before the tariffs were imposed, rising labor costs in China were spurring some companies to shift production from China to places such as Vietnam. But leaving an established supplier can take years. And few places have the scale and expertise China developed over decades with a workforce of 100 million factory workers—equivalent to about a third of the U.S. population.[19]

As the trade discord escalated, corporate investment in everything from research and development to construction of new facilities fell to its lowest level in a decade during the third quarter of 2019, according to a survey of 100 CEOs by The Conference Board, a business think tank that measures their confidence in the economy.

"CEO confidence declined to its lowest level in a decade," said Lynn Franco, senior director of economic indicators at The Conference Board. "Tariffs and trade issues, coupled with expectations of moderating global growth, are causing a heightened degree of uncertainty."[20]

As manufacturers, importers and exporters, economists and trade specialists assess the impact on global supply chains of the U.S.-China trade war, here are some of the questions being discussed:

Are U.S. companies shifting supply chains out of China?

On Aug. 23, 2019, President Trump in a series of tweets urged U.S. companies to move their operations out of China: "The vast amounts of money made and stolen by China from the United States, year after year, for decades, will and must STOP. Our great American companies are hereby ordered to immediately start looking for an alternative to China, including bringing your companies HOME and making your products in the USA."[21]

In fact, rising manufacturing costs in China already had prompted some companies to consider looking elsewhere, such as to Vietnam, Malaysia, the Philippines, India and Mexico, for raw materials,

U.S. Imports from Vietnam Surge as Chinese Trade Declines

The total value of U.S. imports from Vietnam increased nearly 34 percent during the first nine months of 2019 compared to the same period in 2018. The value of imports from China declined 14.5 percent in that period, in part, experts say, due to new U.S. tariffs on a variety of Chinese imports.

Change in U.S. Imports from Major Trading Partners, Jan.–Oct. 2018 to Jan.–Oct. 2019

Country	Change
Vietnam	33.9%
Taiwan	20.1%
France	13.2%
Ireland	7.4%
Switzerland	6.8%
Italy	5.6%
India	5.5%
South Korea	5.2%
United Kingdom	4.8%
Mexico	4.0%
Japan	2.6%
Germany	1.9%
Malaysia	1.7%
Canada	0.7%
China	14.5%

Sources: "Exhibit 4. Exports, Imports, and Trade Balance of Goods by Country and Area, Not Seasonally Adjusted: 2018," U.S. International Trade in Goods in Services (FT900): October 2018, Dec. 6, 2018, United States Census Bureau, https://tinyurl.com/trw3kjk; "Exhibit 4. Exports, Imports, and Trade Balance of Goods by Country and Area, Not Seasonally Adjusted: 2019," U.S. International Trade in Goods in Services (FT900): October 2019, Dec. 5, 2019, https://tinyurl.com/vq32l3x

semifinished and finished goods. [22] But few cited the United States as a realistic alternative due to its comparatively high labor costs.

Some consumer product companies have announced they are moving from China. Action-camera maker GoPro opened a factory in Mexico earlier in 2019. And in October 2019, the maker of fitness tracker Fitbit said it is moving out of China by the end of the year due to the "ongoing threat of tariffs," though it did not say where it was headed. (Google announced it was buying Fitbit for $2.1 billion on Nov. 1.)[23]

"We expect that effectively all trackers and smart-watches starting in January 2020 will not be of Chinese origin," Ron Kisling, Fitbit's chief financial officer, said on Oct. 9, 2019.[24]

Keeping costs down is key to survival for smaller companies, said Nathan Resnick, who runs Sourcify, a company that pairs small and midsize companies with overseas factories. Last year, about 75 percent of Sourcify's partner factories were China-based. This year, that is down to 60 percent, Resnick said in June. The topic of companies moving out of China is mentioned in "pretty much every single conversation we have," Resnick said.[25]

Chinese production costs are climbing as automation becomes more pervasive and education levels in the labor market rise. China is pushing for more complex manufacturing and research and development for its own high-tech products, so companies need high-skilled engineers and scientists rather than assembly line workers, says Jack Buffington, a University of Denver professor specializing in supply chain management.

"China grew as a supply chain power due to its low-cost labor market. So as more manufacturing becomes automated, labor rates in China increased," Buffington says. "There's increasing pressure on politicians to try to understand how a global supply chain can help their people, as opposed to hurt. I think a lot of the politics is superficial. Supply chains operate in an environment where there's always risk and there's always change."

Even before Trump's "hereby" tweet, about 50 companies, including HP Inc., Dell and Nintendo, had said they wanted to move at least some manufacturing outside of China, *The Nikkei Asian Review* reported.[26]

"I would say, on the margin, I'm not aware of a single supplier who is not moving some form of manufacturing

Guests participate in a workout hosted by Fitbit in 2018 in Los Angeles. In October 2019, the maker of the fitness tracker said it is moving production out of China due to the "ongoing threat of tariffs."

Rich Fury/Getty Images for Fitbit

outside of China," Ted Decker, the executive in charge of merchandise for Home Depot, said during an August conference call with analysts.[27]

Apple, the biggest company in the United States by market value (a measure Wall Street calculates using stock price) of more than $1 trillion, considered moving up to 20 percent of its operations outside China, *The Wall Street Journal* reported on June 20, citing unnamed sources.[28]

During a July 30, 2019, conference call with analysts, Apple CEO Tim Cook dismissed a report that Apple planned to move out of China. "I know there's been a lot of speculation around the topic of different moves and so forth," Cook said. "I wouldn't put a lot of stock into those, if I were you."[29]

Apple arguably is the most visible U.S. company intertwined with China through its supply chain. It prints "Designed in California. Assembled in China" on its iPhones, a product that until 2018 accounted for more than half of its profit. And about 20 percent of Apple's sales are to Chinese consumers.[30]

Apple is not alone among U.S. companies pursuing Chinese consumers. Even though China's economic growth rate for the first nine months of 2019 slowed to 6.2 percent—its lowest in 27 years—it is still growing faster than other large economies.[31]

Big multinational companies from the United States, Japan and Europe have long sought to tap that growth. In September 2019 Boeing raised its forecast for the number of planes China will need in the next 20 years. General Motors sells more cars in China than in the United States, though sales declined in 2019. Electric carmaker Tesla is opening a plant near Shanghai. And Caterpillar, the earth-moving equipment maker, makes up to 10 percent of its annual sales from China.[32]

Apple's top 200 suppliers span at least 17 countries. But it would take at least 18 months to move just 5 percent to 7 percent of iPhone production from China to India or Vietnam in a "best-case scenario," securities analyst Daniel Ives wrote in a note to clients on Aug. 13, 2019.[33]

Also in August 2019, the U.S.-China Business Council said only 13 percent of its 220 members operating in China—which include Apple, Boeing, Caterpillar, Coca-Cola and Walmart—planned to move or were already shifting some operations.[34] But only 3 percent planned to move some operations to the United States, a goal of Trump's.

"In short, there is little support for the view that large numbers of foreign firms are fleeing China," wrote Nicholas R. Lardy, a China specialist at the Peterson Institute for International Economics on Sept. 10, 2019. Annual investment in Chinese factories and other nonfinancial spending remain steady, at about $140 billion, rising at about 3 percent a year, Lardy wrote. "A handful of firms leaving China do not confirm a broad trend," he said.[35]

Can companies adjust their global supply chains to Trump's tariffs and still grow?

Trump's sudden trade policy changes are prodding companies to re-examine supply chains for new locations and what economists call resiliency—a way to quickly react to changes.

Researchers at the Massachusetts Institute of Technology, led by Jim Rice, director of the Supply Change Exchange Program, said that is not easy. "Within, say, one month, trade barriers may be erected and removed," the researchers wrote in a June 2019 blog post. "However, supply systems operate much more slowly; cycle times from source to the customer are often measured in months. Today's supply chains lack the agility required to keep pace with trade policy gyrations."[36]

That hurts business confidence and stifles investment, two things needed to keep the economy growing, says Michelle Casario, an assistant professor of economics at Villanova University. (*See Pro/Con.*)

But countries with lower labor costs, such as Vietnam, do not have as many workers or water, power and transportation systems as advanced as those in China. So, while Vietnam's exports to the United States rose nearly 34 percent through August 2019 and China's dropped 14.5 percent, the absolute amount of goods imported from China continues to dwarf that from Vietnam.[37]

"No one offers what China could offer if things were good," Casario says. "So everything seems to be a Plan B, a second best. Some of this is uncharted. Best case, if [companies] start moving supply chains, it could take two to three years" to find efficient and reliable non-Chinese alternative suppliers.

Importing unfinished and semifinished parts from countries with lower labor costs keeps prices down in places such as the United States, Canada and Europe, where consumer spending drives economic growth. And while wages in producing countries are rising, they remain far below those in the United States. Chinese factory workers earn about $5.78 an hour, compared with $4.66 in Mexico and $2.91 in Vietnam. The average manufacturing wage in the United States as of September was $23.65 per hour, according to the Bureau of Labor Statistics.[38]

So Trump's aim to bring traditional manufacturing jobs back to the United States is not likely to happen anytime soon on the scale he promised on the campaign trail in 2016.

Companies want to keep costs low to make their products more attractive to U.S. consumers, whose spending accounts for about 70 percent of economic growth (compared with China's 40 percent).[39] With unemployment in the United States hovering near its lowest level since World War II, consumers remain optimistic, according to a University of Michigan consumer sentiment survey, a measure closely watched by economists. Until September, most products imported from China subject to the tariffs were not sold directly to consumers, and prices had not yet climbed at the cash register.

Consumer sentiment, though down from earlier in the month, remained at very favorable levels, the survey showed. However, "The recent focus of consumers has been on income and job growth, while largely ignoring other news," said Richard Curtin, director of the survey.[40]

For example, The Conference Board, another sampler of consumer confidence, says it has dropped for four straight months and predicted that fourth-quarter economic growth will be weak.[41]

Growth in the U.S. manufacturing sector has officially slowed to a recessionary pace, and the International Monetary Fund predicted in October 2019 that global economic growth will fall to 3 percent in 2020—a pace not seen since the financial crisis a decade ago. It called the outlook "precarious."[42]

"The weakness in growth is driven by a sharp deterioration in manufacturing activity and global trade, with higher tariffs and prolonged trade policy uncertainty damaging investment and demand for capital goods," Gita Gopinath, director of the IMF's research department, wrote in a blog post explaining Census Bureau figures.[43]

Ultimately, U.S. companies will diversify and redesign their supply chains to better weather risk, says Gang Li, an associate professor of management at Bentley University, in Waltham, Mass. In the short term, however, the disruption from tariffs and other trade policies is "going to hurt, no question.

"But if we look at the long term, particularly if we look out five years, my estimate is our supply chain is strong enough to rebound from it," says Li, who expects economic growth to recover. "What doesn't kill you makes you stronger."

Will restrictions on Chinese technology giants protect U.S intellectual property?

From the outset, the Trump administration argued that slashing demand for Chinese exports would act as "an effective tool to pressure China to change its policies" regarding, among other things, the theft of intellectual property, according to a report from the Congressional Research Service.[44] But the White House also has used more direct tools, particularly when it comes to technology supply chains.

Perhaps the most intertwined technology supply chain—and the heart of the contentious trade battle between the United States and China—sits inside mobile phones. Since its inception, the Trump administration has focused on two Chinese telecommunications companies—Huawei and ZTE. To prevent intellectual property theft, Trump officials want the U.S. government to have detailed authority over what parts—such as semiconductor chips and software—are used in equipment made by such tech companies.

In January 2019, the Justice Department announced it was charging Huawei and its chief financial officer, Meng Wanzhou, with violating sanctions against Iran, stealing intellectual property and lying about it to U.S. banks. Meng, who was arrested in Vancouver, Canada, on a U.S. warrant, is fighting extradition.[45]

On May 15, 2019, the U.S. government added Huawei to a blacklist called the Entity List, which means the company cannot purchase or receive hardware, software and other supplies from U.S. firms without the federal government's permission. Later that day, Trump signed an executive order broadening the federal government's power to block transactions linked to information and communications technology (ICT) if those transactions would threaten national security. The move, experts say, was aimed at Huawei because the telecommunications giant's equipment depends heavily on parts from U.S. tech firms, including microchips made by Intel and Qualcomm, as well as mobile software from Google.[46]

Huawei in turn is important to U.S. technology companies because it is the world's biggest supplier of telecom equipment and the second-biggest phone maker, according to the tech website *CNet*.

The Trump administration has relaxed some rules and allowed companies to sell certain equipment to Huawei. About 130 companies applied for licenses to do so. On Dec. 17, 2019, *Bloomberg News* reported the Trump administration was weighing more Huawei restrictions, angering U.S. suppliers.[47]

"Once you take into account the supply chains underpinning Apple and Huawei and the enormous value American firms derive from them, it is easy to see why companies like Apple and Google, Broadcom and Qualcomm want the trade war to end," said Geoffrey Garrett, dean of the Wharton School at the University of Pennsylvania, in a Sept. 5, 2019, blog post.[48]

The quandary for U.S. technology suppliers is this: Can the United States balance the risk of the Chinese stealing technology contained in parts such as semiconductors with the economic boost derived from supplying those goods to China and other foreign customers?[49]

American restrictions may appear to protect U.S. technology, but they also may represent a step toward a "decoupling"—or separation—of the Chinese and U.S. technology supply chains, creating what former Treasury secretary Paulson warned could become an "economic iron curtain" between the two countries.

If the United States no longer has economic interests in China, the risk for more violent kinds of conflict, including military confrontation, increases, said Wharton's Garrett. So, in seeking to protect U.S. technology, a decoupling could "profoundly harm America's national security," he wrote.[50]

On Oct. 11, 2019, President Trump announced that the United States and China had reached "phase one" of a trade deal. On Dec. 13, 2019, the countries announced the broad outlines of the agreement. While it did not include some planned U.S. tariffs on consumer goods, most imports from China were still subject, on average, to tariffs of 19.3 percent, six times higher than before Trump began imposing the levies.[51]

Although the White House said the two sides made progress on some intellectual property issues, such as allegations that China forces U.S. companies to divulge some trade secrets before they can make or sell goods in China, the initial announcement did not address Huawei.[52] Huawei may need two to three years to make up for the damage caused by the U.S. trade ban, CEO Ren Zhengfei told *The Washington Post*.[53]

On Dec. 13, 2019, the United States and China said they would work on further agreements as both sides prepared a detailed version of "phase one." According to a summary from the U.S. trade representative, China will buy some $200 billion in goods over the next several years, including U.S. agricultural products. The agreement also covers technology-sharing requirements for U.S. companies doing business in China and addresses intellectual property concerns. China will also allow U.S. banks and credit card companies to do business in the Chinese consumer market.[54]

In 2018, Congress expanded the power of several administration agencies, working through an interagency body called the Committee on Foreign Investment in the United States, to determine whether foreign investment in a U.S. company poses a risk to national security. The idea is to protect, in addition to intellectual property, critical infrastructure such as electrical grids, ports and military designs.[55] The Commerce Department, through its Bureau of Industry and Security, is reportedly working on how tightly to control intellectual property for emerging and "foundational" technologies such as semiconductors.

The Trump administration is divided over how strictly to control those technologies. Some U.S. researchers and companies seeking to ultimately sell products and technology in China fear restrictions will be so tight that the United States will no longer be an attractive place to create new inventions, in part because the products that emerge will be prohibited for sale to Chinese companies and markets, according to *The New York Times*.[56]

Others, such as Derek Scissors, a China specialist at the conservative American Enterprise Institute think tank, favor decoupling, including as a means of protecting U.S. technology. Any new restrictions on doing business in China, he says, should have "explicit justification" that spells out potential consequences to the United States if such restrictions were not imposed.

The Trump administration pursued restrictions on intellectual property "because it has both economic and military applications," Scissors says. Trump then decided that tariffs were the best way to pressure China into changing its behavior on intellectual property theft.

"[But] we never got to the point of deciding what we should [target to better control intellectual property], so we ended up with across-the-board tariffs the next day, because that's what the president wanted," he says.

BACKGROUND
Shifting Trade Routes

Supply chains—and their disruption—stretch deep into human history.

East-West trade routes, collectively called the Silk Road, began emerging in 130 B.C. during China's Han dynasty. They enabled spices, gold, horses, camels, honey and textiles to travel between China and India, Persia and Europe.

When the Ottoman Empire blocked trade with the West in 1453, wealthy Europeans sent explorers to search for alternative sea routes to the East. After the explorations of Christopher Columbus and Vasco da Gama in the 1490s, an "intercontinental trade boom" ensued.[57]

But until the 1800s, most everyday goods came from a direct supply chain: a farmer grew wheat, took it to a gristmill or ground it at home and sold it nearby. Shipping goods took weeks, months or years. And countries imposed high tariffs to protect their fledgling industries from cheaper imported goods.[58]

During the Industrial Revolution, the steam engine and the telegraph revolutionized supply chains by speeding up trade. In the 1830s a ship took seven weeks to travel from Liverpool to New York, and the return could take more than five. By the 1840s, steam transport cut the trip to two weeks in either direction.

Some economists point to the cotton trade as a good example of how such breakthroughs—combined with the inventions of steel ship hulls, diesel engines and railways—enabled new, faster ways to transport goods. Raw materials, such as cotton, could be shipped to Liverpool's mills from places like the United States and India, refined into fabric and then sent back to be fashioned into finished goods.

But perhaps the most valuable breakthrough for global supply chains came in 1866 with the completion of the first transatlantic telegraph and, later, the telephone.[59]

"The information supplied by the telegraph was like a drug to businessmen, who swiftly became addicted," writes Tom Standage, the author of *The Victorian Internet*. "Suddenly, the price of goods and the speed with which they could be delivered became more important than their geographic location. Tradesmen could have several potential suppliers or markets at their disposal and were able to widen their horizons and deal directly with people whom it would have taken days to reach by mail."[60]

The technology, combined with faster overseas and continental transportation, made imports more common for a wider swath of the population and allowed suppliers to keep less inventory, because orders arrived faster. That freed up cash, making businesses more profitable and allowing increased investment.

In the cotton industry, the telegraph and telephone transformed supply chains, according to Wolfgang Lehmacher, head of the supply chain and transportation industries sections at the World Economic Forum in Geneva. "A broker could actually wire ahead and sell any cotton in transit, well before it arrived in port," Lehmacher wrote in his book *The Global Supply Chain*. "Liverpool became the center of the international cotton trade, connecting raw cotton producers in North and South America, Africa and Asia with manufacturers and consumers of finished goods."[61]

As industrialization spread across Europe, supply chains shifted with technological advances. In 1750, for example, India and China accounted for 73 percent of global manufacturing of finished goods made of cotton, silk and porcelain. By 1913, they accounted for just 7.5 percent, according to Richard Baldwin, a professor of international economics at the Graduate Institute Geneva and author of *The Great Convergence: Information Technology and the New Globalization*.[62]

In addition, from 1790 to 1913, the total value of global trade rose fiftyfold, raising living standards in Europe. "For the first time, products such as sugar, tea and cocoa became widely available," according to Lehmacher. "On the other hand, workers started to become more dependent on developments in other countries and the linkage in international trade."[63]

After the Civil War, the United States retained high tariffs implemented in the early 19th century to protect domestic industries, partly to raise revenue and rebuild U.S. industry decimated by the conflict. But the 1913 Revenue Act lowered the U.S. tariff rate on most imports from 41 percent to 27 percent.[64]

Meanwhile, U.S. manufacturing achieved a major breakthrough when the Ford Motor Co. opened its first moving assembly line in 1913. The Model T's 3,000 parts were grouped into 84 steps performed by different groups of employee as car bodies moved past, pulled by a rope. Assembling a vehicle now took 90 minutes instead of

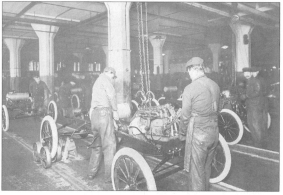

Bettmann/Getty Images

Factory workers at a Ford Motor Co. plant assemble a Model T automobile in 1913. Henry Ford's creation of a moving assembly line that year was a major breakthrough for U.S. manufacturing. The time required to produce a vehicle fell from 12 hours to 90 minutes, and the car's price dropped from $850 to $300.

CHRONOLOGY

1800-1900 *Steam engines and the telegraph fuel an industrial revolution.*

1807 First commercially available steamboat travels from New York City to Albany, leading the way for commercial shipping by water routes.

1837 Samuel Morse is granted a patent for a telegraph machine.

Mid- to late 1800s Transportation by rail, ship and barge allows companies to obtain raw materials and ship products over longer distances, stoking demand for finished goods.

1910s-1930s *U.S. and Europe lower tariffs, reducing prices and expanding trade routes. Technology advances.*

1913 Revenue Act lowers tariff rates on most goods from 41 percent to 27 percent; Ford Motor Co. opens its first moving assembly line.

1927 Ford produces a Model T every 24 seconds.

1929 Stock market crashes in New York, triggering the deepest economic crisis in U.S. history, later known as the Great Depression.

1930 Republican President Herbert Hoover signs the Smoot-Hawley Tariff Act, raising tariffs on 900 products to protect U.S. industries; instead it helps usher in the Great Depression.

1934 To help jump-start the world economy, Democratic President Franklin D. Roosevelt signs the Reciprocal Trade Agreement Act, cutting tariffs on products from 34 countries that agree to reciprocate.

1940s-1960s *Logistics and intermodal containers standardize shipping as post-World War II economy booms.*

1947 The U.S. and Great Britain lead 23 nations in signing the General Agreement on Tariffs and Trade (GATT), a set of international rules lowering tariffs among participating countries.

1948 U.S. Army Master Sgt. Edward A. Guilbert creates a tracking system—the Electronic Data Interchange (EDI)—that uses radio-teletype, telephone or telex, an international telegraph system, to organize the Berlin airlift. It will be used to revolutionize supply chain management.

1961 The International Organization for Standardization sets standard shipping container sizes, boosting efficiency at ports.

1970s-1980s *The modern technology industry emerges, and China joins the world trading system.*

1971 Intel sells the first commercial microprocessor, shrinking space needed for data storage and calculation power.

1979 China and the United States establish diplomatic relations, eventually leading to mutual access to markets for goods and services.

1986 China's "open door" policy encourages foreign investment.

1990-2009 *The rise of the internet and "offshoring" allows companies to produce and track goods more cheaply, expanding global supply chains.*

1993 The European Organization for Nuclear Research puts its World Wide Web project in the public domain.

1994 The United States, Mexico and Canada sign the North American Free Trade Agreement (NAFTA), lowering tariffs among the three nations.

1995 The World Trade Organization (WTO) replaces GATT.

1998 Jack Welch, CEO of General Electric, says companies ideally should put "every plant you own on a barge to move with currencies and changes in the economy."

2001 China is admitted to the WTO.

2008 Lehman Brothers investment bank collapses, triggering worldwide financial crisis.

2009 The 3D printer patent expires, enabling entrepreneurs to develop parts on demand, from rocket engine blades to artificial blood vessels.

2010-Present *Financial crisis gives way to economic growth; a backlash against free trade develops as manufacturing moves out of the United States and robotics and artificial intelligence increasingly replace the need for workers.*

2012 Democratic President Barack Obama pursues free trade agreements, including continuing talks with 11 other Pacific Rim nations to craft a Trans-Pacific Partnership (TPP), begun under Republican President George W. Bush in 2008.

2016 Presidential candidates from both parties attack U.S. trade policy for allegedly eliminating U.S. jobs. . . . Republican Donald Trump wins election, promises to get tough with China and other trading partners, including traditional allies, whom he accuses of taking advantage of U.S. companies. . . . Technology companies test 5G wireless technology, dramatically shrinking download speeds.

2017 Trump withdraws from the TPP, threatens to pull out of NAFTA.

2018 Trump imposes tariffs on solar panels, steel and aluminum and, later, a slew of imported Chinese goods. . . . Negotiators sign an agreement replacing NAFTA called the U.S.-Mexico-Canada Agreement or USMCA (November).

2019 Trump's trade war with China escalates, culminating in plans to impose tariffs on nearly every Chinese-made product. . . . U.S. Trade Representative Robert Lighthizer submits draft agreement of the USMCA to Congress for ratification, but Democrats push for more labor, environmental protections (May). . . . Mexico ratifies the pact (June). . . . Canada says it will move "in tandem" with the United States in approving the deal. House Speaker Nancy Pelosi announces bipartisan changes to the agreement, and the House approves it (December). . . . Senate ratification is not expected until 2020.

12 hours. The price of the car fell from $850 to $300, making it affordable to a wider swath of Americans. Ford also instituted a "$5 workday" wage, up from about $2.25. By 1927, a Model T came off the line every 24 seconds, and Ford had sold 15 million worldwide.[65]

Then, in 1929 the U.S. stock market crashed. In an effort to prop up domestic industry, Congress passed the Smoot-Hawley Tariff Act of 1930, which raised tariffs by an average of 20 percent on 900 imported goods. Most economists say rather than boosting American industry, the law led other countries to implement similar tariffs, and international trade slowed dramatically. The global economy ground to a halt, helping to trigger the Great Depression. Prices of U.S. commodities plummeted by 75 percent and industrial production fell 25 percent during the 1930s; as millions lost their jobs, firms went out of business and demand dried up.[66]

In an attempt to restart the world economy, Democratic President Franklin D. Roosevelt in 1934 signed the Reciprocal Trade Agreement Act, in which 32 countries agreed to cut tariffs. But economic recovery did not really begin until the onset of World War II, when global military production skyrocketed.[67]

During the war the U.S. military made major strides in supply chain logistics, with some armed forces units and divisions developing systems to coordinate transportation, communication, medical services and supplies.[68]

In 1948, three years after the war's end, the Soviet Union cut off food, medicine and other supplies to the Allied-controlled areas of Berlin. A logistics group led by U.S. Army Master Sgt. Edward A. Guilbert created a tracking system using telex, radio-teletype or phone called the Electronic Data Interchange (EDI). It allowed businesses to swap documents such as purchase orders, inventory levels and invoices between mainframe computers. The method enabled what became known as the Berlin airlift—a 13-month effort to drop supplies into the city. Later, Guilbert further refined the EDI methods for use at DuPont, a chemical company, and other companies soon began using it widely.[69]

Tariffs on Cars Are Complicated for Suppliers

"There are really no 100 percent U.S.-built cars. Anywhere."

President Trump is using the broad threat of imposing tariffs on imported cars—invoking national security concerns under a 1962 law—as leverage in negotiating trade deals with Japan, South Korea, the European Union and other places.[1]

The administration wants to increase the percentage of cars and auto parts sold in the United States that are made in America. But the reality is complex.

About one in four vehicles assembled in the United States is made in a foreign-owned factory, says Kristin Dziczek, vice president of research at the Center for Automotive Research, a Michigan-based group that studies the auto industry. For instance, luxury German carmaker BMW's largest plant is in Spartanburg, S.C., where it employs 11,000 people. About 70 percent of the cars assembled there are exported.[2]

Trump's threat carries consequences: Tariffs could disrupt supply chains and slow sales and profits for vehicle and parts makers, potentially costing more than 368,000 factory jobs and another 77,000 jobs at dealerships, the center estimated. And U.S. consumers could pay an average of $2,800 more per car, with fewer model choices, according to the center.[3]

"If they do this, then we are all losers," BMW CEO Oliver Zipse said about the administration's tariff threat during an October automotive conference. "I have the impression [administration officials] are listening carefully. The export model sustains many jobs in the United States."[4]

Although BMW has not cut production at its Spartanburg plant, tariffs could change that, Zipse said.

The White House in November appeared to miss a legal deadline for imposing tariffs based on the 1962 law, first postponed in May. While Commerce Secretary Wilbur Ross said in December that negotiations with individual companies "may or may not" result in tariffs, he evaded questions about the administration's plans.[5]

As a result, the threat of auto tariffs hangs like a sword above negotiations with the Europeans over a broad trade treaty.[6] Tariffs also hover in the background of other negotiations, including a trade agreement with South Korea, signed in 2018, which did not specifically exempt South Korean cars from tariffs under the 1962 law.[7] A U.S.-Japan trade agreement, approved in December, also does not explicitly rule out potential auto tariffs.[8]

The U.S.-Mexico-Canada Agreement (USMCA), a replacement for the North American Free Trade Agreement (NAFTA) negotiated a quarter century ago, mandates that a higher percentage of parts for any vehicle produced in North America be made in one of the three countries.[9] The new agreement has yet to be fully ratified by Congress, but House Speaker Nancy Pelosi in December announced modifications that drew bipartisan approval, and the House passed the new version on Dec. 19. The Senate is expected to vote on the deal in 2020.[10]

Trump reportedly is prepared to hold off on a decision on auto tariffs, preserving the threat but avoiding opening another front in the trade wars. Even if the November deadline has lapsed, the threat remains, because the president could invoke other authority to impose tariffs on auto imports, according to Jennifer Hillman, a Georgetown law professor and former World Trade Organization official.[11]

That would be consistent with Trump's public stance since first threatening the action in 2018. "Auto tariffs are never off the table," Trump said in August. "If I don't get what I want, I'll have no choice but maybe to do that."[12]

Trump in May said he was seeking to protect U.S. automakers from what he characterized as unfair breaks granted to foreign-owned automakers, although industry experts disagree with Trump's characterization.[13]

Tariffs would present problems for auto and parts makers. About half the vehicles sold in the United States are imported, and half of those are made in Mexico or Canada by U.S. companies. At least 40 percent of the parts in most automobiles produced in the United States are made overseas.[14] And some parts, such as steering or braking systems, can cross the U.S.-Mexico border up to six times during the production phase as suppliers add components to pieces before final assembly.[15]

"There are really no 100 percent U.S.-built cars. Anywhere," says Dziczek.

Cars Made in the U.S. Contain Parts from Around the World

Auto manufacturers use parts made in several different countries and sometimes assemble cars in plants overseas. The share of parts coming from each country varies by company and model.

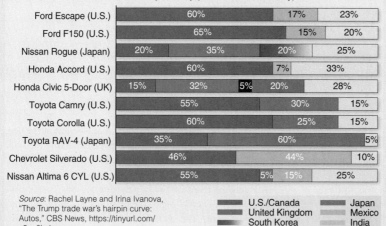

Share of Parts by Country (and Place of Assembly)

	U.S./Canada	United Kingdom	South Korea	Thailand	Japan	Mexico	India	Other
Ford Escape (U.S.)	60%				17%			23%
Ford F150 (U.S.)	65%				15%			20%
Nissan Rogue (Japan)	20%	35%			20%			25%
Honda Accord (U.S.)	60%				7%			33%
Honda Civic 5-Door (UK)	15%	32%	5%		20%			28%
Toyota Camry (U.S.)	55%				30%			15%
Toyota Corolla (U.S.)	60%				25%			15%
Toyota RAV-4 (Japan)	35%				60%			5%
Chevrolet Silverado (U.S.)	46%				44%			10%
Nissan Altima 6 CYL (U.S.)	55%			5%	15%			25%

Source: Rachel Layne and Irina Ivanova, "The Trump trade war's hairpin curve: Autos," CBS News, https://tinyurl.com/y6py6kgb

much more decentralized global footprint."

— Rachel Layne

[1] "Adjusting Imports of Automobiles and Automobile Parts Into the United States," White House, Presidential Proclamation, May 17, 2019, https://tinyurl.com/y5cvjueq.

[2] BMW Group, https://tinyurl.com/s25ab7n.

[3] "Forging a New Path for North American Trade: The Auto Sector," Presentation by the Center for Automotive Research, Federal Reserve Bank of Chicago, Sept. 4-5, 2019.

[4] Edward Taylor, "BMW CEO says trade war could cost U.S. Jobs," *Reuters*, Oct. 25, 2019, https://tinyurl.com/tk4q2x5.

[5] David Shepardson, "U.S. has not ruled out imposing tariffs on imported autos: Commerce chief," *Reuters*, Dec. 3 2019, https://tinyurl.com/ukz4xkq.

[6] Josh Zumbrun, Ben Foldy and Emre Peker, "Threat of Auto Import Tariffs Remains Despite Lapsed Deadline," *The Wall Street Journal*, Nov. 21, 2019, https://tinyurl.com/wzz6xvd.

[7] Esha Dey, "Auto Industry Basks in a 'False Sense of Security' Over Trade," *Bloomberg*, Nov. 25, 2019, https://tinyurl.com/u4r6dy5; "U.S.-Korea Free Trade Agreement fact sheet," U.S. Trade Representative, https://tinyurl.com/vxzr8gz.

[8] Yuri Kageyama, "Trump's US-Japan trade deal wins Japan parliament approval," *The Associated Press*, Dec. 3, 2019, https://tinyurl.com/wgmuvul.

[9] "The United States-Mexico-Canada Agreement Fact Sheet: Automobiles and Automotive Parts," U.S. Trade Representative, https://tinyurl.com/y42voj32; "Proposed U.S.-Mexico-Canada (USMCA) Trade Agreement," Congressional Research Service, Dec. 17, 2019, https://tinyurl.com/t3bp4vf.

[10] Eric Marten, "Mexico's Senate Passes Changes to U.S., Canada Trade Deal," *Bloomberg*, Dec. 10, 2019, https://tinyurl.com/yxxvfbry; Erica Werner, "House passes reworked North American trade deal in victory for Trump, Democrats," *The Washington Post*, Dec. 17, 2019, https://tinyurl.com/sqqadpm.

[11] Jennifer Hillman, Twitter post, Nov. 21, 2019, https://tinyurl.com/rlhhhf4.

[12] Jeff Mason, Andrea Shalal and David Alexander, "Trump says auto tariffs are never off the table in European trade talks," *Reuters*, Aug. 2, 2019, https://tinyurl.com/y2mrj8v8.

[13] David Shepardson, "Trump declares some auto imports pose national security threat," *Reuters*, May 17, 2019, https://tinyurl.com/y6nt7vre.

[14] Rachel Layne and Irina Ivanova, "The Trump trade war's hairpin curve: Autos," *CBS News*, July 19, 2018, https://tinyurl.com/y6py6kgb.

[15] "Section 232 Auto Investigation," Congressional Research Service, June 17, 2019, https://tinyurl.com/y5n3vccv.

[16] *Ibid.*

Auto industry experts cite NAFTA as a major impetus for this trend. Under NAFTA, the free flow of parts, as well as the lower cost of labor in Mexico, made it more attractive for foreign companies to build vehicles for the U.S. market in the United States, Mexico or Canada rather than pay duties on imported finished cars. Since 1992, some 10 foreign-owned manufacturing plants opened in the United States, bringing the total to 17 in 2018. Because more factories were built and autos were more cost-effective to build in the United States, exports doubled.[16]

But because no trade tariffs exist between the three participating countries under NAFTA, it is difficult to determine a finished part's provenance, Dziczek says. "One company does this one piece, it gets sold to somebody else who does some other piece, and so on." So it is "really difficult to trace" an auto part's precise country of origin, she says.

If a tariff regime required automakers to trace their parts, suppliers could be forced to open distribution centers closer to the auto factories, says Charlie Chesbrough, the senior economist at Cox Automotive, an Atlanta-based company that researches the automotive industry and publishes the well-known Kelley Blue Book.

"They're going to have to have facilities and sales people and marketing people in every country where their [automaker] counterpart is going to be having operations," Chesbrough says. "So it probably means higher costs for them just to maintain this

Rising Supply Chain Costs Likely to Hit Consumers

"It is hard to predict how consumers will react to higher prices resulting from tariffs."

Economists predict that existing and proposed tariffs on Chinese-made imports, which range from bicycles to shoes to food, could mean higher prices for those at the end of the supply chain—U.S. consumers.

Although some prices already have gone up, manufacturers, distributors and retailers are scrambling to figure out how much extra the consumer will be willing to pay and how much of the higher costs retailers and suppliers will have to absorb by cutting expenses, such as workers.

"It is hard to predict how . . . consumers will react to higher prices resulting from tariffs," Best Buy CEO Corie Barry said during an Aug. 29, 2019, conference call with analysts.[1]

The Trump administration in August imposed $300 billion in tariffs on Chinese imports. Roughly half of the tariffs went into effect on Sept. 1 and the other half was delayed until Dec. 15, 2019, allowing some retailers to stock up on holiday inventory before the price hikes took effect.[2]

Companies are adopting a variety of strategies for dealing with the tariffs. Walmart, the nation's largest retailer, warned in a letter to the U.S. trade representative in September 2018, a year before the latest tariffs went into effect, that such tariffs would boost prices.

"The immediate impact will be to raise prices on consumers and tax American business and manufacturers," wrote Sarah F. Thorn, a senior director for global government affairs at Walmart.[3]

But Target, a Walmart competitor, told suppliers it would not accept increases in their wholesale prices tied to the tariffs on Chinese goods. In other words, Target expects suppliers to absorb the higher costs due to the tariffs.[4]

As part of the Dec. 13, 2019, announcement of the new trade deal, the administration postponed enacting the final round of tariffs previously scheduled for Dec. 15, 2019.[5]

Holiday sales this year are projected to rise as much as 4.2 percent from 2018, largely due to job growth and higher wages, according to the National Retail Federation, a lobby group for U.S. retailers. However, the group added, "considerable uncertainty" remains around trade issues.[6]

Import volume at the nation's most popular ports for retailers rose in August 2019, indicating that companies were stocking up on supplies ahead of the Sept. 1, 2019, tariffs, according to the National Retail Federation and Hackett Associates, which tracks U.S. port activity.[7]

Barry said the September 2019 tariffs will affect prices of smartwatches, televisions and headphones sold at Best Buy, and the December 2019 tariffs would affect prices of computers, mobile phones and gaming consoles. The company, which gets 60 percent of its goods from China, has lowered its 2019 revenue forecast and is working on "mitigation efforts" to provide a buffer against price increases tied to tariffs, she said.[8]

In 1957, the first ship carrying modified World War II metal containers for commerce landed in Miami from Port Newark, N.J. The containers, later modified and standardized for sea, rail and truck transport, made international trade even more efficient because a single size is easier to stack, maneuver and design equipment such as cranes to handle.[70]

New Trade Rule's

After World War II, the United States helped to create a free trade system among noncommunist countries, in part in reaction to Smoot-Hawley, which most economists

and historians consider had been a major catalyst of the economic turmoil that helped give rise to extremist leaders such as Adolf Hitler and the outbreak of the war.

The Allied nations created postwar economic institutions and rules, culminating in 1944 in the creation of the International Monetary Fund and the World Bank. Discussions ultimately led to the 1947 signing of the General Agreement on Tariffs and Trade (GATT), a set of trade rules aimed at reducing tariffs between countries.[71]

Nearly 50 years later, the World Trade Organization (WTO) replaced the GATT. It promotes free trade by negotiating rules acceptable to its 164 member countries

About 91 percent of U.S. households have smartphones, three-quarters of which are imported from China, according to the Consumer Technology Association, a lobby group representing companies that range from chipmakers to cloud computing service providers. If the December tariffs had been imposed, cellphone prices would climb 14 percent, or about $70 per phone, the group said. Purchases could fall by 28 percent, the group estimated, with low-income households being disproportionately affected.[9]

The situation is starting to harm consumer confidence, an indicator of how consumers might behave in the future. The measurement fell in October to the lowest level since June, its third-straight decline.[10]

It is not just electronics prices that are rising. Some 70 percent of footwear sold in the United States comes from China, much of it subject to the September tariffs, according to the Footwear Distributors & Retailers of America. The industry group represents more than 500 companies, including Easy Spirit, Nike, Crocs and retailers such as DSW.

The group estimated in August that under the new tariffs, prices for a pair of canvas "skate" sneakers would rise from $49.99 to $60.98, while typical hunting boots would climb from $190 to $231.03. A pair of popular running shoes might rise to $193.75 from $150.[11]

Rick Helfenbein, the chief executive officer of the American Apparel and Footwear Association, a lobby group representing manufacturers of accessories, footwear and apparel, says he is concerned that recovery from the next economic downturn will not be as fast as from previous downturns, including the 2007-09 recession.

"In our industry, in retail and apparel, we're the first ones to go in, and we're the first ones to come out" of a recession, Helfenbein says. "What bailed us out in '08 and '09 was the low cost of goods from China. And you know, this time around we're not going to have that."

— *Rachel Layne*

[1] Khadeeja Safdar and Allison Prang, "Best Buy Lowers Sales Forecast, Citing Tariffs' Toll," *The Wall Street Journal*, Aug. 29. 2019, https://tinyurl.com/y6hq4wyv; "Best Buy Co. Inc. Q2 2020 Earnings Call Transcript," *Motley Fool*, Aug. 29, 2019, https://tinyurl.com/y4bukpp2.

[2] Ana Swanson, "U.S. Delays Some Tariffs Until Stores Stock Up for the Holidays," *The New York Times*, Aug. 13, 2019, https://tinyurl.com/y3qd3clb.

[3] Walmart letter to the U.S. Trade Representative, Regulations.gov, Sept. 6, 2018, https://tinyurl.com/y2jshs8f.

[4] William Mauldin and Sarah Nassauer, "Target Tells Its Suppliers to Handle Tariffs Costs," *The Wall Street Journal*, Sept. 4, 2019, https://tinyurl.com/y256t93f.

[5] "United States and China Reach Phase One Trade Agreement," press release, The United States Trade Representative, Dec. 13, 2019, https://tinyurl.com/yk3v5xvr.

[6] "NRF forecasts holiday sales will grow between 3.8 and 4.2 percent," press release, National Retail Federation, Oct. 3, 2019, https://tinyurl.com/y447z9fs.

[7] "Retail imports surging again ahead of more tariffs," press release, National Retail Federation, Sept. 10, 2019, https://tinyurl.com/y2nqn3cs.

[8] Safdar and Prang, *op. cit.*

[9] "Testimony to the U.S. Trade Representative," Consumer Technology Association, June 17, 2019, https://tinyurl.com/yxm6jl6b.

[10] Katia Dmitrieva, "U.S. Consumer Confidence Falls to Lowest Since June," *Bloomberg*, Oct. 29, 2019, https://tinyurl.com/yxg6yah3.

[11] "Pres. Trump's 10% Shoe Tariffs," press release, Footwear Distributors & Retailers of America, Aug. 13, 2019, https://tinyurl.com/tcvkl6v.

and adjudicates disputes that arise when members are accused of violating those regulations.[72] Until Trump's election in 2016, U.S. administrations mainly pursued free trade policies, using tariffs or quotas only occasionally, mostly to protect specific domestic industries.

As information and communications technology developed, the intricacy and speed of supply chains grew, along with multinational corporations.

While technology was advancing in the United States, China's new "open door" policy, adopted seven years after economic reforms began in 1979, encouraged the expansion of a labor pool that was paid more than the average Chinese but less than wages in developed nations. The policy, aimed at pulling China's population out of agrarian poverty, drew investment and business from around the world, including the United States.[73]

Also in the 1980s, foreign auto companies began building plants in the United States and integrating and expanding their supply chains across the globe—in part to avoid import quotas imposed by the Ronald Reagan administration. Japan-based Toyota introduced "just in time" manufacturing techniques to Americans, in which parts are delivered to the factory in time to be used on the day they are delivered. That made smaller factories possible and boosted profits.[74]

By 2019, Japanese companies had invested more than $50 billion in the U.S. auto industry and employed 170,000 Americans. European and South Korean makers had followed suit, and by 2018, some 17 foreign-owned car manufacturing plants were operating in the United States, up from seven in 1992.[75]

The supply chain—called the global value chain—became more closely coordinated, mostly by using special software. It allowed companies—ranging from suppliers of raw, semifinished and finished materials to people transporting those parts and, finally, those assembling the products in a plant—to coordinate their efforts.

Technological Advances

With the advent of the World Wide Web in 1993, businesses began using EDI, personal computing and the internet to produce profound change in global trade and supply chains. These advances helped usher in an ICT revolution, according to Baldwin, of the Graduate Institute in Geneva.[76]

Companies, especially in the world's most advanced economies—known as the Group of Seven (G-7)—saw an opportunity to improve efficiency by moving factories to developing nations. By 1998 Jack Welch, then-CEO of General Electric—the world's largest manufacturer of locomotives, power-plant turbines and jet engines—said the ideal situation would be for companies to put "every plant you own on a barge to move with currencies and changes in the economy."[77]

Just as the steam engine and telegraph had spurred an earlier wave of globalization, the ICT revolution unleashed the next. The supply chain became "denationalized," enabling ideas and factories to be moved across borders, Baldwin said on the podcast *Trade Talks*. "The key wasn't the investment or the offshoring of the jobs. It was know-how. The ICT revolution allows G-7 firms to take their technology, marketing, managerial logistics [and] know-how in manufacturing and move it to nearby developing countries."[78]

Initially, companies chose to make high-tech products in higher-wage G-7 countries, Baldwin said, but within two decades these products could be made anywhere. "The boundaries of competitiveness now become international supply chains, which can cross countries,"

he continued. "GM can take its technology and apply it in Mexico. They can apply the same technology in Thailand, or China, and thereby validate and increase the value of their knowledge."[79]

In 1994, the United States, Mexico and Canada entered into the North American Free Trade Agreement, which cut most tariffs among the three countries, and supply chains for every sector—from agriculture to manufacturing to consumer goods—spread across the continent.

Changes in the U.S. auto industry typify the impact NAFTA had on supply chains. By 2017 the United States was importing more than 4 million vehicles from Mexico, up from 1 million the year the pact was signed. In the same time period, exports of U.S. vehicles doubled.[80]

In addition, some parts, such as steering or braking systems, cross the border up to six times as plants in all three countries add parts. (*See Short Feature.*) About half the vehicles sold in the United States are imported, and half of those imports are made by U.S. companies in Mexico or Canada.[81]

Under Trump, NAFTA has been renegotiated to include a section on digital trade, an issue that didn't exist in the original treaty.[82]

The new pact, called the U.S.-Mexico-Canada Agreement (USMCA), has been revamped by congressional Democrats and Trump administration negotiators for more than a year, securing bipartisan support. USMCA now includes factory inspections by an international panel that will confirm adherence to new provisions for wages and the environment.[83]

The U.S House of Representatives on Dec. 19 voted to approve the new version of the USMCA following Mexico's approval on Dec. 10. Senate approval may not come until 2020, and Canada has said it will follow the United States in ratifying the deal.[84] Earlier in December, some Republican senators said they felt cut out of the deal struck by the House and the Trump Administration.[85]

Protectionist Backlash

China joined the WTO in 2001 with "most-favored nation" status, a controversial decision that allowed it to enjoy the lowest tariffs and the fewest trade barriers between member nations.[86]

Employees check in for the afternoon shift at a mobile phone plant in Sri City, India, in July 2019. Due to rising tariffs and labor costs in China, some companies are moving their assembly plants to India and other lower-wage countries.

The advent of the internet, plus inexpensive labor in China and India, prompted U.S. businesses to close U.S. factories and move the work overseas, a practice called offshoring. Nearly entire industries that are at the start of supply chains, such as textiles, migrated out of the United States.

In 1995, the United States produced 13 percent of the world's textiles, while China made 12 percent. By 2017, China produced 47 percent of global textile output while the United States produced only 3 percent, according to the consulting firm McKinsey & Co.[87]

Between 1999 and 2010, some 6 million manufacturing jobs left the United States. Some economists say the rise of automation and artificial intelligence will continue to exacerbate the loss, but others blame China's rise.[88]

Still, China's rapid growth was fueled by its transformation into the world's biggest exporter. China's share of the global economy, as measured by global gross domestic product (GDP), went from 2 percent in 2001 to 16 percent in 2018, according to McKinsey. Put another way, China went from being the world's 10th-largest exporter in 2000 to the world's biggest exporter in 2017.[89]

In response to China's alleged intellectual property theft and restrictive rules for foreign companies operating inside its borders, Trump began imposing tariffs on Chinese imports in 2018, as leverage to negotiate more-favorable trade agreements. If all the tariffs had been enacted, every import from China would have been subject to tariff levels not seen since the 1930s.

CURRENT SITUATION
Economic Uncertainty

Three years after Trump's election, worldwide trade alliances are in flux, triggering concern among some companies and economists of a looming global economic slowdown.

The vast majority of economists and trade experts oppose the Trump tariffs and predict slower growth as a result. Some numbers are starting to back up that concern. Global trade this year may slump to its slowest pace since the 2007-09 recession, according to the World Trade Organization. On Oct. 1, 2019, the WTO cut its economic growth forecast for 2020, calling it "discouraging but not unexpected."

"Beyond their direct effects, trade conflicts heighten uncertainty, which is leading some businesses to delay the productivity-enhancing investments that are essential to raising living standards," said WTO Director-General Roberto Azevêdo. "Job creation may also be hampered as firms employ fewer workers to produce goods and services for export."[90]

In September, U.S. manufacturing, which accounts for more than 10 percent of the economy and is often a harbinger of the broader economy, slipped into recession (officially measured as two consecutive three-month periods of slowing trade and industrial activity), according to the Institute for Supply Management, which polls purchasing executives.[91]

And the tariffs on goods imported from China alone probably cost some 300,000 U.S. jobs, Mark Zandi, Moody's Analytics' chief economist said in a September report. The figure could hit 900,000 by the end of 2020 if all tariffs are imposed as announced, he wrote.[92]

That is probably why the S&P 500—an index of the daily performance of 500 publicly traded companies—soared to a record on Oct. 28, 2019, when Trump announced his administration may be nearing at least a partial deal with China to end the trade war.[93]

According to the Dec. 13, 2019, announcements from China and the White House, the United States will hold off on tariffs scheduled for $160 billion in mostly imported consumer goods from China and reduce levies imposed in September 2019 from 15 percent to 7.5 percent.[94]

That same week, voters in the United Kingdom elected a government committed to the country's exit

Can global supply chains adjust to Trump's tariffs and still generate economic growth?

YES Gang Li
Associate Professor, Operations Management, Bentley University

Written for *CQ Researcher*, January 2020

The pain caused by President Trump's tariffs is being felt by U.S. consumers and businesses alike. Consumers are seeing price hikes, while companies are busy stockpiling inventory, lowering profit expectations and cutting costs. In the long run, however, the growth of global supply chains will not stagnate, even if Trump's tariff policy continues.

I have spent many years studying the "bullwhip" effect in supply chains, which describes how a small disruption could profoundly impact their performance. True, global supply chains are prone to disruptions, and the disruption caused by high tariffs is by no means "small." However, preparing for the unpredictable and being agile in response to disruptions are requirements for successful supply chain management. Global supply chains have demonstrated their robustness and agility in confronting major disruptions in the past. They will prevail again.

Businesses will continue reshaping their supply chains in today's changing environment. In October, Samsung closed its last mobile phone factory in China and expanded its production capacity in India and Vietnam, while Tesla is fast building its first giant so-called gigafactory in China. Global supply chains have been "shortening" since the global financial crisis of 2008, in order to be closer to end consumers, to reduce complexity and, now, to avoid tariffs. In other words, although Trump's tariff policy is highly unpredictable, businesses have been preparing to prosper in such an environment since a decade ago.

Businesses will increase their investments in emerging technologies such as artificial intelligence, big data and business analytics. For example, Amazon is automating its fulfillment center operations by utilizing mobile robots and drones. Technologies like this help companies reduce operational costs and depend less on labor, thus responding agilely to disruptions. Meanwhile, technologies nurture new demands for global markets and talents, providing the engine for the continued growth of global supply chains. Trump's tariff policy might dampen but certainly cannot kill that trend.

Since the late 1940s, all U.S. presidential administrations, regardless of their political ideologies, have maintained essentially a zero-tariff policy and for good reason: It helps the American economy. Meanwhile, global supply chains have remained strong, despite various disruptions, such as Japan's earthquake and tsunami in 2011.

In summary, if we must put our trust in the continuation of one of them, global supply chains or Trump's tariff policy, which would we pick?

NO Michelle Casario
Assistant Professor, Economics, Villanova University, and Co-Faculty Director, Elenore and Robert F. Moran Sr. Center for Global Leadership

Written for *CQ Researcher*, January 2020

Global supply chains can and have adjusted to the Trump administration's tariffs, but these trade systems are highly integrated and complex, and the relocation process is slow and costly. The disruption of supply chains raises costs for producers, as firms scramble to relocate parts of their production outside of China.

In the long run, diversifying production will benefit U.S. firms, but in the short run, it is costly and inefficient. Firms, especially consumer electronics producers, have deep manufacturing roots in China, developed over decades. Replicating those networks elsewhere, without similar infrastructure, is difficult and could take years.

In addition, the uncertainty surrounding tariffs makes it difficult for firms to undertake long-term planning, forcing U.S. companies to delay investment and reduce capital expenditures. The cancellation of the fourth round of tariffs, scheduled for December 15th, which would have effectively covered all goods imported from China, was a welcome relief for businesses and investors. However, pre-existing tariffs remain in effect on $360 billion worth of Chinese goods, causing a continuous disruption of supply chains and a degree of business uncertainty. This level of prolonged uncertainty regarding trade policy is unprecedented, and firms are looking for clarity.

The recent partial agreement represents a truce in the trade war, but it does not address the main issue that prompted the war: China's subsidies to state-owned enterprises. Without a "phase-two" deal that addresses the fundamental differences between the United States and China, and as long as the threat of tariffs remain, business and investor confidence will not be restored. So, the tit-for-tat tariffs between the United States and China have hurt U.S. producers and consumers without making real progress on legitimate issues such as forced technology transfers and government subsidies.

The most significant consequence of a trade war between the world's two largest economies is the negative impact it has on global trade and growth. The costly disruption of supply chains and the reduction in business investment is showing up in global data. The latest World Trade Organization forecast on trade flows shows just 1.2 percent growth—the lowest annual increase in a decade. This is consistent with the International Monetary Fund's recently downgraded forecast for global growth: It will fall to its slowest rate since the 2007-09 financial crisis. Weaker global growth weighs on U.S. exports and investment spending, demonstrated by the decline in factory activity, which in September hit a 10-year low.

While there is broad agreement regarding China's unfair trade practices, few would argue that escalating trade wars are the solution.

from the European Union, a strong signal the post-World War II era of global trade cooperation is ending, according to a *New York Times* analysis.[95]

For now, American consumers, who drive the U.S. economy, are still spending, as unemployment hovers at the lowest rate in half a century. The National Retail Federation, a lobby group for U.S. retailers, predicted on Oct. 3, 2019, that holiday sales will rise 4.2 percent over last year's holiday season but noted that "considerable uncertainty [exists] around issues including trade."[96]

Some retailers and their suppliers stockpiled goods ahead of tariffs that went into effect on Sept. 1, 2019, electing to accept the risk that the inventory may not sell rather than pay tariffs on imported Chinese goods, the retail federation said on Sept. 10, 2019. "Retailers are still trying to minimize the impact of the trade war on consumers by bringing in as much merchandise as they can before each new round of tariffs takes effect and drives up prices," said Jonathan Gold, the vice president for supply chains and customs policy for the National Retail Federation.[97]

Trump administration trade policy announcements can change within days, often communicated by a presidential tweet. On May 30, 2019, for example, Trump tweeted that he planned to impose a 5 percent tariff on all goods imported from Mexico unless it agreed to changes in immigration policy, an unprecedented link between trade and foreign policy. He rescinded the plan on June 7, 2019.[98]

"Even if there's a truce or deal, that could change," says Villanova's Casario. "It's really a tweet away from the president just saying, 'Nope, we're going to go ahead' with tariffs. There's nothing in this truce or this agreement that says they won't. That is what affects the laptops, the phone, the video game console. All of those [have] been spared up until now."

That kind of uncertainty can shake supply chain managers at companies such as the San Mateo, Calif.-based GoPro, which moved a plant out of China to Mexico in June 2019. "We have moved most of our U.S.-bound camera production to Mexico—Guadalajara to be specific," GoPro Chief Financial Officer Brian McGee said at an investor conference in September 2019. "We are continuing to move lines, and we've adjusted inventory levels ahead of tariffs . . . to effectively neutralize the impact."[99]

GoPro began planning the move in July 2018 after the Office of the U.S. Trade Representative announced some of the first tariffs on imported Chinese goods. The

company is in "pretty good shape," but still had "a little bit more to do in 2020," McGee said.[100]

Preparing for Recession

It is unclear if or how the new partial agreement with China will crack down on a central reason Trump gave for the tariffs in the first place: alleged intellectual property theft and the forced transfer of technology for companies doing business in China.

When pressed by *CBS News*, U.S. Trade Representative Robert Lighthizer said the administration is "right where we hope to be," having gotten "tech transfer, real commitments, IP, real specific commitments" with China. "This is a real structural change. Is it going to solve all the problems? No. Did we expect it to? No. Absolutely not." The full 86-page agreement is expected to be released in January 2020.[101]

Some U.S. companies are cutting investments in supply chains to prepare for a possible recession, just when investment in new technologies may be needed the most.[102]

One remedy under consideration is to blacklist more Chinese companies, particularly those that repeatedly steal intellectual property.[103]

"It's hard to overstate the complexity of supply chain challenges," Robert Mayer, co-chair of the U.S. Department of Homeland Security's Information and Communications Technology Supply Chain Risk Management Task Force, told Congress in October. "For both suppliers and buyers, the potential universe of supply chain vulnerabilities touches all aspects of information technology."[104]

The risk covers "any physical or logical element that can be used to generate, store, manipulate or transport data in digital form," he continued. "That means the billions of new connected objects coming online will expand the risk universe exponentially."[105]

Supply chain managers in North America are breathing a sigh of relief after an agreement was announced in December on terms for the USMCA trade deal.

Another unresolved trade issue involving supply chains concerns tariffs Trump has threatened to impose on every foreign-made automobile or auto part. Economists have warned such taxes could mean hundreds of thousands of layoffs in the United States alone.[106] The new USMCA agreement shields auto imports from Mexico and Canada. (*See Short Feature.*)

OUTLOOK

Rethinking Approaches

What will changes in trade and technology mean for supply chains, the U.S. consumer and the global economy?

No matter what happens with U.S. trade policy, companies will rethink their approach, says Gartner's Raman. That could mean moving 10 percent to 30 percent of their supply chains to a different location or using new technology such as 3D printing to create their own parts and materials closer to consumer markets, she says. "Companies that do business with China have excellent reasons to do so. They will continue doing so. But more and more companies will be forced to at least tweak a portion of their sourcing."

Still, most economists expect protectionist policies to weigh on the global economy this year and next. A survey conducted in September by the National Association for Business Economics predicted that global GDP growth would slip below 2 percent in 2020 and possibly even lower. Eighty-five percent of the economists said they had cut their forecasts because of the trade war.[107]

Despite the partial agreement announced on Dec. 13, 2019, some economists remain skeptical. For one thing, the bulk of tariffs already imposed on imported Chinese goods remain intact under the new deal.

It "remains to be seen if the deal will stick," wrote Julian Evans-Pritchard, a senior China economist at the firm Capital Economics. "China seems to have won larger-than-expected tariff rollbacks for relatively few concessions."[108]

As new technologies such as 5G get closer to widespread use and concerns around intellectual property and security coalesce, trade policy will play an increasing role in how the global economy evolves. If the U.S. and Chinese economies decouple, forcing other countries to take sides, it could even risk triggering military conflict, Wharton's Garrett wrote. Yet technology companies in both places are so intertwined that corporate clout should prevent such escalation, he wrote.

"Advocates promote decoupling in the name of national security. I believe the opposite would be true," Garrett said. "Decoupling would profoundly harm America's national security by reducing the [economic] costs of war with China, hence making military conflict more likely."[109]

He is not alone. The former prime ministers of Australia, New Zealand and Sweden wrote in a *New York Times* opinion piece on Oct. 11, 2019, that decoupling would "present a long-term threat to global peace and security."[110]

Amid the trade war, China is lowering tariffs for other countries while raising them on U.S. imports in retaliation, according to a Sept. 20 analysis from Chad Bown, a senior fellow at the Peterson Institute for International Economics. That encourages U.S. rivals to trade more with China and bolster supply chains and economic relationships that exclude the United States, Bown wrote.[111]

"Trump's provocations and China's two-pronged response mean American companies and workers now are at a considerable cost disadvantage relative to both Chinese firms and firms in third countries," Bown said. "The result is one more eerie parallel to the conditions U.S. exporters faced in the 1930s."[112]

But advocates of decoupling, such as AEI's Scissors, say such predictions are exaggerated. Companies are struggling with relocating supply chains because while "they understand that the world of 2016 is probably gone," it is not yet clear if trade policy will sever the two economies or just invoke restrictions that limit profit growth.

The "short term efficiency losses of the supply chain disruption are extremely low," but in the longer-term the situation is likely to be resolved, Scissors says.

"I understand the distributional effects could be important," he continues. But, he added, "I don't remember the treaty where we promised you indefinite U.S.-China supply chains. There was an opportunity, you took advantage of it, hats off.

"Now the situation is shifting," he points out. "Sorry, that's the way it goes."

NOTES

1. Jeanne Whalen, Abha Bhattarai and Reed Albergotti, "Trump 'hereby' orders U.S. business out of China. Can he do that?" *The Washington Post*, Aug. 24, 2019, https://tinyurl.com/y6aehv7g.

2. "History of the multilateral trading system," World Trade Organization, https://tinyurl.com/y92sle2v; Kevin Rudd, Helen Clark and Carl Bildt, "Former World Leaders: The Trade War Threatens the World Economy," *The New York Times*, Oct. 11, 2019, https://tinyurl.com/y5aqk62x.

3. William Mauldin, "U.S. Tariffs Prompt Anger, Retaliation From Trade Allies," *The Wall Street*

Journal, May 31, 2018, https://tinyurl.com/y4gq28ys.

4. William Mauldin, Lingling Wei and Alex Leary, "U.S., China Agree to Limited Deal to Halt Trade War," *The Wall Street Journal*, Dec. 14, 2019, https://tinyurl.com/vl5bjzd.

5. "Impact of U.S.-China Trade War Felt in Both Countries," "PBS News Hour," Sept. 28, 2019, https://tinyurl.com/y3x66qxs; Rachel Layne, "Who pays tariffs on imported goods: China or U.S. customers?" *CBS News*, Aug. 5 2019, https://tinyurl.com/yy64dpdr; Chad P. Bown, "U.S.-China Trade War: The Guns of August," Peterson Institute for International Economics, Sept. 20, 2019, https://tinyurl.com/y47ayo9e; and Mark Mauer, "U.S. companies preparing for long-term 'confrontational relationship' with China," *The Wall Street Journal*, Oct. 22, 2019, https://tinyurl.com/yygas77g.

6. Josh Zumbrun, "Global Economy on Course for Weakest Growth Since Crisis," *The Wall Street Journal*, Oct. 15, 2019, https://tinyurl.com/yxlwfnoz; Vince Golle, "U.S. Recession Risk Creeps Higher Because of Weak Business Spending," *Bloomberg*, Sept. 17, 2019, https://tinyurl.com/y6lr5tk9; and Josh Chin, "The Internet, Divided Between the U.S. and China, Has Become a Battleground," *The Wall Street Journal*, Feb. 9, 2019, https://tinyurl.com/y52xf4ta.

7. Rudd, Clark and Bildt, *op. cit.*

8. Margaret Brennan, "Transcript: CBS Face The Nation," *CBS News*, May 12, 2019, https://tinyurl.com/yxu56hp2.

9. *Ibid.*

10. Henry Paulson, "Statement from Henry M. Paulson, Jr., Former U.S. Treasury Secretary and Chairman of the Paulson Institute," press release, The Paulson Institute, Dec. 13, 2019, https://tinyurl.com/ws98ek7; Grace Zhu and Chao Deng, "China to Cut Tariffs on Range of Goods Amid Push for Trade Deal," *The Wall Street Journal*, Dec. 23, 2019, https://tinyurl.com/udn5od2.

11. Tom Connors, Mike Byhoff, Jenny Leonard, "How Trump's Trade War Went From Method to Madness," *Bloomberg*, Dec. 5, 2019, https://tinyurl.com/tft27v5.

12. Grant Clark and Shelly Hagan, "QuickTake: What's intellectual property and does China try to steal it?" *Bloomberg News*, March 22, 2018, https://tinyurl.com/y9glysko; World Intellectual Property Organization, https://tinyurl.com/tegh7r8; "United States Trade Representative 2017 Special 301 Report," U.S. Office of the Trade Representative, p. 1, https://tinyurl.com/reexfgw.

13. "Senate Democrats press Trump for China IP, tech transfer commitments," *Reuters*, Feb. 13, 2019, https://tinyurl.com/rv4ya3a.

14. Dennis C. Blair and Jon M. Huntsman Jr., "Update to the IP Commission Report," Commission on the Theft of American Intellectual Property and the National Bureau of Asian Research, 2017, https://tinyurl.com/yyn62c9x; "Current GDP calculator," World Bank, https://tinyurl.com/y63ybe4e.

15. Thilo Hanemann *et al.*, "Two-Way Street: 2019 Update U.S.-China Direct Investment Trends," Rhodium Group, May 8, 2019, https://tinyurl.com/yy3xhwfh.

16. "The Race to 5G," CTIA, https://tinyurl.com/yxg4s65u.

17. Joshua Oliver, "How 3D Printing Will Transform Mass Production," *The Financial Times*, Oct. 6, 2019, https://tinyurl.com/yyxkfbu8; Daniel Oberhaus, "Massive AI-Powered Robots Are 3-D Printing Entire Rockets," *Wired*, Oct. 14, 2019, https://tinyurl.com/y3dybr4a.

18. Elly Cosgrove, "Best Buy follows Amazon, Walmart in next-day delivery push in time for the holidays," *CNBC*, Oct. 22, 2019, https://tinyurl.com/y5ezm9lc; Hiawatha Bray, "From ocean to table, via blockchain," *The Boston Globe*, Oct. 24, 2019, https://tinyurl.com/y4jj6njr; and Edward C. Baig, "Say thank you and please: Should you be polite with your Alexa and the Google Assistant?" *USA Today*, Oct. 10, 2019, https://tinyurl.com/y2qf4pp4.

19. "Manufacturing labor costs per hour for China, Vietnam, Mexico from 2016 to 2020 (in U.S. dollars)," Statista, https://tinyurl.com/y2jtst4; "Table B-8," press release, Bureau of Labor Statistics, Dec. 6, 2019, https://tinyurl.com/gwme9z8; Cissy Zhou,

"Could robotic automation replace China's 100 million workers in its manufacturing industry," *The South China Morning Post*, Feb. 14, 2019, https://tinyurl.com/y2wefsv7; and Niharika Mandhana, "Manufacturers want to quit China for Vietnam. They're finding it impossible," *The Wall Street Journal*, Aug. 21, 2019, https://tinyurl.com/y48jw5wy.

20. "CEO Confidence Declined to Lowest Level in a Decade," press release, The Conference Board, Oct. 2, 2019, https://tinyurl.com/webx6h6.

21. Donald J. Trump, Twitter post, Aug. 23, 2019 https://tinyurl.com/yxwcjbnk.

22. Indermit Gill, "Future Development Reads: China's shifting manufacturing labor pool is creating global dreams—and nightmares," The Brookings Institution, Nov. 17, 2017, https://tinyurl.com/yc48t9tc.

23. Lauren Feiner, "Google to acquire Fitbit, valuing the smartwatch maker at about $2.1 billion," *CNBC*, Nov. 1, 2019, https://tinyurl.com/y2kkac5g.

24. "Fitbit Diversifies its Supply Chain Outside of China," press release, Fitbit, Oct. 9, 2019, https://tinyurl.com/y6ydxlyb.

25. Rachel Layne, "Trump's Mexico tariffs send companies packing—again," *CBS News*, June 5, 2019, https://tinyurl.com/y6h3q3ms.

26. Yoko Kubota and Tripp Mickle, "Apple examines feasibility of shifting some production out of China," *The Wall Street Journal*, June 20, 2019, https://tinyurl.com/y4bzvqd2.

27. "Home Depot Inc. Q2 (2019) Earnings Call Transcript," *The Motley Fool*, Aug. 20, 2019, https://tinyurl.com/y3ubz3um.

28. Kubota and Mickle, *op. cit.*

29. "Apple Q3 2019 Earnings Call Transcript," *The Motley Fool*, July 30, 2019, https://tinyurl.com/y4rvfsln.

30. Stephen Nellis, "Apple's data shows a deepening dependence on China as Trump's tariffs loom," *Reuters*, Aug. 28, 2019, https://tinyurl.com/y26dva8f; "Ben Winck, "Apple surpasses Microsoft as the world's most valuable company," *Business Insider*, Oct. 18, 2019, https://tinyurl.com/y5nk7u4s; "Apple 10K filing for the year 2018," U.S. Securities and Exchange Commission, undated, p. 23, https://tinyurl.com/y4bx3bae; and Austen Hufford and Bob Tita, "Manufacturers move supply chains out of China," *The Wall Street Journal*, July 14, 2019, https://tinyurl.com/yy3dss88.

31. Anna Fifield, "China's Growth Slows to 27-Year Low, but Trump's trade war is only partly to blame," *The Washington Post*, Oct. 18, 2019, https://tinyurl.com/y2m3cag4.

32. Greg Waldron, "Boeing values 20-year Chinese market at $2.9 trillion," *Flight Global*, Sept, 17, 2019, https://tinyurl.com/y6bujqm3; "General Motors annual 10-K filing for 2018," Securities and Exchange Commission, p. 2, https://tinyurl.com/y5gltfvx; "GM's third-quarter China vehicle sales down 17.5%, as U.S. automakers cede ground," *Reuters*, Oct. 10, 2019, https://tinyurl.com/y4yec8ug; Dana Hull and Chunying Zhang, "Elon Musk Set Up His Shanghai Gigafactory in Record Time," *Bloomberg Businessweek*, Oct. 23, 2019, https://tinyurl.com/yxldvuxm; and Thomas Franck, "Two major companies—Caterpillar and Nvidia—on Monday Blamed China for poor earnings," *CNBC*, Jan. 28, 2019, https://tinyurl.com/y8okzgya.

33. "Apple Supplier List," Apple, https://tinyurl.com/ycphlg6q; Daniel Ives, "First Round of Tariffs Likely Absorbed by Cupertino; A Wild Card in FY20," Wedbush Securities, Aug. 13, 2019, https://tinyurl.com/trbeypb.

34. "Member Survey," U.S.-China Business Council, August 2019, https://tinyurl.com/yyjcxmm9.

35. Nicholas R. Lardy, "Are Foreign Companies Really Leaving China in Droves?" Peterson Institute for International Economics, Sept. 10, 2019, https://tinyurl.com/y3ndeuwz.

36. Jim Rice, Kai Trepte and Ken Cottrill, "Trade Policy Whiplash Is the New Norm. How Do Companies Maintain the Integrity of Their Supply Chains?" MIT Center for Transportation and Logistics, June 17, 2019, https://tinyurl.com/y2k5oa7h.

37. "Trade in Goods with China: 2019," U.S. Census Bureau, https://tinyurl.com/k5xumsy.

38. "Manufacturing labor costs per hour for China, Vietnam, Mexico from 2016 to 2020 (in U.S. dollars)," Statista, https://tinyurl.com/https-www-statista-com-stati.

39. "Consumer Spending," Bureau of Economic Analysis, https://tinyurl.com/y48dwxko.

40. "U-M Surveys of Consumers: Confidence depends on favorable job, income prospects," press release, University of Michigan, Oct. 25, 2019, https://tinyurl.com/yycdpaz6.

41. Matt Ott, "Consumer Confidence still high despite November decline," *The Associated Press*, Nov. 26, 2019, https://tinyurl.com/uyz646l.

42. "November 2019 Manufacturing ISM Report On Business," Institute for Supply Management, Dec. 2, 2019, https://tinyurl.com/y285t5me; "World Economic Reports," International Monetary Fund, October 2019, https://tinyurl.com/y5xcnc7a.

43. Gita Gopinath, "The World Economy: Synchronized Slowdown, Precarious Outlook," *IMF blog*, Oct. 15, 2019, https://tinyurl.com/y2ffh9fc.

44. "U.S.-China Tariff Actions by the numbers," Congressional Research Service, Oct. 9, 2019, https://tinyurl.com/rcenlyk.

45. Ellen Nakashima and Devlin Barrett, "Justice Dept. charges Huawei with fraud, ratcheting up U.S.-China tensions," *The Washington Post*, Jan. 29, 2019, https://tinyurl.com/yxppnfr6; "Meng Wanzhou: Huawei CFO seeks halt to extradition after Trump comments," *The Guardian*, May 8, 2019, https://tinyurl.com/y354nx77.

46. Graham Webster, "It's not just Huawei. Trump's new tech sector order could ripple through global supply chains," *The Washington Post*, May 18, 2019, https://tinyurl.com/yym9jjtm; Jon Fingas, "Intel, Qualcomm and other chipmakers cut off supplies to Huawei," *engadget*, May 20, 2019, https://tinyurl.com/y4awaff3.

47. Ana Swanson, "Trump Green-Lights Some Sales to Huawei," *The New York Times*, Oct. 9, 2019, https://tinyurl.com/y6zbgk7n; Sean Keane, "Huawei ban: Full timeline as House bars US goverment from buying Chinese company's gear," *CNet*, Dec. 19, 2019, https://tinyurl.com/yytlvuhk; and Jenny Leonard and Ian King, "Tech Industry Shudders as U.S. Weighs New Limits on Huawei Sales," *Bloomberg*, Dec. 17, 2019, https://tinyurl.com/qlposec.

48. Geoffrey Garrett, "Why U.S.-China Supply Chains Are Stronger than the Trade War," Knowledge@Wharton, Sept. 5, 2019, https://tinyurl.com/y5sf2ty5.

49. Clinton Fernandes, "What's at stake in Trump's war on Huawei: Control of the global computer-chip industry," *The Conversation*, Oct. 1, 2019, https://tinyurl.com/y3aplqbl.

50. Garrett, *op. cit.*

51. Wei and Davis *et al.*, *op. cit.*; "United States and China Reach Phase One Trade Agreement," press release, The United States Trade Representative, Dec. 13, 2019, https://tinyurl.com/yk3v5xvr; and Chad Bown, Twitter post, Peterson International Institute for Economics, Dec. 17, 2019, https://tinyurl.com/rjfwvrv.

52. "Trump announces 'phase one' deal with China," *CBS News*, Oct. 11, https://tinyurl.com/yyopcxrc.

53. Jeanne Whalen and Anna Fifield, "China's Huawei may need two to three years to recover from U.S. trade ban, CEO says," *The Washington Post*, Dec. 12, 2019, https://tinyurl.com/t6kfpl2.

54. "United States and China Reach Phase One Trade Agreement," *op. cit.*

55. Martin Chorzempa, "New CFIUS Regulations: More Powerful, Transparent, and Complex," Peterson Institute for International Economics website, Oct. 10, 2019, https://tinyurl.com/vppxbfb.

56. Ana Swanson, "Trump Officials Battle Over Plan to Keep Technology Out of Chinese Hands," *The New York Times*, Oct. 25, 2019, https://tinyurl.com/y2neabru.

57. Kevin H. O'Rourke and Jeffrey G. Williamson, "After Columbus: Explaining Europe's Overseas Trade Boom, 1500-1800," *Journal of Economic History*, June 2, 2002, pp. 417-456, https://tinyurl.com/y5p3kqfn.

58. Wolfgang Lehmacher, *The Global Supply Chain: How Technology and Circular Thinking Transform Our Future* (2019), https://tinyurl.com/yy3rdzj4l.

59. "Impact of the Telegraph," Samuel F. B. Morse Papers at the Library of Congress, 1793 to 1919, Library of Congress, https://tinyurl.com/y5b6gegt.

60. Tom Standage, *The Victorian Internet: The Remarkable Story of the Telegraph and the Nineteenth Century's On-line Pioneers* (1998), pp. 166-167.

61. Lehmacher, *op. cit.*

62. Richard E. Baldwin, *The Great Convergence: Information Technology and the New Globalization* (2019), pp. 57-58, https://tinyurl.com/y4ropenw.

63. Lehmacher, *op. cit.*

64. "U.S Tariffs and Trade: A Timeline," International Trade Commission, https://tinyurl.com/ycduqwhl.

65. Kat Eschner, "One Hundred and Three Years Ago Today, Henry Ford Introduced the Assembly Line: His Workers Hated It," *Smithsonian.com*, Dec. 1, 2016, https://tinyurl.com/wumgf3w; "100 Years of the Moving Assembly Line," Ford.com, https://tinyurl.com/y4egurga.

66. "U.S Tariffs and Trade: A Timeline," *op. cit.*; Lehmacher, *op. cit.*, p. 9.

67. "U.S Tariffs and Trade: A Timeline," *ibid.*

68. Richard M. Leighton, "Logistics," *Encyclopedia Britannica,* https://tinyurl.com/y36kfze9.

69. Frank Hayes, "The Story So Far," *Computer World*, June 17, 2002, https://tinyurl.com/y53uu7hp.

70. "The birth of 'intermodalism,'" World Shipping Council, https://tinyurl.com/kpa5nbs.

71. "Milestones: 1937-1945," U.S. Office of the Historian, https://tinyurl.com/h3tc5cn.

72. "History of the Multilateral Trading System," World Trade Organization, https://tinyurl.com/y92sle2v.

73. "China Profile Timeline," *BBC*, July 29, 2019, https://tinyurl.com/y5u3kf57.

74. "Toyota production system," Toyota, https://tinyurl.com/y56frrx5.

75. "Section 232 Auto Investigation," Congressional Research Service, June 17, 2019, https://tinyurl.com/y5n3vccv.

76. Baldwin, *op. cit.*, pp. 79-82.

77. "Welcome Home: The outsourcing of jobs to far-away places is on the wane. But this will not solve the West's employment woes," *The Economist*, Jan. 19, 2013, https://tinyurl.com/yyhxpb3s.

78. Baldwin, *op. cit.*, pp. 83-84; Soumaya Keynes and Chad P. Bown, "Trade Talks, Episode 72: Richard Baldwin on Disruption, Technology and Trade," Peterson Institute for International Economics, Feb. 14, 2019, https://tinyurl.com/yxwfx6n9.

79. Keynes and Bown, *ibid.*

80. "Section 232 Auto Investigation," *op. cit.*

81. *Ibid.*

82. "USMCA Fact Sheet," Office of the U.S. Trade Representative, https://tinyurl.com/y4lddw2w.

83. Wei and Davis *et al.*, *op. cit.*

84. Werner, *op. cit.*

85. Seung Min Kim, "Trump's top trade official meets with GOP senators to soothe tensions over final USMCA deal," *The Washington Post*, Dec. 12, 2019, https://tinyurl.com/vsukxlk.

86. "Principles of the trading system," World Trade Organization, https://tinyurl.com/ycf4pbry.

87. Marco Beltrami *et al.*, "The state of fashion 2019," McKinsey & Co, December 2018, https://tinyurl.com/yymtcmgb.

88. Jill Lepore, "Are Robots Competing for Your Job? Probably, but don't count yourself out," *The New Yorker*, Feb. 25, 2019, https://tinyurl.com/y2labwpc; Jeffry Bartash, "China really is to blame for millions of lost U.S. manufacturing jobs, new study finds," *Marketwatch*, May 14, 2018, https://tinyurl.com/y2kosr4c.

89. "World Trade Statistical Review 2019," The World Trade Organization, https://tinyurl.com/y2kuhudl; Jonathan Woetzel *et al.*, "China and the World, inside the dynamics of a changing relationship," McKinsey Global Institute, July 2019, https://tinyurl.com/y6bqndsa.

90. "WTO lowers trade forecast as tensions unsettle global economy," World Trade Organization, Oct. 1, 2019, https://tinyurl.com/y3uenp42.

91. "November 2019 Manufacturing ISM Report On Business," *op. cit.*

92. Mark Zandi *et al.*, "Trade War Chicken: The Tariffs and the Damage Done," Moody's Analytics, September 2019, https://tinyurl.com/t8gdon5.

93. Thomas Heath, "S&P 500 hits all-time high on strong earnings, global trade optimism," *The Washington Post*, Oct. 28, 2019, https://tinyurl.com/t8gdon5.

94. "United States and China Reach Phase One Trade Agreement," *op. cit.*

95. Peter S. Goodman, "Brexit's Advance Opens a New Trade Era," *The New York Times*, Dec. 17, 2019, https://tinyurl.com/serss9g.

96. Patricia Cohen, "Hiring Slowed in September as Unemployment Rate Fell to a 50-Year Low," *The New York Times*, Nov. 1, 2019, https://tinyurl.com/yymtuogb; "NRF forecasts holiday sales will grow between 3.8 and 4.2 percent," press release, National Retail Federation, Oct. 3, 2019, https://tinyurl.com/y447z9fs.

97. "Retail imports surging again ahead of more tariffs," press release, National Retail Federation, Sept. 10, 2019, https://tinyurl.com/y2nqn3cs.

98. Annie Karni, Ana Swanson and Michael D. Shear, "Trump Says U.S. Will Hit Mexico With 5% Tariffs on All Goods," *The New York Times*, May 30, 2019, https://tinyurl.com/ub4cv7n; Michael D. Shear, Ana Swanson and Azam Ahmed, "Trump Calls Off Plan to Impose Tariffs on Mexico," *The New York Times*, June 7, 2019, https://tinyurl.com/txxqch2.

99. "GoPro Reiterates Plans to Move U.S. Bound Camera Production to Mexico," press release, GoPro, May 13, 2019, https://tinyurl.com/y2bb2ly5; "GoPro, Inc. (GPRO) CEO Nicholas Woodman presents at Citi 2019 Global Technology Conference," transcript, GoPro, Sept. 4, 2019, https://tinyurl.com/y3kmkxkw.

100. "USTR Issues Tariffs on Chinese Products in Response to Unfair Trade Practices," press release, Office of the U.S. Trade Representative, June 15, 2018, https://tinyurl.com/y52hunau; "GoPro, Inc. (GPRO) CEO Nicholas Woodman presents at Citi 2019 Global Technology Conference," *ibid.*

101. Margaret Brennan, "Transcript: Robert Lighthizer on 'Face the Nation,' December 15, 2019," *CBS News*, Dec. 15, 2019, https://tinyurl.com/wkorl8z.

102. Golle, *op. cit.*

103. Heather Long, "Trump administration considers blacklisting Chinese companies that repeatedly steal U.S. intellectual property," *The Washington Post*, Oct. 26, 2019, https://tinyurl.com/y4shc7d4.

104. Robert Mayer, written testimony before the House Committee on Homeland Security, Oct. 16, 2019, https://tinyurl.com/y48co4xy.

105. *Ibid.*

106. David Shepardson, "Automakers warn U.S. tariffs will cost hundreds of thousands of jobs, hike prices," *Reuters*, June 27, 2018, https://tinyurl.com/y93lp5f5.

107. "NABE Outlook Survey—October 2019," National Association for Business Economists, undated, https://tinyurl.com/yxg5vdkx.

108. Julian Evans-Pritchard, "US-China trade deal, infrastructure spending," Capital Economics, Dec. 13, 2019, https://tinyurl.com/tv6ttsu.

109. Garrett, *op. cit.*

110. Rudd, Clark and Bildt, *op. cit.*

111. Bown, "U.S.-China Trade War: The Guns of August," *op. cit.*

112. Chad P. Bown, Euijin Jung and Eva (Yiwen) Zhang, "Trump Has Gotten China to Lower Its Tariffs. Just Toward Everyone Else," Peterson Institute for International Economics, June 12, 2019, https://tinyurl.com/y3qv5h5e.

BIBLIOGRAPHY

Books

Baldwin, Richard, *The Great Convergence: Information Technology and the New Globalization,* **Belknap Press, 2019.**
An international economist explains the evolution of trade and supply chains, including breakthroughs in the 1990s that led to a shift in factories, jobs and intellectual property around the globe at a previously unseen pace.

Lehmacher, Wolfgang, *The Global Supply Chain: How Technology and Circular Thinking Transform Our Future*, Springer, 2019.

The head of supply chain and transport industries for the World Economic Forum in Geneva examines the role played by supply chains in the global economy.

Articles

Hufford, Austen, and Bob Tita, "Manufacturers Move Supply Chains Out of China," *The Wall Street Journal*, July 14, 2019, https://tinyurl.com/yy3dss88.

Some global companies are shifting supply chains out of China to avoid paying tariffs imposed in 2018 and 2019.

Kapadia, Shefali, "USMCA promises streamlined shipments and customs—if it passes," *SupplyChainDive*, Sept. 17, 2019, https://tinyurl.com/yypu5rtw.

A supply chain trade publication details changes in cross-border shipping rules proposed in the U.S.-Mexico-Canada Agreement.

Keane, Sean, "Huawei ban: Full timeline as House bars US government from buying Chinese company's gear," *CNet*, Dec. 19, 2019, https://tinyurl.com/yytlvuhk.

A technology publication provides a timeline of the Trump administration's regulation of Chinese telecommunications company Huawei.

Lardy, Nicholas R., "Are Foreign Companies Really Leaving China in Droves?" Peterson Institute for International Economics, Sept. 10, 2019, https://tinyurl.com/y3ndeuwz.

A trade and finance expert argues U.S. tariffs on imported Chinese goods are not slowing China's economy and raising its unemployment there, as President Donald Trump claims.

Webster, Graham, "It's not just Huawei. Trump's new tech sector order could ripple through global supply chains," *The Washington Post*, May 18, 2019, https://tinyurl.com/yym9jjtm.

A policy expert outlines the increased power gained by U.S. authorities over a wide swath of technology companies through new import policies aimed at Chinese suppliers such as telecom company Huawei.

Reports and Studies

"World Development Report 2020: Trading for Development in the Age of Global Value Chains," World Bank Group, October 2019, https://tinyurl.com/yytmza5w.

The institution outlines current trade practices and policies tied to global supply chains.

Dollar, David, et al., "Global Value Chains Development Report 2019: Technological Innovation, Supply Chain Trade, and Workers in a Globalized World," World Bank Group et al., April 15, 2019, https://tinyurl.com/y5m76kjm.

Global trade and economic organizations and regulatory bodies examine the state of technology, supply chains, trade and labor in this annual report.

Kolb, Melina, "What Is Globalization? And How Has the Global Economy Shaped the United States," Peterson Institute for International Economics, 2019, https://tinyurl.com/y6gl87jc.

Economists outline how changes in supply chains, technology, labor and trade have shaped U.S. businesses, workers and consumers.

Schultz, Michael, et al., "U.S. Consumer & Economic Impacts of U.S. Automotive Trade Policies," Center for Automotive Research, February 2019, https://tinyurl.com/y233t9v8.

Experts detail what proposed and enacted U.S. trade policy changes may mean for the auto industry's reliance on complex, cross-border supply chains—and for the U.S. consumer.

Shikher, Serge, et al., "U.S.-Mexico-Canada Trade Agreement: Likely Impact on the U.S. Economy and Specific Industry Sectors," U.S. International Trade Commission, April 2019, https://tinyurl.com/y22323do.

The federal panel that oversees trade policy examines the potential effects of a pact among the United States, Canada and Mexico that, if approved, would replace the North America Free Trade Agreement implemented a quarter century ago.

Williams, Brock R., et al., "Trump Administration Tariff Actions (Sections 201, 232 and 301): Frequently Asked Questions," Congressional Research Service, Feb. 22, 2019, https://tinyurl.com/yxuf7f2g.

The research arm of the U.S. Congress looks at laws authorizing President Trump's tariff actions—and their potential consequences.

Podcasts

Keyes, Soumaya, Chad Bown and Jenny Leonard, "Trump's Mini-Deal with China," *Trade Talks*, **Oct. 14, 2019, https://tinyurl.com/y623gm8c.**
An *Economist* editor (Keyes) and a senior fellow at the Peterson Institute for International Economics (Bown) join *Bloomberg* trade reporter Leonard to discuss a possible U.S.-China trade deal.

THE NEXT STEP

China and Intellectual Property

He, Laura, "China just signaled that it could reform its IP laws. That's good for trade talks," *CNN Business*, **Nov. 25, 2019, https://tinyurl.com/qp9cyxd.**
China released new, stronger guidelines on the protection of intellectual property, which could please the United States as trade negotiations continue.

Lynch, Colum, "China Bids to Lead World Agency Protecting Intellectual Property," *Foreign Policy*, **Nov. 26, 2019, https://tinyurl.com/twn68lv.**
China's drive to lead the United Nations' World Intellectual Property Organization has drawn criticism from trade experts, who cite that country's history of stealing intellectual property.

Zengerle, Patricia, "U.S. agencies lax as China stole intellectual property: Senate report," *Reuters,* **Nov. 18, 2019, https://tinyurl.com/uw3rzcs.**
A Senate subcommittee report found that federal agencies were slow to respond as China stole intellectual property from U.S. university laboratories and research institutions over the past two decades.

Potential Recession

Higgins, Sean, "Trade war presents lingering recession threat," *Washington Examiner,* **Nov. 5, 2019, https://tinyurl.com/uz9z8ap.**
While the ongoing U.S.-China trade war is unlikely to cause a recession on its own, economists say it is influencing business decisions that could ultimately slow U.S. economic growth.

Schulz, Bailey, "Recession in the near future is unlikely, economist says," *Las Vegas Review-Journal*, **Dec. 3, 2019, https://tinyurl.com/u3cfmme.**
Some economists predict economic growth will remain steady in the next two years, but they cite U.S. trade policy and an inverted yield curve—in which long-term interest rates fall below short-term rates—as potential warning signs.

Winck, Ben, "New study shows small businesses are the most optimistic on record, even as trade-war and recession fears swirl," *Markets Insider,* **Dec. 4, 2019, https://tinyurl.com/qtej3tu.**
Even though U.S.-China trade disputes are weighing down the U.S. manufacturing sector, small-business owners are the most optimistic about the economy.

Tariffs

Beech, Kai, "Metal scrappers say their industry is struggling since international tariffs hit," *ABC7 Denver*, **Dec. 11, 2019, https://tinyurl.com/rr8vnbn.**
Scrap metal prices dropped after the Trump administration's tariffs on steel and aluminum came into effect, hurting businesses that buy and sell those materials.

Groom, Nichola, "U.S. solar group says Trump tariffs killing jobs; White House says 'fake news,'" *Reuters*, **Dec. 3, 2019, https://tinyurl.com/uf6ttpg.**
A solar industry trade group warned that the Trump administration's tariffs on imported solar panels could cost the United States 62,000 jobs, a claim the White House disputed.

Thorbecke, Catherine, "Trump administration threatens tariffs of 'up to 100%' on certain French goods," *ABC News*, **Dec. 3, 2019, https://tinyurl.com/wzawvyq.**
After France levied a digital service tax affecting U.S. tech companies, the Trump administration said it would respond with tariffs of up to 100 percent on French products such as wine, cheese, beauty products and handbags.

Trade Deals

"Japan's parliament approves trade deal with U.S.," *Kyodo*, **Dec. 5, 2019, https://tinyurl.com/s3yf4jg.**
Japan's parliament passed a trade deal with the United States that will lower tariffs on U.S. farm goods in Japan

in exchange for a reduction in duties on Japanese industrial goods in the United States.

Leonard, Jenny, and Shuping Niu, "U.S., China Move Closer to Trade Deal Despite Harsh Rhetoric," *Bloomberg*, Dec. 4, 2019, https://tinyurl.com/wzfv8ug.
The United States and China appear close to agreeing on the first phase of a trade deal that would roll back tariffs, even as political disagreements over Hong Kong and China's treatment of the Uighur ethnic group persist.

Rowan, Lisa, "What the USMCA Trade Deal Means for You," *LifeHacker*, Dec. 11, 2019, https://tinyurl .com/vdg73b5.
The benefits of the United States-Mexico-Canada Agreement could include higher wages for autoworkers and quicker access to less expensive generic drugs for American consumers.

For More Information

American Enterprise Institute, 1789 Massachusetts Ave., N.W., Washington, DC 20036; 202-862-5800; aei.org. Conservative think tank promoting free trade and enterprise.

Brookings Institution, 1775 Massachusetts Ave., N.W., Washington, DC 20036; 202-797-6000; brookings.edu. Bipartisan think tank concerned with national and international policy.

Congressional Research Service, 101 Independence Ave., S.E., Washington, DC 20540; 202-707-5000; crsreports. congress.gov. The research arm of Congress that provides nonpartisan briefing papers on major issues.

MIT Center for Transportation and Logistics, 1 Amherst St., MIT E40, Fl 2, Cambridge, MA 02142; ctl.mit.edu. A university division devoted to supply chain management, research and technology.

National Bureau of Economic Research, 1050 Massachusetts Ave., Cambridge, MA 02138-5398; 617-868-3900; nber.org. Private nonpartisan organization that conducts economic research and disseminates the findings to academics, public policymakers and business professionals.

Office of the United States Trade Representative, 600 17th St., N.W., Washington, DC 20508; 202-395-3230; ustr.gov. Federal agency responsible for negotiating, coordinating and resolving trade disagreements, including those affecting U.S. imports and intellectual property protection issues.

Peterson Institute for International Economics, 1750 Massachusetts Ave., N.W., Washington, DC 20036; 202-328-9000; piie.com. Independent think tank that researches and analyzes global trade and economic issues.

U.S. Department of Commerce, 1401 Constitution Ave., N.W., Washington, DC 20230; 202-482-2000; commerce. gov. Federal department that promotes job creation and economic growth for the U.S. economy.

World Trade Organization, Rue de Lausanne, 154 Case Postale, 1211 Genève 2, Switzerland; +41 (0) 22 739 51 11; wto.org. Global organization that oversees international trade rules and resolves trade disputes.

GUILLERMO ARIAS/AFP via Getty Images

An American soldier helps fortify the U.S.-Mexico border in San Diego in 2018. President Trump has called illegal border crossings a "very serious crisis," but immigration advocates say the administration's policies are partly responsible for the problems.

11

Global Migration

Can governments head off another crisis?

By Sarah Glazer

THE ISSUES

Ricci, a 25-year-old farmer from Honduras, and her 4-year-old son arrived at the U.S. border after a harrowing ordeal.

A member of an indigenous group that has long faced discrimination and violence, Ricci fled Honduras after her husband was murdered in December 2018 and she received death threats.

But her troubles were only beginning. While she was in the border city of Ciudad Juárez in Mexico in March, a man tried to kidnap Ricci's son, and she told U.S. asylum officers she feared it would happen again if she did not receive asylum in the United States. (Her last name is being withheld to protect her privacy.) The Trump administration, however, had just introduced its "Remain in Mexico" policy, requiring asylum-seekers to stay in Mexico while their case is adjudicated.

Ricci says she was sent back to Juárez, considered one of the most dangerous cities in the world, to await a decision in her asylum case—a wait that would last five months. Under U.S. and international law, refugees have a right not to be returned to a country where their life or freedom would be threatened, but Ricci says it was not until her third interview that she was allowed to enter the United States.[1]

Then-Homeland Secretary Kirstjen Nielsen said the administration introduced the policy because migrants were trying to "game" the system and disappearing into the United States. Discouraging this "catch and release" practice would reduce incentives for illegal immigration, Nielsen said in announcing the policy in late 2018.[2]

From *CQ Researcher,*
January 17, 2020

Ricci's story illustrates a political divide over immigration that is playing out across the globe. On one side, President Trump and populist politicians in Europe say immigrants are overrunning their countries, changing the culture and abusing laws aimed at providing asylum for the truly persecuted. On the other side, human rights advocates say governments are shirking their obligation under international treaties to provide refuge for those fleeing persecution or violence.

Inherent in this debate is the anxiety expressed by workers and politicians that migrants depress wages and steal jobs. "They're taking our jobs. They're taking our manufacturing jobs. They're taking our money. They're killing us," Trump, speaking of undocumented Mexican immigrants, said at a Phoenix rally during his presidential campaign.[3]

At the same time, many experts say migrants are needed to fill labor shortages in aging populations in Europe and Asia. By 2050, fewer than half of Europeans over 18 will be working—down from about two-thirds now—because Europe's population is graying, according to Michael Clemens, director of migration at the Center for Global Development, a Washington, D.C., think tank. "That's a drastic shift," he says.

The world is witnessing the highest numbers of migrants on record, nearly 272 million in 2019, more than triple the number in 1970. However, the share of migrants as a percentage of world population remains small at 3.5 percent.[4]

"The population of foreign-born people living outside the country of their birth is still at the same level it's been historically," a share that has generally ranged from 2 to 3 percent since 1890, says Justin Gest, assistant professor of public policy and government at George Mason University and co-author of a 2018 book analyzing how 30 countries regulate immigration.[5]

"That's why it's not really a crisis; the crisis is in governance," he says, pointing to the failure of Europe and other nations to deal with the more than 6 million refugees fleeing the Syrian civil war that began in 2011.

Michael Doyle, a political scientist at Columbia University, agrees the global response has been inadequate. "Migrants have not been vilified in these ways since the 1920s," he says. "The refugee system is failing to respond to the needs of millions."

The global migrant population includes:

- **Asylum-seekers**—those who have traveled to another country seeking protection from persecution but whose cases have yet to be adjudicated;
- **Refugees**—those who have met the requirements for protection under international law, according to the United Nations High Commissioner for Refugees, which identifies, screens and in some cases resettles refugees with partner governments to provide protection; and
- **Other migrants**—those who change their country of permanent residence, although there is no accepted definition of migrant in international law.[6]

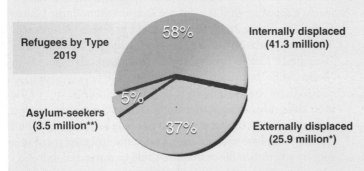

Most Refugees Stay in Their Home Countries

The largest group of refugees—41.3 million—remain within their own countries and are classified by the United Nations as internally displaced. Nearly 30 million others seek protection or asylum elsewhere.

Refugees by Type 2019

- 58% Internally displaced (41.3 million)
- 37% Externally displaced (25.9 million*)
- 5% Asylum-seekers (3.5 million**)

* Figure includes 5.5 million Palestinians defined as refugees.

** Those individuals who have traveled to another country seeking asylum because of persecution but whose cases have yet to be adjudicated. Refugees are defined as those individuals fleeing war, violence or persecution.

Source: "Figures at a Glance," United Nations High Commissioner for Refugees, June 19, 2019, https://tinyurl.com/y4nchokd

Capturing most of the headlines are refugees fleeing violence, war or persecution—70.8 million, according to the United Nations—the highest number since it began tracking refugee movements after World War II. Most refugees have been internally displaced within their own countries—some 41.3 million—while another 20.4 million (not counting Palestinian refugees) have crossed borders, according to the U.N.[7] (*See Graphic.*)

Just three countries account for the majority of refugees, all places where war has dragged on for years: Syria, Afghanistan and South Sudan, the latter an African country racked by civil war since 2013.[8]

Despite attracting most of the attention, refugees are a small minority of all migrants. Most migration is through legal pathways for economic reasons, Gest says, whether it's an American white-collar employee of a multinational firm assigned to London or a Nigerian driving a taxi in Paris. "Most immigration is orderly, safe and regulated," he says.

After the failure of most Western nations to give refuge to Jews during the Holocaust, international compacts sought to help refugees. Under U.S. law, a refugee is a person who is unable or unwilling to return to their home country because of a "well-founded fear of persecution" due to one of five reasons: race, religion, membership in a particular social group, political opinion or national origin. That definition is based on the United Nations' 1951 refugee convention and 1967 Protocol Relating to the Status of Refugees.[9]

However, some experts say this definition, with its individualistic notion of persecution, is too narrow to encompass all who are fleeing more generalized violence or the breakdown of order. For example, the U.N.'s tally of 70 million displaced persons does not include most of the 4 million Venezuelans who have fled the economic collapse and political turmoil in their country.[10] (*See Short Feature.*)

"The 1951 convention standards were designed for the Cold War very explicitly, and they were a political compromise that rested upon a very narrow reed of who is fleeing for emergency purposes—persecution," says Doyle, who recommends the global community broaden the definition of refugees to include those fleeing from any external threat to their life, including climate change.

But most experts, including Doyle, concede that today's anti-immigrant political climate makes a broadened

definition unlikely, and some immigrant advocates fear tinkering with the convention would weaken it.

Under current laws in Europe and the United States, people can only apply for asylum from within the destination country, which often means taking perilous journeys and paying thousands of dollars to smugglers to sneak them across borders. Like Ricci and her son, 70 percent of migrants who cross the Mexico-U.S. border this year will intentionally seek out the U.S. Border Patrol, treating it as an immigration office, and wait to be apprehended, writes David Bier of the Cato Institute, a libertarian think tank in Washington.[11]

"The international refugee regime is fundamentally broken," said T. Alexander Aleinikoff, who served as the U.N. Deputy High Commissioner for Refugees from 2010 to 2015 and now directs the Zolberg Institute on Migration and Mobility at The New School in New York City.[12] He points to European countries like Hungary that have erected fences against refugees.

"We've moved from an era where nations talk about cooperating to shelter refugees and are now talking about cooperation to keep refugees away," says Susan Gzesh, executive director of the Pozen Family Center for Human Rights at the University of Chicago.

In addition, most refugees are "locked in a second exile," languishing in their country of refuge because they are not permitted to work, Aleinikoff says. The majority of refugees live at least five years outside their home territories; half stay over 20 years, according to the U.N.[13]

Today's refugees are often fleeing "forever unsolvable conflicts" based in deep-seated antipathies between people who live side by side but seek power for their ethnic group or religion, says Demetrios G. Papademetriou, co-founder of the Migration Policy Institute, a think tank based in Washington and Brussels.

Papademetriou points to the Syrian civil war, the largest single cause of the migration crisis that sent 1 million people flooding into Europe in 2015. "Suppose [Syrian President Bashar] Assad wins the whole pie?" he asks, "Do we really think Syria will become a society where people will live in harmony?"

Although migrants' share of the world population has risen only slightly since 1960, the number of people moving from the poorer countries of the global south to wealthier Europe and North America more than doubled between 1990 and 2015. Sixty percent of those moving to Europe came from outside the continent.[14]

Increasingly, Doyle says, climate change is influencing the other two main drivers of migration: poverty and civil war. "The Syrian civil war was not caused by drought, but the drought contributed to instability, pushing small farmers into cities [and] delegitimizing the regime. In Central America, the drought has made the viability of small farms much more problematic."

This movement has helped turn public support against immigration, according to University of London migration expert Eric Kaufmann. "Public opinion on immigration tends to sour when [immigrant] numbers increase" and immigrants' ethnicity differs from the nation's majority, he said.[15]

The "appification" of migration is enabling movement.[16] With today's connectivity, "people can see other people's lives and there is much better access to immigration information," says Marie McAuliffe, head of migration policy research for the International Organization for Migration, a U.N.-linked organization in Geneva.

Politicians and critics pushing back against immigration argue that most arrivals are "economic migrants" who fabricate stories of persecution so they can fit the profile of an asylum-seeker.

"Foreign nationals who are seeking irregular entry into the United States are doing so, in most cases, to be able to live and work in this country. A credible fear [of persecution] or asylum claim provides an avenue for them to do so indefinitely," said Andrew R. Arthur, resident fellow in law and policy at the Center for Immigration Studies, a research organization in Washington that advocates for fewer migrants.[17]

But Alexander Betts, professor of forced migration and international affairs at the University of Oxford in England, and Paul Collier, an Oxford economist, have argued there is one good way to tell the difference: Migrants lured by economic hope reach for "honeypots"—rich cities such as New York—while refugees, driven by fear, seek whatever haven they can find.

Except for Germany, the top 10 havens in 2018 were some of the world's poorer nations, chosen for proximity, not economic opportunity: Turkey, Jordan, Lebanon, Pakistan, Iran, Uganda, Sudan, Bangladesh, Ethiopia and Germany.[18]

As migration continues to roil international politics, here are some of the questions the international community, politicians and migration experts are debating:

Is there really a crisis at the U.S.-Mexico border?

"Getting more dangerous. 'Caravans' coming," President Trump tweeted on April 1, 2018, about groups of migrants, many of them mothers with children, traveling together from Central America to the U.S.-Mexico border.[19]

By June of that year, he was describing illegal immigration at the southern border as a "very serious crisis." By October, he said "criminals" were in a caravan and announced he would send the U.S. military to close the border.[20]

The administration and immigration critics noted that arrests of undocumented migrants along the border were surging, reaching nearly 1 million for fiscal 2019, 88 percent more than 2018.[21]

But immigrant advocacy groups and some immigration experts say Trump manufactured the crisis. They note that Trump's crisis declaration occurred at a

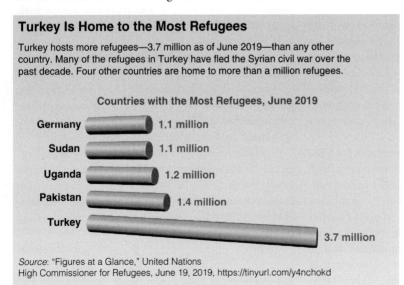

Turkey Is Home to the Most Refugees

Turkey hosts more refugees—3.7 million as of June 2019—than any other country. Many of the refugees in Turkey have fled the Syrian civil war over the past decade. Four other countries are home to more than a million refugees.

Countries with the Most Refugees, June 2019

Germany 1.1 million
Sudan 1.1 million
Uganda 1.2 million
Pakistan 1.4 million
Turkey 3.7 million

Source: "Figures at a Glance," United Nations High Commissioner for Refugees, June 19, 2019, https://tinyurl.com/y4nchokd

time when illegal Mexican immigration at the southern border was in a long-term decline, which most experts ascribed to improving economic conditions in Mexico together with a drop in the growth rate of working-age Mexican men.[22]

In 2017, the number of undocumented immigrants at the southern border reached a more than 40-year low. In 2018, U.S. agents arrested 396,579 people along the border, a 30 percent increase over 2017 but still far below the annual peaks of over 1 million arrested in the 1990s and early 2000s.[23]

"I certainly wouldn't call what's happening at our border a crisis," says Douglas Massey, a professor of sociology and public affairs at Princeton University. "We could deal with what's happening at the border pretty readily if we just admitted them as refugees and asylum-seekers and processed them, just as we did with the Vietnamese boat people who came in the 1970s to '90s. We took in about 1.3 million people. They're all integrated into American society and getting along pretty well."

What created a sense of crisis was not so much the numbers but the change in the kinds of migrants, says Cristobal Ramón, a senior policy analyst at the Bipartisan Policy Center, a Washington think tank that seeks bipartisan solutions to immigration. Central American families with children, a population the U.S. border detention and asylum system was not built to handle, replaced the traditional flow of Mexican male workers, he says.

In addition, a shortage of immigration judges worsened the backlog of cases, which was estimated at more than 1 million as of November 2019, up from about 600,000 in 2017.[24] "That's why the recent arrivals pushed us to the brink," Ramón says.

One reason for the ballooning number of cases is the decision by then-Attorney General Jeff Sessions to effectively put back on the docket more than 320,000 cases previously closed by judges, under a new policy that limits judicial discretion, according to Syracuse University's Transactional Records Access Clearinghouse, which tracks immigration court data.[25]

Under the Obama administration, immigration agencies and judges were directed to prioritize cases that posed threats to border security, national security or public safety from felons.[26] However, the Trump administration removed prosecutorial discretion to decline to prosecute low-priority cases and judicial discretion to

close such cases; this change increased waiting times, says David FitzGerald, co-director of the Center for Comparative Immigration Studies at University of California, San Diego: "U.S. government policy is largely responsible for producing that crisis."

Arthur of the Center for Immigration Studies praises the Trump administration's shift away from the Obama approach of closing cases administratively. "All too often under the Obama administration, this procedure became nothing more than a 'back-door amnesty' for aliens who entered illegally," he wrote.[27]

Ariana Sawyer, a researcher at Human Rights Watch, an international watchdog group, says the Trump administration was wrong to frame the influx as a security crisis of dangerous criminals. "But there is a crisis of families fleeing really serious violence and persecution in Central American countries," she says, citing people she has interviewed who were plagued by gangs that terrorize shopkeepers and their families.

In addition, the administration's "Remain in Mexico" policy has exacerbated the crisis, according to Human Rights Watch. Many families and children are living in unsanitary tent camps while they wait weeks or months in Mexico for their asylum court date. Along the Mexican side of the border, Sawyer says, "we've seen a rise in violence" from criminal Mexican cartels vying for power or territory.

ORLANDO SIERRA/AFP via Getty Images

A caravan of Honduran migrants crosses the Guatemalan border on its way to the United States in January 2019. While President Trump tweeted in 2018, "Getting more dangerous. 'Caravans' coming," human rights advocates say migrants are fleeing persecution at home.

Cartel members will kidnap asylum-seekers, then scroll through their cellphones for numbers of U.S. relatives or friends from whom they demand ransoms of thousands of dollars, she says. "The Trump administration is almost directly enriching these cartels."

The vast majority of Central American asylum-seekers have family members or friends in the United States willing to shelter them in their homes, according to Sawyer, and under previous administrations they could have awaited their court dates with them.

However, the Trump administration contends that policy just led to more undocumented immigrants disappearing into the United States and never showing up for their court dates. Trump condemned the previous process: "Somebody comes into our country . . . and we have to catch them. . . . We then take their names and we bring them to a court—can you believe this?—and we release them. . . . And they go into our country, and . . . then you say, 'Come back in three years for your trial.' " Trump claimed that only 2 percent of those released show up for their immigration hearing. However, Trump administration officials say about 50 percent do, while immigration advocates and some researchers put the figure higher.[28]

"The data show they do show up at pretty reasonable rates," says Ramón, the Bipartisan Policy Center analyst.

Arthur says the main draw for the recent wave of families is the 1997 federal court settlement in *Flores v. Reno*, which limited the time that children could be kept in detention to 20 days and was extended to parents with children. "So it encourages migrants to bring a kid in

anticipation of release," he says. "We need to close the Flores loophole." A federal judge in September 2019 rejected a Trump administration rule that would have put an end to the Flores settlement.[29]

In December 2019, the number of migrants crossing the border dropped for the seventh straight month—by 75 percent from its high point in May 2019, a declining trend for which the administration has claimed credit, although some experts say the drop may reflect usual seasonal trends. "The administration's strategies have brought dramatic results. . . . We have essentially ended catch and release along the southwest border," Customs and Border Patrol acting commissioner Mark Morgan said in October.[30]

Many migrants arrive for economic reasons, not legitimate asylum claims, Arthur says, because the U.S. wage advantage can be as much as 16 times what they can earn at home.

Cato's Bier agrees that many in the current surge are coming for economic reasons, but said the fundamental reason is that asylum is "the only legal process available to them" because waiting for a green card takes up to 65 years.[31]

The solution, he argues, would be to increase the number of temporary work visas, as the United States did under the bracero program for seasonal Mexican farmworkers, which together with tough enforcement led to a dramatic drop in illegal immigration between 1954 and 1964.[32] Until that happens, he says, Central American immigrants will continue to "pound square pegs into round holes" by claiming asylum to gain access to the U.S. job market.

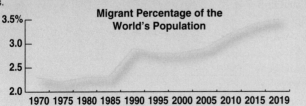

Migrant Share of Population Rises

Migrants make up a larger percentage of the world's population today than they did 50 years ago, but their share remains small. In 1970, 2.3 percent of people worldwide, or 84.5 million people, were migrants. In 2019, 3.5 percent—271.6 million—were migrants.

Migrant Percentage of the World's Population

Source: "World Migration Report 2020," Table 1, International Organization for Migration, Nov. 27, 2019, p. 21, https://tinyurl.com/yj66wo2k

Are Europe's efforts to reduce migration a model for the U.S. and other countries?

The photographs are eerily similar. In one, Oscar Martinez's 23-month-old daughter clings to him as they float in the Rio Grande River after both drowned while trying to cross into the United States in June. In the other, Alan Kurdi, a 3-year-old Syrian, lies face down on a Turkish beach after drowning while trying to cross the Mediterranean in 2015.[33] It was the photo of Alan, some say, that

A woman holds a picture of 3-year-old Alan Kurdi, who drowned in the Mediterranean in 2015, during a rally that year for refugees in Marseille, France. The boy's death produced an outpouring of international sympathy and helped publicize the plight of migrants.

awakened Germany's conscience and led Chancellor Angela Merkel to open Germany's doors to Syrian migrants—if temporarily.

Oxford's Betts said Europe's experience holds lessons for the United States, both negative and positive.

Mexico's agreement to help enforce the Trump administration's Remain in Mexico policy mirrors Europe's failed attempt to set up a similar system to process asylum-seekers outside Europe in Libya and elsewhere, Betts said.[34]

At its embassy in Beirut, Italy annually screens about 1,000 Syrian asylum-seekers who are then flown to Italy if they meet Italian standards, according to the University of California's FitzGerald. "The purpose is to create an illusion that it's possible for refugees to travel safely," he says of these small numbers.

Over the past two and a half years, the European Union (EU) has paid the Libyan coast guard to intercept tens of thousands of migrants and asylum-seekers at sea who were trying to reach Italy. Libya has housed them indefinitely in detention centers with "inhuman and degrading conditions," including sexual exploitation, according to Human Rights Watch.[35]

Betts argued that other policies helped to end Europe's migrant crisis by 2017, and these policies could be a positive model for the United States, notably a 6 billion euro ($6.7 billion) package for Turkey in exchange for its hosting 3.7 million Syrian refugees and

preventing them from continuing to Europe. This deal, together with aid packages to Africa and Jordan to create jobs for refugees, "removed some of the 'push' factors" that caused migrants to flee home and transit countries, he said.[36]

But former U.N. official Aleinikoff calls the Turkey deal "shameful."

"This was business as usual—the global north buying off the global south to keep refugees where they are," he says. "It's a poor model." Instead, the EU and other countries should have agreed that each country would take a share of Syrian refugees, before migrants risked their lives to reach Europe's shores, he argues.

The Turkey deal "has definitely become the model" for the Trump administration's recent "safe third-country" agreements negotiated with Guatemala, Honduras and El Salvador, three nations known collectively as the Northern Triangle, says Columbia University's Doyle, who is critical of those accords. Under the agreements and new Trump administration rules, migrants will not be permitted to apply for asylum at the U.S.-Mexican border unless they have applied for asylum to the first "safe" country they traveled through—namely in the Northern Triangle.[37]

The American Civil Liberties Union (ACLU) and human rights groups are challenging those rules in court. The Trump policy "effectively ends asylum at the southern land border, because everyone but Mexicans transits through a third country," says ACLU attorney Lee Gelernt. "When you learn that Guatemala has only five asylum officers, and the same gangs that persecuted people in El Salvador are there in Guatemala, you understand why that's not a realistic option."

The logic behind a safe third-country agreement is that "it's reasonable to expect a refugee to go to the first country where their life is not in danger," says Arthur of the Center for Immigration Studies, who supports Trump's policy. "Otherwise you're forum-shopping for the best country, and if you pass through a number of countries, that suggests you're an economic migrant"—not a refugee.

But none of those Northern Triangle countries meets the definition under international or U.S. law of a "safe" country, which must have a fair asylum process and be a place where a refugee's life would not be threatened by persecution, according to Gzesh of the Pozen Family Center for Human Rights.[38]

"Those are all countries people are trying to get out of because of fundamental failures of the state to protect human life," she says, noting high levels of government corruption. El Salvador has the highest homicide rate of any country in the world, and Honduras the fourth highest.[39]

Although superficially similar, the U.S. agreements with Central American countries actually bear little resemblance to Europe's agreement with Turkey, says the Migration Policy Institute's Papademetriou. Most of the money for Turkey, he says, went to the refugees themselves—for example as debit cards to pay for rent and groceries—which "demonstrates to the local population that these newcomers are contributors, not just fakers" and helps integrate them into Turkish society. By contrast, critics say, the estimated $143 million in foreign aid that Trump first threatened to withhold and then released in exchange for the Northern Triangle countries' signing the agreements likely will not go to the refugees.[40]

The Trump administration defends the agreements as an effort to share the distribution of hundreds of thousands of asylum claims. "The U.S. asylum system remains overtaxed," the administration said, noting that people from the Northern Triangle countries account for half of asylum claims.[41]

Europe may be facing a new migration crisis, Germany recently warned, stemming from migrants traveling from Turkey to Greece, where migrant camps are already overloaded. Arrivals to Greece in 2019 rose more than 30 percent from 2018. Europe has been unable to come up with an allocation system everyone can agree to, despite the urging of Germany's previously anti-immigrant Interior Minister Horst Seehofer.[42]

The spike may be the result of Turkish President Recep Tayyip Erdogan "again demonstrating he holds the key to how many people can leave," Papademetriou says. Erdogan's government has long complained that it has not received enough money to support its more than 3 million refugees and has disputed that it received all 6 billion euros promised.[43] Erdogan has twice threatened publicly to send refugees on to Europe, most recently as he invaded Syria in October 2019 to create a Turkish-controlled zone there.

"It seems like Erdogan's getting what he wants in money, safe haven and lack of monitoring" of his abuses of democracy, says the University of California's FitzGerald. "That's a pretty high political price that the EU is paying."

Erdogan's behavior demonstrates the danger of such agreements, says the Bipartisan Policy Center's Ramón: "These countries that are buffers may hit a point where they say, 'We can't do this anymore unless you give us more resources.' That's the real issue the Trump administration will face."

Are developed countries doing enough to address the causes of increased migration?

Ever since the 2015 migration crisis, European political leaders have talked increasingly about giving foreign aid to migrants' countries of origin as one way to reduce the "push" factor of poverty and other root causes of emigration.

But the Migration Policy Institute's Papademetriou says Europe's foreign development aid has been too small to make a difference.

And it takes at least a generation before such aid will reduce migration, he and other experts say. The development of a middle class, which requires improved government services, is vital to improving an economy to the point where fewer workers leave—something that has already occurred in the decades-long drop of Mexican migrant workers to the United States.

Yet during this developmental period, Papademetriou says, emigration continues to be a rite of passage for young people who take the view, " 'My father left 30 years ago and found a job in the U.S.; my brother left five years ago. . . . I'm waiting to become 14, 15, 16 to follow the same path.' "

The conundrum is that rising incomes in poor countries almost always lead to more migration, researchers at the Center for Global Development, a Washington think tank, concluded in a review of 71 poor countries whose per capita income has grown since 1960.[44]

When people have more money in their pockets, they invest it in whatever they calculate will improve their lives the most, and sometimes that is migration, says the Center for Global Development's Clemens. That calculation can have surprising results. For example, low-income Guatemalans are using microfinance loans not

Danilo Campailla/SOPA Images/
LightRocket via Getty Images

A young migrant who fled Africa and was rescued by the Italian coast guard waits to be processed in Pozzallo, Italy, in October 2019. The European Union has paid Libya and Turkey to keep migrants and asylum-seekers in their countries.

for their intended purpose of starting small businesses, but to pay smugglers to get them to the United States.[45]

Improving economic conditions also usually lead to better health, with more children surviving to working age, Clemens notes. But the population rise can outstrip the growth in jobs. As countries get wealthier and develop economic links with richer countries, young working-age people are "more likely to have an uncle in Paris or a cousin in Lisbon," Clemens says, and are more savvy about the opportunities abroad.

However, a German study of 25 donor countries and 129 recipient nations found that a different type of aid—improving public services, such as schools, health care and air quality—was associated with falling emigration rates. At the same time, the researchers warned, an "unrealistically large" doubling of aid for public services would be needed to lower emigration rates by 10 to 15 percent.[46]

In Central America, where gang violence is an important spur to the exodus, "there are definitely opportunities to reduce migration pressure," Clemens says. He points to a U.S.-funded neighborhood mentoring program that helped keep youths out of gangs. The program halved the rate of reported homicides in neighborhoods where it operated, according to the study.[47]

Youth jobs programs can reduce emigration modestly in the short term in countries that remain poor, a survey of research by Clemens and his associates found. But no study has found such programs capable of reducing youth

unemployment on a large scale, according to the Center for Global Development's review of the literature.[48]

The more than $2 billion sent by the United States and other donors to Central America over the last few years has not slowed migration, according to Sarah Bermeo, associate director of the Duke University Center for International Development. Much of that aid has been aimed at the donor governments' more immediate self-interests, such as countering narcotics traffic, she said. Even if governments seek to reduce organized crime and corruption, improvements probably will not happen fast enough for parents who "worry about children being raped or killed on the way to school," she wrote.[49]

Efforts to help farmers by, among other things, combating drought and climate change could also reduce pressure to migrate, but those areas have received little foreign aid: Of all the U.S. aid to Guatemala from 2015 to 2017, only 16 percent went to agriculture; the figure in Honduras was 14 percent, and in El Salvador, it was less than 1 percent.[50]

Even more skeptical of aid is Nayla Rush, a researcher at the Center for Immigration Studies, who wonders whether the funds ever reach their intended targets because of corruption. "The West is good at signing blank checks, but it should be more careful about accountability," she says.

Experts say reducing migration caused by civil war or suppression of human rights is difficult. In a review of 19 studies on the impact of aid on violence in countries affected by civil war, Christoph Zürcher, a professor of public and international affairs at the University of Ottawa, concluded, "Aid in conflict zones is more likely to exacerbate violence than dampen violence." He cited instances where those invested in violence have sabotaged aid projects in order to disrupt cooperation between the local population and the government or have even stolen the aid.[51]

Development aid can positively affect human rights and democracy, but the impact "dissipates quickly," according to the Center for Global Development.[52]

Clemens has calculated that raising economic growth by just 1 percentage point a year in an average poor country would require aid equal to 10 percent of the country's GDP, and that a high level of growth would need to be sustained for three generations before it would begin to discourage migration.

"The evidence we have implies that aid would need to act in unprecedented ways, at much higher levels of funding, over generations, to greatly affect some of the most important plausible drivers of emigration," Clemens and co-author Hannah M. Postel wrote.[53]

BACKGROUND

European Emigration

In the 19th century, both colonialism and the desire to secure a better life spurred the movements of people.

By the late 1800s, France, Britain and the Netherlands had gained control over much of the world's Muslim territories: France conquered Algiers in 1830 and later took control of Morocco and Tunisia, along with eight predominantly Muslim countries in West Africa. The British colonized Nigeria and India, which included modern-day Pakistan and Bangladesh. The Dutch dominated trade in Southeast Asia.[54]

During this period, France began importing low-paid workers from Algeria and other African territories, while other European countries recruited workers from their colonies and territories.

Many Europeans also emigrated to the United States. Spurred by the potato famine of 1845-49, more than 2 million Irish left for North America between 1845 and 1855 in overpacked cargo ships, some dying along the way.[55]

By 1853, Boston's population was 40 percent Irish, and a majority were foreign-born. In response to this change, native-born Protestants founded the anti-Catholic, anti-immigrant party dubbed the "Know Nothings" because members took an oath of secrecy. Their goal was to reduce immigration and introduce a 21-year residency requirement for citizenship.[56]

But the first legislation to embody anti-immigrant sentiment was aimed at Chinese laborers, who were recruited by railroad magnates in the 1860s to help build the transcontinental railroad, at one-third the pay of white workers. The Chinese Exclusion Act of 1882, pushed by the Irish Catholic-led Workingmen's Party in California, suspended Chinese immigration for 10 years and declared Chinese immigrants ineligible for citizenship.[57]

Aside from this prohibition, however, open immigration prevailed until the 1920s, says the University of California's FitzGerald. Today's distinction between refugees and economic migrants did not exist, because "if anyone could come in, there was no reason to have a separate refugee policy," he says. At Ellis Island, the immigration station that began operating in New York Harbor in 1892, "the inspectors didn't care if you were fleeing persecution or wanted a better job or were coming to join your family," he notes.

This period saw waves of Italian, Polish, Jewish and other European immigrants arrive in the United States.

But as anti-immigrant sentiment rose, Republican President Warren Harding in 1921 signed the Emergency Immigration Act, which set quotas for European countries at 3 percent of their representation in the 1910 immigration population, thus slashing immigration from Poland by 70 percent and from Italy by 82 percent.[58]

In 1924, the National Origins Quota Act was even more favorable to Northern and Western Europeans by pegging quotas to the 1890 immigration population: one-half of the quota went to immigrants from Britain.[59]

A major justification for these restrictions was the pseudoscience of eugenics, which had captured the imagination of some leading intellectuals and politicians by confirming ethnic stereotypes and ranking people from Eastern and Southern Europe as genetically inferior to Western Europeans.[60]

Republican President Calvin Coolidge, who signed the Quota Act, had previously declared as vice president: "America must be kept American. Biological laws show . . . that Nordics deteriorate when mixed with other races."[61]

1930s, World War II and the Aftermath

The Great Depression made the United States a less attractive destination in the 1930s. Support for the quotas remained strong, even as German leader Adolf Hitler began his campaign of persecution against Jews that ended in genocide. In one of the most shameful incidents, the United States in 1939 refused to let the *St. Louis*, a ship carrying more than 900 mainly Jewish refugees from Germany, land on American shores, and the vessel was forced to return to Europe. More than 250 passengers eventually died in the Holocaust.

Keystone/Hulton Archive/Getty Images

Refugees crowd the deck of the *St. Louis* as it sailed to the United States in June 1939. Jewish refugees were seeking a haven from Nazi persecution, but the ship was denied entry and it returned to Europe.

Jews trying to flee Europe were restricted by the national origin quotas; three months before the *St. Louis* sailed, a bill had died in Congress that would have permitted 20,000 German Jewish children to enter in an exception to the existing quota.[62]

During World War II, which was fought from 1939 to 1945, some 175 million people were displaced in both Asia and Europe, amounting to almost 8 percent of the world's population, according to historians.

Six million European Jews died in the Holocaust. At the end of the war, hundreds of thousands of Jews emerged from concentration camps and hiding places to a world where they no longer had homes. The failure to protect Jews from the Nazis, combined with growing Western concern about Soviet suppression of dissidents during the Cold War, galvanized the global community.

In 1951, the recently formed United Nations adopted the Convention Relating to the Status of Refugees, which has been signed by 145 nations, outlining the rights of refugees and nations' obligations to protect them. For the first time, refugees received a distinct legal status. The convention defined refugees as people with a "well-founded fear of being persecuted" who are unable or unwilling to return to their former country. Member countries cannot return refugees against their will to a country where they would be in danger, under a provision known as "non-refoulement."[63]

However, those nations did not agree to a binding legal obligation to receive a certain number of refugees in their territory. "The absence of any such mechanism is a driving force behind the . . . present-day dysfunction" of the refugee system, former U.N. official Aleinikoff and co-author Leah Zamore wrote.[64]

The United States did not sign the 1951 convention, instead adopting its own laws protecting selected groups of refugees. The 1953 Refugee Relief Act allowed in approximately 190,000 refugees, many from Communist regimes, before it expired in 1956.[65]

In 1965, Democratic President Lyndon Johnson signed the Immigration and Nationality Act. It replaced quotas based on national origin with preferences based largely on family connections. At the time, the bill's sponsors assured members of Congress that the legislation would not lead to any change in the composition of immigrants, who were then mainly European. "Few imagined that the legislation would lead the country to become increasingly non-European in origin in the ensuing decades," writes the University of London's Kaufmann.[66]

In 1960, nearly 75 percent of U.S. immigration was from Europe, but by 2010 more than 80 percent was from Latin America or Asia.[67]

The United Nations Refugee Protocol in 1967 established current international refugee standards for 146 countries, including the United States. It expanded the definition of refugee beyond those who had been displaced in Europe before 1951, but allowed member nations to define for themselves how they would evaluate refugee status. By ratifying the protocol, the United States bound itself to the 1951 Refugee Convention.[68]

Postwar Immigration Trends

Europe did not become a major immigrant destination until the 1950s, when it began recruiting workers from

CHRONOLOGY

19th Century *European colonialism presages later migration.*

1830 France conquers Algeria; its North African colonization lays groundwork for 20th-century migration of Algerian, Moroccan and Tunisian workers to France seeking better living conditions.

1845 Potato famine leads to migration of more than 2 million Irish to North America over the decade.

1882 Chinese Exclusion Act suspends Chinese immigration to United States for 10 years.

1920s-1970s *After global failure to protect Jews during Holocaust, treaties seek to shield refugees from persecution.*

1921 In the United States, Emergency Immigration Act sets quotas for European countries at 3 percent of 1910 immigration population, slashing immigration from Eastern and Southern Europe.

1924 U.S. Quota Act limits migrants from Eastern and Southern Europe even further, favoring immigrants from Britain and Northern Europe.

1939 The U.S. refuses to let the *St. Louis*, a ship carrying more than 900 mainly Jewish refugees from Germany, land on American shores; after the vessel is forced to return to Europe, more than 250 passengers die in the Holocaust.

1951 United Nations adopts Convention Relating to the Status of Refugees, signed by 145 nations, outlining rights of refugees.

1953 U.S. Refugee Relief Act admits refugees, many from Communist regimes.

1965 U.S. Immigration and Nationality Act eliminates national origin quotas and introduces preferences based on family connections, resulting years later in an upsurge of immigration from Latin America and Asia.

1967 U.N. Refugee Protocol establishes current international refugee standards for 146 countries, including the United States; expands the definition of

refugee beyond those displaced in Europe before 1951 but allows member nations to define how to evaluate refugee status.

1975 Vietnamese refugees arrive in United States after fall of South Vietnam to the Communist North.

1980s-2000s *Terrorist attacks, rising immigration raise opposition to migrants in Europe and United States.*

1980 Cuban leader Fidel Castro allows thousands to leave for the United States in Mariel boatlift.

1986 Republican President Ronald Reagan signs Immigration Reform and Control Act, combining tougher border enforcement with amnesty for undocumented immigrants.

2001 Al Qaeda attacks World Trade Center in New York City and the Pentagon near Washington, killing 3,000. Republican President George W. Bush suspends refugee admissions for several months.

2005 U.S. Congress rejects bipartisan bill combining more border enforcement with a temporary worker program and path to citizenship for undocumented immigrants.

2009 Democrat Barack Obama becomes president, pledging immigration reform.

2010-Present *Syrian civil war spurs refugee flight to Europe, which aims to stem flow.*

2010 Ordinances in 370 U.S. jurisdictions require police to check immigrant status of those stopped. . . . Anti-immigration parties make unprecedented electoral gains in Europe. . . . Immigration reform bill fails again in U.S. Congress.

2011 Syrian exodus begins as civil war intensifies. . . . Libya becomes hub for smuggling refugees.

2013 Immigration reform fails once again in U.S. Congress.

2014 Refugee crossings of Mediterranean to Europe increase.

2015 European migration crisis intensifies as thousands of refugees drown in Mediterranean. Hungary announces it will build fence on border with Serbia. . . . European Union (EU) adopts refugee quota scheme, but Hungary, Poland and Czech Republic refuse to participate.

2016 Under deal with the EU, Turkey agrees to stop refugees heading to Europe. . . . New York Declaration signed at U.N. presages 2018 Global Compacts to cooperate on migration and refugees. . . . Republican Donald Trump wins presidency on anti-immigrant platform. . . . For first time, more non-Mexicans than Mexicans are arrested trying to cross southwest U.S. border illegally.

2017 EU declares European migration crisis over. . . . Mexicans are no longer the majority of undocumented

immigrants living in the United States, but are still the dominant group, followed by Central Americans and Asians.

2018 President Trump declares "crisis" on Mexican border; the administration refuses to sign U.N. Global Compacts on migration or refugees, saying they violate U.S. sovereignty. In December, family members make up more than half of arrests at southern border, most of them from El Salvador, Guatemala and Honduras.

2019 U.S. plans to admit only 18,000 refugees in fiscal 2020, a historically low number. . . . Civil rights groups challenge Trump administration rules restricting asylum-seekers at Mexican border and sending most to wait in Mexico. . . . House passes bill giving migrant farmworkers path to citizenship.

abroad to rebuild cities and economies ravaged by World War II. West Germany, Belgium and Sweden initiated guest-worker programs, recruiting laborers first from Italy and Spain and later from North Africa and the Middle East. However, many of the workers recruited to West Germany wanted to stay, and corporations pressured the government to make guest-worker contracts renewable and allow family members to join them.[69]

By the late 1960s and early '70s, Europe's industries were declining, and its need for overseas manpower was dwindling. As unemployment rose, anti-immigrant sentiment grew.[70]

During the 1970s and 1980s, the United States took in selected groups of immigrants fleeing Communist regimes. In 1975, the fall of South Vietnam to the Communist North sent a surge of Vietnamese and Cambodians to the United States, many fleeing in flimsy boats. In response, Congress passed a law in 1975 permitting 130,000 Vietnamese to enter the United States. In 1977 Democratic President Jimmy Carter allowed 15,000 of these "boat people" to become permanent residents. The Refugee Act of 1980 laid out procedures for admission of refugees and remains in effect.[71]

In April 1980, Cuban leader Fidel Castro announced that all Cubans wishing to leave the Caribbean island for

the United States were free to board boats at the port of Mariel west of Havana. Thousands took boats to Florida, but the Mariel boatlift became a political problem for Carter once it was revealed that Castro had freed many of the immigrants from jails and mental hospitals. The exodus ended in October 1980 by mutual agreement between Cuba and the United States.[72]

In 1986, Republican President Ronald Reagan signed the Immigration Reform and Control Act. It combined tougher border enforcement and penalties for employers who hired undocumented people with legalization for unauthorized immigrants. The legalization section, often described as an amnesty, allowed undocumented immigrants who had been in the country for five years or more to apply for temporary legal status, which could lead to permanent legal status. A separate program also permitted those who had performed seasonal agricultural service during the previous year to legalize their status. In signing the bill, Reagan said it would permit undocumented workers to come out of the shadows and "step into the sunlight."[73]

Rising Anti-Immigrant Sentiment

The dramatic increase in U.S. immigration from 300,000 per year in 1965 to more than 1 million by the 1990s—together with an increasingly Latin American

Working-Class Alienation Sparks Anti-Immigrant Mood

Feelings of displacement drive support for right-wing populism.

"All these Eastern Europeans that are coming in, where are they flocking from?"

Gillian Duffy, a white working-class woman from Rochdale, one of England's poorest towns, asked Prime Minister Gordon Brown that question during the 2010 election campaign. After their broadcast conversation had ended, Brown forgot to turn off his microphone and described Duffy to an aide as "a bigoted woman."

When that comment became public, Brown was widely criticized, and he later apologized to Duffy. The episode was a sign that the cultural mood was shifting away from the view that criticism of immigration was always bigoted, and toward a more sympathetic portrayal of white working-class concerns, wrote Eric Kaufmann, a professor of politics at the University of London, in his 2019 book, *Whiteshift: Populism, Immigration, and the Future of White Majorities.*[1]

Justin Gest, assistant professor of public policy and government at George Mason University and the author of a 2018 book called *The White Working Class*, says working-class whites are "aware of their political abandonment by the parties on the left, which once championed unions and the white working class—and no longer do so." He says many center-left parties turned away from their traditional advocacy of economic justice for workers and focused more on racial and social justice for minorities. "As a result, it is only natural that some white working-class people may perceive that they've been displaced by people of immigrant origins."

Kaufmann's and Gest's books are among several recently published that try to explain why much of the white working class has shifted to the right politically. Kaufmann analyzes research showing that in continental Europe, Great Britain and the United States, change in the ethnic makeup of a neighborhood or region—not economics—"nearly always predicts increased anti-immigration sentiment and populist-right voting."[2]

In a city, region or country, support for right-wing populism tends to rise as the immigrant or minority share of the population increases, 27 studies found. A majority of studies said native white opposition to immigration or support for the populist right was linked to ethnic change over time, according to a meta-analysis co-authored by Kaufmann.

For individuals Kaufmann describes as "psychological conservatives"—those who judge their nation according to the world they knew growing up—"ethnic changes are particularly jarring as they disrupt the sense of attachment to locale, ethnic group and nation," Kaufmann wrote.[3]

In the aftermath of the 2016 Brexit vote backing the United Kingdom's departure from the European Union (EU), journalist David Goodhart tried to explain the outcome of the referendum to shocked liberals in his book *The Road to Somewhere.*

He calls pro-Brexit voters the "Somewheres"—people "nostalgic for a lost Britain," rooted in their place of birth, who identify as a Scottish farmer or Cornish housewife and place a high value on familiarity, he wrote. They often lack higher education, "have lost economically with the decline of well-paid jobs" for people without a college degree and "feel uncomfortable about many aspects of cultural and economic change," such as mass immigration, he said. By contrast,

and Asian population seen as culturally distant from the nation's white Christian majority—led to rising anti-immigrant sentiments, according to Kaufmann. In 1965, Gallup polls showed 33 percent of Americans wanted a decrease in immigration; by 1993 that figure had risen to 65 percent.[74]

Terrorist attacks, particularly by Islamic radicals, fueled new fears of migrants in both Europe and the United States. After the Sept. 11, 2001, attacks on the World Trade Center in New York City and the Pentagon near Washington, Republican President George W. Bush suspended refugee admissions for several months. Caps on refugees accepted by the United States remained around 80,000 per year from 2001 to 2015.[75]

By 2010, 370 American jurisdictions had passed Illegal Immigration Relief Ordinances, many of which

"Anywheres" are voters who support remaining in the EU and tend to be university-educated with white-collar jobs. They feel comfortable living in almost any cosmopolitan city abroad—and they are not bothered by immigration.[4]

When liberals propose to make it easier for young Africans to move to Western Europe to supply its aging population's labor needs, Goodhart has argued, those liberals ignore the fact that good societies are typified by high levels of trust, and that "increasing diversity can also reduce the readiness to share"—particularly in societies with generous social welfare programs.[5]

Oxford University economist Paul Collier, who grew up in the dying English steel town of Sheffield, recalls how a neighbor lost his job and a relative ended up with a job cleaning toilets. In his 2018 book *The Future of Capitalism*, he sees widening economic inequality and high youth unemployment behind the growing power of right-wing, anti-immigrant parties such as the Alternative for Germany (AfD) and the National Rally party in France headed by Marine Le Pen.[6]

But some researchers say racism, rather than fear of losing jobs, explains white working-class support for anti-immigration policies and politicians. In England, white working-class support for Brexit was linked more to hostility toward black and brown immigrants than to opposition to immigrants from other EU countries, some polls indicate.[7]

An anti-migrant poster unveiled by the pro-Brexit UK Independence Party (UKIP) during the Brexit campaign showed a stream of Middle Eastern and other mostly non-white migrants and refugees. The poster urged voters to "break free of the EU and take back control of our borders." Trade union officials branded it as "an attempt to incite racial hatred."[8]

Collier said the working class has been left out of the "fashionable 'victim' groups" for which the left has advocated assistance, adding that what he calls traditional working-class values, such as respect for meeting obligations and "a shared sense of belonging to place," have fallen out of policy discussions.[9]

To avert a far-right takeover, countries should try to find a balance in immigration policy, Kaufmann argued. "Immigration will need to be slower than is economically optimal, but the result should be a more harmonious society," he wrote.[10]

A century from now, Kaufmann says, societies that are currently majority-white are likely to become more multi-ethnic through intermarriage and the successful integration of minorities. In the United States, where half of newborns are Latino, Asian or black, the nation is projected to become "majority minority" in the 2040s.[11]

His prediction: "When the majority sees itself as having a largely mixed-race future, it may become more open to immigration."[12]

— Sarah Glazer

[1] Eric Kaufmann, *Whiteshift: Populism, Immigration, and the Future of White Majorities* (2019), pp. 179-180.

[2] *Ibid.*, p. 18.

[3] *Ibid.*, pp. 218-19, 69.

[4] David Goodhart, *The Road to Somewhere: The Populist Revolt and the Future of Politics* (2017), p. 19.

[5] *Ibid.*, pp. 21-22.

[6] Paul Collier, *The Future of Capitalism: Facing the New Anxieties* (2018), pp. 5, 7.

[7] Kaufmann, *op. cit.*, pp. 182-183.

[8] Heather Stewart and Rowena Mason, "Nigel Farage's anti-migrant poster reported to police," *The Guardian*, June 16, 2016, https://tinyurl.com/zhj5m8a.

[9] Collier, *op. cit.*, pp. 16, 212.

[10] Kaufmann, *op. cit.*, p. 28.

[11] William H. Frey, "New Projections Point to a Majority Minority Nation in 2044," Brookings Institution, Dec. 12, 2014, https://tinyurl.com/y9c4qgy3.

[12] Kaufmann, *op. cit.*, p. 28.

required police to check the immigration status of those apprehended or questioned. Many of these areas had experienced rapid ethnic change with the arrival of Hispanic immigrants. At the same time, nearly 100 state and local governments declared their support of unauthorized immigrants by establishing "sanctuaries," places where they refused to check immigrants' documents.

In Europe, politics turned more quickly anti-immigrant than in the United States. By the early 2000s, anti-immigrant political parties had gained enough support from voters to bargain for concessions from coalitions of mainstream parties in Austria, Norway, the Netherlands, Denmark and Italy.

Across Europe, the crisis of 2015, when more than 1 million asylum-seekers reached European shores from

Venezuelan Exodus Could Become World's Largest

More than 4 million flee failing economy, dire social conditions.

When her parents arrived in Westchester County, N.Y., from Venezuela for a visit two years ago, Angelica Arrayago was shocked by their physical condition. Her father was "almost blind" from diabetes that had gone untreated because the country's hospitals had run out of insulin; her mother was skinny and "blackened from the sun" after spending as long as six hours in line waiting for government-subsidized rice.

Conditions in Venezuela have only worsened as the country has suffered from record inflation rates of 1.7 million percent. Under the authoritarian rule of socialist Nicolás Maduro, who became president in 2013, the economy has collapsed and violence has increased.[1]

Some 4.6 million people, about 16 percent of Venezuela's population, have fled the country over the past four years, and that figure could rise to 6.5 million by the end of 2020, according to the United Nations High Commissioner for Refugees, the world body's refugee agency.[2] Ninety percent of the country lives below the poverty line, and only 3 percent of Venezuelans can afford to eat three meals a day. Hospitals have run out of the most basic supplies—even paper on which to take medical notes.[3]

"There's no medicine; babies die, and pregnant women come [to Peru] because there's no postnatal care," says Luisa Feline Freier, assistant professor of political science at Universidad del Pacífico in Lima, Peru, who recently interviewed 2,000 Venezuelans in Peru. "Many children have not been in school for months or years because all their teachers have migrated. This is survival migration. These are middle-class people who sold all their belongings maybe to get a bus ticket—in order not to have to walk."

So far the Venezuelan exodus has received far less attention and foreign aid than other refugee crises around the world, even though experts at the Brookings Institution think tank in Washington have predicted it could soon outpace the Syrian crisis and is "one of the worst humanitarian crises this hemisphere has ever seen."[4]

That is partly because neighboring South American countries, which have been receiving most of the refugees, have been comparatively welcoming. *The Economist* magazine calculated that outside donors have given just $100 for each Venezuelan migrant compared with $5,000 for each of the 5.6 million refugees from the conflict in Syria.[5]

But recently, anti-immigrant sentiment has been rising in neighboring countries. Crimes committed by Venezuelan immigrants have been sensationalized in the media, and many recent migrants are poorer than earlier arrivals. In August, Ecuador became the latest country to tighten entry requirements, joining Peru and Chile in requiring most Venezuelans to present a passport and evidence of a clean criminal record.[6]

However, passports are almost impossible to obtain in Venezuela, Freier says. Applicants have to pay up to $5,000 under the table, wait times are long and there is not enough paper on which to print documents, she says.

Nearly 80 percent of Venezuelan refugees are in Latin American and Caribbean countries, according to the U.N. refugee agency; the top four destinations are Colombia, Peru, Ecuador and Chile.[7]

Brazil and Colombia have kept their borders open so far. However, Daphne Panayotatos, an advocate at Refugees International, a refugee advocacy organization, calls Colombia "a ticking time bomb," pointing to recent street protests against corruption, government-proposed cuts in pensions and police violence as well as the prominence of drug and trafficking groups on the border who prey on migrants.

South American countries have been more generous than Europe or the United States in dealing with migrant surges. But "they've been less generous than they should have been," Freier says, citing the broad refugee definition South American countries adopted under the 1984 Cartagena Declaration on Refugees. The definition includes people fleeing "circumstances which have seriously disturbed public order."[8]

Under that declaration, governments cannot deport anyone who qualifies for refugee status until the situation in their home country improves, and refugees would have access to health care and education. However, Venezuela's neighboring governments have not applied the Cartagena declaration due to a "huge increase in xenophobic sentiment" among the public and politicians' fears about a political backlash, Freier says.

The Cartagena definition is broader than the one used by most countries, including the United States, under the United Nations' 1951 Convention on Refugees. That treaty restricts the definition to those who fear persecution. Nevertheless, under pressure from human rights activists, the U.N. refugee agency in May said it considered most Venezuelan migrants to be refugees in need of international protection.[9]

In November 2019, the U.N. agency began a campaign to raise $1.35 billion to help Venezuelan refugees and their host countries with health care and education, calling on nations to donate. However, previous funding efforts have fallen short.

"The Syrian crisis is much more immediate for Europe—it is much closer than the Venezuelan crisis for them," said Eduardo Stein, the joint special representative for Venezuelan refugees and migrants for both the United Nations High Commissioner for Refugees and the International Organization for Migration, an intergovernmental organization that aids migrants and governments.[10]

Since 2017, the Trump administration has imposed sanctions to choke off revenues to Venezuela's government in an effort aimed at toppling the Maduro regime.[11] In August, President Trump imposed new sanctions freezing the property and assets of the Venezuelan government, citing the "continued usurpation of power" by Maduro and his attempts to undermine opposition leader Juan Guaidó, who last year declared himself interim president with the support of the Trump administration.[12]

New York Times columnist Nicholas Kristof recently asked whether U.S. sanctions on Maduro's government were making the situation worse. He cited an economic analysis that found decreases in oil revenues produced by the sanctions led to a loss of $17 billion a year for the economy and deteriorating living conditions. Although the sanctions were intended to undermine the Maduro regime, Kristof wrote, they "have failed to drive Maduro from power, inflicting anguish instead on vulnerable Venezuelans."[13]

Gustav Brauckmeyer, a Venezuelan business consultant living in Lima, disagrees: "There's no stopping the migrant crisis unless there's a change in government, and that's why there has to be more regional pressure. The feeling people have in Venezuela is, if we don't do it soon, we'll be stuck for a long time."

— Sarah Glazer

[1] Alexander Betts, "Nowhere to Go," *Foreign Affairs*, November/December 2019, https://tinyurl.com/r6aa9e2.

[2] Danny Bahar and Meagan Dooley, "Venezuela refugee crisis to become the largest and most underfunded in modern history," Brookings Institution, Dec. 9, 2019, https://tinyurl.com/uvlq7sv.

[3] "Joint IOM-UNHCR Press Release: USD 1.35 billion Needed to Help Venezuelan Refugees and Migrants and Host Countries," International Organization for Migration, Nov. 13, 2019, https://tinyurl.com/qqs6h34; Betts, *op. cit.*; and Nicholas Kristof, "Venezuela's Kids Are Dying. Are We Responsible?" *The New York Times*, Nov. 23, 2019, https://tinyurl.com/vq2w7os. Also see, Luisa Feline Freier and Nicolas Parent, "The Regional Response to the Venezuelan Exodus," *Current History*, February 2019, pp. 56-61, https://tinyurl.com/w5vm7ve.

[4] Bahar and Dooley, *op. cit.*

[5] "Millions of refugees from Venezuela are straining neighbours' hospitality," *The Economist*, Sept. 12, 2019, https://tinyurl.com/y2rykatc.

[6] *Ibid.*

[7] "U.S. $1.35 billion needed to help Venezuelan refugees and migrants and host countries," U.N. High Commissioner for Refugees, Nov. 13, 2019, https://tinyurl.com/uzxqj3e.

[8] Betts, *op. cit.*

[9] "Majority fleeing Venezuela in need of refugee protection—UNHCR," U.N. High Commissioner for Refugees, May 21, 2019, https://tinyurl.com/ru58v36.

[10] "Venezuelan migrants will need $1.35b in 2020 for basic services, say aid groups," *Reuters*, Nov. 14, 2019, https://tinyurl.com/ry3qqgb.

[11] "Venezuela: Overview of U.S. Sanctions," Congressional Research Service, Oct. 16, 2019, https://tinyurl.com/uf2m3c2.

[12] Michael Crowley and Anatoly Kurmanaev, "Trump Imposes New Sanctions on Venezuela," *The New York Times*, Aug. 6, 2019, https://tinyurl.com/sl3xh72.

[13] Francisco Rodríguez, "Trump Doesn't Have Time for Starving Venezuelans," *The New York Times*, July 10, 2019, https://tinyurl.com/uu9yfm3; Kristof, *op. cit.*

the Middle East and Africa, gave populist right-wing parties "a shot in the arm," Kaufmann said. But anti-immigrant feeling had already been building on the continent. In nine of 10 European countries, support for populist right-wing parties closely tracked rising immigration rates.[76]

In the United States, divisions in Congress stymied efforts at immigration reform. In 2005, a bipartisan bill that would have combined stricter border enforcement with a temporary worker program, a path to citizenship and the so-called Dream Act to legalize the status of immigrants who entered the country as children failed to pass Congress. Democratic President Barack Obama took office in 2009 promising to forge an immigration compromise. But in 2010 and 2013 immigration reform bills were defeated again.[77]

In September 2016, Obama hosted a meeting on the global refugee crisis at the U.N. General Assembly. He called for world leaders to double the number of refugees they resettled and to provide more aid. The nations signed the New York Declaration, expressing their intent to initiate two new conventions, one on refugees and a second on migration, to foster more sharing of burdens, but neither was legally binding.[78]

In 2016, real estate tycoon Donald Trump campaigned for the Republican presidential nomination on an anti-immigrant platform, blaming Mexican immigrants for a crime wave (contrary to evidence) and claiming many of them were "drug dealers, criminals and rapists."[79]

After Trump's election, his administration refused to sign the U.N. Global Compact on Migration, which was adopted by representatives of 164 nations in December 2018, or the Global Compact on Refugees, adopted that same month by 181 countries.[80]

The U.S. ambassador to the United Nations at the time, Nikki Haley, wrote later that the deal breaker for the administration was the migration compact's advocacy for international law, rather than individual countries, to govern migration. "Only we will decide how best to control our borders and who will be allowed to enter our country," she wrote, adding the compact was "headed toward creating an international right to migration, which . . . is not compatible with U.S. sovereignty."[81]

CURRENT SITUATION
New European Crisis

Fears of another European migration crisis are growing following a spike in the number of migrants arriving in Greece from Turkey. Nearly 44,000 migrants traveled that route between January and November of 2019, about one-third more than all of 2018 but still far below the levels of 2015 and 2016.[82]

Expressing frustration with the EU's inability to come up with a system to allocate asylum-seekers country-by-country once again this year, German Interior Minister Seehofer said in October, "If there is no common European asylum policy, there is a danger that uncontrolled immigration will once again take place throughout Europe."[83]

More Afghans are fleeing their country after 2018 turned out to be the country's deadliest year to date, and Turkish policies are making it harder for refugees to stay there. Turkey has carried out mass deportations of Afghans in the past two years, tightened residency requirements and changed its asylum procedures to make it harder for Afghans to gain legal status. Many are making their way to Greece.

With tens of thousands of Afghan and Syrian migrants packed onto the Greek islands in miserable conditions, the Council of Europe's commissioner for human rights, Dunja Mijatovic, called the situation "explosive." Over human rights groups' objections, the Greek government passed legislation on Oct. 31, 2019, that would speed up asylum procedures and permit it to return more migrants to Turkey.[84]

In recent months, Turkey's Erdogan has repeatedly threatened to "open the gates" of migration to pressure Europe to support his goal of a "safe zone" in northern Syria that would be free of Kurdish fighters, a threat he made again in October 2019 in the face of European opposition to his invasion to create such a zone. Thousands of Syrian Kurds have fled to Iraq; the Turkish military campaign displaced some 200,000 people.[85]

In September 2019, German's interior ministry urged Greece to step up deportations to Turkey and called for a more comprehensive implementation of the 2016 EU-Turkey deal, under which Turkey agreed to stop migrants from leaving its shores for Europe in exchange for 6 billion euros. The EU-Turkey deal was set to expire at the end of 2019, and a new deal is being negotiated.[86]

In Libya, the other country that Europe tasked with holding migrants, the United Nations announced a second airlift of children and other vulnerable migrants in October out of detention centers to Rwanda. Earlier in July, the U.N. called for all Libyan detention centers to be closed, describing conditions as "awful."[87]

The European Court of Justice, Europe's highest court, is expected to rule early this year on its Advocate General's opinion that three countries—Poland, Hungary and the Czech Republic—broke EU law when they refused to participate in the EU's 2015 quota scheme for migrants. The court usually follows the advocate's opinions.[88]

As the EU continues to struggle with efforts to allocate migrants among its members, the Migration Policy Institute's Papademetriou says it should take a lesson from its "Pyrrhic victory" in passing an allocation formula in 2015: "Those who lost told everyone to take a walk." He says a refugee-sharing solution should not be imposed but negotiated country-by-country so governments can select the migrants they want. For example, "If countries don't want to take Muslims, maybe they can take Christians," he says.

U.S. Developments

President Trump continues to take a hard line on the entry of both refugees and migrants, but several of his most controversial changes face legal challenges.

Under the U.N. refugee resettlement program, the United States plans to admit a maximum of 18,000 refugees in fiscal 2020, down from a presidentially imposed ceiling of 30,000 for the fiscal year ending in September 2019—the third consecutive year the administration has lowered the cap. This would be the fewest number of refugees resettled by the United States in a single year since 1980, when Congress created the resettlement program.[89]

The Trump administration has cited "enormous security challenges" posed by refugees and said it needs to focus on the influx of asylum-seekers at the Mexican border. However, refugee groups say under the resettlement program, U.S. authorities are turning away thousands of refugees who have already been screened and vetted by the U.N. and the State Department. Refugees under the U.N. resettlement program apply from outside the United States, whereas asylum-seekers apply from inside the country.[90]

In November 2019, U.S. officials began deporting some asylum-seekers at the Mexican border to Guatemala, including families and children, under a new rule preventing anyone from seeking asylum in the United States if they have passed through Guatemala, Honduras or El Salvador without seeking asylum there first.[91]

Although the ACLU and other civil liberties groups are challenging the rule, the Supreme Court said in September that the administration can enforce it while the legal fight works its way through other courts.[92]

In Guatemala, new President Alejandro Giammattei had criticized the Trump administration agreement with the outgoing government to accept deported asylum-seekers and make them seek asylum there first. He took office on Jan. 14, 2020, and has said he will review the agreement.[93]

Under the Trump administration's Remain in Mexico policy, more than 50,000 asylum-seekers at the southern border have been returned to Mexico to await the adjudication of their cases. A federal appeals court in May ruled that the government may continue to implement that policy while the court reaches a decision on the merits of legal challenges. Immigration advocacy groups challenging the policy presented arguments in October 2019 before the 9th Circuit Court of Appeals.[94]

Human rights groups also have criticized the government's policy of limiting the number of people who can apply for asylum each day at the southern border, adding to squalid conditions at encampments in northern Mexico. The policy, known as metering, kept an additional 21,398 asylum-seekers on waitlists in 11 Mexican border cities in November, the University of Texas' Strauss Center for International Security and Law and the Center for U.S.-Mexican Studies reported.[95]

In December, the U.S. House passed the bipartisan Farm Workforce Modernization Act to give thousands of undocumented migrant farmworkers temporary work permits and a pathway to citizenship. Undocumented workers make up about half the farm workforce. The bill passed 260-165, with 34 Republicans supporting it. Although it has backing from both liberals and

AT ISSUE

Is the Trump administration justified in accepting fewer refugees than in the past?

YES

Nayla Rush, Ph.D.
Senior Researcher, Center for Immigration Studies

Written for *CQ Researcher*, January 2020

Those outraged by lower refugee ceilings under the Trump administration are less mindful of its efforts to assist millions of refugees overseas and address the lingering U.S. asylum backlog.

Away from alarming stands, let's try to put matters (or numbers) into perspective.

Out of some 26 million refugees worldwide, and the 1.2 million refugees in need of resettlement according to the U.N. High Commissioner for Refugees (UNHCR), only 81,337 were referred for resettlement in 2018 (0.3 percent of all refugees and 7 percent of those considered to be in need of resettlement).

Despite dropping admissions, the United States under the Trump administration remains the top country for refugee resettlement in the world.

Resettlement is just the tip of the iceberg of refugee protection. The United States remains the leading donor of humanitarian assistance. In fiscal 2018 alone, the U.S. contribution to UNHCR reached a high of $1.6 billion.

U.S. humanitarian efforts include assisting thousands of asylum-seekers already present on American soil. These are vulnerable people seeking relief under the same standard as refugees. The United States received the greatest number of new asylum applications worldwide in calendar years 2017 and 2018 and anticipates receiving 350,000 new asylum claims in fiscal 2020.

The current debate about resettled refugees often revolves around numbers (how many should be allowed in?) while little attention is given to the fairness of the selection process and the scope of U.S integration practices (what happens after they get here?).

Resettlement must be a ticket out only for refugees who are genuinely at risk in the countries hosting them. But contrary to common claims, for most resettlement is not a matter of life and death. Only 17 percent of UNHCR global resettlement submissions in 2018 were urgent or emergency ones. A refugee ceiling of 18,000 would cover most if not all the U.N.'s urgent and emergency submissions worldwide this coming year.

Moreover, resettled refugees should be provided with every tool possible for successful integration. Admitting fewer refugees but spending more on each one can ensure they receive the

NO

Jen Smyers
Director of Policy and Advocacy, Immigration and Refugee Program, Church World Service

Written for *CQ Researcher*, January 2020

For centuries, advocates of immigration restrictions have relied on the same four arguments to keep out generations of immigrants: scare tactics, economic scapegoating, perceived scarcity and false choices. These tired excuses, used in an attempt to justify drastic cuts to refugee resettlement, are just as factually inaccurate and morally bankrupt now as when they were used to slander the ancestors of the majority of people reading this essay.

By definition, refugees have fled their country due to persecution based on their race, religion, nationality, political opinion or social group. Resettlement is the last resort for refugees who cannot safely return home or rebuild their lives where they first fled, and less than 1 percent of refugees will ever be resettled.

Each year President Trump has set a new historic low for refugee resettlement: 45,000 in fiscal 2018, 30,000 in fiscal '19 and 18,000 in fiscal '20. This is an 81 percent reduction from the average refugee cap of 95,000 since Congress passed the 1980 Refugee Act. And the president also has issued an executive order requiring states and localities to provide consent for refugee resettlement to continue in their jurisdictions. There drastic cuts come precisely when the world is facing the largest displacement crisis in history. There is no legitimate justification for the dramatic cuts this administration has made to the lifesaving refugee program.

The U.S. government handpicks the refugees who are resettled here, knowing precisely who they are and verifying their information before issuing them a travel loan and booking their flight. Each refugee is thoroughly screened by government agencies before they arrive, including biometric screenings, medical exams, interagency checks and in-person interviews with specially trained Homeland Security officers.

Once they arrive here, refugees start working right away, contributing to local economies, filling labor shortages, paying taxes, starting businesses and revitalizing neighborhoods.

The U.S. effort in this area pales In comparison to countries that are hosting hundreds of thousands—in some cases millions—of refugees, including Jordan, Turkey, Lebanon, Kenya, Uganda and Sudan. Canada, Sweden and Germany all welcome significantly more refugees per capita than the United States.

appropriate help necessary to build a successful life in the United States. This is not a negligible expense; the government spent an average of $32,533 on resettlement for each refugee brought here in fiscal 2019 and will spend $49,555 in fiscal 2020.

Refugee resettlement should not be used as a political tool or a conscience alleviator. Focusing instead on the best way to help refugees, whether inside or outside the United States, is the commendable thing to do.

Some might say we should resettle fewer refugees because there are more asylum-seekers at our southern border. But the administration is keeping them out too, forcing them back to Mexico and other dangerous countries. We're actually admitting far fewer refugees and asylum-seekers than we were in the 1980s. Last year, the administration admitted 30,000 refugees, showing that the asylum backlog is a false excuse, and proving that xenophobia and politics are what truly underlay the cruel cut to 18,000.

conservatives, the legislation could face opposition in the Republican-controlled Senate.[96]

Experts agree that comprehensive immigration legislation stands little chance of enactment. The Bipartisan Policy Center's Ramón says the recently passed farmworker bill shows "there is support for reform that is employment-based." But, he says, "when it comes to the Mexico border issue, it doesn't seem there is much consensus. There's a lot of conflict over whether people should get asylum or there should be restrictions on asylum to deter them."

OUTLOOK

Demographic Changes

Most experts expect more movement as young people in poorer countries feel greater economic pressure to find work abroad. So far, much of the world has been focused on the conflicts in Syria and Afghanistan that have spurred some of the biggest waves into Europe and the Middle East.

But demographic changes, particularly in Africa, could shift the direction of migration significantly. As wealthier societies age and produce fewer children, demand in the West for workers to care for the elderly and to perform manual labor will provide a strong "pull" factor, while the combination of a population boom and low wages in poorer countries will provide a strong "push" factor for migration.[97]

Sub-Saharan Africa will see 800 million new workers entering the labor force over the next 30 years—about 24 times the current labor force in Britain, the Center for Global Development's Clemens calculates.[98]

"It's not possible for such an epic demographic change to happen and for people to simply remain in Ethiopia or Chad," he says. Clemens points to Japan, traditionally anti-immigrant, which recently changed its laws to allow hundreds of thousands of migrant workers to fill labor shortages and is bringing in 300,000 Indian workers to work in elder care and manufacturing.[99]

"That's a harbinger for Europe in the future," Clemens says.

George Mason University's Gest predicts that rich nations may try to satisfy both anti-immigrant attitudes and their need for more labor by handing out temporary work visas while being more restrictive about citizenship. This "uberization" trend in immigration policy is already evident in the 30 nations he analyzes in his book *Crossroads*.[100]

The United States is the exception to this trend, relying on its undocumented immigrants for additional labor rather than legal work permits. "If 12 million undocumented immigrants suddenly disappeared overnight, it would probably paralyze the United States," Gest says. "We have a policy system stuck in formaldehyde."

While the United Nations has proposed more global cooperation in hosting refugees, there does not seem to be much political appetite among nations to invite significantly more foreigners to settle permanently. In Europe, if mainstream center-right parties fail to control immigration levels or another flood of refugees results, "the populist right could surge yet again, perhaps winning outright majorities," the University of London's Kaufmann has predicted.[101]

At the same time, Kaufmann said, young Europeans, who have grown up in more ethnically diverse societies than their elders, tend to be more tolerant of immigration, and their entry into the electorate could lead to a liberalization of attitudes.

"It's an opportunity of epic proportions that there are all these energetic young workers available" from regions like Africa, says Clemens.

NOTES

1. The 1951 Convention on Refugees prohibits the removal of a refugee to any country where "the alien's life or freedom would be threatened in that country because of the alien's race, religion, nationality, membership in a particular social group, or political opinion." See "Brief of Amicus Curiae Local 1924," in *Innovation Law Lab v. Department of Homeland Security*, U.S. Court of Appeals in the 9th Circuit, June 26, 2019, https://tinyurl.com/rgjeyv2.

2. "Secretary Kirstjen M. Nielsen Announces Historic Action to Confront Illegal Immigration," Department of Homeland Security, Dec. 20, 2018, https://tinyurl.com/y7587ozs.

3. Ben Schreckinger, "Donald Trump storms Phoenix," *Politico*, July 11, 2015, https://tinyurl.com/ukad5o8.

4. "World Migration Report 2020," Table 1, International Organization for Migration, November 2019, p. 21, https://tinyurl.com/w7j2mt7.

5. Anna K. Boucher and Justin Gest, *Crossroads: Comparative Immigration Regimes in a World of Demographic Change* (2018).

6. "Master Glossary of Terms," U.N. High Commissioner for Refugees, 2006, https://tinyurl.com/wkw6l8n; "Recommendations on Statistics of International Migration," United Nations, 1998, https://tinyurl.com/uebk6r2.

7. "Figures at a Glance," Statistical Yearbooks, U.N. High Commissioner for Refugees, June 19, 2019, https://tinyurl.com/y4nchokd.

8. *Ibid.*

9. "An Overview of U.S. Refugee Law and Policy," American Immigration Council, January 2020, https://tinyurl.com/qolkv6e.

10. Nick Cumming-Bruce, "Number of People Fleeing Conflict Is Highest Since World War II, U.N. Says," *The New York Times*, June 19, 2019, https://tinyurl.com/yxz86kz3.

11. David Bier, "Legal Immigration Will Resolve America's Real Border Problems," Cato Institute, Aug. 20, 2019, https://tinyurl.com/ucluse7.

12. T. Alexander Aleinikoff and Leah Zamore, *The Arc of Protection: Reforming the International Refugee Regime* (2019), p. 3.

13. Alexander Betts and Paul Collier, *Refuge: Transforming a Broken Refugee System* (2018), p. 8.

14. Eric Kaufmann, *Whiteshift: Populism, Immigration, and the Future of White Majorities* (2019), p. 16.

15. *Ibid.*, pp. 68-69.

16. Marie McAuliffe, "The appification of migration," Asia & the Pacific Policy Society, Jan. 20, 2016, https://tinyurl.com/ryebw9g.

17. Andrew R. Arthur, "DHS and DOJ Issue Rule on Third-Country Asylum Agreements," Center for Immigration Studies, Nov. 21, 2019, https://tinyurl.com/wxo6hla.

18. Betts and Collier, *op. cit.*, pp. 30-31. For the 2018 list, see "World Migration Report 2020," *op. cit.*, p. 40.

19. Kirk Semple, "Trump Transforms Immigrant Caravans in Mexico Into Cause Célèbre," *The New York Times*, April 2, 2018, https://tinyurl.com/y7h4pc4u.

20. Linda Qiu, "Trump's Evidence-Free Claims About the Migrant Caravan," *The New York Times*, Oct. 22, 2018, https://tinyurl.com/y9rqcedm; "President Trump Meeting with Cabinet," *C-Span*, June 21, 2018, https://tinyurl.com/wspreb5; and Julie Hirschfield Davis and Thomas Gibbons-Neff, "Trump Considers Closing Southern Border to Migrants," *The New York Times*, Oct. 25, 2018, https://tinyurl.com/uarm777.

21. Nick Miroff, "Nearly 1 million migrants arrested along Mexico border in fiscal 2019, most since 2007," *The Washington Post*, Oct. 8, 2019, https://tinyurl.com/yybr2rkd.

22. Michael Clemens and Kate Gough, "Can Regular Migration Channels Reduce Irregular Migration?" Center for Global Development, February 2018, https://tinyurl.com/rqnuhc7.

23. "Southwest Border Sectors," U.S. Border Patrol, https://tinyurl.com/y5rg8efs.

24. "Backlog of Pending Cases in Immigration Courts as of November 2020," Transactional Records Access Clearinghouse, https://tinyurl.com/qpglbbx.

25. "Immigration Court's Active Backlog Surpasses One Million Cases," Transactional Records Access Clearinghouse, Sept. 18, 2019, https://tinyurl.com/tbna9o4.

26. "Prosecutorial Discretion All But Dead as Immigration Remedy, Owing to Trump Order," Nolo, https://tinyurl.com/v43rng6.

27. Andrew R. Arthur, "Attorney General Orders Review of Administrative Closure," Center for Immigration Studies, Jan. 9, 2018, https://tinyurl.com/rwzf2e2.

28. Eugene Kiely, "Trump's Bogus 'Catch and Release' Statistic," Factcheck.org, Jan. 25, 2019, https://tinyurl.com/unc8a6l.

29. Katie Reilly and Madeleine Carlisle, "The Trump Administration's Move to End Rule Limiting Detention of Migrant Children Rejected in Court," *Time*, Sept. 30, 2019, https://tinyurl.com/y3wwwpgp.

30. Robert Moore and Abigail Hauslohner, "Trump administration working to close immigration 'loopholes'—but border is still a crisis, officials say," *The Washington Post*, Oct. 20, 2019, https://tinyurl.com/vhd98bl; Michelle Hackman and Alicia A. Caldwell, "Arrests at U.S. Border With Mexico Drop for Seventh Straight Month," *The Wall Street Journal*, Jan. 9, 2020, https://tinyurl.com/wkzyk2h.

31. Bier, *op. cit.*

32. Clemens and Gough, *op. cit.*

33. Alexander Betts, "Nowhere to Go," *Foreign Affairs*, November/December 2019, https://tinyurl.com/r6aa9e2.

34. Betts, *ibid.*; "EU migrant crisis: France plans asylum 'hotspots' in Libya," *BBC News*, July 27, 2017, https://tinyurl.com/s48krqt.

35. "No escape from hell: EU policies contribute to abuse of migrants in Libya," Human Rights Watch, Jan. 21, 2019, https://tinyurl.com/seuhouv; Sally Hayden, "The U.N. Is Leaving Migrants to Die in Libya," *Foreign Policy*, Oct. 10, 2019, https://tinyurl.com/u4oz23t.

36. Betts, *op. cit.*

37. "Trump Administration's Third Country Transit Bar is an Asylum Ban that Will Return Refugees to Danger," Human Rights First, Sept. 13, 2019, https://tinyurl.com/th58yoq.

38. Susan Gzesh, "'Safe Third Country' Agreements with Mexico and Guatemala would be Unlawful," Just Security, July 15, 2019, https://tinyurl.com/rself23.

39. "Murder Rate by Country," World Atlas, https://tinyurl.com/y4lcp3vp.

40. Daniel Trotta, "U.S. restores aid to Central America after reaching migration deals," *Reuters*, Oct. 16, 2019, https://tinyurl.com/w8t62na.

41. "Implementing Bilateral and Multilateral Asylum Cooperative Agreements Under the Immigration and Nationality Act," Department of Homeland Security, Nov. 19, 2019, https://tinyurl.com/w54d4z2.

42. Emer Scully, "Germany warns of repeat of 2015 European migration crisis," *The Daily Mail*, Oct. 8, 2019, https://tinyurl.com/ru3lx6n; Nikolia Apostolou, "Briefing: How will Greece's new asylum law affect refugees," *The New Humanitarian*, Nov. 4, 2019, https://tinyurl.com/yxy8ba69.

43. Scully, *Ibid.*

44. Michael Clemens and Hannah Postel, "Deterring Emigration with Foreign Aid: An Overview of Evidence from Low-Income Countries," Center for Global Development, Feb. 12, 2018, p. 10, https://tinyurl.com/tl57pj4.

45. Kevin Sieff, "The migrant debt cycle," *The Washington Post*, Nov. 4, 2019, https://tinyurl.com/rme8g6p.

46. "Development aid alone will not reduce migration," IFW/Kiehl Institute for the World Economy, Jan. 15, 2019, https://tinyurl.com/tyc7tn9.

47. "Impact Evaluation of USAID's Community-Based Crime and Violence Prevention Approach in Central America," USAID, Oct. 29, 2014, https://tinyurl.com/s3k6bqg.

48. Clemens and Postel, *op. cit.*

49. Sarah Bermeo, "Could foreign aid help stop Central Americans from coming to the U.S.?" *The Washington Post*, June 18, 2019, https://tinyurl.com/rltxqhm.

50. *Ibid.*

51. Christoph Zürcher, "What Do We (Not) Know about Development Aid and Violence? A Systematic Review," World Development, October 2017, pp. 506-22, https://tinyurl.com/vgsynte.

52. Clemens and Postel, pp. 7-8.

53. *Ibid.*, p. 8.

54. Sarah Glazer, "European Migration Crisis," *CQ Researcher*, July 31, 2015, https://tinyurl.com/qqcpm3s.

55. *Ibid.*

56. Kaufmann, *op. cit.*, p. 36.

57. *Ibid.*, pp. 40-41; "Chinese Exclusion Act," History.com, Sept. 13, 2019, https://tinyurl.com/y6wx9zww.

58. Daniel Okrent, *The Guarded Gate: Bigotry, Eugenics, and the Law That Kept Two Generations of Jews, Italians, and Other European Immigrants Out of America* (2019), pp. 286-88.

59. Kaufmann, *op. cit.*, pp. 44-45.

60. *Ibid.*

61. Daniel J. Kevles, *In the Name of Eugenics: Genetics and the Uses of Human Heredity* (1985), Kindle edition, location 2219.

62. "Voyage of the *St. Louis,*" Holocaust Encyclopedia, https://tinyurl.com/yxuokmmb.

63. "United States Immigration and Refugee Law, 1921-1980," Holocaust Encyclopedia, https://tinyurl.com/yamrb7sz. For the text, see "The 1951 Refugee Convention," U.N. High Commissioner for Refugees, https://tinyurl.com/yxwf5vf3.

64. Aleinikoff and Zamore, *op. cit.*, p. 13.

65. "United States Immigration and Refugee Law, 1921-1980," *op. cit.*

66. Kaufmann, *op. cit.*, pp. 57-58.

67. Julie Hirschfeld Davis and Michael D. Shear, *Border Wars: Inside Trump's Assault on Immigration* (2019), p. 114.

68. "United States Immigration and Refugee Law, 1921-1980," *op. cit.*

69. Glazer, *op. cit.*

70. *Ibid.*

71. "United States Immigration and Refugee Law, 1921-1980," *op. cit.*

72. "Castro announces Mariel Boatlift," This Day in History: April 20, 1980, https://tinyurl.com/tudy54s.

73. Muzaffar Chishti, Doris Meissner and Claire Bergeron, "At Its 25th Anniversary, IRCA's Legacy Lives On," Migration Policy Institute, Nov. 16, 2011, https://tinyurl.com/y2kh2l5e.

74. Kaufmann, *op. cit.*, pp. 68-74.

75. Claire Felter and James McBride, "Backgrounder: How Does the U.S. Refugee System Work?" Council on Foreign Relations, Oct. 10, 2018, https://tinyurl.com/y98lollf.

76. Kaufmann, *op. cit.*, pp. 211, 246.

77. *Ibid.*, pp. 107-09.

78. Davis and Shear, *op. cit.*, p. 151.

79. Scott Neuman, "During Roundtable, Trump Calls Some Unauthorized Immigrants 'Animals,'" *NPR*, May 17, 2018, https://tinyurl.com/yczf3yqo.

80. "Governments adopt UN global migration pact to help 'prevent suffering and chaos,'" *UN News*, Dec. 10, 2018, https://tinyurl.com/rqlhode; Margaret Besheer, "UN States Adopt Global Compact on Refugees," *Voice of America*, Dec. 17, 2018, https://tinyurl.com/wdv8flm.

81. Nikki R. Haley, *With All Due Respect: Defending America with Grit and Grace* (2019), p. 242.

82. Apostolou, *op. cit.*

83. Gabriela Baczynska, "Germany warns of repeat of 2015 EU migration chaos," *Reuters*, Oct. 8, 2019, https://tinyurl.com/qu7n3g5.

84. Apostolou, *op. cit.*

85. Eric Reidy, "Briefing: Behind the new refugee surge to the Greek islands," *The New Humanitarian*,

Oct. 30, 2019, https://tinyurl.com/qk3ubd7; Patrick J. McDonnell, "'How long can we live like this?': Kurds in growing refugee camp plead for help, end to losses, suffering," *Los Angeles Times*, Oct. 20, 2019, https://tinyurl.com/wl6e5kc.

86. "Germany pressures Greece to step up migrant deportations to Turkey," *Deutsche Welle*, Sept. 12, 2019, https://tinyurl.com/yyp8ac85.

87. "Second life-saving evacuation of vulnerable refugees from Libya lands in Rwanda," U.N. High Commissioner for Refugees, Oct. 11, 2019, https://tinyurl.com/sccqjyc; "UN calls for Libyan migrant detention centres to be shut," *BBC News*, July 14, 2019, https://tinyurl.com/y2yapswn.

88. Jonas Ekblom, "Poland, Hungary broke EU laws by refusing to host migrants," *Reuters*, Oct. 31, 2019, https://tinyurl.com/qnx69mo.

89. Jens Manuel Krogstad, "Key facts about refugees to the U.S.," Pew Research Center, Oct. 7, 2019, https://tinyurl.com/yxccd5ha.

90. "Donald Trump has cut refugee admissions to America to a record low," *The Economist*, Nov. 4, 2019, https://tinyurl.com/torrbf9.

91. Molly O'Toole, "In a first, U.S. starts pushing Central American families seeking asylum to Guatemala," *Los Angeles Times*, Dec. 10, 2019, https://tinyurl.com/wdvy5uu.

92. Adam Liptak, "Supreme Court Says Trump Can Bar Asylum Seekers While Legal Fight Continues," *The New York Times*, Sept. 11, 2019, https://tinyurl.com/y5bh38fa.

93. Adriana Beltrán, "Guatemala Is No Safe Third Country," *Foreign Affairs*, Sept. 25, 2019, https://tinyurl.com/tpm7so7.

94. Camilo Montoya-Galvez, "Judge grills government lawyer on potential violations of international refugee law," *CBS News*, Oct. 1, 2019, https://tinyurl.com/y5xyxvck; "Ninth Circuit Stay Ruling," ACLU, May 7, 2019, https://tinyurl.com/usnbr5z.

95. "Metering Update," Strauss Center for International Security and Law and the Center for U.S.-Mexican Studies, November 2019, https://tinyurl.com/wnf8caa; "US Move Puts More Asylum Seekers at Risk," Human Rights Watch, Sept. 25, 2019, https://tinyurl.com/vldoalm.

96. Chantal Da Silva, "House Praised for Passing Bill Giving Undocumented Farm Workers Pathway To Citizenship: 'Bipartisanship Lives,'" *Newsweek*, Dec. 12, 2019, https://tinyurl.com/sawpg3s.

97. Kaufmann, *op. cit.*, p. 16.

98. Clemens and Gough, *op. cit.*

99. "Japan eases immigration rules for workers," *BBC News*, Dec. 8, 2018, https://tinyurl.com/ybgjvhvu; Malini Goyal, "Why countries like Switzerland, Singapore, Sweden and Japan are focused on making more Indians employable," *Economic Times*, Oct. 22, 2017, https://tinyurl.com/sxq2y2j.

100. Boucher and Gest, *op. cit.*

101. Kaufmann, *op. cit.*, p. 263.

BIBLIOGRAPHY

Books

Aleinikoff, T. Alexander, and Leah Zamore, *The Arc of Protection: Reforming the International Refugee Regime*, Stanford University Press, 2019.
A professor specializing in migration at The New School in New York City (Aleinikoff) and a senior policy analyst at New York University's Center on International Cooperation (Zamore) examine today's refugee system, which they call "dysfunctional." They propose a global sharing of responsibility for refugees.

Betts, Alexander, and Paul Collier, *Refuge: Transforming a Broken Refugee System*, Penguin Books, 2018.
A migration expert at the University of Oxford in England (Betts) and Oxford economist (Collier) say support for asylum in developed countries has collapsed and a stronger effort is needed to provide jobs to refugees languishing in camps and countries to which they have fled.

Davis, Julie Hirschfeld, and Michael D. Shear, *Border Wars: Inside Trump's Assault on Immigration*, Simon & Schuster, 2019.
Two *New York Times* reporters trace President Trump's immigration policies from early closed-door meetings with his advisers.

Kaufmann, Eric, *Whiteshift: Populism, Immigration, and the Future of White Majorities*, Abrams Press, 2019.
A professor of politics at the University of London surveys the history of immigration and the rise of right-wing populism in the United States, Britain, Europe and Canada, finding that rising immigration fuels the rightward shift of white majorities.

Articles

Apostolou, Nikolia, "Briefing: How will Greece's new asylum law affect refugees," *The New Humanitarian*, Nov. 4, 2019, https://tinyurl.com/yxy8ba69.
An Athens-based journalist reports on a new law in Greece, passed as rising numbers of refugees arrived in the country, which would speed deportations of asylum-seekers to Turkey. Human rights groups say the law will violate refugees' rights.

Bermeo, Sarah, "Could foreign aid help stop Central Americans from coming to the U.S.?" *The Washington Post*, June 18, 2019, https://tinyurl.com/rltxqhm.
The more than $2 billion sent by the United States and other donors to Central America over the past few years has not stemmed migration, writes the associate director of the Duke University Center for International Development.

Betts, Alexander, "Nowhere to Go," *Foreign Affairs*, November/December 2019, https://tinyurl.com/r6aa9e2.
A professor of forced migration and international affairs at the University of Oxford says Europe's handling of its 2015 migration crisis holds lessons for the United States as it confronts a crisis at the Mexican border.

Bier, David, "Legal Immigration Will Resolve America's Real Border Problems," Cato Institute, Aug. 20, 2019, https://tinyurl.com/ucluse7.
An immigration policy analyst at Cato, a libertarian think tank in Washington, argues that the United States could control the influx of migrants at the Mexican border if it expanded guest-worker programs and other paths to legalization.

Gzesh, Susan, "'Safe Third Country' Agreements with Mexico and Guatemala would be Unlawful," *Just Security*, July 15, 2019, https://tinyurl.com/rself23.
The executive director of a human rights center at the University of Chicago says agreements the United States has been negotiating to deport asylum-seekers to Central America would violate U.S. and international law.

Hayden, Sally, "The U.N. Is Leaving Migrants to Die in Libya," *Foreign Policy*, Oct. 10, 2019, https://tinyurl.com/u4oz23t.
A journalist reports on deaths and victimization among refugees and migrants in Libya's detention camps, quoting aid officials who say the United Nations is "ignoring or downplaying systemic abuse and exploitation" there.

Reports and Studies

"Projected Global Resettlement Needs 2020," United Nations High Commissioner for Refugees, July 1-2, 2019, https://tinyurl.com/yxy6ttgs.
The U.N. refugee agency projects that the refugees most at risk and in need of resettlement in 2020 are Syrians (40 percent), followed by South Sudanese (14 percent) and those from the Democratic Republic of Congo (11 percent).

"World Migration Report 2020," International Organization for Migration, November 2019, https://tinyurl.com/w7j2mt7.
This comprehensive report published by a U.N.-linked organization that provides migration services and information has the latest figures on global migration and refugees, with sections covering climate change, asylum, child migration and other topics.

Clemens, Michael, and Hannah Postel, "Deterring Emigration with Foreign Aid: An Overview of Evidence from Low-Income Countries," Center for Global Development, Feb. 12, 2018, https://tinyurl.com/tl57pj4.
A Washington think tank analyzes research on foreign aid to low-income countries and concludes that it generally does not deter migration.

THE NEXT STEP
Foreign Aid

Lamble, Lucy, and Karen McVeigh, "Less than 10% of EU aid reaches world's poorest countries, study finds," *The Guardian*, Nov. 21, 2019, https://tinyurl.com/twl9jy7.

The European Union and its member states, which have been seeking to head off migration to the continent, supplied over half the foreign aid in the world in 2018, but the world's 16 poorest countries received only 8 percent of European aid.

Larson, Ren, "Trump's plan to cut aid to Central America could push more migrants to come to US," *USA Today*, Sept. 23, 2019, https://tinyurl.com/uktdcom.
Some experts say more people will flee Guatemala, El Salvador and Honduras if the United States cuts aid to those countries.

Mashal, Mujib, "Afghanistan Needs Billions in Aid Even After a Peace Deal, World Bank Says," *The New York Times*, Dec. 5, 2019, https://tinyurl.com/rjkf9k8.
Experts at the World Bank warn that Afghanistan's economy could collapse if the United States stops providing foreign aid to the country, which has one of the largest refugee populations.

Internally Displaced People

"Nearly 100 displaced by ISIS return home to Iraq's disputed Kirkuk," *Kurdistan 24*, Dec. 17, 2019, https://tinyurl.com/v6ta98p.
Two years after the defeat of the Islamic State terrorist group in an Iraqi province, dozens of refugees will finally return home.

Bilak, Alexandra, "Africa is the crucible of the global internal displacement challenge," *The Africa Report*, Dec. 18, 2019, https://tinyurl.com/tkapkmo.
The displacement of Africans due to violence or conflict has reached unprecedented levels, according to new research by the Internal Displacement Monitoring Centre, a Geneva-based group that studies migration.

Bouscaren, Durrie, "The world closed its doors to Syrian refugees. Now Turkey wants to send them back," *PRI*, Oct. 29, 2019, https://tinyurl.com/st5cpyz.
Turkey, which hosts more Syrian refugees than any other nation, plans to resettle the refugees in a Turkish-occupied section of Syria.

U.S.-Mexico Border

Attanasio, Cedar, and Philip Marcelo, "Brazilians arrive in waves at the US-Mexico Border," *The*

***Associated Press*, Dec. 13, 2019, https://tinyurl.com/srdcx24.**
Some 18,000 Brazilians were apprehended after crossing the U.S-Mexico border in fiscal 2019, a 600 percent increase from the previous high in 2016, as many fled unfavorable economic conditions, corruption and violence in their home country.

Laporta, James, "Exclusive: Military documents about US-Mexico border are now classified to prevent leaks, limit media coverage," *Newsweek*, Dec. 17, 2019, https://tinyurl.com/td6c8a8.
Previously unclassified orders and communications between the U.S. Department of Homeland Security and the Defense Department regarding military operations at the border are now sent over a secret network to avoid leaks and media coverage.

Long, Colleen, "Immigration official says US-Mexico border crisis not over," *The Associated Press*, Oct. 29, 2019, https://tinyurl.com/y4q43lz9.
A top U.S. Border Patrol official says that resources at the border are still stretched thin, even as the number of migrants crossing has dropped in recent months.

U.S. Refugee Policy

Frost, Natasha, "Not a single refugee was resettled in the US last month," *Quartz*, Nov. 3, 2019, https://tinyurl.com/y4epowxz.
October was the first month since record-keeping began in 1980 in which no refugees were admitted into the United States.

Rao, Maya, "Minnesota refugee aid center's future in flux at 100," *Minneapolis Star-Tribune*, Dec. 16, 2019, https://tinyurl.com/rmktckk.
A century-old refugee institute in St. Paul, Minn., is struggling with funding, because it is paid by the federal government per refugee and the Trump administration has significantly reduced the number of refugees being resettled in the United States.

Smith, Mitch, and Miriam Jordan, "Trump Said Local Officials Could Block Refugees. So Far, They Haven't," *The New York Times*, Dec. 9, 2019, https://tinyurl.com/vyz68rr.
No state or local government has taken advantage of a new option offered by President Trump to refuse to take in refugees in 2020.

For More Information

Center for Global Development, 2055 L St., N.W., Suite 500, Washington, DC 20036; 202-416-4000; cgdev.org/. Research and action group that works to reduce poverty in developing countries.

Center for Immigration Studies, 1629 K St., N.W., Suite 600, Washington, DC 20006; 202-466-8185; cis.org/. Research organization that advocates for stricter limits on immigration in the United States.

International Organization for Migration, 17 Route des Morillons, PO Box 17, CH-1211 Geneva 19, Switzerland; +44 22-717-9111; iom.int/. U.N.-related organization that provides migration services to governments and migration information to the public.

Migration Policy Institute, 1400 16th St., N.W., Suite 300, Washington, DC 20036; 202-266-1940; migrationpolicy.

org/. Nonpartisan research institute that focuses on North America and Europe.

Refugee Council USA, 1628 16th St., N.W., Washington, DC 20009; 212-319-2102; https://rcusa.org/. Coalition of 26 U.S.-based organizations dedicated to welcoming refugees under the U.S. refugee resettlement program.

Refugees International, PO Box 3306, Washington, DC 20033; 202-828-0110; refugeesinternational.org/. Independent advocacy group that seeks to improve the lives of displaced people around the world.

United Nations High Commissioner for Refugees, Case Postale 2500, CH-1211 Genève 2 Dépôt, Switzerland; +41 22 739 8111; unhcr.org/en-us/contact-us.html. The U.N. agency charged with aiding and protecting refugees.

12

Global Protest Movements

Can they lead to lasting change?

By Bill Wanlund

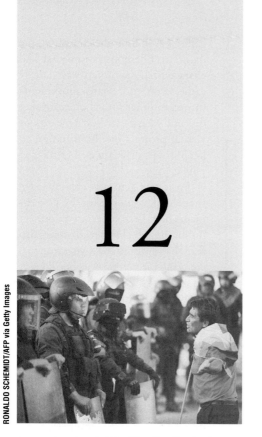

A supporter of ousted President Evo Morales faces off against police during a protest in Cochabamba, Bolivia, in November 2019. Demonstrations for and against Morales were part of a worldwide wave of protests in 2019.

From *CQ Researcher,*
May 1, 2020

THE ISSUES

Enraged Lebanese took to the streets last Oct. 18, 2019, when their government announced a $6-a-month tax on calls made via WhatsApp and other online apps. One of the protesters in Beirut, Rayya Haddad, says, "As I was walking to my parents' house, a friend texted me about the demonstrations starting, so I went. There were blocked streets, burning tires—all the country was up in revolt."

Within hours, the Cabinet scrapped the tax proposal, which was supposed to help ease a lingering economic crisis and rescue Lebanon's ailing telecommunications industry. But the demonstrations continued, and the "WhatsApp tax" protests morphed into what Haddad and her fellow protesters began calling a revolution.

On Oct. 29, 2019, 11 days after the protests began, Prime Minister Saad Hariri resigned—but even that did not satisfy anti-government demonstrators, who had swelled into the hundreds of thousands. "The protests . . . continued because people are fed up with government corruption and incompetence," Haddad says.

Lebanon's protests bear many of the characteristics of those that roiled the world last year: Seemingly mundane local events, like a WhatsApp tax, spark demonstrations, which in turn unleash anger about more fundamental grievances such as government incompetence or social and economic inequality. A report by the Center for Strategic and International Studies, a Washington think tank, found that more than 37 countries experienced massive

Protests Worldwide Grew More Frequent

During the decade between 2009 and 2019, the number of protests increased worldwide by 11.5 percent annually, according to an analysis by the Center for Strategic and International Studies. Protests increased the most in sub-Saharan Africa, by just under 24 percent.

Increase in Protests Annually, 2009–19

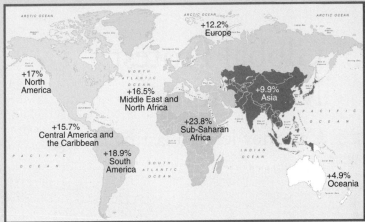

Source: Samuel J. Brannen, Christian S. Haig and Katherine Schmidt, "The Age of Mass Protests," Center for Strategic and International Studies, March 2020, https://tinyurl.com/wgceft8

anti-government movements in the last few months of 2019 alone. This continued a decade-long trend, during which mass political protests increased by an annual average of 11.5 percent, the center reported.[1]

"Protesters have taken to the streets to speak out about corruption, economic injustices, environmental questions, repression and a range of particular local issues," Richard Youngs, a senior fellow at Carnegie Europe, a part of the Carnegie Endowment for International Peace think tank, wrote last fall. "Several protests have driven political leaders out of office; some have triggered draconian government reprisals. Mass mobilizations have occurred in democracies and nondemocracies and advanced and developing economies alike. They are now a major feature of global politics."[2]

Maria Stephan, director of the Program on Nonviolent Action at the U.S. Institute of Peace in Washington, puts it this way: "We are probably living in the most contentious time in recorded history."

But early this year, as the deadly coronavirus spread rapidly around the world and governments instituted social distancing requirements and bans on public gatherings to limit the contagion, the mass street demonstrations that had characterized the protest wave largely came to an end. Many movements turned to other means of expressing dissent, such as strikes, boycotts or virtual protests on the internet, to keep their grievances before the public.[3]

Protesters generally acknowledge that the measures taken by governments have been necessary to protect public health. However, some also fear that authoritarian governments are using the coronavirus breakout as an excuse to exert powers to quash legitimate dissent. "We could have a parallel epidemic of authoritarian and repressive measures [closely] following . . . a health epidemic," said Fionnuala Ní Aoláin, the United Nations special rapporteur on counterterrorism and human rights.[4]

Lebanon's protests followed a predictable pattern. Demonstrations often progress from small, discrete issues to larger, more encompassing ones, says Kai Thaler, a professor of global studies at the University of California, Santa Barbara. The movements "start out with small causes. Then, some people make the case for wider protests, and other people see the opportunity to express their own grievances, and things snowball."

Recent examples include:

- France's *gilets jaunes* (yellow vests) protests, named for the high-visibility safety jackets that French motorists must carry, were triggered by a proposed increase in the national fuel tax in 2018. The tax was abandoned in April 2019.[5] The size of the protests dwindled, but they continued as part of a wider anti-government movement.
- Protests erupted in Hong Kong in March 2019 when many citizens felt the city's limited autonomy from mainland China was threatened by a proposed extradition law in the Hong Kong Legislature. After five months of protests, the bill

Fewer Believe State Benefits All Citizens

The view that the state is run for the benefit of everyone is losing popularity in many countries, according to polling by the Pew Research Center. In Italy, the proportion holding this view fell from 88 percent in 2002 to 30 percent last year. In the same period, the share in the United States dropped from 65 percent to 46 percent.

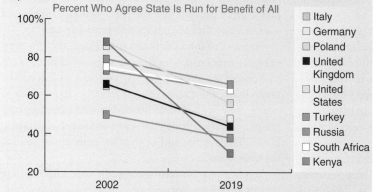

Percent Who Agree State Is Run for Benefit of All

Legend: Italy, Germany, Poland, United Kingdom, United States, Turkey, Russia, South Africa, Kenya

Source: Richard Wike and Shannon Schumacher, "Democratic Rights Popular Globally but Commitment to Them Not Always Strong," Pew Research Center, Feb. 27, 2020, https://tinyurl.com/y9yjlhm4

was withdrawn—but protests continued, with expanded demands for democratic guarantees.[6] The emergence of the coronavirus diminished the size of the demonstrations, although movement participants vow to continue pressing their demands.[7] (*See Short Feature.*)

- Bolivians took to the streets in October to protest once-popular President Evo Morales' extralegal effort to seek a fourth term in office. After three weeks, Morales fled the country, but demonstrations continued against his conservative interim successor, Jeanine Áñez, until coronavirus safety measures suspended street protests.[8]

- In Chile, student demonstrations in October over a 30-peso (4-cent) rise in rush-hour subway fares mushroomed into a protest against economic mismanagement and inequality that drew a million participants.[9] The national Congress agreed to call a referendum (now postponed) in April on the question of creating a new constitution, meeting a key protester demand. President Sebastián Piñera promised to increase pensions. Demonstrations continued, however, amid complaints of harsh repressive tactics by police: According to press

reports at least 30 demonstrators have been killed, though no official figure is available.[10] The Office of the U.N. High Commissioner for Human Rights reported some 28,000 were jailed.[11]

- In November, increased fuel costs triggered protests in Iran. Then, in January, the government's lack of transparency over its reporting of the downing of a Ukrainian airliner led to another nationwide protest. Security forces quelled both; neither protest led to noticeable change in government policies.[12]

Experts see the trend toward more protests as signaling an erosion of faith in governments' ability to solve problems, and even in democracy itself.

"More people are motivated to engage in nonviolent mobilization because of a seeming inability of governments around the world to address major challenges of our time," says Erica Chenoweth, a professor of human rights and international affairs at Harvard University's Kennedy School of Government. "People believe our political institutions are not equipped to address national problems that also affect people locally."

Chenoweth adds, "There's also a rising tide of authoritarianism. There are fewer democracies in the world than there were 10 years ago, and more democracies at risk today than in a very long time. People are resisting this authoritarian march."

Although the number of protests has increased dramatically, there is no guarantee that they will achieve their objectives. Political analyst Youssef Cherif, deputy director of Columbia University's Global Center in Tunisia, said, "Staging [demonstrations] is no longer the difficult part. The problem is what to do after the protests, how to make your point and achieve the goals you're protesting for. . . . You can break off part of a system, but it's very hard to break the whole structure . . . of institutions and networks."[13]

Authoritarian regimes often resort to violence to end opposition protests.

In Iran, which is controlled by a theocratic Islamist regime, the human rights group Amnesty International said it had seen credible reports that security forces killed at least 208 protesters during last year's protests.[14] The U.S. State Department, pointing to unspecified "international media reports," put the number killed at approximately 1,500.[15]

Hadi Ghaemi, executive director of the New York-based Center for Human Rights in Iran, believes repression will not stop the protests. "The future of Iran is completely tied to whether the government will represent the people's interests or try to suppress them," he says. "If they continue to kill and to refuse to tolerate any dissent, we're sure to see more dissent and more violence in the future."

And even nominally democratic governments, such as Chile's, can adopt harsh measures. Alexa Schaeffer Quintero, an American working in Santiago, who took part in some of the protests there, says, "As the weeks passed, the police's repressive tactics got worse—the police used rubber and metal bullets that caused hundreds of flesh wounds and eye injuries. During protests the water tanks sprayed a yellowish water that caused a burning sensation. . . . My fear was never of the actions of other protesters, only of the police and their excessive and unnecessary use of force."

Today, as in earlier times, there is lively debate over whether violent acts can advance the goals of protesters or will prove counterproductive.

To protest police use of pellet guns, Chilean demonstrators hold placards depicting eyes in Santiago in December 2019. The pellets caused numerous eye injuries during anti-government protests last fall.

Thaler, the University of California scholar, said violence can help further a movement's cause. "In Chile, protesters' willingness to fight with police and burn buildings, in addition to nonviolent tactics, helped push the government to make serious concessions," he said. And violent protests pushed Bolivia's Morales to step down "amid unhappiness with his ignoring the results of a referendum and allegations of electoral fraud."[16]

Stephan, of the U.S. Institute of Peace, says any benefits violence might lend to an otherwise nonviolent movement are short-lived. "If you add violence," she says, "in the short term you get more media covering it, or you may get a morale boost, but over time you may see participation levels decrease, more people staying home. That, at the end of the day, ends up weakening the movement."

While many protests are specific to a single society and its problems, some issues catalyze far-flung cross-border protests. Two examples are climate change and violence against women.

Millions of students around the world have rallied to demand climate action in both physical and online protests. Many were inspired by Greta Thunberg, the Swedish teenager who called for action to end climate-damaging practices in high-profile appearances at the United Nations and the World Economic Forum in Davos, Switzerland.[17]

A movement against femicide—gender-based killing of women—has spread across Latin America and to other continents as well. According to the United Nations, some 87,000 women and girls were murdered worldwide in 2017—50,000 by a spouse, partner or close family member.[18]

As nations and their citizens confront both rising social tensions and a virulent virus, here are some of the questions they are asking:

Is the current protest wave a sign that democracy is failing?

It is no coincidence that the wave of protests has occurred at a time when there is also an upsurge in authoritarian regimes and rulers and increasing skepticism about democratic governance, Stephan says.

"This resurgent authoritarianism is probably linked to growing global inequality and sense of disenfranchisement," she says. "People orient to those populist leaders who say they have the solutions to the problem. They're giving up on the traditional legislative and judicial processes that are seen to be ineffective, and look to the autocratic strongman to bring solutions."

Some recent studies echo these views. According to the latest survey by Freedom House, a Washington-based organization that researches issues pertaining to democracy, last year 64 countries experienced a deterioration in political rights and civil liberties while just 37 experienced improvements. "The unchecked brutality of autocratic regimes and the ethical decay of democratic powers are combining to make the world increasingly hostile to fresh demands for better governance," the group said.[19]

And a 2020 Pew Global Research study found "considerable dissatisfaction with the way democracy is working in many countries." Across the 34 nations polled, 52 percent of respondents said they were dissatisfied with how their democracy was functioning. The biggest complaint was the feeling that political leaders were out of touch; Pew found that 64 percent "believe elected officials do not care what people like them think." In the United States, 71 percent feel that way. Overall, the Pew study found that 59 percent of Americans are dissatisfied with the way democracy is working in the United States.[20]

"I think we're living through an anti-establishment wave, and public frustration is at play," says Chenoweth of Harvard's Kennedy School. "A lot of people think the electoral system isn't as representative as it should be, or perhaps as it used to be, and that institutions aren't responsive to urgent issues."

She adds, "There's also a sense of gridlock, that public polarization has infected government institutions in ways that keep them from moving. The public is divided, so the institutions are divided, so much so that there's no wiggle room."

Another gloomy assessment comes from the University of Cambridge in England. Its 2020 "Global Satisfaction with Democracy" report, which reviewed dozens of international surveys between 1995 and this year, found that "dissatisfaction with democracy has risen over time, and is reaching an all-time global high." It said last year represented "the highest level of democratic discontent on record."

The report marks 2005 as the high point for global satisfaction with democracy. Since then, it said, "democratic institutions around the world have faced setbacks ranging from military coups, to domestic crises, to the election of populist or authoritarian leaders willing to use their office to erode the independence of parliament, courts and civil society."[21]

The Cambridge study's principal author, Roberto Foa, a lecturer in politics and public policy, says global democracy is in "a state of deep malaise." He says, "In transitional democracies in Africa, Latin America, parts of Asia, many of the hopes and expectations that were raised during the democratic transition—better delivery of public services, better rule of law, more control over corruption—have been disappointed."

In developed democracies, Foa says, "it's more to do with the consequences of the [2007-09] financial crisis and the eurozone crisis and the economic frustrations that created, and the feeling of being left behind without a voice."

But Monica de Bolle, director of Latin American studies and emerging markets at the Johns Hopkins University School of Advanced International Studies, says there is no evidence that democracy is dying.

"Nothing is linear," she says. "We make progress, we take a step back, we make progress. To infer that democracy and democratic institutions are going away on the basis of what's been going on in the past very few years is overly pessimistic, even irresponsible."

Democracy is complicated, de Bolle says. "Institutions need to be modernized, and they will modernize when there's discontent with what's happening. That's what will move things forward."

Erica Frantz, a Michigan State University political science assistant professor, believes government institutions are falling short of their promise. "On one hand, it's cause for optimism that people are hitting the streets and protesting," she says. "At the same time, the underlying cause of their frustration is that they don't feel their governments are delivering. If there is some sort of ideological battle between democracy and authoritarianism at the moment, it's up to these democratic governments to prove they can provide, and do all those things democracies are supposed to do."

Haddad, the protester in Beirut, describes Lebanon as a "schizophrenic" democracy. "We have an open, free press," she says. "That's why the government didn't put a blackout on the internet, it would have been unconstitutional. But we don't really have free speech—people have been imprisoned for criticizing the president."

Support for Free Speech Rising in Many Nations

Support for the view that people should be able to say what they want without government censorship rose between 2015 and 2019 in most countries surveyed by the Pew Research Center. The biggest increase was in Turkey, where support jumped 22 percentage points. Israel and India experienced declines.

Share Who Say Free Speech Is Very Important

Country	2015	2019	Change
Turkey	43%	65%	+22
France	67%	83%	+16
Hungary*	74%	87%	+13
United Kingdom	57%	68%	+11
Argentina	77%	87%	+10
Mexico	65%	73%	+8
Indonesia	29%	37%	+8
United States	71%	77%	+6
Philippines	50%	56%	+6
Israel	58%	51%	-7
India	44%	32%	-12

* Hungary was polled in 2016.

Source: Richard Wike and Shannon Schumacher, "Democratic Rights Popular Globally but Commitment to Them Not Always Strong," Pew Research Center, Feb. 27, 2020, https://tinyurl.com/y9yjlhm4

Thomas Carothers, founder and director of the Democracy and Rule of Law Program at the Carnegie Endowment for International Peace, says the surge of protests "is not a crisis of democracy per se, though a lot of democracies are facing pressure from their citizens— as are a lot of autocracies. Part of the paradox of governing is, the more you satisfy [citizens], the more demands they have. Sometimes good performance leads to high expectations, and you fail to meet them. It isn't a straight line between bad performance and failure to meet expectations."

And for all the turmoil and discontent, Stephan sees the protests as a sign of democracy's health. "People finding voice and employing it in institutional, extralegal ways is arguably very good for democracy—people believing they can bring about change through collective action," she says. "That's a hopeful aspect of what we're seeing around the world: an exertion of agency."

Is social media responsible for the recent wave of protests?

One thread linking recent mass protests is the use of social media as a recruitment and organizing tool.

Haddad, who participated in the WhatsApp tax protests in Lebanon, says social media played a huge role.

"It unites the people, people send flyers and documents, tell where the next protest is, when to meet, where people are gathering, what to bring," she says. "People share stories, or photos. It's much more accurate than TV or other traditional media for following what's happening."

Most scholars agree that social media has played an important part in modern movements, but add that there are limits to its value. "There's no question that social media is an accelerator of protest, but I wouldn't point to it as an original cause," says Carothers of the Carnegie Endowment. "I think it's an accelerator of underlying causes."

Social media has played an important role in the Hong Kong protests, activist and lawyer Angeline Chan says. Two platforms that have been especially important are Telegram, a Dubai-based messaging app that describes itself as heavily encrypted, and a Hong Kong forum, LIHKG, she says.

"These platforms are where people can come together and brainstorm and make plans," Chan says. "They can get people together from all districts of Hong Kong, for example to form a human chain, or to start online petitions, for circulating posters—they're really the place to go for information."

Michigan State's Frantz, who studies authoritarianism, says that "access to new technologies facilitates more protests and helps reduce barriers to collective action. Protests are on the increase, and there's good evidence that it's due to the rise of social media."

At the same time, she says, "dictatorships are using this technology to repress dissent—shutting down the internet, for example, or surveilling people online."

And Frantz says that reliance on social media may, perversely, be undermining the ultimate success of protests.

"The logic behind this is that, before social media, to organize a protest you had to work hard to develop your organization and get feet on the ground," she says. "Now, because it's easier to spread the word about a protest, the organizations that are backing them are weaker and less cohesive than in the past. . . . Opposition movements could become more resilient by strengthening their organizations offline and mimicking opposition movements of the past that didn't rely on social media to get going."

Under an authoritarian regime, it can be difficult to use the internet to facilitate protests. That is the case in Iran, says Garrett Nada, program officer at the U.S. Institute of Peace's Center for the Middle East & Africa. In order to communicate more safely, he says, Iranian protesters must use a virtual private network, which allows a user to make an encrypted connection to a public network to block monitoring and bypass censorship.

"Most popular foreign social media platforms are banned, such as Telegram, Facebook, YouTube and Twitter," Nada says. "During the November 2019 protests, the regime resorted to shutting down the internet for five days to limit communications."

At the same time, social media can create a diffusion of inspiration, ideas and tactics across borders—a "global contagion," in the words of David Gordon, senior adviser in the Washington office of the International Institute for Strategic Studies, a research organization. "Seeing protests in other places motivates people to be willing to go to the streets in their own countries," Gordon said.[22]

But Dawn Brancati, a research scholar at Yale University's MacMillan Center for International and Area Studies, says pro-democracy protests in one nation are unlikely to be replicated in adjoining countries, because protests arise primarily from unique domestic conditions such as fraudulent elections or economic crises.

"Democracy protests can even dampen prospects for protests in neighboring countries," Brancati says. "After all, national leaders watch the same regional developments that activists do, and can take steps to block protests in their own countries, like shutting down internet access and pre-emptively arresting activists."

The 2011 Arab Spring, a wave of pro-democracy uprisings across the Arab world, began in Tunisia. The protests, widely shared on Facebook and other social media, led within weeks to the resignation of the country's president and, subsequently, to democratic elections.

Tunisia has been cited as an example of how a successful protest in one country can, thanks to social media, inspire similar events in another.

"The protests that brought down Tunisia's leader had an immediate impact—people in other Arab countries said, 'Wow, we can do the same thing,'" says Kurt Weyland, professor of government at the University of Texas at Austin.

But while the unrest soon spread to Egypt, Libya, Syria, Yemen and other countries in the region, it ultimately failed to achieve its fundamental goal of a democratic transformation in the Arab world.

"If change is not inspired by a country's own domestic reasons, then that change isn't likely to succeed," Weyland says. "The Arab Spring brought democratization to one country: Tunisia. In the others it didn't succeed. Diffusion is a prediction of probable failure."

Can protests bring about lasting change?

Several of 2019's protests have led to major changes. In Algeria, Sudan, Lebanon, Iraq and Bolivia, leaders were forced out. Governments in Chile, France, Ecuador and Hong Kong made significant concessions in response to demonstrators' initial demands.

However, most of these protests have yet to produce the fundamental changes many protesters had sought. Bolivia's Morales was ousted for suspected election corruption, but replaced by an unpopular right-wing politician; new elections were scheduled for May but then postponed over coronavirus concerns. The Hong Kong extradition legislation, which would have allowed mainland China to extradite criminal defendants, was withdrawn, but the protesters' wider demands for greater democracy remain unfulfilled. Demonstrators' success in overthrowing Sudan's longtime dictator, Omar al-Bashir, has been thrown into question by repressive tactics on the part of the interim military government that succeeded Bashir.[23]

Youngs of Carnegie Europe believes what activists do after an action can determine the movement's success or failure. "What happens in the immediate aftermath of a protest is just as crucial as what occurs during the protest," he said. "It is a major factor in determining whether mass protest becomes a force to restructure politics or ultimately remains a dramatic yet ineffective interlude in the status quo."

Sudanese protesters wave the national flag in Khartoum in February 2020. Demonstrations last year toppled President Omar al-Bashir, but repressive tactics by an interim military government have sparked new protests.

Youngs is the editor of "After Protest: Pathways Beyond Mass Mobilization," a Carnegie Europe report in which educators and other experts analyze 10 major recent domestic conflicts and how the choices made by the activists affected the outcomes.[24]

In Egypt, Youngs wrote, activists were ready for revolution but not prepared to govern in the aftermath. "Civic activist strategies after the 2011 revolution that ousted President Hosni Mubarak became highly polarized around a division between secularists and Islamists," and a repressive authoritarian government filled the vacuum, he wrote.

Ukrainians, on the other hand, generally chose to work—albeit warily—with their new government after toppling President Viktor Yanukovych in 2014. Activists "moved into new roles of supporting the formally democratic [new] government but also sought ways to resist the government's growing reluctance to reform fully," said Youngs. "The largest activist group has focused on local-level volunteering and community-organizing. . . ."[25]

Whether a protest movement will succeed is difficult to forecast. "Nonviolent popular uprisings are among the least predictable events we see in humankind," says Harvard's Chenoweth.

Stephan of the Institute of Peace says successful movements typically share a few central attributes. She says the key questions are: "Is the protest growing and bringing in new participants from different parts of society?

How are they dealing with violent repression? Can they maintain nonviolent discipline? Are there loyalty shifts among key pillars of regime support, such as workers and security forces?"

In addition, she says, a successful protest will display "innovative, dispersed and coordinated use of tactics—more than just street protests, for example."

Stephan notes one striking trend: "The overall success rate of nonviolent campaigns has decreased noticeably. Twenty years ago, about 70 percent of nonviolent campaigns succeeded in achieving their goals. Starting in the 2000s, that rate dropped to 30 percent. That's a staggering decline," she says, one she attributes to an increase in authoritarian governments, which tend to use repressive tactics against protesters.

George Lakey, a retired professor in peace and conflict studies at Swarthmore College, says one thing is certain: A single protest is not sufficient to bring about change.

"In a one-off demonstration, your opponent knows perfectly well at the end of the day you're going to go back home, so the next day they continue doing what they've been doing," says Lakey.

As a case in point, Lakey—who is also a longtime activist in support of progressive causes—recalls the massive Feb. 15, 2003, global protest against U.S. plans to go to war against Iraq. Perhaps as many as 11 million people gathered in at least 650 cities around the world—the largest one-day protest in history.[26]

But the demonstrations ultimately had no impact on the Bush administration's war plans, because other actions did not follow, he says.

"It was an amazing expression of public opinion, and it had very little impact," Lakey says. "The one-off may persuade more people to agree with the protesters' point of view, but the newly convinced don't have a place to go without a campaign—a sustained series of actions."

BACKGROUND
Peasants and Protestants

For centuries, social and economic inequality has been at the heart of protest. England's Peasants' Revolt of 1381 challenged the conditions of serfdom—heavy taxes, bondage to the land and a government-enforced income cap. The nobility quelled the uprising, but because the revolt demonstrated peasants' potential power, historians say it helped break down England's feudal system.[27]

The Protestant Reformation, sparked in 1517 by German monk Martin Luther, challenged the authority of the Roman Catholic Church (and gave "protest" its modern meaning). Luther questioned the church's right to define Christian practice. The Reformation, supported by princes seeking to replace the church's authority with their own, spread through much of Europe, resulting in Protestant dominance of much of the northern part of the continent by 1648.[28]

By preaching the leveling notion of a "priesthood of all believers," Luther unintentionally inspired discontented agrarian workers to challenge social and political hierarchies, leading to another rebellion, the German Peasants' War of 1524-25. Like England's, it sprang from the social and economic inequality that were hallmarks of feudalism—and, like England's, it was put down by nobles' armies.[29]

In the late 18th century, colonists in British North America also chafed under what they regarded as unequal treatment, in that they were heavily taxed by Parliament but had no political representation in England. As taxes and trade restraints on the colonies increased, so did American resentment. Battles between British troops and American militias broke out in 1775 and the 13 colonies formally declared their independence in 1776. Britain's superiority in manpower and materiel was negated by its long, unreliable supply lines and the hemorrhaging effects of the rebels' guerrilla tactics. With the Treaty of Paris in 1783, the United States had secured its independence.[30]

Encouraged by the American example but motivated by their own grievances, French citizens rose up against their monarchy in 1789. Social inequality and onerous taxation were core concerns. In a bloody revolution, French citizens eliminated the absolute monarchy and the feudal system, adopting a new constitution in 1791. However, the ensuing government, inefficient and corrupt, was overthrown in 1799 in a coup d'etat led by Napoleon Bonaparte, who crowned himself emperor in 1804.[31]

Expanding literacy helped spread the writings of political thinkers and philosophers throughout Europe, and by 1848 the idea of revolution had taken hold throughout the continent. In January, Sicilians threw out the ruling Bourbon monarchy; revolutions in the states of the Italian peninsula erupted later that year. In February, the French overthrew their constitutional monarchy and replaced it with the Second Republic under Louis-Napoléon, nephew of Bonaparte. Revolution spread to the German states and to Austria, Denmark and Hungary in March.

The revolutions of 1848 enjoyed limited success; the dethroned monarchs soon returned to power. However, the upheavals resulted in some victories: Hungary gained autonomy within the Hapsburg Empire, the Italian states made progress toward a unified government, Austria ended the feudal system and abandoned press censorship and the German state of Prussia established an elective assembly.

Other European countries avoided 1848's revolutionary turmoil. Some had undergone earlier revolutions or civil wars and enacted reforms.[32] Others pre-emptively instigated reforms demanded elsewhere and successfully avoided violent unrest; in the Netherlands, King William II voluntarily authorized a new constitution, including direct elections, and ceded royal authority.[33]

Birth of Nonviolent Resistance

Mohandas Gandhi, a 24-year-old Indian-born lawyer, moved to Natal, a British colony in present-day South Africa, in 1893. There, he quickly discovered the discrimination against people of Indian descent. When Indians lost the right to vote in 1894, he led protests against the colonial government.

Gandhi developed satyagraha, a philosophy of nonviolent resistance, and in 1915 brought it home to India. Although the British imprisoned him several times, he was instrumental in winning support for India's independence, and eventually became known as mahatma, or great soul. Gandhi, although himself a Hindu, was assassinated in January 1948 by a Hindu extremist because of his tolerance of India's Muslims, five months after India became independent from Great Britain.[34]

Gandhi's nonviolent philosophy and the struggle for racial equality came together in the U.S. civil rights movement. Martin Luther King Jr., an admirer of Gandhi, became a dominant figure in the movement, which sought full political, economic and social rights for African Americans. King's nonviolent strategy and powerful oratory helped build sympathy for the

CHRONOLOGY

14th Century *Peasants unite to seek better life.*

1381 English peasants march on London seeking relief from serfdom.

18th-19th Centuries *An age of revolutions opens.*

1776 Protesting "taxation without representation," American colonists declare independence from Britain.

1783 After a long war, Britain recognizes American independence.

1789 Revolution topples the French monarchy, establishes a republic three years later.

1848 Revolutions sweep across Europe, toppling monarchs; most return to power, but with concessions to demands. . . . The Seneca Falls Declaration asserts U.S. women's right to full citizenship.

1894 Mohandas Gandhi leads Indian-rights protests in South Africa.

1915-1945 *Nonviolent protests arise.*

1915 Gandhi brings nonviolent resistance to India's campaign for independence from Britain.

1930 Gandhi leads a "salt march," a civil disobedience protest over British colonial treatment of India; he and 60,000 other protesters are arrested.

1945 As World War II ends, the Soviet Union begins to expand its influence in Eastern Europe. . . . Vietnamese communists and other nationalists declare their country independent from France, triggering conflict with French forces.

1950s-1970s *Racism and war take people into the streets.*

1954 The U.S. Supreme Court rules racial segregation in schools is unconstitutional. . . . Nationalists defeat French forces in Vietnam; Geneva Accords ending the war result in division of the country into a communist-controlled North and noncommunist South.

1955 Rosa Parks, a black activist, is arrested for refusing to yield her seat to a white bus rider in Montgomery, Ala., touching off a monthslong boycott in protest. . . . United States sends 700 military advisers to train South Vietnamese forces, the beginning of a commitment in which more than 2.7 million service members would serve in Vietnam by war's end.

1960 Security forces at Sharpeville, South Africa, massacre 69 black demonstrators, spotlighting the injustice of South Africa's rigid system of racial separation known as apartheid.

1963 The Rev. Martin Luther King Jr. leads a civil rights March on Washington and delivers "I have a dream" speech to 250,000 at Lincoln Memorial.

1964 President Lyndon B. Johnson signs Civil Rights Act, guaranteeing full citizenship rights to black Americans.

1965 Johnson orders bombing of North Vietnam and sends U.S. combat troops to South Vietnam in an effort to help defeat North Vietnamese and Vietcong forces. The war, popular at first, becomes increasingly controversial as casualties rise.

1968 King is assassinated in Memphis, touching off riots and rebellions in hundreds of cities. . . . Anti-war protesters battle police outside Democratic convention in Chicago. . . . Anti-government student protests paralyze France. . . . Soviet military invasion of Czechoslovakia ends brief Prague Spring liberalization. . . . Mexico City police kill dozens of students demonstrating for greater freedoms.

1970 An estimated 20 million Americans observe the first Earth Day to call attention to the environment; Congress authorizes creation of the Environmental Protection Agency.

1980s-1990s *Democracy takes center stage.*

1989 Pro-democracy demonstrations at Tiananmen Square in Beijing call attention to Chinese desire for democracy, but end in bloody suppression. . . . Soviet bloc convulses as Berlin Wall falls. The following year, communist East Germany disappears and Germany reunites.

1991 Soviet Union dissolves, and its constituent republics become independent nations.

1999 Anti-globalization demonstrators disrupt World Trade Organization meeting in Seattle.

2000-Present *New voices speak out against political, economic and social grievances.*

2003 As many as 11 million people take part in a worldwide protest against the impending U.S. invasion of Iraq, the largest single-day protest in history; the United States invades anyway.

2011 Pro-democracy Arab Spring protests sweep the Middle East. . . . Occupy Wall Street protests against economic inequality emerge in New York, spread across the United States and overseas.

2013 Black Lives Matter movement organizes to protest police killings of African Americans.

2017 Marches around the country, sparked by Donald Trump's comments about women, protest his inauguration as president.

2018 Students protest gun violence after a mass shooting at a Florida high school. . . . Swedish teenager Greta Thunberg's protests calling for greater action against climate change engage millions of students around the world.

2019 Protests against the lack of democracy or persistent social grievances engulf dozens of countries, ranging from Lebanon to France and Hong Kong.

2020 Government stay-at-home orders to diminish the coronavirus threaten to halt global protest movements. . . . As economic pressure tightens, protests to end government lockdown restrictions erupt in dozens of U.S. states.

movement, as did the tactics employed by its participants, including acts of civil disobedience such as sit-ins— peaceful occupation by blacks of whites-only facilities— along with marches, boycotts and letter-writing campaigns.

Violence, or at least the fear of it, was also present in the movement, embodied by Malcolm X, who sought a separate society for African Americans. In 1964 he urged blacks "to fight whoever gets in our way . . . and bring about the freedom of [people of African descent] by any means necessary."[35] He was assassinated in 1965 while giving a speech in Harlem. Three members of the Nation of Islam, a group that Malcolm X once helped lead but had split from, were convicted of his murder. Many years later, amid doubts about the case, New York authorities reopened the investigation into his death.[36]

The Black Panther Party, formed in 1966, supported black nationalism, socialism and "armed self-defense."[37]

Civil rights activism played a key role in bringing about several laws enacted in the 1960s to protect the rights of black Americans. The Civil Rights Act of 1964 outlawed racial segregation in schools, at the workplace and in facilities such as stores, restaurants and hotels that

Young civil rights demonstrators in Birmingham, Ala., in 1963 are flattened against a wall by fire hoses. The images of police brutality against the marchers created widespread sympathy for their cause.

served the general public.[38] In 1965, the Voting Rights Act made it illegal to deny the right to vote based on race and set up a system of federal registrars to ensure that blacks could vote.[39] The Fair Housing Act of 1968 outlawed racial discrimination in the sale, rental or financing of housing.[40]

King was assassinated in 1968; a white man with a racist past, James Earl Ray, was convicted of the crime.[41]

Hong Kong Protesters Confront Beijing's Power

"They're fighting because they feel they have no choice."

In 2018, a Hong Kong teenager visiting Taiwan, Chan Tong-kai, allegedly killed his girlfriend. He then returned to Hong Kong. Chan subsequently confessed to police, but Hong Kong has no extradition treaty with Taiwan, a separately-governed island off the Chinese mainland, so the killing could not be prosecuted.[1]

This tawdry murder case set off a chain of events that led to an eruption of dissent among Hong Kong citizens who feared the encroachment of the People's Republic of China and its authoritarian government. The result has been massive and at times violent street demonstrations, a significant electoral victory for the protesters, but also lingering questions about what they have ultimately achieved as the coronavirus and its restrictions now force protesters off the streets.

The year after the killing, the Hong Kong government cited Chan's case when it proposed legislation permitting case-by-case extradition to countries with which it does not have formal agreements—including the People's Republic.[2] This triggered alarm that such a law could lead to arbitrary imprisonment of Hong Kong residents who dissent against the Chinese government. Pro-democracy activists responded by organizing protests against the proposed law.

The dispute was rooted in the laws that govern relations between Hong Kong and the mainland. The 1,108-square-mile Hong Kong Special Administrative Region enjoys special economic, political and legal status until at least 2047, the result of the agreement by which Great Britain ceded Hong Kong to China in 1997. Under the agreement, which applies a principle called "one country, two systems," Hong Kong has maintained the free-market economic system that makes it an important world financial center, and its citizens enjoy civil and political rights unheard of in mainland China.[3]

"Extraditing people from Hong Kong into China would break down the 'one country, two systems' firewall," says Angeline Chan, a Hong Kong lawyer who took part in the pro-democracy movement that opposed the legislation.

The protests peaked on June 9 with a crowd estimated by police at 240,000 and by organizers at more than 1 million.[4] The protests continued during the summer.

On Sept. 4, 2019, Hong Kong Chief Executive Carrie Lam withdrew the extradition bill, saying she was doing so "to eradicate the worries of [the] people" of Hong Kong.[5] But her move came too late to quell the movement. By that time the protesters had broadened their demands and hardened their position.

They said they would not end the demonstrations until the government met four other demands in addition to withdrawing the extradition bill: cease defining the protests as rioting, grant amnesty for arrested protesters, conduct an independent inquiry into police violence and give Hong Kong citizens more say in choosing their government. At present, residents elect a territorial council with limited authority, but the powerful chief executive is chosen by an electoral council made up of 1,194 representatives of various sectors of Hong Kong society who are approved by Beijing.[6]

Protesters criticized Hong Kong's security forces for using unreasonable force. "We've seen police violence used regularly—tear gas, beanbag rounds, pepper spray, batons, with hardly any police held to account," Chan says. "The focus of the protests has shifted from the extradition bill to the fact that the police are acting with impunity."

But protesters too have used violence. During a standoff at Hong Kong Polytechnic University in November 2019, barricaded students used firebombs and bows and arrows against police—who themselves had used tear gas, rubber bullets and water cannons.[7]

The protesters can claim some credit for a major political shift in Hong Kong. In November 2019's territorial council elections, pro-democracy candidates won 389 of

452 seats; previously they held 124. Pro-Beijing candidates took just 58 seats, down from 300.[8] "This election [was] totally a de facto referendum for the protests," said Samson Yuen, an assistant professor of political science at Hong Kong's Lingnan University.[9]

A survey by the Hong Kong Public Opinion Research Institute taken March 17-20, 2020, indicated substantial public support for protesters' demands, with those backing the protests outnumbering opponents by 58 percent to 28 percent.[10]

But Richard Bush, a China specialist and senior fellow in foreign policy at the Brookings Institution, a centrist Washington think tank, says the movement is probably failing in fulfilling its objectives.

"If the goal is to get Beijing to create a more democratic system, then it has failed," he says. "If the goal was to deal with the extradition bill and then return to more normal circumstances, it failed by following up with unreasonable demands that would lead Beijing, the Hong Kong government and the Hong Kong elite to conclude the movement really didn't want a mutually acceptable solution."

However, he adds, "if the goal is to keep Hong Kong in a permanent state of instability, the movement succeeded, and will probably be back for more once the coronavirus subsides."

Without a doubt, the pandemic is complicating the pro-democracy movement. Hong Kong's first coronavirus death was confirmed Feb. 4, and the city instituted quarantines and other preventive measures. Since then, demonstrations have been sporadic, and smaller.[11]

Albert Ho, a pro-democracy leader, said authorities appear to be using the respite to prevent large demonstrations, including rounding up protest organizers. "They have to do everything to deter the social organizers from continuing to organize marches and demonstrations on a big scale," Ho said.[12]

The coronavirus outbreak may dampen enthusiasm for street demonstrations, but in the long run it could help fuel the protest movement, whose leaders see the government's failure to cope with the virus as an opportunity to rally support.

"Street protests are just a part of the movement," said Eric Lai Yan-ho, deputy convener of the Civil Human Rights Front. Yan-ho's group, which organized rallies, also helped gather more than 35,000 online signatures in a city-wide campaign to protest the government's handling of the virus crisis. Unions added to the pressure by engaging in Hong Kong's largest-ever medical strike.[13]

Chan, the lawyer-activist, says the cause is vital to Hong Kong residents. "A lot of the protesters I come into contact with feel that if they don't resist, the way of life we know in Hong Kong will disappear," she says. "They're fighting because they feel they have no choice."

— *Bill Wanlund*

[1] Cindy Sui, "The murder behind the Hong Kong protests: A case where no-one wants the killer," *BBC*, Oct. 23, 2019, https://tinyurl.com/y8fjl24o.

[2] Daniel Victor and Tiffany May, "The Murder Case That Lit the Fuse in Hong Kong," *The New York Times*, June 15, 2019, https://tinyurl.com/y6qz8cx3.

[3] Eleanor Albert, "Democracy in Hong Kong," Council on Foreign Relations, Sept. 20. 2019, https://tinyurl.com/ybw2yd7r.

[4] Eric Kleefeld, "Hundreds of thousands attend protest in Hong Kong over extradition bill," *The South China Morning Post*, June 9, 2019, https://tinyurl.com/y2pmzr65.

[5] "Hong Kong: Carrie Lam withdraws controversial extradition bill," *Deutsche Welle*, Sept. 4, 2019, https://tinyurl.com/y967uqfw.

[6] "How Hong Kong picks its chief executives," *The Economist*, March 21, 2017, https://tinyurl.com/y7fp2723.

[7] Edward Wong *et al.*, "Hong Kong Violence Escalates as Police and Protesters Clash at University," *The New York Times*, Nov. 17, 2019, https://tinyurl.com/voa6lwq.

[8] Keith Bradsher, Austin Ramzy and Tiffany May, "Hong Kong Election Results Give Democracy Backers Big Win," *The New York Times*, Nov. 24, 2019, https://tinyurl.com/qk33gms.

[9] Casey Quackenbush, "Hong Kong democrats score historic victory amid ongoing protests," *Al-Jazeera*, Nov. 24, 2019, https://tinyurl.com/uzr3v9w.

[10] Felix Tam and Clare Jim, "Exclusive: Support for Hong Kong protesters' demands rises even as coronavirus halts rallies: poll," *Reuters*, March 27, 2020, https://tinyurl.com/y87z8vsp.

[11] James Griffiths, "Hong Kong appeared to have the coronavirus under control, then it let its guard down," *CNN*, March 23, 2020, https://tinyurl.com/ws6xhhq.

[12] Helen Davidson, "Hong Kong: with coronavirus curbed, protests may return," *The Guardian*, March 15, 2020, https://tinyurl.com/s664gyy.

[13] Natalie Wong and Tony Cheung, "A new strain of resistance? How the coronavirus crisis is changing Hong Kong's protest movement," *The South China Morning Post*, Feb. 10, 2020, https://tinyurl.com/yddyq8t3.

Parkland Protesters Meld Power of Youth, Social Media

"People are caring a lot more about what young people want."

On Feb. 14, 2018, a gunman killed 17 people at Cameron Kasky's high school. Almost immediately, Kasky, then 17, became one of the leaders of a national movement to end gun violence.

"One Wednesday everything changed," says Kasky. "And by Sunday we were living a completely different life that had a different structure to it."

The shooting at Marjory Stoneman Douglas High School in Parkland, Fla., was neither the first nor the most lethal in a string of recent mass shootings in the United States, but it inspired the largest protests against gun violence nationwide.

Exactly one month after the Parkland shooting, thousands of students across the country walked out of class in a coordinated protest against gun violence. Ten days after that, hundreds of thousands of protesters descended on Washington for the March for Our Lives, which became the name of an organization that continues to organize against gun violence.

"To the leaders, skeptics and cynics who told us to sit down, stay silent and wait your turn, welcome to the revolution," Kasky told the protesters.[1]

David S. Meyer, a professor of sociology and political science at the University of California, Irvine, says it is not unusual for political movements to take off after a push from younger people. And he says the Parkland students were in a kind of sweet spot: young enough so they had no political background that opponents could attack, but old enough to be able to speak for themselves—unlike the students at Sandy Hook Elementary School in Newtown, Conn., where 20 first graders and six staffers died in a 2012 shooting.

In addition, Meyer says, "these kids went to one of the best-funded schools in Florida." Because they were more likely to be children of professionals, they had access to resources that others in their situation might not have had, he says.

Despite his rhetoric at the Washington march, Kasky says he does not want to fan the flames of generational resentment. "It always made me upset when people made things a generational battle," he says.

In the two years that have followed the initial burst of activism, the Parkland activists have compiled a mixed record of achievements. Their demands for new federal gun laws remain unfulfilled, and some movement leaders, such as David Hogg and Kasky, became targets for criticism themselves. Their critics say they ignore the constitutional rights of gun owners and unfairly ascribe illegitimate motives to their opponents.

"The student activists presume that there is a ready solution to mass shootings that everyone knows, and the only reason why someone might not act on this universally accepted policy is malice or corruption," wrote Rich Lowry, editor of *National Review*, a conservative publication.[2]

They have had more success at the state level and in the private sector, and participation by younger voters—one of the organization's goals—has recently increased. In the 2018 midterm elections, turnout among 18-to-29-year-olds surged to almost 36 percent from 20 percent in 2014.[3]

From the start, the young Parkland survivors relied heavily on social media to tell their stories, spread the hashtag #NeverAgain and inspire others to join them.[4]

"The March for Our Lives movement started using social media during the shooting itself," says Errol

King's assassination sparked riots and rebellions in nearly 200 cities across the United States.[42]

Also in 1968, protests against the U.S. war in Vietnam swept the world. That was the year when the number of American troops in Vietnam peaked, and also when American public opinion turned against the war.[43] Tens of thousands of mostly young demonstrators protested the war at the Democratic Party's national convention in Chicago. Violence outside the convention—later termed a "police riot" by the head of an investigating commission—and rancor and confusion within the hall crippled the Democrats and helped Republican nominee Richard Nixon win the presidency in November.[44]

Salamon, a postdoctoral teaching associate in media and popular culture at the University of Minnesota who attended the 2018 Washington march. "And they were using tools on social media that people could identify with."

Salamon says the consistent use of Twitter was essential to the movement's growth. But while the methods of communication may be new, youth activism has been a staple of American politics for decades, he says.

"Young people have long been in protest movements, and this extends back as far as the countercultural movement of the 1960s," Salamon says.

While the Parkland movement did not persuade a Republican-controlled Congress to enact gun laws such as a new assault weapons ban, the movement has had lasting effects in other ways. Several state legislatures have taken up the issue of gun control, passing laws designed to prevent another Parkland.[5]

Florida raised the legal age to purchase a firearm to 21 shortly after the shooting. (The Parkland gunman was 19.)[6] Several states, including Colorado, Nevada and Hawaii, have passed "red flag" laws, which allow police or family members to petition a state court to temporarily remove firearms from someone who may pose a danger to themselves or others.[7]

Kasky says federal action is still needed to prevent potential perpetrators of gun violence from buying weapons in other states. "We can pass strong gun laws in one state, but there are always going to be people taking advantage of that," he says.

Despite the lack of new federal legislation, Kasky says the movement and its message have motivated some businesses to take action in order to appear socially responsible in the eyes of younger consumers. "People are caring a lot more about what young people want and what young people have to say," Kasky says.

One company that changed its policy was Dick's Sporting Goods, which stopped selling the type of semi-automatic rifle used in the Parkland shooting and raised the age required to purchase any firearm at its stores to 21. The chain's CEO, Ed Stack, said he was personally moved by the Parkland tragedy and the young survivors' response.[8]

But it may be hard to maintain momentum during the coronavirus pandemic. In the current era of social distancing, in-person protests may be dangerous, frowned upon or even illegal.

Parkland survivors believe their movement can adjust, because many activists have been sharing their message on social media for years. "It's very much online already right now," Kasky says.

Yet while the movement may have spread on Twitter early on, Salamon says it is unlikely it would have gotten so far without a physical presence. "It could not have just been a hashtag movement," he says. "People needed to be there in person."

— *Brock Hall*

[1] Ray Sanchez, "Student marchers call Washington's inaction on gun violence unacceptable," *CNN*, March 23, 2018, https://tinyurl.com/y8qrjf8s.

[2] Rich Lowry, "The Teenage Demagogues," *National Review*, March 27, 2018, https://tinyurl.com/y8vj7adv.

[3] Tara Golshan, "Young people, women, voters in cities: how Democrats won in 2018, by the numbers," *Vox*, April 26, 2019, https://tinyurl.com/y6yxz8k4.

[4] "Timeline: How the #NeverAgain Movement Gained Momentum After Parkland," *NBC Philadelphia*, Feb. 14, 2019, https://tinyurl.com/y9gza2u8.

[5] Rep. David N. Cicilline, "H.R. 5087—Assault Weapons Ban of 2018," Congress.gov, Feb. 26, 2018, https://tinyurl.com/ydcl9uv3; Steven Melendez, "Here's a list of gun control laws passed since the Parkland shooting," *Fast Company*, Feb. 14, 2019, https://tinyurl.com/y83juh79.

[6] Patricia Mazzei, "Florida Governor Signs Gun Limits Into Law, Breaking With the N.R.A.," *The New York Times*, March 9, 2018, https://tinyurl.com/ybu7f4mu.

[7] Jonathan Levinson and Lisa Dunn, "What is a Red Flag Law?" *WAMU*, Aug. 5, 2019, https://tinyurl.com/y8vsh6jg.

[8] Alina Selyukh, "Soul-Searching After Parkland, Dick's CEO Embraces Tougher Stance On Guns," *NPR*, Feb. 12, 2019, https://tinyurl.com/ybo8fv8s.

Other events led some observers to compare 1968 to 1848 in the global sweep of the protests:

- In May, much of France shut down as tens of thousands of students, later joined by millions of workers, protested capitalism, consumerism and the Vietnam War.[45]

- Soviet troops invaded Czechoslovakia in August to end the Prague Spring, the government reforms instituted by Czech leader Alexander Dubček. Thousands of Czechs protested, but the Soviet military prevailed.[46]

- That summer, inspired in part by the French protests and the anti-Vietnam War demonstrations, students in Mexico City protested for greater freedom. At a rally on Oct. 2, just days before Mexico hosted the Summer Olympics, soldiers fired into a crowd of thousands of students. Dozens died; the actual number killed is still in dispute. The protests and the violent reaction of the authorities are often cited as a key moment in the development of Mexican democracy.[47]

A Democratic Moment

By the late 1980s, two decades after the Soviet crackdown in Prague, demands for political change were again rising within the communist world. This hunger for democratic reforms underpinned two major events in 1989.

In China, pressure was building for greater freedoms and an end to government corruption. That spring, protesters began gathering in Beijing's Tiananmen Square— perhaps as many as 1 million at one point. After weeks of internal Communist Party debate about how to handle the protests, the Chinese military forcibly cleared the square with tanks and troops. The government estimated the death toll at 200 civilians and several dozen security personnel; other casualty estimates ranged as high as 10,000.[48] The Tiananmen Square events failed to democratize China, and they remain a sensitive issue for the authorities to this day—government internet censors still block content related to the protest.[49]

Also in 1989, Soviet leader Mikhail Gorbachev, who had come to power four years earlier pledging greater openness, began loosening Moscow's control over its Eastern European satellites. Seeing an opportunity for independence, trade unions in Poland negotiated free elections. In November, after months of protests in Soviet-dominated East Germany, the wall separating communist East Berlin from democratic West Berlin was breached; Czechoslovakia overthrew its pro-Moscow government and, in the coming months, other Soviet allies broke away. In December 1991, the Soviet Union itself ceased to exist and its constituent states became independent.

Arab Spring and Grassroots Protests

In December 2010, police forbade a 26-year-old Tunisian street vendor to sell his produce because he had no official permit. Unable to make a living, the man,

Mohamed Bouazizi, publicly immolated himself. Sympathy demonstrations evolved into nationwide anti-government protests that toppled the regime of longtime President Zine el-Abidine Ben Ali. It marked the start of the Arab Spring, a wave of pro-democracy demonstrations around the Middle East.[50]

When the Arab Spring ended, Tunisia's rebellion was the only clear success. Although the protests also brought about the downfall of leaders in Egypt and Libya, their successors proved no more democratic. Protests led to bloody civil wars in Libya, Syria and Yemen.[51] The Arab Spring showed the power of social media to communicate, organize and mobilize, but also its limits in sustaining a movement.[52]

In 2007 a financial crisis brought about by risky practices by U.S. financial institutions spawned a global recession that lasted until 2009, the deepest slump since the Great Depression of the 1930s. In the United States, a plummeting stock market, mortgage foreclosures and widespread unemployment contributed to the rise of populist movements on both the left and right in opposition to the political elite.[53]

In 2009 fiscally conservative Americans formed the Tea Party movement. Rallies in many states voiced opposition to what participants called big government and wasteful economic policies. In the 2010 midterm elections, the Tea Party helped end Democratic control of the House of Representatives and pushed the Republican Party further to the right, widening political polarization, fostering distrust of the federal government and helping to enable Donald Trump's election as president in 2016.[54]

On the left side of the spectrum, on Sept. 17, 2011, hundreds of demonstrators marched into a small park in New York City to protest what they called corporate greed and economic inequality. The Occupy Wall Street movement spread to other cities across the United States; it also had a presence in Canada, Europe, Australia and elsewhere. While it did not produce major structural changes, it made economic and social equality a part of the national political debate and helped fuel support for the 2016 and 2020 presidential campaigns of Sen. Bernie Sanders of Vermont, a self-described democratic socialist.[55]

Other grassroots protest movements arose in the United States during and after the presidency of

Democrat Barack Obama, who served from 2009 to 2017. The Black Lives Matter movement was founded in 2013 in response to the acquittal of George Zimmerman, a white man accused of killing Trayvon Martin, a 17-year-old African American who Zimmerman said was acting suspiciously.[56] By publicizing shootings of unarmed blacks by white police officers, the movement has "forced [America] to confront its deep-rooted problems with race and inequality," said a World Economic Forum report.[57]

Trump's 2016 election angered many who were upset by what they regarded as his demeaning attitude toward women.[58] A Women's March on Jan. 21, 2017, the day after Trump's inauguration, drew hundreds of thousands of protesters to Washington and large crowds to events in other cities.[59] Subsequent annual rallies were held, although the number of participants steadily declined.[60] However, the movement is credited with encouraging women to run for political office; a record 117 women were elected to Congress in 2018.[61]

Frightened and angered by shootings in U.S. schools and frustrated by the lack of legislative action to prevent them, students began to protest. The March For Our Lives movement was started by students at Marjory Stoneman Douglas High School in Parkland, Fla., who were galvanized into action after a gunman walked into their school on Feb. 14, 2018, and killed 17 classmates and faculty members. The organization tries to maintain public attention through group protests and student walkouts.[62] (*See Short Feature.*)

Gun owners and enthusiasts also have taken a stand. The National Rifle Association (NRA) and other gun-rights groups have lobbied with considerable success against state and federal legislation that would restrict and regulate gun ownership.[63] After Virginia's state elections in 2019 gave control of the Legislature to Democrats, and lawmakers then proceeded to enact stricter gun laws, a large crowd of pro-gun-rights protesters gathered at the state Capitol in Richmond on Jan. 20, 2020. The demonstration was peaceful.[64]

CURRENT SITUATION
Coronavirus Impact

The wave of protests in 2019 had been expected to continue and even expand as protesters dug in, and new

movements formed, to press demands for government action on corruption, economic reform and other issues.

But the emergence of the coronavirus altered the landscape. While government responses to protesters' demands have blunted some protests and refocused others, public fear of the coronavirus and strictures imposed by governments as disease preventative measures have led to a decline in protesters' participation and enthusiasm.

In the Middle East, during what the Carnegie Endowment's Middle East expert Michele Dunne calls "the second wave of the Arab Spring," pro-democracy protests in 2019 toppled longtime dictators Abdelaziz Bouteflika in Algeria and Bashir in Sudan and forced the resignations of prime ministers Hariri of Lebanon and Adel Abdul-Mahdi in Iraq.

Despite these apparent successes, demonstrations continued because "the sense lingers of a job left unfinished," said Bobby Ghosh, former editor of New Delhi's *Hindustan Times*, who writes about the Middle East. "The political systems in all four countries remain largely intact, in the hands of the elites that enabled the misrule protesters were hoping to end."[65]

But in March, amid the threat of the coronavirus and strictly enforced government restrictions on public gatherings, the protests in the Middle East were largely suspended. Algerians ended their string of Friday protests after 56 consecutive weeks.[66]

On March 10, 2020, Lebanese protesters formed a human chain around the Palace of Justice in the capital of Beirut, but they wore masks and gloves and kept a distance from one another. On March 21, 2020, the government ordered security services to enforce social distancing and stay-at-home measures and to "prevent gatherings."[67] Since then, virtual outreach has replaced physical demonstrations: Activists livestream information sessions, stage social media campaigns and solicit funds.

Protests in other regions also were affected by the coronavirus. In Chile, protests over economic inequities, which ebbed at the end of 2019, resumed in early March, only to be dampened weeks later by the pandemic. "Plaza Dignidad, a place that has been the point of congregation for daily protests in Santiago since October 19th, is now completely empty," says Schaeffer Quintero in Santiago.

On March 15, 2020, President Sebastián Piñera declared a 90-day "state of catastrophe," giving the govern-

Is violence an effective tool for protest?

YES

Benjamin Ginsberg
David Bernstein Professor of Political Science, Johns Hopkins University

Written for *CQ Researcher*, May 2020

Violence is the driving force of politics. The importance of violence derives from the dominance it usually manifests over other forms of political action, from its destructive and politically transformative power and from the capacity of violence to serve as an instrument of political mobilization. These three factors explain why Chinese leader Mao Zedong was correct in his assertion that political power emanated from the gun barrel.

Political forces willing and able to employ violence to achieve their goals will generally best their less bellicose adversaries, overturning the results of elections, negating the actions of parliamentary bodies and riding roughshod over peaceful expressions of political opinion. Indeed, the mere threat of violence is often enough to instill fear in, and compel acquiescence by, those unwilling or unable to forcefully defend themselves. Violent groups can usually be defeated only by adversaries able to block their use of mayhem or to employ superior force against them. Those who cannot or will not make use of violence seldom achieve their goals over the opposition of those who are not similarly constrained. As Machiavelli observed, things have seldom turned out well for unarmed prophets.

Much attention, of course, is given to the putative effectiveness of nonviolence as a political method. In actuality, though, far from being nonviolent, the protest tactics—strikes, boycotts, demonstrations and the like—employed by such leaders as Mahatma Gandhi and Dr. Martin Luther King were designed to produce economic and social disruption and, in some instances, to actually provoke violent responses from their opponents. Violent attacks on apparently peaceful protesters would, it was hoped, elicit sympathy for the innocent victims of bloodshed and perhaps encourage powerful external forces to intervene on their behalf. Their success was predicated upon the availability of allies who could be drawn into the fray.

In the United States, nationally televised images of the violence unleashed upon peaceful protesters generated enormous sympathy for the civil rights cause and helped create the setting for enactment of the 1965 Voting Rights Act, which sent an army of federal law enforcement officials into the South with the power to suppress white resistance to the registration of black voters. In essence, nominally nonviolent protest succeeded because the protesters' allies had an even greater capacity for violence than their foes. Where, as in the case of China's Tiananmen Square in 1989, powerful allies are not available to deploy or at least threaten the use of force, nonviolent protest is almost always doomed to failure.

NO

Jonathan Pinckney
Program on Nonviolent Action, U.S. Institute of Peace

Written for *CQ Researcher*, May 2020

To answer whether violence is an effective tool for protest, one needs to first ask how protest works. Public protests are only one of a broad set of tactics employed by social movements such as strikes or boycotts. Protest is effective when it is strategically deployed alongside these additional tactics to undermine an opponent's power by prompting defections from their supporters. This defection process varies. A movement against a polluting company, for instance, might convince investors to divest, or customers to boycott. A pro-democracy movement might convince security forces to disobey orders to violently crack down.

Does violence help this process? While the impact of violence varies across cases, on average there are strong reasons to believe that it cannot.

First, violence tends to increase and legitimize government repression. Violent protests face much higher levels of government violence in response. While violent government repression of nonviolent protesters may spark backlash and condemnation, government repression of violent protesters is more likely to be seen as legitimate. Governments more easily paint violent protests as dangerous to social order and worthy of state violence in return. This tends to demobilize movements, leading to lower effectiveness.

Second, violence reduces who can reasonably participate in protests and other social movement tactics. Protest violence is overwhelmingly the province of young men, and when movements turn to violence their size and diversity tend to drop precipitously. This further undermines the protesters' legitimacy, as well as their potential points of connection with regime supporters. Without these points of connection, inducing defection among the opponent's supporters becomes more difficult.

Third, on average violence undermines mobilization of and external support for a movement. Numerous studies in political science and social psychology have shown that when movements use more violence, observers become less sympathetic and less likely to join or support them. This mobilization disadvantage is likely to undermine movements' attempts to achieve their goals.

There are certainly exceptions to these general trends. Some studies indicate that large social movements may have sufficient momentum that they are unaffected by peripheral incidents of violence. And in some specific cases, violence may have a highlighting effect, drawing attention to otherwise neglected causes. But when looking at movements as a whole, there are few good reasons to believe that violence is an effective tool, and many good reasons to believe that it directly undermines movements' effectiveness.

ment powers to restrict freedom of movement and secure supply lines for food and medical supplies.[68] The government also postponed for six months the scheduled April 26, 2020, referendum on whether to write a new constitution—a key protester demand—because of the virus.[69]

In Bolivia, elections to choose the successor to Morales had been scheduled for May 3, 2020, but the government postponed them, citing coronavirus concerns. The Bolivian electoral tribunal has proposed new dates between June 7 and Sept. 6.[70]

In Hong Kong, protests waned after the coronavirus arrived in the city. Organizers are exploring alternate ways of pressuring the government for change. (*See Short Feature.*) However, protesters began to defy the government's pandemic-related ban on public gatherings of more than four people. On April 24, 2020, 100 pro-democracy activists demonstrated at a Hong Kong shopping mall; on April 26, 300 demonstrators targeted another mall.[71]

Yellow vest protesters in France—which is among the nations hit hardest by the coronavirus—defied a government public health ban on gatherings of more than 100 people to demonstrate on March 14, 2020, the eve of local elections.[72] Prime Minister Edouard Philippe banned yellow vest protests on the Champs-Élysées in central Paris and in two other cities after 18 weeks of violent demonstrations.[73]

Lebanese activists suspect their government is using the virus as an excuse to suppress dissent. They say the emergency measures enacted March 15, 2020, that mandated stay-at-home restrictions and closed offices and businesses failed to include basic practices to safeguard public health.

"The government activated criminal laws to arrest and charge people [but] did not stop flights from [coronavirus] epicenters like Iran and ignored taking necessary measures to protect the people," said activist Jad Yateem.[74] The government eventually stopped airline flights from Iran, some three weeks after Lebanon's first reported coronavirus victim—who had returned from Iran.[75]

Global Climate Campaign

The coronavirus also has affected the global movement to fight climate change undertaken by Swedish teenager Thunberg. The Fridays for Future (FFF) movement she inspired, in which students took Fridays off from school

to agitate for cutting greenhouse gas emissions, had drawn millions of protesters to demonstrate in cities around the world.

But the pandemic has closed schools and driven the campaign indoors, robbing it of publicity, draining its influence and forcing its leaders to change tactics. FFF in many countries has suspended public demonstrations, instead using social media and the internet to get its message out.[76] On March 13, 2020, Thunberg, who said she believed she had the virus, tweeted, "In a crisis we change our behaviour and adapt to the new circumstances for the greater good of society."[77]

With public demonstrations off the table in most countries, a coalition of environmental organizations held a three-day continuous livestream "mobilization to stop the climate emergency" called Earth Day Live, April 22-24, 2020. The event included teach-ins, musical performances and a voter registration drive for U.S. audiences. The Future Coalition, an organizer of Earth Day Live, said 2.75 million people viewed the event.[78]

One online tactic is the "digital strike," in which activists post a picture of themselves and a sign bearing a slogan on social media. Joe Hobbs, 17, a student and FFF-United States activist from Columbia, Md., says, "Before [the virus struck] we would have physical strikes—protesting at the White House or the Capitol or the Library of Congress—once a month, and once a week we'd strike digitally, on social media. Now, we're going for all-digital strikes."

FABRICE COFFRINI/AFP via Getty Images

A student in Davos, Switzerland, participates in a January 2020 school strike demanding action against climate change. Inspired by teenage Swedish activist Greta Thunberg, students around the world have joined climate demonstrations.

Dana Fisher, a professor of sociology at the University of Maryland who researches activism, said social media campaigns "end up . . . amplifying within an echo chamber, which is really different from what the movement wants." Twitter hashtags do not get the visibility and publicity that large public demonstrations do, she said. However, she acknowledged that the young climate-change protesters are skilled at using social media to advance their cause.[79]

Hobbs says that "a digital strike, like a physical strike, raises awareness among your followers and anyone else who sees it." He says, "A lot of people thought that, because of the coronavirus, our numbers [of supporters] would go down, but actually they've gone up—more people are staying at home and able to interact with us online."

But online protests have drawbacks. Akshaya Kumar, director of crisis advocacy at Human Rights Watch, sees "a huge issue with . . . the digital divide—questions about who's able to get online and the bandwidth limitations for people based on their economic situation." She added, "It's certainly not as [accessible] as participating in a street protest, which is available to people regardless of their socioeconomic status."[80]

The coronavirus has had profound effects on the global economy. Stock market values have plunged, as have industrial production and retail sales, and unemployment has soared. The disease and governments' attempts to combat it have themselves become the target of protesters as the desire to slow the rate of infection conflicts with citizens' fears that the economic slowdown will leave them unable to make a living.[81] In Kenya, police killed 12 people while enforcing a dusk-to-dawn curfew which began March 27, 2020—more than the 11 that had been officially reported killed by the virus itself as of April 16.[82]

In the United States, hundreds protested in state capitals against stay-at-home measures and other safeguards imposed by governors, arguing the restrictions were no longer necessary and infringed on constitutional liberties. President Trump had declared the preventative measures to be the province of the state governors rather than the federal government, but he also encouraged the protests by criticizing governors for obstructing the nation's economic recovery, saying they've "gone too far." Targeted governors responded that they lacked the data

that would justify relaxing the measures.[83] *The Washington Post* reported that the state protests, though appearing spontaneous, had actually been orchestrated in a Facebook campaign by far-right activists.[84]

Between mid-March and mid-April, 2020, more than 22 million Americans filed for unemployment benefits, a record number.[85] As of April 25, the U.S. Centers for Disease Control and Prevention was reporting 928,619 coronavirus cases, with 52,459 deaths from the disease.[86]

Foreign Protests and U.S. Policy

Trump won the gratitude of the Hong Kong protesters when he signed legislation allowing the United States to levy sanctions on those who violate human rights in the city. Protesters draped themselves in American flags and waved pro-Trump banners in demonstrations celebrating the president's Nov. 27, 2019, signing of the Hong Kong Human Rights and Democracy Act, which also requires the State Department to conduct an annual review of Hong Kong's special trade status.[87]

The Chinese Foreign Ministry called the law "a severe interference in Hong Kong affairs, which are China's internal affairs. It is also in serious violation of international law and basic norms governing international relations."[88]

Another new law forbids U.S. companies to sell rubber bullets, pepper spray, tear gas and other crowd management munitions to Hong Kong police.[89]

Trump also inserted himself into Iran's January 2020 protests over the downing of a Ukrainian airliner when, in a series of tweets, he expressed solidarity with the demonstrators and warned the government, "DO NOT KILL YOUR PROTESTERS."[90] In response, Iranian Supreme Leader Ali Khamenei tweeted, "The villainous US [government] repeatedly says that they are standing by the Iranian [people]. They lie. If you are standing by the Iranian [people], it is only to stab them in the heart with your venomous daggers."[91]

Joseph Nye, former dean of Harvard's Kennedy School of Government and former chair of the U.S. National Intelligence Council, which provides long-term strategic analysis to government officials, says supporting protests in other countries "is useful if it's in the context of a general advancement or protection of human rights. But if it's seen as a weapon used against some countries but turning a blind eye to similar events in other countries, then it's viewed as hypocrisy."

"If President Trump wants to defend protesters in Iran, he has to reconcile that with his excusing the dismemberment of [Jamal] Khashoggi in the Saudi Arabian consulate in Istanbul," Nye says, referring to the Saudi dissident and *Washington Post* columnist who was murdered there. "Those responses don't fit together very well."

Frantz of Michigan State University says, "Both mainland China and the Iranian regime are very adept at putting forth the narrative that the U.S. is an agent provocateur. In some ways any U.S. involvement is just fodder for these regimes to put out this propaganda and help them withstand the [protesters'] challenge. If the U.S. is not willing to put up the resources to back up its words, it's empty rhetoric."

OUTLOOK
Democracy in Peril?

As the coronavirus spreads rapidly around the world, governments have imposed strict social distancing requirements and limitations on public gatherings to mitigate the impact of the virus and protect public health. But some protesters and civil liberties advocates fear governments might also use the new laws to suppress dissent and that autocratic leaders could assume dictatorial powers that do not expire when the virus threat subsides.

"The pandemic may well lead to a serious decline in democracy around the world," said Florian Bieber, professor of Southeast European history and politics at the University of Graz in Austria.

"Emergency laws or declared states of emergency [are] a tactic autocrats can use to consolidate power," Bieber said. He acknowledged that restricting gatherings and postponing elections are valid public health practices, noting that "French municipal elections held on March 15 might have accelerated the spread of the coronavirus." But he added: "Postponing elections for months might deprive governments of their legitimacy and allow autocrats to" strengthen their power.[92]

Democracy experts Crothers and David Wong of the Carnegie Endowment for International Peace wrote that "some governments are capitalizing on the crisis to enhance their ability to quash protest." But despite this challenge, they said, "the global protest wave is by no means moribund. Government responses to the virus have already sparked a spate of new protests. Prisoners in Lebanon and Italy have rioted over unsanitary conditions and overcrowding, and Brazilian and Colombian citizens have banged pots and pans from their windows to protest their leaders' public health response."

Moreover, they said, "the unfolding economic devastation resulting from the virus and the governance crises it has triggered may also sow the seeds for future protests. By exposing governments' incompetence in key areas such as public health and socioeconomic justice, the global pandemic could reinvigorate existing protests or even ignite demonstrations in new contexts."[93]

Hong Kong may be a case study for the theory. While the coronavirus has stalled public protests, a survey by the independent Hong Kong Public Opinion Research Institute found that three-quarters of Hong Kong residents believe the city did not do enough to stop the illness.[94] "The handling of the crisis by the government has been extremely poor," said activist Nathan Law. "[P]ublic anger is still growing and . . . the movement will revive when the outbreak is ended."[95]

Dunne of Carnegie believes many more protests are in store for the Middle East, too. "The whole economic structure of the region is crumbling," she says. "World energy markets are changing. There's a lot of oil and gas in the region, but it's not worth what it was."

Yet as the region's economic situation worsens, its population is growing and its people are increasingly aware of inequality, Dunne says. "I would say virtually every country in the region is vulnerable."

Stephan of the U.S. Institute of Peace says the future for peaceful protest movements is cloudy. "It's very disconcerting when considering the future of nonviolent movements," she says. "My worst fear is that we will see a strengthening of authoritarianism and a backsliding of democracies around the world."

But, she adds, "My optimistic side says people know how to organize and push back, and they can learn from each other. There's a competition going on between democracy and authoritarianism, and it remains to be seen who prevails."

NOTES

1. Samuel J. Brannen, Christian S. Haig and Katherine Schmidt, "The Age of Mass Protests: Understanding

an Escalating Global Trend," Center for Strategic and International Studies, March 2020, https://tinyurl.com/wgceft8.

2. Richard Youngs, ed., "After Protest: Pathways Beyond Mass Mobilization," Carnegie Europe, Oct. 24, 2019, https://tinyurl.com/y938awr4.

3. Jonathan Pinckney and Miranda Rivers, "Nonviolent Action in the Time of Coronavirus," U.S. Institute of Peace, March 25, 2020, https://tinyurl.com/y93qxzdo.

4. Selam Gebrekidan, "For Autocrats, and Others, Coronavirus Is a Chance to Grab Even More Power," *The New York Times*, March 30, 2020, https://tinyurl.com/yd4xfrp9.

5. James McAuley, "'Yellow vest' anniversary: What happened to the movement that shook France?" *The Washington Post*, Nov. 16, 2019, https://tinyurl.com/u8599be.

6. Tara John, "Why Hong Kong is protesting: Their five demands listed," *CNN*, Aug. 30, 2019, https://tinyurl.com/y2prgjze.

7. Brian C.H. Fong, "Where Does Hong Kong's Protest Movement Stand Amid Coronavirus Fears?" *The Diplomat*, Feb. 24, 2020, https://tinyurl.com/ycgyjud2.

8. Lucien Chauvin and Anthony Faiola, "As the U.S.-backed government in Bolivia unleashes a wave of political persecution, the Trump administration remains silent," *The Washington Post*, March 6, 2020, https://tinyurl.com/yarmjdfj.

9. Charis McGowan, "Chile protests: What prompted the unrest?" *Al-Jazeera*, Oct. 30, 2019, https://tinyurl.com/yypf9obg.

10. "Violence resurgence in Chile: three deaths, looting and torched supermarkets," *MercoPress*, Feb. 1, 2020, https://tinyurl.com/ycprltzp.

11. J. Patrice McSherry, "Chile's Struggle to Democratize the State," North American Congress on Latin America, Feb. 24, 2020, https://tinyurl.com/yb6fvokz.

12. Andy Gregory, "'They are killing us slowly': Iranian security forces used 'unlawful force against plane protesters,'" *The Independent*, Jan. 15, 2020, https://tinyurl.com/ycstf6s7.

13. Michael Safi *et al.*, "Protests rage around the world—but what comes next?" *The Guardian*, Oct. 25, 2019, https://tinyurl.com/yxjdm74k.

14. "Iran: Death toll from bloody crackdown on protests rises to 208," Amnesty International, Dec. 2, 2019, https://tinyurl.com/y7pbyakj.

15. "Iran 2019 Human Rights Report," U.S. Department of State, March 2020, https://tinyurl.com/ya6u7mb7.

16. Kai Thaler, "Violence Is Sometimes the Answer," *Foreign Policy*, Dec. 5, 2019, https://tinyurl.com/ya7xpcsb.

17. Shola Lawal, "Coronavirus Halts Street Protests, but Climate Activists Have a Plan," *The New York Times*, March 19, 2020, https://tinyurl.com/r4nm8bv.

18. "Femicide: A global scourge," *Agence France-Presse*, Nov. 19, 2019, https://tinyurl.com/yaoo75bc.

19. Sarah Repucci, "A Leaderless Struggle for Democracy," Freedom House, 2020, https://tinyurl.com/qwh9ek8.

20. Richard Wike and Shannon Schumacher, "Democratic Rights Popular Globally but Commitment to Them Not Always Strong," Pew Research Center, Feb. 27, 2020, https://tinyurl.com/y9yjlhm4.

21. R.S. Foa *et al.*, "The Global Satisfaction with Democracy Report 2020," University of Cambridge, January 2020, https://tinyurl.com/vcof6j3.

22. Robin Wright, "The Story of 2019: Protests in Every Corner of the Globe," *The New Yorker*, Dec. 30, 2019, https://tinyurl.com/v5ptgme.

23. Danna Takriti, "Sudan just took a step backward on its path to democracy," *Vox*, Feb. 21, 2020, https://tinyurl.com/yadm8sok.

24. Youngs, *op. cit.*

25. *Ibid.*

26. Paul Blumenthal, "The Largest Protest Ever Was 15 Years Ago. The Iraq War Isn't Over. What Happened?" *Huffpost*, March 17, 2018, https://tinyurl.com/y89as2hj.

27. Kim Milone, "The English Peasants' Revolt of 1381," *Loyola University Student Historical Journal 1986-87*, https://tinyurl.com/y9wx6azz.

28. Tara Isabella Burton, "The Protestant Reformation, explained," *Vox*, Nov. 2, 2017, https://tinyurl.com/y742lygk.

29. "The Reformation," History.com, https://tinyurl.com/yb9pk6xq.

30. Robert Longley, "The Road to the American Revolution," ThoughtCo., Jan. 14, 2019, https://tinyurl.com/ybbx62xv.

31. "French Revolution," History.com, Feb. 21, 2020, https://tinyurl.com/ybvhnauh.

32. "Revolutions of 1848" *Encyclopedia Britannica,* Jan. 20, 2019, https://tinyurl.com/y5ctwqkl.

33. "William II: King of the Netherlands," *Encyclopedia Britannica,* March 13, 2020, https://tinyurl.com/y7bcb5zt.

34. Erin Blakemore, "How Mahatma Gandhi changed political protest," *National Geographic*, Sept. 27, 2019, https://tinyurl.com/y6rp2hae.

35. "Malcolm X's Speech at the Founding Rally of the Organization of Afro-American Unity," *Blackpast*, Oct. 15, 2007, https://tinyurl.com/y7d5j3gu.

36. John Leland, "Who Really Killed Malcolm X?" *The New York Times*, Feb. 6, 2020, https://tinyurl.com/ychcls9q.

37. "The Black Panther Party," National Archives, https://tinyurl.com/r963yzu.

38. "Transcript of Civil Rights Act (1964)," National Archives, https://tinyurl.com/s5yev7x.

39. "Transcript of Voting Rights Act (1965)," National Archives, https://tinyurl.com/ycmpcm3t.

40. "Fair Housing Act," U.S. Department of Justice, https://tinyurl.com/y72pxabo.

41. "The Assassination of Martin Luther King, Jr.," Stanford University, https://tinyurl.com/yawhf47c.

42. Lorraine Boissoneault, "Martin Luther King Jr.'s Assassination Sparked Uprisings in Cities Across America," *Smithsonian Magazine*, April 4, 2018, https://tinyurl.com/yawab8aa.

43. Daniel S. Levy, "Behind the Anti-War Protests That Swept America in 1968," *Time*, Jan. 19, 2018, https://tinyurl.com/y9ycgrsw.

44. Joel Achenbach, "'A party that had lost its mind': In 1968, Democrats held one of history's most disastrous conventions," *The Washington Post*, Aug. 24, 2018, https://tinyurl.com/y7h6s584.

45. Alissa J. Rubin, "May 1968: A Month of Revolution Pushed France Into the Modern World," *The New York Times*, May 5, 2018, https://tinyurl.com/y7j7onro.

46. Robert Tait, "Prague 1968: lost images of the day that freedom died," *The Guardian*, Aug. 19, 2018, https://tinyurl.com/y4vplqzk.

47. Elizabeth Malkin, "50 Years After a Student Massacre, Mexico Reflects on Democracy," *The New York Times*, Oct. 1, 2018, https://tinyurl.com/y78w7gen.

48. "Tiananmen Square: What happened in the protests of 1989?" *BBC*, June 4, 2019, https://tinyurl.com/y8ujo2fr.

49. Cate Cadell, "China's internet censors are on high alert ahead of the anniversary of the Tiananmen Square protests," *Reuters, Business Insider*, May 26, 2019, https://tinyurl.com/y9h4oz7e.

50. "The Arab Spring: A Year Of Revolution," *National Public Radio*, Dec. 17, 2011, https://tinyurl.com/ybxw7ggh.

51. Erin Blakemore, "What was the Arab Spring and how did it spread?" *National Geographic*, March 29, 2019, https://tinyurl.com/yy4ae9eh.

52. Jessi Hempel, "Social Media Made the Arab Spring, But Couldn't Save It," *Wired*, Jan. 26, 2016, https://tinyurl.com/yag4o99f.

53. Gautam Mukunda, "The Social and Political Costs of the Financial Crisis, 10 Years Later," *Harvard Business Review*, Sept. 25, 2018, https://tinyurl.com/y7n5ykzj.

54. Jeremy W. Peters, "The Tea Party Didn't Get What It Wanted, but It Did Unleash the Politics of Anger," *The New York Times*, Aug. 28, 2019, https://tinyurl.com/y2gfhafq.

55. Megan Leonhardt, "The Lasting Effects of Occupy Wall Street, Five Years Later," *Money*, Sept. 16, 2016, https://tinyurl.com/y8pn4p7y; Emily Stewart, "We are (still) the 99 percent," *Vox*, April 30, 2019, https://tinyurl.com/y4qk58wz.

56. "Herstory," Black Lives Matter, https://tinyurl.com/t7r4x8b.

57. Alem Tedeneke, "The Black Lives Matter movement explained," World Economic Forum, Aug. 11, 2016, https://tinyurl.com/y42dadhu.

58. Ritu Prasad, "How Trump talks about women—and does it matter?" *BBC*, Nov. 29, 2019, https://tinyurl.com/s2rzvrh.

59. Anemona Hartocollis and Yamiche Alcindor, "Women's March Highlights as Huge Crowds Protest Trump: 'We're Not Going Away,'" *The New York Times*, Jan. 21, 2017, https://tinyurl.com/jb5ouxu.

60. Austa Somvichian-Clausen, "After low attendance, is the Women's March still relevant?" *The Hill*, Jan. 22, 2020, https://tinyurl.com/yah6o7fe.

61. Li Zhou, "A historic new Congress will be sworn in today," *Vox*, Jan. 3, 2019, https://tinyurl.com/yc3a56sr.

62. "We Want Change!" March for our Lives, https://tinyurl.com/yaz2fsxa.

63. Dominic Rushe, "Why is the National Rifle Association so powerful?" *The Guardian*, May 4, 2018, https://tinyurl.com/y7bxcd4o.

64. Alan Suderman and Sarah Rankin, "Pro-gun Rally by Thousands in Virginia Ends Peacefully," *The Associated Press*, Jan. 20, 2020, https://tinyurl.com/ueg4zp3.

65. Bobby Ghosh, "Coronavirus blunts momentum of second Arab Spring," *The Eagle*, March 27, 2020, https://tinyurl.com/y8y4ffuk.

66. "Coronavirus: Algeria protests called off for first time in a year," *BBC*, March 20, 2020, https://tinyurl.com/yc6eyeht.

67. "Lebanon calls in army to enforce coronavirus lockdown," *Agence France-Presse*, March 3, 2020, https://tinyurl.com/ycu7sht2.

68. Dave Sherwood, "Chile's Pinera Declares 90-Day State of Catastrophe Over Coronavirus Outbreak," *Reuters*, March 18, 2020, https://tinyurl.com/y7pabzpt.

69. Charis McGowan, "Chile moves to postpone constitutional referendum amid coronavirus crisis," *The Guardian*, March 19, 2020, https://tinyurl.com/u2v9oak.

70. Sergio Limachi, "Bolivia election body proposes June-to-September window for coronavirus-delayed vote," *Reuters*, March 26, 2020, https://tinyurl.com/yc35rjcf.

71. Julia Fioretti and Iain Marlow, "Hong Kong Police Disperse Protesters Gathered at City Mall," *Bloomberg*, April 26, 2020, https://tinyurl.com/y957oph6.

72. John Irish and Marine Pennetier, "Teargas, clashes in Paris as Yellow Vests' protesters defy coronavirus ban," *Reuters*, March 14, 2020, https://tinyurl.com/sef5dul.

73. Victoria Albert, "France's Prime Minister Edouard Philippe Bans Yellow Vest Protests After Saturday Riots," *The Daily Beast*, March 18, 2019, https://tinyurl.com/yaeqcgxf.

74. Nisan Ahmado, "Lebanese Activists Fear Hezbollah-led Government Is Using Coronavirus to Solidify Power," *Voice of America*, March 30, 2020, https://tinyurl.com/y8638ocw.

75. "Hezbollah Shifts Attention From Syria Fight to Battle Virus," *The Associated Press*, March 30, 2020, https://tinyurl.com/yd22f6my.

76. Paul Hockenos, "Shifting Gears: The Climate Protest Movement in the Age of Coronavirus," *Yale Environment 360*, March 26, 2020, https://tinyurl.com/yc8xe85e.

77. Greta Thunberg, Twitter post, March 20, 2020, https://tinyurl.com/ydfdpup4.

78. "Earth Day Live," https://tinyurl.com/ydbpdf4c; Anna Belle Peevey, "Video: Covid-19 Drives Earth Day Anniversary Online, Inspiring Creative New Tactics For Climate Activists," *Inside Climate News*, April 26, 2020, https://tinyurl.com/y9eje4s5.

79. Lawal, *op. cit.*

80. Max de Haldevang, "Coronavirus has crippled global protest movements," *Quartz*, April 1, 2020, https://tinyurl.com/y86rfg7e.

81. Liz Sly, "Stirrings of unrest around the world could portend turmoil as economies collapse," *The Washington Post*, April 19, 2020, https://tinyurl.com/yay7vnab.

82. Rael Ombuor and Max Bearak, "'Killing in the name of corona': Death toll soars from Kenya's curfew crackdown," *The Washington Post*, April 16, 2020, https://tinyurl.com/yccp6kg2.

83. Brett Samuels, "Trump: Some governors have gone too far on coronavirus restrictions," *The Hill*, April 19, 2020, https://tinyurl.com/y8ct9py9.

84. Isaac Stanley-Becker and Tony Romm, "Pro-gun activists using Facebook groups to push anti-quarantine protests," *The Washington Post*, April 19, 2020, https://tinyurl.com/yahe9k6h.

85. Heather Long, "U.S. now has 22 million unemployed, wiping out a decade of job gains," *The Washington Post*, April 16, 2020, https://tinyurl.com/yby2yet3.

86. "Cases of Coronavirus Disease (COVID-19) in the U.S.," U.S. Centers for Disease Control and Prevention, accessed April 25, 2020, https://tinyurl.com/qqt3aq6.

87. Deanna Paul and Shibani Mahtani, "Hong Kong protesters wave 'Swole Trump' posters at Thanksgiving rally," *The Washington Post*, Nov. 29, 2019, https://tinyurl.com/vecjv74.

88. "Statement of the Ministry of Foreign Affairs," People's Republic of China, Nov. 28, 2019, https://tinyurl.com/y83jfupp.

89. David Brunnstrom, "Trump approves legislation backing Hong Kong protesters," *Reuters*, Nov. 27, 2019, https://tinyurl.com/y7thythp.

90. Donald Trump, Twitter post, Jan. 11, 2020, https://tinyurl.com/yx82xbea; Donald Trump, Twitter post, Jan. 12, 2020, https://tinyurl.com/y8lj72gkl; and Donald Trump, Twitter post, Jan. 13, 2020, https://tinyurl.com/yczu63rt.

91. Ali Khamenei, Twitter post, Jan. 17, 2020, https://tinyurl.com/ycpt2ezp.

92. Florian Bieber, "Authoritarianism in the Time of the Coronavirus," *Foreign Policy*, March 30, 2020, https://tinyurl.com/ycohshj8.

93. Thomas Carothers and David Wong, "Misunderstanding Global Protests," Carnegie Endowment for International Peace, April 1, 2020, https://tinyurl.com/yc8fbkp2.

94. "Coronavirus widens Hong Kong anger at government, China," *Reuters*, Feb. 21, 2020, https://tinyurl.com/y8bhl8k8.

95. Dawn Brancati, "Coronavirus and the Hong Kong Protests," *Political Violence at a Glance*, Feb. 20, 2020, https://tinyurl.com/ybwccury.

BIBLIOGRAPHY

Books

Brancati, Dawn, *Democracy Protests: Origins, Features, and Significance*, Cambridge University Press, 2016.
A scholar at Yale University's MacMillan Center for International and Area Studies examines why major protests get started and how economic crises can trigger them.

Chenoweth, Erica, and Maria Stephan, *Why Civil Resistance Works: The Strategic Logic of Nonviolent Conflict*, Columbia University Press, 2011.
Two political scientists use statistical analysis and case studies to explain why some protest movements succeed and others fail, concluding that nonviolent campaigns have a better record than violent ones.

Kendall-Taylor, Andrea, Natasha Lindstaedt and Erica Frantz, *Democracies and Authoritarian Regimes*, Oxford University Press, 2020.
Three scholars look at the challenges facing democracy today, including populism and the rise of authoritarian regimes.

Articles

"COVID-19 and Conflict: Seven Trends to Watch," International Crisis Group, March 24, 2020, https://tinyurl.com/spu4kzy.
Analysts from a foreign affairs think tank discuss the coronavirus and its potential impact on world political events even after the danger of contagion has passed.

Karam, Zeina, "The New Mask: Wave of Global Revolt Replaced by Virus Fear," *The Associated Press*, March 12, 2020, https://tinyurl.com/rlsylp3.
Journalists for a global news agency report on how the coronavirus put 2019's wave of political protests on hold.

Kendall-Taylor, Andrea, Erica Frantz and Joseph Wright, "The Digital Dictators: How Technology Strengthens Autocracy," *Foreign Affairs*, March-April 2020, https://tinyurl.com/yaz9x3f6.
The director of the trans-Atlantic security program at the Center for a New American Security (Kendall-Taylor) and two political science professors explain how artificial intelligence, social media and other technologies are helping authoritarian leaders stay in power.

Kennon, Isabel, and Grace Valdevitt, "Women protest for their lives: Fighting femicide in Latin America," Atlantic Council, Feb. 24, 2020, https://tinyurl.com/qvnk5zj.
Two intern-researchers at the Atlantic Council examine gender-based violence directed at women and what governments are doing about it, and provide recommendations for more action.

Wright, Robin, "The Story of 2019: Protests in Every Corner of the Globe," *The New Yorker*, Dec. 30, 2019, https://tinyurl.com/v5ptgme.
In a pre-coronavirus report, a joint fellow at the U.S. Institute of Peace and the Woodrow Wilson Center discusses the protests that spanned the world last year.

Reports and Studies

Brannen, Samuel J., Christian S. Haig and Katherine Schmidt, "The Age of Mass Protest: Understanding an Escalating Global Trend," Center for Strategic and International Studies, March 2, 2020, https://tinyurl.com/y86cm553.
Researchers from a Washington foreign affairs think tank examine the causes and outcomes of the current global wave of protests and why it is likely to continue and expand.

Foa, R.S., *et al.,* "The Global Satisfaction with Democracy Report 2020," Centre for the Future of Democracy, Bennett Institute for Public Policy, January 2020, https://tinyurl.com/vcof6j3.
In this survey of surveys, researchers from the United Kingdom's University of Cambridge found global dissatisfaction with democracy in 2019 reached the highest level since measurements began 25 years ago.

Repucci, Sarah, "Freedom in the World 2020: A Leaderless Struggle for Democracy," Freedom House, https://tinyurl.com/y743l3xn.
In its most recent annual report on political rights and civil liberties, the research and advocacy organization finds democracy in decline around the world for the 14th straight year.

Youngs, Richard, ed., "After Protest: Pathways Beyond Mass Mobilization," Carnegie Endowment for International Peace, 2019, https://tinyurl.com/ydhbzqkk.
Local experts in civic activism analyze protests in 10 countries to explain what happens to protesters after their movement has ended.

Websites

"Global Protest Tracker," Carnegie Endowment for International Peace, last updated April 1, 2020, https://tinyurl.com/ybrgyaee.
A Washington think tank launched an interactive site in April that provides details on causes, triggers, duration and sizes of protests around the world since 2017.

Chenoweth, Erica, and Christopher Wiley Shay, "List of Campaigns in NAVCO 1.3," Harvard University, last updated March 17, 2020, https://tinyurl.com/y7ugzjhz.
Harvard researchers identify 622 major resistance campaigns, violent and nonviolent, from 1900 to 2019, by name, location, date, objective and outcome.

THE NEXT STEP
Coronavirus-Related Protests

Dougherty, Conor, and John Eligon, "Protesting Without Gathering, Tenant Organizers Get Creative," *The New York Times*, April 23, 2020, https://tinyurl.com/yc6c4jmz.
Housing activists are decorating their cars in support of a protest movement that wants rents canceled during the pandemic.

Selyukh, Alina, "Amazon Workers Stage New Protests Over Warehouse Coronavirus Safety," *NPR*, April 21, 2020, https://tinyurl.com/ydym9b32.
Hundreds of Amazon warehouse workers staged a nationwide walkout to protest the lack of paid sick leave and to support further measures to protect employees from contracting the coronavirus.

Wang, Vivian, Maria Abi-Habib and Vivian Yee, "'This Government Is Lucky': Coronavirus Quiets Global Protest Movements," *The New York Times*, April 23, 2020, https://tinyurl.com/y888ly69.
Millions of protesters are forced to stay at home worldwide because of the coronavirus, but dissent over some pandemic-related restrictions could lead to future demonstrations.

International Protests

Davidson, Helen, "China to prosecute first foreign national over Hong Kong protests," *The Guardian*, April 24, 2020, https://tinyurl.com/y97aev5h.
China is prosecuting a Belizean national for his participation in the 2019 Hong Kong protests.

McGowan, Charis, "How quarantined Chileans are keeping their protest movement alive," *Al-Jazeera*, April 14, 2020, https://tinyurl.com/y7cm8ont.
Chilean protesters bang pots and create virtual art to continue protesting inequality during the coronavirus pandemic restrictions.

Saleh, Walid, "Lebanon cities erupt against economic hardship, one protester killed in Tripoli," *Reuters*, April 27, 2020, https://tinyurl.com/yagj83y4.
One demonstrator was killed as protests erupted in Lebanon over worsening economic hardship.

Social Media

Overly, Steven, "Republicans attack Facebook as network shuts down anti-lockdown protests," *Politico*, April 20, 2020, https://tinyurl.com/y72ou2vt.
Facebook is blocking anti-quarantine protesters from organizing on their platform because they say the protests will violate states' stay-at-home orders, and some conservatives are criticizing the move.

Serhan, Yasmeen, "The Common Element Uniting Worldwide Protests," *The Atlantic*, Nov. 19, 2019, https://tinyurl.com/y767qppt.
Social media allows movements to operate in a decentralized way, which can benefit protesters facing suppression.

Tucker, Margaret, "A Guide to Chile's Revolutionary Social Media Slang," *Slate*, Dec. 17, 2019, https://tinyurl.com/qtxfe2w.
Chilean protesters have developed online slang and jokes to needle the government, such as dubbing President Sebastián Piñera, who was seen eating pizza shortly before ordering a crackdown, "El Pizza."

U.S. Protests

Gabbatt, Adam, "US anti-lockdown rallies could cause surge in Covid-19 cases, experts warn," *The Guardian*, April 20, 2020, https://tinyurl.com/y7per7jq.
Some health care workers are worried that anti-quarantine protests could allow the virus to spread faster.

Hauck, Grace, and Chris Woodyard, "Outraged Americans condemn US actions in Iraq and Iran: 'Enough with this nonsense,'" *USA Today*, Jan. 4, 2020, https://tinyurl.com/sey3dyz.
Protests against the Trump administration's killing of an Iranian general took place across the United States in an effort to prevent war with Iran.

Vogel, Kenneth P., Jim Rutenberg and Lisa Lerer, "The Quiet Hand of Conservative Groups in the Anti-Lockdown Protests," *The New York Times*, April 21, 2020, https://tinyurl.com/ycj3k39r.
Political groups founded during the Tea Party protests a decade ago are helping organize demonstrations against states' stay-at-home orders.

For More Information

Belfer Center for Science and International Affairs, 79 John F. Kennedy St., Cambridge, MA 02138; 617-495-9858; belfercenter.org. A center at Harvard University's Kennedy School of Government that performs research and training in international security and diplomacy, environmental and resource issues.

Carnegie Endowment for International Peace, 1779 Massachusetts Ave., N.W., Washington, DC 20036-2103; 202-483-7600; carnegieendowment.org. Independent think tank that researches and reports on issues pertaining to world peace.

Center for Security and International Studies, 1616 Rhode Island Ave., N.W., Washington, DC 20036; 202-887-0200; csis.org. Think tank examining trends and developments in international security.

Centre for the Future of Democracy, Bennett Institute for Public Policy, Department of Politics and International Studies, Alison Richard Building, 7 West Road, Cambridge, CB3 9DT England; +44-(0)1223-767233; bennettinstitute.

cam.ac.uk. Part of England's University of Cambridge, the center conducts research into challenges facing democracy and democratic societies.

Peterson Institute for International Economics, 1750 Massachusetts Ave., N.W., Washington, DC 20036-1903; 202-328-9000; piie.com. Research institution dealing with economic aspects of current and emerging international issues.

United States Institute of Peace, 2301 Constitution Ave., N.W., Washington, DC 20037; 202-457-1700; usip.org. Congressionally funded independent organization that researches and promotes nonviolent conflict resolution and mitigation.

Woodrow Wilson Center, One Woodrow Wilson Plaza, 1300 Pennsylvania Ave., N.W., Washington, DC 20004-3027; 202-691-4000; wilsoncenter.org. Nonpartisan think tank conducting research into, and disseminating information about, international issues and U.S. policy.

ANWAR AMRO/AFP via Getty Image

Christians from Syria and Iraq who fled their homelands in the face of insurgency and civil war attend a Mass in Lebanon on Christmas Day 2015.

13

Christians in the Mideast

Is the decline reversible?

By Sara Toth Stub

THE ISSUES

Hala Warda left Iraq in 2008 when, as part of its small native Christian community, she and her family felt threatened by Islamist insurgency movements that arose after the 2003 U.S. invasion. Eventually, in 2014, Islamic State militants ravaged her native city of Mosul and targeted many Iraqi Christians, in addition to Muslims.

But now Warda, 40, a graduate student, plans to return to Iraq from Steubenville, Ohio, and help establish a new Christian university as part of a project with Franciscan University of Steubenville.[1]

She is part of a movement of some Iraqi Christians who are returning to their home country and hoping to re-establish a presence there, despite heavy challenges. The obstacles include ongoing violence and fear of stigmatization as they accept aid from foreign governments and charities in an area already wracked by sectarian divisions.[2]

Iraq, which has lost about 83 percent of its Christian population since the American invasion, is not alone: Throughout the Middle East, Christians and other religious minorities face declining numbers and increased persecution.[3] Experts say this is not only a significant human rights crisis but a possible indicator that pluralism and democracy have failed in the conflict-ridden region.[4]

From *CQ Researcher,*
May 29, 2019

Christian Share of Population Dropping in Several Mideast Countries

The share of the population identifying as Christian has fallen and is projected to continue declining through 2025 in Egypt, Iraq and Israel. Christians are expected to remain less than 1 percent of the population of Iran. In the United Arab Emirates, the Christian population rose from just under 6 percent in 1970 to 12.6 percent in 2010 and is expected to hold steady.

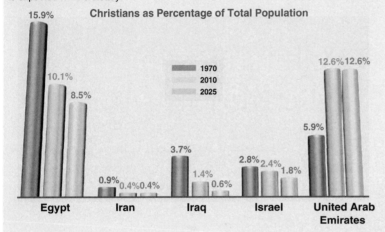

Christians as Percentage of Total Population

Legend: 1970, 2010, 2025

Egypt: 15.9%, 10.1%, 8.5%
Iran: 0.9%, 0.4%, 0.4%
Iraq: 3.7%, 1.4%, 0.6%
Israel: 2.8%, 2.4%, 1.8%
United Arab Emirates: 5.9%, 12.6%, 12.6%

Source: Todd M. Johnson and Gina A. Zurlo, "Ongoing Exodus: Tracking the Emigration of Christians from the Middle East," *Harvard Journal of Middle Eastern Politics and Policy*, Table 1, p. 44, https://tinyurl.com/yaelsgng

The decline also means the loss of some of the oldest Christian communities in the world, as well as a piece of history.

"Historically, this region has been hugely diverse, and the cradle of some of the world religions of today," says Gerard Russell, a former British diplomat in the region and the author of *Heirs to Forgotten Kingdoms*, a book about religious minorities in the Middle East. "But this diversity is in danger and severely diminishing."

Christians will make up just 3.6 percent of the region's population in 2025, down from 13.6 percent in 1910, according to the Center for the Study of Global Christianity at the Gordon-Conwell Theological Seminary in Hamilton, Mass.[5]

"The entire Christian presence is facing an existential threat," says Nina Shea, director of the Center for Religious Freedom at the Hudson Institute, a Washington think tank.

The decline in the number of Christians ultimately means that Middle Eastern societies will be less pluralistic and stable, experts say. The fact that so many people from a religion born in the region have been forced out, or

suffer discrimination and violence, implies it could be difficult for anyone who differs from the majority culture to live there safely; and it means that increasingly homogenous societies will struggle to interact with a diverse world.[6]

"A loss of pluralism can lead also to a reduction in security and stability for the society itself," says Jeremy Barker, senior program officer and director of the Middle East Action Team at the Religious Freedom Institute, a Washington-based group. "In this sense, religious minorities are often a test of a society's tolerance of the 'other,' however that is defined. Christians often are the proverbial canary in the coal mine."

Christians have been declining as a percentage of the Middle East population for many decades due mainly to emigration to North America and Europe to escape violence and to find better financial opportunities or more personal freedom. Christians also have had lower birth rates than local Muslim populations.[7]

But more recent and ongoing events—the U.S. invasion of Iraq, the subsequent rise of Islamist militant groups such as the Islamic State (ISIS), the fallout of the 2011 Arab Spring uprisings and the Syrian civil war—have increased the pressure on minority groups.[8] All of these events have contributed to the emergence of extremist groups whose actions include targeting minorities and contributing to general violence.[9]

"The situation in many places is worse, but not necessarily from government actions; rather it has often stemmed from the breakdown of the rule of law," says Philip Luther, Middle East and North Africa research and advocacy director at Amnesty International, the global human rights group.[10]

In Iraq, the vacuum left after U.S. troops overthrew longtime autocrat Saddam Hussein created years of local violence and the rise of ISIS and other militant groups that later spread throughout the region.[11]

Tunisians demonstrate against President Zine El Abidine Ben Ali in 2011, at the start of the Arab Spring uprisings that swept through the Middle East. The upheavals had the unintended consequence of removing protections for Christians and other religious minorities.

After Saddam's government fell, "the minorities found themselves without the umbrella of the state to protect them," says Saad Salloum, an assistant professor of political science at the University of Mustansiriyah in Baghdad. "And then ISIS destroyed what little had remained for the minorities after the invasion."

In Iraq, in addition to targeting foreigners and anyone who did not adhere to its principles, Islamic State took aim at Christians and other minorities. These included the Yazidis, a Kurdish group that practices an ancient faith, about 10,000 of whom were killed or captured in a single ISIS attack in August 2014.[12] The United States later labeled these actions, as well as ISIS attacks in Syria, as genocide.[13]

As the war in Iraq raged, the Arab Spring uprisings, which began with calls for democracy, transformed the region by toppling governments in Egypt, Tunisia, Libya and Yemen.[14] The upheaval led to civil war in Libya, Yemen and Syria, and the emergence of extreme Islamist groups that authoritarian regimes had long tamped down.[15]

These developments meant that many minority communities lost the stability and limited protection they had enjoyed under autocratic leaders, even as those leaders often curtailed freedom in general and committed severe human rights abuses.[16] For example, in Egypt, where authoritarian President Hosni Mubarak was ousted in 2011, Coptic Christians, who made up 10 percent of the population in 2010, were subsequently targeted by ISIS-affiliated groups and others. This spurred many to flee abroad or to other parts of the country.[17]

"People are running for their lives," said Mina Thabet, an official at the Egyptian Commission for Rights and Freedoms, a human rights group based in Cairo.[18]

And in Syria, where the Islamic State gained a stronghold and also is accused of genocide against minorities, about two-thirds of the country's Christian population has left since 2011—leaving behind empty villages and a sense of hopelessness about the future among those who remained.[19]

In fact, the Arab Spring upheavals resulted in increased challenges and threats to religious minorities in almost every affected country, according to Daniel Philpott, professor of political science at the University of Notre Dame, who studies the role of religion in conflict and politics. The one exception is Tunisia, where religious tolerance has increased slightly, Philpott said.[20] "Although that was not their intention, these uprisings ultimately made things worse," he says.

Government policies that discriminate against religious minorities and curtail their rights are more prevalent in the Middle East than other regions, according to the Pew Research Center, a Washington research group.[21] In Iran and Saudi Arabia, government restrictions on religion remain among the most severe in the world, Pew found.[22]

In addition to severely limiting non-Islamic practices, Iran and Saudi Arabia have targeted minority Muslim groups—Sunnis in Iran and Shiites in Saudi Arabia. The two countries are on opposite sides of a Sunni-Shiite schism that first emerged almost 14 centuries ago in Islam's early days over which descendants of the Prophet Muhammad should lead the new religion and empire. The divide has deepened today, with both religious and political ramifications.[23]

"The geostrategic rivalry between the two [countries] has exacerbated the extent to which authorities in both places have seen religious and ethnic minorities as political opponents," Amnesty International's Luther says.

In Iran, where the official religion since the 1979 revolution has been a specific stream of Shiite Islam, the government gives limited protections only to native Jews, some Christians and followers of the ancient religion of Zoroastrianism. According to the U.S. State

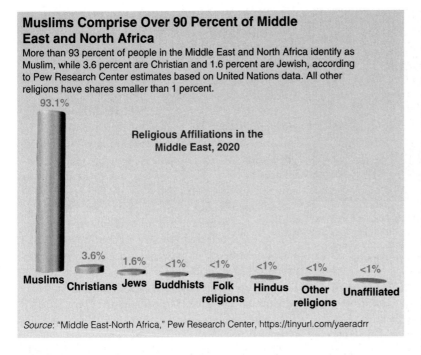

Muslims Comprise Over 90 Percent of Middle East and North Africa

More than 93 percent of people in the Middle East and North Africa identify as Muslim, while 3.6 percent are Christian and 1.6 percent are Jewish, according to Pew Research Center estimates based on United Nations data. All other religions have shares smaller than 1 percent.

Religious Affiliations in the Middle East, 2020

93.1% Muslims
3.6% Christians
1.6% Jews
<1% Buddhists
<1% Folk religions
<1% Hindus
<1% Other religions
<1% Unaffiliated

Source: "Middle East-North Africa," Pew Research Center, https://tinyurl.com/yaeradrr

Department, there are ongoing reports of arrests of members of nonrecognized groups, including converts to evangelical Christianity.[24] Proselytizing for any religion outside the official version of Shiite Islam is punishable by death.[25]

"Discriminatory policies are enshrined in the constitution," says Shahin Milani, a human rights lawyer and the executive director of the Iran Human Rights Documentation Center, a Connecticut-based group. Over the last decade, the Iranian government has executed and carried out extrajudicial killings and arrests of Sunni Muslims, who make up about 9 percent of the country's population, often accusing them of having ties with Sunni terrorist groups such as al Qaeda and ISIS, Milani says.[26]

In Saudi Arabia, public non-Muslim religious practice remains banned, even though a large number of foreign diplomats, businesspeople and laborers are present in the kingdom. Shiites have suffered in recent years from persecution ranging from execution without trial to social discrimination and public insults, human rights groups such as Amnesty International said.[27]

Even in parts of the Middle East not ruled by religious regimes or mired in full-blown wars, such as

Lebanon, Jordan, Israel and the Palestinian territories, economic challenges and underlying political tensions continue to encourage Christians to emigrate.

However, there is a countertrend: an influx from the Philippines and India of Roman Catholic and other Christian foreign workers, especially to the wealthier Persian Gulf countries and Israel.[28] Although in many of these places, including Bahrain, Kuwait and the United Arab Emirates, religion remains highly restricted for citizens, such foreign communities are allowed to have churches.[29] (*See Short Feature.*)

In December 2018, an Egyptian Coptic bishop celebrated a Mass in Saudi Arabia, the first instance in that country of a public Christian ceremony.[30] In 2019, Pope Francis became the first pontiff to visit the United Arab Emirates, where the government subsequently announced the building of a mosque-church-synagogue complex, called the Abrahamic Family House, a space for prayer services and interfaith dialogue.[31]

"You do see some little encouraging signs," says Russell, the former British diplomat, although he adds that the overall picture for religious minorities remains grim, especially for those native to the region.

BACKGROUND
Christianity's Origins

When Christianity first emerged in the Middle East 2,000 years ago, the followers of this new religion were small in number and heavily persecuted under the Roman Empire that ruled the region.[32] But when Emperor Constantine personally converted to Christianity in 312 and lifted legal restrictions on it the following year, the religion grew and eventually became the majority faith in a region stretching from North Africa to the Persian Gulf and across the Mediterranean.[33]

CHRONOLOGY

1900s-1930s *Secular states arise.*

1922 Ottoman Empire falls; Turkish leader Kemal Ataturk begins era of secular governments in the Middle East.

1928 Muslim Brotherhood is founded in Egypt as a pan-Islamic social welfare political movement, the first of several such initiatives in the region that often use violence and are largely repressed by ruling powers.

1940s-1990s *Sectarian tensions escalate.*

1948 Establishment of the state of Israel sets off war with neighboring Arab countries, as well as a wave of immigration of Jews from other Middle Eastern countries to the new state.

1975 Civil war begins in Lebanon, pitting religious groups against each other and sparking emigration to Europe and the United States.

1979 Militants establish the Islamic Republic in Iran after the overthrow of the Shah.

1981 Shiite Islamic group Hezbollah carries out its first suicide bombing in Lebanon, ushering in an era of religiously motivated terrorist attacks.

1990 Iraq invades and occupies Kuwait; U.S. intervention leads to the first Persian Gulf War, which results in Iraq's defeat.

1991 Kurds and Shiite Muslims in Iraq rise up against Iraqi leader Saddam Hussein, but are quickly and violently subdued, demonstrating the enduring power of Saddam's authoritarian Sunni government.

2000-2006 *U.S. role in the Middle East increases amid rising sectarian tensions.*

2003 U.S. troops invade Iraq and quickly topple Saddam's regime.

2006 Islamic militant Hamas party wins Palestinian elections, ending years of secular leadership. . . . Sectarian

tensions and violence increase in Iraq, setting off years of fighting and terrorism.

2010-Present *Arab Spring uprising and chaos in Iraq trigger violence against religious minorities.*

2010 Arab Spring uprisings begin in Tunisia and spread the following year to Egypt, Syria, Libya, Yemen, Bahrain and other places.

2011 Egypt's regime falls, and civil war breaks out in Syria. . . . Egypt's Coptic Christian minority suffers the first of many fatal violent attacks as order breaks down in the country.

2012 Muslim Brotherhood leader Mohamed Morsi wins the Egyptian presidency.

2013 Egyptian military ousts Morsi, killing at least 1,000 people with alleged ties to Islamist extremists.

2014 The Islamic State (ISIS) ramps up armed offensives in Iraq and Syria. It also targets religious minorities, killing thousands of Yazidis and others.

2016 The United States declares ISIS's actions to be genocide. . . . Saudi Arabia curbs power of its religious police, but non-Islamic public worship remains illegal.

2017 ISIS begins to lose large amount of its territory in Syria and Iraq. . . . Churches begin to help Christians who had fled ISIS return to Iraq and rebuild.

2018 U.S. begins withdrawing troops from Syria, where civil war has killed at least 400,000 since 2011; the departure worries Kurds and other minorities that Turkey could fill the vacuum and target them.

2019 Pope Francis visits United Arab Emirates in first pontifical visit to the Persian Gulf.

2020 Some Christians and other religious minorities continue returning to Iraq despite fears of the resurgence of ISIS and other terrorist groups; the coronavirus pandemic threatens further economic downturn in the region.

Influx of Asian Christians Boosts the Faith in Middle East

"It's one Mass after the other on weekends."

Every Friday evening, hundreds of migrant workers gather for Mass in a residential neighborhood of Tel Aviv, Israel's bustling commercial center. The site, Our Lady Woman of Valour, opened in 2014 and is the first Roman Catholic church in the mainly Jewish city. It includes a daycare center and religious education programs for children of foreign laborers and asylum-seekers who have come to Israel over the last two decades.

"It's one Mass after the other on weekends," says the Rev. Rafic Nahra, coordinator for pastoral care of migrants and patriarchal vicar for Hebrew-speaking Catholics of the Vicariate of St. James in Israel, which oversees Our Lady Woman of Valour. "It is essential that the church be here to help these people, because many are here alone, and need support at all levels, psychiatric, economic."

This community is part of the growing stream of foreign Christians flowing into the Middle East, even as the religion struggles locally with emigration and persecution.[1]

"There are two competing trends in the region as it relates to Christianity," says Gina A. Zurlo, co-director of the Center for the Study of Global Christianity at the Gordon-Conwell Theological Seminary in Hamilton, Mass. The number of Christians indigenous to the region has been declining for more than a century, with steeper falls in recent years due to wars in Iraq, Syria and Yemen, along with a documented increase of persecution of religious minorities in the midst of the Arab Spring uprisings.[2]

But in many other countries, including majority-Muslim Bahrain, Saudi Arabia and Oman, the number of Christians has risen sharply.[3] This is due mainly to the influx of foreigners from places such as the Philippines and India taking jobs as domestic workers in the increasingly wealthy Persian Gulf countries, Zurlo says. These workers come from Roman Catholic, Pentecostal and Protestant backgrounds, she says. While conversion to Christianity remains illegal for locals in Gulf countries, these foreign workers are allowed to build and attend churches—except in Saudi Arabia, where they must gather privately if at all.[4]

"Where churches are allowed, it is definitely a sign that those countries want to be seen as more modern," says Nina Shea, director of the Center for Religious Freedom at the Hudson Institute, a Washington think tank. Much of this openness to foreigners practicing their religions has roots in the economic and business concerns of Gulf economies, which rely heavily on foreign migrant labor.[5]

In 2019, for example, the emirate of Abu Dhabi formally recognized 17 churches for foreigners and established a special department to deal with expatriates' religious affairs.[6] Similarly, since 2008, Qatar has allowed churches to be built, mainly to serve foreigners.[7]

While many kinds of Christian communities have grown up around the migrants, the Roman Catholic Church has been especially active in creating organizational structures to minister to these flocks. The Vatican established the Apostolic Vicariate of Northern Arabia in 2011 to serve the approximately 1.7 million Catholics in Bahrain, Qatar, Kuwait and Saudi Arabia.[8] In Bahrain, that organization is building a cathedral called Our Lady of Arabia, which will seat more than 2,000 people and include a five-story conference center and room for 6,000 in an outdoor courtyard.[9]

In 2019, Pope Francis became the first pontiff to visit the region when he traveled to the United Arab Emirates, at the invitation of Abu Dhabi's crown prince Sheikh Mohammed bin Zayed Al Nahyan, to participate in an interfaith event and celebrate a Mass for the thousands of foreign Catholics working there.[10]

But challenges remain. "Restriction on the number of priests, too few churches and limited space in the churches are the difficulties that we face," in addition to a strict ban on outreach to local Muslims, the Vicariate of Northern Arabia said on its website.[11]

The Catholic Church has also had a department in Israel since 2011 to serve growing numbers of foreign workers and asylum-seekers in that country, most of them from the Philippines, India and Africa.[12]

The number of foreign Christians in Israel—about 150,000 migrant workers and asylum seekers—is now nearly equal to those native to the country, about 160,000, according to the vicariate. Although the Israeli government allows only religious marriage, has strict requirements for conversion to Judaism and has been accused of unfairly curtailing some Islamic groups, by law freedom of worship is permitted.[13]

Many large old churches in Israel that had emptied over the years as local Christian communities shrank now celebrate many Masses in multiple languages.[14]

"When you see this presence of these people, it gives life to the church," says Nahra, the patriarchal vicar. But he adds that the communities of foreign Christians are transient by nature and remain separate from local Arabic-speaking Christians.

"I don't think it will change the balance for Christianity," Nahra says. The migrants and asylum-seekers still face large challenges, including economic insecurity and the threat of deportation for those who are undocumented or have overstayed their visas. "The current coronavirus pandemic puts this community even more at risk, with many who are out of work now, but also without any insurance," he says.

In many Gulf countries, thousands of Asian migrant workers have already been put out of work because of the pandemic, depriving their relatives of the much-needed remittance payments they often send back home. In fact, some workers have started returning to their home countries.[15]

While Nahra says the presence of Catholic domestic workers can contribute to a positive perception of Christianity in the Middle East, he and others say the temporary nature of migrants and lack of integration limits their influence on a society and its levels of tolerance.

"It is important to remember that the migrants live lives of marginalization wherever they go," says the Rev. David Neuhaus, the former patriarchal vicar, who is still involved with the migrant community. "Even in Israel, they are not really part of or really benefiting from any democratic nature of the society."

—Sara Toth Stub

[1] *World Christian Encyclopedia*, 3rd edition (2020), p. 933.

[2] *Ibid.*

[3] *Ibid.*

[4] Declan Walsh and Jason Horowitz, "Why Pope Francis' Historic Visit to the Gulf Matters," *The New York Times*, Feb. 3, 2019, https://tinyurl.com/yaw8larl.

[5] Taylor Luck, "Can Religious Tolerance Help an Aspiring Muslim Power?" *The Christian Science Monitor*, June 11, 2019, https://tinyurl.com/y8zs2ece.

[6] Ramola Talmar Badam, "Abu Dhabi churches and temples to receive new legal status on Sunday," *The National*, Sept. 21, 2019, https://tinyurl.com/y7zy7j66.

[7] Sebastian Castelier and Clément Pouré, "In Qatar Christianity Grows on the Fringes," *The New Arab*, Dec. 21, 2018, https://tinyurl.com/ybwkkcyw.

[8] "Welcome to The Cathedral of Our Lady of Arabia," Apostolic Vicariate of Northern Arabia, 2020, https://tinyurl.com/y9364nzy.

[9] *Ibid.*

[10] Harriet Sherwood, "Pope faces critics over Yemen on first papal visit to UAE," *The Guardian*, Feb. 2, 2019, https://tinyurl.com/ybl2s8k7; Walsh and Horowitz, *op. cit.*

[11] "Welcome to The Cathedral of Our Lady of Arabia," *op. cit.*

[12] "Pastoral of the local Catholic Church towards migrants and asylum seekers in Israel," St. James Vicariate for Hebrew Speaking Catholics in Israel, 2020, https://tinyurl.com/ycppyxs5.

[13] Ilanit Chernick, "State Department report: concerns over religious freedom in Israel," *The Jerusalem Post*, July 8, 2019, https://tinyurl.com/yd25r52a.

[14] Sara Toth Stub, "New Life Breathed into Israel's Churches by Expats and Immigrants," *The Wall Street Journal*, Jan. 8, 2016, https://tinyurl.com/y7phmr4q.

[15] Rory Jones, "Jobless Migrants Flee Oil-Rich Countries to the Chagrin of Their Home Countries," *The Wall Street Journal*, May 23, 2020, https://tinyurl.com/ybrgdcnq.

A 19th-century depiction of Roman Emperor Constantine's conversion to Christianity in 312. Constantine removed legal restrictions on Christians, facilitating the spread of the religion throughout his empire.

Even after Islam began to spread through the Middle East starting in the 7th century, large Christian communities remained throughout the region. But the Crusades—a series of religiously motivated European invasions of the Middle East that began in the late 11th century—triggered Muslim suspicion of local Christian communities and increased discrimination against them.[34]

It was not until the Middle Ages, between the 12th and 14th centuries, that places such as Syria-Palestine and Egypt became majority Muslim.[35] New religious communities also continued to develop, including the Druze, people who follow a monotheistic faith that emerged in 11th-century Egypt and who now live mainly in Israel, Syria and Lebanon; and the Baha'i religion, which grew out of Shiite Islam in 19th-century Persia (now Iran).[36] While there were many periods of persecution, many of these smaller communities survived by living in mountainous or isolated areas, Russell says.

Under various Islamic rulers, most Jews and Christians were given some amount of protection and independence in education, marriage and inheritance regulations.[37]

"The Christians and other minorities also tended to be transnational, and were important for trade, diplomacy and spreading new ideas," Russell says. As European colonialism increased in the 19th century, Western governments, churches and missionaries were among those to establish some of the most renowned universities and hospitals in the region, including the American University of Beirut.[38]

Secular Regimes

Following World War II and the decline of European colonialism, secular nationalistic regimes rose in Egypt, Iraq and Syria. Those regimes repressed and limited the practice of Islam—but gave religious minorities, including Jews and Christians, certain rights and protections. "Islam was seen as anti-modern and backward by these secular governments that wanted to focus on economic development and modernization," says Philpott, the Notre Dame political scientist.

But when the state of Israel was created in 1948, long-established Jewish populations in Middle Eastern and North African countries became the targets of an upsurge in violence, and most fled to the newly created Jewish state.[39]

By the 1960s, Islam as a political alternative to Arab nationalism began to gain strength throughout the region.[40] In Iran, the religious forces eventually prevailed, establishing an Islamic Republic in 1979 in what had long been a secular country; this rise of a Shiite regime inspired rivalry in Sunni-majority countries.[41] But in many places, from Egypt to Iraq to Libya, dictators suppressed Islamist forces, resulting in societies where religious identity was de-emphasized. This often worked to the benefit of religious minorities, even as human rights abuses continued.[42]

"Christians often saw they had no choice but to support the dictatorships, simply to survive," Philpott says.

When these regimes began to fall, beginning in 2003 with Saddam in Iraq, the region's minorities were suddenly vulnerable to the forces that had previously been suppressed.

The aftermath of the American invasion in Iraq also highlighted how strong the Sunni-Shiite tensions had become, as the country descended into sectarian violence that became a civil war.[43] These tensions ultimately became a strong recruiting tool for Sunni-oriented ISIS.[44] They also came to the forefront in other places amid the collapse of established powers following the Arab Spring uprisings, including in the war between Iranian and Saudi proxies in Yemen, where Christians and other minorities have been targets.[45]

"It's really quite shocking that Christians lived in relative stability in the region as religious minorities for many centuries, up until the 21st century," says Gina A. Zurlo, co-director of the Center for the Study of Global Christianity.

CURRENT SITUATION

Hurdles to Overcome

While the wars in Iraq and Syria have lessened in intensity, religious minorities face steep challenges throughout the region, mainly due to lack of protection from governments and a continuation of threats from sectarian violence and armed groups. In Iraq, ethno-religious minorities are in an "unprecedented state of crisis," wrote Salloum, the political scientist. While more than 1.7 million people have returned home to heavily devastated areas of northern Iraq, the rates of return are lower for the Christian and Yazidi minorities, Salloum said.[46]

Those who do return face high security and economic hurdles, including threats from local militias, worries that ISIS could re-emerge and lack of jobs.[47] The U.S. government is redirecting aid money for general recovery directly to minority communities—an effort that may have domestic political ramifications as the Trump administration seeks to please a conservative evangelical Christian voting base at home.[48]

At the same time, it is increasingly difficult for Iraqi Christians to get asylum status in the United States, the news site ProPublica reported earlier this year. The Trump administration has argued that they are not eligible for asylum because the Iraqi government is now protecting Christians—a view disputed by some experts on the region and even one administration official.[49]

"The responsibility of Western nations is very real and indisputable," said Ignace Joseph III Younan, the patriarch of the Syriac Catholic Church. "Their opportunism created conflicts that have led to chaos."[50]

In Egypt, the Coptic Christian community is struggling to navigate the post-Arab Spring world amid fears of violence from Islamist militant groups and mixed feelings about President Abdel-Fattah el-Sissi, who some see as taking only symbolic steps to support minorities.[51]

El-Sissi, who promised to protect Copts during his election campaign in 2014, continues to publicly support them, recently inaugurating the largest cathedral in the Middle East in Cairo and becoming the first Egyptian leader to attend a Mass.[52] But more than 140 Copts have

Egyptian President Abdel-Fattah el-Sissi greets worshippers at a Mass near Cairo in January 2020. Some Egyptian Christians have mixed feelings about el-Sissi, saying he has not always fulfilled his promises to protect religious minorities.

been killed in attacks by ISIS-related groups and others since 2015.[53]

"Egypt is suffering from terrorism, but sometimes Copts feel they are paying the price more than others," said Bishop Anba Makarios, the head of the Coptic diocese in the province of Minya, south of Cairo.[54] In addition, rules about church-building that have come into effect during the past year, at first touted as helpful to Copts, have ultimately proved to further limit the building of new churches and to close existing churches, according to the Egyptian Initiative for Personal Rights, a local nongovernmental organization.[55] In some cases, local authorities have used these rules to fan sectarian violence and persecution of Christians, according to a report from Minority Rights Group International, a British group that promotes the inclusion and fair treatment of minorities around the world.[56]

In addition, Egyptian forces arrest those who speak out about attacks on minorities—including the Coptic activist Ramy Kamel, who remains jailed on charges of spreading false news and joining a terrorist group in connection with his sharing footage on social media of sectarian violence targeting Christians.[57] The United States has called for his release.[58]

"The [el-Sissi] government is waging a war against its opposition, rather than a war against terrorism," said Thabet, of the Egyptian Commission for Rights and Freedoms.[59]

Should government and private foreign aid programs target religious minorities?

YES
Jeremy P. Barker
Director, Middle East Action Team and Senior Program Officer, Religious Freedom Institute

Written for *CQ Researcher*, May 2020

The humanitarian imperative of "need not creed" is vital, yet the reality is that in many conflict or crisis situations *creed exacerbates need.*

Religious identity often leads to heightened vulnerability and need. Many aid and development programs fail to account for religious identity and therefore fail to ensure that their assistance addresses the specific needs of religious minorities and other marginalized communities.

The key point: Religious identity should neither lead to special treatment nor to special burdens when providing aid. And particular needs and vulnerabilities may be relevant when helping members of a persecuted group.

Why is this the case?

First, generic, location-based programs may fail to account for pre-existing inequalities that are frequently heightened in times of conflict or crisis. As recent Pew Forum data on religious restrictions show, more than 80 percent of the world's population lives in countries with high government restrictions or social hostilities. These factors disproportionately affect religious minorities, converts from a majority religion and atheists, bringing about societal inequalities. Even when religious identity is not the primary driver of a conflict or crisis, it can interact with other factors to increase vulnerability and need. These factors should encourage aid workers and donors to give explicit attention to how these inequalities are addressed through assistance programs.

Second, a general approach to assistance often overlooks the needs of vulnerable communities. A targeted, person-centered approach puts the individual as the primary concern for aid and development programs. Emphasizing the individual requires paying attention to not just material needs such as food, water and shelter but also to religious identity and practice. Without explicit attention to these factors, the needs of minorities often go unaddressed.

Finally, one-size-fits-all approaches fail to address barriers to inclusion of vulnerable communities. Simply tying programs to a shared geographic space will not ensure equal access to and participation of diverse populations. As efforts to help gender and physical disabilities have shown, a twin-track approach that includes both targeted efforts and the inclusion of vulnerable groups in general programs is often necessary. Monitoring, evaluation and learning programs should be structured to ensure, rather than assume, that desired outcomes are being met.

While the United Nations' 1951 Refugee Convention recognized religious persecution as one of the reasons for refugee status, it is often overlooked as a vulnerability criterion in foreign aid assistance programs today. Both donors and aid providers would do well to consider this factor in their assistance efforts.

NO
Hady Amr
Nonresident Senior Fellow, Brookings Institution; Adjunct Senior Fellow, Center for a New American Security

Written for *CQ Researcher*, May 2020

Minority groups may certainly need our help. But targeting them with bespoke foreign aid may do more harm than good. Here's why:

Imagine if a foreign country like China or Mexico decided that Americans of Asian or Latin origin were unfairly discriminated against in the United States. And also imagine that China or Mexico decided to target its foreign aid to benefit Asian American or Latin American communities. How would other Americans, especially those who were struggling in life, feel about foreign aid that excluded them? Would they be thrilled? Or would they be resentful that they could not benefit? And would that resentment create an even more threatening environment for these disadvantaged communities?

It is undeniable that across the Middle East and around the world religious and ethnic groups face significant discrimination. But even if we want to focus our aid on only one of these groups, singling them out for support also singles them out for resentment by their fellow citizens.

The best way to help a group is to seek to lift up as many disadvantaged groups as possible in that society. In health care, for example, the foreign aid program should provide help to the individuals or communities with the worst health care outcomes—including but not only the target group. In education, it should provide assistance to the schools with the worst educational outcomes. And if it is in basic income, it should provide economic assistance to those most in need.

If we believe there really is systematic discrimination at the legal or government policy level against a particular group—even a religious group—then we should address it right there with frank conversations with government and the judiciary about the need to make the law and government practice more fair and nondiscriminatory.

The only exception to this approach might be for programs that seek to empower women or youths, because such aid benefits large swaths of society.

While it is true that some societies have set up affirmative action programs, such programs only stand the chance of not engendering resentment if they are the outcome of genuine *internal* societal discussion. And even then, we must admit they have also, unfortunately, engendered some—though likely far less—resentment. An *external* aid program would be far more likely to sow social divisions.

A better way to help those in need, including and especially religious minorities in the Middle East, would be to vigilantly design our aid programs to help the neediest—not only those who pray in a particular way.

Converts Threatened

In Iran, government authorities are increasingly targeting those who convert to Christianity, an act classified as illegal and punishable by death.[60] This comes as ties to religious practices other than the official Shiite Islam are viewed as political statements and signs of disloyalty to the state rather than traditional religious offenses, such as apostasy, says Milani, the human rights lawyer.

"The Assyrian and Armenian Christians, along with Zoroastrians, are generally left alone because they do not attract converts," Milani says. "But those who seek converts are seen differently." The number of those converting to Christianity is not clear, but "it is enough to create concern in the government," says Sara Afshari, who has studied the issue as part of her doctoral thesis at the University of Edinburgh.[61]

She says that motivations for Christian converts vary in Iran: Some who plan to emigrate choose to embrace Christianity in order to feel more Western; others are motivated primarily by the spiritual truth they find in it; and still others see it as a way to reject the Islamic regime. American and other foreign evangelical groups also try to encourage the practice. The government regularly raids underground churches, mainly held in homes, and practitioners are often charged with security offenses, including having ties to Israel or other foreign governments.[62]

A growing number of Iranian evangelical Christians have fled to Turkey, where they then request that the United Nations settle them as refugees in a third country; but aid workers there say that U.N. officials have grown distrustful of the motivations of such people and few are successful in moving elsewhere.[63]

OUTLOOK
Waning Hope

Religious minorities remain skeptical that they will ever regain the levels of stability and protection they enjoyed earlier. Because of widespread lawlessness and other problems, few have faith that local governments or foreign powers will do enough to make a difference, many Middle East Christians say.

"We are facing a total extinction, I assume," Maryam Binyamen, an Iraqi Christian, said, explaining that her community fears the re-emergence of ISIS. "Not the church nor the government can do anything about it."[64]

Minorities will only be protected if "countries are able to develop effective, inclusive, transparent governance for all citizens," says Barker of the Religious Freedom Institute. "Protection for religious freedom is a key element of that governance and, among many others, will come in the form of rescinding anti-conversion laws, blasphemy laws and a variety of forms of discrimination against religious communities outside the majority faith," he adds. The barriers to such action, including violent extremist groups, are huge, he says. Studies predict further violence against minorities in the Middle East, and more emigration for those who have that option.[65]

Shea, at the Hudson Institute, says that the coronavirus pandemic, if it spreads quickly in refugee camps and jails and causes economic damage, will also likely hurt Christians and other minorities. An economic downturn would make many Christians in places such as Lebanon, Israel and the West Bank especially vulnerable, as many rely on small businesses and tourism for their livelihoods.[66]

"These Christians often have the connections abroad, through their churches, and a big diaspora abroad, so more could leave," Shea says.

NOTES

1. Peter Jesserer Smith, "Iraqi Catholic Student at Franciscan Vows to Rebuild Christianity in Iraq," *National Catholic Register*, March 10, 2020, https://tinyurl.com/ycte5y6t.

2. Emma Green, "The Impossible Future of Christians in the Middle East," *The Atlantic*, March 23, 2019, https://tinyurl.com/yxbj9jkr; Yeganeh Torbati, "How Mike Pence's Office Meddled in Foreign Aid to Reroute Money to favored Christian Groups," *ProPublica*, Nov. 6, 2019, https://tinyurl.com/y54w9tbr.

3. Frank Gardner, "Iraq's Christians 'close to extinction,'" *BBC*, May 23, 2019, https://tinyurl.com/y63s5sel; Maria Abi-Habib, "Christians, in an epochal shift, are leaving the Middle East," *The Wall Street Journal*, May 12, 2017, https://tinyurl.com/y7brdqxc.

4. Brian Katulis, Rudy deLeon and John B. Craig, "The Plight of Christians in the Middle East," Center for American Progress, March 12, 2015, https://tinyurl.com/ybqwcabq.

5. Todd M. Johnson and Gina A. Zurlo, "Ongoing Exodus: Tracking the Emigration of Christians from the Middle East," *Harvard Journal of Middle Eastern*

Politics and Policy, Table 1, https://tinyurl.com/yaelsgng.

6. Katulis, deLeon and Craig, *op. cit.*, p. 2.

7. *Ibid.*; "Middle East North Africa," Pew Research Center, April 2, 2015, https://tinyurl.com/y9p5uv8k.

8. *World Christian Encyclopedia*, 3rd edition (2020); Daniel Philpott, *Religious Freedom In Islam* (2019); Katulis, deLeon and Craig, *op. cit.*

9. Katulis, deLeon and Craig, *ibid.*

10. "Middle East still home to the highest levels of restrictions on religion, although levels have declined since 2016," Pew Research Center, July 15, 2019, https://tinyurl.com/y85nn2q9.

11. Stephen Kinzer, "Among the Casualties of US Wars in the Middle East: Christianity," *The Boston Globe*, Dec. 24, 2019, https://tinyurl.com/rnv5k3y.

12. Matthew Rosenberg, "Citing Atrocities, John Kerry Calls ISIS Actions Genocide," *The New York Times*, March 17, 2016, https://tinyurl.com/y8z42j3a; Valeria Cetorelli and Sareta Ashraph, "A demographic documentation of ISIS's attack on the Yazidi village of Kocho," The London School of Economics Middle East Centre, June 2019, p. 6, https://tinyurl.com/yd58g82c.

13. "U.S. Decries ISIS 'Genocide' of Christians, Other Groups," *The Associated Press/NBC News*, Aug. 15, 2017, https://tinyurl.com/yb2647x3.

14. Erin Blakemore, "What was the Arab Spring and how did it spread?" *National Geographic*, accessed April 27, 2020, https://tinyurl.com/yy4ae9eh.

15. Katulis, deLeon and Craig, *op. cit.*, p. 11.

16. Philpott, *op. cit.*

17. Declan Walsh and Mohamed Ezz, "ISIS Says it was Behind Deadly Attack on Christians in Egypt," *The New York Times*, Nov. 2, 2018, https://tinyurl.com/ycy7a2j8.

18. Tamer El-Ghobashy and Dahlia Kholaif, "Egyptian Christians Fearing Terror Flee Sinai," *The Wall Street Journal*, Feb. 26, 2017, https://tinyurl.com/y76bczcu.

19. Ben Hubbard, "'There are no girls left': Syria's Christian Villages Hollowed out by ISIS," *The New York Times*, Aug. 15, 2018, https://tinyurl.com/y7qxqg8o; John Pontifex, "Christians in Syria hit new low," *The Sunday Times*, April 7, 2018, https://tinyurl.com/yawlnspl.

20. Philpott, *op. cit.*

21. "Middle East still home to the highest levels of restrictions on religion, although levels have declined since 2016," *op. cit.*

22. "Social Hostilities Index Score in 2016," Pew-Templeton Global Religious Futures Project, 2016, https://tinyurl.com/y85m5xow.

23. Jonathan Marcus, "Why Saudi Arabia and Iran are bitter rivals," *BBC*, Sept. 16, 2019, https://tinyurl.com/yc2nuf27.

24. "Iran 2018 International Religious Freedom Report," U.S. Department of State, 2019, p. 2, https://tinyurl.com/yd8wka2b.

25. *Ibid.*, p. 5.

26. "Iran," Minority Rights Group International, accessed April 27, 2020, pp. 11-12, https://tinyurl.com/ttmrzkt; "Iran 2018 International Religious Freedom Report," *op. cit.*, pp. 11-12.

27. Rory Jones, "Saudi Arabia Executes 37 Citizens, Drawing Fire From Rights Groups," *The Wall Street Journal*, April 23, 2019, https://tinyurl.com/y8g58ewd; Ahmed Al Omran and Margherita Stancati, "Standoff with Iran Inflames Anti-Shiite Feelings in Saudi Arabia," *The Wall Street Journal*, Aug. 31, 2016, https://tinyurl.com/y9sxcnk4.

28. Declan Walsh and Jason Horowitz, "Why Pope Francis' Historic Visit to the Gulf Matters," *The New York Times*, Feb. 3, 2019, https://tinyurl.com/yaw8larl.

29. *Ibid.*; Masako Ishii *et al.*, eds., *Asian Migrant Workers in the Arab Gulf States: The Growing Foreign Population and Their Lives* (2019), p. 184.

30. "For First Time Ever, Christian Mass Held Openly in Saudi Arabia," Middle East Media Research Institute, Dec. 6, 2018, https://tinyurl.com/yclvkqa8.

31. Walsh and Horowitz, *op. cit.*; Sophie Tremblay and Jessie Gretener, "Mosque, church and synagogue to share home in Abu Dhabi," *CNN*, Sept. 26, 2019, https://tinyurl.com/y4twwukz.

32. Colin Chapman, "Christians in the Middle East—Past, Present and Future," *Transformation*, May 17, 2012, https://tinyurl.com/y7gn2376.

33. *Ibid.*

34. *Ibid.*

35. "How Did the Christian Middle East Become Predominantly Muslim?" *Oxford Arts Blog*, Sept. 17, 2018, https://tinyurl.com/yb7wah3g.

36. "Druze," *Encyclopedia Britannica,* https://tinyurl.com/y8kg5cdm; "Origins of Baha'i History," *BBC*, Sept. 28, 2009, https://tinyurl.com/y8vj74k7.

37. Ceren Belge and Ekrem Karakoc, "Minorities in the Middle East: Ethnicity, Religion, and Support for Authoritarianism," *Political Research Quarterly*, May 2015, p. 4, https://tinyurl.com/y9odztle.

38. "History," American University in Beirut, https://tinyurl.com/ybf74btj.

39. "Israel said to seek $250b Compensation for Jews Forced out of Arab countries," *The Times of Israel*, Jan. 5, 2019, https://tinyurl.com/y98sym3q.

40. John Moore, "The Evolution of Islamic Terrorism," *Frontline*, https://tinyurl.com/yc7zydaq.

41. "Modern Sunni-Shia Tensions," Council on Foreign Relations, 2020, https://tinyurl.com/y9znamht.

42. Belge and Karakoc, *op. cit.*; Katulis, deLeon and Craig, *op. cit.*, pp. 7-8.

43. Kenneth M. Pollack, "The Fall and Rise and Fall of Iraq," Brookings Institute Middle East Memo, July 2013, https://tinyurl.com/gtdghxx.

44. Zack Beauchamp, "The conflict between Iraqi Sunnis and Shias sustains ISIS," *Vox*, Nov. 17, 2015, https://tinyurl.com/ybhpzstw.

45. Belkis Wille, "Christians Among The Victims in an Unstable Yemen," Human Rights Watch, May 10, 2016, https://tinyurl.com/y9us2mpc.

46. Saad Salloum, "Barriers to Return for Ethno-Religious Minorities in Iraq," International Organization for Migration, January 2020, p. 6, https://tinyurl.com/yc3waauv.

47. John Pontifex, "In northern Iraq, a ravaged Christian village comes back to life," *Aleteia*, March 13, 2020, https://tinyurl.com/ybspoqom; Green, *op. cit.*; Xavier Bisits, "How Iran-backed fighters are making life hell for Iraq's Christians," *America*, March 30, 2020, https://tinyurl.com/ybkhduqb; Lorraine Mallinder, "Mosul's new masters: After Isis, came the mafia," *The Irish Times*, March 14, 2020, https://tinyurl.com/yadvfpfj; and Emily Judd, "Iraq Christians fear future holds 'total extinction,' ISIS resurgence," *Al Arabiya*, Feb. 23, 2020, https://tinyurl.com/y9jf9vtg.

48. Jessica Donati and Peter Nicholas, "With Evangelicals Behind Him, Vice President Mike Pence Takes Prominent Role in Foreign Policy," *The Wall Street Journal*, Feb. 19, 2019, https://tinyurl.com/yy2upysa; Green, *op. cit.*; and Yeganeh Torbati, "The Trump Administration Calls Iraq Dangerous for Christians—Until It Wants to Deport Them," *ProPublica*, March 4, 2020, https://tinyurl.com/r43wvdg.

49. Torbati, "The Trump Administration Calls Iraq Dangerous for Christians—Until It Wants to Deport Them," *ibid.*

50. Doreen Abi Raad, "Christians Are Slowly Returning to Iraq, Says Syriac Patriarch," *Assyrian International News Agency*, Jan. 8, 2020, https://tinyurl.com/y8mslxzv.

51. Charlie Hoyle, "Saviour or Dictator: Copts in Sisi's Egypt Trapped by a Strongman's Balancing Act," *Al Arabiya*, Feb. 4, 2020, https://tinyurl.com/ydazn2n7.

52. *Ibid.*

53. Amira El-Fekki and Jared Malsin, "Anti-Christian Violence Surges in Egypt, Prompting an Exodus," *The Wall Street Journal*, April 26, 2019, https://tinyurl.com/ya9h4pt2.

54. *Ibid.*

55. "EIPR criticizes slow rate of church legalization: Three years later, the church construction law has failed to resolve sectarian tensions related to worship," Egyptian Initiative for Personal Rights, Jan. 6, 2020, https://tinyurl.com/txux3e2.

56. "Justice Denied, Promises Broken: The Situation of Egypt's Minorities Since 2014," Minority Rights International, January 2019, p. 2, https://tinyurl.com/y766p9bw.

57. "Egypt arrests Coptic activist on terror charges," *Middle East Monitor*, Nov. 26, 2019, https://tinyurl.com/ybtlrydq.

58. "USCIRF Condemns Egypt's Arrest of Coptic Activist Ramy Kamel," United States Commission on International Religious Freedom, Dec. 13, 2019, https://tinyurl.com/y9gyxguo.

59. "Egypt jails Coptic rights activist on charges of 'terrorism,'" *Middle East Eye*, Nov. 25, 2019, https://tinyurl.com/y7bp7otp.

60. "Promotion and protection of human rights: human rights situations and reports of special rapporteurs and representatives," United Nations General Assembly, Oct. 30, 2019, p. 4, https://tinyurl.com/ycydp5zm.

61. "Iran 2018 International Religious Freedom Report," U.S. Department of State, 2019, pp. 19-20, https://tinyurl.com/ycn7g6lb; "Iran: Christian converts and house churches (1)—prevalence and conditions for religious practise," Landinfo, Norwegian Country of Origin Information Centre, November 2017, https://tinyurl.com/y95oygmj.

62. Lela Gilbert, "For Iran's Imprisoned Christians, coronavirus is a new danger," *Newsweek*, March 29, 2020, https://tinyurl.com/y9ddql59.

63. Fariba Nawa, "Iranians Are Converting To Evangelical Christianity In Turkey," *NPR*, Dec. 14, 2018, https://tinyurl.com/y845s5fx.

64. Judd, *op. cit.*

65. Gina Zurlo and Todd Johnson, "Ongoing Exodus: Tracking the Emigration of Christians from the Middle East," *Harvard Journal of Middle East Politics and Policy*, January 2014, https://tinyurl.com/y8cmdxtc.

66. Ellen Francis, Issam Abdallah and Walid Saleh, "Lebanese protesters return to streets in car convoys amid coronavirus lockdown," *Reuters*, April 21, 2020, https://tinyurl.com/y87nr24p; Bruce Riedel, "Jordan's unique coronavirus challenge," Brookings Institution, April 16, 2020, https://tinyurl.com/yajqxd3p; and Paul Cochrane, "Coronavirus: Egypt, Lebanon, Jordan suffer economic pain amid falling remittances," *Middle East Eye*, April 16, 2020, https://tinyurl.com/y8f22t62.

BIBLIOGRAPHY

Books

Murad, Nadia, *The Last Girl: My Story of Captivity and My Fight Against the Islamic State,* **Tim Duggan Books, 2017.**
A young Yazidi woman, who was later awarded the Nobel Peace Prize, writes about her kidnapping and enslavement by the ISIS terrorist group in Iraq.

Philpott, Daniel, *Religious Freedom in Islam: The Fate of a Universal Human Right in the Muslim World Today,* **Oxford University Press, 2019.**
A University of Notre Dame political scientist examines religious freedom in the contemporary Middle East and its connections to democracy, women's rights and terrorism.

Russell, Gerard, *Heirs to Forgotten Kingdoms: Journeys Into the Disappearing Religions of the Middle East,* **Basic Books, 2014.**
A former British diplomat in the Middle East explores a variety of small faiths and ancient cultures whose numbers are shrinking rapidly in the region.

Sanasarian, Eliz, *Religious Minorities in Iran,* **Cambridge, 2000.**
A political science professor at the University of Southern California offers a rare overview of the cultural makeup of Iran and the relationships between non-Muslims and the state.

Articles

Belge, Ceren, and Ekrem Karakoc, "Minorities in the Middle East: Ethnicity, Religion and Support for Authoritarianism," *Political Research Quarterly,* **2015, https://tinyurl.com/y9odztle.**
Two political scientists analyze how some threatened religious minorities in the Middle East have been more likely to support authoritarian governments than democracies.

El-Fekki, Amira, and Jared Malsin, "Anti-Christian Violence Surges in Egypt, Prompting an Exodus," *The Wall Street Journal,* **April 26, 2019, https://tinyurl.com/ya9h4pt2.**
Journalists describe the struggles of Coptic Christians in Egypt.

Green, Emma, "The Impossible Future of Christians in the Middle East," *The Atlantic*, May 23, 2019, https://tinyurl.com/yxbj9jkr.
A journalist describes the phenomenon of Christians fleeing Iraq after the 2003 U.S. invasion and the subsequent rise of militant groups, including the Islamic State (ISIS).

Hubbard, Ben, "'There Are No Girls Left': Syria's Christian Villages Hollowed Out by ISIS," *The New York Times*, April 15, 2018, https://tinyurl.com/y7qxqg8o.
A journalist reports from villages trying to rebuild after civil war and attacks by ISIS.

Johnson, Todd, and Gina Zurlo, "Ongoing Exodus: Tracking the Ongoing Emigration of Christians from the Middle East," *Harvard Journal of Middle East Politics and Policy*, January 2014, https://tinyurl.com/y8cmdxtc.
Demographers evaluate the trend of Christians leaving the Middle East from the early 20th century through the post-Arab Spring period.

Katulis, Brian, Rudy deLeon and John Craig, "The Plight of Christians in the Middle East: Supporting Religious Freedom, Pluralism and Tolerance During a Time of Turmoil," Center for American Progress, 2015, https://tinyurl.com/yde9obz7.
A public policy research organization documents challenges for Christians in the Middle East, how U.S. policy could help and how the decline of religious minorities indicates a general erosion of pluralism and tolerance.

Torbati, Yeganeh, "The Trump Administration Calls Iraq Dangerous for Christians—Until It Wants to Deport Them," *ProPublica*, March 4, 2020, https://tinyurl.com/r43wvdg.
An investigative report argues the Trump administration uses Christians in Iraq to justify various conflicting political positions.

Walsh, Declan, and Jason Horowitz, "Why Pope Francis' Historic Visit to the Gulf Matters," *The New York Times*, Feb. 3, 2019, https://tinyurl.com/yaw8larl.
Two reporters describe the implications of the influx of Christian workers to the Persian Gulf.

Reports and Studies

"A Closer Look at How Religious Restrictions Have Risen Around the World," Pew Research Center, July 2019, https://tinyurl.com/y5srlcn5.
A Washington think tank identifies new and continuing trends in governmental and societal repression of religion around the world.

"Iran: Christian converts and house churches (1)—prevalence and conditions for religious practise," Landinfo, Norwegian Country of Origin Information Centre, November 2017, https://tinyurl.com/y95oygmj.
A Norwegian government report looks at the dangers Iranian Muslims who convert to evangelical Christianity face.

"Justice Denied, Promises Broken: The Situation of Egypt's Minorities since 2014," Minority Rights Group International, Jan. 25, 2019, https://tinyurl.com/ybgjt9yb.
An international human rights organization documents the increasing struggles of Egypt's religious and cultural minorities since the country adopted a new constitution in 2014.

"2018 Report on International Religious Freedom," U.S. Department of State, July 2019, https://tinyurl.com/ybpeqkq6.
The State Department analyzes global trends on religious freedom and U.S. efforts to promote such freedom.

Salloum, Saad, "Barriers to Return for Ethno-Religious Minorities in Iraq," International Organization for Migration, January 2020, https://tinyurl.com/yc3waauv.
An intergovernmental group evaluates the challenges facing Christians, Yazidis and other minorities who are trying to rebuild in Iraq after years of Islamic State violence.

THE NEXT STEP

Christians in Syria

Arraf, Jane, "It's a Dangerous Time for Christians in Northeastern Syria," *NPR*, Feb. 12, 2020, https://tinyurl.com/sajsba4.
As Christians in northeastern Syria face attacks from ISIS, they are also wary of Turkish forces that recently invaded the country.

Frantzman, Seth J., "US Congressman Abraham visits eastern Syria to see Christians and Kurds," *The Jerusalem Post*, Feb. 23, 2020, https://tinyurl.com/yaxvea2t.
A Louisiana congressman met with Christian militias battling ISIS in Syria.

Gavlak, Dale, "Advocates to Trump: Don't desert Christians, Yazidis, Kurds in Syria," *National Catholic Reporter*, Oct. 11, 2019, https://tinyurl.com/yalkr585.
Worried about the safety of Christians in northeastern Syria as Turkey invades the region, Christian advocates in the United States asked President Trump to reconsider his decision to pull U.S. troops out of the area.

Refugees

Macchi, Victoria, "US Hits Lowered Refugee Cap for 2019 as Another Decrease Looms," *Voice of America News*, Oct. 1, 2019, https://tinyurl.com/y9wno6hh.
Christians make up a growing share of refugees admitted to the United States under the Trump administration.

Tremblay-Boire, Joannie, and Aseem Prakash, "Why Americans appear more likely to support Christian refugees," *The Conversation*, April 9, 2019, https://tinyurl.com/y7m7oc4k.
In a study, Americans were more inclined to donate to a refugee organization if it specified that it helped Christians in the Middle East.

Williams, Hattie, "Covid-19 catastrophic for refugees, charities warn," *Church Times*, March 24, 2020, https://tinyurl.com/ycpc6puz.
Christian groups are raising concerns about the potential spread of the coronavirus in refugee camps.

U.S. Action

Huby, Chris, "Christians in northeast Syria living in fear as Turkish forces, IS group active in region," *France 24*, Feb. 7, 2020, https://tinyurl.com/s3v3gm7.
U.S. troops took up positions defending Christian villages in Syria in January after ISIS sleeper cells were reactivated and targeted the Christian minority in the region.

Lin, Christina, "Willful ignorance hurts Christian militia in Iraq," *Asia Times*, Jan. 2, 2020, https://tinyurl.com/yb8g2akt.
The United States launched a retaliatory rocket attack against an Iraqi force that included Christian militias.

Nissenbaum, Dion, and Nazih Osseiran, "U.S. Withholds Support for New Lebanon Government," *The Wall Street Journal*, Jan. 22, 2020, https://tinyurl.com/yaqvbb7x.
The Trump administration said it was not certain it could work with the new Lebanese government, which is dominated by Hezbollah and excludes a Christian political group.

Violence

"Vatican urges visiting Iraqi president to protect Christians," *The Associated Press*, Jan. 25, 2020, https://tinyurl.com/y9n6uuxu.
Pope Francis discussed the security of Christians in Iraq with the nation's president as tensions rose between the United States and groups in Iraq believed to be associated with Iran.

Bandow, Doug, "A New Ranking of Nations Where Christians Are Persecuted the Most," *National Review*, Jan. 28, 2020, https://tinyurl.com/sjk5q84.
Afghanistan, Yemen and Iran are ranked as some of the countries where persecution and violence against Christians is worst, according to a nonprofit religious group.

Lederer, Edith M., "UN team reports new evidence against Islamic State in Iraq," *The Associated Press*, May 19, 2020, https://tinyurl.com/y88tq6zy.
The United Nations has established two field investigation units in Iraq to study crimes committed by ISIS against Christian communities and other minorities in the country.

For More Information

Aid to the Church in Need, 725 Leonard St., Brooklyn, NY 11222; 800-628-6333; churchinneed.org. International Roman Catholic charity that provides humanitarian assistance to churches around the world.

Amnesty International, 1 Easton St., London WC1X 0DW, UK; +44 20 7413 5500; amnesty.org. Advocacy group that promotes and tracks civil liberties and human rights internationally.

Free Yezidi Foundation, 14 Pennsylvania Plaza, #1010, New York, NY 10122; freeyezidi.org, info@freeyezidi.org. Nonprofit that runs programs to help this religious minority in Iraq and raises awareness of their plight internationally.

Hudson Institute Center for Religious Freedom, 1201 Pennsylvania Ave., N.W., Suite 400, Washington, DC 20004; 202-974-2400; hudson.org/policycenters/7-center-for-religious-freedom. Think tank that researches, tracks and promotes religious freedom around the world.

Minority Rights Group International, 54 Commercial St., London E1 6LT, UK; +44 20 7422 4200; minorityrights. org. Advocacy group that campaigns for rights of disadvantaged minorities worldwide.

Open Doors, PO Box 27001, Santa Ana, CA 92799; 888-524-2535; opendoorsusa.org. Nondenominational organization tracking discrimination against Christians; also supports Christians in more than 70 countries.

Pew Research Center, 1615 L St., N.W., Suite 800, Washington, DC 20036; 202-419-4300; pewresearch. org. Nonpartisan organization gathering data and research on religion and other aspects of public life around the world.

Religious Freedom Institute, 316 Pennsylvania Ave., S.E., Suite 501, Washington, DC 20003; 202-838-7734; religiousfreedominstitute.org. Organization working for freedom of religion around the world.

Under Caesar's Sword, University of Notre Dame, 2034 Nanovic Hall, Notre Dame, IN 46556; ucs.nd.edu. University-based project that researches and tracks Christian responses to persecution globally.

14

Extreme Weather

Will global warming produce more disasters?

By Stephen Ornes

Kyle Rivas/Getty Images

Farm equipment and debris lie scattered near a damaged home after a tornado passed through Linwood, Kan., on May 29, 2019. The month of May brought one of the most active streaks of tornado activity in U.S. history.

At first, people living on Ocracoke Island in North Carolina thought they had been spared the worst of Hurricane Dorian's fury.

"We were all on social media laughing about how we'd done well and there was really no flooding at all, just rain, typical rain," recalled Steve Harris, one of hundreds of people who defied orders to evacuate Ocracoke as Dorian approached on Sept. 6, 2019.[1]

The sense of relief was short-lived. A storm surge from the hurricane sent what Harris described as a "wall of water" cascading down local roads as people scrambled to get into their attics. "I've been through every storm," said Ocracoke resident Dan Garrish, 66. "I've never seen water come in like this."[2]

The hurricane, which flattened communities in the Bahamas as a Category 5 storm on its way to the U.S. East Coast, was just one example of the extreme weather the country and much of the world have experienced this year.

New national records for total rainfall in a 12-month period in the United States have been set three times since Jan. 1, with torrential downpours causing massive flooding along the Missouri River and ruining crops. Record cold hit the Midwest in January 2019. A 13-day period in May 2019 brought one of the most active streaks of tornado activity in the country's history, with at least eight twisters per day. Worldwide, July 2019 was the hottest month on record. The temperature in Paris reached 108.7 degrees Fahrenheit on July 25, and Germany, Belgium and the Netherlands also broke heat records.[3]

From *CQ Researcher,*
September 20, 2019

Scientists are increasingly convinced that some extreme weather events are becoming more frequent and more intense as a result of global warming caused by greenhouse gas emissions.

"Scientists have long predicted we would eventually reach a point where human-caused climate change altered Earth's system to such a degree that we would begin to see weather and climate events that would not have been possible without human contributions," said Stephanie Herring, a climate scientist with the Center for Weather and Climate at the National Oceanic and Atmospheric Administration (NOAA).[4]

Outside the scientific community, arguments that extreme weather events are tied to carbon emissions are politically divisive, with many conservatives and other skeptics disputing any connection. They say Democrats and environmentalists are using worst-case theories about extreme weather to feed alarmism over climate change and that, in any case, communities will adapt to whatever weather-related changes the country experiences.

Recent extreme weather events also have heightened the debate about whether the federal government should continue subsidizing the post-disaster rebuilding of homes and businesses in areas particularly vulnerable to weather-related disasters, such as coastal flooding. Repeated rebuilding in disaster-prone regions wastes taxpayer dollars and puts lives at risk, say critics of the subsidy programs. They note that, as of July 9, 2019, the United States had experienced six extreme weather-related events this year (two floods and four severe storms) with losses exceeding $1 billion each. Hurricane Dorian is certain to bring the number to seven.[5]

Supporters of the subsidies counter that many people living in areas affected by extreme weather cannot afford to leave, and that damaged communities can rebuild in ways that protect them from disastrous damage in future events. "You can't just pick up people and say, 'You have to go somewhere else,'" former New Orleans Mayor Mitch Landrieu said. "The world doesn't work that way."[6]

Scientists define extreme weather events as those that fall into the most unusual 10 percent of a particular region's meteorological history, often causing extensive damage or deaths. They include unusually severe heat waves, droughts, tornadoes, wildfires, flooding, blizzards, freezes and hurricanes.[7]

Such events have occurred throughout history and can result from natural variability in the weather. But scientists say some trends are becoming more apparent:

- Heat waves are happening more often. The average heat wave season across 50 major U.S. cities is 47 days longer than in the 1960s, according to the U.S. Global Change Research Program, a federal initiative that coordinates government research on global environmental conditions. Those cities now experience an average of six heat waves annually, up from two a year in the 1960s.[8]
- Extreme precipitation events are more frequent, especially in the Midwest and Northeast. "In recent years, a larger percentage of precipitation has come in the form of intense single-day events," the U.S. Environmental Protection Agency said.[9]
- Wildfires in California are getting bigger. "Since the early 1970s, California's annual wildfire extent increased fivefold, punctuated by extremely large and destructive wildfires in 2017 and 2018," university researchers said in a study published in July. Scientists say rising temperatures are drying out soil, leaving trees and vegetation parched and primed to fuel fires.[10]
- Hurricanes are not occurring more often, but they appear to be becoming more powerful. Between 1988 and 2017, the average power of major hurricanes around the world, as measured by wind speed and duration, increased 41 percent compared to the previous 30-year period, according to an Associated Press analysis. "There's no question that the storms are stronger than they were 30 years ago," said James Kossin, an atmospheric research scientist at NOAA.[11]

Hurricanes also are moving more slowly than they used to because climate change is decreasing the speed of winds high in the atmosphere that propel the storms along, researchers say. They cite Hurricane Dorian, which remained parked over the Bahamas for 40 hours this past Labor Day weekend. "This is yet another example of the kind of slow-moving tropical systems that we expect to see more often as a response to climate change," Jennifer Francis, a scientist with the Woods Hole Research Center in Falmouth, Mass., said of Dorian.[12]

Slower hurricanes produce more rain. Hurricane Harvey, which slammed Texas as a Category 4 storm in 2017, dropped more than 60 inches of rain on an area northeast of Houston, breaking the U.S. total storm rainfall record of 52 inches set in 1950.[13]

As extreme weather events become more frequent, long-term trends show they also are becoming deadlier and more costly, experts say. The 14 most destructive weather and climate disasters in the United States in 2018 killed at least 247 people and cost the government an estimated $91 billion. The toll in 2017 was even worse, with 16 billion-dollar disasters that killed 362 and caused a record-setting $306 billion in damage.[14]

"We know that the costs of extreme events are rising," says Noah Diffenbaugh, a climate scientist at Stanford University.

As recently as 15 years ago, scientists were reluctant to link specific extreme weather events to climate change, but advances in computer modeling and data collection have made it possible to measure that connection. Researchers who are part of a new scientific field called climate attribution now feel comfortable saying global warming increases the likelihood and severity of certain events—such as heat waves, thunderstorms and coastal flooding from rising sea levels. Higher temperatures, they say, are melting glaciers and putting more moisture into the air through evaporation, which increases rainfall.[15]

Even periods of bitter cold, such as the record low temperatures parts of the United States experienced in

January 2019, are tied to global warming, climate experts say. They say climate change is destabilizing an area of atmospheric low pressure over the Arctic known as the polar vortex and bringing cold air southward. Overall, however, scientists say such freezes are becoming less common with climate change.[16]

Linking climate change to some weather events is complicated and uncertain, scientists acknowledge. Data on tornadoes, for example, does not go back far enough for researchers to detect clear patterns in frequency and severity. But tornadoes do appear to be more clustered than in the past, with outbreaks of multiple twisters occurring more often, and they seem to be forming more often in unexpected locations, researchers say.[17]

Climate experts warn that global warming caused primarily by the burning of fossil fuels will lead to an increase in extreme weather events around the world. In the United States, the Northeast and Midwest will

Billion-Dollar Disasters on the Rise

Six of the weather-related disasters the United States experienced during the first half of 2019 each caused damages exceeding $1 billion. Hurricane Dorian is expected to be this year's seventh billion-dollar disaster. The average annual number of such disasters between 2016 and 2018 was more than double the long-term average. Government scientists attribute that to increased development in vulnerable areas, which heightens damage costs, and to climate change.

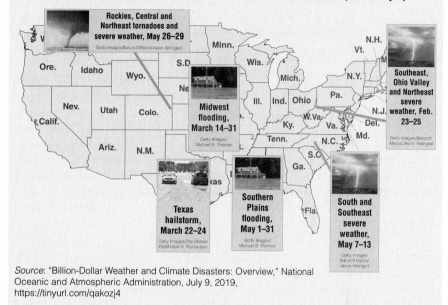

Billion-Dollar U.S. Weather and Climate Disasters, 2019 (as of July 9)

Source: "Billion-Dollar Weather and Climate Disasters: Overview," National Oceanic and Atmospheric Administration, July 9, 2019, https://tinyurl.com/qakozj4

Parisians try to cool off in a fountain near the Eiffel Tower during a July 2019 heat wave in which the temperature hit a record-setting 108.7 degrees Fahrenheit.

see more heat waves and heavy downpours, while the Southeast and Northwest will experience more wildfires and insect outbreaks threatening crops and human health, according to the Global Change Research Program.[18]

"More frequent and intense extreme weather and climate-related events . . . are expected to continue to damage infrastructure, ecosystems, and social systems that provide essential benefits to communities," the program said in its "Fourth National Climate Assessment" released last year.[19]

Climate change skeptics, including President Trump, dismiss such concerns, arguing that weather patterns fluctuate constantly due to factors unrelated to greenhouse gas emissions. They say activists use the term "extreme weather" to stoke fear about climate change as part of a political agenda. "It used to be called global warming. That wasn't working," the president said in a June 2019 interview on a British television program. "Then it was called climate change. Now it's actually called extreme weather because with extreme weather you can't miss."[20]

Politics largely determines how individual Americans view extreme weather in context with climate change, surveys show. "Partisan affiliation . . . powerfully shapes individual perceptions of extreme weather events," said Wanyun Shao, an assistant professor of geography at the University of Alabama. "Where Democrats perceive rising air temperatures and an increasing number of hurricanes, droughts and floods, Republicans are less

likely to agree that climate conditions are changing or that extreme weather is increasing."[21]

Extreme weather affects Americans from all socioeconomic and ethnic backgrounds, but research shows it can be particularly devastating for low-income and minority Americans. A 2013 study by researchers at the University of California, Berkeley, found that blacks were 52 percent more likely than whites to live in the hottest parts of U.S. cities, with the least tree cover. And a 2018 study by sociology professors at the University of Pittsburgh and Rice University in Houston found that, because of how disaster aid is distributed, black victims of extreme weather events tend to lose wealth after a disaster while white victims tend to gain wealth. The researchers cited evidence from prior studies showing that blacks had lower access to government aid and were more likely to experience housing and income losses due to an extreme weather event.[22]

Building standards also are improving in areas repeatedly hit by severe weather. Since 2008, when an insurance industry research group created a set of construction standards designed to make homes hurricane-proof, the number of homes built to those standards in "a handful of hurricane-prone states" has increased from 1,122 to more than 12,500, according to *Insurance Journal*, an online industry publication.[23]

As climatologists, policymakers and researchers weigh the significance of recent trends in extreme weather, here are some of the questions they are asking:

Will extreme weather events become more frequent?

Climate experts have warned for decades that unless greenhouse gas emissions fall drastically, certain extreme weather events—especially heat waves, droughts and torrential downpours—will increase around the world. Such events will occur more frequently, they say, even if countries meet their commitments under the 2015 Paris Agreement on climate change.

"Many areas are still likely to experience substantial increases in the probability of unprecedented [weather] events," researchers at Stanford University, Columbia University and Washington State University said in a study published in February 2018.[24]

North America, Europe and East Asia, for example, should expect to see more "record-setting hot, wet, and/

or dry events," the study said. A special report issued in October 2018 by the Intergovernmental Panel on Climate Change (IPCC), a United Nations group that assesses the science related to global warming, reached similar conclusions.[25]

Officials in California say extreme weather caused by climate change is taking an increasing toll there, noting that the state's six worst wildfire years since 1950 (in total acres burned) have all occurred since 2006.[26]

"There's no debate about whether climate change is or isn't impacting extremes," says climate scientist Stephanie Herring at NOAA's Center for Weather and Climate.

But the difficulties involved in separating natural climate cycles from aberrant weather patterns have led climate change skeptics to challenge the consensus view that severe weather will happen more often as the planet warms.

"Researchers from many different subject areas study extreme events," university researchers said in one 2018 study. "However . . . researchers from different backgrounds may use very different words to communicate about these events and different ways of deciding what makes an extreme event 'extreme.'"[27]

Some political conservatives say there is little or no evidence that severe weather will get more frequent. They cite language in the IPCC's fifth report, finalized in 2014, noting a lack of "robust trends" in the annual number of tropical storms and hurricanes over the past 100 years in the North Atlantic. The IPCC also said last year it had only "medium confidence" that a temperature increase of 1.5 degrees Celsius (2.7 degrees Fahrenheit) would bring more intense, more frequent droughts.[28]

"Overall, we are not seeing more floods, droughts, tornadoes or hurricanes in spite of the steady rise in the small amount of carbon dioxide, and in spite of the mild warming of the planet," said David W. Kreutzer, an economist and former senior research fellow at the Heritage Foundation, a conservative think tank in Washington. "The data show that there is no significant upward trend in any of these weather events."[29]

Even within the climate science community, a small minority of experts say the computer models that the vast majority of climatologists use to predict future extreme weather trends grossly exaggerate the amount of global warming and, by extension, the likelihood of future extreme weather events.

"Climate models are overwhelming the system," says John Christy, a climate scientist at the University of Alabama in Huntsville who also serves as the state's climatologist. "They are not trustworthy in determining what is going to happen in the future."

The vast majority of climate experts defend the computer models as scientifically sound, but they acknowledge that the models have limitations. "For some event types, we have a much higher degree of confidence in our understanding of how those events are changing than for other types," Herring says.

The Paris Agreement's top goal is to limit increases in the average global surface temperature to "well below" 2 degrees Celsius (3.6 degrees Fahrenheit) above levels predating the start of the Industrial Revolution in the late 1700s, and to "strive for" an increase of no more than 1.5 degrees Celsius. Already, the Earth has warmed by 1 degree Celsius (1.8 degrees Fahrenheit) since the 1800s.[30]

Many experts doubt that the 1.5 degree Celsius goal is achievable. "Stabilizing global warming at 1.5C will be extremely difficult if not impossible at this point," said Michael Mann, a climatologist who runs the Earth System Science Center at Pennsylvania State University.[31]

The Washington Post reported on Sept. 11, 2019, that its analysis of temperature data from around the world shows that many locations already have warmed by at least 2 degrees Celsius over the past century.[32]

Many climate scientists expect the world to warm by at least 3 degrees Celsius over pre-industrial levels by 2100. That would increase the risk of extreme hot, wet and dry events between threefold and fivefold in much of the world, according to the February 2018 study report by university researchers.[33]

Predictions regarding trends in extreme weather vary depending on the type of event. NOAA predicts "more frequent and intense droughts," as well as increases in flooding events. It also says future hurricanes will likely dump more rainfall than they do now, and it has "medium confidence" that hurricanes will become more intense, with higher wind speeds.[34]

Dorian, for example, was the strongest storm ever to hit the Bahamas and one of the most powerful to occur in the Atlantic, with sustained winds of 185 mph when it made landfall in the Abaco Islands on Sept. 1, 2019.[35]

Predicting future tornado activity is more difficult, scientists say, due to a lack of reliable, long-term historical data. Recent research has found that, although the number of tornadoes each year has remained relatively constant, tornado patterns are shifting, with more in the Midwest and Southeast and fewer in portions of the central and southern Great Plains that are traditionally considered part of Tornado Alley. Researchers could not explain the reasons for the shift.[36]

"Both tornado reports and tornado environments indicate an increasing trend in portions of Mississippi, Alabama, Arkansas, Missouri, Illinois, Indiana, Tennessee and Kentucky," the National Weather Service says on its website.[37]

Will extreme weather events become more destructive?

2018 was remarkable for weather-related havoc around the world. Wildfires killed more than 80 people in Greece. A heat wave killed 65 in a single week in Japan, which also experienced record rainfall and flooding. Extreme heat was blamed for up to 70 deaths in Quebec in July.[38]

In the United States, 14 weather-related disasters, each of which did at least $1 billion in damage, killed 247 people and cost about $91 billion. Those disasters included two devastating Atlantic hurricanes—Florence and Michael—and California wildfires that burned 1.8 million acres. One wildfire alone, the Camp Fire, killed at least 85 people and destroyed an entire town. The country fared even worse in 2017, with 16 billion-dollar disasters—including floods, hurricanes, droughts and wildfires—that killed more than 300 people and cost $306 billion.[39]

The long-term trend in billion-dollar disasters is especially alarming, experts say. The annual average number of such disasters in 2016, 2017 and 2018 was more than double the long-term average, according to NOAA.[40]

"The number of billion-dollar weather disasters has been increasing, and the total

cost associated with those disasters has been increasing," says Diffenbaugh at Stanford University.

But experts disagree about the role that climate change plays in the rising cost of extreme weather events—in both damage to infrastructure and loss of life—and about the best ways to respond. Most scientists say there is clear evidence that climate change caused by greenhouse gas emissions from cars, power plants and other sources is creating hotter, dryer conditions that have made heat waves more intense, expanded the acreage burned in wildfires and increased the amount of rainfall from hurricanes.[41]

"Climate change is adding to what's going on naturally, and it's that extra stress that causes things to break," said Kevin Trenberth, a scientist at the National Center for Atmospheric Research in Boulder, Colo. "It takes the experience well outside anything that's been experienced before. . . . As a result, things break, people die, and things burn."[42]

Other experts say that a variety of other factors unrelated to climate change influence the potential impact of severe weather. They note, for example, that an increasing number of people live in areas vulnerable to hurricanes, flooding and wildfires. Forty percent of the nation's population lives on a coast, and one in 12 homes in California is at high risk from wildfires.[43]

In addition, building codes in many locations have not been updated to require that homes and other structures withstand a severe weather event. A 2018 report by

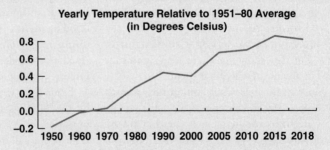

Global Temperatures Heating Up

The global average surface temperature last year was 0.82 degrees Celsius (1.5 degrees Fahrenheit) higher than the 1951-80 average, according to data from NASA. Eighteen of the 19 warmest years have occurred since 2001, with 1998 being the 19th. The warmest year on record was 2016.

Yearly Temperature Relative to 1951–80 Average (in Degrees Celsius)

Source: "Global Temperature," NASA, Aug. 28, 2019, https://tinyurl.com/hsrjbmr

the Insurance Institute for Business & Home Safety, an organization in South Carolina and Florida that works to minimize insurance losses from severe weather, cited a "concerning lack of progress in the adoption and enforcement of updated residential building code systems" in some coastal states.[44]

Climate change skeptics say some global warming studies make wild predictions about the destructiveness of future weather-related disasters as a way to justify proposals such as a tax on carbon emissions or the Green New Deal proposed by progressive Democrats in Congress that would require dramatic actions by the federal government and the private sector to reduce carbon emissions.[45]

"Investing in . . . preparation for extreme weather events can be worthwhile," said Nicolas Loris, an economist and research fellow at the Heritage Foundation. "However, the combination of fearmongering and offering solutions that would require a takeover of the global economy are unrealistic and counterproductive."[46]

Jeff Berardelli, a meteorologist and extreme-weather expert in New York City, said warmer ocean water caused by climate change clearly is fueling stronger storms, which he cited as the reason Dorian was the fifth Category 5 storm to form in the Atlantic over the past four years.[47]

"The more heat that there is in the ocean, especially near the surface of the ocean, the stronger these systems tend to get," he said.[48]

Public opinion on connections between climate change and the destructive power of extreme weather events can depend largely on personal experience. Studies show that people who have lived through an event are more likely to believe that climate change played a role. That is especially true when extreme weather severely damages whole communities, according to a study published in May by researchers at Duke University and the University of Colorado, Denver.[49]

"How our community or neighborhood fares—the damages it suffers—may have a stronger and more lasting effect on our climate beliefs than individual impacts do," said Elizabeth A. Albright, assistant professor of the practice of environmental science and policy methods at Duke's Nicholas School of the Environment. "We found that damage at the zip code level . . . was positively associated with stronger climate change beliefs even three or four years after the extreme flooding event our study examined."[50]

At the same time, however, people who experienced extreme temperatures repeatedly over an extended period—generally between two and eight years—came to view it as normal, according to a study published in February 2019 by government and academic researchers.

"The definition of 'normal weather' shifts rapidly over time in a changing climate," the researchers said. And people who no longer consider extreme weather to be unusual may also be less likely to consider climate change a pressing issue, they said.[51]

Should government subsidize rebuilding in vulnerable areas?

After Hurricane Harvey left one-third of Houston underwater in 2017, a familiar pattern played out. Area residents whose home or business had flooded filed a claim with the National Flood Insurance Program (NFIP), waited for their checks to arrive, then financed repairs with the money. The program eventually paid out about $9 billion on more than 90,000 Harvey-related claims.[52]

Many of the homes in the storm's path had flooded multiple times before. An investigation by the *Houston Chronicle* found that Houston is home to seven of 10 homes throughout the country that experience substantial flooding most frequently. One home in Kingwood, Texas, has received more than $2.5 million in flood insurance payouts on 22 claims since 1979, the investigation found.[53]

Wildfire victims also can count on government help. In the wake of California's devastating 2018 wildfire season, the Federal Emergency Management Agency (FEMA) and the Small Business Administration (SBA) approved grants and loans totaling $500 million to help victims rebuild, including in areas at high risk for future wildfires. And new homes continue to go up in those same areas. University researchers predicted in 2014 that an estimated 1 million new homes will be built in fire-prone zones in California by 2050.[54]

With scientists predicting that climate change will make weather-related calamities more frequent and more intense, many disaster management experts say it makes no sense for taxpayers to continue absorbing the cost of letting homeowners rebuild in vulnerable areas.

"If you want to rebuild in an area where there's a good chance your home is going to burn down again, go for it," said Ian Adams, a policy analyst at the R Street

Institute, a free-market think tank in Washington. "But I don't want to be subsidizing you."[55]

Many environmentalists say planning efforts should focus on discouraging people from moving into disaster-prone areas and either building new homes or buying those of people already there. This allows the vacated property to be turned into parks or, in the case of areas prone to flooding, wetlands.[56]

"We can begin by shifting development away from areas that are or will soon be subject to frequent flooding," the Environmental Defense Fund, an advocacy group in Washington, says on its website. "Immediately after a flood event is a good time to make this shift with property buyouts, but before the next flood is even better."[57]

Many people living or working in disaster-prone areas, however, have developed strong personal or financial ties to their communities and cannot imagine moving. Robert and Janice Jucker, owners of Three Brothers Bakery in Houston, have seen their business flood at least five times since 2001, including after Hurricane Harvey. They rebuilt using SBA loan money and said last year they had no plans to move. "We've become really good at disasters," Robert Jucker said. "How do we survive without our customers? We can't."[58]

Policymakers, moreover, often are reluctant to tell individual homeowners they cannot rebuild in areas susceptible to a weather-related disaster.

"One could make the argument that people were not meant to live in those environments," said Susan Gorin, a member of the Board of Supervisors in Sonoma County, Calif. But, she added, "it is very difficult for governments or anyone to tell another person, another property owner, that they could not, should not, rebuild."[59]

Joseph T. Edmiston, executive director of the Santa Monica Mountains Conservancy, which works to protect open space and wildlife in Southern California, disagrees. He has suggested that people whose houses have been destroyed twice by wildfire should be ineligible to receive additional federal rebuilding money. "I think two strikes is enough and they ought to be bought out," he said.[60]

Some disaster experts see buyouts in flood-prone areas as a way to minimize further losses for the National Flood Insurance Program, which is $20.5 billion in debt. "Rebuilding out of harm's way can help avoid future devastation in a way that flood insurance cannot," said David Maurstad, who heads the program as FEMA's deputy associate administrator for insurance and mitigation.[61]

But critics say buyout programs can leave communities pockmarked with blighted properties and are hampered by delays and other problems. In flood-prone areas, such programs "are extremely expensive, extremely disruptive, and many of the attempts have not gone well," said former FEMA Administrator Craig Fugate.[62]

Over the past 30 years, federal and local government officials have spent more than $5 billion buying vulnerable properties across the country from homeowners who volunteer to sell, according to an Associated Press analysis of data from FEMA and the Department of Housing and Urban Development. In most cases, local and state governments take over ownership of the properties.[63]

Other options aimed at minimizing repeated rebuilding in disaster-prone areas include charging people fees to build homes in those areas, and using federal money to buy land before people move there to maintain it as open space.[64]

"It's a wicked dilemma, for sure," Donald Falk, fire specialist with the University of Arizona's School of Natural Resources and the Environment, said of the debate over whether to continue subsidizing rebuilding in disaster-prone areas. "We at least like to think that we take care of people who have been exposed to disaster. Does that compassion lead us to simply do the same dance over and over again?"[65]

Some experts say congressional disaster aid packages should require that communities repeatedly victimized by weather-related disasters adopt tougher building codes. And homeowners are increasingly asking architects to design houses that can survive floods, wildfires and other disasters.[66]

Sean Jennings, for example, built his house in Lake County, Calif., out of polystyrene foam, steel and concrete. He said that explains how the building survived a 2015 wildfire that destroyed everything else in the area. "I wanted something that was fireproof, earthquake proof, flood proof," Jennings said. "Future proof, basically."[67]

BACKGROUND

Ancient Disasters

The extreme weather events that countries around the world are experiencing today are mild compared to the changes in climate that occurred millions of years ago as a result of volcanic activity, widespread cooling with the formation of glaciers, fluctuating sea levels and asteroid collisions. Those events drastically elevated carbon levels in the atmosphere—the same process that climate scientists say is occurring today with the release of greenhouse gases—and some killed most life on the planet.[68]

"Major mass extinctions of species closely coincided with abrupt rises of atmospheric carbon dioxide and ocean acidity," said Andrew Glikson, a climate scientist at Australian National University in Canberra, Australia. "These increases took place at rates to which many species could not adapt."[69]

Some researchers also have theorized that certain mass extinction events, including the one that wiped out dinosaurs 66 million years ago, could have started with an asteroid impact that then produced hypercanes, giant hurricanes with winds of 675 miles per hour that would have suffocated animals and plants by drastically lowering air pressure. The storms would have been caused by superheated ocean water, possibly due to underwater volcanic eruptions.[70]

Such eruptions were a major cause of extreme weather in the ancient world. One of the world's oldest known weather reports, written 3,500 years ago on a stone block in Egypt, describes torrential rain and refers to "the sky being in storm without cessation, louder than the cries of the masses." Scholars believe those conditions could have been caused by a volcanic eruption on an island in the Mediterranean Sea.[71]

Extreme weather also may have played a role in the collapse of entire civilizations. Some studies blame a prolonged drought for wiping out the Mayan Empire around A.D. 900 in what is now Guatemala. Researchers at the University of California, Davis, said such a drought "likely corresponded with crop failures, death, famine [and] migration." And environmental historians believe the ancient Khmer empire of Angkor in Cambodia collapsed in the early 15th century due to a severe drought followed by unusually intense monsoon rains that caused massive flooding and destroyed the city's infrastructure.[72]

A period known as the Little Ice Age began around 1300 and lasted until about 1850, possibly caused by a series of volcanic eruptions in the tropics that ejected clouds of sulphate particles into the upper atmosphere. The particles reflected heat from the sun back into space, lowering temperatures on Earth enough to expand ice sheets. The period brought bitterly cold winters to North America and Europe, leading to crop failure and famine.[73]

Centuries ago, people were less able to prepare for extreme weather, resulting in huge loss of life. The Great Hurricane in October 1780, for example, killed more than 20,000 people in the Caribbean and sank British and French warships fighting in the American Revolutionary War.[74]

Links to Pollution

In the 1820s, Jean Fourier, a French mathematician, became the first scholar to explain that the Earth's atmosphere retains heat radiation. Decades later, John Tyndall, a natural historian in Britain, discovered that water vapor and carbon dioxide (CO_2) are effective at trapping heat.[75]

Tyndall's research led Svante Arrhenius, a Swedish chemist, to perform experiments establishing that carbon dioxide, not water vapor, is the key to regulating the Earth's temperature. In 1896, Arrhenius said burning fossil fuels could eventually double CO_2 levels in the atmosphere, raising average global temperatures up to 4 degrees Celsius. Other scientists dismissed his findings as implausible.[76]

In the United States, extreme weather killed hundreds of people during the 1800s. A fast-moving Arctic cold front created the so-called Children's Blizzard that killed 235 people, including many children walking home from school, across the Great Plains on Jan. 12, 1888. Another blizzard in March that year killed more than 400 people in the Northeast, the nation's highest death toll from a winter storm. In October 1871, following an unusually dry summer, the most destructive forest fire in the country's history—the Peshtigo Fire—raged through parts of Wisconsin, killing at least 1,200 people.[77]

In 1849, the Smithsonian Institution, established to expand scientific and other knowledge, began supplying weather instruments to telegraph companies. By the end of the year, volunteers were reporting on weather conditions across the country.[78]

The next century brought new record-setting weather events. The Great Galveston Hurricane of 1900 on the Gulf Coast of Texas killed more than 6,000 people and still stands as the deadliest hurricane in U.S. history. The country's most lethal tornado killed almost 700 people in 1925, destroying entire towns in the Midwest with 300-mile-per-hour winds. A series of droughts crippled large parts of the United States during the 1930s, causing cropland to dry up and inspiring the term "Dust Bowl" to describe the south-central part of the country.[79]

Around the world, meanwhile, temperatures set new records in 1937, a development that climate scientists say would have been virtually impossible without rising levels of carbon in the atmosphere due to greenhouse gas emissions.[80]

In 1938, Guy Callendar, a steam engineer in Britain, said his research on the atmosphere and global weather patterns showed that burning fossil fuels had raised global temperatures by increasing carbon dioxide in the atmosphere. Callendar saw this as a benefit, saying the warming effect would help prevent the return of "deadly glaciers." As with Arrhenius before him, his contributions were considered improbable by other scientists at the time.[81]

After rising rapidly during the early decades of the 20th century, average global temperatures began dropping after 1940 and remained low until 1970. Many scientists attributed the cooler period to aerosols that had entered the atmosphere due to volcanic eruptions and increased industrial activity after World War II. They said sulfates in the aerosols reflected solar energy back into space, lowering surface temperatures on Earth. Temperatures began rising quickly again after new anti-pollution laws around the world reduced aerosol emissions.[82]

In 1981, scientists at Columbia University announced findings that they said confirmed the warming effect of carbon dioxide pollution entering the atmosphere. Their report followed another by scientists at NASA noting increases in global temperatures since 1880.[83]

New Research

In response to such discoveries, the United Nations and the World Meteorological Organization, located in Geneva, created the IPCC in 1988 "to provide a comprehensive summary of what is known about the drivers of climate change, its impacts and future risks, and how adaptation and mitigation can reduce those risks."[84]

A year later, Republican President George H.W. Bush established the U.S. Global Change Research Program. Congress codified the program the following year to help the nation and the world "understand, assess, predict and respond to" climate change from human and natural causes.[85]

In its first climate assessment report, issued in 2000, the program said that "Climate change is likely to decrease the number of some types of weather extremes, while increasing others," and predicted that rising temperatures likely would lead to "greater frequency of both very wet and very dry conditions."[86]

Five years later, Hurricane Katrina became the costliest hurricane to hit the United States. Damage from Katrina, which overwhelmed levees in New Orleans and caused massive flooding, totaled $161 billion. In 2012, Hurricane Sandy, also known as Superstorm Sandy, hit the U.S. East Coast, affecting 24 states. It set records for storm surge and caused about $71 billion in damage.[87]

The Global Change Research Program's first report was tentative in describing links between greenhouse gas emissions and extreme weather, but by 2014, the group was expressing greater confidence that the two were connected.[88]

"Changes in extreme weather and climate events, such as heat waves and droughts, are the primary way that most people experience climate change," the 2014 report said. "Human-induced climate change has already increased the number and strength of some of these extreme events. Over the last 50 years, much of the U.S. has seen increases in prolonged periods of excessively high temperatures, heavy downpours, and in some regions, severe floods and droughts."[89]

CHRONOLOGY

1800s *The U.S. government makes its first efforts to monitor and predict extreme weather.*

1849 Smithsonian Institution establishes a national weather-monitoring network.

1870 President Ulysses S. Grant signs a bill establishing a national weather warning service under the federal Department of War.

1871 The Peshtigo Fire in Wisconsin kills 1,200 people, making it the deadliest wildfire in U.S. history.

1890 The national weather warning service is named the U.S. Weather Bureau and is transferred to the Department of Agriculture.

1900-1940s *Scientists see early signs of global warming.*

1900 Hurricane strikes Galveston, Texas, and kills at least 6,000 people, becoming the deadliest extreme weather event in U.S. history.

1920 Meteorologist Charles Franklin Brooks founds the American Meteorological Society in Massachusetts to advance the study of weather.

1925 The Tri-State Tornado, the deadliest in U.S. history, kills nearly 700 people in Missouri, Illinois and Indiana. Some observers estimate it at a mile wide.

1935 Congress approves money to improve hurricane warning services, including new forecast centers in Jacksonville, Fla., New Orleans, Puerto Rico and Boston.

1938 Guy Callendar, a British engineer and inventor, links carbon dioxide emissions to rising global temperatures, but his work goes largely unnoticed.

1940 U.S. Weather Bureau is moved to the Department of Commerce.

1950s-1990s *Satellites make weather monitoring more accurate as scientists warn of global warming.*

1950 U.S. Weather Bureau begins issuing tornado alerts.

1960 NASA launches TIROS-1, the first successful weather satellite, which takes pictures of Earth's cloud cover for 78 days and paves the way for an orbiting weather-monitoring network used worldwide.

1968 Congress establishes the National Flood Insurance Program, which offers insurance to people living in areas at high risk for flooding.

1970 U.S. Weather Bureau, now part of the National Oceanic and Atmospheric Administration, is renamed the National Weather Service.

1975 NASA launches the first Geostationary Operational Environmental Satellite (GOES), a "hurricane hunter" that tracks tropical cyclones.

1981 Scientists report a warming in global temperatures since 1880 and attribute the trend to carbon emissions entering the atmosphere.

1990 The Intergovernmental Panel on Climate Change (IPCC) issues its first assessment, laying the groundwork for international efforts to predict the effects of global warming.

2000-Present *As billion-dollar disasters occur more often, scientists and policymakers seek ways to predict and prepare for extreme weather.*

2004 In one of the first studies linking climate change to a specific weather event, British scientists say a 2003 record-setting heat wave in Europe that killed 35,000 people was made twice as likely by climate change.

2005 Hurricane Katrina overwhelms levees in New Orleans and causes about $161 billion in damage, becoming the most expensive weather disaster in U.S. history.

2011 *The Bulletin of the American Meteorological Society* begins publishing a special issue highlighting studies on links between climate change and extreme weather events.

2017 Sixteen weather-related disasters costing at least $1 billion each in the U.S. kill 362 people and cause $306 billion in damage.

2018 The Camp Fire in California kills 85 people, burns more than 150,000 acres and destroys more than 18,000 buildings, becoming the deadliest and most destructive fire in the state's history—and the deadliest in the country since 1918.

2019 U.S. experiences six billion-dollar weather disasters by July 9 with a combined death toll of 15. . . . Hurricane Dorian hits the Bahamas as a Category 5 storm and stalls over the islands for two days, killing dozens of people and causing massive destruction.

Farmers Face Difficult Odds as Extreme Weather Grows

"Dry areas will get even dryer, and wet areas will get even wetter."

Kate Glastetter, a 25-year-old Missouri farmer, likened her fields this past spring to lakefront property. "The fields are washing away," she said.[1]

A combination of heavy rains and melting snow led to historic flooding throughout much of the United States last spring, especially in areas that drain into the Missouri or Mississippi Rivers. By March 2019, some regions had received more than twice their yearly rainfall average, according to the National Oceanic and Atmospheric Administration.[2]

The floods forced farmers such as Glastetter's neighbors to delay planting, and by mid-May 2019, for the first time in recorded U.S. history, less than half the nation's corn fields had been planted, according to the U.S. Department of Agriculture (USDA).

Sam Gray, who manages a farm in North Easton, Mass., drives along a flooded road on May 14, 2019. Climate scientists say rising global temperatures will bring increasing episodes of both intense rain and severe droughts, threatening crops around the world.

The Farm Bureau, an organization that represents agricultural interests, estimated spring flooding damage to stored crops, livestock, fields, farm buildings and equipment in Nebraska and Iowa, among the most affected states, at more than $3 billion.[3]

And flooding damage in the central part of the country was only the beginning. Although the effects of high water had begun to abate by late June 2019, with most fields planted by then, according to the USDA, a new peril loomed. In late July a heat wave threatened to stunt root development and further decrease crop yields.[4]

Climate scientists have long predicted that climate change would spur increases in severe droughts and floods like those that have occurred this year. Computer models still cannot accurately predict when or where such events will occur, but the models do suggest that the future will see an increase in drastic weather swings.

"Dry areas will get even dryer, and wet areas will get even wetter," says climate scientist Jhordanne Jones, a doctoral student at Colorado State University in Fort Collins who focuses on predicting tropical cyclones.

Farmers cannot plant in fields that are too saturated or too dry, and massive flooding can spoil stored crops before they are sold. Excessive rain or heat also promotes the growth of destructive pests, weeds and fungi.

A drought in 2012 sent corn yields nationwide more than 26 percent below predictions, and farm income decreased by nearly $5 billion nationwide. The drought also drove the Mississippi River to record low levels, making it impossible for grain-carrying barges to deliver their cargo. Animals that feed on grain also were affected.[5]

A July report by the USDA's Economic Research Service predicted that U.S. corn and soybean yields could fall by as much as 80 percent in the next 60 years due to weather extremes driven by climate change.[6]

In a June 2018 study published in the *Proceedings of the National Academy of Sciences*, researchers estimated that corn production by the top four corn-producing countries—the United States, China, Brazil and Argentina—will drop significantly if the average global temperature rises by 4 degrees Celsius (7 degrees Fahrenheit).[7]

Agricultural production in tropical regions will be hit hardest, according to other studies.[8] "That's where you have the weakest institutions in terms of helping farmers," says Dan Blaustein-Rejto, senior food and agriculture analyst at the Breakthrough Institute, an environmental research center in San Francisco.

The USDA report predicted that declining yields will sharply drive up the cost of wheat, corn and soybeans as well as the cost of crop insurance. As of July 15, the department had spent about $300 million on insurance on 2019 crops; the report predicted that in six decades that will climb to more than $10 billion.[9] As much as 85 percent of a farmer's land is protected against natural disasters or market fluctuations by crop insurance subsidized by the federal government, which covers an average of 62 percent of the insurance premiums.[10]

Experts also predict that extreme weather events will lead to periods of food scarcity. After studying five decades of data on crops, livestock, aquaculture and fisheries, an international team of researchers in January reported that food-scarcity episodes have been increasing in recent years, especially in developing countries, because of extreme weather.[11]

As researchers look for ways to deal with the effects of extreme weather on agriculture, information from the USDA has become harder for them to find, according to an investigation by *Politico*, an online news publication. It found that the Trump administration has "refused to publicize dozens of government-funded studies that carry warnings about the effects of climate change, defying a longstanding practice of touting such findings by the Agriculture Department's acclaimed in-house scientists."[12]

Many researchers and policymakers see some hope in biotechnology. Scientists have been developing crop seeds genetically modified to resist pests, drought and floods, but Blaustein-Retjo says funding for crop research in the United States has fallen in the last 20 years. In addition, a complicated approval process and public mistrust of genetically modified organisms—including seeds and livestock—have slowed research.

— *Stephen Ornes*

[1] Emily Moon, "'The Fields are Washing Away': Midwest Flooding is Wreaking Havoc on Farmers," *Pacific Standard*, June 6, 2019, https://tinyurl.com/y3maxvlz.

[2] "January-May Precipitation," National Climate Report, National Oceanic and Atmospheric Administration, May 2019, https://tinyurl.com/y4p2qxnl.

[3] Jessie Higgins, "Midwestern farmers devastated by uninsured flood losses," UPI, March 29, 2019, https://tinyurl.com/y6973lhz; Matthew Schwartz, "Nebraska Faces over $1.3 Billion in Flood Losses," *NPR*, March 21, 2019, https://tinyurl.com/y22gm5nb.

[4] Mark Weinraub, "U.S. corn plantings top expectations despite floods; prices sink," *Reuters*, June 28, 2019, https://tinyurl.com/y6ax4bk6; Emma Newburger, "'It never stops': US farmers now face extreme heat wave after floods and trade war," *CNBC*, July 20, 2019, https://tinyurl.com/yy9ffb6w.

[5] Ben Foster, "Drought and the Mighty Mississippi," *Property and Environment Research Center Magazine*, Vol. 35, No. 2, 2016, https://tinyurl.com/yyzz4m33.

[6] Andrew Crane-Droesch *et al.*, "Climate Change and Agricultural Risk Management into the 21st Century," U.S. Department of Agriculture, July 2019, https://tinyurl.com/y2zlwtdz.

[7] Michelle Tigchelaar *et al.*, "Future warming increases probability of globally synchronized maize production shocks," *Proceedings of the National Academy of Sciences*, Vol. 115, No. 26, pp. 6644-6649, June 11, 2018, https://tinyurl.com/y4dqnftn.

[8] *Ibid.*

[9] Crane-Droesch, *op. cit.*; Kirk Maltais, "USDA Report Sees Dire Climate-Change Impact on U.S. Crops," *The Wall Street Journal*, July 23, 2019, https://tinyurl.com/y42r9cx3.

[10] Maltais, *ibid.*

[11] Richard Cottrell *et al.*, "Food production shocks across land and sea," *Nature Sustainability*, Vol. 2, pp. 130-137, Jan. 28, 2019, https://tinyurl.com/y2mz6nvv.

[12] Helena Bottemiller Evich, "Agriculture Department buries studies showing dangers of climate change," *Politico*, June 23, 2019, https://tinyurl.com/yxbzqhnq.

Insurers React as Extreme Weather Boosts Claims

Many raise rates and reassess risk in response to changing climate.

As extreme weather events become more frequent and powerful, insurance companies are changing how they price homeowner policies and determine what to cover.

The change has occurred largely because recent extreme weather has led to record annual payouts by insurers to cover losses. Insured losses from disasters around the world in 2017 totaled $140 billion, higher than ever before, according to German reinsurance company Munich Re Group. Those losses included at least one event not tied to the weather, a severe earthquake in Mexico. Munich Re said losses in the United States dominated the statistics.[1]

Insured losses worldwide dropped to $80 billion in 2018, which Munich Re noted was still "substantially higher than the long-term average." Again, earthquakes accounted for some of those losses. Claims in 2017 were driven up by the costliest Atlantic hurricane season on record. The single most expensive event in 2018 was a wildfire, the Camp Fire in California, Munich Re said.[2]

A Nationwide Mutual Insurance Co. survey of 100,000 claims in 2017 found that the number and amount of claims have climbed significantly in recent years. Between 2014 and 2016, a period of unusually warm winters and other unexpected weather events, including massive flooding, the average claim amount was 26 percent higher than in the seven-year period between 2007 and 2013.[3]

Many insurers have raised rates in recent years in response to extreme weather events.[4] Others have stopped insuring homeowners in certain high-risk areas, or raised premiums in those locations. At least one carrier, USAA, offers discounts to homeowners who live in communities that are at risk of fire but have taken precautions, such as consulting with fire experts and clearing flammable debris and vegetation near buildings.[5]

"Few sectors of the economy play a role as intense in catastrophe recovery as insurance," said Anna Maria D'Hulster, then-secretary general of the Geneva Association, an international insurance think tank in Geneva.[6]

The availability—or lack—of insurance coverage can induce homeowners to make better decisions about preparation and even about where to live, experts say. Pricing premiums according to weather risk, for example, can help shape the real estate market.

"If it's expensive to insure a house on the coast, individuals will have an incentive to live elsewhere," three University of Southern California economists wrote in an article for *Harvard Business Review.* "If insurers offer a discount for climate-proofing homes, homeowners will likewise have an incentive to make that investment."[7]

JOSH EDELSON/AFP/Getty Images

Cars and homes burn as the Camp Fire roars through Paradise, Calif., in November 2018. Experts say the number of acres burned by wildfires in California has increased fivefold since the early 1970s, one of many events driving up insurance losses.

The economists said insurers increasingly use tools that more precisely assess the risk of damage to individual houses. In coastal communities, for example, houses built closer to the shore or at lower elevations typically are at greater risk than those on hills or further inland.

Insurance companies also have developed new modeling and pricing tools that explicitly take into consideration the latest scientific findings and predictions about weather. In particular, they are exploring ways to account for extremes due to climate change.

Catastrophic-loss models have traditionally been defined by long-term climate data, averaged over time. They have treated the climate as a stationary, or unchanging, influence. But a 2014 report by Lloyd's of London, the British insurance firm, said Atlantic hurricane risk varies dramatically over time, due to natural variation and also due to human activities. Lloyds concluded that new models need to reflect a changing climate to better predict future losses.[8]

Extreme weather is an issue for crop insurance, which farmers use to recover from disasters. Insurance can shield farmers against low yields of crops such as wheat, soybeans and corn and unexpected drops in market prices. If extreme weather events become more severe and common, insurance will become increasingly important in protecting farmers' livelihoods, experts say.

However, crop insurance raises questions of responsibility. The U.S. government pays 60 percent of farmers' premiums.[9] Critics argue that the Federal Crop Insurance Program favors large farms and rewards farmers for using practices known to diminish land resiliency, such as planting a single crop rather than rotating crops.

"The current U.S. crop insurance program encourages farmers to adopt production practices that will not be sustainable in the face of climate change, and in the short term contribute to greenhouse gas emissions," said Montana State University agricultural economist Vincent Smith. "Crop insurance encourages people to adopt production practices that are riskier, and by definition, reduce resiliency."[10]

That is similar to arguments made against other government-subsidized insurance programs, such as the National Flood Insurance Program (NFIP) and Florida's Citizens Property Insurance Corp., a nonprofit insurance company created in 2002 by the Florida Legislature that offers property insurance to people unable to get a policy from a private insurer. These government-subsidized programs insure people living in high-risk areas, but they may distort a homeowner's perception of the danger, some researchers say.

"Once the government subsidizes the risk, then people view it as less costly than it is to live in a risky area," says Omri Ben-Shahar, a law professor at the University of Chicago who has studied the effects of government subsidies in relation to extreme weather. He says programs such as the NFIP encourage people to build and live in places known to be at high risk of damage from extreme weather.

"Sometimes the answer isn't to build a wall two feet higher, but not to live somewhere at all," he says.

— Stephen Ornes

[1] "Natural catastrophe review: Series of hurricanes makes 2017 year of highest insured losses ever," Munich Re, Jan. 4, 2018, https://tinyurl.com/y7y9jhc6; "Extreme storms, wildfires and droughts cause heavy nat cat losses in 2018," Munich Re, Jan. 8, 2019, https://tinyurl.com/yakmgnpd.

[2] "Natural catastrophe review," *ibid.*

[3] "Nationwide Warns of Widening Gap Between Disaster Risks and Business Preparedness," press release, Nationwide, Feb. 28, 2017, https://tinyurl.com/y259efox; Don Jergler, "Nationwide Says Extreme Weather Brings Bigger Claims, Need for Disaster Plans," *Insurance Journal*, March 2, 2017, https://tinyurl.com/y6ztwrun.

[4] Jeff Blyskal, "How Climate Change Could Affect Your Homeowners Insurance Coverage," *Consumer Reports*, Sept. 20, 2017, https://tinyurl.com/y3bgx4ob.

[5] "Firewise USA," National Fire Protection Association, accessed Sept. 5, 2019, https://tinyurl.com/y5v4hfef.

[6] "Managing Physical Climate Risk: Leveraging Innovations in Catastrophe Risk Modeling," The Geneva Association, November 2018, https://tinyurl.com/y4ny64vw.

[7] Matthew Kahn, Brian Casey and Nolan Jones, "How the Insurance Industry Can Push us to Prepare for Climate Change," *Harvard Business Review*, Aug. 28, 2017, https://tinyurl.com/yblbjhgg.

[8] "Catastrophe Modelling and Climate Change," Lloyd's of London, 2014, https://tinyurl.com/yywur4gn.

[9] "Reduce Subsidies in the Crop Insurance Program," Option for Reducing the Deficit, Congressional Budget Office, Dec. 13, 2018, https://tinyurl.com/y3yspdvw.

[10] Georgina Gustin, "U.S. Taxpayers on the Hook for Insuring Farmers Against Growing Climate Risks," *Inside Climate News*, Dec. 31, 2018, https://tinyurl.com/y863tvos.

The report also said that:

- Climate change from human activity "has generally increased the probability of heat waves" and "prolonged (multimonth) extreme heat has been unprecedented since the start of reliable instrumental records in 1895."
- The amount of rain falling in the United States in very heavy precipitation events has been significantly above average since 1991.
- The intensity, frequency and duration of Atlantic hurricane activity has significantly increased since the early 1980s. "Quantifying the relative contributions of natural and human-caused factors is an active focus of research," the report said.

In December the following year, the United States and 194 other countries signed the Paris Agreement on climate change as part of a global effort to reduce carbon emissions and limit the temperature increases that scientists blamed for the increasing frequency and severity of some types of extreme weather.[90]

Disaster Costs Grow

Improvements in computer climate models allowed scientists to increasingly link specific extreme weather events to climate change. Research published in the *Bulletin of the American Meteorological Society* in December 2018, for example, found that three extreme weather-related events that took place in 2017: droughts in the U.S. northern Plains and East Africa, floods in South America, China and Bangladesh, and heat waves in China and the Mediterranean—were all made more likely because of greenhouse gas emissions.[91]

The report also said that certain ocean heat events, including severe marine heat waves in the Tasman Sea, were "virtually impossible" without climate change caused by human activity.

The year 2017 was notable in the United States for a record number of billion-dollar weather-related disasters. The 16 events included hurricanes (Harvey, Irma and Maria), eight severe storms and two inland floods. In June that same year, President Trump announced that the United States would withdraw from the Paris Agreement in November 2020, citing "the draconian

financial and economic burdens the agreement imposes on our country."[92]

The president's critics, however, cite reports showing the federal government has spent more than $430 billion since 2005 on humanitarian assistance following weather-related disasters in the country. A report from the Government Accountability Office (GAO), the investigative arm of Congress, predicts such costs will grow.

"The costliness of disasters is projected to increase as extreme weather events become more frequent and intense due to climate change," the GAO said in March. It also noted that government officials since 2017 have rolled back policies designed to deal with climate change.[93]

The Center for Climate Security, which advocates for action on climate change to protect national security, said the GAO report "makes a strong case that the U.S. is moving backwards in that effort, despite the regular warnings coming from the defense, intelligence and science agencies of our government, and the broader national security community."[94]

CURRENT SITUATION
Flood Insurance Future

This year's wet-weather extremes—including storm surge and heavy downpours in North Carolina as a result of Hurricane Dorian and torrential rain and flooding in the Midwest and Southeast—focused new attention on attempts to reform the National Flood Insurance Program. The program is set to expire—and run out of money—on Sept. 30, 2019, unless Congress acts to reauthorize it.[95]

Critics of the program, which provides about $1.3 trillion in coverage for about 5 million homes across the country, say it charges premiums that are too low for some homeowners and too high for others, produces shoddy flood maps and encourages rebuilding in areas that are sure to flood repeatedly.[96]

"Here you have a program that is subsidizing people to live and develop in harm's way," said Steve Ellis, vice president of Taxpayers for Common Sense, a budget watchdog group in Washington.[97]

Completely overhauling the program would require congressional approval. In the meantime, FEMA, which oversees the NFIP, has proposed changing how the program calculates premiums to make sure they accurately reflect an individual home's flood risks.[98]

Congress last reauthorized the program in May, the 12th reauthorization since the fall of 2017. Without new legislation extending it, FEMA will stop issuing new flood insurance policies for millions of homes across the country, potentially threatening 40,000 home-sale closings each month.[99]

"NFIP reauthorization is an opportunity for Congress to take bold steps to reduce the complexity of the program and strengthen the NFIP's financial framework," FEMA said in a statement.[100]

Reform proposals include a measure introduced by Sen. Bob Menendez, D-N.J., in July that would reauthorize the flood insurance program for five years. It would cap annual premium increases at 9 percent, boost funding for flood maps and for grants to homeowners who want to relocate or elevate their homes, and close loopholes that the NFIP has used in the past to deny reimbursement to flood victims. At least four Republicans have signed on as co-sponsors. Menendez is a member of the Senate Banking Committee that oversees the NFIP and sits on a Senate task force formed in 2015 to improve FEMA's handling of flood claims related to Hurricane Sandy, which caused extensive damage to his state.[101]

A rival bill introduced by Rep. Maxine Waters, D-Calif., chairwoman of the House Financial Services Committee, also would reauthorize the NFIP for five years but does not include other provisions Menendez is pushing.[102]

Administration Actions

The Trump administration, meanwhile, continues acting to minimize the role of climate change science in government policy:

- In May 2019, James Reilly, director of the U.S. Geological Survey, ordered his office to use computer-generated climate models that project conditions only through 2040 instead of the end of the century. Scientists see that as a move to ignore the time period when they say the effect of climate change on weather conditions will be most apparent.[103]
- Administration officials have decided that the next national climate assessment from the Global

Change Research Program will not include worst-case scenarios such as a temperature increase of 8 degrees Fahrenheit that would result in a drastic rise in sea levels and a sharp increase in devastating storms and droughts.[104] "The previous use of inaccurate modeling that focuses on worst-case emissions scenarios, that does not reflect real-world conditions, needs to be thoroughly re-examined and tested if such information is going to serve as the scientific foundation of nationwide decision-making now and in the future," said James Hewitt, a spokesman for the Environmental Protection Agency.

- William Happer, a physicist and a member of the White House National Security Council, is working to create a new panel inside the White House that would challenge the science behind global warming, including evidence that climate change is causing more incidents of extreme weather.[105]
- Last year, FEMA removed references to climate change from its four-year strategic plan, and a section in the plan titled "Emerging Threats" includes no references to extreme weather. The agency's public affairs director said the plan "fully incorporates future risks from all hazards regardless of cause."[106]
- The administration has abandoned its former practice of announcing the result of studies by scientists at the Agriculture Department warning of the effects of climate change, including severe weather events.[107]

"The intent is to try to suppress a message—in this case, the increasing danger of human-caused climate change," said Mann at Penn State. "Who loses out? The people, who are already suffering the impacts of sea level rise and unprecedented super storms, droughts, wildfires and heat waves."[108]

Climate scientists also castigated the administration recently for what they view as actions intended to politicize government weather forecasting. On Sept. 8, NOAA's acting chief scientist, Craig McLean, said he will investigate whether the agency violated its own ethical policies when it defended the president's inaccurate

Should the federal government subsidize rebuilding in areas vulnerable to extreme weather?

YES
Alan Rubin
Principal, Blank Rome Government Relations LLC

Written for *CQ Researcher*, September 2019

The question of where development can take place in the United States has always been a controversial one. Cities, municipalities, counties and states have looked to property taxes and other taxes to support their growth and pay for social programs. Environmentalists, social scientists and green advocates have always advocated for a minimalist approach to development to prevent what they view as the destruction of ecosystems and natural resources.

As the country has grown and population densities have increased, these priorities have not been kept in balance. However, people in areas where natural disasters have occurred have attempted to rebuild with the intention of "building back better." Because 60 percent of the population lives along or near the coast, intelligent recovery and the use of zoning laws and unique construction designs must be implemented. In the recovery and resiliency process, we must recognize the potential for repetitive natural and man-made disasters.

With that as a premise, federal programs should allow for rebuilding in areas that are prone to extreme weather events. The key is making sure the redevelopment utilizes all of the innovative concepts and latest strategies in the legislative toolkit.

Examples include reauthorizing the National Flood Insurance Program for five to 10 years as opposed to the current practice of reauthorizing the program after it runs out of money following a natural disaster. As a part of this reauthorization, there should be an annual limit on premium increases that would exclude catastrophic-loss years. Additionally, a formula for increased rates would apply to the most expensive properties. And of course, there would need to be a means test for affordability and low income in setting rates.

Multiple programs at the local, state and federal levels can be used to facilitate rebuilding in areas devastated by natural disasters. These include:

- Mold mitigation assistance grants.
- Hazard mitigation grants.
- Elevation requirements for commercial and residential buildings.
- Mapping modernization and implementation.
- Revolving loan funds for affected areas.

NO
Josiah Neeley
Senior Fellow and Energy Policy Director, R Street Institute

Written for *CQ Researcher*, September 2019

When it comes to practicing medicine, doctors try to follow a simple rule set forth in the Hippocratic Oath: First, do no harm. Government should follow the same rule, but it often doesn't.

A clear example of this is the way government subsidizes building in storm-prone areas.

We've all seen the damage that storms like Hurricanes Harvey and Sandy can cause. And such storms are expected to become more dangerous in the future. A recent study by the Risky Business Project, which assesses the economic risks to the United States from climate change, concluded that in the Southeast alone, between $48.2 billion and $68.7 billion worth of existing coastal property will be below sea level by 2050. By the end of the century, some parts of Louisiana may be at least 4.3 feet below sea level. Yet even as the danger from flooding and storms grows, the number of people moving to flood-prone areas is increasing.

Why are people moving into the path of future storms? Part of the answer is that the government encourages them to do so. Take, for example, the National Flood Insurance Program (NFIP). The NFIP was founded in 1968 as a means of providing flood insurance to properties that simply couldn't qualify for flood insurance from the private insurance market. The rates the NFIP charges, however, are far below what are necessary to pay out expected claims. Unsurprisingly, this has led the NFIP to incur chronic financial difficulties. The NFIP is currently more than $20 billion in debt, and that's after Congress canceled $16 billion in debt in 2017.

Beyond these financial problems, the NFIP's artificially low rates create perverse incentives for developers. Prices convey information. If the cost to insure property in a given area is prohibitively high, that is a signal that the risks of building in that area are similarly high. By subsidizing rates, the NFIP sends a false signal that building in flood-prone areas is far less risky than it really is, leading to overdevelopment. The NFIP is one of many such programs that subsidize risky development.

People should be free to live where they want, of course. But the rest of us shouldn't have to pay for it. Ending government

- Mandatory business interruption insurance.
- Mold damage identification.

Many of these items are being addressed. Certainly, improved zoning laws, buffer zones and architectural designs that prevent repetitive damage are all important weapons in legislating new and successful rules to help rebuilding in areas that have been or could be affected by extreme weather.

It is possible to successfully recover and prevent additional damage. This is required in order to coexist in a period of climate change and massively destructive storms.

subsidies for building in disaster-prone areas won't eliminate risk, but it will give people a better sense of the true costs and help us all be better prepared for when the rains come.

claim on Sept. 1, 2019, that Alabama was in the path of Hurricane Dorian.[109]

Many national security experts also fear that political motivations are increasingly driving the government's reaction to extreme weather caused by climate change.

"When extreme weather hits the United States, it degrades the fighting force," 58 former military and national security leaders wrote to President Trump in March. "We support the science-driven patriots in our national security community who have rightly seen addressing climate change as a threat reduction issue, not a political one."[110]

In January 2019, then-Director of National Intelligence Dan Coats warned in a report about national security dangers across the globe that heat waves, droughts and floods are a growing threat to food and water supplies, "increasing the risk of social unrest, migration and interstate tension in countries such as Egypt, Ethiopia, Iraq and Jordan."[111]

"Extreme weather events, many worsened by accelerating sea level rise, will particularly affect urban coastal areas in South Asia, Southeast Asia and the Western Hemisphere," Coats' report said. "Damage to communication, energy and transportation infrastructure could affect low-lying military bases, inflict economic costs, and cause human displacement and loss of life."[112]

On Sept. 12, 2019, the Internal Displacement Monitoring Centre, an agency in Geneva that estimates the number of people displaced around the world by disasters, conflict and other causes, reported that weather disasters displaced a record 7 million people during the first half of 2019.[113]

"In today's changing climate, mass displacement triggered by extreme weather events is becoming the norm," the report said.[114]

A poll conducted in July and August this year by *The Washington Post* and the Kaiser Family Foundation, a private research group located in San Francisco and Washington, found that about eight in 10 Americans—and 60 percent of Republicans—believe human activity fuels climate change. Nearly 40 percent of Americans said climate change has reached "crisis" levels, up from less than 25 percent five years ago. And 67 percent of those surveyed said they are unhappy with how President Trump has handled climate change.[115]

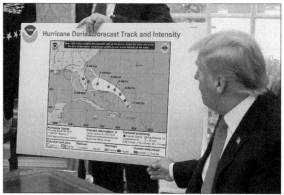

President Trump displays a map of Hurricane Dorian's predicted path that appears to have been altered to validate his earlier, incorrect statement that Dorian was expected to hit Alabama. Scientists say some of Trump's actions have politicized government weather forecasting.

Chip Somodevilla/Getty Images

Campaign Issue

Extreme weather and its link to climate change caused by carbon emissions is a key issue for candidates vying for the Democratic presidential nomination in 2020.

Most of the candidates—20 were still in the race as of mid-September—have strategies, costing trillions of dollars, to reduce greenhouse gas emissions. A number, for example, have expressed support for a tax on emissions. That includes the three candidates who were leading in the polls at the time—former Vice President Joseph Biden, Sen. Elizabeth Warren of Massachusetts and Sen. Bernie Sanders of Vermont, an independent who caucuses with Democrats.[116]

Sen. Kamala Harris of California supports a "progressively increasing fee" targeting companies that pollute. Julián Castro of Texas, former Housing and Urban Development secretary, argues for an emissions fee for the "biggest . . . industrial scale polluters." Former Rep. Beto O'Rourke, also of Texas, supports a cap-and-trade plan that would impose a limit on carbon pollution and let polluters buy and sell allowances for emissions within that limit.[117]

Virtually all of the 10 Democratic candidates who spoke at a *CNN* town hall on climate change issues on Sept. 4 said the United States should remain committed to the Paris Agreement.[118]

The Green New Deal, or something similar to it, is widely supported by the Democratic field. The sweeping proposal, which is pending in Congress, aims to cut U.S. greenhouse gas emissions in half by 2030. It would dramatically increase reliance on renewable energy sources to address climate change while providing jobs and economic security for low-income Americans. Biden has offered qualified support but says the plan lacks specifics about its goals.[119]

Republican critics of the plan say it would result in soaring energy costs, and even some moderate Democrats say its goals are too ambitious.[120]

Mental Health

New research finds that people whose homes are damaged by extreme weather are more likely to experience serious mental health issues such as depression. A study published in September 2019 by researchers in Britain, for example, found that people who had experienced storm and flood damage were about 50 percent more likely to suffer poorer mental health.

"This is reflective of the huge impact storms and flooding have on people's lives, as alongside the physical damage to homes and businesses, there is the emotional damage to the sense of security that many people derive from their home," said Hilary Graham, a professor at the Department of Health Sciences at the University of York and the study's lead author.[121]

Researchers said in a study published in August that recent Atlantic hurricanes—Harvey, Irma and Maria in 2017, and Florence and Michael in 2018—led to increased rates of common mental disorders such as depression and post-traumatic stress disorder among storm victims. "As hurricanes become increasingly severe, health care systems may expect to see more mental illness related to these extreme storms," the authors said.[122]

Tools used to forecast extreme weather, meanwhile, continue to improve. In June, NOAA announced a significant upgrade to its Global Forecast System software used by meteorologists around the world. The agency says the upgrade should allow forecasters to more accurately predict the track and intensity of hurricanes, as well as rainfall amounts.[123]

Experts warn that the damaging impact of extreme heat on mental health around the world will become an increasing problem as the world continues to warm. They anticipate higher rates of violent conflict, suicide, depression and cognitive impairment.[124]

"By 2050 there may be between 9,000 to 40,000 additional suicides in the U.S. and Mexico," the *Psychiatric Times* reported in July. "These rates are comparable to the effects on suicide incidence due to economic recessions and unemployment and offset gains in suicide prevention programs and gun control policies."[125]

OUTLOOK

Worsening Trends

Climate scientists expect some forms of extreme weather to worsen later this century. Floods so severe they would normally occur just 1 percent of the time will take place every year in New England and every 1 to 30 years along the southeast Atlantic and Gulf of Mexico coastlines, according to a study published in August by researchers from the Stevens Institute of Technology in Hoboken, N.J., Princeton University and the Massachusetts Institute of Technology. The researchers based their prediction on an analysis of how hurricanes and rising sea levels combine to produce coastal flooding.[126]

"Current flood risk mapping from the U.S. Federal Emergency Management Agency (FEMA) has not accounted for the effects of climate change," the authors said.[127]

Other researchers predict that within 60 years, the climate in 540 urban areas in North America—with a combined population of 250 million—will shift to essentially duplicate the climate of cities much farther to the south. In 2080, for example, living in Washington, D.C., could feel as hot as living near Greenwood, Miss., feels now, according to researchers at the University of Maryland and North Carolina State University. That would mean an increase of 8 degrees Fahrenheit in average temperature.[128]

"Cities in the northeast will tend to feel more like the humid subtropical climates typical of parts of the Midwest or southeastern U.S. today . . . whereas the climates of western cities are expected to become more like those of the desert Southwest or southern California," the researchers said.[129]

NOTES

1. Jack Healy, "They Rode Out Dorian in the Outer Banks. Now Comes the Hard Part," *The New York Times*, Sept. 8, 2019, https://tinyurl.com/yxut5k7a.

2. *Ibid.*

3. Max Golembo, "US sets rain record for 3rd time this year as Gulf prepares for tropical system," *ABC News*, July 9, 2019, https://tinyurl.com/yxh93npc; Allison Mollenkamp, "Floods That Hit The Midwest In March Continue To Affect The Farm Economy," *NPR*, May 21, 2019, https://tinyurl.com/yx9fpdzl; "Global Climate Report—July 2019," National Oceanic and Atmospheric Administration, August 2019, https://tinyurl.com/y3ggxd3z; Jonathan Watts, "Holiday heat headlines not focusing enough on climate crisis reality—experts," *The Guardian*, Aug. 27, 2019, https://tinyurl.com/y366fets; Amanda Schmidt, "May 2019 could be historic month for tornadoes after unprecedented twister streak finally ends at 13 days," AccuWeather, July 12, 2019, https://tinyurl.com/y6p2rols; and Doyle Rice, "Paris sets new temperature record at 108 as Europe heat wave continues to sizzle," *USA Today*, July 25, 2019, https://tinyurl.com/yxhnwl53.

4. James Rainey, "Global warming can make extreme weather worse. Now scientists can say by how much," *NBC News*, Aug. 19, 2018, https://tinyurl.com/ybdu6obc.

5. "Billion-Dollar Weather and Climate Disasters: Overview," National Oceanic and Atmospheric Administration, July 9, 2019, https://tinyurl.com/qakozj4; Jeff Dahdah, "Dorian set to be the seventh billion dollar hurricane for U.S. in four years," Spectrum News1, Sept. 10, 2019, https://tinyurl.com/y4735rl2.

6. John Schwartz, "After a Natural Disaster, Is It Better to Rebuild or Retreat?" *The New York Times*, Dec. 13, 2018, https://tinyurl.com/yauxhdmv.

7. Kimberly Amadeo, "Extreme Weather, Its Effect on the Economy and You," *the balance*, June 25, 2019, https://tinyurl.com/y2pmohzp; "Extreme Events," National Oceanic and Atmospheric Administration, undated, https://tinyurl.com/y6zymaqz.

8. "U.S. heat wave frequency and length are increasing," U.S. Global Change Research Program, 2018, https://tinyurl.com/yxf4kg86.

9. "Extreme Precipitation and Climate Change," Center for Climate and Energy Solutions, undated, https://tinyurl.com/y6hsgpzn; "Climate Change Indicators: Heavy Precipitation," U.S. Environmental Protection Agency, undated, https://tinyurl.com/yyywbum4.

10. A. Park Williams *et al.*, "Observed Impacts of Anthropogenic Climate Change on Wildfire in California," *Earth's Future*, Vol. 7, No. 8, July 15, 2019, https://tinyurl.com/yxucv5h6; Robinson Meyer, "California's Wildfires Are 500 Percent Larger Due to Climate Change," *The Atlantic*, July 16, 2019, https://tinyurl.com/y4lln8qz.

11. Seth Borenstein, "Science Says: Era of Monster Hurricanes Roiling the Atlantic," The Associated Press/WeatherBug, Sept. 10, 2019, https://tinyurl.com/yy7ahmeu.

12. Emma Newburger, "A signal of climate change: Hurricane Dorian stalls over Bahamas, causing massive destruction," *CNBC*, Sept. 3, 2019, https://tinyurl.com/y6fh74jy; Jason Samenow and Andrew Freedman, "Hurricane Dorian poised to slam the Carolinas after scraping the coasts of Florida and Georgia," *The Washington Post*, Sept. 4, 2019, https://tinyurl.com/y26gz2fa; and John Schwartz, "How Has Climate Change Affected Hurricane Dorian?" *The New York Times*, Sept. 3, 2019, https://tinyurl.com/yxvh6yvf.

13. Giorgia Guglielmi, "Hurricanes slow their roll around the world," *Nature*, June 6, 2018, https://tinyurl.com/y6pgnsx3; Merrit Kennedy, "Harvey The 'Most Significant Tropical Cyclone Rainfall Event In U.S. History,'" *NPR*, Jan. 25, 2018, https://tinyurl.com/yyc3qzub.

14. Brady Dennis and Chris Mooney, "Wildfires, hurricanes and other extreme weather cost the nation 247 lives, nearly $100 billion in damage during 2018," *The Washington Post*, Feb. 6, 2019, https://tinyurl.com/y89avatx; Doyle Rice, "Natural disasters caused record $306 billion in damage to U.S. in 2017," *USA Today*, Jan. 8, 2018, https://tinyurl.com/yatrtw3h.

15. Nicola Jones, "Wild Weather and Climate Change: Scientists Are Unraveling the Links," *YaleEnvironment360*, May 9, 2017, https://tinyurl.com/y2ldlq2g; Rainey, *op. cit.*; "The Science Connecting Extreme Weather to Climate Change," Union of Concerned Scientists, undated, https://tinyurl.com/yyafc9ly; Justin Fox, "Climate Change Definitely Probably Caused This Heat Wave," *Bloomberg*, July 26, 2019, https://tinyurl.com/y6kuu4rg; and "Hurricanes and Climate Change," Union of Concerned Scientists, June 25, 2019, https://tinyurl.com/ybo2282m.

16. Ethan Siegel, "This Is Why Global Warming Is Responsible For Freezing Temperatures Across The U.S.," *Forbes*, Jan. 30, 2019, https://tinyurl.com/y5wjotj5; "Future Days Below Freezing," *Climate Central*, Jan. 23, 2019, https://tinyurl.com/y2dbswzt.

17. Zeke Hausfather, "Tornadoes and climate change: what does the science say?" *CarbonBrief*, May 31, 2019, https://tinyurl.com/yyeyoh57; Kevin Williams and Alan Blinder, "Kansas City-Area Tornadoes Add to 12 Straight Days of Destruction," *The New York Times*, May 28, 2019, https://tinyurl.com/yxtuhgve; and Nsikan Akpan, "Is climate change making U.S. tornadoes worse?" *WETA*, March 5, 2019, https://tinyurl.com/y6lo3pt5.

18. "Overview and Report Findings," Global Change Research Program, 2014, https://tinyurl.com/y6rdpkbv.

19. "Fourth National Climate Assessment," Global Change Research Program, 2018, https://tinyurl.com/ybw3k3rr.

20. "Trump says 'climate change goes both ways,'" *BBC News*, June 5, 2019, https://tinyurl.com/y4grp2cj.

21. Wanyun Shao, "Can 2018's extreme weather convince skeptics that the climate is changing?" *The Washington Post*, Dec. 7, 2018, https://tinyurl.com/yxotlvk8.

22. Bill M. Jesdale, Rachel Morello-Frosch and Lara Cushing, "The Racial/Ethnic Distribution of Heat Risk—Related Land Cover in Relation to Residential Segregation," *Environmental Health Perspectives*, July 1, 2013, https://tinyurl.com/y5hh3nzz; Rachel Leven, "Natural Disasters Are Getting Worse. People With The Least Power Are More At Risk," The Center for Public Integrity, April 25, 2019, https://tinyurl.com/yxmogb62; and Junia Howell and James R. Elliott, "As Disaster Costs Rise, So Does Inequality," *Socius*, 2018, https://tinyurl.com/y6sahsqz.

23. Jim Efstathiou Jr. and Prashant Gopal, "How Homes Are Being Built, Raised to Withstand Extreme Weather," *Insurance Journal*, May 13, 2019, https://tinyurl.com/y5e997gt.

24. Noah S. Diffenbaugh, Deepti Singh and Justin S. Mankin, "Unprecedented climate events: Historical changes, aspirational targets, and national

commitments," *Science Advances*, Feb. 14, 2018, https://tinyurl.com/y25we8rd.

25. *Ibid.*; "Summary for Policymakers," Intergovernmental Panel on Climate Change, Oct. 8, 2018, https://tinyurl.com/y4wh6cka.

26. Alex Barnum and Sam Delson, "Impacts of climate change in California significant and increasingly stark, new report says," California Environmental Protection Agency, May 9, 2018, https://tinyurl.com/y6sf56jm.

27. Lauren E. McPhillips *et al.*, "Defining Extreme Events: A Cross-Disciplinary Review," *Earth's Future*, Vol. 6, No. 3, Feb. 22, 2018, https://tinyurl.com/y5bpwgwc.

28. David W. Kreutzer, "Hurricane Florence Is Not an Omen About Climate Change," The Heritage Foundation, Sept. 13, 2018, https://tinyurl.com/yxvot24b; "Observations: Atmosphere and Surface," Intergovernmental Panel on Climate Change, 2014, https://tinyurl.com/l4lhs8f; and "Global Warming of 1.5° C," Intergovernmental Panel on Climate Change, Oct. 8, 2018, https://tinyurl.com/ydxvgtdl.

29. Kreutzer, *ibid.*

30. "Global Warming of 1.5° C," *op. cit.*; Brad Plumer and Nadja Popovich, "Why Half a Degree of Global Warming Is a Big Deal," *The New York Times*, Oct. 7, 2018, https://tinyurl.com/yad3lzj7.

31. Stephen Leahy, "Climate change impacts worse than expected, global report warns," *National Geographic*, Oct. 7, 2018, https://tinyurl.com/y97cm5aq.

32. Chris Mooney and John Muyskens, "Dangerous new hot zones are spreading around the world," *The Washington Post*, Sept. 11, 2019, https://tinyurl.com/y26ctye5.

33. Diffenbaugh, Singh and Mankin, *op. cit.*

34. "Future Drought," National Oceanic and Atmospheric Administration, August 2019, https://tinyurl.com/y34r437l; "Global Warming and Hurricanes," Geophysical Fluid Dynamics Laboratory, National Oceanic and Atmospheric Administration, Aug. 15, 2019, https://tinyurl.com/yxerocox.

35. Ian Livingston, "Hurricane Dorian has smashed all sorts of intensity records in the Atlantic Ocean," *The Washington Post*, Sept. 1, 2019, https://tinyurl.com/y5qjhcj3.

36. Kate Wheeling, "Is Climate Change Creating More Tornadoes?" *Pacific Standard*, March 5, 2019, https://tinyurl.com/y2g9mecq; Vittorio A. Gensini and Harold E. Brooks, "Spatial trends in United States tornado frequency," Climate and Atmospheric Science, 2018, https://tinyurl.com/y5obtdmt; and "US tornado frequency shifting eastward from Great Plains," *Science Daily*, Oct. 17, 2018, https://tinyurl.com/yazee2fz.

37. "Is tornado frequency increasing in parts of the U.S.?" National Weather Service, undated, https://tinyurl.com/y5f9qtkt.

38. Joel Achenbach and Angela Fritz, "Climate change is supercharging a hot and dangerous summer," *The Washington Post*, July 26, 2018, https://tinyurl.com/ycywsq88.

39. Charles Duncan, "Hurricane Florence was among the costliest disasters on record. Here's NOAA's tally," *The News & Observer*, Feb. 8, 2019, https://tinyurl.com/y3jcxz6b; "Billion-Dollar Weather and Climate Disasters: Overview," *op. cit.*; Dennis Romero, "California had nation's worst fire season in 2018," *NBC News*, March 9, 2019, https://tinyurl.com/y5rhpm9s; Angela Fritz, "The cost of natural disasters this year: $155 billion," *The Washington Post*, Dec. 26, 2018, https://tinyurl.com/y56urlqz; Laura Santhanam, "2017 is on track to be a record-setting year for massive natural disasters in the U.S.," *WETA*, Oct. 13, 2017, https://tinyurl.com/y87gqfq5; and Adam B. Smith, "2017 U.S. billion-dollar weather and climate disasters: a historic year in context," National Oceanic and Atmospheric Administration, Jan. 8, 2018, https://tinyurl.com/ybkume5y.

40. Adam B. Smith, "2018's Billion Dollar Disasters in Context," National Oceanic and Atmospheric Administration, Feb. 7, 2019, https://tinyurl.com/y6mnyk5o.

41. "Billion-Dollar Disasters Trending Up," *Climate Central*, Dec. 5, 2018, https://tinyurl.com/yyzcefzn.

42. Joel Achenbach, "Extreme weather in 2018 was a raging, howling signal of climate change," *The Washington Post*, Dec. 31, 2018, https://tinyurl.com/yd2eaj52.

43. "Areas At Severe Risk of California Wildfires Are Home to 2.7 Million People, Analysis Finds," The Associated Press and The Weather Channel, April 11, 2019, https://tinyurl.com/y2o7gr4l; "Economics and Demographics," Office for Coastal Management, National Oceanic and Atmospheric Administration, undated, https://tinyurl.com/y4vepfln.

44. "Rating the States," Insurance Institute for Business and Home Safety, March 2018, https://tinyurl.com/y6gdgbsb.

45. Nicolas Loris, "4 Problems With the New Climate Change Report," The Heritage Foundation, Nov. 27, 2018, https://tinyurl.com/yyp4emfo.

46. Nicolas Loris, "Climate Alarmists Admit They Want to Dismantle Our Free-Enterprise System," The Heritage Foundation, Oct. 11, 2018, https://tinyurl.com/yxw8pnuj.

47. Samenow and Freedman, *op. cit.*; Ailsa Chang, "When It Comes To Recent Powerful Storms, Hurricane Dorian Is 1 Of Many," *NPR*, Sept. 2, 2019, https://tinyurl.com/yyff54uv.

48. Chang, *ibid.*

49. "Community impacts from extreme weather shape climate beliefs," *Science Daily*, May 31, 2019, https://tinyurl.com/yxb5p66k.

50. *Ibid.*

51. Frances C. Moore *et al.*, "Rapidly declining remarkability of temperature anomalies may obscure public perception of climate change," *PNAS*, Feb. 25, 2019, https://tinyurl.com/y67sr8ar; Kendra Pierre-Louis, "Extreme Weather Can Feel 'Normal' After Just a Few Years, Study Finds," *The New York Times*, Feb. 26, 2019, https://tinyurl.com/y5lcotbr.

52. "NFIP Proof of Loss claim deadline is just weeks away," Federal Emergency Management Agency, July 24, 2018, https://tinyurl.com/y4ewxn6m.

53. Mark Collette, "Flood Games," *Houston Chronicle*, undated, https://tinyurl.com/y33frbes.

54. "Whom to Call, Where to Go When FEMA Can't Help," Federal Emergency Management Agency, July 29, 2019, https://tinyurl.com/y5b6cw2y; Michael L. Mann *et al.*, "Modeling residential development in California from 2000 to 2050: Integrating wildfire risk, wildland and agricultural encroachment," *Science Direct*, November 2014, https://tinyurl.com/y6nnrwd9.

55. Christopher Flavelle, "Why Is California Rebuilding in Fire Country? Because You're Paying for It," *Bloomberg Businessweek*, March 1, 2018, https://tinyurl.com/yamyoca8.

56. Stephen Paulsen, "Flood the market," *grist*, Aug. 27, 2019, https://tinyurl.com/y4rok79a.

57. "4 ways to strengthen coastal communities' resilience before the next storm," Environmental Defense Fund, April 12, 2019, https://tinyurl.com/y3g9ltup.

58. Sahil Chinoy, "The Places in the U.S. Where Disaster Strikes Again and Again," *The New York Times*, May 24, 2018, https://tinyurl.com/ybc4zd45; Greg Morago, "The 'King and Queen of Disaster' look back at Harvey flooding," *Houston Chronicle*, Aug. 27, 2018, https://tinyurl.com/y32gk5h6.

59. Flavelle, *op. cit.*

60. Doug Smith, "After California's most destructive fire season, a debate over where to rebuild homes," *Los Angeles Times*, Dec. 16, 2017, https://tinyurl.com/y56tc7gq.

61. John Schwartz, "As Floods Keep Coming, Cities Pay Residents to Move," *The New York Times*, July 6, 2019, https://tinyurl.com/y4alwa75.

62. Jen Schwartz, "Surrendering to Rising Seas," *Scientific American*, Aug. 1, 2018, https://tinyurl.com/y9hodsj5.

63. David A. Lieb, "AP: Flood Buyout Costs Rise as Storms Intensify, Seas Surge," *U.S. News & World Report*, May 28, 2019, https://tinyurl.com/yy5kgo3w.

64. "A Brief Introduction to the National Flood Insurance Program," Congressional Research Service, Aug. 14, 2019, https://tinyurl.com/y6rulye2; Doug Smith, *op. cit.*

65. Doug Smith, *ibid.*

66. Cathleen Kelly, Kristina Costa and Sarah Edelman, "Safe, Strong, and Just Rebuilding after Hurricanes Harvey, Irma and Maria," Center for American Progress, Oct. 3, 2017, https://tinyurl.com/ya2ectbp.

67. Anna Bahney, "These homes can withstand hurricanes, earthquakes and fires," *CNN Business*, Oct. 8, 2018, https://tinyurl.com/ycgvbz5u.

68. Mishana Khot, "The Five Deadly Extinctions In Earth's History," The Weather Channel, July 13, 2018, https://tinyurl.com/y4s3jxfw.

69. Andrew Glikson, "Another link between CO_2 and mass extinctions of species," *The Conversation*, March 21, 2013, https://tinyurl.com/y3uly4hp.

70. "675 m.p.h. 'Hypercanes' May Be Cause Of Ancient Mass Extinctions," *Chicago Tribune*, Sept. 10, 1995, https://tinyurl.com/y2dzg4c4; Kerry A. Emanuel *et al.*, "Hypercanes: A possible link in global extinction scenarios," *Journal of Geophysical Research: Atmospheres*, July 20, 1995, https://tinyurl.com/y2mnefpw.

71. "Ancient stormy weather: World's oldest weather report could revise bronze age chronology," University of Chicago and *Science Daily*, April 1, 2014, https://tinyurl.com/y3ahf2vn.

72. Stefan Lovgren, "Angkor Wat's Collapse From Climate Change Has Lessons for Today," *National Geographic*, April 5, 2017, https://tinyurl.com/y2xfzp9x; "Extreme weather preceded collapse of ancient Maya civilization," University of California-Davis and *Science Daily*, Nov. 8, 2012, https://tinyurl.com/y6nfgfus; and Catie Leary, "5 ancient civilizations that were destroyed by climate change," *MNN*, May 12, 2016, https://tinyurl.com/y6lumeza.

73. K. Jan Oosthoek, "Little Ice Age," Environmental History Resources, June 5, 2015, https://tinyurl.com/yawyxwf7; Richard Black, "Volcanic origin for Little Ice Age," *BBC News*, Jan. 30, 2012, https://tinyurl.com/yynx2dxu.

74. "Great Hurricane of 1780," *History*, April 12, 2019, https://tinyurl.com/yx9rkd9n.

75. Hans Kaper, "The Discovery of Global Warming," Rutgers University and American Institute of Physics, undated, https://tinyurl.com/y4sxulg2; "1820-1930: Fourier to Arrhenius," CO_2.earth, undated, https://tinyurl.com/y3gj22yq.

76. Elisabeth Crawford, "Svante Arrhenius," Encyclopaedia Britannica, undated, https://tinyurl.com/y4sbe4mz; "Svante Arrhenius," *Famous Scientists*, undated, https://tinyurl.com/y49kcjpc.

77. "Blizzard brings tragedy to Northwest Plains," *History*, Nov. 13, 2009, https://tinyurl.com/y5b9h53j; Becky Oskin, "The 10 Worst Blizzards in US History," LiveScience, Feb. 8, 2013, https://tinyurl.com/y5a9j8rn; and Kim Estep, "The Peshtigo Fire," *Green Bay Press-Gazette* and National Weather Service, undated, https://tinyurl.com/y4mkstjb.

78. "History of the National Weather Service," National Weather Service, undated, https://tinyurl.com/yxunvecn.

79. Adam Augustyn, "Tri-State Tornado of 1925," *Encyclopaedia Britannica,* undated, https://tinyurl.com/y9bpzycr; "The Dust Bowl," National Drought Mitigation Center, University of Nebraska, undated, https://tinyurl.com/yylowsng.

80. John Upton, "Scientists Trace Climate-Heat Link Back to 1930s," *Climate Central*, March 9, 2016, https://tinyurl.com/y9k269t8.

81. Charles C. Mann, "Meet the Amateur Scientist Who Discovered Climate Change," *Wired*, Jan. 23, 2010, https://tinyurl.com/y98t5etp; James Rodger Fleming, "The Callendar Effect," American Meteorological Society, 2007, https://tinyurl.com/y4j99qek.

82. "From A Dimmer Past to a Brighter Future?" NASA, Nov. 5, 2007, https://tinyurl.com/y9q2alsy; Catherine Brahic, "Climate myths: The cooling after 1940 shows CO_2 does not cause warming," *New Scientist*, May 16, 2007, https://tinyurl.com/jfbg79a.

83. Robert Reinhold, "Evidence is Found of Warming Trend," *The New York Times*, Oct. 19, 1981, https://tinyurl.com/y36fm27e.

84. "About the IPCC," Intergovernmental Panel on Climate Change, undated, https://tinyurl.com/y328s33m.

85. "Legal Mandate," U.S. Global Change Research Program, Nov. 16, 1990, https://tinyurl.com/y4ytzqsr.

86. U.S. Global Change Research Program, *Climate Change Impacts on the United States: The Potential Consequences of Climate Variability and Change* (2000), https://tinyurl.com/hc349th.

87. "Hurricane Costs," National Oceanic and Atmospheric Administration, July 10, 2019, https://tinyurl.com/y6ouof2s; "Hurricane Sandy Fast Facts," *CNN*, Oct. 29, 2018, https://tinyurl.com/ybd7unn8.

88. *Climate Change Impacts on the United States, op. cit.*

89. "Extreme Weather," U.S. Global Change Research Program, 2014, https://tinyurl.com/y93s6fkm.

90. "Historic Paris Agreement on Climate Change: 195 Nations Set Path to Keep Temperature Rise Well Below 2 Degrees Celsius," United Nations, Dec. 13, 2015, https://tinyurl.com/yy5jlmq7.

91. "Explaining Extreme Events from a Climate Perspective," American Meteorological Society, December 2018, https://tinyurl.com/hdktbd4.

92. Adam Smith, *op. cit.*; Robinson Meyer, "The Indoor Man in the White House," *The Atlantic*, Jan. 13, 2019, https://tinyurl.com/yxcqcwy6.

93. "High-Risk Series: Substantial Efforts Needed to Achieve Greater Progress on High-Risk Areas," Government Accountability Office, March 2019, https://tinyurl.com/y5qbs2fq.

94. Caitlin Werrell and Francesco Femia, "GAO Report: U.S. Government Has Regressed on Managing Climate Change Risks," The Center for Climate and Security, March 8, 2019, https://tinyurl.com/y54nvvmh.

95. Umair Irfan, "The severe floods soaking the Midwest and Southeast are not letting up," *Vox*, June 11, 2019, https://tinyurl.com/y52a5kqy; Richard Fausset, Nicholas Bogel-Burroughs and Patricia Mazzei, "Carolinas Hit by Winds, Floods and Tornadoes," *The New York Times*, Sept. 6, 2019, https://tinyurl.com/y2tacrj2; and "National Flood Insurance Program: Reauthorization," Federal Emergency Management Agency, June 11, 2019, https://tinyurl.com/y4dazchr.

96. "The National Flood Insurance Program: Critical Issues and Needed Reforms," Environmental and Energy Study Institute, undated, https://tinyurl.com/y6bcwawu; Michelle Cottle, "Can Congress Bring the National Flood Insurance Program Above Water?" *The Atlantic*, Aug. 5, 2017, https://tinyurl.com/yayynsyn; and "Menendez Co-Leads Bipartisan Push for Comprehensive Flood Insurance Reforms," press release, Office of Sen. Bob Menendez, May 23, 2019, https://tinyurl.com/y284fco4.

97. Cottle, *ibid.*

98. "NFIP Transformation and Risk Rating 2.0," Federal Emergency Management Agency, May 22, 2019, https://tinyurl.com/y56jrf72.

99. Kathleen Howley, "Congress approves a 4-month rescue of flood insurance program," *Housing Wire*, June 4, 2019, https://tinyurl.com/yy8ryojl.

100. "National Flood Insurance Program: Reauthorization," *op. cit.*

101. David Levinsky, "Menendez unveils bill to reform federal flood insurance program, cap premium hikes," *Burlington County Times*, July 17, 2019, https://tinyurl.com/y2jtna8a; "S.2187—National Flood Insurance Program Reauthorization and Reform Act of 2019," Congress.gov, undated, https://tinyurl.com/yyezebcv; and "NJ, NY Senators Convene Sandy Task Force," press release, Office of Sen. Bob Menendez, April 28, 2015, https://tinyurl.com/y6ejntaw.

102. Levinsky, *ibid.*

103. Coral Davenport and Mark Landler, "Trump Administration Hardens Its Attack on Climate Science," *The New York Times*, May 27, 2019, https://tinyurl.com/y2v5s9ff.

104. *Ibid.*

105. *Ibid.*

106. Richard Gonzales, "FEMA Drops 'Climate Change' From Its Strategic Plan," *NPR*, March 15, 2018, https://tinyurl.com/y8tkdhg4.

107. Helena Bottemiller Evich, "Agriculture Department buries studies showing dangers of climate change," *Politico*, June 23, 2019, https://tinyurl.com/yxbzqhnq.

108. *Ibid.*

109. Kayla Epstein *et al.*, "NOAA's chief scientist will investigate why agency backed Trump over its experts on Dorian, email shows," *The Washington Post*, Sept. 9, 2019, https://tinyurl.com/y296hv6u.

110. "Letter to the President of the United States: 58 Senior Military and National Security Leaders Denounce NSC Climate Panel," The Center for Climate and Security, March 5, 2019, https://tinyurl.com/yx8vzv67.

111. "Worldwide Threat Assessment of the U.S. Intelligence Community," Daniel R. Coats, Director of National Intelligence, Jan. 29, 2019, https://tinyurl.com/y9r6kkhu.

112. *Ibid.*

113. "Internal Displacement From January To June 2019," Internal Displacement Monitoring Center, Sept. 12, 2019, https://tinyurl.com/y4h5bk75.

114. *Ibid.*

115. Brady Dennis, Steven Mufson and Scott Clement, "Americans increasingly see climate change as a crisis, poll shows," *The Washington Post*, Sept. 13, 2019, https://tinyurl.com/yyvcrnv8.

116. Aylin Woodward, "What the 10 Democrats running for president each think the US should do about climate change," *Business Insider*, Sept. 7, 2019, https://tinyurl.com/yykejxey.

117. "How cap and trade works," Environmental Defense Fund, undated, https://tinyurl.com/p9dp6qy.

118. Woodward, *op. cit.*

119. *Ibid.*; Matt Mossman, "Renewable Energy Debate," *CQ Researcher*, March 15, 2019, https://tinyurl.com/yywe9rhy.

120. *Ibid.*

121. "Extreme weather events linked to poor mental health," *Science Daily*, Sept. 5, 2019, https://tinyurl.com/y3rglofr.

122. Zelde Espinel *et al.*, "Forecast: Increasing Mental Health Consequences From Atlantic Hurricanes Throughout the 21st Century," *Psychiatric Services*, Aug. 12, 2019, https://tinyurl.com/y5eomgpr.

123. Henry Fountain, "A Software Upgrade (After 40 Years) Aims to Improve U.S. Weather Forecasts," *The New York Times*, June 12, 2019, https://tinyurl.com/y2go7sl3.

124. Robin Cooper, "The Impacts of Extreme Heat on Mental Health," *Psychiatric Times*, July 30, 2019, https://tinyurl.com/y3eeahgr.

125. *Ibid.*

126. Jen A. Miller, "'100-year' floods will happen every one to 30 years, according to new coastal flood prediction maps," Princeton University, Aug. 27, 2019, https://tinyurl.com/y5kac9yc; Reza Marsooli *et al.*, "Climate change exacerbates hurricane flood hazards along US Atlantic and Gulf Coasts in spatially varying patterns," *Nature Communications*, Aug. 22, 2019, https://tinyurl.com/y4hatwjm.

127. *Ibid.*

128. Matthew C. Fitzpatrick, "Contemporary climatic analogs for 540 North American urban areas in the late 21st century," *Nature Communications*, Feb. 12, 2019, https://tinyurl.com/y37ls2v9; "U.S. climate data," usclimatedata.com, 2019, https://tinyurl.com/y5uuvp48.

129. Fitzpatrick, *ibid.*

BIBLIOGRAPHY

Books

Blum, Andrew, *The Weather Machine: A Journey Inside the Forecast*, Ecco, 2019.
A science journalist shows how weather observation and meteorological theory merged to produce the contemporary approach to weather forecasting.

Brannen, Peter, *The Ends of the World: Volcanic Apocalypses, Lethal Oceans, and Our Quest to Understand Earth's Past Mass Extinctions,* **Ecco, 2017.**

A science journalist offers a lively telling of how ancient climate and weather conditions led to the five mass extinctions in Earth's history.

Kolbert, Elizabeth, *Field Notes from a Catastrophe: Man, Nature, and Climate Change,* **Bloomsbury USA, 2006.**

This modern environmental classic by an award-winning writer at *The New Yorker* reports on the frontiers of climate change, from rapidly changing Inuit villages to policymaking circles in Washington, D.C.

Wallace-Wells, David, *The Uninhabitable Earth: Life After Warming,* **Tim Duggan Books, 2019.**

A deputy editor at *New York* magazine offers a vivid and alarming narrative about how climate change can bring about future weather catastrophes, as well as transform global and human progress.

Articles

"Climate Change Is Sinking the National Flood Insurance Program," Natural Resources Defense Council, 2017, https://tinyurl.com/y3rd7xh2.

An environmental advocacy group highlights ongoing problems with a national program that subsidizes flood insurance premiums for people who live in areas at high risk of extreme weather.

Campbell, SueEllen, "Farm Bureau shows little concern about climate change ag effects," Yale Climate Connections, April 16, 2019, https://tinyurl.com/y3xhca5m.

An environmental writer and retired English professor says that despite recent droughts and excess rainfall that have imperiled crops, the American Farm Bureau Federation, the most influential agricultural organization in the nation, remains unconvinced that human-caused climate change is real "and disapproves of nearly all proposed means of lessening its impacts."

Comen, Evan, "Here are 20 places where weather is getting worse because of climate change," *24/7 Wall Street and USA Today,* **Aug. 4, 2019, https://tinyurl .com/y2uodpmh.**

Researchers interview climate scientists and examine evidence connecting recent extreme weather events to climate change.

Robinson, Meyer, "How Climate Change Could Trigger the Next Global Financial Crisis," *The Atlantic,* **Aug. 1, 2019, https://tinyurl.com/ y2huu3qd.**

In an interview, Adam Tooze, an author and economic historian at Columbia University, describes potential financial pitfalls of climate change.

Simon, Ruth, "One House, 22 Floods: Repeated Claims Drain Federal Insurance Program," *The Wall Street Journal,* **Sept. 15, 2017, https://tinyurl.com/ yd7atzoa.**

A reporter focuses on a Texas homeowner who received more than $1.8 million from the National Flood Insurance Program to repeatedly rebuild his $800,000 home in the wake of hurricanes.

Reports and Studies

"Attribution of Extreme Weather Events in the Context of Climate Change," National Academies of Sciences, Engineering and Medicine, 2016, https:// tinyurl.com/y6q3kh2r.

Experts provide an overview of how scientists are connecting climate change to extreme weather events.

"Extreme Weather and Climate Change," Center for Climate and Energy Solutions, 2019, https://tinyurl .com/y8gpmt9u.

This interactive infographic shows major weather disasters and how scientists believe those events are linked to climate change.

"Fourth National Climate Assessment Volume II: Impacts, Risks, and Adaptation in the United States," U.S. Global Change Research Program, 2018, https:// tinyurl.com/ybw3k3rr.

This federally mandated report summarizes recent research in the wake of destructive hurricanes, wildfires and other events and suggests that extreme weather could worsen.

"Special Report on climate change, desertification, land degradation, sustainable land management, food security, and greenhouse gas fluxes in terrestrial

ecosystems," Intergovernmental Panel on Climate Change, Aug. 8, 2019, https://tinyurl.com/y6dlmvog.

A report from a United Nations group that assesses the science related to global warming includes contributions from more than 100 scientists in 52 countries and focuses on how land systems will be affected by climate change and extreme weather.

Herring, Stephanie, *et al.*, "Explaining Extreme Events of 2017 from a Climate Perspective," *Bulletin of the American Meteorological Society*, Feb. 15, 2019, https://tinyurl.com/hdktbd4.

The most recent issue of the society's annual report on extreme weather includes studies that quantify the impact of climate change on droughts, floods and hurricanes worldwide.

THE NEXT STEP

Climate Change

Mann, Michael, and Andrew E. Dessler, "Global heating made Hurricane Dorian bigger, wetter—and more deadly," *The Guardian*, Sept. 4, 2019, https://tinyurl.com/yxlxhyl9.

Two climate experts explain how warmer ocean waters may have strengthened Hurricane Dorian.

Minchin, Rod, and Phoebe Weston, "Harsh winters are not triggered by loss of Arctic sea ice, study finds," *The Independent*, Aug. 12, 2019, https://tinyurl.com/y4urbsab.

Weather experts in Europe determined that random fluctuations in atmospheric circulation, not the loss of Arctic sea ice, likely caused unusually cold winters in more moderate latitudes.

Myers, Chad, "I am a CNN meteorologist. I used to be a climate crisis skeptic," *CNN*, Sept. 4, 2019, https://tinyurl.com/y249ojwb.

A CNN meteorologist explains how he became convinced that greenhouse gas emissions affect the climate and lead to extreme weather events.

Climate Modeling

"New climate model for the IPCC," Alfred Wegener Institute and Phys.org, Sept. 6, 2019, https://tinyurl.com/yxdl7ysv.

A German research institute explains how its global climate model works and announces plans to make its data part of the next global climate assessment issued by an international panel on climate change.

Snowden, Scott, "Greenland's Massive Ice Melt Wasn't Supposed to Happen Until 2070," *Forbes*, Aug. 16, 2019, https://tinyurl.com/y26euwrm.

Greenland's ice sheet is melting at a rate that was not supposed to happen until 2070, according to many climate models.

Temple, James, "Climate change or just crazy weather? How improving tools make it easier to tell," *MIT Technology Review*, Aug. 15, 2019, https://tinyurl.com/yyfxsud2.

Climate models have improved enough in just the past few years to give scientists a better understanding of the relationship between global warming and extreme weather.

Disaster-Proof Homes

Barlyn, Suzanne, "How Insurers Help Design High-End Homes That Mitigate Disaster Risk," *Insurance Journal*, Aug. 30, 2019, https://tinyurl.com/y452227f.

Some insurers offer to help design luxury properties to withstand disasters, a service that will become more popular if extreme weather events become more frequent.

Lazarus, Eli, and Evan B. Goldstein, "Why are Atlantic and Gulf coast property owners building back bigger after hurricanes?" *The Conversation*, July 23, 2019, https://tinyurl.com/y62o7mpf.

Two climate experts say building codes that require storm-proofing send mixed signals about which areas are safe for development.

Peters, Adele, "This hurricane-proof home is made from 600,000 plastic bottles," *Fast Company*, July 2, 2019, https://tinyurl.com/yyvacmfa.

A Canadian startup company recently unveiled a prototype of a house in Nova Scotia that is environmentally friendly and can withstand extreme weather.

National Flood Insurance Program

"Editorial: People keep building and waters keep rising," *The* (Fredericksburg, Va.) *Free Lance-Star*, Sept. 4, 2019, https://tinyurl.com/y5j9ejfk.

Editors at a Virginia newspaper say state and federal officials should provide subsidies to local governments to help them absorb tax revenue losses they incur by discouraging development in flood-prone areas.

Brodsky, Robert, "How 2020 revamp of federal flood insurance rates could affect you," *Newsday,* **April 6, 2019, https://tinyurl.com/y6zaz8sd.**
The Federal Emergency Management Agency's planned revamp of flood insurance assessments is expected to increase premiums for expensive waterfront homes and decrease premiums for less expensive homes farther inland.

Lucas, Dave, "Schumer Seeks Changes to National Flood Insurance Program," WAMC, Sept. 6, 2019, https://tinyurl.com/y2l48a8g.
Sen. Chuck Schumer, D-N.Y., stood with homeowners in flood zones to promote his proposal to limit premium increases under the National Flood Insurance Program.

For More Information

350.org, 20 Jay St., Suite 732, Brooklyn, NY 11201; 802-448-0839; 350.org. Organization that advocates for ways to decrease fossil fuel use and address climate change.

American Farm Bureau Federation, 600 Maryland Ave., S.W., Suite 1000 W, Washington DC 20024; 202-406-3600; fb.org. Organization that advocates on behalf of agricultural interests.

California Department of Forestry & Fire Protection, 1416 Ninth St., P.O. Box 944246, Sacramento, CA 94244-2460; 916-653-5123; fire.ca.gov. State agency that monitors wildfires and provides real-time updates on them.

Intergovernmental Panel on Climate Change, World Meteorological Organization, 7 bis Avenue de la Paix, C.P. 2300, CH-1211 Geneva 2, Switzerland; +41 22 730 8208/54/84; ipcc.ch. International organization of scientists that focuses on climate change.

National Flood Insurance Program, c/o FEMA, 500 C St., S.W., Washington, DC 20472; 800-621-FEMA; floodsmart.gov. Government program that provides flood insurance for homes in high-risk areas.

National Oceanic and Atmospheric Administration, 1401 Constitution Ave., N.W., Room 5128, Washington, DC 20230; 301-427-9855; noaa.gov. Scientific agency within the Commerce Department that monitors weather and climate.

National Weather Service, 1325 East West Highway, Silver Spring, MD 20910; 828-271-4800; weather.gov. Federal agency that supports weather research, monitors weather conditions and issues warnings for extreme weather events.

15

Climate Change and Health

Is the threat to humans growing?

By Lola Butcher

Protesters in Kyiv, Ukraine, in September demand action on climate change, which has been linked to human health problems. A 2018 survey found that people in 13 out of 26 countries polled ranked climate change as the top threat facing their nation.

THE ISSUES

Shakira Franklin of Baltimore was driving to work on a scorching July day in 2018 when she started having trouble breathing. "Before I knew it, I was gasping for air," said Franklin, who has asthma.[1]

She was not alone. As Baltimore's temperature hovered near 100 degrees that day, emergency calls from people struggling with heat stroke, cardiac arrest and high blood pressure poured in. The same situation was playing out across a large swath of the world that summer, with more than 1,600 deaths associated with heat waves and wildfires in Europe, Japan and the United States.[2]

Deadly for some, these heat and extreme-weather events also are creating or worsening health issues for millions of people around the globe. And a growing number of experts say there is a connection between such weather events and changes in the climate. Scientists have linked climate change to, among other problems, allergies, premature births, stroke, kidney problems, malnutrition, mental health problems and the spread of malaria, dengue, Lyme disease and West Nile virus.[3]

Until recently, climatologists and meteorologists were reluctant to attribute the severity of an individual weather event—a heat wave, an ice storm or a hurricane, for example—to climate change, says Dr. Georges C. Benjamin, executive director of the American Public Health Association, a Washington-based organization working to mitigate climate change. But as scientific

From *CQ Researcher,*
November 29, 2019

evidence has accumulated, the United Nations' Intergovernmental Panel on Climate Change (IPCC) has made that connection—and many experts agree that climate change's direct impact on human health is becoming clearer.

"People are now connecting the dots," Benjamin says. "As the health effects of climate change to date have become more visible, the discussion is shifting from protecting polar bears to protecting people."

Members of the public who might have lacked a sense of urgency about addressing climate change when they viewed it solely as an environmental threat are becoming more engaged now that they see it as a threat to their health, Benjamin says. Climate activists say governments must do more to reduce greenhouse gas emissions associated with fossil fuels, but beyond that, consensus is lacking about how to protect people's health.

The health threats associated with climate change—and their severity—differ from one location to the next. The World Health Organization (WHO), the U.N.'s public health agency, summarizes the global risk in stark terms: "A changing, more variable climate . . . presents a clear and present danger to health security."[4]

An estimated 157 million more people in every region of the world were exposed to extreme heat in 2017 than in 2000, according to the Lancet Countdown: Tracking Progress on Health and Climate Change, an interdisciplinary research collaboration among 27 leading academic institutions, the United Nations and intergovernmental agencies. Experts say Europe and the eastern Mediterranean appear more vulnerable to heat than Africa and Southeast Asia, probably because their populations are older and more urban.[5]

Prolonged droughts in large areas of South America, Africa and Southeast Asia are causing malnutrition, stunting the growth of children and contributing to premature deaths. Floods, attributable to heavy rains and rising seas due to global warming, can be deadly and have longer-term effects, including the spread of infectious disease from unclean water and worsening of mental illness as flooding displaces victims, according to the Lancet Countdown.

The list goes on: Deaths from dengue fever—a mosquito-borne tropical disease—are increasing in Southeast Asia and the Americas because the warming climate allows mosquitoes to thrive in more parts of the world. Mortality rates for malignant melanoma, associated with exposure to the sun's ultraviolet radiation, have increased in Europe, the Americas and the western Pacific.[6]

In 2017, the United States had 16 extreme-weather disasters—including hurricanes and wildfires—that killed nearly 3,300 people, according to a climate change review conducted for the American Public Health Association. Cases of Lyme disease, West Nile virus and other vector-borne illnesses transmitted by insects that have spread to the United States tripled between 2004 and 2016.[7]

Making what it calls "a highly conservative estimate," WHO said climate change globally will cause 250,000 additional deaths each year between 2030 and 2050. Of those, 38,000 will be elderly people exposed to heat, 48,000 will be victims of diarrhea and 60,000 will die from malaria and 95,000 from childhood undernutrition.[8]

But climatologist Patrick Michaels, a senior fellow at the Competitive Enterprise Institute, a public policy organization in Washington, disputes these forecasts, saying projecting the health effects of climate change is folly because people will adapt to changing conditions. He says his research shows that although heat killed hundreds of people in the Chicago area in 1995 and thousands in Paris in 2003 during heat waves, similar

PHILIPPE HUGUEN/AFP via Getty Images

Mosquito-borne diseases, including Zika and dengue fever, are increasing in Southeast Asia and elsewhere. Experts say warmer temperatures in temperate climates are enabling mosquitoes, which thrive in tropical regions, to migrate into other regions and to live for longer seasons each year.

Disease-Carrying Insects Thrive on a Warming Planet

The number of cases of diseases spread by mosquitoes, ticks and fleas in the United States more than tripled over 12 years, rising from 27,388 in 2004 to 96,075 in 2016. Scientists say higher temperatures due to climate change allow these organisms to spread.

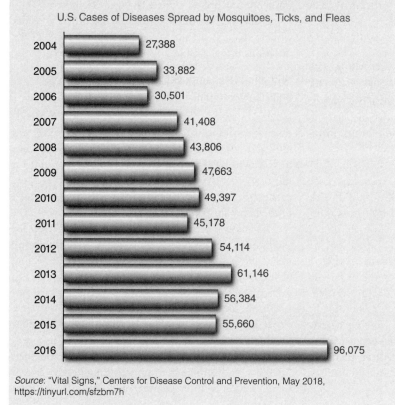

U.S. Cases of Diseases Spread by Mosquitoes, Ticks, and Fleas

Year	Cases
2004	27,388
2005	33,882
2006	30,501
2007	41,408
2008	43,806
2009	47,663
2010	49,397
2011	45,178
2012	54,114
2013	61,146
2014	56,384
2015	55,660
2016	96,075

Source: "Vital Signs," Centers for Disease Control and Prevention, May 2018, https://tinyurl.com/sfzbm7h

events in each city a few years later killed far fewer people. People had learned from experience, he says.

In the United States, heat warnings increased public awareness, cooling centers opened in large cities and health officials advised people to check on their elderly neighbors, Michaels says; in France, air conditioning became a priority.

"People decided that getting an air conditioner to plug into the window was maybe not such a bad idea for grandma's room," says Michaels. "So there was both technological adaptation and social adaptation."

Polling shows the public is increasingly concerned about climate change. A 2018 Pew Research Center survey found that climate change ranked as the top threat—higher than terrorism and other common worries—in 13 of 26 countries polled.[9] Polling conducted in April by the Yale Program on Climate Change Communication, a university-affiliated research center in New Haven, Conn., found that 62 percent of Americans are at least "somewhat worried" about climate change; 38 percent think climate change already is harming Americans.[10]

Mona Sarfaty, director of the Program for Climate and Health at George Mason University in Virginia, says the Yale survey, conducted twice a year, documents a rise in concern among the U.S. public. "We see a real shift, with people starting to feel that 'Gee, people right near me may be impacted,'" she says.

But polling also shows a large partisan divide: Only 27 percent of Republicans consider climate change a major threat, while 83 percent of Democrats do, according to the 2018 Pew survey. President Trump, a Republican, once called climate change a hoax and continues to question the scientific consensus on global warming. When a 2018 study produced by 13 federal agencies and 300 leading climate scientists warned about the impact of climate change, Trump responded: "I don't believe it." Younger Republicans, however, apparently diverge from their elders: A survey from Ipsos and Newsy found that some 77 percent of Republicans between 18 and 38 said climate change is a serious threat, slightly higher than Democrats in the same age group.[11]

After years of debate, representatives from 196 countries signed the Paris Agreement on climate change in 2015, pledging to take steps to hold the increase in global average temperature to well below 2 degrees Celsius above preindustrial levels.[12] However, Trump announced in 2017 that the United States would withdraw from the agreement, calling it a "draconian" deal that would harm the U.S. economy and impose unfair environmental standards on American businesses and workers. On Nov. 4, Trump issued a formal notification of withdrawal, beginning a one-year process of U.S. departure from the accord.[13]

The Lancet Countdown, established by the British medical journal *The Lancet* to monitor climate change, said many nations are failing to meet the Paris accord's goal: "A lack of progress in reducing emissions and building adaptive capacity threatens both human lives and the viability of the national health systems they depend on, with the potential to disrupt core public health infrastructure and overwhelm health services."[14]

The fossil fuel industry is the biggest source of greenhouse gas emissions; 20 oil, gas and coal companies have contributed more than one-third of all carbon dioxide and methane emissions worldwide since 1965, according to the Climate Accountability Institute, an independent research institute in Colorado.[15]

But the American Petroleum Institute (API), a Washington-based organization that represents oil and gas companies, argues that the U.S. energy sector is doing its part to reduce emissions by becoming the world's largest supplier of natural gas, which generates about half the carbon emissions of coal when used to generate electricity.[16] "As a cleaner-burning fuel, it is essential to climate progress," Reid T. Porter, an institute spokesperson, said in an email.

Most industries could do more to address global warming, including the health care industry, which contributes nearly 10 percent of U.S. greenhouse gas emissions, says Jessica Wolff, U.S. director of climate and health for Health Care Without Harm, an international organization that seeks to reduce the environmental footprint of the health care sector. "Health care has a healing mission, but at the same time, its operations are significantly contributing to climate change and the very diseases they are trying to treat," she says.

A group of 19 U.S. health systems that represent about 10 percent of the nation's hospitals have joined Health Care Without Harm's climate council, committing to reduce their carbon emissions and help their communities become more resilient to climate change. Internationally, about 18,000 hospitals and health systems have signed on to Health Care Without Harm's global climate challenge, promising to be leaders in tackling the climate crisis.

"The health care sector has both the opportunity and the obligation to use its ethical, economic and political influence to work on climate change," Wolff says.

As doctors, scientists, politicians and others consider climate change's impact on health, here are some of the questions they are asking:

Will climate change set off a global health catastrophe?

When David Attenborough, a longtime British broadcaster known for his natural-history documentaries, was invited to speak at the U.N. Climate Change Conference in Katowice, Poland, in December 2018, he did not mince words. "If we don't take action," he warned, "the collapse of our civilizations and the extinction of much of the natural world is on the horizon."[17]

His fellow Briton, Rupert Read, a spokesperson for the Extinction Rebellion, a global organization pushing for climate action, disagrees with that time frame. "Dangerous climate change is already causing a health catastrophe in parts of the world," says Read, a philosophy professor at the University of East Anglia.

Both are correct, according to the WHO. It has compiled a list of catastrophes that have occurred in recent decades, such as a 2003 heat wave that killed more than 70,000 across Europe. In Ethiopia, droughts have caused famines along with high levels of child undernutrition since the 1980s. In 2010 alone, 6 million people in Pakistan needed urgent medical care from floods, which had destroyed more than 200 health care facilities.[18]

The WHO projects an even higher level of catastrophe in coming years, including increasing incidences of respiratory and cardiovascular disease; injuries and deaths from extreme-weather events; the spread of infectious diseases; and food and water shortages stemming from ecological changes caused by global warming.[19]

Worried about rising sea levels, the leaders of small, island nations asked the United Nations to take a new look at the consequences of climate change. In late 2018, scientists convened by the world body said that without immediate action to reduce greenhouse gas emissions, increased coastal flooding may displace millions by 2040.[20]

The IPCC, a group of more than 100 scientists from 36 countries, reported that some 50 million people living in the United States, Bangladesh, China, Egypt, India, Indonesia, Japan, the Philippines and Vietnam will be affected by increased coastal flooding if the atmosphere warms by 2.7 degrees Fahrenheit (1.5 degrees Celsius) above preindustrial levels—and such warming could happen by 2040.[21]

Previously, the scientists had focused on the damage resulting from an average temperature increase of 3.6 degrees Fahrenheit (2 degrees Celcius), the threshold that had been considered to trigger the most severe effects of climate change. The IPCC's report says that if that threshold were reached, a "rapid evacuation" will occur in the tropics.

"In some parts of the world, national borders will become irrelevant," said Aromar Revi, director of the Indian Institute for Human Settlements, an education institute that focuses on urbanization, and an author of the report. "You can set up a wall to try to contain 10,000 and 20,000 and 1 million people, but not 10 million."[22]

Michaels, at the Competitive Enterprise Institute, says it is wrong to focus on the IPCC's worst-case scenario. The IPCC analysis gives "multiple lines of evidence" to expect the scope and pace of global warming will be less worrisome than the most dire scenario depicted, he says. "Yes, global warming is real and people have something to do with it," says Michaels, a past president of the American Association of State Climatologists. "But the magnitude of the warming that we are going to see is going to be at the low end of the projected range."

Rep. Buddy Carter, R-Ga., a member of the House Select Committee on the Climate Crisis, agrees. Climate change "is something that needs to be addressed, but it certainly isn't a 'doomsday' scenario," he said in an email. "The climate is changing, but it's been changing since day one. Instead of forecasting doom, we need to be working on innovation, mitigation and adaptation to actually address the issue."

Michaels points to hydraulic fracking—the process of extracting oil and gas from subterranean rock by injecting liquid under high pressure to create fractures—as an example of how technological innovation can address climate change in unforeseen ways. Less than two decades ago, the consensus that the United States had depleted its natural gas deposits was upended when fracking technology improved. For the past decade, the nation has been the world's leading producer of natural gas, which emits less carbon dioxide than coal when burned in power plants.

"Imagine if we had passed a law in some fit of hyper-environmentalism, saying, 'There shall be no more exploration for new sources of fossil fuels,'" he says. "What would we have forgone as a result of that? A lot."

Representing people who live on Georgia's coastline, Carter advocates mitigation measures such as using federal grants to elevate houses in flood-prone areas. "We need to be focused on things like ensuring homes, bridges and roadways are in positions where they won't be flooded," he says.

Wolff, at Health Care Without Harm, agrees that planning can mitigate some health effects of climate change. "We have to do some adaptation and become resilient to the changes that are going to happen because the atmosphere has already warmed," she says.

For example, after a 2010 heat wave killed more than 1,300 people in Ahmedabad, India, leaders developed a heat action plan that included training health care staff, distributing water and painting roofs with white reflective paint to reduce the heat in homes. When a similar heat wave hit in 2015, fewer than 20 people died.[23]

But adaptation strategies will not undo the climate change that has already been put in motion by carbon dioxide pumped into the atmosphere, Read, the Extinction Rebellion spokesperson, says. The only hope is for an immediate and dramatic reduction in greenhouse gas emissions.

"So things are bound to get worse for a long time to come on a human scale whatever we do," he says. "And if we don't rise up to the kind of challenge that people like [teen activist] Greta Thunberg and Extinction Rebellion are laying down now, then things will get worse basically forever."

Should doctors take responsibility for educating the public about the health effects of climate change?

When her patient—a 64-year-old with asthma that worsens during allergy season—asked why her eyes and nose were running for longer periods every year, Dr. Mary Rice, a pulmonologist at Beth Israel Deaconess Medical Center in Boston, had the answer ready.[24]

At-Risk Cities Are Least Ready for Climate Change

The U.S. cities most threatened by climate change are the ones least prepared for global warming, according to an analysis by the real estate website Clever. Coastal cities are the most vulnerable to climate change-related hazards, such as flooding and sea level rise. Scientists have linked climate change to numerous health problems, including allergies, premature births and stroke.

Cities Most Vulnerable and Most Prepared for Climate-Related Hazards

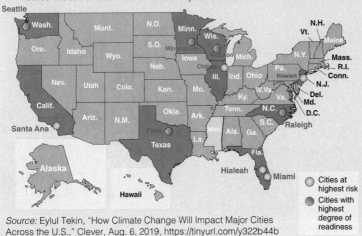

Source: Eylul Tekin, "How Climate Change Will Impact Major Cities Across the U.S.," Clever, Aug. 6, 2019, https://tinyurl.com/y322b44b

"Because of global warming, the plants are flowering earlier in the spring," she said. "After hot summers, the trees are releasing more pollen the following season. And the ragweed—it's extending longer into the fall."

For that reason, Rice said, her patient may need stronger medicines, more air filters in her home and more days wearing a mask.[25]

The Medical Society Consortium on Climate and Health at George Mason University—composed of the American College of Physicians and other medical societies—seeks to encourage doctors to educate themselves and others about climate change. In 2014, Sarfaty, its director, surveyed three groups of U.S. doctors—allergists, pulmonologists and physicians who belong to the National Medical Association, which represents African American doctors—to ask if they treated patients whose health was affected by climate change. "About 70 percent said that they did—and 50 percent said patients' health was impacted to a 'great' or 'moderate' extent," she says.

But attempts by health officials and scientists in recent years to sound the alarm about the health effects of climate change have not always resonated with the public.

Patients need to hear from their own physicians, says Molly Rauch, public health director for Moms Clean Air Force, a New York City-based coalition of more than 1 million parents working to promote healthy air.

"We need to be hearing these messages from the people to whom we entrust our health and our children's health," Rauch says. "We need to get information from the people who are already talking to us about smoking and bike helmets. That's going to be much more powerful than experts releasing a report or health officials issuing a brochure."

The 2018 Lancet Countdown brief for the United States agrees. "Given that the bedrock of public health is education about threats to health, it is critical that health providers inform their patients, communities, and policy makers about the health harms of climate change," the report said.[26]

Its authors pointed to research showing that primary care providers are among the most trusted voices to deliver a message about the health effects of climate change, outranking family and friends, government agencies and climate scientists.[27]

Some physicians are on board, and organizations such as Florida Clinicians for Climate Action are emerging to encourage them.[28] That group, formed in 2018, urges physicians and nurses to educate the public and policymakers about the health effects of climate change in Florida and the United States, and one goal is to "move public opinion."[29]

Such education is appropriate only if the context is right, says Dr. Aaron Bernstein, co-director of the Center for Climate, Health and the Global Environment at Harvard University, who also is a pediatrician at Boston Children's Hospital. "Our first obligation as [health care] providers is to meet people where they're at," he says. "Our job is not to convince them that climate change is happening, and our job is not to use people's illnesses as a means to educate them on climate change or any other potential topics."

Ragweed Pollen Season Lengthens in Central North America

Because of a warming climate, the length of the season for ragweed pollen, a common allergen, increased for many locales across central North America between 1995 and 2015. The one exception was in Austin, Texas, where the length of the season was shortened by one day.

Change in Length of Ragweed Pollen Season, 1995–2015

Source: "Climate Change Indicators: Ragweed Pollen Season," Environmental Protection Agency, August 2016, https://tinyurl.com/t5fx29q

Through the center, Bernstein works to address the causes of climate change with the goal of improving the health of children around the world. If he's caring for a child hospitalized for, say, an infection unrelated to climate, he does not proselytize. "But if someone is asking, and it matters to their understanding of what they are going through, then yes," Bernstein says. "And it does come up."

Sarfaty says some physicians—particularly those who treat children, patients with lung problems and older people—find that discussing climate change is essential to helping patients cope with specific medical conditions.

"But I would say that most physicians feel that there's no time," she says.

Physicians responding to a consortium survey in 2016 identified lack of time and lack of payment as obstacles to discussing climate change with their patients, Sarfaty says. Those two issues are related; insurers require that physicians do several specific things to get paid for an office visit, and discussing climate change is not on the list.

Rauch says environmental activists disagree on what climate change messages physicians should be giving to their patients. Some want health professionals to encourage their patients to call lawmakers and become activists, but she has a different view.

As the mother of three children, Rauch says she wants her pediatrician to provide action items relative to a specific health threat. Not all parents or patients know, for example, that they need to pay attention to heat advisories, drink a lot of water and keep kids indoors during a heat wave.

"And, as he's talking to me about this, I want him to say, 'You know, we're going to be seeing more and more of these because of climate change. And climate change is something that is caused by the pollution that people are creating. And until that pollution is prevented, we need to be very aware of these health impacts,'" Rauch says.

Is climate change causing or worsening mental health problems?

In a comparison of 67 developed nations, Australia ranks as one of the most vulnerable to global warming because of its struggles with stronger storms, rising seas and growing frequency of brush fires, according to a report by the global bank HSBC. Sarah Udin, an Australian in her 20s, suffers from knowing that. "Sometimes I wake up from nightmares of the dystopian future that's becoming more of a reality for our children," she said.[30]

She is not alone. Researchers for the Lancet Countdown said both gradual climate change and extreme-weather events take a toll on mental health. Heat is the single biggest culprit. "Because of their rapidly growing frequency, duration and intensity, heat waves are of particular concern, with strong evidence linking their occurrence to increases in population distress, hospital psychiatric admissions and suicides," *The Lancet* report said.[31]

Certain groups—the elderly, pregnant women, people with pre-existing mental illness, the economically disadvantaged and tribal and indigenous communities—are most vulnerable to the mental health effects of climate change, according to the most recent U.S. national climate assessment, a periodic report to Congress and the president. People living in a household that experienced a flood are more likely to experience depression and anxiety, even years after the event, than those who did not, and high temperatures are associated with an increase in aggressive behaviors, including homicide.[32]

The problem is particularly worrisome for mental health professionals working in communities that historically have had a high prevalence of depression, such as those above the Arctic Circle. A recent survey found that 76 percent of Greenland's residents said they had personally experienced the effects of global warming in their daily lives. Some, for example, reported that because of shorter winters and growing economic troubles they had to euthanize their sled dogs; others fear traveling on thinning ice.[33]

"There is no question, Arctic people are now showing symptoms of anxiety, 'ecological grief' and even post-traumatic stress related to the effects of climate change," said Dr. Courtney Howard, board president of the Canadian Association of Physicians for the Environment. "Many of these islanders are in mourning for a disappearing way of life."[34]

The psychiatric profession has no validated methods to screen individuals for mental health issues associated with climate change, so the prevalence of the problem is unknown, says Dr. Carissa Cabán-Alemán, a psychiatrist at Florida International University and a member of the Climate Psychiatry Alliance. She says more people will seek treatment as they become aware that mental health

Joe Raedle/Getty Images

Jerry Norton lives in Kivalina, Alaska, an island village more than 80 miles above the Arctic Circle that is threatened by sea level rise due to melting ice. Dr. Courtney Howard said indigenous Arctic peoples are showing symptoms of anxiety and "ecological grief" because of climate change.

professionals have tools to help. Psychological first aid—a technique developed in the field of disaster psychiatry—might be used in some situations; medications, psychotherapy and mindfulness-based stress reduction also might be appropriate, she says.

In the aftermath of Hurricane Maria in Puerto Rico in 2017, Cabán-Alemán has worked with CrearConSalud, a nonprofit organization composed of Puerto Rican psychiatrists practicing in the U.S. mainland, to help disaster victims. Her primary technique is to promote "transformational resilience," a proactive response to the anxiety caused by climate change.

"We are giving the tools to people to empower themselves, to seek out the resources that they need for themselves and to demand the governmental resources that they need to confront climate change adequately and to mitigate the effects it is having," she says.

Extreme anxiety and depression about climate change is rational and can even be helpful, according to Extinction Rebellion's Read. "More and more people are going to be stricken with eco-anxiety, which is simply a terror about the future, horror at what we've done and grief over what we've destroyed and lost," he says. "But these people, among whom I include myself, are actually the lucky ones because we are ahead of the curve."

Thunberg, a Swedish teenager, has said global warming was one cause of the depression she experienced

Warming Planet Affects Farmworkers the Most

Dangerous heat from climate change is taking a toll on laborers' health, and also on their ability to work: In 2017, a total of 153 billion labor hours were lost globally due to heat exposure, up 62 billion from 2000, according to a study published in *The Lancet*, a British medical journal. The agricultural sector lost the most—122 billion labor hours.

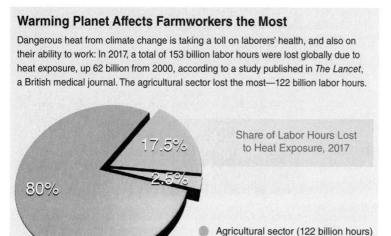

Share of Labor Hours Lost to Heat Exposure, 2017

17.5%

2.5%

80%

● Agricultural sector (122 billion hours)
● Industrial sector (27 billion hours)
● Service sector (4 billion hours)

Source: "The Lancet: Proportion of population vulnerable to heat exposure is rising globally," EurekAlert!, Nov. 28, 2018, https://tinyurl.com/vxefso6

before she became one of the world's most visible activists for governmental action against climate change.[35]

The American Psychological Association agrees that the changing environment is a legitimate source of distress that threatens society's ability to deal with the problem at hand. "To compound the issue, the psychological responses to climate change, such as conflict avoidance, fatalism, fear, helplessness and resignation are growing," the association said. "These responses are keeping us, and our nation, from properly addressing the core causes of and solutions for our changing climate, and from building and supporting psychological resiliency."[36]

But eco-anxiety is not a bad thing if, instead of paralyzing its victims, it motivates them to take action, said David Austern, a clinical psychologist at NYU Langone Health in New York City. "Is it more pathological for someone to be so worried about climate change or is it actually more pathological that people are not more worried about it?'" he asked.[37]

BACKGROUND

Warming in the Dark

The idea that gases in the Earth's atmosphere trap heat from the sun, keeping the planet warm, was first theorized by French physicist Joseph Fourier in 1824.[38]

In 1904, Swedish scientist Svante Arrhenius concluded that human use of fossil fuels was causing carbon dioxide to build up in the atmosphere and increasing the Earth's temperature—a positive development, in his view, because he thought warmer climes would increase crop production and make some regions more habitable.[39]

The connection between higher concentrations of carbon dioxide and global warming was confirmed by British engineer Guy S. Callendar when he calculated that the mean global temperature had risen close to 0.3 degrees Celsius (0.5 degrees Fahrenheit) over the previous 50 years. In 1938, he concluded that atmospheric carbon dioxide concentrations, which had increased by about 10 percent since 1900, were the cause.[40]

In the 1950s, scientists began measuring carbon dioxide in the atmosphere and in ocean surface waters. Using an instrument atop the volcanic Mauna Loa peak in Hawaii, American scientist Charles Keeling was able to measure carbon dioxide concentrations in the atmosphere far away from human sources of the gas.[41]

Writing in *Scientific American* in 1959, physicist Gilbert Plass predicted that global temperatures would rise by perhaps 3 degrees Fahrenheit (1.7 degrees Celsius) by the end of the century. The magazine's editorial staff, aware of the public's growing concern about pollution, illustrated the article with a photograph of industrial coal smoke captioned, "Man upsets the balance of natural processes by adding billions of tons of carbon dioxide to the atmosphere each year."[42]

In 1963, a few months after her book, *Silent Spring*, about the environmental harms of pesticides became a bestseller, Rachel Carson warned a congressional subcommittee about the dangers of pollution. "Our heedless and destructive acts enter into the vast cycles of the Earth and in time return to bring hazard to ourselves," she said.[43]

The public's concern about environmental degradation was behind the first Earth Day, held in 1970. After the Massachusetts Institute of Technology asked about

CHRONOLOGY

1900s-1950s *Amid industrialization, researchers study effects of greenhouse gas emissions on the Earth's atmosphere.*

1904 Svante Arrhenius of Sweden becomes the first scientist to theorize that the human use of fossil fuels is causing carbon dioxide to build up in the atmosphere and increase the Earth's temperature; he considers it a positive development that will enable the world "to enjoy ages with more equable and better climates."

1938 British engineer Guy S. Callendar presents evidence supporting Arrhenius' belief that humans' burning of fossil fuels was behind global warming; he calculates that the mean global temperature had risen close to 0.3 degrees Celsius over the previous century.

1957 Scientist Roger Revelle tells a U.S. congressional committee that global warming might someday turn parts of the U.S. into "real deserts" and that the Arctic Ocean might become ice-free.

1960s-1980s *Carbon dioxide in the atmosphere is accurately measured for the first time.*

1963 After a meeting convened by the private Conservation Foundation, scientists begin framing greenhouse warming as an environmental problem that could endanger human health.

1970 The first Earth Day highlights a growing awareness about global environmental degradation.

1972 Fears about climate change emerge when severe droughts spread across Africa as well as India and Ukraine, creating a world food crisis.

1902 Scientists document strong global warming since the mid-1970s, with 1981 the warmest year on record since collection of temperature data began.

1988 With international concern about climate change growing, the United Nations creates the Intergovernmental Panel on Climate Change (IPCC) to conduct research on environmental and health effects.

1990s-Present *As extreme weather becomes more common, awareness of climate change's impact on health grows.*

1995 The IPCC documents evidence that human activity is contributing to global warming and declares that serious warming is likely within the next century.

2005 Hurricane Katrina, a Category 5 storm, devastates the U.S. Gulf Coast, triggering debate over whether global warming increases storm intensity.

2007 A Gallup survey finds that about 40 percent of adults in 119 countries have never heard of climate change.

2009 Experts warn that global warming is arriving at a faster and more dangerous pace than anticipated just a few years earlier.

2014 A survey by the Yale University Program on Climate Change Communication finds that 61 percent of respondents had given little or no thought to how global warming might affect people's health until they took the survey.

2015 The Lancet Commission on Health and Climate Change, a collaboration of the U.N., research institutions and governments, cites a "widespread lack of awareness of climate change as a health issue" and says health professionals must mobilize to protect the health of future generations. . . . Representatives from 195 countries, including the U.S., and the European Union sign the Paris Agreement on climate change, pledging to hold the increase in global average temperature to well below 2 degrees Celsius above preindustrial levels.

2016 The U.S. government says the effects of climate change worsen a wide range of chronic conditions—Alzheimer's disease, asthma, chronic obstructive pulmonary disease, diabetes, cardiovascular disease, mental illness and obesity.

2017 Hurricane Maria slams Puerto Rico, killing thousands and damaging the island's health care infrastructure. Global warming contributed to the storm's ferocity, scientists say. . . . Republican President Trump announces he will withdraw the U.S. from the Paris Agreement, saying the pact hurts economic growth.

2018 The IPCC says limiting global warming to 1.5 Celsius above preindustrial levels is "possible within the laws of chemistry and physics but doing so would require unprecedented transitions in all aspects of societies." . . . Seventeen state governors who belong to the U.S. Climate Alliance pledge to fulfill Paris accord goals and announce initiatives to cut carbon emissions by more than 26 percent by 2025.

2019 More than 70 U.S. medical societies say climate change constitutes the "greatest public health challenge of the 21st century" and urge policymakers to take immediate action to stem greenhouse gas emissions (June). . . . At a U.N. Climate Action Summit, the World Bank and others pledge to invest more than $650 million in the next three years to help 300 million small farmers in developing countries address the impact of climate change on food production and thus forestall malnutrition (September).

40 scientists to consider environmental issues, they reported the rise of carbon dioxide and the associated risk of global warming was "so serious that much more must be learned about future trends of climate change."[44]

Not all scientists believed the planet was warming. In 1974, the U.S. government reported a growing consensus among leading climatologists that the world was undergoing a cooling trend that might affect global food supplies. A report produced for the CIA that year cited an increase in Arctic ice and a shortened English growing season since the 1940s. British climatologist Hubert Lamb said 22 of 27 forecasting methods he reviewed predicted a cooling trend through the rest of the 20th century.[45]

This view proved to be short-lived. In 1981, NASA predicted global warming of "almost unprecedented magnitude" in the coming decades.[46]

The Intergovernmental Panel on Climate Change said in 1990 that the danger of greenhouse gases was real, human activity contributed to climate change and both global temperatures and sea levels will continue to rise.[47]

Initially, climate change was not a partisan issue in the United States. A Gallup Poll in 1997 found almost identical proportions of Democrats and Republicans—46 percent of the former and 47 percent of the latter—said "the effects of global warming have already begun." A decade later, only 41 percent of Republicans held that view, while 76 percent of Democrats agreed with the statement.[48]

Health Connection Emerges

The European heat wave of 2003 caught people off guard. Temperatures topped 100 degrees for a full week, imperiling low-income residents living in old apartment buildings without air conditioning. People did not realize they needed to check on their elderly neighbors, and public health officials did not recognize the need for cooling centers to provide water and air conditioning. Nearly 12,000 people died in Paris alone.[49]

Vacationers on an Alaskan cruise in 2004 became ill after eating local shellfish, and the culprit was identified

ROBYN BECK/AFP via Getty Images

An aerial view of New Orleans' 9th Ward in September 2005 shows flooding from Hurricane Katrina. In addition to causing some 1,200 deaths, according to a federal government estimate, the catastrophic storm, which scientists say intensified due to warmer water temperatures in the Gulf of Mexico, left deep emotional scars on city residents.

On a Warming Planet, Heat Waves Are Becoming More Dangerous

Deaths will rise if nations don't help people adapt, expert warns.

During a heat wave in Boston last summer, an elderly man showed up at Massachusetts General Hospital's emergency department in the middle of the night with a core temperature of more than 105 degrees Fahrenheit.

"The ambulance crew said his apartment was the hottest they had ever been in," said Dr. Renee Salas, the physician who treated him. "It was on the top floor with only one window—no air conditioning and no fan."[1]

Extreme heat is the most widespread health threat associated with climate change, with 157 million more people around the world exposed to heat wave events in 2017 than in 2000, according to the Lancet Countdown: Tracking Progress on Health and Climate Change, an interdisciplinary research collaboration between 27 leading academic institutions, the United Nations and intergovernmental agencies.[2]

That is deadly news, says nurse Adrienne Wald, a member of the Alliance of Nurses for Healthy Environments, an advocacy group based in Mount Rainier, Md.

"Heat waves are the deadliest of any extreme weather-related events in the United States—more deadly than tornadoes, hurricanes, earthquakes and floods combined," says Wald, an associate professor of nursing at the College of New Rochelle in New York who studies how climate change affects health.

The U.S. Global Change Research Program, which coordinates federal government research on climate change, defines a heat wave as two or more consecutive days in which daily lows exceed the 85th percentile of historical July and August temperatures. By that definition, the number of heat waves in 50 American cities has tripled since the 1960s.[3]

A relatively slight change in average annual temperature translates into a big increase in extreme heat events. "A warming of 1 degree Celsius [1.8 degrees Fahrenheit], which is what we've seen thus far, can lead to a tenfold increase in the frequency of 100-degree days in New York City, for example," said Michael Mann, director of the Earth System Science Center at Pennsylvania State University.[4]

The most severe heat-related illness is heatstroke, defined as a core temperature above 104 degrees Fahrenheit, which can be fatal. Less serious problems range from mild heat cramps to heat exhaustion, which may include headache and nausea.[5]

Beyond that, higher temperatures contribute to conditions that spread vector- and water-borne diseases, including dengue fever and malaria. Heat waves also are associated with increased aggression and violence, according to the American Public Health Association. The health effects of extreme heat disproportionately affect vulnerable people, including children and the elderly, pregnant women, low-income individuals and families, people who have chronic illnesses and outdoor workers.[6]

The impact of heat-related illness extends beyond those who get sick. In 2017, 153 billion hours of labor were lost because of heat, nearly double the amount in 2000.[7] Dr. Georges C. Benjamin, executive director of the American Public Health Association, says employers have to be more careful about protecting workers than in the past.

as *Vibrio parahaemolyticus*, a bacterium whose natural habitat is coastal ocean waters in warm climates. Rising ocean temperatures allowed the pathogens carrying subtropical diseases to spread northward.[50]

Hurricane Katrina—a Category 5 storm—struck New Orleans in 2005, causing catastrophic damage to the city, which did not have the appropriate infrastructure and evacuation plan in place to limit the devastation. A survey of affected residents a month after the hurricane found

that 49.1 percent of respondents were experiencing anxiety-related mood disorders. A longer-term evaluation of the mental health impact on Katrina victims said the prevalence of post-traumatic stress disorder and attempts at self-harm and suicide increased over time.[51]

An Inconvenient Truth, a documentary about former U.S. Vice President Al Gore's campaign to educate the public about global warming, was screened at the Sundance Film Festival in 2006; it became an

"Increasingly, if you're a farmer with workers in the field, you're probably seeing more days when it's too hot to work or when you have to do more things to protect your workers," he says.

Heat waves are likely to get steadily worse as the planet warms, according to new research by the Union of Concerned Scientists, a science advocacy organization in Cambridge, Mass. Its researchers used computer modeling to project how many days the United States will experience a heat index—a National Weather Service measure of how hot it really feels when temperature is combined with humidity—of 100 degrees Fahrenheit or greater. They produced what they called a relatively conservative estimate: the number of days in which the heat index hits 100 degrees could double and the number of days with a reading of 105 could triple by the middle of the century.[8]

Currently, people—particularly those older than 65 years—in Europe and the eastern Mediterranean are much more vulnerable to heat exposure than those in Africa and Southeast Asia probably because their populations are older and more urban.[9] Computer modeling techniques have also been used to project that heat-related deaths outside of Europe, particularly in Colombia, the Philippines, Brazil and other tropical countries, will rise sharply.[10]

"If we cannot find a way to mitigate the climate change and help people adapt to heat waves, there will be a big increase of heat-wave-related deaths in the future, particularly in the poor countries located around the equator," said Yuming Guo, a physician researcher at Monash University in Australia.[11]

In the United States, at least, heat waves do not need to mean death, says Wald, the nursing professor.

"You don't have to die of heat stroke," she says. "It's 100 percent preventable if it's identified early and treatment is initiated immediately."

Local communities have to develop climate action plans specific to their own population, and residents must be educated about how to avoid heat stroke, she says.

"We're going to have to educate employers about occupational health," Wald says. "You can't have people out doing agricultural work and construction work during a heat wave without taking rest breaks and hydrating and other things to stay safe."

— *Lola Butcher*

[1] "Interview with Dr. Renee Salas on the effects of climate change on human health and health systems," *The New England Journal of Medicine*, 2019, https://tinyurl.com/y64s5l4y.

[2] Nick Watts *et al.*, "The 2018 report of the Lancet Countdown on health and climate change: shaping the health of nations for centuries to come," *The Lancet*, Nov. 28, 2018, https://tinyurl.com/ya76m2nl.

[3] "Heat Waves," U.S. Global Change Research Program, https://tinyurl.com/yxf4kg86.

[4] Kendra Pierre-Louis, "Heat Waves in the Age of Climate Change: Longer, More Frequent and More Dangerous," *The New York Times*, July 18, 2019, https://tinyurl.com/y6qfo35a.

[5] Adrienne Wald, "Emergency Department Visits and Costs for Heat-Related Illness Due to Extreme Heat or Heat Waves in the United States: An Integrative Review," ResearchGate, January/February 2019, https://tinyurl.com/y3oshuc7.

[6] Watts *et al.*, *op. cit.*; Renee Salas, Paige Knappenberger and Jeremy Hess, "Lancet Countdown on Health and Climate Change Brief for the United States of America," American Public Health Association, Nov. 28, 2018, https://tinyurl.com/y57msg92.

[7] Watts *et al.*, *ibid.*

[8] Jamie Ducharme, "Scientists Predict Climate Change Will Make Dangerous Heat Waves Far More Common," *Time*, July 16, 2019, https://tinyurl.com/y44a9xn7.

[9] Watts *et al.*, *op. cit.*

[10] Sebastian Malo, "Scientists predict major increase in heatwave deaths as world warms," *Reuters*, July 31, 2018, https://tinyurl.com/y44sl7dc.

[11] "Heatwave deaths will rise steadily by 2080 as globe warms up," *ScienceDaily*, Aug. 1, 2018, https://tinyurl.com/y9hy74qj.

international box office success and won two Academy Awards. In 2007, Gore and the IPCC were jointly awarded the Nobel Peace Prize to recognize "their efforts to build up and disseminate greater knowledge about man-made climate change."[52]

In late 2007, the Yale Program on Climate Change conducted the first-ever in-depth study of the public's perceptions of risks associated with climate change by surveying New York City residents. A large majority said

they were convinced that global warming was happening and was caused mainly by human activities. Sixty percent said they worried either a great deal or a fair amount about global warming, but most respondents said they believed that global warming was a greater threat to species, people and places relatively far away.[53]

Public views changed relatively little over the next six years: A national survey in November 2013 found that 63 percent believed global warming was happening, but

Climate Change Exacts High Physical, Emotional Toll in Puerto Rico

Repeated storms have battered the U.S. territory.

In Puerto Rico, the hits from climate change just keep coming.

First came a sea level rise of more than six inches since 1880, which contributed to nearly 80 floods in the past 25 years.[1]

Then came a growing number of extreme-heat days, followed by more-devastating hurricanes, including Irma and Maria in 2017, which struck the U.S. territory within two weeks of each other and left the island without power and potable water for months. The health impact of these weather events on Puerto Ricans, according to experts, has been diverse and devastating.

"There is property in several municipalities that has already been invaded by the sea where people are not able to live anymore," says Carissa Cabán-Alemán, a psychiatrist at Florida International University in Miami. Research after Hurricane Katrina, the Category 5 storm that struck New Orleans and the Gulf Coast in 2005, found that displaced populations have increased health risks and psychosocial challenges.[2]

Heavy rains and flooding also increase the risk of insect-borne illnesses such as Zika, which is transmitted by mosquitoes. In 2016, Puerto Rico experienced almost 35,000 cases of Zika infection in which symptoms were present, compared with 6,218 cases elsewhere in the United States and its territories.[3]

Besides water-borne illnesses, Puerto Rico has experienced an increase of 1.5 degrees Fahrenheit in average annual temperature since 1950, imperiling those with cardiovascular disease, diabetes and other conditions exacerbated by high temperatures. Puerto Rico's childhood asthma rate is the highest of any U.S. state or territory.[4]

Hurricane Maria, meanwhile, produced the "single largest maximum rainfall event" in Puerto Rico since researchers started keeping records in 1956, according to a study by the American Geophysical Union, a Washington-based organization that studies the atmosphere. Climate change does not cause hurricanes, but warmer ocean temperatures can result in hurricanes dropping extraordinarily high amounts of rain. In the case of Maria, the devastating amount of rainfall—41 inches in a single day—was linked to global warming, said David Keellings, a geographer at the University of Alabama, Tuscaloosa, who was the study's lead author.[5]

Damage to buildings was so extensive that, a year later, some hospitals were not operating at full capacity. The Puerto Rican island of Vieques is still using a temporary hospital and patients must travel to the main island to seek specialty care.[6]

"Most people who need to go to the [big] island for medical service try to get on the first boat that leaves," said Elda Carrasquillo, who coordinates health workshops in Vieques through a group called Taller Salud that works to improve women's access to health care.[7]

The health impact is perhaps most visible in the death toll—and the difficulty of even measuring it. Three months after the hurricane, Puerto Rico's Department of Public Safety listed just 64 deaths, reflecting the fact that government agencies were too damaged to get an accurate count. One 2018 survey that included "indirect deaths" resulting from water and electricity shortages, worsened chronic conditions and delayed medical treatment estimated 2,975 fatalities; another calculated 5,740 deaths.[8]

Puerto Rico's experience shows the danger of a common climate-change effect: reduced access to clean water. After the hurricane, some people drank or used water from ponds, lakes and streams, risking exposure to disease-causing microbes. Local health care providers reported increases in vomiting, diarrhea, pink eye, asthma and scabies related to unclean water. A month after the storm, Puerto Rico had tallied 121 cases of, and four confirmed deaths from, leptospirosis, a bacterial illness caused by unclean water. The island normally records about 60 cases a year.[9]

An estimated 130,000 Puerto Ricans left the islands after the hurricane. According to a 2018 article in the medical journal *BMC Medicine*, displaced populations face increased health risks, including food insecurity and the spread of infectious diseases.[10] Agnes Torres Rivera, a graduate student at the University of Puerto Rico, was one of nearly 2,200 island residents who moved to Connecticut in the hurricane's wake. "It forced thousands of people like myself to flee home and build a new life on the United States mainland," she said.[11]

Beyond the physical damage, the hurricane took a heavy emotional toll. Studies found that in the first six months after Maria, suicides increased by 26 percent over the same period from the year before. A survey of more than 96,000 schoolchildren several months after the hurricane found that 7.2 percent suffered post-traumatic stress disorder (PTSD).[12]

The team that conducted the survey said they had expected the PTSD rate to be even higher, prompting the suggestion that Puerto Rico's cultural value of *familismo*—the importance of family and community—may be at work. "Puerto Ricans place a high value on these social connections," said Regan Stewart, a clinical psychologist at the Medical University of South Carolina who was part of the team. "We know from the literature that social support may be a protective factor after a traumatic event."[13]

Since the hurricane, psychiatrist Cabán-Alemán has worked in several underserved, mostly rural communities in Puerto Rico to facilitate healing and emotional recovery. She says residents are coping with a long-term socioeconomic crisis, problems with the government—Gov. Ricardo Rosselló resigned under fire in August—and the myriad effects of climate change.[14] But, she adds, the hurricane's destruction galvanized some people to work for positive change. She points to emerging agroecology projects—methods to produce food without damaging natural resources—as one example.

"Amidst all that they are going through, there are many initiatives to do all kinds of projects," she says. "I have a lot of hope, and I am very excited about all of the empowerment that Puerto Rican communities have engaged since Hurricane Maria."

— Lola Butcher

[1] Jane Palmer, "How to survive climate change: a lesson from Hurricane Maria," *Mosaic*, March 21, 2018, https://tinyurl.com/ydes8rbz.

[2] Renee Salas, Paige Knappenberger and Jeremy Hess, "2018 Lancet Countdown on Health and Climate Change Brief for the United States of America," American Public Health Association, Nov. 28, 2018, https://tinyurl.com/y4xk545v.

[3] Josh Michaud and Jennifer Kates, "Public Health in Puerto Rico after Hurricane Maria," Issue Brief, The Henry J. Kaiser Family Foundation, Nov. 17, 2017, https://tinyurl.com/yct2rejw.

[4] Jennifer Runkle, Kenneth Kunkel and Laura Stevens, "Puerto Rico and the U.S. Virgin Islands State Climate Summary," NOAA Technical Report NESDIS 149-PR, 2018, https://tinyurl.com/y3mjexsv; Palmer, *op. cit.*

[5] "Climate change to blame for Hurricane Maria's extreme rainfall," American Geophysical Union, *ScienceDaily*, April 16, 2019, https://tinyurl.com/yyoq3f39.

[6] Steven Ross Johnson, "Puerto Rico's slow recovery leaves health system exposed for next major storm," *Modern Healthcare*, Sept. 8, 2018, https://tinyurl.com/yxo73ydl; Nicole Avecedo, "The Puerto Rican island of Vieques still has no hospital. Democrats demand answers from FEMA," *NBC News*, May 16, 2019, https://tinyurl.com/y6jax4ek.

[7] Avecedo, *ibid.*

[8] Salas, Knappenberger and Hess, *op. cit.*

[9] Michaud and Kates, *op. cit.*

[10] John Sutter, "130,000 left Puerto Rico after Hurricane Maria, Census Bureau says," *CNN*, Dec. 19, 2018, https://tinyurl.com/yx35x445; Patricia Schwerdtle, Kathryn Bowen and Celia McMichael, "The health impacts of climate-related migration," *BMC Medicine*, 2018, https://tinyurl.com/y4eod7xn.

[11] Agnes M. Torres Rivera, "Hurricane Maria Made Me A Climate Change Refugee," *Teen Vogue*, May 7, 2018, https://tinyurl.com/y8wegnoe.

[12] Salas, *op. cit.*; Helen Adams, "Psychologists release results of survey of 'Maria generation' kids," *ScienceDaily*, April 30, 2019, https://tinyurl.com/y3oulde8.

[13] Adams, *ibid.*

[14] Patricia Mazzei and Frances Robles, "Ricardo Rosselló, Puerto Rico's Governor, Resigns After Protests," *The New York Times*, July 24, 2019, https://tinyurl.com/y5jzgy9l.

23 percent disagreed—up 7 percentage points from April of that year. Although most Americans believed climate change would harm future generations of people, plants and other animal species, only 38 percent said they personally would be harmed "a moderate amount" or a "great deal" by global warming.[54]

Calls for Action

Humankind's impact on the Earth has been on the international agenda since 1972, when the U.N. Conference on Human Environment convened in Stockholm. The World Commission on Environment and Development, established in 1983, concluded that the future of humanity was at risk if growth and development continued at an unsustainable rate.[55]

In June 1992, some 20,000 people, including more than 100 heads of states, gathered in Brazil for the Earth Summit to debate solutions to environmental threats, including climate change.[56]

The Kyoto Protocol, an international agreement setting emission reduction targets, was adopted in 1997 and went into effect in 2005. Initially, 37 industrialized countries and the European Community agreed to reduce greenhouse gas emissions by an average of 5 percent below 1990 levels between 2008 and 2012. Subsequently, a different group of countries committed to reduce emissions by at least 18 percent below 1990 levels by 2020. Although 191 nations and the European Union have ratified the protocol, the United States never did and dropped out of the process in 2001.[57]

Leaders from nearly 200 countries who gathered at the U.N. Framework Convention on Climate Change in 2015 signed the Paris Agreement, the first climate agreement to win broad global support. Its targets: limit global temperature rise to well below 2 degrees Celsius and pursue efforts to keep warming to no more than 1.5 degrees Celsius above preindustrial levels. WHO leaders have called the pact "potentially the strongest health agreement of this century."[58]

The next year, more than 100 experts representing eight U.S. federal agencies reviewed a scientific assessment of climate change as part of the President's Climate Action Plan and issued a report warning that "climate change threatens human health and well-being in the United States."

The report documented how certain groups—children, the elderly, individuals with pre-existing health conditions and those with low socioeconomic status—are the most vulnerable to health effects attributed to climate change. Further, the scientists identified a wide range of conditions—Alzheimer's, asthma, chronic obstructive pulmonary disease, diabetes, cardiovascular disease, mental illness, obesity and disability—that are worsened by the effects of climate change.[59]

At its annual meeting in Taiwan in 2016, the World Medical Association, a confederation of 114 national medical societies, adopted a policy statement calling on its members to educate health scientists, businesses and governments about the health benefits of reducing greenhouse gas emissions. The association urged health organizations to replace their investments in energy companies that rely on fossil fuels with investments in enterprises that generate energy from renewable sources.[60]

In June 2017, President Trump announced that the United States would withdraw from the Paris Agreement because he said its economic costs were too high. Two months later, he rolled back standards that required the federal government to account for climate change and sea level rise when building infrastructure.[61]

Meanwhile, physician groups in 2017 created the U.S. Medical Society Consortium on Climate and Health to inform the American public and policymakers about the health harms of climate change and the health benefits of climate solutions. They were following the lead of the UK Health Alliance on Climate Change, a coalition of British medical and nursing colleges and health institutions that has a similar mission.[62]

Also in 2017, two research groups—one at the U.S. Department of Energy's Lawrence Berkeley National Laboratory, the other an international coalition of scientists known as World Weather Attribution—said climate change was likely a factor in the devastating rainfall of Houston's Hurricane Harvey earlier that year. Harvey was a Category 4 storm that caused catastrophic flooding.[63]

In conjunction with international talks to advance the Paris Agreement, Health Care Without Harm recruited 129 institutions in 31 countries to sign a call to action for the health sector to play a leadership role in tackling climate change. The document urged hospitals, drugmakers and other health care stakeholders around the world to reduce their carbon footprint, build greater health system resiliency and step up as leaders to protect "public and planetary health from climate change."[64]

Scientists' messages about the health effects of climate change grew more urgent in 2018, when the U.S. Global Change Research Program, consisting of 13 federal agencies that conduct or use climate change research, issued a report. Its key messages:

- Climate change is already affecting Americans' health and well-being, and the adverse consequences will worsen with additional climate change.
- Exposure and resilience vary across populations, with children, communities of color, low-income communities and older adults the most vulnerable.
- Proactive adaptation policies and programs reduce the risks and effects from climate-sensitive health outcomes and disruptions in health care services.
- Reducing greenhouse gas emissions directly saves lives and produces economic benefits.[65]

Trump said he did not believe the report's finding, which included the warning that the U.S. economy will suffer substantially from global warming. His administration is proposing changes to the way projections are made in reports, prompting Philip B. Duffy, the president of the Woods Hole Research Center, a think tank that studies climate change, to decry "a pretty blatant attempt to politicize the science."[66]

In response to Trump's decision to withdraw the United States from the Paris Agreement, 17 state governors belonging to the U.S. Climate Alliance announced initiatives in 2018 to cut carbon pollution by more than 26 percent by 2025, fulfilling their share of the U.S. commitment to the accord. In addition to capping emissions from vehicles and power plants, the states seek to change the way power is bought and sold. The governors' goal is to create incentives for clean energy projects and reduce the most dangerous greenhouse gases.[67]

In October 2018, the IPCC reported that the short-term consequences of climate change were more dire than believed. If greenhouse gas emissions continue at the current rate, it said, the atmosphere will warm by as much as 2.7 degrees Fahrenheit above preindustrial levels by 2040, intensifying flooding, droughts and poverty.[68]

CURRENT SITUATION
United Nations and WHO

The U.N. Intergovernmental Panel on Climate Change on Sept. 25, 2019, released a report saying that it is too late to stop at least some sea level rise from occurring because of global warming.

Rapidly melting glaciers and ice sheets will, by 2050, make floods that used to occur once a century become annual events in low-lying coastal areas that are home to as many as 680 million people, the report said.[69]

The health effects include a major loss of food production as ocean warming reduces the habitats for fish, an important dietary staple for many people in the tropics. Speaking at a U.N. Climate Action Summit in late September, Lionel Aingimea, president of the tiny country of Nauru, said the loss of the tuna fishery will mean "economic Armageddon" for this Pacific island northeast of Australia. He said he is focusing on building resilience, including a new port and an initiative to move houses and infrastructure inland.[70]

Also at the U.N. summit, nearly 30 global initiatives to speed action on climate change were introduced. Among them: a commitment by the Bill & Melinda Gates Foundation, the World Bank, the European Commission and five nations—the United Kingdom,

Spencer Platt/Getty Images

World Bank President David R. Malpass, Microsoft co-founder Bill Gates and Tuntiak Katan, an indigenous leader from the Amazon (left to right), attend the U.N. Climate Action Summit in New York City in September 2019. Gates and other leaders pledged to invest more than $650 million in the next three years to help farmers in developing countries address the impact of climate change on food production.

Will climate change set off a global health catastrophe?

YES

Rupert Read
Associate Professor of Philosophy, University of East Anglia, and Spokesperson for Extinction Rebellion

Written for *CQ Researcher*, November 2020

Dangerous anthropogenic climate change is having a very real impact on the lives of many people around the world, especially those living in climates that are already hot. But that's just the tip of the (melting) iceberg.

Tragically, the situation is virtually guaranteed to get much worse, whatever we do, for about the next 30 to 40 years. When you put carbon into the atmosphere, it stays there for decades or even for centuries, and this is likely to set off further massive ice loss and methane release. So the climate disasters that we are already seeing are a result primarily of carbon that was released before 1990. Since 1990, we've emitted the same amount of carbon as in the entire previous existence of the human race.

That obviously means that even in the best-case scenario, there will be health disasters around the world. Here is what the World Health Organization says: "Climate change is impacting human lives and health in a variety of ways. It threatens the essential ingredients of good health—clean air, safe drinking water, nutritious food supply and safe shelter— and has the potential to undermine decades of progress in global health."

We are staring down the barrel of the uncontrolled collapse of our civilization, and whether that occurs through water shortages or food shortages or other means, you will see the mother of all health catastrophes.

It's too late to find a way of perpetuating a civilization organized as our civilization is currently organized. We needed to switch to genuinely renewable energies about a generation ago. All there is time for now is a very rapid bringing down of our deadly emissions and a cessation of our destruction of natural habitats. We have to rapidly reduce our impacts on the Earth now, or our civilization will simply collapse, within a generation or so, maybe less.

Is that collapse really likely to happen? Common sense would say no, but previous "common sense"—an economy based on fossil fuels could keep growing forever, for example—could be said to have actually gotten us into this extreme crisis.

I am incredibly encouraged by the waking up that now seems to be occurring around the world: the climate strikes, Extinction Rebellion and more. It's not too late to make a difference. So it's time for us to try, as a last-ditch effort, to save ourselves.

NO

Jessica Wolff
U.S. Director of Climate and Health, Health Care Without Harm

Written for *CQ Researcher*, November 2020

Climate change is already affecting health, but preventing a global health catastrophe will depend on the decisions we make today. In 2018, the Special Report on Climate Change by the United Nations Intergovernmental Panel on Climate Change estimated that continuing with a "business as usual" emissions scenario will likely have catastrophic impacts on human health.

However, the report also found that by limiting warming to below 1.5 degrees Celsius, we can dramatically reduce the risks to the climate and human health. To achieve this target, we must cut greenhouse gas emissions 45 percent by 2030 and reach "net-zero" emissions by midcentury. The good news is, many of the actions we need to reduce emissions by roughly half within the next decade are already underway around the world. We just need greater ambition to accelerate and scale up these solutions.

The Lancet said tackling climate change could be the "greatest global health opportunity of the 21st century," as many of the solutions that mitigate climate change will also create opportunities for reducing poverty and promoting health equity worldwide.

In addition, the health care industry can be a climate-smart, innovative sector that protects public health from climate change, while using its purchasing power to lead the transition to a low-carbon economy. Representing 18 percent of the U.S. economy and 10 percent of the global economy, the health care sector can have a substantial impact by investing in sustainable energy, food and transportation systems for every community.

For example, members of the U.S. Health Care Climate Council, a group of 19 health systems representing 500 hospitals, are implementing innovative climate solutions in their facilities, building climate resilience in the communities they serve and using their trusted voice and purchasing power to move policy and markets. At the global level, our health care climate challenge includes 18,000 health facilities in 30 countries pledging to adopt this "climate-smart health care" approach by committing to reduce their carbon emissions and helping their communities become more resilient to climate change.

If we focus on adapting to the changes already happening, we can safeguard those who are most vulnerable, while also reducing the emissions that worsen climate change and threaten health. As anchor institutions and major employers, hospitals can take many vitally important actions that build resilience, such as transitioning to renewable electricity and investing in a sustainable local food economy. Taking action now will produce immediate and sustained benefits to human health around the globe.

the Netherlands, Switzerland, Sweden and Germany—to invest more than $650 million in the next three years to help 300 million small farmers in developing countries address the impact of climate change on food production.[71]

A few days before the summit, the World Health Organization pledged to increase its financial support to address the health effects of climate change. In a statement issued Sept. 11, 2019, WHO Director-General Tedros Adhanom Ghebreyesus said less than 0.5 percent of international finance for climate change is directed to health, while small-island states—whose residents are most affected by climate change—receive only a fraction of that.[72]

In November 2019, more than 11,000 scientists from some 150 countries declared a "climate emergency" and warned of "untold suffering" if immediate action is not undertaken. Writing in *Bioscience*, they listed six issues that must be addressed to prevent the most catastrophic scenarios: replacing fossil fuels, cutting greenhouse gas emissions, eating less meat, restoring and protecting ecosystems, building a carbon-free economy and stabilizing population growth.[73]

Trump Administration

The Trump administration and a bipartisan group of state governors continue to disagree on whether U.S. energy policies should focus on climate change.

The administration announced on Sept. 18, 2019, that it will curtail California's authority to set its own vehicle emission standards allowed via its long-standing waiver under the Clean Air Act. Those standards have allowed California to require more-efficient cars than required by federal regulations. Two days later, California and several other states sued the administration to stop the revocation.[74]

Whether abolishing California's tailpipe emissions waiver will affect human health is a matter of debate. The move "could have devastating consequences for our kids' health and the air we breathe, if California were to roll over," said California Gov. Gavin Newsom, a Democrat. "But we will not."[75]

By contrast, administration officials said the Environmental Protection Agency improperly granted California's waiver because greenhouse gases do not cause specific local problems, such as asthma or lung disease, that are associated with smog and other pollutants. Abolishing California's authority to set its own emission

standards "meets President Trump's commitment to establish uniform fuel economy standards for vehicles across the United States, ensuring that no state has the authority to impose its policies on everybody else in our whole country," said Transportation Secretary Elaine Chao.[76]

On Nov. 4, 2019, the administration formally notified signatories that it will withdraw from the Paris climate accord in November 2020. "In international climate discussions, we will continue to offer a realistic and pragmatic model—backed by a record of real-world results—showing innovation and open markets lead to greater prosperity, fewer emissions and more secure sources of energy," Secretary of State Mike Pompeo said. "We will continue to work with our global partners to enhance resilience to the impacts of climate change and prepare for and respond to natural disasters."

But critics noted the administration has been cutting environmental protections and condemned the decision to withdraw. "Abandoning the Paris Agreement is cruel to future generations, leaving the world less safe and productive," said Andrew Steer, president of the World Resources Institute, a global research organization based in Washington.[77]

Despite the administration's plan to exit the agreement, city, regional and business entities are on track to achieve about half of the U.S. commitment to cut carbon emissions, according to the American Public Health Association. More than 3,500 governmental entities, businesses, universities, tribes and other organizations have joined the "We Are Still In" movement, committing to do their part to hit America's Paris Agreement pledge.[78]

In June, more than 75 public health groups, including the American Medical Association, the American Academy of Family Physicians and the American Academy of Pediatrics, issued a call to action that urged government, business and community leaders to take action that promotes health by fighting climate change. Calling climate change the "greatest public health challenge of the 21st century," the signers said leaders should comply with the Paris Agreement; transition from fossil fuels to renewable energy; encourage people to drive less; support sustainable agriculture; make sure all communities have safe and sustainable supplies of drinking water; and ensure a "just transition" for workers and communities hurt by climate change.[79]

In a report released on Nov. 18, 2019, the U.S. Government Accountability Office warned that climate change threatens 60 percent of the nation's Superfund sites—federally designated sites contaminated by toxic waste. Extreme weather worsened by climate change, including flooding from sea level rise and more intense hurricanes, increases the risk of toxic substances being washed into waterways, communities and farmland, according to the report. Wildfires also increase the chance that health-harming pollutants will become airborne.[80]

Extreme Weather

Recovery from Hurricane Dorian, which hit parts of the Bahamas in September 2019, is going slowly because electricity and running water were not fully restored more than a month later. Five health clinics were destroyed on the islands of Abaco and Grand Bahama, affecting some 75,000 people. When WHO Director-General Ghebreyesus toured the devastation on Oct. 1, 2019, the official death toll was 56 and about 600 people were still missing.[81]

"Hurricane Dorian is another urgent reminder that we must address the drivers of climate change and invest more in resilient communities," he said. "The longer we wait, the more people will suffer."[82]

Even before Dorian, 2019 was on pace to be one of the most disastrous years, weather-wise, in almost two decades. During the first six months of the year, an estimated 7 million people were forced out of their homes because of floods, landslides or other extreme-weather events, according to the Internal Displacement Monitoring Centre, an independent organization based in Geneva. This figure included 3.4 million evacuated from their homes in India and Bangladesh because of Cyclone Fani in May 2019. Two months earlier, 617,000 people were displaced across Mozambique, Malawi, Zimbabwe and Madagascar when Cyclone Idai struck, killing more than 1,000 people.[83]

Acknowledging that further health effects of climate change are unavoidable, some world leaders are pivoting to focus on resilience-building efforts.

In September 2019, the Global Commission on Adaptation—consisting of leaders from 19 countries and headed by former U.N. Secretary-General Ban Ki-moon; Bill Gates, co-chair of the Bill & Melinda Gates Foundation; and Kristalina Georgieva, chief executive officer of the World Bank—issued a "call for action" to invest in resilience initiatives. "Global actions to slow climate change are promising but insufficient," the commission said. "We must invest in a massive effort to adapt to conditions that are now inevitable: higher temperatures, rising seas, fiercer storms, more unpredictable rainfall and more acidic oceans."[84]

The commission began a series of initiatives in September, several of which are focused on the health effects of global warming. One example: investments in early-warning systems, especially in the least-developed countries and small-island states, so that millions more people can protect themselves from storms or heat waves.[85]

Los Angeles in July 2019 became the first U.S. city to form a Climate Emergency Mobilization Department to address local effects of climate change. Among other things, the department will help workers displaced by climate change find jobs.[86]

An analysis of the 100 most populated U.S. cities identified Santa Ana, Calif., as the most vulnerable to climate change because it is likely to experience an "extreme climate event" in the next two decades and it is poorly prepared to handle it. Most of the cities with high vulnerability and low preparation to cope with such an event are in Florida, California and along the coasts of New York and New Jersey.[87] (*See Graphic.*)

In April, New York City began a local version of the federal Green New Deal proposal; the city plans to invest $14 billion in initiatives to reduce greenhouse gas emissions by 30 percent by 2030. Democratic Mayor Bill de Blasio announced that the program will complement the city's $20 billion resiliency plan to address the threats stemming from climate-induced storms, sea level rise, extreme heat and increased precipitation.[88]

OUTLOOK
Threats to Multiply?

Among those who monitor the health effects of climate change, the short-term forecast is not good.

"There's no question that in the next 10 years, we will continue to see what we've seen over the last few and most likely to a greater extent," says Sarfaty, director of the Medical Society Consortium on Climate and Health. "In other words, more hot days—more scorching, searing-heat days—more souped-up storms, more torrential rains, more long, large fire seasons. More issues with food supply as the areas that are being affected by drought grow. More issues with the availability of fish and other food that comes from the sea as the waters get warmer."

Benjamin, the American Public Health Association's executive director, agrees that the health effects of climate change will get worse before they get better.

"But it will get better," he says. "I'm confident that America is waking up. In fact, the whole world is waking up more and more on this."

It remains to be seen whether people are waking up—and taking action—quickly enough to avert disaster. Jessica Wolff, U.S. director of climate and health for Health Care Without Harm, points to clear guidance from the IPCC: To avoid climate disaster, global warming must be limited to 1.5 degrees Celsius, which requires a 45 percent decrease in carbon dioxide emissions from 2010 levels by 2030.[89]

"The future could be really bright, and in fact, solving climate change would allow us to address serious health equity and energy equity issues around the world," she says. "There's opportunity that we could actually improve health by addressing climate. It's just a question if we're able to do that."

Harvard's Bernstein says that some simple steps can mitigate climate change, build resilience and promote health. One example: planting trees, which reduces carbon dioxide in the atmosphere.[90] Replacing concrete with green space reduces air temperature in cities, he says.

"We also have an ever-growing pile of evidence that exposure to green space improves health, mental health, school performance and a whole suite of other stuff," he says. "So helping people think about protecting themselves ties into the solutions for climate change itself."

Climatologist Michaels at the Competitive Enterprise Institute says such predictions are fanciful: "Anybody who thinks that we can quote-unquote 'stop global warming' is either deceiving themselves or, if they are saying it in public while they know better, deceiving others."

That said, he says many experts frequently overstate the magnitude and pace of climate change and that, in affluent countries, people will adapt to the warmer world, averting the worst health effects.

Rep. Carter, of the House Select Committee on Climate Change, expects the U.S. energy sector to be part of that adaptation. He says the country's success in coal, oil and gas development gives him confidence the United States can become a leader in renewable energy. "We need to create and incentivize new technology and infrastructure in the most efficient and affordable ways possible and in a way that creates new American jobs and keeps America ahead," he says.

Rauch of Moms Clean Air Force takes encouragement from the work being done at the city and state levels. "There's this incredible movement to have cities and states basically take ownership of their climate pollution," she says. "And they are moving to power their economies with renewable energy and to build incentives into their urban planning that have people using less gas and less electricity."

That kind of commitment keeps Benjamin from despairing. "It's not so overwhelming a problem that we can't start working on it today," he says. "My point is: Do what you can to reduce your own carbon footprint, and then, advocate for changes at work, home and community."

NOTES

1. Meg Anderson and Sean McMinn, "As Rising Heat Bakes U.S. Cities, The Poor Often Feel It Most," *NPR*, Sept. 3, 2019, https://tinyurl.com/y3jmtyxr.

2. *Ibid.*; "State of the Climate in 2018 shows accelerating climate change impacts: Report," press release, United Nations, March 28, 2019, https://tinyurl.com/y6ch2kdv.

3. Emily Holden, "'Like a sunburn on your lungs': how does the climate crisis impact health?" *The Guardian*, Sept. 16, 2019, https://tinyurl.com/y3fqfh8h.

4. "COP24 Special report: Health & Climate Change," World Health Organization, 2018, https://tinyurl.com/y38usnzn.

5. Nick Watts *et al.*, "The 2018 report of the Lancet Countdown on health and climate change: shaping the health of nations for centuries to come," *The Lancet*, Nov. 28, 2018, https://tinyurl.com/ya76m2nl.

6. *Ibid.*

7. Renee Salas, Paige Knappenberger and Jeremy Hess, "2018 Lancet Countdown on Health and Climate Change Brief for the United States of America," American Public Health Association, 2018, https://tinyurl.com/y4xk545v.

8. "COP24 Special report: Health & Climate Change," *op. cit.*

9. Moira Fagan and Christine Huang, "A look at how people around the world view climate change," Pew Research Center, April 18, 2019, https://tinyurl.com/y53ebt7w.

10. Anthony Leiserowitz *et al.*, "Climate Change in the American Mind: April 2019," Yale Program for Climate Change Communication, June 27, 2019, https://tinyurl.com/y3pm9ery.

11. Fagan and Huang, *op. cit.*; Chris Cillizza, "Donald Trump doesn't think much about climate change, in 20 quotes," *CNN*, Aug. 8, 2017, https://tinyurl.com/ycgw6alq; Chris Cillizza, "Donald Trump buried a climate change report because 'I don't believe it,'" *CNN*, Nov. 27, 2018, https://tinyurl.com/y9bnwkza; and Kate Yoder, "On climate change, younger Republicans now sound like Democrats," *Grist*, Sept. 9, 2019, https://tinyurl.com/y248nrpc.

12. Camila Domonoske, "So What Exactly Is In The Paris Climate Accord?" *NPR*, June 1, 2017, https://tinyurl.com/y57dke37.

13. Michael Shear, "Trump Will Withdraw U.S. From Paris Climate Agreement," *The New York Times*, June 1, 2017, https://tinyurl.com/y8zgpmsa; Lisa Friedman, "Trump Serves Notice to Quit Paris Climate Agreement," *The New York Times*, Nov. 4, 2019, https://tinyurl.com/y3s62mqu.

14. Watts *et al., op. cit.*

15. Matthew Taylor and Jonathan Watts, "Revealed: the 20 firms behind a third of all carbon emissions," *The Guardian*, Oct. 9, 2019, https://tinyurl.com/y28jdhwa.

16. "How much carbon dioxide is produced when different fuels are burned?" U.S. Energy Information Administration, June 4, 2019, https://tinyurl.com/kypxsun.

17. "Sir David Attenborough Launches UN Campaign to Promote Climate Action by the People," United Nations, Dec. 3, 2018, https://tinyurl.com/y2zfj22n; David Wallace-Wells, "Time to Panic," *The New York Times*, Feb. 16, 2019, https://tinyurl.com/y3jobsmm.

18. "COP24 Special report: Health & Climate Change," *op. cit.*

19. "Health benefits far outweigh the costs of meeting climate change goals," press release, World Health Organization, Dec. 5, 2018, https://tinyurl.com/ycez4m4h.

20. Coral Davenport, "Major Climate Report Describes a Strong Risk of Crisis as Early as 2040," *The New York Times*, Oct. 7, 2018, https://tinyurl.com/y8kv9gfo.

21. *Ibid.*

22. *Ibid.*

23. "Adapt Now: A Global Call for Leadership on Climate Resilience," Global Commission on Adaptation, 2019, https://tinyurl.com/y4lshmnz.

24. Martha Bebinger, "Has Your Doctor Talked To You About Climate Change?" *NPR*, July 13, 2019, https://tinyurl.com/yyr86mz7.

25. *Ibid.*

26. "Lancet Report: Education is Key to Climate Change Response," Columbia University, Nov. 29, 2018, https://tinyurl.com/y6cymb89.

27. Salas, Knappenberger and Hess, *op. cit.*

28. Lulu Garcia-Navarro, "How Climate Change Is Affecting Residents' Health in Miami," *NPR*, March 24, 2019, https://tinyurl.com/y4aymjuf.

29. "About Us," Florida Clinicians for Climate Action, https://tinyurl.com/yym4ym2h.

30. Cole Latimer, "Australia one of the countries most exposed to climate change, bank warns," *Sydney Morning Herald*, March 22, 2018, https://tinyurl.com/y77zr9zy; Katie Hill, "'Eco-Anxiety' Is Very Real And It's On The Rise," *10 Daily*, July 20, 2019, https://tinyurl.com/yxvtjjs7.

31. Watts *et al., op. cit.*

32. David Reidmiller *et al.*, "2018: Impacts, Risks, and Adaptation in the United States: Fourth National Climate Assessment, Volume 2," U.S. Global Change Research Program, 2018, https://tinyurl.com/ybw3k3rr; "Extreme weather events linked to poor mental health," *ScienceDaily*, Sept. 5, 2019, https://tinyurl.com/y3rglofr; and Arun Rath, "Heat And Aggression: How Hot Weather Makes It Easy For Us To Offend," *WGBH*, July 11, 2018, https://tinyurl.com/wjjvpox.

33. Dan MacDougall, "'We need to talk about ecological grief': Greenlanders traumatised by climate emergency," *The Guardian*, Aug. 12, 2019, https://tinyurl.com/y6xg2tem.

34. *Ibid.*

35. Jonathan Watts, "Greta Thunberg, schoolgirl climate change warrior: 'Some people can let things go. I can't,'" *The Guardian*, March 11, 2019, https://tinyurl.com/yyfeo6z3.

36. Zoë Schlanger, "We need to talk about 'ecoanxiety': Climate change is causing PTSD, anxiety, and depression on a mass scale," *Quartz*, April 3, 2017, https://tinyurl.com/kgg8yuk.

37. Isobel Whitcomb, "The Barrage of Bad News About Climate Change Is Triggering 'Eco-Anxiety,' Psychologists Say," *Live Science*, July 2, 2019, https://tinyurl.com/yylo7fyk.

38. David Wogan, "Why we know about the greenhouse gas effect," *Scientific American*, May 16, 2013, https://tinyurl.com/y8fehazt.

39. Steve Graham, "Svante Arrhenius (1859-1927)," NASA Earth Observatory, Jan. 18, 2000, https://tinyurl.com/y9vhbo6d.

40. Ed Hawkins, "Global temperatures: 75 years after Callendar," *Climate Lab Book*, April 22, 2013, https://tinyurl.com/vf947kw; Spencer Weart, The Discovery of Global Warming, January 2017, https://tinyurl.com/yybpcajn; James Fleming, "The Callendar Effect: The Life and Work of Guy Stewart Callendar (1898-1964), the Scientist Who Established the Carbon Dioxide Theory of Climate Change," American Meteorological Society, 2007, https://tinyurl.com/sog9q4b.

41. Weart, *Ibid.*

42. *Ibid.*

43. Eliza Griswold, "How 'Silent Spring' Ignited the Environmental Movement," *The New York Times Magazine*, Sept. 21, 2012, https://tinyurl.com/y8xzln8l.

44. Weart, *op. cit.*

45. "Potential Implications of Trends in World Population, Food Production, and Climate," CIA, made available through The Black Vault, August 1974, https://tinyurl.com/yc36rosb.

46. Walter Sullivan, "Study Finds Warming Trend That Could Raise Sea Levels," *The New York Times*, Aug. 22, 1981, https://tinyurl.com/ycc88cp2.

47. J.T. Houghton, G.J. Jenkins and J.J. Ephraums, eds., "Climate Change: The IPCC Scientific Assessment," U.N. International Panel on Climate Change, Cambridge University Press, 1990, https://tinyurl.com/y6hyrc6w.

48. Riley E. Dunlap, "Partisan Gap on Global Warming Grows," Gallup, May 29, 2008, https://tinyurl.com/y7toqhw8.

49. Jay Lemery and Paul Auerbach, *Environmedics: The Impact of Climate Change on Human Health* (2017).

50. *Ibid.*

51. *Ibid.*

52. Pete Hammond, "Al Gore, Paramount And Participant Celebrate Oscar Winner 'An Inconvenient Truth's' 10th Anniversary," *Deadline*, May 25, 2016, https://tinyurl.com/yy7x553g; "The Nobel Peace Prize 2007," Nobel Prize, 2007, https://tinyurl.com/y354f3mh.

53. "New York City Global Warming Survey," Yale Program on Climate Change Communication, May 13, 2008, https://tinyurl.com/y5atqghu.

54. "Climate Change in the American Mind: Americans' Global Warming Beliefs and Attitudes in November 2013," Yale Program on Climate Change Communication, Jan. 16, 2014, https://tinyurl.com/y4qvc33m.

55. Paul Brown, "From the archive, 3 June 1992: Earth Summit: Long and troubled road to Rio," *The Guardian*, June 13, 2012, https://tinyurl.com/wlz87o8.

56. "Back in time: What was Rio 1992?" United Nations Regional Information Centre for Western Europe, https://tinyurl.com/vcj3qgb.

57. "Kyoto Protocol Fast Facts," *CNN* Library, March 21, 2018, https://tinyurl.com/yc5q3xlu; "What Is the Kyoto Protocol?" U.N. Framework Convention on Climate Change, https://tinyurl.com/r8pk7n8.

58. Justin Worland, "World Approves Historic 'Paris Agreement' to Address Climate Change," *Time*, Dec. 12, 2015, https://tinyurl.com/v7cbodk; Monica Dean, "4 Key Findings on Climate Change and Health," United Nations Foundation, Jan. 9, 2019, https://tinyurl.com/tus4wah.

59. A. Crimmins *et al.*, "The Impacts of Climate Change on Human Health in the United States: A Scientific Assessment," U.S. Global Change Research Program, 2016, https://tinyurl.com/jydxwaz.

60. "Health Organisations Urged to Divest From Fossil Fuels," World Medical Association, Oct. 22, 2016, https://tinyurl.com/y4ywghhe.

61. Michael Shear, "Trump Will Withdraw U.S. From Paris Climate Agreement," *The New York Times*, June 1, 2017, https://tinyurl.com/y8zgpmsa; Lisa Friedman, "Trump Signs Order Rolling Back Environmental Rules on Infrastructure," *The New York Times*, Aug. 15, 2017, https://tinyurl.com/y4kk2x9e.

62. Erin Blakemore, "Doctors Warn That Climate Change Makes People Sick," *Smithsonian.com*, March 16, 2017, https://tinyurl.com/y5sbhsby; Watts *et al.*, *op. cit.*

63. Henry Fountain, "Scientists Link Hurricane Harvey's Record Rainfall to Climate Change," *The New York Times*, Dec. 13, 2017, https://tinyurl.com/y97pehuy.

64. "Health Care Worldwide Calls for Action on Climate Change," Medical Society Consortium on Climate & Health, Nov. 14, 2017, https://tinyurl.com/y2m4rjbg.

65. Kristie L. Ebi *et al.*, "Fourth National Climate Assessment, Vol. II: Impacts, Risks, and Adaptation in the United States, Chapter 14: Human Health," U.S. Global Change Research Program, 2018, https://tinyurl.com/y2fxpoq9.

66. Emily Holden, "Trump on own administration's climate report: 'I don't believe it,'" *The Guardian*, Nov. 26, 2018, https://tinyurl.com/s4yfbde; Coral Davenport and Mark Landler, "Trump Administration Hardens Its Attack on Climate Science," *The New York Times*, May 27, 2019, https://tinyurl.com/y4cyllfv.

67. Jeremy Deaton, "States Promised to Fulfill the Paris Agreement. Here's How They're Going to Do It," *NexusMedia*, June 1, 2018, https://tinyurl.com/yc6bszwx.

68. Davenport, "Major Climate Report Describes a Strong Risk of Crisis as Early as 2040," *op. cit.*

69. Drew Kann, "Landmark UN report warns sea levels will rise faster than projected by 2100," *CNN*, Sept. 25, 2019, https://tinyurl.com/y3tk8c4p.

70. *Ibid.*; "Nauru President warns of possible climate change 'economic Armageddon,'" *U.N. News*, Sept. 26, 2019, https://tinyurl.com/yy4ey6fs.

71. Megan Rowling, "12 global initiatives that could help us beat back climate threats," Global Center on Adaptation, Sept. 26, 2019, https://tinyurl.com/yyzppf2f.

72. "WHO Director-General urges world leaders to protect health from climate change," World Health Organization, Sept. 11, 2019, https://tinyurl.com/y4888r2c.

73. Emma Tobin and Ivana Kottasová, "11,000 scientists warn of 'untold suffering' caused by climate change," *CNN*, Nov. 6, 2019, https://tinyurl.com/y4facfm7.

74. Vivian Ho *et al.*, "Trump to block California from setting vehicle emissions rules," *The Guardian*, Sept. 17, 2019, https://tinyurl.com/y3mex29j; Paul Eisenstein, "Trump axes California's right to set own auto emission standards," *NBC News*, Sept. 18, 2019, https://tinyurl.com/y65gsl9g.

75. Scott Neuman, "Trump Says California's Ability To Set Its Own Emissions Standards Will Be

Revoked," *NPR*, Sept. 18, 2019, https://tinyurl .com/y22unrqn.

76. Coral Davenport, "California Sues the Trump Administration in Its Escalating War Over Auto Emissions," *The New York Times*, Sept. 20, 2019, https://tinyurl.com/rmkzfzu.

77. Brady Dennis, "Trump makes it official: U.S. will withdraw from the Paris climate accord," *The Washington Post*, Nov. 4, 2019, https://tinyurl.com/ y497dgr9.

78. Salas, Knappenberger, and Hess, *op. cit.*; "About," We Are Still In, https://tinyurl.com/y4d7mdfr.

79. Olivia Rosane, "77 Health Organizations Call for Climate Action to Fight Public Health Emergency," *EcoWatch*, June 25, 2019, https://tinyurl.com/ y4t43u6p.

80. Phil McKenna, "60% of Toxic Superfund Sites Threatened by Climate Change, GAO Finds," *Inside Climate News*, Nov. 19, 2019, https://tinyurl .com/yxx6m2vo.

81. Jason Beaubien, "A Month After Hurricane Dorian Hit The Bahamas, Recovery Is Slow And Uneven," *NPR*, Oct. 2, 2019, https://tinyurl.com/y2qf3l6s; "WHO chief underscores need to address climate change following visit to Bahamas," *UN News*, Oct. 2, 2019, https://tinyurl.com/y4pgjayq.

82. "WHO chief underscores need to address climate change following visit to Bahamas," *ibid.*

83. Somini Sengupta, "Extreme Weather Displaced a Record 7 Million in First Half of 2019," *The New York Times*, Sept. 12, 2019, https://tinyurl.com/ y2cyrmne.

84. Adele Peters, "Bill Gates and Ban Ki-moon: Investing in climate solutions could generate $7.1 trillion," *Fast Company*, Sept. 10, 2019, https:// tinyurl.com/yy5t22jb; "Adapt Now: A Global Call for Leadership on Climate Resilience," *op. cit.*

85. "Adapt Now: A Global Call for Leadership on Climate Resilience," *ibid.*

86. "New Department Is Set to Assist Communities Affected by Climate Change," *KNBC*, July 3, 2019, https://tinyurl.com/y6slrqm3.

87. Eylul Tekin, "How Climate Change Will Impact Major Cities Across the U.S.," Clever, Aug. 6, 2019, https://tinyurl.com/y322b44b; Brentin Mock, "What U.S. Cities Facing Climate Disaster Risks Are Least Prepared?" CityLab, Aug. 19, 2019, https://tinyurl.com/y3vuyl87.

88. Mock, *ibid.*; "Action on Global Warming: NYC's Green New Deal," press release, New York City, April 22, 2019, https://tinyurl.com/y4sflsne.

89. Davenport, "Major Climate Report Describes a Strong Risk of Crisis as Early as 2040," *op. cit.*

90. Stephen Leahy, "How to erase 100 years of carbon emissions? Plant trees—lots of them," *National Geographic*, July 4, 2019, https://tinyurl.com/ y674uhqb.

BIBLIOGRAPHY

Books

Kenner, Alison, *Breathtaking: Asthma Care in a Time of Climate Change*, University of Minnesota Press, 2018.
An ethnographer examines how a changing climate affects asthma and its treatment.

Lemery, Jay, and Paul Auerbach, *Environmedics: The Impact of Climate Change on Human Health*, Rowman & Littlefield, 2017.
Emergency medicine physicians use patients' case studies to illustrate the effects of environmental change on human health.

Wallace-Wells, David, *The Uninhabitable Earth: Life After Warming*, Tim Duggan Books, 2019.
A *New York* magazine columnist describes a range of current and anticipated crises—food shortages, refugee emergencies, economic turmoil and more—attributable to climate change.

Articles

Anderson, Meg, "As Rising Heat Bakes U.S. Cities, The Poor Often Feel It Most," *NPR*, Sept. 3, 2019, https://tinyurl.com/y3jmtyxr.
An interactive tool shows that low-income neighborhoods, because of their lack of green cover, are more likely to be hotter than their wealthier counterparts.

Fialka, John, "Reducing China's CO$_2$ Emissions Would Curb Deadly Air Pollution in the U.S.," *Scientific American*, July 26, 2019, https://tinyurl.com/y6peyco7.

China's efforts to curb air pollution could mean nearly 2,000 fewer premature deaths in the United States by 2030, a Massachusetts Institute of Technology study found.

Holden, Emily, "'Like a sunburn on your lungs': how does the climate crisis impact health?" *The Guardian*, Sept. 16, 2019, https://tinyurl.com/y3fqfh8h.

A roundup of health effects shows that climate change affects virtually every medical specialty, from heart and lung diseases to digestive illnesses.

Koh, Howard K., and Gina A. McCarthy, "Private and Public Sector Responses to Climate Change," *JAMA Forum*, March 28, 2018, https://tinyurl.com/y355j73f.

Two experts say urgency is growing across the globe to deal with climate change and its impact on health.

Newkirk, Vann R. II, "How Climate Change Is Challenging American Health Care," *The Atlantic*, Dec. 6, 2018, https://tinyurl.com/y5nacm3e.

An international collaboration tracks how climate change is degrading human health and suggests ways to mitigate damage from a warming planet.

Pierre-Louis, Kendra, "Heat Waves in the Age of Climate Change: Longer, More Frequent and More Dangerous," *The New York Times*, July 18, 2019, https://tinyurl.com/y6qfo35a.

Heat waves are increasingly threatening people's health, especially the elderly and young.

Reports and Studies

Campbell-Lendrum, Diarmid, *et al.*, "COP24 Special Report: Health and Climate Change," World Health Organization, 2018, https://tinyurl.com/y4vd3xoe.

The United Nations health agency warns that residents in poorer nations and on small islands are especially vulnerable to the health hazards of climate change.

Crimmins, A., *et al.*, "The Impacts of Climate Change on Human Health in the United States: A Scientific Assessment," U.S. Global Change Research Program, 2016, https://tinyurl.com/jydxwaz.

Experts representing eight federal agencies document scientists' understanding of how climate change affects public health.

Cutler, David, and Francesca Dominici, "A Breath of Bad Air: Cost of the Trump Environmental Agenda May Lead to 80,000 Extra Deaths per Decade," *JAMA Forum*, June 12, 2018, https://tinyurl.com/yxhsm2wk.

Two Harvard University economics professors list more than 60 U.S. environmental rules that the Trump administration has reversed or proposed to reverse and projects the health effects that will likely result.

Eckelman, Matthew J., and Jodi D. Sherman, "Estimated Global Disease Burden from US Health Care Sector Greenhouse Gas Emissions," *American Journal of Public Health*, April 2018, https://tinyurl.com/y4clw6jr.

Environmental engineers project how greenhouse gas emissions from the health care industry will contribute to malnutrition and other health harms.

Ghebreyesus, Tedros, "Health, environment and climate change," World Health Organization, April 18, 2019, https://tinyurl.com/y3zupkk5.

The organization offers its vision on how the world and the medical community need to respond to environmental health risks and challenges between now and 2030.

Watts, Nick, *et al.*, "The 2018 report of the Lancet Countdown on health and climate change: shaping the health of nations for centuries to come," *The Lancet*, Nov. 28, 2018, https://tinyurl.com/ya76m2nl.

Researchers from every continent assess progress on 41 indicators tracking the health effects of climate change.

THE NEXT STEP

Doctors

Abbott, Brianna, "Medical Schools Are Pushed to Train Doctors for Climate Change," *The Wall Street Journal*, Aug. 7, 2019, https://tinyurl.com/y4b2dmy4.

As changing climates increasingly affect health outcomes, medical schools are beginning to include climate-related education in their curriculums.

Bains, Camille, "Doctors say political activism part of their jobs on issues affecting health," *National Observer*, Oct. 7, 2019, https://tinyurl.com/y65ld3lw.
Canadian doctors are becoming more vocal about efforts to curb climate change as the negative health effects become apparent.

Howard, Beth, "The rising health threats of a hot planet," Association of American Medical Colleges, Oct. 8, 2019, https://tinyurl.com/y5t4hnzl.
Some doctors have noticed that increasing temperatures and decreasing air quality have worsened symptoms among patients, particularly those with chronic obstructive pulmonary disease.

Extreme Weather

Adams, Helen, "Psychologists release results of survey of 'Maria generation' kids," *ScienceDaily*, April 30, 2019, https://tinyurl.com/y3oulde8.
A study found that 7 percent of children who survived Hurricane Maria suffered from post-traumatic stress disorder (PTSD).

Berlinger, Joshua, "Nearly 1,500 deaths linked to French heat waves," *CNN*, Sept. 9, 2019, https://tinyurl.com/y694gjhu.
Heat waves brought about the highest recorded temperature ever in France this summer and contributed to nearly 1,500 deaths.

Farge, Emma, "Climate change hampers progress on fighting epidemics: Global Fund," *Reuters*, Oct. 22, 2019, https://tinyurl.com/y646annd.
Warmer temperatures and more-intense cyclones are driving an increase in malaria cases in Africa.

Health Trends

Jagannathan, Meera, "How climate change could contribute to racial maternal-health disparities," *MarketWatch*, Oct. 21, 2019, https://tinyurl.com/yy589f2d.
Pregnant women's exposure to extreme heat increases their chance of being hospitalized—and as temperatures rise in coming decades, maternal health for women of color and for the poor, who are less likely to have access to air conditioning, could be particularly affected.

Schumaker, Erin, "Why climate change is also a public health problem," *ABC News*, Sept. 25, 2019, https://tinyurl.com/yya78p2g.
Health experts say that an increase in extreme-weather events could worsen mental health outcomes and lead to a lack of access to medical care when hospitals are damaged in storms.

Thompson, Dennis, "Experts: Climate Change 'Threat to Human Well-Being'" *HealthDay News*, Nov. 5, 2019, https://tinyurl.com/r5qd4te.
A global coalition of scientists warns that climate change would cause "untold human suffering" and that negative health effects, such as the spread of infectious diseases, have already begun.

Mental Health

Ro, Christine, "The harm from worrying about climate change," *BBC Future*, Oct. 10, 2019, https://tinyurl.com/y6nm8oa8.
Psychologists are divided on how to best treat mental health struggles that stem from people worrying about climate change.

Wetsman, Nicole, "How Communities Can Build Psychological Resilience to Disaster," CityLab, Nov. 7, 2019, https://tinyurl.com/y3lr2fe3.
Mental health experts say being informed, volunteering and staying socially conscious will help communities prepare for disasters that could lead to trauma.

Wulfhorst, Ellen, "Climate change-fueled US wildfires take toll on those who fight them," *Reuters*, Nov. 8, 2019, https://tinyurl.com/y3ghk87e.
A study found that nearly half of U.S. firefighters experience sleep troubles, emotional fatigue and other health problems, and PTSD is a growing problem for firefighters battling California wildfires.

For More Information

American Medical Association, AMA Plaza, 330 N. Wabash Ave., Suite 39300, Chicago, IL 60611; 312-464-4782; ama-assn.org. Association of physicians that educates doctors about how climate change affects health.

American Public Health Association, 800 I St., N.W., Washington, DC 20001; 202-777-2742; apha.org. Organization that advocates policies to mitigate climate change.

Center for Climate, Health and the Global Environment, 401 Park Drive, 4th Floor West, Suite 415, Boston, MA 02215; 617-384-8350; hsph.harvard.edu/c-change. Harvard University research unit that seeks to inform climate policy.

Environmental Change and Security Program, Woodrow Wilson Center, Ronald Reagan Building and International Trade Center, 1 Woodrow Wilson Plaza, 1300 Pennsylvania Ave., N.W., Washington, DC 20004-3027; 202-691-4000; wilsoncenter.org/program/environmental-change-and-security-program. Nonpartisan policy research organization that examines the connections between climate change and health.

Health Care Without Harm, 12355 Sunrise Valley Drive, Suite 680, Reston, VA 20191; 703-860-9790; noharm-uscanada.org. Global organization working to make the health care industry more sustainable.

Moms Clean Air Force, 257 Park Ave. South, New York, NY 10010; 917-887-0146; momscleanairforce.org. Parents' group advocating for a healthier environment.

U.S. Energy Information Administration, 1000 Independence Ave., S.W., Washington, DC 20585; 202-586-8800; eia.gov. Branch of the U.S. Department of Energy that publishes statistics about energy use worldwide.

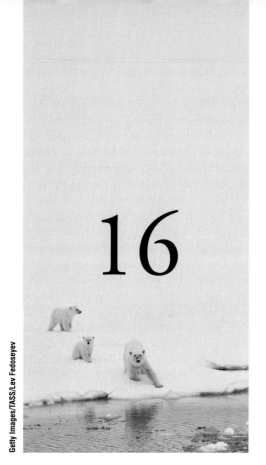

Getty Images/TASS/Lev Fedoseyev

A polar bear and her cubs walk on an Arctic ice floe. Polar bears use offshore floes for hunting platforms, but as a warming climate depletes Arctic ice, they can be forced to swim longer distances to reach floes.

16

Fuel Efficiency Standards

Will Trump's rollbacks increase greenhouse gas emissions?

By Reed Karaim

THE ISSUES

On March 31, 2020, President Trump turned to his favorite means of communication, Twitter, to laud his administration's just-announced decision to roll back automobile fuel efficiency standards implemented under his predecessor, Barack Obama.

"Great news!" Trump tweeted. "American families will now be able to buy safer, more affordable, and environmentally friendly cars with our new SAFE VEHICLES RULE."[1]

But Trump's Safer Affordable Fuel-Efficient (SAFE) Vehicles rule quickly generated opposition from critics, including some within his own Environmental Protection Agency — and in May 2020, 23 states, led by California, filed suit to block the order. They were joined by a dozen environmental and consumer groups suing separately to block the SAFE rule.[2]

"Because of this change, we will breathe more polluted air, suffer more premature deaths and see a net loss of jobs in the automobile industry," said Mary Nichols, chair of the California Air Resources Board, a state entity charged with fighting air pollution and climate change, in a statement announcing the lawsuit.[3]

The court cases are the latest round in a heated battle between the Trump administration and both states and environmental groups over a key question: How efficient and clean-running should U.S. vehicles be to limit their impact on climate change and protect the public from pollution? The battle is

From *CQ Researcher,*
June 29, 2020

being waged not only over the automobile regulations known as Corporate Average Fuel Economy (CAFE) standards, but also California's long-standing authority to set emission rules stricter than those of the federal government.[4]

Trump's SAFE standard replaces rules the Obama administration negotiated with automakers in 2012 that required a 5 percent annual increase in vehicle fuel efficiency. The Trump standards mandate only a 1.5 percent annual increase. Under the Obama plan, an automaker's vehicle fleet would have averaged about 54 mpg by 2025. Under the SAFE rule, the standard will be 40 mpg by 2026.[5]

The clash over the greenhouse gases and pollutants that come out of vehicles' tailpipes has consequences for automobile manufacturers, car buyers, public health and the global climate. It has divided the major automakers, with some supporting Trump's new rule and others agreeing to the stricter CAFE standards set by California, which several other states also follow.[6]

It also presents a stark contrast between the environmental positions of Trump and presumptive Democratic presidential nominee Joe Biden as they head into the November 2020 election. Trump has hailed the new car standards as part of his administration's broader reversal of Obama-era environmental regulations he says stifled American business.[7] Biden has promised to impose standards even stricter than those under Obama to tackle climate change and accelerate the country's move to clean, renewable energy.[8]

The Trump administration and its supporters say the SAFE rule still provides adequate environmental protection, while lowering the cost of cars for consumers because manufacturers will no longer have to spend as much on technology to boost mileage. The administration maintains the new rule will save automakers up to $100 billion in compliance costs and will reduce the average price of a new vehicle by $1,000.

That price cut, they say, will spur Americans to buy new, safer and cleaner-running cars, which will not only improve air quality but save thousands of lives. "This rule reflects the Department's No. 1 priority—safety—by making newer, safer, cleaner vehicles more accessible for Americans who are, on average, driving 12-year-old cars," said U.S. Transportation Secretary Elaine Chao. "By making newer, safer, and cleaner vehicles more

accessible for American families, more lives will be saved and more jobs will be created."[9]

Opponents of weakening the standards say the administration's claims are built on a series of flawed estimations. "The federal agencies used questionable science, faulty logic and ludicrous assumptions to justify what they wanted from the start: to gut and rewrite the single most important air regulation of the past decade," said Nichols, the California Air Resources Board chair.[10]

Federal CAFE standards are developed through a collaboration between the National Highway Traffic Safety Administration (NHTSA) and the Environmental Protection Agency (EPA). Opponents note the EPA's internal review of the SAFE rule disputed several of the administration's public arguments, including the central assertion that it would reduce tailpipe pollutants and emissions that cause climate change compared to "the absence of regulation." According to documents obtained by Sen. Tom Carper, D-Del., the EPA review stated, "This is not correct. 'The absence of regulation' . . . would be the existing EPA standards, which are more stringent than those finalized in this action."[11]

The EPA assessment dismissed another key contention: that weaker standards would lead automakers to build cheaper cars and thus spur consumers to buy newer vehicles with better safety features. The EPA said this argument was built on the unfounded assumption "that it's necessary to give up fuel savings to get other attributes" in vehicle design. Anticipating the possibility of court challenges, an EPA staffer wrote in an internal email that the rule had "numerous factual inaccuracies which litigants can easily disprove."[12]

An EPA spokesperson described the documents as part of the internal deliberative process between the federal agencies. EPA Administrator Andrew Wheeler has publicly supported the SAFE rule, saying it "strikes the right regulatory balance that protects our environment, and sets reasonable targets for the auto industry. The rule supports our economy, and the safety of American families."[13]

Analysts on both sides of the debate say the severe economic downturn tied to the COVID-19 pandemic has upended certainty about the impact that the revised standards could have on the industry and the car-buying public. Some believe car shoppers are likely to be even more price-sensitive, while others say Americans are unlikely to be buying new cars under any circumstances.

The shutdown imposed due to the coronavirus pandemic produced a dramatic improvement in Los Angeles' air quality, as this view of MacArthur Park and downtown in April 2020 showed. Advocates of tougher auto emissions standards say this indicates what can be accomplished through regulatory action.

it had to apply for a waiver in each case.[16] That authority remained in effect for nearly half a century. The Trump administration revoked it last year, claiming it gave California de facto power to set national standards because several states followed its lead, forcing automakers to build more-expensive vehicles overall.[17]

California officials say courts have upheld their state's right to set emissions standards and contend the Trump administration is acting illegally in revoking the authority.[18] Analysts say the different lawsuits involving emissions policies could end up before the U.S. Supreme Court.

The key underlying issue is climate change. Transportation of all kinds, from automobiles to trucks to airplanes, is the United States' single largest source of the greenhouse gases—predominantly carbon dioxide (CO_2)—that almost all scientists accept are warming the planet. Transportation accounted for 29 percent of such

Ironically, the pandemic-triggered quarantines and business shutdowns have led to the cleanest air in decades, just as the issue of vehicle efficiency and emissions is being hotly debated. In late March and early April of 2020, Los Angeles, which historically has had some of the worst air pollution in the country, recorded its longest stretch of clean air since the EPA began recording data in the early 1970s.[14]

Los Angeles and California have long been at the center of America's battle to reduce the pollution coming out of tailpipes. California was the first state to regulate vehicle emissions in the 1960s.[15]

The 1970 federal Clean Air Act recognized California's unique challenge by giving the state authority to set stricter standards than the federal government, although

Transportation Is Most Common Emissions Source

The transportation sector accounted for 29 percent of U.S. greenhouse gas emissions in 2017, according to the Environmental Protection Agency. Light-duty vehicles were the biggest source of transportation emissions, generating 59 percent of emissions in that sector.

U.S. Greenhouse Gas Emissions by Sector, 2017*

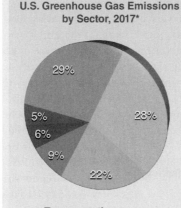

- Transportation
- Electricity
- Industry
- Agriculture
- Commercial
- Residential

U.S. Transportation Greenhouse Gas Emissions by Source, 2017

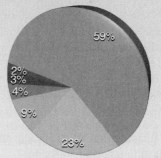

- Light-duty vehicles
- Medium and heavy-duty trucks
- Aircraft
- Other
- Ships and boats
- Rail

* Totals may not add to 100 percent due to rounding.
Source: "Fast Facts on Transportation Greenhouse Gas Emissions," Environmental Protection Agency, July 16, 2019, https://tinyurl.com/y2vqneto

emissions in 2017. The power industry was second at 28 percent.[19]

Within the transportation sector, so-called light-duty vehicles—essentially the cars, sport utility vehicles and pickup trucks Americans love to drive—produce the biggest share, 59 percent, of those emissions.[20] More than 284 million cars and trucks are registered in the United States.[21] A typical gasoline-powered passenger vehicle emits 4.6 metric tons of carbon dioxide per year.[22] Improving the fuel efficiency to reduce greenhouse gas emissions is key to limiting climate change, according to environmentalists and others concerned by how the planet is warming.

"Based on what the science is telling us, we have a limited amount of time to act," says Andrew Linhardt, former deputy director of advocacy for the clean transportation program at the Sierra Club, an environmental group. "Getting vehicles to be as efficient as possible [and] moving into a market where vehicles are electrified is the only way we're going to be able to tackle the climate crisis."

But the administration and many supporters of rolling back CAFE standards say the issue of climate change is less pressing — or dismiss it outright.

Nicolas Loris, an energy and environmental policy fellow at the Heritage Foundation, a conservative think tank in Washington, does not fall into the dismissal camp. But when considering the difference between Obama's and Trump's fuel efficiency standards, he says, "The overall impact on climate change would be trivial."

As the Trump administration and its opponents battle over fuel efficiency and emissions standards, here are some questions central to the debate:

Were Obama's fuel efficiency standards an effective approach to reducing emissions?

When the Obama White House announced that the administration's clean car fuel efficiency standards had been finalized in 2012, the official statement emphasized the difference the new rule would make in the battle against climate change.

The standards would cut greenhouse gases coming from U.S. cars and light trucks—trucks weighing 8,500 pounds or less—in half by 2025, the administration said, reducing emissions by 6 billion metric tons, more than the total amount of carbon dioxide emitted by the United States in 2010.[23] The White House also said the rules would save a total of 12 billion barrels of oil, reducing consumption by more than 2 million barrels a day by 2025.[24]

By 2030, the standards would have produced a reduction in greenhouse gases equivalent to shutting down 140 coal-fired power plants for an entire year, according to the Union of Concerned Scientists, a science advocacy group based in Cambridge, Mass.[25]

Environmental activists say discarding the Obama fuel efficiency requirements will have a significant impact on climate change. "The standards President Trump is rolling back represent the single biggest step any nation has ever taken against global warming," says Dan Becker, director of the Safe Climate Transport Campaign at the Center for Biological Diversity. The campaign is an advocacy group working to reduce greenhouse gases.

Trump's SAFE rule, Becker says, makes American air quality worse. Even though tailpipe exhaust is far cleaner than it was decades ago, it still contains nitrogen oxides, particulate matter and other compounds that can hurt human health. Lower fuel efficiency standards mean more exhaust as Americans burn more gasoline, he says.[26]

"It makes everything worse," Becker says. "It means more of the stuff that you breathe that makes you sick. And that's just the direct health effects. In addition, in a way we can't quantify as easily, it makes global warming worse, which makes the likelihood of all the consequences of global warming worse—sea level rise, flooding, droughts, you name it."

But the Heritage Foundation's Loris says the United States accounts for only about 14 percent of global greenhouse gas emissions, and the transportation sector even less. Rather than mandate changes in fuel efficiency standards that raise the price of vehicles, he says, a more effective approach to tackling climate change would be to focus on bringing down the costs of technologies that can reduce emissions, which could speed their adoption both in the United States and abroad.

"If you're increasing the cost, whether it's new vehicles or . . . other energy technology, you're only going to disincentivize the investment in those projects," Loris says. "The best way to be a leader is to lower the cost so that

[U.S.] consumers and consumers in other countries can more readily adopt them."

The Trump administration's analysis of the SAFE rule acknowledges it will lead to an increase of 2 to 3 percent in U.S. oil consumption, which would amount to half a million more barrels a day. However, it says that will amount to an increase in global temperatures of only three-thousandths of a degree Celsius by 2100.[27]

"The opponents of the rule try to portray it as if terrible things are going to happen imminently . . . and the numbers certainly do not support that kind of assessment, to put it charitably," says Marlo Lewis Jr., a senior fellow at the Competitive Enterprise Institute, a public policy group based in Washington dedicated to promoting free markets. Lewis' group says it will sue to weaken the fuel efficiency standards even further.

But a research paper published in *Science*, the peer-reviewed journal of the American Association for the Advancement of Science, concluded the Trump administration's projections about the rule's impact are based on faulty underlying assumptions.

Antonio Bento, a professor of public policy and economics at the University of Southern California and a lead author of the paper, told a U.S. House committee that one significant error is a large undercount in the number of vehicles the administration projects to be on the road by 2029. This means there will be more miles driven than the administration forecasts, he said, and "increased driving translates into increases in gasoline

consumption and the external effects" of greenhouse gas emissions and local air pollution.[28]

Other analysis indicates that even the Trump forecast for the increase in greenhouse gas emissions with the new rule is equivalent to about four years' worth of those emissions from the entire U.S. transportation sector, not just vehicles.[29]

The Sierra Club's Linhardt says the effect of greenhouse gases is cumulative, with a growing impact that becomes harder to mitigate over time. "Billions of tons of CO_2 is nothing to dismiss as small," he says. "Transportation emissions are not small and tackling them now is essential."

Other advocates of the Obama rules say focusing on greenhouse gases neglects the fact that reducing emissions also cuts other pollutants coming out of tailpipes, and even small changes make a difference. "California has 26 million passenger vehicles, and we drive about 350 billion miles a year in those 26 million vehicles," says Steven Cliff, deputy executive officer of the California Air Resources Board. "So the incremental pollution from each vehicle is extremely important."

Did Obama's stricter standards impose an undue financial burden on automakers?

The fuel efficiency standards set out in Obama's 2012 clean car rule were the result of lengthy negotiations with 13 major foreign and U.S. automakers, including General Motors, Ford and Chrysler, which all agreed to the annual increases in efficiency outlined in the rule.

But Lewis, of the Competitive Enterprise Institute, says the Obama rule was partly based on a faulty forecast. "The fuel economy standards and even the CO_2 standards are based on expectations of what fuel prices will be over the next 13 years," he says, with those estimates determining "how much fuel savings are worth to consumers and, thus, how much it is reasonable for consumers to invest in fuel-saving technology."

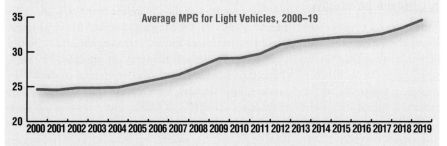

Fuel Efficiency Rises in U.S.

Fuel efficiency for light vehicles—which include cars, sport utility vehicles and light trucks—has increased by 10 mpg to 34.6 mpg over the past two decades, according to an analysis by the Rhodium Group, a New York City research institute.

Average MPG for Light Vehicles, 2000–19

Source: Zeke Hausfather, "Analysis: How Trump's rollback of vehicle fuel standards would increase US emissions," Carbon Brief, July 10, 2019, https://tinyurl.com/y8y2lzvf

The forecasts saw gasoline prices reaching $4.50 a gallon by 2025, he says. However, the growth of U.S. production from shale oil fields has helped keep fuel prices below predicted levels, he says, which has changed the equation and made it more difficult for auto manufacturers to meet the standard.

"They forecast that one way people would deal with rising fuel costs, which they expected, was to buy compact cars, coupes and sedans," Lewis says. "Because consumers decided they wanted more heavier, taller vehicles than the agencies forecast, it meant that it was more difficult for the automakers to comply with the 2012 standards."

But Ann Carlson, a professor of environmental law at UCLA, says the technological capability to meet the Obama standards exists and the case for the effort still holds. "Both California and the EPA took a really careful look at the question and concluded that automakers could meet those standards, and that seemed quite justifiable to me," she says.

Carlson says that when car manufacturers first approached the Trump administration, they were not asking for a big rollback of standards. "The automakers didn't ask for a freeze, and they didn't ask for the cuts the Trump administrations has agreed to," she says. "What they were arguing for was little tweaks around the edges."

That was essentially the message Bob Holycross, then global director for sustainability and vehicle environmental matters at Ford, delivered at a hearing held by federal regulators in 2018. "Let me be clear: We do not support standing still," Holycross said. "Clean-car standards should increase year over year, with the inclusion of provisions that promote ongoing investment in technology that will further drive greenhouse gas reductions."[30]

Carlson adds that five automakers have reached a separate agreement with California to meet stricter emissions requirements than those in the SAFE rule. This undermines the case that the Obama rule was an undue burden, she says.

However, Brett Smith, technology director at the Center for Automotive Research, a nonprofit group based in Ann Arbor, Mich., says there were signs the Obama standards were going to be harder for automakers to meet going forward.

Under the complicated system that exists for meeting efficiency rules, car companies can bank credits for overperforming in early years and can also trade credits—so Ford, for example, could buy credits from Hyundai to meet the standards in a given year if Hyundai had credits to spare. Car companies are using up their credits, Smith says, and could have trouble meeting the standards in the next few years while still providing the vehicles consumers want.

"If you look at the data, if you look at the credits available, and if you look at how severe [the Obama rule] gets for pickup trucks in next few years, the car companies were probably going to be in trouble," Smith says.

Thomas Pyle, president of the American Energy Alliance, a Washington-based public interest group that promotes market-oriented energy and environmental policies, says the efficiency requirements backed by Obama and California distort the car market and hurt sales. "By making the mpg mandate so high, they're forcing the auto industry to make cars that currently consumers don't want or can't afford," says Pyle. "Consumers are buying crossovers and SUVs and pickup trucks. That's what their preferences are. That's what they want."

Advocates of stricter fuel efficiency standards sharply dispute the idea they are restricting either carmakers or consumer choice. "Nobody is being forced into any kind of car. Look—on the market, there's a wide range of vehicles available," says Bill Magavern, policy director of the Coalition for Clean Air, a California organization that works to promote air quality.

"The auto companies were making the same arguments in the 1970s; they were saying the consumers wouldn't be able to buy full-size vehicles, they would be too expensive—all that was proven false," he says. "The CAFE standards that were enacted in the 1970s were a huge success. Cars got safer and much more efficient, and that was without any sacrifice in consumer choice."

More recently, Magavern says, automakers have been prospering under the Obama rules while selling plenty of bigger vehicles. "They recovered from the [2007-09] recession, and they were having their best years, even as the fuel efficiency standards were going up under that agreement."

Will Trump's rollback on standards spur a move to newer, cleaner cars?

The biggest single influence on car sales this spring had nothing to do with fuel efficiency or pollution control costs. Sales tumbled an estimated 53 percent in April for major automakers, in a collapse that analysts say was the result of the severe economic downturn resulting from the pandemic.[31]

Given the economy's uncertain future, analysts say, it is hard to determine what impact other factors, including sticker price and fuel efficiency ratings, might have on car sales. "It's all going to depend on what the recovery looks like and what consumer confidence looks like," says the Heritage Foundation's Loris.

But even before the pandemic, analysts were casting doubt on the Trump administration's claim that the reduction in fuel efficiency requirements would lead to lower vehicle prices that would spur a car-buying spree. "The cost per vehicle to meet the fuel efficiency requirements is relatively small in the overall cost of a new car," says the Sierra Club's Linhardt. "Depending on the model, it's somewhat like $800 to $1,200 per vehicle, and [when] you compared those numbers to [the cost of] all the new bells and whistles, it's not that much."

The average cost of a new car in the United States in January was $37,851, according to analysts at Kelley Blue Book, the car pricing firm.[32]

Pyle, of the American Energy Alliance, says the cost of meeting fuel efficiency standards built into that price does inhibit buyers. "What this is doing is making it harder to buy a new car. It's pricing people

out of the purchasing deal, and who gets hit the hardest? It's the poor," says Pyle. "It's preventing poor people from having the freedom and mobility of a new, safer car."

The money automakers will save by meeting the SAFE rule instead of the more stringent Obama standards will bring new vehicles within range of more Americans, Pyle says. "If you don't have [a lot] of disposable income and you need a car, if a new car is more affordable, then at least it's an option for you," he says.

Linhardt, however, doubts consumers will see savings from the SAFE rule. "If anyone thinks that automakers are going to lower the cost of their vehicles because they're not doing fuel efficiency, they haven't been paying attention to the auto industry for the last 30 years," he says.

Loris says the issue is how much prices will increase. "One of the benefits of the SAFE rule compared to the Obama era standards is that it's less aggressive. The 1.5 percent increase is pretty modest comparatively, so it shouldn't result in as much investment in changing

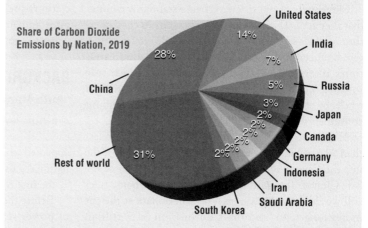

China, U.S. Are World's Top Carbon Emitters

China was responsible for 28 percent of all the carbon dioxide emitted globally in 2019, according to the Union of Concerned Scientists. The United States was second at 14 percent, and India was third at 7 percent.

Share of Carbon Dioxide Emissions by Nation, 2019

United States 14%
India 7%
Russia 5%
Japan 3%
Canada 2%
Germany 2%
Indonesia 2%
Iran 2%
Saudi Arabia 2%
South Korea 2%
Rest of world 31%
China 28%

Source: "Each Country's Share of CO$_2$ Emissions," Union of Concerned Scientists, May 11, 2020, https://tinyurl.com/yyxgukld

vehicle technology and design," he says. "In that regard, I think automakers will be better off in terms of how they can meet the standard in a way that doesn't significantly raise prices."

Supporters of the stricter Obama standards counter that they actually provided greater benefits to consumers through fuel savings, making automobiles more attractive financially. They point to the Trump administration's internal analysis that showed the SAFE rule rollback would lower the price of new cars and light trucks by about $1,000, but would increase the amount consumers would pay for gasoline by $1,400.[33]

Even though gasoline prices fell to an average of less than $2 a gallon this spring and have not increased at the rate the Obama administration predicted, Becker of the Safe Climate Transport Campaign says the Obama rules still would "save consumers a trillion dollars at the gas pump long-term, and that's down from $1.7 trillion before gas prices fell."

The $1.7 trillion figure was the savings the Obama administration projected from their 2012 efficiency standards.[34] Critics of those standards say the projection was always unrealistic because it included accumulated savings over an excessively long period of time and assumed ever higher gasoline prices.

The critics also question how much consumers actually value the savings they get from higher fuel efficiency when shopping for a new vehicle. The Center for Automotive Research's Smith says it only has a limited impact. "Consumers are interested in saving money at the pump, but it's not a high priority," he says. "It's just not that big a deal for most people. With gas relatively inexpensive, [car shoppers feel] 'I'd rather have that sunroof' or the newest tech or something else."

Researchers have reached contradictory conclusions on the effect of fuel savings on sales. The National Bureau of Economic Research, a nonpartisan group that distributes economic research to policymakers and others, found buyers steeply discount fuel efficiency when making price considerations and are willing to pay only $380 extra for $1,000 savings in fuel costs.[35] However, a study by Consumers Union, a public interest advocacy group, found car buyers were willing to pay $1,000 more for a vehicle to save $100 per year in fuel costs.[36]

The National Automobile Dealers Association, which supports Trump's SAFE rules, feels the rollback

has more value than the fuel savings from Obama's standards and will boost car sales. "Regulatory standards that embrace marketplace realities will accelerate, not inhibit, fleet turnover," said Peter Welch, the association's president and CEO, "and ensure that newer, safer and more fuel-efficient cars and trucks get on America's roads."[37]

BACKGROUND
"Auto Mania"

America's love affair with the automobile began early in the 20th century, when the first "horseless carriages" appeared on the nation's roads. But it exploded into a national passion with the arrival of Henry Ford's Model T, the first relatively affordable, mass-produced car.

Before the Model T, automobiles came with a variety of power sources, including steam engines, alcohol-fueled motors and even battery-powered electric vehicles. Tom McCarthy, author of *Auto Mania: Cars, Consumers, and the Environment*, a history of the car in American society, says that some of today's concerns about the gasoline engine were present in the earliest days of the automobile.

"I was amazed . . . to find people who, from the very beginning, were picking up on these problems," says McCarthy, a historian at the U.S. Naval Academy in

Getty Images/PhotoQuest

Model Ts fresh off the assembly line are parked outside the Ford plant in Highland Park, Mich., in 1913. Ford built 15 million Model Ts between 1908 and 1927, helping to make automobiles ubiquitous.

Annapolis, Md. "There was a whole big debate on electric versus gasoline versus alcohol: 'Shouldn't we burn alcohol? It's so much cleaner.'"

In 1900, most of the roughly 8,000 automobiles on U.S. roads were steam-powered. About a quarter of the vehicles built in America were electric powered. But the power and range advantage gasoline-fueled engines enjoyed gave them the edge over other power sources. By the time Henry Ford designed the Model T, they had already come to dominate automobile design.[38]

The initial Model T rolled off the assembly line on Oct. 1, 1908. Between that year and 1927, Ford built about 15 million of them.[39] Their sales, along with those of models from General Motors, formed in 1908, and other companies, would transform the nation.

In 1908, the United States had fewer than 200,000 motor vehicles. Twenty years later, more than 24 million cars and trucks were on the nation's roadways. By 1948, that number had grown to more than 41 million, and more rapid growth was ahead in the prosperous decades of the 1950s and 1960s.[40]

The original Model T got up to 21 mpg, but as cars grew heavier and more powerful, fuel efficiency shrank.[41] By 1950, average mileage was down to slightly under 13 mpg.[42] More cars burning more gasoline meant much more automobile exhaust. But as millions of vehicles crowded roadways, officials were slow to connect the growth in traffic with the increasingly dirty air in major metropolitan areas.

Reckoning in California

In the summer of 1943, a thick blanket of smog—a combination of fog and atmospheric pollutants—descended on Los Angeles, limiting visibility to only three blocks and leaving people with burning eyes and lungs and nausea. Officials at first thought a local chemical plant was to blame. But when the plant was shut down, the smog continued.[43]

In 1947, Los Angeles County formed a special board to control air pollution, the first such body in the United States. But the city's smog continued despite the board's effort to regulate power plants, oil refineries and other industrial sites it thought might be to blame.[44]

In the 1950s, Arie Haagen-Smit, a bio-organic chemistry professor working for the Los Angeles air district, finally connected the smog to automobile exhaust. He

determined that airborne hydrocarbons and nitrogen oxides released when gasoline was burned in car engines were responsible for the polluted air.[45]

His conclusions were disputed by oil companies, which hired their own experts to challenge his findings.[46] But by the 1960s, the connection had been established and California began to build a regulatory framework to control auto exhaust. In 1966, the state created the first tailpipe emissions standards in the United States and, a year later, launched the California Air Resources Board to work for clean air.[47]

On the national level, growing environmental awareness and rising concern about air pollution led to the 1970 Clean Air Act. The law authorized the development of regulations to limit vehicle emissions. The EPA was created the same year to implement the law.[48] Recognizing California's earlier efforts and pollution challenges, the Clean Air Act also authorized the state to set emissions regulations that were stricter than federal standards by applying for a waiver from the EPA.[49]

Shift to Fuel Efficiency

From 1950 to 1975, American cars grew bigger, more powerful and more luxurious—but slightly less fuel efficient. In 1950, U.S. vehicles averaged 12.8 mpg, according to the U.S. Energy Information Administration. By 1975, that had fallen to 12.2 mpg, with mild ups and downs along the way.[50]

The inattention to fuel efficiency was made possible by a sustained era of relatively cheap fuel. From 1950 to 1975, the average gasoline price in the United States climbed from 27 cents a gallon to 57 cents a gallon. Yet when adjusted for inflation, gasoline was cheaper in 1975 that it had been 25 years earlier.[51]

But by then, the price was already climbing as a result of events in the Middle East. For decades, the United States had been growing increasingly dependent on oil from that region to feed its gasoline habit. By the mid-1970s, about one-third of the oil refined into gasoline was coming from outside the United States.[52]

When Israel faced off against Egypt and Syria in a 1973 war, Arab oil-producing nations imposed an embargo on sales to the United States in retaliation for U.S. support of Israel. The embargo would lead to a quadrupling of oil prices, gasoline shortages, long lines at filling stations and the nation's first fuel efficiency standards.[53]

CHRONOLOGY

1943-1967 *California leads the way in regulating tailpipe emissions.*

1943 Severe smog in Los Angeles reduces visibility and causes burning eyes and lungs, but scientists do not consider automobiles to be the cause.

1950 California Institute of Technology chemistry professor Arie Haagen-Smit identifies automobile tailpipe emissions as the cause of Los Angeles' smog.

1966 With air pollution worsening, California establishes the first tailpipe emissions standards in the nation.

1967 Gov. Ronald Reagan creates California's Air Resources Board to address pollution.

1970-1975 *Concerns about the environment, auto safety and dependence on foreign oil spur regulation.*

1970 Congress passes the Clean Air Act, requiring a 90 percent reduction in harmful emissions from new automobiles by 1975. The law gives California the authority to set its own standards.

1973 The Environmental Protection Agency (EPA) releases a study confirming that lead from automobile exhaust threatens public health and issues regulations to reduce the metal in gasoline. . . . An oil embargo by Arab nations sends U.S. gasoline prices soaring, spurring interest in more-efficient vehicles, which boosts sales of smaller four-cylinder Japanese models.

1975 The Energy Policy and Conservation Act sets the first fuel economy goals through the Corporate Average Fuel Economy (CAFE) program.

1981-1996 *Growing focus on tailpipe emissions' health hazards sparks further action.*

1981 A new generation of catalytic converters with sensors and onboard computers appears in new cars, reducing pollutants from tailpipes.

1985 EPA issues regulations to cut the amount of lead in gasoline by 90 percent starting Jan. 1, 1986.

1992 Senate approves and President George H.W. Bush signs the United Nations Framework Convention on Climate Change, committing countries to fight global warming.

1996 EPA completes its 25-year mission to completely remove lead from gasoline, banning it from gasoline as of Jan. 1.

2003-2012 *Rising fuel prices and global warming concerns lead to renewed focus on fuel efficiency.*

2003 A spike in gasoline prices that would last until 2008 spurs interest in hybrid and electric vehicles.

2007 The U.S. Supreme Court rules that the EPA has authority to regulate carbon dioxide and other greenhouse gas vehicle emissions as pollutants under the Clean Air Act.

2008 Federal government offers a tax credit of up to $7,500 to purchasers of qualified plug-in electric vehicles.

2012 The Obama administration finalizes standards to increase fuel economy standards to roughly 54 mpg for cars and light-duty trucks by 2025.

2017-Present *President Trump vows to reduce government regulation and boost the U.S. oil industry.*

2017 President Trump tells autoworkers he will review fuel efficiency standards that automakers had agreed to during the Obama administration.

2018 California Gov. Jerry Brown commits the state to getting nearly 5 million electric vehicles on the road by 2030 to reduce greenhouse gas emissions.

2019 The Trump administration revokes the waiver giving California the authority to set its own, stricter vehicle emission standards, which are also followed by several other states. . . . California sues the Trump administration in federal court over the revocation of its emissions waiver.

2020 The Trump administration finalizes rules rolling back fuel efficiency standards to 40 miles mpg by 2026, saying the change will lower car costs (March). . . . Twenty-three states, the District of Columbia and a dozen environmental and consumer groups file suit to block the administration's decision to weaken fuel efficiency standards (May).

In 1975, President Gerald Ford signed the Energy Policy and Conservation Act, which included a provision establishing mandatory fuel efficiency standards for automakers that would gradually rise to 27.5 mpg for 1985-model cars.[54]

The requirement spurred a revolution in U.S. automobile design, says Smith, of the Center for Automotive Research. Manufacturers switched from heavier body-on-frame construction, in which the car's body is mounted on a rigid frame, to lighter unibody construction, in which the vehicle's body and chassis are integrated into a single structure. They also shifted more production to smaller cars.

In both cases, Japanese and European automakers had an edge, because they were already making smaller, more fuel-efficient unibody cars. "It took [U.S. automakers] a long time to get really good at unibody cars," Smith says, "and over that time, they lost a lot of market share to international companies."

At the time, U.S. automakers complained the fuel efficiency mandate would mean the end of full-sized cars and would destroy their business. A Ford executive testified before Congress in 1974 that the standards "would result in a Ford product line consisting . . . of all sub-Pinto-sized vehicles." (The Pinto was a small Ford hatchback.)[55]

Larger vehicles did not disappear, and the 1975 mandate succeeded in raising fuel efficiency. By 1985, average mileage for cars had reached 27.5 mpg. But the rule had a separate, lower standard of 19.5 mpg for light trucks, which included minivans and sport utility vehicles as well as pickup trucks. In 1986 automakers successfully lobbied President Ronald Reagan's administration to lower the standard to 26 mpg for cars. At the same time, two of the vehicles designated as light trucks were taking off in popularity: The first minivan was introduced by Chrysler in 1983 and become an immediate hit, while SUVs grew in popularity in the 1990s.[56]

The consumer shift toward these less efficient vehicles, along with a lack of interest on Capitol Hill in increasing standards, stalled fuel efficiency for two decades. In 1995, Democratic President Bill Clinton tried to raise light truck efficiency standards, but a Republican-controlled Congress responded by stripping the administration's authority to increase vehicle efficiency. The withdrawal of authority remained in place until 2000.[57]

Removing Lead

The Clinton administration was more successful in continuing the effort to make vehicle exhaust cleaner. In 1996, the EPA completed a 25-year effort to remove lead, a human health hazard, from gasoline. Two years later, the administration, automakers and Northeastern states agreed to put cleaner cars on the roads before it was mandated under the Clean Air Act. The cars produced under this National Low Emission Vehicle program first become available in New England in 1999.[58]

California continued on its own aggressive path, starting a "zero emissions" vehicle program in 1990 requiring automakers to offer a specific number of the very cleanest vehicles available, including electric vehicles and some hybrids—vehicles powered by both gasoline and batteries.[59]

In 2000, oil prices again soared, renewing interest in stricter federal fuel efficiency standards. The Clinton administration modestly raised the light truck requirements that year, but oil prices continued to be high, and in 2007 Congress passed the Energy Independence and Security Act, raising CAFE standards for cars and light trucks by 40 percent.

When Obama took office in 2009, he accelerated those improvements, requiring automakers to reach a fleetwide average of 35.5 mpg by 2016. He also took steps to bring federal standards in lines with California's,

President Barack Obama announces his administration's new fuel emissions standards in 2011 in an event with auto executives, including Jim Lentz (left), then president and chief operating officer of Toyota Motor Corp.'s U.S. sales unit.

U.S. Lags in Fuel Economy

China, EU are moving aggressively to cut tailpipe emissions.

President Trump's rollback of U.S. fuel efficiency standards will leave the United States far behind most of the developed world in reducing tailpipe emissions over the next decade.

The European Union (EU) has forged ahead with an ambitious—critics say unrealistic—schedule to cut the vehicle greenhouse gases responsible for climate change, requiring cars to average the equivalent of 57 mpg by 2021 and 92 mpg by 2030.[1] Trump's fuel efficiency rule requires that automakers' U.S. vehicle fleets reach 40 mpg by 2026.[2] (Trump rolled back a more ambitious standard set by the Obama administration, calling it overly burdensome; critics say the rollback is unneeded and will result in greater pollution.)

China has made a major commitment to developing, building and promoting the use of electric vehicles, setting a goal that 25 percent of automobiles and trucks sold in the country will be zero-emission, meaning primarily electric, by 2025. That goal increases to 50 percent by 2030.[3]

In addition, China has adopted stricter fuel efficiency requirements than the United States. The average for new vehicles sold in China in 2018 was already 41 mpg, exceeding the U.S. 2026 requirement.[4] Japanese standards also exceed U.S. requirements.[5]

Europe, the United States and China use different methods to track the progress limiting greenhouse gases from vehicles. The Europeans record and publish grams per kilometer of carbon dioxide (CO_2), the principal greenhouse gas. China also focuses on the volume of certain tailpipe gases. The United States uses miles per gallon as a way to determine the amount of emissions.

"But the bottom line is, our [standards] are worse. They're worse than the 'godless communists' in China. They're worse than Europe," says Dan Becker, director of the Safe Climate Transport Campaign at the Center for Biological Diversity. The campaign is an advocacy group that works to reduce greenhouse gases.

China, the United States and the EU are the world's three largest automobile markets, in that order, with Japan a distant fourth. Climate change activists consider drastically reducing the CO_2 that comes from vehicles a key part of limiting climate change.

The global commitment to cutting emissions is strong enough that a study by the International Council on Clean Transportation (ICCT), a global environmental think tank, concluded, "An increasing number of local and national governments are signaling their intention to phase out combustion-engine-powered vehicles altogether."[6]

China invested nearly $60 billion between 2009 and 2017 in electric vehicles. About 450 manufacturers working on electric vehicles are registered with the Chinese government, including domestic and foreign companies. Tesla, the leading U.S. electric car manufacturer, recently announced plans to increase production of its Model 3 electric cars to 4,000 vehicles a week at a plant in Shanghai.[7]

China's electric vehicles industry has been hurt by the global recession tied to the coronavirus pandemic, as well as a decision by the Chinese government to trim subsidies.[8]

a move referred to as "harmonization," which ended an ongoing concern of automakers that they would be required to meet two separate standards.[60]

In 2011, after lengthy negotiations with automakers, the Obama administration announced even stricter CAFE requirements, which reflected growing concern about the role that the greenhouse gases in auto exhaust, particularly CO_2, were playing in climate change.

When Obama's clean car standards were announced in 2011, 13 auto executives joined Obama on stage for the announcement. Margo Oge, director of the EPA's office of transportation and air quality and a lead EPA negotiator of the agreement, remembered the scene:

"A fleet of shiny new cars, SUVs, and pickup trucks serves as a gleaming backdrop for President Obama as he strides across a brightly lit convention center stage. He quickly shakes the hands of thirteen smiling auto CEOs and senior executives before stepping to the lectern and announcing some of the stiffest new regulations on automobiles in decades. The executives sit

But analysts believe the country's leaders remain committed to the industry long-term.

The EU's clean-vehicle goals include stiff fines for automakers that fail to meet the emissions requirements. The European Automobile Manufacturers Association has called the standards unrealistic, saying they "are driven purely by political motives, without taking technological and socioeconomic realities into account."[9]

Those realities, said Erik Jonnaert, the association's secretary general in 2019, are the still higher-than-average cost of electric vehicles (EVs) and the shortage of charging stations to make EVs widely acceptable to consumers.[10]

But some European countries already are transitioning to electric vehicles. In March, nearly 60 percent of all cars purchased in Norway were fully electric, continuing a trend that has the country on course to meet its goal of phasing out gasoline- and diesel-powered vehicles by 2025.[11]

Aggressive government policies have helped make EVs popular in Norway. Norwegians who go electric get an exemption from the country's steep vehicle purchase tax, as well as a 50 percent discount on tolls, ferries and parking rates (originally 100 percent). They also can use the traffic lanes reserved for buses if they have one passenger.[12]

Nic Lutsey, who directs the ICCT's electric vehicle program, says setting emissions requirements for manufacturers that lead them to invest in clean-car technology and offer more zero-emission models, combined with purchasing incentives for consumers, are the keys to getting the public to try EVs. He adds that electric vehicles are cheaper to operate than gasoline-powered cars. "Every market has found the same thing: Consumers don't naturally take up that offering, but it overwhelmingly offers a cost benefit for consumers when they do," Lutsey says.

In Norway, the combination appears to be working. "It's actually quite amazing how fast the mindset's changed," said Christina Bu, secretary general of the Norwegian Electric Vehicle Association. "Even in 2013 or 2014, people were skeptical. Now, a majority of Norwegians will say: 'My next car will be electric.'"[13]

— Reed Karaim

[1] Ethan N. Elkind, "Trump's Flawed Rollback of Fuel Economy Rules," *Regulatory Review*, May 18, 2020, https://tinyurl.com/y77f2bqs.

[2] Coral Davenport, "Trump Calls New Fuel Economy Rule a Boon. Some Experts See Steep Costs," *The New York Times*, March 31, 2020, https://tinyurl.com/rvjbasw; David Shepardson, "U.S. to finalize fuel efficiency rewrite through 2026: sources," *Reuters*, March 30, 2020, https://tinyurl.com/y857alev.

[3] Elkind, *op. cit.*

[4] *Ibid.*

[5] Zifei Yang and Dan Rutherford, "Japan 2030 fuel economy standards," International Council on Clean Transportation, Sept. 27, 2019, https://tinyurl.com/y32v93zj.

[6] "The end of the road? An overview of combustion-engine car phaseout announcements across Europe," International Council on Clean Transportation, May 2020, https://tinyurl.com/ybu864do.

[7] Eleanor Albert, "Can China's Electric Car Industry Weather the COVID-19 Storm?" *The Diplomat*, May 8, 2020, https://tinyurl.com/y8vwjc2o.

[8] *Ibid.*

[9] "Auto industry reacts to deal on CO_2 targets for cars and vans," European Automobile Manufacturers Association, Dec. 17, 2018, https://tinyurl.com/y9zuo5bw.

[10] *Ibid.*

[11] Jon Henley and Elisabeth Ulven, "Norway and the A-ha moment that made electric cars the answer," *The Guardian*, April 19, 2020, https://tinyurl.com/yblyo6t4.

[12] *Ibid.*

[13] *Ibid.*

listening agreeably, even proudly, to the plan that would compel their companies—representing 90 percent of the American market—to double the fuel efficiency of their products and cut greenhouse gas emissions in half by 2025."[61]

The Center for Automotive Research's Smith, however, says the automakers agreed to the new rules only reluctantly. "They knew going in, it was going to be really, really hard, especially if fuel prices didn't drastically increase because most people don't value fuel efficiency, and certainly at that time very few people understood or valued" lowering greenhouse gas emissions, he says.

But an EPA report found that through 2018 automakers scored record-breaking gains in fuel efficiency and in limiting greenhouse gas emissions under the Obama rules. In 2018, average fuel economy reached a record 25.1 mpg and CO_2 emissions from new U.S. vehicles fell to the lowest level ever recorded. The EPA projected further gains for 2019.[62]

Electric Vehicle Boosters Eye Greater Growth

California leads with an ambitious goal for 2030.

When climate change activists envision a future where greenhouse gas emissions have been brought under control, electric vehicles play a critical part.

"Between 2040 and 2050, getting to all zero-emission vehicles is basically what the science would say is needed for climate change mitigation," says Nic Lutsey, who directs the electric vehicle program for the International Council on Clean Transportation, a global think tank that provides research to fight climate change.

Electric vehicle advocates believe a significant transition to electric vehicles (EVs) in the United States is possible within the next few decades. "I like to think in 10 years we'll be closing in on all new sales of vehicles being electric or highly efficient," says Andrew Linhardt, former deputy director of advocacy for the clean transportation program at the Sierra Club, an environmental group.

But electric vehicle skeptics doubt EVs can gain sufficient traction to seriously dent the market for gasoline-powered vehicles. "There is a market for EVs. It's a niche market, and it should not be forced on people," says Thomas Pyle, president of the American Energy Alliance, a Washington-based group that works to promote market-oriented energy policies.

California has led the charge in the United States for electric vehicles, setting an ambitious goal to have 5 million zero-emission vehicles on the road by 2030, up from about 700,000 this year.[1] Those vehicles would almost all be purely electric vehicles or plug-in hybrids, in which a battery-powered electric motor drives the wheels but a gasoline-fueled engine can charge the battery when it starts to run down. Cars or trucks powered by hydrogen fuel cells could account for a small portion of zero-emission vehicles.

In early 2020, California had roughly half of all zero-emission vehicles in the United States.[2] A more than sevenfold increase would be required to meet the state's 2030 goal.

California is committing significant resources to making that happen. By the end of 2019, the state had about 21,000 electric vehicle charging stations. The California Air Resources Board, whose mission includes fighting climate change, has committed nearly $1.1 billion to EV projects, the bulk of it going to charging stations.[3] By 2025, the state hopes to have 250,000 such stations in place.[4]

California's zero-emissions vehicle program, largely adopted by 10 other states, requires that a certain number of the vehicles sold in the state by any manufacturer be zero-emission vehicles, with the number linked to their total California sales.[5]

Last year, President Trump revoked California's authority to set its own emission standards, including its zero-emissions vehicle program. The state is challenging Trump's move in court.

The program does seem to have spurred EV sales. The number of zero-emission vehicles in California has grown by 30 percent annually in the last two years.[6]

The agency also found that automakers were developing a range of approaches to meet the standards. "Technological innovation in the auto industry has led to a wide array of technology available to manufacturers to achieve CO_2 emissions, fuel economy and performance goals," the report stated.[63]

All the major automobile manufacturers were in compliance with the Obama clean car standards at the end of 2018, the EPA said. The wider use and refinement of established technologies such as turbocharged engines and gasoline direct injection—in which fuel is injected directly into the combustion chamber, improving efficiency—contributed. So did newer approaches such as cylinder deactivation that uses only part of an engine when less power is necessary and stop/start systems that shut down the engine entirely at idle, the EPA

The rest of the country, however, lags far behind. Electric vehicle sales have been less than 3 percent of U.S. sales overall, even with federal tax credits and additional incentives offered by some states.[7]

EV skeptics say consumers simply prefer the gasoline-powered vehicles they are familiar with, and which are still cheaper to buy on average. They say consumers are unfamiliar with EV technology, and worry about how far electric vehicles can go on a charge and whether they will be able to find a charging station when needed.

Lutsey, of the International Council on Clean Transportation, acknowledges significant barriers remain to widespread adoption of EVs. The foremost remains cost, he says, with EVs selling at a price premium compared with gasoline-powered vehicles, but he says that could change soon: "Our analysis indicates that cost parity will happen before 2030."

The two largest U.S. automakers say they remain committed to producing electric vehicles. Ford is reportedly investing $11 billion to produce 20 new EV models by 2023, including the Mustang Mach-E, which brings the company's most venerated model name to an electric compact sport utility vehicle. General Motors says it will spend $20 billion in the next three years on EVs, with 60 percent of its research and development going to developing new EV technology and vehicles.[8]

Currently, one company, Tesla, sells 80 percent of all the EVs bought in the United States. The relative paucity of available electric vehicle models compared to gasoline models is one of the barriers to wider adoption, Lutsey says, which the investments by GM, Ford and other large automakers could address.

Vehicle range, once a limiting factor, is becoming less important as battery power and range increase, he says. Several models from different manufacturers can now go more than 200 miles on a single charge.[9]

But a lack of consumer knowledge about electric vehicles remains a problem, Lutsey says. "Some people don't know that EVs exist. People confuse EVs and hybrids," he says. "There are all these barriers in just understanding what the technology is."

Still, studies forecast U.S. EV sales will grow significantly in the coming decades, despite a temporary downturn associated with the coronavirus, and will account for as much as one-third of sales in the 2030s.[10] EVs already have taken off in parts of Europe, largely as a result of government policies encouraging adoption, says Lutsey. (*See Short Feature.*)

In the United States, he says, maintaining the zero-emission standards established by California is key to the future. "Taking that away," Lutsey says, "would be a massive deterrent to electric vehicles."

— *Reed Karaim*

[1] David Shepardson, "California looks to ramp up electric vehicle sales," *Reuters*, Jan. 26, 2018, https://tinyurl.com/yd375vpc; Skip Descant, "Reaching California's EV Goals Will Take Policy, Partnerships," *Government Technology*, March 6, 2020, https://tinyurl.com/y7pye5wc.

[2] *Ibid.*

[3] Rob Nikolewski, "California electric vehicle sales are up. But will we reach the 5 million goal by 2030?" *Los Angeles Times*, Dec. 1, 2019, https://tinyurl.com/ycfb5spx.

[4] Shepardson, *op. cit.*

[5] "What is ZEV?" Union of Concerned Scientists, Sept. 12, 2019, https://tinyurl.com/ybf9a9uc.

[6] Nikolewski, *op. cit.*

[7] "Electric Vehicle Sales: Facts and Figures," Edison Electric Institute, October 2019, https://tinyurl.com/y8ve634u.

[8] Henry Payne, "As GM and Ford ramp up for EVs for U.S., Europeans retreat," *The Detroit News*, March 11, 2020, https://tinyurl.com/yaceuqy3.

[9] Kelly Lin, "Longest-Range Electric Cars of 2020: 19 EVs That Can Go the Distance," *Motor Trend*, Dec. 23, 2019, https://tinyurl.com/y9hymuhw.

[10] "Electric Vehicle Outlook 2020, Executive Summary," *BloombergNEF*, May 19, 2020, https://tinyurl.com/ybzo4wmh.

said. In addition, the growth of hybrid and all-electric vehicles contributed to the gains.[64]

To allay concerns about the new standards, however, the administration had agreed to a midterm review. In the review, the Obama administration concluded the standards were still reasonable—but at the request of some automakers, the Trump administration reopened the review shortly after taking office.[65]

The reassessment was part of a larger review of environmental regulation, which Trump had criticized during the 2016 campaign as stifling business. The Trump administration initially floated the idea of freezing fuel efficiency standards, but some automakers opposed the proposal, causing a split within the industry.[66]

The administration then began considering the 1.5 percent annual increase they finalized this March, which provides automakers regulatory relief while still allowing the car companies to say they are steadily improving fuel efficiency and fighting climate change.[67]

CURRENT SITUATION
Final Rule

Trump's SAFE rule is scheduled to go into effect on June 29. The impact will not be felt immediately as automakers work on car designs years ahead. Court challenges could also derail the regulation.

But the final order, posted April 30 in the *Federal Register*, outlines the requirements automakers will be expected to meet if the rule stays in force. As was the case with the earlier CAFE and greenhouse gas emission standards established by the Obama administration, the requirements are partly "vehicle-footprint-based," which means they take the number of larger, less efficient vehicles automakers produce into account when calculating the requirements for each manufacturer's vehicle fleet. As the standards become more stringent each year, they move the entire vehicle fleet toward the required average.[68]

In concluding the new rule will save automakers money and lower new-car costs, NHTSA and EPA said they "believe their analysis of the final rule represents the best available science, evidence and methodologies for assessing the impacts of changes in CAFE and CO_2 emission standards."[69]

Even before the rule was formally announced, however, Carper, the senior Democrat on the Senate Environment and Public Works Committee, had asked the EPA's inspector general to open an investigation into how the rule was put together. Carper said he had received reports that EPA political appointees may have violated the law by avoiding the required steps associated with finalizing the rule, "including potential efforts to conceal documents that should eventually be made public."[70]

Carper is now asking the inspector general to expand its investigation based on new evidence he said shows his concerns were justified. "My previous request to you observed that an effort to conceal further interagency disagreement could result in the concealment of embarrassing and legally risky information related to flaws in the final rule," the senator wrote to the inspector general. "I have learned that this is exactly what has occurred."[71]

Court Action

At least four different lawsuits are pending concerning fuel efficiency standards and the Trump administration's decision to revoke California's authority to set stiffer rules.

The most recent is the suit filed by 23 states, four cities and the District of Columbia on May 27 2020, challenging the Trump administration's plan to relax the fuel efficiency requirements established by the Obama administration through Trump's SAFE rule.[72]

The suit, filed in the U.S. Court of Appeals for the District of Columbia Circuit, contends the Trump rule violates the Clean Air Act as well as procedures for rulemaking established in the Administrative Procedure Act.[73] "The EPA and NHTSA improperly and unlawfully relied on an analysis riddled with errors, omissions and unfounded assumptions in an attempt to justify their desired result," said California Attorney General Xavier Becerra when announcing the lawsuit.[74]

NHTSA did not comment on the lawsuit, while the EPA restated earlier comments that its rule "provides a sensible, single national program that strikes the right regulatory balance, protects our environment and sets reasonable targets for the auto industry, while supporting our economy and the safety of American families."[75]

The suit will not be heard until 2021, says Craig Segall, assistant chief counsel at the California Air Resources Board. The case is expected to end up before the U.S. Supreme Court. "There's no world in which this is resolved before the election," says Segall.

Twelve environmental and consumer groups are also suing the administration over the SAFE rules based on largely the same contentions. They include the Sierra Club, the Natural Resources Defense Council, the Union of Concerned Scientists and the Consumer Federation of America.[76]

In a separate action filed last year, California, 23 other states and the cities of Los Angeles and New York are suing to overturn the administration's decision to revoke California's authority to set its own emission standards. The suit contends NHTSA's decision exceeds the authority granted the agency by Congress and is based on arguments rejected by the courts in the past.[77]

Segall says final arguments are expected before the Court of Appeals for the District of Columbia Circuit sometime after October.

Finally, the Competitive Enterprise Institute, the libertarian think tank, announced in May it is suing the administration because it did not roll back the fuel efficiency standards far enough. The institute contends the government's analysis indicates the public would benefit if the standards were weakened further or frozen entirely.[78]

The Alliance for Automotive Innovation, a newly formed group that represents all the major automobile manufacturers, has announced it will oppose the Competitive Enterprise Institute lawsuit, saying automakers support continued improvements in the standards.[79] However, several members of the alliance are supporting the Trump administration in the lawsuit over whether California has the right to set stricter emission and fuel efficiency standards.[80]

California's Separate Deal

Volvo is joining four other major automakers who have struck a separate deal with California to follow stricter fuel efficiency and emission standards than those in the Trump SAFE rule.[81]

Volkswagen, Ford, BMW and Honda earlier agreed to meet higher standards negotiated with the state. The deal negotiated between the state and the companies stretches out the original schedule in the Obama rules by one year to 2026 and lowers the required annual reduction in greenhouse gas emissions from 4.7 percent to 3.7 percent, says Cliff, the deputy executive officer of the California Air Resources Board. The agreement "basically does what the Obama standards would have done in four years in five," he says.

The agreement could boost the average fuel efficiency of an automaker's fleet to about 50 mpg by 2026, below the Obama standard's goal of 54.5 mpg but significantly higher than the 40 mph in Trump's SAFE rule.[82]

Cliff says the state plans to go ahead with its new standards even if it loses the suit to overturn the SAFE rule in court. "The outcome of any of this litigation is really not important for the purpose of this agreement," he says. "The automakers are agreeing to this outcome no matter what happens."

The same is true if California loses its other lawsuit against the Trump administration in which it seeks to regain authority to set its own emission standards. "These are fairly robust agreements," which would still be in force, says Segall.

Trump lashed out at the original four automakers who reached an agreement with California, dismissing them as "politically correct" and calling their leaders "Foolish executives!" He reiterated administration claims that the SAFE rule would lead to safer, cheaper cars with very little impact on the environment.[83]

In a joint statement, the four automakers said the deal was driven by a need for the predictability and reduced costs that come with embracing one standard and a wish to be good environmental stewards.[84]

Legislative and Administrative Policy

The Clean and Efficient Cars Act of 2019, a bill sponsored by 75 House Democrats that would restore the Obama fuel efficiency rules, is one of several pieces of legislation introduced in Congress that would require the government to support cleaner, more efficient vehicles.[85]

They include bipartisan legislation in the House and Senate called the Driving America Forward Act. The measure would extend and restore tax credits for electric vehicle purchases and encourage vehicles fueled by hydrogen fuel cells, a technology that releases only water vapor into the air.[86] The electric vehicle credit, which can reach $7,500 for some vehicles, currently phases out as a manufacturer sells 200,000 electric vehicles.[87] For example, the federal tax credit for Tesla, manufacturer of the most popular U.S. electric vehicle models, expired at the start of this year.[88]

Rep. Alexandria Ocasio-Cortez, D-N.Y., announces introduction of the Green New Deal legislation to address climate change in 2019, joined by co-sponsor Sen. Ed Markey, D-Mass. (right) and other lawmakers.

Will Trump's fuel efficiency standards harm efforts to contain climate change?

YES

Dan Becker
*Director, Safe Climate Transport Campaign,
Center for Biological Diversity*

James Gerstenzang
*Editorial Director, Safe Climate Transport
Campaign, Center for Biological Diversity*

Written for *CQ Researcher*, June 2020

President Trump's rollback of clean-car rules halts the biggest single step any nation has taken to cut global warming pollution. The rules took effect in 2012 and would deliver a new-car fleet in 2025 that averages 37 mpg, while cutting auto emissions in half. By trashing the rules, the president is leaving the world at far greater risk of the climate catastrophes we are already witnessing.

Before Trump gutted them, the rules not only reduced pollution—they were saving Americans hundreds of billions of dollars at the pump. Even after paying for the gasoline-saving improvements—more-efficient transmissions and safe, light-weight materials—consumers would come out $4,000 to $6,000 ahead because their cars would need less fuel.

Each gallon of gasoline we burn pumps 25 pounds of carbon dioxide (CO_2), the primary global warming pollutant, into the atmosphere. The stringent standards were designed to prevent release of 6 billion tons of CO_2 by eliminating our need for 12 billion barrels of oil.

CO_2 creates an invisible heat-trapping blanket close to Earth. The energy from that heat is making tropical storms and wildfires more frequent and fierce. The heat is helping spread tropical diseases to once-temperate climates and is making increasing swaths of the globe unfit for human habitation.

Ignoring science, Trump is ending widely popular rules that would improve the cars we drive for years to come and keep as much CO_2 out of the atmosphere as shutting all U.S. coal-fired power plants for more than a year.

By adopting these responsible rules, the United States had signaled it was committed to tackling the planet's biggest environmental threat—rather than burying its head in the warming sand.

Trying to justify the rollback, the Trump administration falsely claimed that stronger rules would make us less safe on the road. As we wrote in *The New York Times*:

"This is auto mechanics, not rocket science. Ford proved that efficiency and safety go hand in hand when it converted the steel bodies of its F-150 pickups to aluminum. It lopped 700 pounds from America's best-selling model and helped lift mileage by 4 mpg. The [government] upgraded the truck to a five star safety rating."

NO

Marlo Lewis
*Senior Fellow in Energy and Environmental
Policy, Competitive Enterprise Institute*

Written for *CQ Researcher*, June 2020

The Trump administration's Safer Affordable Fuel-Efficient (SAFE) Vehicles rule is deregulatory compared to the 2012 Obama administration rule it replaces. The SAFE rule increases the stringency of corporate average fuel economy (CAFE) standards by 1.5 percent annually. If still in effect today, the 2012 rule would increase regulatory stringency by 5 percent annually.

California and its allies tout the 2012 rule as a "climate solution" and slam the SAFE rule as a planet wrecker. In fact, both rules are irrelevant to the climate.

Under the SAFE rule, national gasoline consumption and the associated carbon dioxide (CO_2) emissions will decline by 32 percent during 2020-50, whereas consumption and emissions would decline by 43 percent under the 2012 rule. Will the SAFE rule's slower rate of decline doom humanity to planetary ruin? Will future generations pay a terrible price for the Trump agencies' deregulatory ambitions? No.

Compared to the 2012 rule, the SAFE rule will, in 2100, increase CO_2 concentrations by 0.66 parts per million, global average temperatures by 0.003 of a degree Celsius, and sea levels by 0.06 centimeters—about two-hundredths of an inch. Those numbers come from the Environmental Protection Agency's standard climate policy calculator, a model called MAGICC.

Climate sensitivity—the long-term change in global average surface temperature after a doubling of atmospheric CO2 concentration—is a key variable in climate assessments. The Intergovernmental Panel on Climate Change estimates that climate sensitivity is "likely in the range of 1.5 degrees-4.5 degrees Celsius."

Accordingly, the Trump agencies used sensitivities of 1.5 to 4.5 degrees Celsius and 6.0 degrees Celsius to estimate the SAFE rule's potential climate effects. Even under the least stringent regulatory option considered (freezing CAFE standards at model year 2020 levels) and assuming the highest sensitivity (6.0 degrees Celsius), the global mean surface temperature in 2100 is only 0.006 of a degree Celsius higher than under the 2012 rule.

Six-thousandths of a degree Celsius is 13 times smaller than the margin of error for measuring changes in annual average global temperatures. That tiny temperature increase 80 years from now would have no discernible impact on weather patterns, crop yields, species habitat or any other environmental condition people care about.

Yet while touting "safety," the administration ignored deadly air pollution from refineries needed to keep more gas guzzlers on the road. This will kill an estimated 18,000 people.

To justify its attack, the Trump administration has fabricated a false conflict between safe cars and a safe climate. Americans can and must have both.

The SAFE rule's alleged evisceration of "critical climate protections" is political theater. In contrast, the rule's reduction in vehicle ownership costs is real. By helping middle-income families afford new, safer, more fuel-efficient vehicles, the SAFE rule will benefit people more than the rule it replaces.

The most high-profile piece of environmental legislation that concerns vehicle emissions is the Green New Deal, which lays out a multiyear roadmap for tackling the causes of climate change and includes investing in electric vehicles. The Green New Deal is often mischaracterized as mandating changes, but the bill that was introduced last year by Rep. Alexandria Ocasio-Cortez, D-N.Y., and Sen. Ed Markey, D-Mass., is a nonbinding resolution, so its provisions would not become law without further legislative action.[89]

Congressional observers say none of this legislation is likely to become law in this congressional session given the bitter divisions between the two political parties over the need to address climate change, a phenomenon about which many Republicans are skeptical. Instead, the direction of fuel efficiency and emissions policy is likely to continue to be set by regulatory action by the executive branch, which will be determined by the upcoming presidential election.

The Trump campaign website, as of early June, did not include a section outlining plans to address vehicle emissions or climate change. But in an "Energy and Environment" section listing Trump's achievements, it notes that the administration has "rescinded many costly Obama-era regulations."[90]

Biden, the presumptive Democratic nominee, has called the Green New Deal "a crucial framework for meeting the climate challenges we face."[91] His environmental plan, which his campaign site calls "a Clean Energy Revolution," includes several proposals to dramatically reduce vehicle emissions, with the goal of getting to a 100 percent clean energy economy by 2050.[92]

Those plans include developing new fuel economy standards that not only reverse the Trump SAFE plan but go "beyond what the Obama-Biden administration put in place" and are aimed at ensuring 100 percent of new sales for light- and medium-duty vehicles will be electrified.

Biden also promises to "work with our nation's governors and mayors to support the deployment of more than 500,000 new public charging outlets by the end of 2030." In addition, his administration would restore the "full electric vehicle tax credit to incentivize the purchase of these vehicles."[93]

OUTLOOK
An Inevitable Change?

With stark differences between Biden and Trump toward climate change and federal regulation, analysts say the 2020 election obviously will play a huge role in determining the direction of fuel emissions and efficiency policy over the next four years.

Still, several advocates of stronger policies believe a longer-term shift to cleaner, even zero-emission vehicles is inevitable. The Safe Climate Transport Campaign's Becker says the need for U.S. automakers to compete globally—particularly in China, which is making a commitment to shift to electric vehicles—along with gasoline prices he expects to rise again, mean that vehicles will be much cleaner and burn much less—or no—gasoline in the next decade. "I think we're on a one-way street toward cleaner, more efficient vehicles after the detour and stall of the Trump administration is behind us," he says.

But Smith, at the Center for Automotive Research, says there is a good chance the U.S. market goes its own way and, when it comes to electric vehicles and fuel efficiency, the United States could become "a technology backwater. We already are in some ways."

That would simply reflect the desire of American consumers for larger, less fuel-efficient vehicles, says Smith. "The reality is the markets are different and they're going to be different for a long time. . . . The U.S. consumer, at least until there's a real change in beliefs on greenhouse gases, which is slowly happening, we're not going to value [greenhouse gases] as much as Europe does," he says. "We're not going to value [a government-established] industrial policy as much as China does. They're going to be different models."

UCLA's Carlson sees policy at the state level, supported by several automakers, continuing to move the United States toward a zero-emissions future. "I do think the push to electrify the transportation sector is going to continue," she says. "We're seeing investments in infrastructure, and I don't think California will back away."

Electric vehicles, whether purely electric or plug-in hybrids that also burn gasoline, accounted for less than 3 percent of automobile sales last year, but surveys show that nearly a third of Americans now say they would consider an electric vehicle for their next purchase.[94]

The Coalition for Clean Air's Magavern believes that sentiment means the transportation industry could be on the verge of a dramatic shift. "In 10 years we'll have seen the transition really pick up steam and, at that point, it will appear inevitable that we'll be going to fully electric vehicles," he says.

Cliff, at the California Air Resources Board, says the investments automakers are making in the next generation of zero-emission vehicles to respond to global concerns about climate change have created a momentum within the industry that shifts in U.S. federal regulations cannot derail. "There's really no going back at this point," he says.

But other experts say the American public, which has valued style, convenience and price more than environmental considerations, does not share the same urgency. McCarthy, the author and historian, believes concern about climate change has become more dominant in recent years, but the attitudes that govern vehicle purchases are likely to remain largely the same, with fuel efficiency or emissions not the primary concern for many buyers.

"Consumers quite understandably have other priorities than solving world problems when buying automobiles," McCarthy says. "You're really talking about having to transform an entire culture, how you think about the world, what we value in the world and how we should value it. That's a pretty big step."

NOTES

1. Coral Davenport, "Trump Calls New Fuel Economy Rule a Boon. Some Experts See Steep Costs," *The New York Times*, March 31, 2020, https://tinyurl.com/rvjbasw.

2. Rebecca Beitsch, "States, green groups sue Trump over rollback of Obama fuel efficiency regulations," *The Hill*, May 27, 2020, https://tinyurl.com/yd2k5w8g.

3. "California and 22 other states take Trump Administration to court over vehicle emissions rollback," California Air Resources Board, May 27, 2020, https://tinyurl.com/ydbuswdy.

4. "Attorney General Becerra Files Lawsuit Against EPA for Attacking California's Advanced Clean Air Standards," State of California Department of Justice, Nov. 15, 2019, https://tinyurl.com/y7p7g7q8.

5. Davenport, *op. cit.*; David Shepardson, "U.S. to finalize fuel efficiency rewrite through 2026: sources," *Reuters*, March 30, 2020, https://tinyurl.com/y857alev.

6. David Shepardson and Ben Klayman, "California, four automakers defy Trump, agree to tighten emission rules," *Reuters*, July 25, 2019, https://tinyurl.com/y5v8u2ol.

7. "Energy and Environment, President Donald J. Trump achievements," Donald Trump for President, accessed June 11, 2020, https://tinyurl.com/uzjt-kmk.

8. "Climate: Joe's Plan for a Clean Energy Revolution and Environmental Justice," Joebiden.com, accessed June 11, 2020, https://tinyurl.com/y65rc9fr.

9. "U.S. DOT and EPA Put Safety and American Families First with Final Rule on Fuel Economy Standards," National Highway Traffic Safety Administration, March 31, 2020, https://tinyurl.com/yas28cx4.

10. "California and 22 other states take Trump Administration to court over vehicle emissions rollback," *op. cit.*

11. Rebecca Beitsch, "New documents show EPA rolled back mileage standards despite staff, WH concerns," *The Hill*, May 20, 2020, https://tinyurl.com/yauwkpte.

12. *Ibid.*

13. "U.S. DOT and EPA Put Safety and American Families First with Final Rule on Fuel Economy Standards," *op. cit.*

14. Ann Carlson, "Los Angeles Air Quality in the Time of Covid-19," *LegalPlanet*, April 21, 2020, https://tinyurl.com/ybvfsgha.

15. "History," California Air Resources Board, 2020, https://tinyurl.com/ycs3awya.

16. *Ibid.*; "Vehicle Emissions California Waivers and Authorizations," U.S. Environmental Protection Agency, Feb. 20, 2020, https://tinyurl.com/ycgt4ntm.

17. Kevin Liptak and Gregory Wallace, "Trump revokes waiver for California to set higher auto emission standards," *CNN*, Sept. 18, 2019, https://tinyurl.com/yyxm2yxb.

18. Dino Grandoni and Juliet Eilperin, "California sues Trump administration over revoking authority to limit car pollution," *The Washington Post*, Sept. 20, 2019, https://tinyurl.com/y3ozv9zu.

19. "Fast Facts on Transportation Greenhouse Gas Emissions," U.S. Environmental Protection Agency, July 16, 2019, https://tinyurl.com/y2vqneto.

20. *Ibid.*

21. "U.S. Vehicle Registration Statistics," Hedges & Company, 2020, https://tinyurl.com/ycnkclv4.

22. "Greenhouse Gas Emissions from a Typical Passenger Vehicle," U.S. Environmental Protection Agency, May 10, 2018, https://tinyurl.com/yad7qmts.

23. "Obama Administration Finalizes Historic 54.5 MPG Fuel Efficiency Standards," The White House, Aug. 28, 2012, https://tinyurl.com/r5jej4u.

24. *Ibid.*

25. "A Brief History of U.S. Fuel Efficiency Standards," Union of Concerned Scientists, Dec. 6, 2017, https://tinyurl.com/y89wtz6q.

26. "Smog, Soot and Other Air Pollution from Transportation," U.S. Environmental Protection Agency, March 18, 2019, https://tinyurl.com/y7zhkty4.

27. "The Safer Affordable Fuel-Efficient (SAFE) Vehicles Rule Model Year 2021-2026 Passenger Cars and Light Trucks, Final Environmental Impact Statement," National Highway Traffic Safety Administration, March 2020, https://tinyurl.com/ydaaooql.

28. Antonio M. Bento, "Written Testimony," U.S. House Committee on Oversight and Reform, Subcommittee on Environment, Oct. 29, 2019, https://tinyurl.com/ych8xhy9.

29. Jessica McDonald, "The Facts on Fuel Economy Standards," Factcheck.org, May 3, 2019, https://tinyurl.com/yxrzjvb7.

30. Michael Wayland, "Ford, UAW voice opposition to freezing fuel economy standards," *Automotive News*, Sept. 25, 2018, https://tinyurl.com/y9u3q97c.

31. Michael Wayland, "Coronavirus pandemic tanks U.S. auto sales in April," *CNBC*, May 1, 2020, https://tinyurl.com/y8xnqa8l.

32. "Average New-Vehicle Prices Up 3.5% Year-Over-Year in January 2020 on Sales Mix, According to Kelley Blue Book," *PR Newswire*, Feb. 18, 2020, https://tinyurl.com/y7rspfk6.

33. Coral Davenport, "U.S. to Announce Rollback of Auto Pollution Rules, a Key Effort to Fight Climate Change," *The New York Times*, March 30, 2020, https://tinyurl.com/yx5j28bg.

34. "Obama Administration Finalizes Historic 54.5 MPG Fuel Efficiency Standards," *op. cit.*

35. Simon Constable, "Detroit's Headache: Car Buyers Don't Seem to Care About Fuel Efficiency," *Forbes*, June 10, 2019, https://tinyurl.com/ydbqo6tj.

36. "New Study Finds Consumers Are Willing to Pay More for Fuel Economy as Auto Regulators Look to Roll Back Efficiency Standards," *Consumer Reports*, June 12, 2018, https://tinyurl.com/y7cnlzpm.

37. "NADA Supports Right-Sizing Fuel Economy Standards for Current Market Realities," National Automobile Dealers Association, March 31, 2020, https://tinyurl.com/yd44s89u.

38. Martin Melosi, "The Automobile and the Environment in American History," Automobile in American Life and Society, 2010, https://tinyurl.com/ycjmc2o5.

39. "Ford Motor Company unveils the Model T," *History*, 2020, https://tinyurl.com/qquqmjy.

40. "State Motor Vehicle Registrations by Years, 1900-1995," U.S. Department of Transportation Federal Highway Administration, https://tinyurl.com/ycx-l9xz3.

41. Meredith Bennett-Smith, "From Model T to Prius: 13 big moments in fuel efficiency history," *The Christian Science Monitor*, March 7, 2012, https://tinyurl.com/y9c7yk78.

42. "Table 2.8—Motor Vehicle Mileage, Fuel Consumption, and Fuel Economy, 1949-2010," U.S. Energy Information Administration, Sept. 27, 2012, https://tinyurl.com/ya3pzyr7.

43. "History," California Air Resources Board, *op. cit.*

44. *Ibid.*

45. *Ibid.*

46. "Fifty Years of Clearing the Skies," *CalTech*, April 25, 2013, https://tinyurl.com/ybjgvqcd.

47. "History," California Air Resources Board, *op. cit.*

48. "Evolution of the Clean Air Act," U.S. Environmental Protection Agency, Jan. 3, 2017, https://tinyurl.com/ydhc27nt.

49. "History," California Air Resources Board, *op. cit.*

50. "Table 2.8—Motor Vehicle Mileage, Fuel Consumption, and Fuel Economy, 1949-2010," *op. cit.*

51. "Fact #915: March 7, 2016 Average Historical Annual Gasoline Pump Price, 1929-2015," Office of Energy Efficiency and Renewable Energy, Energy.gov., March 7, 2016, https://tinyurl.com/y6gdo8zk.

52. "Table 5.1a—Petroleum and Other Liquids Overview, Selected Years, 1949-2011," U.S. Energy Information Administration, Annual Energy Review, 2011, https://tinyurl.com/yd2brk2l.

53. "Energy Crisis (1970s)," *History*, Aug. 21, 2018, https://tinyurl.com/y7ekxmyx.

54. Philip Shabecoff, "Ford Signs Bill on Energy that Ends Policy Impasse and Cuts Crude Oil Prices," *The New York Times*, Dec. 23, 1975, https://tinyurl.com/ycjxybxl.

55. "History of Fuel Economy—One Decade of Innovation, Two Decades of Inaction," The Pew Environment Group, April 2011, https://tinyurl.com/y7eokqu7.

56. Bob Sorokanich, "30 Years Ago Today, Chrysler Invented the Minivan, And Changed History," *Gizmodo*, Nov. 2, 2013, https://tinyurl.com/y88ow4um.

57. "History of Fuel Economy—One Decade of Innovation, Two Decades of Inaction," *op. cit.*

58. "Timeline of Major Accomplishments in Transportation, Air Pollution and Climate Change," U.S. Environmental Protection Agency, Jan. 10, 2017, https://tinyurl.com/ybv4ocht.

59. "Zero-Emission Vehicle Program," California Air Resources Board, 2020, https://tinyurl.com/ycxy-hyxy.

60. John M. Broder, "Obama to Toughen Rules on Emissions and Mileage," *The New York Times*, May 18, 2009, https://tinyurl.com/yam3er9b.

61. Margo T. Oge, "Driving the Future: Combating Climate Change with Cleaner, Smarter Cars," Arcade, 2015, Kindle edition, location 2613.

62. "The 2019 EPA Automotive Trends Report, Executive Summary," U.S. Environmental Protection Agency, March 2020, https://tinyurl.com/y9fpf8ss.

63. *Ibid.*

64. *Ibid.*

65. Steven Overly and Juliet Eilperin, "President Trump to reopen review of Obama-era fuel economy standards," *The Washington Post*, March 13, 2017, https://tinyurl.com/zazs4fz.

66. Rebecca Beitsch, "Trump administration backing off plans to freeze fuel economy: WSJ," *The Hill*,

Oct. 31, 2019, https://tinyurl.com/yc4gvg6b; Wayland, "Ford, UAW voice opposition to freezing fuel economy standards," *op. cit.*

67. *Ibid.*

68. "A Rule by the Environmental Protection Agency and the National Highway Traffic Safety Administration on 04/30/2020," *Federal Register*, April 30, 2020, https://tinyurl.com/ya3tsz8x.

69. *Ibid.*

70. "After Reviewing New Documents, Carper Urges Expansion of EPA Inspector General Investigation into the SAFE Vehicles Rule," U.S. Senate Committee on Environment and Public Works, May 19, 2020, https://tinyurl.com/yd3tutow.

71. *Ibid.*

72. Jace Lington, "Group of states and cities sue Trump administration over rollback of Obama administration fuel efficiency standards," Ballotpedia News, June 2, 2020, https://tinyurl.com/ycjx9t3o.

73. *Ibid.*

74. "Attorney General Becerra Files Lawsuit Challenging Trump Administration's Reckless Rollback of America's Clean Car Standards," State of California Department of Justice, May 27, 2020, https://tinyurl.com/y9ybz3sq.

75. Beitsch, "States, green groups sue Trump over rollback of Obama fuel efficiency regulations," *op. cit.*

76. "Trump Administration Sued for Gutting Clean Car Standards," Natural Resources Defense Council, May 27, 2020, https://tinyurl.com/y93nbq9f.

77. "Attorney General Becerra Files Lawsuit Challenging Trump Administration's Attempt to Trample California's Authority to Maintain Longstanding Clean Car Standards," State of California Department of Justice, Sept. 20, 2019, https://tinyurl.com/y9hh9bv2.

78. Rebeca Beitsch, "Conservative group sues administration, arguing rollback of Obama mileage rule wasn't aggressive enough," *The Hill*, May 1, 2020, https://tinyurl.com/y82lt98j.

79. "Auto Innovators Intervenes in Fuel Economy Litigation," Alliance for Automotive Innovation, May 22, 2020, https://tinyurl.com/ybwu6pvp.

80. Tom Krisher and Ellen Knickmeyer, "Automakers side with Trump in legal fight with California," *The Associated Press*, Oct. 29, 2019, https://tinyurl.com/y843ktp7.

81. Bradley Berman, "Volvo joins automakers siding with California on emissions, opposing Trump administration," electrek, April 7, 2020, https://tinyurl.com/vko97bo.

82. Brakkton Booker and Jennifer Ludden, "Trump Administration Challenges California And Automakers On Fuel Economy," *NPR*, Sept. 6, 2019, https://tinyurl.com/y662orgk.

83. "Trump Lashes Out After Automakers Agree to California's Standards," *Bloomberg/IndustryWeek*, Aug. 21, 2019, https://tinyurl.com/yc7ge6ub.

84. Juliet Eilperin and Brady Dennis, "Major automakers strike climate deal with California, rebuffing Trump on proposed mileage freeze," *The Washington Post*, July 25, 2019, https://tinyurl.com/yyho54u8.

85. "Matsui Introduces Legislation that Pushes Back on the Trump Administration Attempts to Roll Back the Fuel Economy and Vehicle Emissions Standards," press release, Office of Rep. Doris Matsui, Feb. 5, 2019, https://tinyurl.com/yajb8rab.

86. "Stabenow, Alexander, Peters, Collins, Kildee Introduce Bipartisan Bill to Expand Electric Vehicle and Hydrogen Fuel Cell Tax Credits," press release, Office of Sen. Debbie Stabenow, April 10, 2019, https://tinyurl.com/yaha29fy.

87. "Federal Tax Credits for New All-Electric and Plug-in Hybrid Vehicles," U.S. Department of Energy, Office of Energy Efficiency and Renewable Energy, May 14, 2020, https://tinyurl.com/nba8gs2.

88. Eric Walz, "Tesla is Without the Federal EV Tax Credit for the First Time Since the Introduction of the Model S in 2012," *FutureCar*, Jan. 2, 2020, https://tinyurl.com/yafzjn92.

89. Lisa Friedman, "What Is the Green New Deal? A Climate Proposal, Explained," *The New York Times*, Feb. 21, 2019, https://tinyurl.com/y4kw8pmz.

90. "Energy and Environment, President Donald J. Trump Achievements," Donald Trump for President, *op. cit.*

91. "Climate: Joe's Plan for a Clean Energy Revolution and Environmental Justice," Joebiden.com, *op. cit.*

92. *Ibid.*

93. *Ibid.*

94. "Electric Vehicle Sales: Facts and Figures," Edison Electric Institute, October 2019, https://tinyurl.com/y8ve634u; "New Survey Shows Strong Support for Electric Vehicles Across Economic Spectrum," Union of Concerned Scientists, July 18, 2019, https://tinyurl.com/ya5vkatn.

BIBLIOGRAPHY

Books

Doyle, Jack, *Taken for a Ride: Detroit's Big Three and the Politics of Pollution,* **Four Walls Eight Windows, 2000.**
A former analyst with the Environmental Policy Institute, a Washington think tank, documents a 50-year history of General Motors, Ford and Chrysler resisting anti-pollution technology.

Gardiner, Beth, *Choked: Life and Breath in the Age of Air Pollution,* **University of Chicago Press, 2019.**
A journalist examines air pollution and the toll it takes on human health around the world, including pollution from automobiles, and the efforts underway to get to a future of zero-emission vehicles.

McCarthy, Tom, *Auto Mania: Cars, Consumers, and the Environment,* **Yale University Press, 2007.**
A historian looks at America's love affair with the car, particularly large, less fuel-efficient vehicles, and how that and the efforts of automakers have made effective environmental regulation of automobiles difficult.

Oge, Margo T., *Driving the Future: Combating Climate Change with Cleaner, Smarter Cars,* **Arcade, 2015.**
A former director of the federal Office of Transportation and Air Quality recounts the story behind the Obama administration's 2012 deal with automakers to double vehicle fuel efficiency.

Articles

Dennis, Brady, and Juliet Eilperin, "GM, Toyota and Chrysler side with White House in fight over California fuel standards, exposing auto industry split," *The Washington Post,* **Oct. 28, 2019, https://tinyurl.com/y4hv3cku.**
A group of automobile manufacturers, including General Motors and Toyota, backed the Trump administration's effort to restrict California's authority to set stricter vehicle emission standards, while other carmakers, including Ford and Volkswagen, agreed to follow California's standards.

Meyer, Robinson, "Trump's New Auto Rollback Is an Economic Disaster," *The Atlantic,* **April 13, 2020, https://tinyurl.com/ybtyfgqu.**
According to the government's own analysis, the Trump administration's fuel efficiency rollback will not create auto industry jobs as the president has stated, but instead will eliminate nearly 13,500 jobs.

Shepardson, David, "Trump finalizes rollback of Obama-era vehicle fuel efficiency standards," *Reuters,* **March 31, 2020, https://tinyurl.com/yak2rg6f.**
The Trump administration reduced the annual requirement for automakers to improve the fuel efficiency of their vehicle fleets from 5 percent to 1.5 percent through 2026, a move it said will cut the cost of a car; critics said the change will lead to more harmful vehicle emissions.

Tabuchi, Hiroko, "States Sue to Block Trump From Weakening Fuel Economy Rules," *The New York Times,* **May 27, 2020, https://tinyurl.com/ybyvwvsq.**
Twenty-three states, led by California, are suing the Trump administration over its new vehicle fuel efficiency standards, arguing the move is based on bad science.

Reports and Studies

"Final Regulatory Impact Analysis, The Safer Affordable Fuel-Efficient (SAFE) Vehicles Rule for Model Year 2021-2026 Passenger Cars and Light Trucks," National Highway Traffic Safety Administration and the Environmental Protection Agency, March 2020, https://tinyurl.com/yb4cjxyh.
Two federal agencies' analysis of the Trump administration's rollback of vehicle fuel efficiency standards

concludes that the benefits to consumers and the auto industry in reduced costs outweigh the increased emissions of greenhouse gases and pollutants.

Harto, Chris, Shannon Baker-Branstetter and Jamie Hall, "The Un-SAFE Rule: How a Fuel-Economy Rollback Costs Americans Billions in Fuel Savings and Does Not Improve Safety," *Consumer Reports*, August 2019, https://tinyurl.com/yb54awmc.
A study by a consumer advocacy organization finds that the administration's pullback on fuel efficiency standards will not improve vehicle safety and will cost consumers billions in extra costs at the gas pump through increased consumption.

Reidmiller, David, *et al.*, "Fourth National Climate Assessment Volume II: Impacts, Risks, and Adaptation in the United States," U.S. Global Change Research Program, 2018, https://tinyurl.com/y93ha5f5.
The latest U.S. government assessment of climate change predicts increasingly severe consequences for the nation, including heat waves, reduced crop yields, flooding, severe storms and hundreds of billions of dollars in economic damage.

Smith, Brett, "Fuel Economy and Greenhouse Gas Regulation in the United States: Change is Coming," Center for Automotive Research, March 19, 2019, https://tinyurl.com/ydxkajt5.
The director of propulsion technologies and energy infrastructure at the Center for Automotive Research examines Trump's fuel efficiency rule and the possible outcomes from the new standard.

THE NEXT STEP

Electric Vehicles

"A Million-Mile Battery From China Could Power Your Electric Car," *Bloomberg*, June 7, 2020, https://tinyurl.com/y7v4pnoe.
A Chinese company that produces batteries for Tesla and Volkswagen electric cars has developed a battery that lasts for 16 years and 1.24 million miles.

Geman, Ben, "Tesla says air quality jumps from coronavirus lockdowns make case for electric vehicles," *Axios*, June 9, 2020, https://tinyurl.com/y8lko4e5.
The coronavirus shutdowns show how much air quality would improve if electric cars replaced gasoline-powered vehicles, Tesla argues.

Stevens, Pippa, "Meet Nikola, the speculative electric vehicle stock that traders believe is as valuable as Ford," *CNBC*, June 9, 2020, https://tinyurl.com/yadbvogn.
An electric vehicle company that has not generated any revenue currently has about the same market capitalization as Ford.

Emissions During the Pandemic

Cohan, Daniel, "The COVID-19 shutdown leaves the air cleaner, but it isn't getting cooler," *MarketWatch*, May 11, 2020, https://tinyurl.com/ybe89ks6.
Air quality is improving during the COVID-19 shutdowns because of falling carbon emissions, but temperatures will continue to rise until the planet reaches net-zero emissions, according to an atmospheric scientist.

Fox, Alex, "Carbon Emissions Are Decreasing During the Pandemic but Could Bounce Back Fast," *Smithsonian Magazine*, May 22, 2020, https://tinyurl.com/ybh57f9w.
At the height of the coronavirus shutdowns in April, global carbon emissions dropped 17 percent year-over-year, but quickly began to rebound.

Plumer, Brad, and Nadja Popovich, "Traffic and Pollution Plummet as U.S. Cities Shut Down for Coronavirus," *The New York Times*, March 22, 2020, https://tinyurl.com/tebno2n.
Satellites detected significant declines in emissions in metropolitan areas during the shutdowns.

Environmental Protection Agency

Beitsch, Rebecca, "House Oversight seeks docs from oil giant Marathon after Trump mileage rollback," *The Hill*, May 28, 2020, https://tinyurl.com/y7hyaw6n.
The Democratic-led House Oversight and Reform Committee asked Marathon Petroleum for documents regarding meetings with Environmental Protection Agency (EPA) officials and the U.S. Department of Transportation after the Trump administration revised Obama-era fuel efficiency regulations.

Daly, Matthew, "Democrats decry 'pandemic of pollution' under Trump's EPA," *The Associated Press*, **May 20, 2020, https://tinyurl.com/y95rlqog.**
Sen. Ed Markey, D-Mass., said the Trump administration has turned the EPA into "Every Polluter's Ally"—a charge agency Administrator Andrew Wheeler denied.

Eilperin, Juliet, and Brady Dennis, "EPA staff warned that mileage rollbacks had flaws. Trump officials ignored them," *The Washington Post*, **May 19, 2020, https://tinyurl.com/ybm45tts.**
Government documents show that political appointees sidelined EPA officials when the EPA officials questioned revised mileage standards.

New Rules

Beitsch, Rebecca, "Automakers fight effort to freeze fuel efficiency standards," *The Hill*, **May 22, 2020, https://tinyurl.com/y8t9ddwo.**

A conservative organization has filed suit arguing that the Trump administration's fuel efficiency standards are actually too ambitious—but a group of automakers is opposing the lawsuit.

Chuang, Tamara, "Colorado, Denver join 25 other cities and states in suing EPA for relaxing clean-car rule," *The Colorado Sun*, **May 27, 2020, https://tinyurl.com/yb6fm9na.**
Concerned that lower clean-car standards could undercut the state's zero-emissions policy, Colorado joined a lawsuit against the Environmental Protection Agency.

Shaw, Adam, "Trump administration eases Obama-era regs on vehicle fuel economy," *Fox News*, **March 31, 2020, https://tinyurl.com/ybvpequn.**
Trump administration officials argue the new fuel efficiency rules will save hundreds of lives and balance environmental concerns with affordability, but Democrats disagree.

For More Information

Alliance for Automotive Innovation, 1050 K St., N.W., Suite 650, Washington, DC 20001; 202-326-5500; autosinnovate.org. Advocacy group that represents the auto industry, including its suppliers.

American Energy Alliance, 1155 15th St., N.W., Suite 900, Washington, DC 20005; 202-621-2940; americanenergyalliance.org. Alliance that works to enlist consumers to support anti-regulatory, free market policies regarding U.S. energy and fuels.

California Air Resources Board, 1001 I St., Sacramento, CA 95814; 800-242-4450; https://ww2.arb.ca.gov. State agency charged with protecting Californians from the harmful effects of air pollution and developing programs to fight climate change.

Competitive Enterprise Institute, 1310 L St., N.W., 7th Floor, Washington, DC 20005; 202-331-1010; cei.org.

Libertarian think tank that opposes government actions to limit climate change, including regulation of greenhouse gas emissions.

Environmental Protection Agency, 1200 Pennsylvania Ave., N.W., Washington, DC 20460; 202-564-4700; epa.gov. Federal agency whose mission is to ensure that Americans have access to clean air, water and land.

International Council on Clean Transportation, 1500 K St., N.W., Suite 650, Washington, DC 20005; 202-798-3986; theicct.org. Research organization that seeks to improve the environmental performance of all modes of transportation.

National Highway Traffic Safety Administration, 1200 New Jersey Ave., S.E., Washington, DC 20590; 888-327-4236; nhtsa.gov. Federal agency charged with enforcing vehicle safety and performance standards.

Safe Climate Transport Campaign, Center for Biological Diversity, 1411 K St., N.W., Suite 1300, Washington, DC 20005, 202-494-5577, safeclimatecampaign.org. Advocacy group that fights global warming by lobbying for measures to reduce greenhouse gas emissions, including slashing auto emissions and cutting U.S. oil use in half.

Sierra Club, 2101 Webster St., Suite 1300, Oakland, CA 94612; 415-977-5500; sierraclub.org. Leading environmental organization that seeks to mitigate climate change.

Union of Concerned Scientists, 2 Brattle Square, Cambridge, MA 02138; 800-666-8276; ucsusa.org. Science advocacy group that favors more stringent fuel efficiency standards.